DATE DUE

T3-BNO-899

THIRD EDITION

CONTEMPORARY ISSUES IN SOCIAL PSYCHOLOGY

THIRD EDITION

CONTEMPORARY ISSUES IN SOCIAL PSYCHOLOGY

Edited by

John C. Brigham
Florida State University

and

Lawrence S. Wrightsman
University of Kansas

Brooks/Cole Publishing Company
Monterey, California
A Division of Wadsworth Publishing Company, Inc.

Printed in the United States of America

10 9 8 7 6 5 4 3 2 1

Library of Congress Cataloging in Publication Data

Main entry under title:

Contemporary issues in social psychology.

In earlier editions Wrightsman's name appeared first on the title page.
Includes bibliographies.
1. Social psychology—Addresses, essays, lectures.
2. United States—Social conditions—Addresses, essays, lectures. I. Brigham, John Carl, 1942-
II. Wrightsman, Lawrence Samuel, comp. Contemporary issues in social psychology.
HM251.W77   1977   301.1'08   76-43315
ISBN 0-8185-0210-X

Production Editor: *John Bergez*
Interior and Cover Design: *John Edeen*

PREFACE

In creating this third edition of *Contemporary Issues in Social Psychology,* we have attempted to bring together the best of the research efforts in the most important and central areas of social psychology. In doing so, we have resisted the temptation to delve into oversimplistic "pop psychology," striving instead to provide the reader with material that is interesting and relevant to contemporary problems but that is also scientifically and conceptually sound.

We believe that social psychology's greatest contribution to understanding of our contemporary world is through the analysis of its theoretical concepts. Such topics as helping behavior, interpersonal attraction, obedience, aggression, attribution processes, sexism, and so on provide concepts around which our knowledge is organized. This volume concentrates on ten of these concepts. For each, three articles are reprinted; generally one article is a statement of theory or review of research, a second is a report of research generated by the theory, and a third is a review of the accumulated research on the topic. (However, we have chosen to deviate from that format when the topic demanded a different mix of articles.)

As editors, we have tried both to select the best group of articles available on the most important areas in contemporary social psychology and to provide a frame of reference that will be valuable to students in reading, understanding, and interpreting these articles. To achieve this latter aim, we have included an introductory piece on how to read a scientific article, developed a comprehensive Glossary of terms that might otherwise be somewhat unfamiliar to some readers, and written Introductions and Summaries for each of the ten Sections. Each Introduction contains a brief review of the conceptual and empirical issues leading up to the research included in that Section. Each Summary, in addition to summarizing the findings described in the articles, also attempts to establish the place of these findings within the broader framework of social psychology and to suggest directions in which future research and theorizing are likely to go.

The use of the volume along with a standard text for an undergraduate course in social psychology can expose the student to greater depth in theory, methodology, and analysis. Or, if the instructor prefers to use lecture material to give the extensive continuity that many textbooks provide, *Contemporary Issues in Social Psychology* can serve as the basic text. An additional use of the volume is to acquaint graduate students in a proseminar course with current research in social psychology.

In selecting the articles to be used in this third edition, we have had invaluable aid from a panel of ten expert reviewers, eminent social psychologists who have used the first and second editions of this book in their own classes and were well aware of the strengths and shortcomings of the material included in the earlier editions. In the end we retained ten articles that appeared in the second edition and brought together twenty new ones. Hence, while there is continuity with the earlier editions, there is also a great deal of new material in the third edition.

We also listened to our reviewers for advice on which Sections to include, expand, or delete. Of the ten Sections in the present volume, eight were also part of the second edition (many of them including different articles), while two—Interpersonal Attraction and Group Processes: Deindividuation, Group-think and War—are new. The ten Sections in this third edition appear to us to deal with concepts and issues that are at the forefront of social-psychological research and knowledge.

Many people have been of invaluable aid in helping us to produce this volume. Our thanks must go first to the authors and publishers of the material included in this collection for permitting us to reprint their work here. Claire Verduin, Bill Hicks, and John Bergez at Brooks/Cole have provided support, encouragement, ideas and occasional sharp nudges—all of which have been much appreciated. The students who read and studied from the first two editions have not been hesitant to give us the benefit of their opinions about the strengths and weaknesses of the book. Though such feedback has occasionally been painful to us, it has always been valuable. Helen Nanashko in Tallahassee and Doreen Lovelace in Nashville have provided not only their typing skills but also their observations on the clarity and appropriateness of the Introductions and Summaries.

Finally, we would like to thank the reviewers of this third edition. They are: Leonard Bickman, Loyola University (Chicago); Ray Bixler, University of Louisville; Keith E. Davis, University of South Carolina; Charles G. McClintock, University of California (Santa Barbara); Sam McFarland, Western Kentucky University; Richard Noel, California State University (Bakersfield); Robert D. Nye, State University College (New Paltz, N. Y.); Ronald W. Rogers, University of Alabama; Joseph E. Trimble, Oklahoma City University; and Robert Wicklund, University of Texas (Austin).

Reviewers of the first edition were: Georgia Babladelis, California State College; Daryl J. Bem, Stanford University; Earl R. Carlson, California State College; Philip S. Gallo, Jr., San Diego State College; Chester A. Insko, University of North Carolina; Bhuwan Joshi, University of California, Santa Cruz; and Harry C. Triandis, of the University of Illinois.

The reviewers of the second edition were Les Herold, California State College at San Bernardino; Lance K. Canon, University of Washington; Robert Wicklund, University of Texas (Austin); Samuel Komorita, Indiana University; Philip Gallo, San Diego State College; Harry C. Triandis, University of Illinois; Dalmas Taylor, University of Maryland; Daryl J. Bem, Stanford University; and Frances Hill, University of Montana.

John C. Brigham
Lawrence S. Wrightsman

TO THE STUDENT

The past two decades have witnessed massive upheavals and transitions in United States and Canadian society. On the international front, the Vietnam War of the 1960s and early 1970s brought the tragic realities of war to the forefront of national consciousness. The tragic My Lai massacre in 1968, involving Lt. William Calley and other United States soldiers, shocked and revolted many citizens—even while similar actions were ignored because of lack of publicity. On a more analytical level, many people wondered how the "best and brightest" minds in the government of the United States could have conceived and approved the disastrous invasion of Cuba at the Bay of Pigs in 1961 or involved the nation in the escalating conflict that became the Vietnam War.

On the national front, a series of tragic and seemingly senseless events have raised painful questions about our society, its institutions, and the factors that help to determine our behavior. The assassinations of national political leaders—John F. Kennedy, Martin Luther King, Jr., and Robert Kennedy—and the attempted assassinations of George Wallace and Gerald Ford have made us more acutely aware of the role that aggression and violence continue to play in contemporary society. The massacre at Attica Prison in New York in 1971, where 34 inmates were killed by police, national guardsmen, and prison guards, has confronted us with the still unresolved issue of how to control the violence and feelings of dehumanization associated with institutions such as prisons. News accounts describing provocative cases in which people were injured or killed because no one came forth to help them, such as the widely publicized murder of Kitty Genovese in New York in 1964, have raised other, equally disturbing questions about the structure of our society and the behavior of our fellow citizens.

In the past two decades, major social movements also swept through the United States and Canada. Although perhaps not as spectacular as the incidents we have mentioned above, they will likely have an even greater influence on the restructuring of contemporary society. In particular, the civil rights movement and the "women's liberation" movement have had a dramatic impact on the attitudes and behavior of men and women, majority- and minority-group members alike. In academic circles, much controversy and acrimony have been sparked by the recent debate over the role of intelligence-test scores in predicting achievements of minority-group members. Since the publication of Arthur Jensen's controversial article in 1968, much has been said and written about the role of "Jensenism" in creating or denying conditions of equal educational opportunity for all citizens.

The concepts of *conformity, compliance,* and *attitude change* have become particularly prominent in the political and social realm. Both the commercial use of increasingly sophisticated advertising techniques and their application to mass-media campaigns and the "selling" of political candidates have raised new questions about the efficacy and morality of available persuasion techniques. The concept of attitude change has also been noteworthy in the more frightening sense of the "brainwashing" of political or military prisoners. For many of us this became a particularly salient issue when, during the Vietnam War, captured U. S. military men were subjected to Communist propaganda barrages, and when North Korean forces captured—and elicited "confessions" from—the crew of the United States spy ship *Pueblo* in 1968.

Finally, the Watergate scandal of the early 1970s, which eventually led to the resignation of President Nixon and the conviction of a number of high campaign and government officials for various wrongdoings, has brought the concepts of conformity and obedience into still sharper focus. The question was asked again and again: how could intelligent, hard-working people have been drawn into this disastrous caper and its aftermath?

In recent years social psychologists have been actively involved in seeking answers to the questions raised by events such as these. The articles we have chosen for inclusion in this book not only represent high-quality research—well-written, interesting, and conceptually and methodologically sound—but also represent attempts by social psychologists to grapple with important contemporary issues. The "logical leap" between interpreting the results of a laboratory research study and understanding societal events is obviously a large one. Nevertheless, the knowledge obtained from research like that described in this book can provide both invaluable data and an objective frame of reference for increasing our understanding of the complexities of our society.

CONTENTS

HOW TO READ A SCIENTIFIC RESEARCH REPORT

Each article reprinted in this book was written by a psychologist or group of psychologists with the intent of communicating their theories or findings to their peers. Scientific writing, like all other forms, has its specific style and format. The undergraduate student who has not read many scientific journal articles in the past may profit from studying this brief section before starting to read the articles reprinted in this book. Although all the articles in this book are scientific in intent, some are review articles or speculative pieces, whereas others report empirical findings in detail. The first type is easier to read; such articles may possess some personal style, and there is permitted some deviation from the formal restrictions of style and format that must be maintained in the reports of empirical findings. It is the reading of the second type, called the research report, that we will discuss in detail here.

Notice that every research report is organized as follows:

1. An introduction, which sets forth the purpose of the study, defines terms, reviews relevant past research, and sets forth hypotheses that will be tested by the study.
2. A Procedure section, which describes the subjects who participated in the study, the methods used to test the hypotheses, and the instruments (tests, equipment, and so on) employed.
3. A Results section, which employs statistical techniques to determine and report the outcomes of the hypotheses. Basically, the Results section reports whether each of the study's hypotheses was confirmed or disconfirmed. Other important empirical findings are also presented in the Results section.
4. A Discussion section, which evaluates and interprets the findings presented in the Results section. Here is the place where the findings are put "in context"; for example, they may be related to the findings of other studies. Particularly if hypotheses are not confirmed, the Discussion section is the appropriate place for the researcher to offer explanations for the findings. And the Discussion section almost inevitably ends with something to the effect that, before we have a complete understanding of the phenomenon under study, "further research is necessary."

The Results and Discussion sections are sometimes collapsed together. Some articles contain a Summary and Conclusions section, and all articles end with a list of references.

It is suggested that, when you are ready to read a research report in this book, you do the following:

1. Read the title of the article and then quickly skim through it to obtain a general idea of the researcher's purpose and findings.
2. Next, reread the Section Introduction and the Section Summary, which will usually deal succinctly with the main points in each of the articles in that section.
3. At this point you should identify the hypotheses of the study and be sure you understand them. Then you should determine, for each hypothesis, whether the

Adapted from *Reading for Meaning in College and After*, by J. R. Strange and S. M. Strange. Copyright © 1972 by Wadsworth Publishing Company, Inc. Reprinted by permission of the publisher, Brooks/Cole Publishing Company, Monterey, California. We wish to thank Jack and Sallie Strange for giving us permission to adapt their suggestions.

findings confirmed or disconfirmed it. This is done by reading relevant sections of the Results and Discussion sections. In addition, you should attempt to understand the study's experimental design and controls, its procedures, and its instruments.

4. Now carefully read the article in its entirety. The organization of the article—the reason for the sections appearing as they do—should be more apparent now. You may find that utilization of the references at the end of the article is necessary if you wish a thorough understanding of procedures, data analyses, and findings. Because space is limited in journals, a research report will often refer the reader to an earlier article that used the same procedure, rather than reprint it in detail. Likewise, the justifiability of certain statistical techniques may be indicated by references to other articles or books.

5. Last of all, underline the important points of the research report. Preparing a brief summary of the article, which deals with the hypotheses, procedures, results, and conclusions, is a good way of developing an integrated understanding of the study.

The statistical techniques and analyses in some of the articles may be beyond your level of training. However, if you follow the above suggestions, you should still be able to understand the thrust of the article.

SECTION I

HELPING BEHAVIOR

INTRODUCTION

In our complex, urbanized, and fast-paced society, we all depend on others a great deal. The study of the factors that may facilitate or inhibit such interdependence has become of prime interest to social scientists. One important aspect of this picture is the study of the conditions under which people will choose to help or refuse to help others.

Much recent attention has focused on helping behavior within one very specific context: that of an emergency situation. This research interest has stemmed rather directly from the grave concern and puzzlement produced by reports in recent years of seemingly bizarre events—tragic cases in which individuals in dire need of help from others have gone unaided, even as dozens of people witnessed their plight. The end result of this failure to give aid has often been the further injury or even the death of the person in the emergency situation.

Probably the most widely known case of this sort occurred in 1964, when Kitty Genovese was murdered near her home in New York City at 3:30 A.M. Her assailant took more than half an hour to murder her, and her screams for help were heard by at least 38 of her neighbors. Nobody came directly to her aid; in fact, no one even called the police. (Rosenthal [1964] has written a book about this incident.) Do occurrences such as this reflect growing apathy, callousness, and lack of concern for others in modern urban society? Or are there other factors that may contribute to such an appalling lack of response?

Bibb Latané and John Darley, two social psychologists who were then at Columbia University and New York University, respectively, initiated a program of research to attempt to answer such questions. They began by trying to identify the special characteristics that differentiate an emergency situation from a nonemergency situation (Latané & Darley, 1969, 1970): (1) An emergency involves threat or harm. There are relatively few positive payoffs for the witness who makes a successful action in an emergency; usually, the best that can be hoped for is a return to the status quo. (2) Emergencies are unusual and rare events, and people will have had little personal experience in handling such situations. (3) Emergencies differ widely from one another. Each emergency (for example, a drowning, a fire, an assault) presents a different type of problem, and each requires a different type of action by the witness. (4) Emergencies are unforeseen; they emerge suddenly and without warning. Hence they must be handled without the benefit of forethought or planning. (5) An emergency requires instant action; the witnesses must come to a decision before they have had time to consider their alternatives. It places each of them in a condition of stress. All of these characteristics provide good reasons for a person *not* to intervene. As Latané and Darley (1969) have commented, "the bystander to an emergency situation is in an unenviable position. It is perhaps surprising that anyone should intervene at all" (p. 247).

In the first article in this Section, Latané and Darley describe three studies that they carried out to assess the effects of different situational variables on the likelihood of bystander intervention in emergencies. As you will see, their results suggest that *apathy* is not a wholly accurate term for describing cases in which bystanders do not intervene. Rather, they propose, there are two distinct *social processes—pluralistic ignorance* and *diffusion of responsibility*—that play a major role in emergency situations. Both of these processes involve the effect of *other* bystanders on the likelihood that a bystander will help in an emergency. The presence of these other bystanders may affect both the amount of responsibility for helping that an individual feels and whether he or she even interprets an ambiguous situation as a real emergency.

But the presence or absence of other bystanders is not the only important aspect of an emergency situation. The second article, by Russell D. Clark, III, and Larry E. Word of Florida State University, highlights the crucial importance of *ambiguity*— that is, how clear it is that a real emergency is taking place. Clark and Word found, in this study as well as in an earlier one (Clark & Word, 1972), that when an emergency situation was not ambiguous almost everyone helped. When the emergency situation *was* ambiguous, Clark and Word found some evidence of the social processes described by Latané and Darley.

The numerous forces inherent in urban living are discussed on a broader scale in the article by Stanley Milgram, who is now at the Graduate Center of the City University of New York. The key concept that he describes is *overload,* the inability of a system (such as a person) to process inputs from the environment because they are too numerous to cope with or because they arrive in too rapid succession. Milgram points out that lack of trust, lack of civility, and bystander nonintervention may all be adaptive responses by city dwellers to such overload.

REFERENCES

Clark, R. D., III, & Word, L. E. Why don't bystanders help? Because of ambiguity? *Journal of Personality and Social Psychology,* 1972, *24,* 392–400.

Latané, B., & Darley, J. M. Bystander "apathy." *American Scientist,* 1969, *57,* 244–268.

Latané, B., & Darley, J. M. *The unresponsive bystander: Why doesn't he help?* New York: Appleton-Century-Crofts, 1970.

Rosenthal, A. M. *Thirty-eight witnesses.* New York: McGraw-Hill, 1964.

ARTICLE 1

Social determinants of bystander intervention in emergencies[1]

Bibb Latané
John M. Darley

Almost 100 years ago, Charles Darwin wrote: "As man is a social animal, it is almost certain that he would . . . from an inherited tendency be willing to defend, in concert with others, his fellow-men; and be ready to aid them in any way, which did not too greatly interfere with his own welfare or his own strong desires" *(The Descent of Man).* Today, although many psychologists would quarrel with Darwin's assertion that altruism is inherited, most would agree that men will go to the aid of others even when there is no visible gain for themselves. At least, most would have agreed until a March night in 1964. That night, Kitty Genovese was set upon by a maniac as she returned home from work at 3:00 A.M. Thirty-eight of her neighbors in Kew Gardens came to their windows when she cried out in terror; but none came to her assistance, even though her stalker took over half an hour to murder her. No one even so much as called the police.

Since we started our research on bystander response to emergencies, we have heard about dozens of such incidents. We have also heard many explanations: "I would assign this to the effect of the megalopolis in which we live, which makes closeness very difficult and leads to the alienation of the individual from the group," contributed a psychoanalyst. "A disaster syndrome," explained a soicologist, "that shook the sense of safety and sureness of the individuals involved and caused psychological withdrawal from the event by ignoring it." "Apathy," others claim. "Indifference." "The gratification of unconscious sadistic impulses." "Lack of concern for our fellow men." "The Cold Society." These explanations and many more have been applied to the surprising failure of bystanders to intervene in emergencies—failures which suggest that we no longer care about the fate of our neighbors.

From *Altruism and Helping Behavior,* by J. R. Macaulay and L. Berkowitz (Eds.). Copyright 1970 by Academic Press, Inc. Reprinted by permission.

[1]The research reported in this paper was supported by National Science Foundation Grants GS1238, GS1239, GS2292, and GS2293, and was conducted at Columbia University and New York University.

But can this be so? We think not. Although it is unquestionably true that the witnesses in the incidents above did nothing to save the victim, "apathy," "indifference," and "unconcern" are not entirely accurate descriptions of their reactions. The 38 witnesses of Kitty Genovese's murder did not merely look at the scene once and then ignore it. Instead they continued to stare out of their windows at what was going on. Caught, fascinated, distressed, unwilling to act but unable to turn away, their behavior was neither helpful nor heroic; but it was not indifferent or apathetic either.

Actually it was like crowd behavior in many other emergency situations; car accidents, drownings, fires, and attempted suicides all attract substantial numbers of people who watch the drama in helpless fascination without getting directly involved in the action. Are these people alienated and indifferent? Are the rest of us? Obviously not. It seems only yesterday we were being called overconforming. But why, then, do we not act?

Paradoxically, the key to understanding these failures of intervention may be found exactly in the fact that so surprises us about them: so many bystanders fail to intervene. If we think of 38, or 11, or 100 individuals, each looking at an emergency and callously deciding to pass by, we are horrified. But if we realize that each bystander is picking up cues about what is happening and how to react to it from the other bystanders, understanding begins to emerge. There are several ways in which a crowd of onlookers can make each individual member of that crowd less likely to act.

DEFINING THE SITUATION

Most emergencies are, or at least begin as, ambiguous events. A quarrel in the street may erupt into violence or it may be simply a family argument. A man staggering about may be suffering a coronary, or an onset of diabetes, or he simply may be drunk. Smoke pouring from a building may signal a fire, but on the other hand, it may be simply steam or airconditioner vapor. Before a bystander is likely to take action in such ambiguous situations, he must first define the event as an emergency and decide that intervention is the proper course of action.

In the course of making these decisions, it is likely that an individual bystander will be considerably influenced by the decisions he perceives other bystanders to be taking. If everyone else in a group of onlookers seems to regard an event as nonserious and the proper course of action as nonintervention, this consensus may strongly affect the perceptions of any single individual and inhibit his potential intervention.

The definitions that other people held may be discovered by discussing the situation with them, but they may also be inferred from their facial expressions or behavior. A whistling man with his hands in his pockets obviously does not believe he is in the midst of a crisis. A bystander who does not respond to smoke obviously does not attribute it to fire. An individual, seeing the inaction of others, will judge the situation as less serious than he would if alone.

But why should the others be inactive? Probably because they are aware that other people are also watching them. The others are an audience to their own reactions. Among American males, it is considered desirable to appear poised and collected in times of stress. Being exposed to the public view may constrain the actions and expressions of emotion of any individual as he tries to avoid possible ridicule and embarrassment. Even though he may be truly concerned and upset about the plight of a victim, until he decides what to do, he may maintain a calm demeanor.

If each member of a group is, at the same time, trying to appear calm and also looking around at the other members to gauge their reactions, all members may be led (or misled) by each other to define the situation as less critical than they would if alone. Until someone acts, each person sees only other nonresponding bystanders and is likely to be influenced not to act himself. A state of "pluralistic ignorance" may develop.

It has often been recognized that a crowd can cause contagion of panic, leading each person in the crowd to overreact to an emergency to the detriment of everyone's welfare. What we suggest here is that a crowd can also force inaction on its members. It can suggest by its passive behavior that an event is not to be reacted to as an emergency, and it can make any individual uncomfortably aware of what a fool he will look for behaving as if it is.

*Where There's Smoke, There's
(Sometimes) Fire*[2]

In this experiment we presented an emergency to individuals either alone or in groups of three. It was our expectation that the constraints on behavior in public combined with social influence processes would lessen the likelihood that members of three-person groups would act to cope with the emergency.

College students were invited to an interview to discuss "some of the problems involved in life at an urban university." As they sat in a small room waiting to be called for the interview and filling out a preliminary questionnaire, they faced an ambiguous but potentially dangerous situation. A stream of smoke began to puff into the room through a wall vent.

Some subjects were exposed to this potentially critical situation while alone. In a second condition, three naive subjects were tested together. Since subjects arrived at slightly different times, and since they each had individual questionnaires to work on, they did not introduce themselves to each other or attempt anything but the most rudimentary conversation.

As soon as the subjects had completed two pages of their questionnaires, the experimenter began to introduce the smoke through a small vent in the wall. The "smoke," copied from the famous Camel

cigarette sign in Times Square, formed a moderately fine-textured but clearly visible stream of whitish smoke. It continued to jet into the room in irregular puffs, and by the end of the experimental period, it obscured vision.

All behavior and conversation were observed and coded from behind a one-way window (largely disguised on the subject's side by a large sign giving preliminary instructions). When and if the subject left the experimental room and reported the smoke, he was told that the situation "would be taken care of." If the subject had not reported the smoke within 6 minutes from the time he first noticed it, the experiment was terminated.

The typical subject, when tested alone, behaved very reasonably. Usually, shortly after the smoke appeared, he would glance up from his questionnaire, notice the smoke, show a slight but distinct startle reaction, and then undergo a brief period of indecision, perhaps returning briefly to his questionnaire before again staring at the smoke. Soon, most subjects would get up from their chairs, walk over to the vent and investigate it closely, sniffing the smoke, waving their hands in it, feeling its temperature, etc. The usual Alone subject would hesitate again, but finally would walk out of the room, look around outside, and, finding somebody there, calmly report the presence of the smoke. No subject showed any sign of panic; most simply said: "There's something strange going on in there, there seems to be some sort of smoke coming through the wall. . . ." The median subject in the Alone condition had reported the smoke within 2 minutes of first noticing it. Three-quarters of the 24 people run in this condition reported the smoke before the experimental period was terminated.

Because there are three subjects present and available to report smoke in the Three Naive Bystanders condition as compared to only one subject at a time in the Alone condition, a simple comparison between the two conditions is not appropriate. We cannot compare speeds in the Alone condition with the average speed of the three subjects in a group because, once one subject in a group had re-

---

[2]A more complete account of this experiment is provided in Latané and Darley (1968). Keith Gerritz and Lee Ross provided thoughtful assistance in running the study.

ported the smoke, the pressures on the other two disappeared. They could feel legitimately that the emergency had been handled and that any action on their part would be redundant and potentially confusing. Therefore, we used the speed of the first subject in a group to report the smoke as our dependent variable. However, since there were three times as many people available to respond in this condition as in the Alone condition, we would expect an increased likelihood that at least one person would report the smoke by chance alone. Therefore, we mathematically created "groups" of three scores from the Alone condition to serve as a baseline.[3]

In contrast to the complexity of this procedure, the results were quite simple. Subjects in the three-person-group condition were markedly inhibited from reporting the smoke. Since 75% of the Alone subjects reported the smoke, we would expect over 98% of the three-person groups to include at least one reporter. In fact, in only 38% of the eight groups in this condition did even one person report ($p < .01$). Of the 24 people run in these eight groups, only one person reported the smoke within the first 4 minutes before the room got noticeably unpleasant. Only three people reported the smoke within the entire experimental period. Social inhibition of reporting was so strong that the smoke was reported faster when only one person saw it than when groups of three were present ($p < .01$).

Subjects who had reported the smoke were relatively consistent in later describing their reactions to it. They thought the smoke looked somewhat "strange." They were not sure exactly what it was or whether it was dangerous, but they felt it was unusual enough to justify some examination. "I wasn't sure whether it was a fire, but it looked like something was wrong." "I thought it might be

steam, but it seemed like a good idea to check it out."

Subjects who had not reported the smoke were also unsure about exactly what it was, but they uniformly said that they had rejected the idea that it was a fire. Instead, they hit upon an astonishing variety of alternative explanations, all sharing the common characteristic of interpreting the smoke as a nondangerous event. Many thought the smoke was either steam or airconditioning vapors, several thought it was smog, purposely introduced to simulate an urban environment, and two actually suggested that the smoke was a "truth gas" filtered into the room to induce them to answer the questionnaire accurately! Predictably, some decided that "it must be some sort of experiment" and stoically endured the discomfort of the room rather than overreact.

The results of this study clearly support the prediction. Groups of three naive subjects were less likely to report the smoke than solitary bystanders. Our predictions were confirmed—but this does not necessarily mean that our explanation of these results is the correct one. As a matter of fact, several alternative explanations center around the fact that the smoke represented a possible danger to the subject himself as well as to others in the building. For instance, it is possible that the subjects in groups saw themselves as engaged in a game of "chicken" in which the first person to report would admit his cowardliness. Or it may have been that the presence of others made subjects feel safer, and thus reduced their need to report.

To rule out such explanations, a second experiment was designed to see whether similar group inhibition effects could be observed in situations where there is no danger to the individual himself for not acting. In this study, male Columbia University undergraduates waited either alone or with a stranger to participate in a market research study. As they waited they heard a woman fall and apparently injure herself in the room next door. Whether they tried to help and how long they took to do so were the main dependent variables of the study.

---

[3]The formula for calculating the expected proportion of groups in which at least one person will have acted by a given time is $1 - (1 - p)^n$ where p is the proportion of single individuals who acted by that time and n is the number of persons in the group.

The Fallen Woman[4]

Subjects were telephoned and offered $2 to participate in a survey of game and puzzle preferences conducted at Columbia by the Consumer Testing Bureau (CTB), a market research organization. When they arrived, they were met at the door by an attractive young woman and taken to the testing room. On the way, they passed the CTB office, and through its open door they were able to see a desk and bookcase piled high with papers and filing cabinets. They entered the adjacent testing room, which contained a table and chairs and a variety of games, and they were given questionnaires to fill out. The representative told subjects that she would be working next door in her office for about 10 minutes while they were completing the questionnaire and left by opening the collapsible curtain which divided the two rooms. She made sure that subjects were aware that the curtain was unlocked and easily opened and that it provided a means of entry to her office. The representative stayed in her office, shuffling papers, opening drawers, and making enough noise to remind the subjects of her presence. Four minutes after leaving the testing area, she turned on a high fidelity stereophonic tape recorder.

The Emergency. If the subject listened carefully, he heard the representative climb up on a chair to reach for a stack of papers on the bookcase. Even if he were not listening carefully, he heard a loud crash and a scream as the chair collapsed and she fell to the floor. "Oh, my God, my foot . . . I . . . I . . . can't move . . . it. Oh . . . my ankle," the representative moaned. "I . . . can't get this . . . thing . . . off me." She cried and moaned for about a minute longer, but the cries gradually got more subdued and controlled. Finally she muttered something about getting outside, knocked over the chair as she pulled herself up and thumped to the door,

[4]This experiment is more fully described in Latané and Rodin (1969).

closing it behind her as she left. The entire incident took 130 seconds.

The main dependent variable of the study, of course, was whether the subjects took action to help the victim and how long it took them to do so. There were actually several modes of intervention possible: a subject could open the screen dividing the two rooms, leave the testing room and enter the CTB office by the door, find someone else, or most simply, call out to see if the representative needed help. In one condition, each subject was in the testing room alone while he filled out the questionnaire and heard the fall. In the second condition, strangers were placed in the testing room in pairs. Each subject in the pair was unacquainted with the other before entering the room and they were not introduced.

Across all experimental groups, the majority of subjects who intervened did so by pulling back the room divider and coming into the CTB office (61%). Few subjects came the round-about way through the door to offer their assistance (14%) and a surprisingly small number (24%) chose the easy solution of calling out to offer help. No one tried to find someone else to whom to report the accident.

Since 70% of the Alone subjects intervened, we should expect that at least one person in 91% of all two-person groups would offer help if members of a pair had no influence upon each other. In fact, members did influence each other. In only 40% of the groups did even one person offer help to the injured woman. Only eight subjects of the 40 who were run in this condition intervened. This response rate is significantly below the hypothetical baseline ($p < .001$). Social inhibition of helping was so strong that the victim was actually helped more quickly when only one person heard her distress than when two did ($p < .01$).

When we talked to subjects after the experiment, those who intervened usually claimed that they did so either because the fall sounded very serious or because they were uncertain what had occurred and felt they should investigate. Many talked about intervention as the "right thing to do" and asserted they would help again in any situation.

Many of the noninterveners also claimed that they were unsure what had happened (59%), but had decided that it was not too serious (46%). A number of subjects reported that they thought other people would or could help (25%), and three said they refrained out of concern for the victim—they did not want to embarrass her. Whether to accept these explanations as reasons or rationalizations is moot— they certainly do not explain the differences among conditions. The important thing to note is that noninterveners did not seem to feel that they had behaved callously or immorally. Their behavior was generally consistent with their interpretation of the situation. Subjects almost uniformly claimed that in a "real" emergency they would be among the first to help the victim.

These results strongly replicate the findings of the Smoke study. In both experiments, subjects were less likely to take action if they were in the presence of others than if they were alone. This congruence of findings from different experimental settings supports the validity and generality of the phenomenon; it also helps rule out a variety of alternative explanations suitable to either situation alone. For example, the possibility that smoke may have represented a threat to the subject's personal safety and that subjects in groups may have had a greater concern to appear "brave" than single subjects does not apply to the present experiment. In the present experiment, nonintervention cannot signify bravery. Comparison of the two experiments also suggests that the absolute number of nonresponsive bystanders may not be a critical factor in producing social inhibition of intervention; pairs of strangers in the present study inhibited each other as much as did trios in the former study.

Other studies we have done show that group inhibition effects hold in real life as well as in the laboratory, and for members of the general population as well as college students. The results of these experiments clearly support the line of theoretical argument advanced earlier. When bystanders to an emergency can see the reactions of other people, and when other people can see their own reactions, each individual may, through a process of social influence, be led to interpret the situation as less serious than he would if he were alone, and consequently be less likely to take action.

These studies, however, tell us little about the case that stimulated our interest in bystander intervention: the Kitty Genovese murder. Although the 38 witnesses to that event were aware, through seeing lights and silhouettes in other windows, that others watched, they could not see what others were doing and thus be influenced by their reactions. In the privacy of their own apartments, they could not be clearly seen by others, and thus inhibited by their presence. The social influence process we have described above could not operate. Nevertheless, we think that the presence of other bystanders may still have affected each individual's response.

DIFFUSION OF RESPONSIBILITY

In addition to affecting the interpretations that he places on a situation, the presence of other people can also alter the rewards and costs facing an individual bystander. Perhaps most importantly, the presence of other people can reduce the cost of not acting. If only one bystander is present at an emergency, he carries all of the responsibility for dealing with it; he will feel all of the guilt for not acting; he will bear all of any blame others may level for nonintervention. If others are present, the onus of responsibility is diffused, and the individual may be more likely to resolve his conflict between intervening and not intervening in favor of the latter alternative.

When only one bystander is present at an emergency, if help is to come it must be from him. Although he may choose to ignore them out of concern for his personal safety, or desire "not to get involved," any pressures to intervene focus uniquely on him. When there are several observers present, however, the pressures to intervene do not focus on any one of the observers; instead, the responsibility for intervention is shared among all the on-lookers and is not unique to any one. As a result, each may be less likely to help.

Potential blame may also be diffused. However much we wish to think that an individual's moral behavior is divorced from considerations of personal punishment or reward, there is both theory and evidence to the contrary. It is perfectly reasonable to assume that under circumstances of group responsibility for a punishable act, the punishment or blame that accrues to any one individual is often slight or nonexistent.

Finally, if others are known to be present, but their behavior cannot be closely observed, any one bystander may assume that one of the other observers is already taking action to end the emergency. If so, his own intervention would only be redundant—perhaps harmfully or confusingly so. Thus, given the presence of other onlookers whose behavior cannot be observed, any given bystander can rationalize his own inaction by convincing himself that "somebody else must be doing something."

These considerations suggest that even when bystanders to an emergency cannot see or be influenced by each other, the more bystanders who are present, the less likely any one bystander would be to intervene and provide aid. To test this suggestion, it would be necessary to create an emergency situation in which each subject is blocked from communicating with others to prevent his getting information about their behavior during the emergency.

A Fit to Be Tried[5]

A college student arrived in the laboratory, and was ushered into an individual room from which a communication system would enable him to talk to other participants (who were actually figments of the tape recorder). Over the intercom, the subject was told that the experimenter was concerned with

[5]Further details of this experiment can be found in Darley and Latané (1968).

the kinds of personal problems faced by normal college students in a high-pressure, urban environment, and that he would be asked to participate in a discussion about these problems. To avoid embarrassment about discussing personal problems with strangers, the experimenter said, several precautions would be taken. First, subjects would remain anonymous, which was why they had been placed in individual rooms rather than face-to-face. Second, the experimenter would not listen to the initial discussion himself, but would only get the subject's reactions later by questionnaire.

The plan for the discussion was that each person would talk in turn for 2 minutes, presenting his problems to the group. Next, each person in turn would comment on what others had said, and finally there would be a free discussion. A mechanical switching device regulated the discussion, switching on only one microphone at a time.

The Emergency. The discussion started with the future victim speaking first. He said he found it difficult to get adjusted to New York and to his studies. Very hesitantly and with obvious embarrassment, he mentioned that he was prone to seizures, particularly when studying hard or taking exams. The other people, including the one real subject, took their turns and discussed similar problems (minus the proneness to seizures). The naive subject talked last in the series, after the last prerecorded voice.

When it was again the victim's turn to talk, he made a few relatively calm comments, and then, growing increasingly loud and incoherent, he continued:

I er I think I I need er if if could er er somebody er er er er er er er give me a little er give me a little help here because I er I'm er er h-h-having a a a a real problem er right now and I er if somebody could help me out it would er er s-s-sure be sure be good . . . because er there er er a cause I er I uh I've got a a a one of the er sei . . . er er things coming on and and and I could really er use some help so if somebody would er give me a little h-help uh er-er-er-er-er c-could somebody er er help er uh uh uh (Choking sounds). . . . I'm gonna die er er I'm . . . gonna die er help er er seizure (chokes, then quiet).

The major independent variable of the study was the number of people the subject believed also heard the fit. The subject was led to believe that the discussion group was one of three sizes: a two-person group consisting of himself and the victim; a three-person group consisting of himself, the victim and the other person; or a six-person group consisting of himself, the victim, and four other persons.

The major dependent variable of the experiment was the time elapsed from the start of the victim's seizure until the subject left his experimental cubicle. When the subject left his room, he saw the experimental assistant seated at the end of the hall, and invariably went to the assistant to report the seizure. If 5 minutes elapsed without the subject's having emerged from his room, the experiment was terminated.

Ninety-five percent of all the subjects who ever responded did so within the first half of the time available to them. No subject who had not reported within 3 minutes after the fit ever did so. This suggests that even had the experiment been allowed to run for a considerably longer period of time, few additional subjects would have responded.

Eighty-five percent of the subjects who thought they alone knew of the victim's plight reported the seizure before the victim was cut off; only 31% of those who thought four other bystanders were present did so. Every one of the subjects in the two-person condition, but only 62% of the subjects in the six-person condition ever reported the emergency. To do a more detailed analysis of the results, each subject's time score was transformed into a "speed" score by taking the reciprocal of the response time in seconds and multiplying by 100. Analysis of variance of these speed scores indicates that the effect of group size was highly significant ($p < .01$), and all three groups differed significantly one from another ($p < .05$).

Subjects, whether or not they intervened, be-

lieved the fit to be genuine and serious. "My God, he's having a fit," many subjects said to themselves (and we overheard via their microphones). Others gasped or simply said, "Oh." Several of the male subjects swore. One subject said to herself, "It's just my kind of luck, something has to happen to me!" Several subjects spoke aloud of their confusion about what course of action to take: "Oh, God, what should I do?"

When those subjects who intervened stepped out of their rooms, they found the experimental assistant down the hall. With some uncertainty but without panic, they reported the situation. "Hey, I think Number 1 is very sick. He's having a fit or something." After ostensibly checking on the situation, the experimenter returned to report that "everything is under control." The subjects accepted these assurances with obvious relief.

Subjects who failed to report the emergency showed few signs of the apathy and indifference thought to characterize "unresponsive bystanders." When the experimenter entered her room to terminate the situation, the subject often asked if the victim was all right. "Is he being taken care of?" "He's all right, isn't he?" Many of these subjects showed physical signs of nervousness; they often had trembling hands and sweating palms. If anything, they seemed more emotionally aroused than did the subjects who reported the emergency.

Why, then, didn't they respond? It is not our impression that they had decided not to respond. Rather, they were still in a state of indecision and conflict concerning whether to respond or not. The emotional behavior of these nonresponding subjects was a sign of their continuing conflict, a conflict that other subjects resolved by responding.

The fit created a conflict situation of the avoidance-avoidance type. On the one hand, subjects worried about the guilt and shame they would feel if they did not help the person in distress. On the other hand, they were concerned not to make fools of themselves by overreacting, not to ruin the ongoing experiment by leaving their intercoms, and not to destroy the anonymous nature of the situation, which the experimenter had earlier stressed as important. For subjects in the two-person condition, the obvious distress of the victim and his need for help were so important that their conflict was easily resolved. For the subjects who knew that there were other bystanders present, the cost of not helping was reduced and the conflict they were in was more acute. Caught between the two negative alternatives of letting the victim continue to suffer or rushing, perhaps foolishly, to help, the nonresponding bystanders vacillated between them rather than choosing not to respond. This distinction may be academic for the victim, since he got no help in either case, but it is an extremely important one for understanding the causes of bystanders' failures to help.

Although subjects experienced stress and conflict during the emergency, their general reactions to it were highly positive. On a questionnaire administered after the experimenter had discussed the nature and purpose of the experiment, every single subject found the experiment either "interesting" or "very interesting" and was willing to participate in similar experiments in the future. All subjects felt that they understood what the experiment was all about and indicated that they thought the deceptions were necessary and justified. All but one felt they were better informed about the nature of psychological research in general.

CONCLUSION

We have suggested two distinct processes which might lead people to be less likely to intervene in an emergency if there are other people present than if they are alone. On the one hand, we suggested that the presence of other people may affect the interpretations each bystander puts on an ambiguous emergency situation. If other people are present at an emergency, each bystander will be guided by their apparent reactions in formulating his own impressions. Unfortunately, their apparent reactions may not be a good indication of their true feelings. It is possible for a state of "pluralistic ignorance" to develop, in which each bystander is led by the apparent lack of concern of the others to interpret the situation as being less serious than he would if alone. To the extent that he does not feel the situation is an emergency, he will be unlikely to take any helpful action.

Even if an individual does decide that an emergency is actually in process and that something ought to be done, he still is faced with the choice of whether he himself will intervene. Here again, the presence of other people may influence him—by reducing the costs associated with nonintervention. If a number of people witness the same event, the responsibility for action is diffused, and each may feel less necessity to help.

"There's safety in numbers," according to an old adage, and modern city dwellers seem to believe it. They shun deserted streets, empty subway cars, and lonely dark walks in dark parks, preferring instead to go where others are or to stay at home. When faced with stress, most individuals seem less afraid when they are in the presence of others than when they are alone.

A feeling so widely shared should have some basis in reality. Is there safety in numbers? If so, why? Two reasons are often suggested: individuals are less likely to find themselves in trouble if there are others about, and even if they do find themselves in trouble, others are likely to help them deal with it. While it is certainly true that a victim is unlikely to receive help if nobody knows of his plight, the experiments above cast doubt on the suggestion that he will be more likely to receive help if more people are present. In fact, the opposite seems to be true. A victim may be more likely to get help, or an emergency be reported, the fewer the people who are available to take action.

Although the results of these studies may shake our faith in "safety in numbers," they also may help us begin to understand a number of frightening incidents where crowds have heard but not answered a call for help. Newspapers have tagged these incidents with the label, "apathy." We have become indifferent, they say, callous to the fate of suffering of others. Our society has become "dehumanized" as it has become urbanized. These glib phrases may contain some truth, since startling cases such as the Genovese murder often seem to occur in our large cities, but such terms may also be misleading. Our studies suggest a different conclusion. They suggest that situational factors, specifically factors involving the immediate social environment, may be of greater importance in determining an individual's reaction to an emergency than such vague cultural or personality concepts as "apathy" or "alienation due to urbanization."

They suggest that the failure to intervene may be better understood by knowing the relationship among bystanders rather than that between a bystander and the victim.

REFERENCES

Darley, J. M., & Latané, B. Bystander intervention in emergencies: Diffusion of responsibility. *Journal of Personality and Social Psychology,* 1968, **8,** 377–383.

Latané, B., & Darley, J. M. Group inhibition of bystander intervention. *Journal of Personality and Social Psychology,* 1968, **10,** 215–221.

Latané, B., & Rodin, J. A lady in distress: Inhibiting effects of friends and strangers on bystander intervention. *Journal of Experimental Social Psychology,* 1969, **5,** 189–202.

ARTICLE 2

Where is the apathetic bystander? Situational characteristics of the emergency

Russell D. Clark, III
Larry E. Word[1]

In the past few years there has been a growing interest among social psychologists concerning the failure of bystanders to help a person in distress. Much of the original research in this field can be attributed to Latané and Darley in a series of unique experiments using male subjects in the New York metropolitan area (Darley & Latané, 1968; Latané & Darley, 1968, 1969, 1970a, 1970b; Latané & Rodin, 1969). The results of their experiments indicate that the failure of individuals in groups to help in emergencies can be attributed either to a process of diffusion of responsibility whereby the presence of others reduces the costs associated with nonintervention or to a process of social influence whereby the presence of others, particularly when they are acting in a calm manner, causes a given individual to misinterpret an ambiguous emergency as nonserious. With either process the likelihood that a given individual will render aid decreases as the number of observers increases.

Most, if not all, of the variables that have been investigated involve relationships among bystanders, that is group size (Latané & Darley, 1970b; Schwartz & Clausen, 1970), group composition (Borofsky, Stollak, & Messé, 1971; Kazdin & Bryan, 1971; Latané & Darley, 1970b; Schwartz & Clausen, 1970; Wispé & Freshley, 1971), perceived responsibility (Bickman, 1971; Korte, 1969; Midlarsky, 1968; Staub, 1970a; Tilker, 1970), and modeling (Bryan & London, 1970; Bryan & Test, 1967; Test & Bryan, 1969). There is no doubt that these factors are very useful in predicting the behavior of persons in emergencies. Yet, there is no a priori reason to assume that they are the most important or the only factors determining whether an individual will help. An illustration of this point would be the evidence that a sizable percentage of alone subjects have failed to intervene

Reprinted and slightly abridged from *Journal of Personality and Social Psychology,* 1974, *29,* pp. 279–287. Copyright 1974 by the American Psychological Association. Reprinted by permission.

[1] The authors deeply appreciate the statistical advice provided by Douglas A. Zahn. Additional thanks go to William Haythorn and Michael Rashotte for their helpful criticisms of an earlier version of this article.

in many laboratory experiments, for example, 25% in Latané and Darley's (1968) smoke study, 30% in Latané and Rodin's (1969) lady in distress study, and 68% in Staub's (1970b) development study. In these conditions the effects of social influence and diffusion of responsibility are negligible.

These results must be contrasted with those obtained by Piliavin, Rodin, and Piliavin (1969). Victims who feigned sickness received help in 62 of 65 sessions even before a "helping model" could be employed. A major difference in this field study and most laboratory situations could be the nonambiguous nature of the emergency.

Evidence of the importance of the situational characteristics of the ambiguity and seriousness of consequences of the emergency to the victim was demonstrated by Clark and Word (1972). They found 100% helping among subjects alone, in two-person groups, and in five-person groups who were exposed to an unmistakable emergency (overhearing a maintenance man fall and cry out in agony). Similar subjects who were confronted with an ambiguous emergency (overhearing an identical fall without the verbal cues indicating that the victim was injured) helped approximately 30% of the time. In the latter condition, when a correction was made for the fact that more persons were present to help in the group conditions, the results demonstrated that alone subjects were more likely to help and responded faster than either the two- or five-person-group helpers. Thus, the inhibiting influence of groups on helping that has been typically found by Latané and Darley (1970b) only occurred in groups who were exposed to an ambiguous emergency. Bystanders who were exposed to a nonambiguous emergency did not misinterpret the event, and, consequently, their behavior was not affected by the presence of others.

Another situational characteristic of emergencies that has been relatively ignored in the literature, yet obviously acts as a suppressant on helping behavior, is the cost of intervention. Depending on the nature of the event in question, the price that a bystander may be forced to pay in order to help another can range from mere inconvenience or possible embarrassment to grave physical harm. This consideration operates as the individual makes his decision whether to help and, in cases where he does react, may mediate his exact response (Piliavin et al., 1969). A study by Denner (1968) revealed that subjects who had witnessed a staged attempted theft and then failed to report it invariably mentioned that they were unsure of what they had seen and feared possible embarrassment. In the Piliavin et al. experiment, the victim who feigned drunkenness was helped less often than the victim who simulated a heart attack. In a similar experiment Piliavin and Piliavin (1972) further demonstrated that a bloody victim received help less often than did a nonbloody victim. These studies suggest that the relative cost involved may inhibit helping behavior.

The purpose of the present experiments was to investigate the effect of ambiguity in a situation where the consequences are severe for the victim and the potential cost for helping by the bystander(s) is high. It was hypothesized that the rate of helping would decrease as the level of ambiguity rose and that the presence of others would lower the probability that a given individual in a moderately ambiguous situation would render aid to the victim. Based on the cost-reward model proposed by Piliavin et al. (1969), we predicted more indirect help when the immediate consequences for helping were high.

OVERVIEW OF EXPERIMENTS 1 AND 2

The subjects, either alone or in two-person groups, were brought to the laboratory ostensibly to validate a test of mental ability. As the subjects were leaving the laboratory upon completing this task, they were exposed to a contrived emergency in which a male technician appeared to receive a severe electric shock. The main independent variables were group size and the magnitude of ambiguity present in the emergency situation. The subjects were exposed to one of three emergencies: *nonambiguous*, *moderate ambiguity*, and *high ambiguity*.

High and low danger for intervening was manipulated only in Experiment 1. The dependent measure in both experiments was the number of trials in which the victim received help in any form.

EXPERIMENT 1

Method

Subjects. A total of 108 male undergraduates at Florida State University participated in the experiment, 11 for each of the four alone conditions and 8 pairs for each of the four group conditions. All were volunteers and received research credits for their participation.

Procedure. The subjects were met in a faculty member's office by one of two female undergraduates who introduced themselves as research assistants. The participants were then informed that they would be validating a test of mental ability originated by the U.S. Navy to screen recruits for clerical skills. The subjects were told that other tests were being administered concurrently and that use of available testing rooms was being coordinated through the faculty member's office. The experimenter then led them to a small laboratory on the floor above where the written test was to be completed. As the subjects reached the top of the stairs they were able to observe a laboratory filled with various items of electronic equipment. Just inside the door a male technician could be seen adjusting a cathode ray oscilloscope.

Within this room various items of electronic equipment were arranged to give the impression of an elaborate operational setup. The apparatus included a Tektronix cathode ray oscilloscope resting on a portable cart just inside the door. A power source, a switchboard, and a receiver from an SB 82/SSR ship radio were located on the floor close to the cart. A John Fluke power supply, an Empire microwave signal generator, and a timing device used for multiple physiological measuring instruments were placed along a shelf against the wall, so that all of the equipment was arranged in a semicircle facing the doorway into the main hall. A series

of wires and cables ran along the floor and appeared to connect the equipment. Although all of the equipment was inoperable, several items had indicator lights that were functioning. The oscilloscope screen was illuminated and obviously visible from the hallway. Numerous high-voltage signs were placed inside and outside of the room.

The room where the test validation was to occur was located 30 feet farther down the hall and around the corner. After the subjects were seated, the experimenter explained the required task in more detail, indicating that an attempt was being made to correlate the Navy test as a predictor of academic achievement and to determine the optimum time limit to be allotted for the measure. To give this task more credibility, the subjects were asked to sign a form that would permit the researchers to obtain their official transcripts for future evaluation. They were further informed that the current session would be under a "minimum time" condition with a limit of 10 minutes in which to complete as many questions as possible. The subjects were aware that other conditions included 30- and 45-minute sessions. The actual test items were taken from the Otis intelligence test. The subjects were told that a large number of individuals were needed to validate the test and that the experimenter would be busy orienting other participants and would not remain with them in the room. The experimenter indicated that an automatic timer would be used to signal the end of the test at which time the subjects were free to leave. She then signed the subjects' credit slips, set the timer, and departed from the room.

The sound of the timer, which could be heard some distance down the hallway, afforded the victim approximately 45 seconds warning of the subjects' approach. The subjects necessarily passed the laboratory when they exited from the building. As they turned the corner just prior to descending the stairs they were facing directly into the laboratory and could observe the victim on his knees with his back to the door making repairs on the small switchboard. The female experimenter was located behind a door within the laboratory where she could clearly see and record the behavior of both the victim and the subjects. When the subjects reached a point outside the laboratory where they could unmistakably view the victim, a signal that was not visible in the hallway was initiated by the experimenter to begin the "emergency." Where helping occurred, both subjects always entered the room to render aid to the victim.

Experimental Conditions. Either one or two subjects were randomly assigned to one of four experimental conditions. In one condition, the nonambiguous, dangerous situation, the subjects observed and heard the victim sustain what appeared to be a serious shock simulated by a flash of light and a dull buzzing sound that emanated from the equipment. The visual cue was produced using a Megalume 7 portable electric flash unit (100-watt-second flash). The "shorting-out" sound resulted from passing 110-volt ac current through a dc relay attached to an empty can. Both of these items were encased in the chassis of a Kepko power supply and connected in series to a push-button switch located on the equipment that the victim appeared to be repairing. The combination of these effects created the distinct impression that an electrical malfunction had occurred within the power supply. Simultaneously, the victim would stiffen his body while giving out a sharp cry of pain, upset the apparatus and his tools, then collapse in a prone position on the floor. The victim feigned unconsciousness and could be observed lying on several wires with one hand resting in the switchboard and the other holding an electronic probe. This condition represented a clear emergency that could be potentially dangerous for the bystander(s).

The second condition, nonambiguous and nondangerous, was identical to the first with the exception that the victim fell completely separated from any portion of the equipment or wiring. Again the subjects perceived a nonambiguous event; however, the potential physical danger of touching the victim was eliminated.

In the third variation of the emergency, moderate ambiguity, the victim was located in one corner of the laboratory out of the subjects' field of vision. The cues perceived from the equipment were identical to the other conditions, but the only information presented to the subjects by the victim was his cry of pain.

The fourth condition, high ambiguity, closely resembled the moderately ambiguous condition with the exception that the verbal cue from the victim was eliminated. Thus, the sound of the victim and the equipment falling was the only direct indication that the laboratory was occupied. In the conditions of moderate and high ambiguity, a subject investigating the situation would be confronted with the victim lying unconscious in contact with the equipment, constituting potential danger.

Dependent Measure. The dependent measure was the percentage of subjects either aiding the victim directly, seeking assistance from others, or leaving the area. Those subjects who rendered immediate and direct aid to the victim by touching him or attempting to interrupt the flow of electrical current were credited with direct help. The subjects who left the scene of the emergency either to report the incident or to obtain assistance from others were considered to have helped the victim indirectly. If a subject passed the series of occupied offices (on the floor below) without attempting to report anything he had seen or heard, it was assumed that no help would be forthcoming. In this event, the downstairs observer would follow the subjects to the ground floor where they were stopped and asked to return to the laboratory to fill out some "additional forms."

Results and Discussion

Two basic questions may be asked when one compares individuals and groups. First, one can ask which is more efficient, the group or the individual. That is, is the victim more likely to receive help if a single bystander is present or if *n* others are present? Here the percentage of alone subjects helping is compared to the number of times that at least one

TABLE 1. Observed and corrected percentages of helping for eight conditions in Experiment 1.

Group size	Levels of ambiguity			
	Nonam-biguous/dangerous	Nonam-biguous/non-dangerous	Moderate ambiguity	High am-biguity
Alone	91	100	36	18
Two-person	100	100	50	50
Corrected two-person	99.9	100	59	33

member helps in a group of n size. The second question is concerned with what effect the presence of others has on an individual's behavior. In terms of reaction to emergency situations, does the group have any inhibiting effect on the probability of an individual within the group helping the victim? As the number of bystanders increases one would expect the percentage of helping to increase on the basis of chance alone. The data were analyzed to answer both questions.

Efficiency Question. The first two rows of Table 1 contain the percentages of help (direct and indirect) afforded by at least one subject per trial to the victim under the eight experimental conditions. . . . More helping occurred in the nonambiguous conditions than in conditions of moderate or high ambiguity ($\chi^2 = 11.69$ and 16.84, respectively, $df = 1$, $p < .001$). In contrast to predictions, the difference between moderate and high ambiguity was less than 1. In short, the results indicated that complete elimination of the visual stimulus (the victim), which indicated that someone was hurt, dramatically lowered the rate of helping.[2]

[2] A prior analysis included the variables of experimenters and type of help (direct help, indirect help, and no help). The main effect and interactions for experimenters were statistically insignificant. The main effects of type of help and ambiguity and their interaction were significant. There was a tendency for subjects to help directly. Sixty-three percent of the helpers did so directly ($\chi^2 = 3.40$, $df = 1$, $p < .10$). However, direct and indirect help did not interact with either group size or levels of ambiguity.

Effect of the Group on the Individual. To determine what effect, if any, the group may have had on the individual, it was necessary to correct the percentages obtained from the two-person-group conditions in order to account for the fact that there were more persons physically present who could potentially react to the emergency. The formula $1 - (1 - p)^n$, where p is the probability of the behavior occurring in the alone condition and n is the size of the group, was used to estimate the corrected percentage assuming that each individual's behavior is independent of others in the group (Latané & Darley, 1968). The second and third rows of Table 1 show the observed and corrected percentages of helping behavior for the group conditions.

In the nonambiguous-group conditions, the observed percentages of helping (100%) were identical to the expected percentages. The corresponding values in the condition of moderate ambiguity (50% and 59%) were insignificant when subjected to a binomial test ($p = .43$). The largest discrepancy occurred for groups in the highly ambiguous condition. However, this difference was in the opposite direction than that found in previous studies; that is, more helping occurred (50%) than was expected (33%), although the difference was not statistically significant (binomial test, $p = .25$). Thus, in each of the four experimental conditions, the presence of another individual did not significantly affect the likelihood that a given individual would help.

The relatively low rate of helping observed in the moderately ambiguous conditions was puzzling. In reevaluating the debriefing comments of individuals exposed to moderately ambiguous emergencies, it could not be determined if all of the subjects heard the verbal cue from the victim. It is possible that the noise of the overturning equipment may have masked this important stimulus in some cases. Also, the nature of the dependent measure (the initial touching of the victim) may not have allowed for a complete behavioral assessment of the subjects' perception of cost. Attempts were made to eliminate these problems in the following experiment.

EXPERIMENT 2

Method

Subjects. Seventy-two male subjects were recruited from the general student population at Florida State University with 8 subjects being assigned to each of the three alone conditions and 8 pairs to each of the three group conditions. Prospective subjects were approached at random on campus and asked to participate in a validation of a mental ability test to be used by the university administration for evaluating first-year students. Individuals were told that a $2 fee would be paid for the single session and were asked to make a convenient appointment. To insure against friends signing up for the group conditions, the subjects were approached individually.

Procedure. The procedure was very similar to the one used in Experiment 1. Therefore, only the changes made are reported. First, the rooms used for the experimental setting were shifted to the opposite end of the same building. The relationship as well as the approximate distances between the laboratory where the staged accident occurred and the room in which the unrelated task was conducted were virtually identical. Second, the two female experimenters and the victim were different from those in the previous experiment. Third, to insure that the discriminating stimulus in the moderately ambiguous conditions was heard by all of the subjects, the victim was careful to separate his cry of pain from the sounds of the overturning equipment. A check on the consistency of this procedure was provided by the observer on the stairway below the laboratory. No trial was acceptable unless the verbal cues were heard by that individual. None were deleted. Fourth, since results from the nonambiguous/dangerous and nonambiguous/nondangerous conditions did not differ in Experiment 1, this manipulation was eliminated; all of the conditions in the present experiment were "potentially"

dangerous. Finally, for those subjects who helped directly, the experiment was terminated only after the victim was separated from contact with the equipment and wires. Hence, the subjects either alone or in pairs were varied orthogonally across conditions of nonambiguity, moderate ambiguity, and high ambiguity.

Results

Efficiency Question. The observed frequencies of helping behavior across conditions of ambiguity and group size may be seen in the first and second rows of Table 2. . . .

TABLE 2. Observed and corrected percentages of helping for six conditions in Experiment 2.

Group size	Levels of ambiguity		
	Non-ambiguous	Moderate ambiguity	High ambiguity
Alone	88	75	13
Two-person	100	75	38
Corrected two-person	98.6	93.8	24.3

There were no significant differences between the nonambiguous and moderately ambiguous conditions (Fisher exact test, $p = .14$). Significant differences were evident, however, between the conditions of nonambiguity and high ambiguity ($\chi^2 = 16.53$, $df = 2$, $p < .001$) and between the conditions of moderate ambiguity and high ambiguity ($\chi^2 = 7.72$, $df = 2$, $p < .05$). Thus, the only factor that influenced the probability of whether the victim would receive assistance in the present experiment was the degree of ambiguity of the emergency.[3]

[3] As with Experiment 1, an additional analysis included the variables of experimenters and type of help. No effects due to experimenters were found. The main effects of types of help and ambiguity and their interaction were significant. Seventy-one percent of the helpers rendered aid directly to the victim ($\chi^2 = 5.46$, $df = 1$, $p = .02$). However, direct and indirect help did not interact with the experimental conditions.

Effect of the Group on the Individual. To evaluate possible effects of the group on the individual, comparisons of the observed percentages of helping in two-person groups were made with those expected after correcting for the increased number of bystanders. The second and third rows of Table 2 illustrate these percentages. Results very similar to those reported in Experiment 1 were found. There was virtually no discrepancy between observed and expected percentages of helping in the nonambiguous-group condition (100% and 98.6%, respectively). Again, the subjects who were exposed to a highly ambiguous emergency helped at a greater rate (38%) than would be expected from the correction (24%), although the difference was not statistically significant (binomial test, $p = .30$). In the moderately ambiguous condition, there was less helping than was expected. Since 75% of the alone subjects helped, we would expect that 94% of the groups would include at least one person who would help. However, the observed percentage was only 75%. This difference reached borderline significance (binomial test, $p = .08$, one-tailed).

Individuals who reported having either formal training or experience with electronic equipment were considered to be "competent," whereas individuals who reported having only a slight knowledge or no knowledge of electronic equipment were classified as "less competent." In the group conditions, the person having the most training or experience was included in the sample. With this procedure 10 subjects were classified as competent and 36 subjects as less competent. Ninety percent of the competent subjects reacted to the emergency across all conditions, while only 58% of those with little or no skill did so. Fisher's exact test, employed because of low expected frequencies, yielded a statistically significant difference ($p = .05$). Furthermore, all of the competent subjects helped in a safe manner, whereas only 57% of the less competent subjects did so (Fisher's exact test, $p = .02$). All but one of the competent helpers rendered assistance directly to the victim.

POSTEXPERIMENTAL INVESTIGATIONS

All of the subjects were given a thorough debriefing, which usually required more time than the original experiment. A written questionnaire was administered to elicit responses regarding (*a*) the degree of arousal felt during the emergency and after the debriefing, (*b*) the importance of the research, and (*c*) the necessity for the use of deception. If one considers only the 78 subjects who were exposed to the nonambiguous conditions in Experiments 1 and 2, 25% indicated they were very upset, 43% were mildly upset, and 32% were not upset at the time of the emergency.[4] Upon completion of the debriefing only 1 subject indicated that he was still very upset. The overwhelming majority of subjects either agreed or strongly agreed that this type of research is valuable (95%) and that the deception practiced was unavoidable (94%).

These data are open to question, since the experimenter demand was rather explicit and obvious. However, an attempt was made to contact as many subjects as possible under fictitious auspices (the University Committee on Undergraduate Affairs) to further determine their reactions to participating in psychology experiments. The time elapsed since participation was approximately six months for the subjects in Experiment 1 and three months for the subjects in Experiment 2. The experimenters were able to contact by phone or mail 50% of the present subjects and an additional 50 subjects who had participated in other psychology experiments. The latter subjects served as a control group.

The overwhelming majority of our subjects (92%) and control subjects (94%) reported that they did not feel their rights were violated in psychology experiments and/or that they were not induced to do

---

[4] Across conditions in Experiment 2, 91% of subjects reporting being upset helped, as compared to 38% of those not reporting being upset ($\chi^2 = 11.57$, $p < .01$). These results were consistent with the cost-reward model proposed by Piliavin et al. (1972).

something that they would rather have avoided. The few subjects who agreed with these items were more likely to describe other experiments that used aversive stimulation rather than the present experiments. Thus, exposure to a relatively stressful situation was brief and mild, having virtually no reported negative effects.[5]

GENERAL DISCUSSION

These studies demonstrate that the salience of the cues perceived by the bystander concerning a potential emergency are important bits of information processed by the individual as he interprets the event. In both Experiment 1 and Experiment 2, whether the victim received help or not depended directly on the level of ambiguity presented in the emergency situation. When the subjects clearly heard and observed the accident, the victim received help 96% of the time. When the subjects were denied any feedback from the victim and exposed to only the sounds of the malfunctioning and falling equipment (high ambiguity), he received help in only 29% of the cases. Demonstration of a medium level of ambiguity proved to be more difficult. In Experiment 1 some subjects reported that they heard no cry of pain in the conditions of moderate ambiguity. This cue was apparently masked by the noise of the equipment. The helping rate in these trials proved to be strikingly similar to that found in highly ambiguous conditions. In the second experiment where the cry of pain was distinctly separated from the sound of the equipment, the helping rate rose from 36% to 75% in the alone condition and from 50% to 75% in the two-person condition. These percentages more closely parallel those obtained in the nonambiguous conditions. The problem encountered in manipulating moderate ambiguity illustrates dramatically how a single cue may be crucial to the interpretation process.

The only inhibiting effect of group size occurred

in the moderately ambiguous condition of Experiment 2. This result is consistent with Latané and Darley's (1969) social influence hypothesis. This view suggests that when individuals in a group are confronted with an ambiguous event, they are often influenced by one another's behavior. In these experiments a fellow subject's failure to act may have convinced the subject that nothing unusual had occurred. However, the lack of significant differences between the observed and the estimated percentages of helping for the other conditions suggests some limitations to the usefulness of the social influence hypothesis. When a situation is clearly perceived either as a definite emergency or as a normal occurrence not requiring particular attention, interpretation of that event may be based solely on the stimulus cues of the event itself. However, if the stimuli are unusual but sufficiently vague to defy interpretation, then another observer's interpretation of them may be solicited and integrated in order to make a decision. This notion implies that an upper and a lower boundary of situational ambiguity may exist beyond which social influence is of little importance.

The situational characteristics of the emergency probably take on even greater importance in real-life settings. The occurrence of distracting and irrelevant stimuli that interfere with the accurate interpretation of an event increases in larger urban environments. Milgram (1970) proposed two adaptive behaviors used by city dwellers to counter stimulus overload that are applicable to this discussion. First, there is a tendency to screen out low-priority inputs. When moving about in a city, a sort of "tunnel vision" may be developed by the individual in which he attends only to those stimuli necessary to assure his safe and efficient passage from one point to another. Surely a person fully adapted in this respect is less likely to notice or interpret an ambiguous event occurring on his periphery. Second, less time may be allocated to the interpretation of each input. This may lead an individual to regard a situation as nonserious when a number of reasonable explanations for the event

[5]Further details concerning debriefing and results of the follow-up study can be obtained from the first author.

may exist that do not necessarily constitute an emergency. When these additional factors are present, it is much more likely that an even greater percentage of onlookers might fail to intervene in a genuine emergency.

While the cost of intervention in these situations did not affect the probability that the victim would receive help, there was no doubt that most subjects were aware of the cost of intervening. In Experiment 2, 79% of the subjects reported that they interpreted the situation to be dangerous for themselves. This was demonstrated by the fact that 71% of the subjects who helped did so in a variety of ways that would reduce or eliminate their chances of being injured (42% directly helped and 29% indirectly helped). It is interesting to note that all but one of the subjects who touched the victim with their hands indicated later that they realized the ''inappropriateness'' of their actions, but at the time they acted so quickly that no consideration was given to the possible harm involved.

The failure to obtain more indirect than direct help is not particularly damaging to the Piliavin et al. (1969) model. If, as in the present case, many individuals perceived that they could directly assist a victim in a safe manner, one would not necessarily predict more indirect help. A more adequate test of their hypothesis would involve creating a dangerous emergency where most subjects would perceive that they were unable to help directly in a safe manner. The possibility that severe consequences for the bystander may at least modify a subject's responses in different situations can be demonstrated by comparing the results of Experiment 2 with those obtained by Clark and Word (1972). In the latter experiments, the subjects helped the victim directly 100% of the time, whereas in 29% of the sessions in Experiment 2, the subjects who helped did so indirectly ($\chi^2 = 10.53$, $df = 1$, $p = .002$). Thus, the cost of intervention may well mediate the type of helping (or if help actually occurs), but further research must concretely establish this and gauge its relative importance.

Special skills that have been acquired by an individual may also affect the intervention process. The subjects in Experiment 2, who were considered competent in terms of their experience with electronic equipment, were not only more likely to help the victim but did so with less risk to themselves. These results are consistent with those obtained by Form and Nosow (1958), Kazdin and Bryan (1971), and Midlarsky (1968).

It can be concluded from these studies that the probability of a victim receiving help is high when an individual is exposed to a situation which (a) can clearly be interpreted as an emergency, (b) presents serious consequences for another, and (c) allows the bystander to help in a manner that is safe for him. However, these results indicate only some of the necessary conditions for intervention to occur. It must be realized that the factors mentioned are insufficient by themselves to explain the failure of bystanders to help in emergencies. Other variables such as derogation of a victim (Lerner, 1970), norms dealing with privacy or noninvolvement, as well as diffuson of responsibility, operate in situations to further reduce the likelihood of intervention. Notwithstanding these social processes, the situational characteristics of the emergency are crucial variables determining whether a victim will receive help.

REFERENCES

Bickman, L. The effect of another bystander's ability to help on bystander intervention in an emergency. *Journal of Experimental Social Psychology*, 1971, **7**, 376–379.

Borofsky, G. L., Stollak, G. E., & Messé, L. A. Sex differences in bystander reactions to physical assault. *Journal of Experimental Social Psychology*, 1971, **7**, 313–318.

Bryan, J. H., & London, P. Altruistic behavior by children. *Psychological Bulletin*, 1970, **73**, 200–211.

Bryan, J. H., & Test, M. A. Models and helping: Naturalistic studies in aiding behavior. *Journal of Personality and Social Psychology*, 1967, **6**, 400–407.

Clark, R. D., III, & Word, L. E. Why don't bystanders help? Because of ambiguity? *Journal of Personality and Social Psychology*, 1972, **24**, 392–400.

Darley, J. M., & Latané, B. Bystander intervention in emergencies. *Journal of Personality and Social Psychology,* 1968, **3**, 377–383.

Denner, B. Did a crime occur? Should I inform anyone? A study of deception. *Journal of Personality,* 1968, **36**, 454–465.

Form, W. H., & Nosow, S. *Community in disaster.* New York: Harper, 1958.

Kazdin, A. E., & Bryan, J. H. Competence and volunteering. *Journal of Experimental Social Psychology,* 1971, **7**, 87–97.

Korte, C. Group effects on help-giving in an emergency. *Proceedings of the 77th Annual Convention of the American Psychological Association,* 1969, **4**, 383–384. (Summary)

Latané, B., & Darley, J. M. Group inhibition of bystander intervention in emergencies. *Journal of Personality and Social Psychology,* 1968, **10**, 215–221.

Latané, B., & Darley, J. M. Bystander apathy. *American Scientist,* 1969, **57**, 224–268.

Latané, B., & Darley, J. M. Social determinants of bystander intervention in emergencies. In J. M. Macaulay & L. Berkowitz (Eds.), *Altruism and helping behavior.* New York: Academic Press, 1970. (a)

Latané, B., & Darley, J. M. *The unresponsive bystander.* New York: Appleton-Century-Crofts, 1970. (b)

Latané, B., & Rodin, J. A lady in distress: Inhibiting effects of friends and strangers on bystander intervention. *Journal of Experimental Social Psychology,* 1969, **5**, 189–202.

Lerner, M. J. Desire for justice and reactions to victims. In J. Macaulay & L. Berkowitz (Eds.), *Altruism and helping behavior.* New York: Academic Press, 1970.

Midlarsky, E. Some antecedents of aiding under stress. *Proceedings of the 76th Annual Convention of the American Psychological Association,* 1968, **3**, 385–386. (Summary)

Milgram, S. The experience of living in cities. *Science,* 1970, **167**, 1461–1468.

Piliavin, J. A., & Piliavin, I. M. Effect of blood on reactions to a victim. *Journal of Personality and Social Psychology,* 1972, **23**, 353–361.

Piliavin, I. M., Rodin, J., & Piliavin, J. A. Good samaritanism: An underground phenomenon. *Journal of Personality and Social Psychology,* 1969, **13**, 289–299.

Schwartz, S. H., & Clausen, G. T. Responsibility, norms, and helping in an emergency. *Journal of Personality and Social Psychology,* 1970, **16**, 299–310.

Staub, E. A child in distress: The effect of focusing responsibility on children on their attempts to help. *Developmental Psychology,* 1970, **2**, 152–153. (a)

Staub, E. A child in distress: The influence of age and number of witnesses on children's attempts to help. *Journal of Personality and Social Psychology,* 1970, **4**, 130–140. (b)

Test, M. A., & Bryan, J. H. The effects of dependency, models, and reciprocity upon subsequent helping behavior. *Journal of Social Psychology,* 1969, **78**, 205–212.

Tilker, H. A. Socially responsible behavior as a function of observer responsibility and victim feedback. *Journal of Personality and Social Psychology,* 1970, **14**, 95–100.

Wispé, L. G., & Freshley, H. B. Race, sex, and sympathetic helping behavior: The broken bag caper. *Journal of Personality and Social Psychology,* 1971, **17**, 59–65.

ARTICLE 3

The experience of living in cities: A psychological analysis

Stanley Milgram[1]

When I first came to New York it seemed like a nightmare. As soon as I got off the train at Grand Central I was caught up in pushing, shoving crowds on 42nd Street. Sometimes people bumped into me without apology; what really frightened me was to see two people literally engaged in combat for possession of a cab. Why were they so rushed? Even drunks on the street were bypassed without a glance. People didn't seem to care about each other at all.

This statement represents a common reaction to a great city, but it does not tell the whole story. Obviously, cities have great appeal because of their variety, eventfulness, possibility of choice, and the stimulation of an intense atmosphere that many individuals find a desirable background to their lives. Where face to face contacts are important, the city is unparalleled in its possibilities. It has been calculated by the Regional Plan Association (1969) that in Nassau county, a suburb of New York City, an official can meet 11,000 others with whom he may do business within 10 minutes of his office by foot or car. In Newark, a moderate-sized city, he could see more than 20,000 persons. But in midtown Manhattan an office worker can meet 220,000 persons within 10 minutes of his desk. There is an order of magnitude increment in the communication possibilities offered by a great city. That is one of the bases of its appeal and, indeed, of its functional necessity. The city provides options that no other social arrangement permits. But there is a negative side also, as we shall see.

Reprinted and abridged from F. F. Korten, S. W. Cook, and J. I. Lacey (Eds.), *Psychology and the Problems of Society,* American Psychological Association, 1970. This article is a slightly revised version of an article appearing in *Science,* March 13, 1970. Copyright © 1970 by the American Association for the Advancement of Science and reprinted with their permission and the permission of the author.

[1]Barbara Bengen worked closely with the author in preparing the present version of this paper, and its expository values reflect her skill. The author wishes to express thanks to Gary Winkel, editor of *Environment and Behavior,* for useful suggestions and advice.

Granted that cities are indispensable in a complex society, we may still ask what contribution psychology can make to understanding the experience of living in them. What theories are relevant? How can we extend our knowledge of the psychological aspects of life in cities through empirical inquiry? If empirical inquiry is possible, along what lines should it proceed? In short, where do we start in the construction of urban theory and in laying out lines of research?

Observation is the indispensable starting point. Any observer in the streets of midtown Manhattan will see: (*a*) large numbers of people, (*b*) high density, and (*c*) heterogeneity of population. These three factors need to be at the root of any sociopsychological theory of city life, for they condition all aspects of our experience in the metropolis. Wirth (1938), if not the first to point to these factors, is nonetheless the sociologist who relied most heavily on them in his analysis of the city. Yet, for a psychologist there is something unsatisfactory about Wirth's theoretical variables. *Numbers, density,* and *heterogeneity* are demographic facts, but they are not yet psychological facts. They are external to the individual. Psychology needs an idea that links the individual's *experience* to the demographic circumstances of urban life.

One link is provided by the concept of *overload.* This term, drawn from systems analysis, refers to the inability of a system to process inputs from the environment because there are too many inputs for the system to cope with, or because successive inputs come so fast that Input A cannot be processed when Input B is presented. When overload is present, adaptations occur. The system must set priorities and make choices. Input A may be processed first while B is kept in abeyance, or one input may be sacrificed altogether. City life, as we experience it, constitutes a continuous set of encounters with adaptations to overload. Overload characteristically deforms daily life on several levels, impinging on *role performance,* evolution of *social norms, cognitive functioning,* and the *use of facilities.*

The concept has been implicit in several theories of urban experience. Simmel (1950) pointed out that since urban dwellers come into contact with vast numbers of people each day, they conserve psychic energy by becoming acquainted with a far smaller proportion of people than their rural counterparts and by maintaining more superficial relationships even with these acquaintances. Wirth (1938) points specifically to "the superficiality, the anonymity, and the transitory character of urban social relations," and to the loss of community that produces "the state of *anomie,* or the social void." Simmel notes as well that the high density of cities encourages inhabitants to create distance in social contacts to counteract the overwhelming pressures of close physical contact. The greater the number and frequency of human contacts the less time, attention, and emotional investment one can give to each of them, thus, the purported blasé and indifferent attitude of city dwellers toward each other.

One adaptive response to overload, therefore, is that *less time is given to each input.* A second adaptive mechanism is that *low priority inputs are disregarded.* Principles of selectivity are formulated so that the investment of time and energy is reserved for carefully defined inputs (e.g., the urbanite disregards a drunk, sick on the street, as he purposefully navigates through the crowd). Third, *boundaries are redrawn in certain social transactions so that the overloaded system can shift the burden to the other party in the exchange;* for example, harried New York bus drivers once made change for customers, but now this responsibility has been shifted to the client who must have the exact fare ready. Fourth, *reception is blocked off prior to entering a system;* city dwellers increasingly use unlisted telephone numbers to prevent individuals from calling them, and a small but growing number resort to keeping the telephone off the hook to prevent incoming calls. More subtly, one blocks inputs by assuming an unfriendly countenance, which discourages others from initiating contact. Additionally, *social screening devices are interposed between the individual and environmental inputs* (in a town of 5,000 anyone can drop in to chat with the mayor, but in the metropolis organizational screening devices deflect inputs to other destinations). Fifth, the *intensity of inputs is diminished by filtering devices* so that only weak and relatively superficial forms of involvement with others are allowed. Sixth, *specialized institutions are created to absorb inputs that would otherwise swamp the individual* (e.g., welfare departments handle the financial needs of a million individuals in New York City, who would otherwise create an army of mendicants continuously importuning the pedestrian). The interposition of institutions between the individual and the social world, a characteristic of all modern society and most acutely present in the large metropolis, has its negative side. It deprives the individual of a sense of direct contact and spontaneous integration in the life around him. It simultaneously protects and estranges the individual from his social environment.

Many of these adaptive mechanisms apply not only to individuals, but to institutional systems as well, as Meier (1962) has so brilliantly shown in connection with the library and the stock exchange.

In summary, the observed behavior of the urbanite in a wide range of situations appears to be determined largely by a variety of adaptations to overload. We shall now deal with several specific consequences of responses to overload, which come to create a different tone to city and town.

SOCIAL RESPONSIBILITY

The principal point of interest for a social psychology of the city is that moral and social involvement with individuals is necessarily restricted. This is a direct and necessary function of excess of input over capacity to process. Restriction of involvement runs a broad spectrum from refusal to become involved in the needs of another person, even when the person desperately needs assistance (as in the Kitty Genovese case), through refusal to do favors, to the simple withdrawal of courtesies (such as offering a lady a seat, or saying "sorry"

when a pedestrian collision occurs). In any transaction more and more details need to be dropped as the total number of units to be processed increases and assaults an instrument of limited processing capacity. There are myriad specific situations dealing with social responsibility. Specific incidents can be ordered in terms of two dimensions. First, there is the dimension of the importance of the action in question. Clearly, intervening to save someone's life rates higher than tipping one's hat, though both imply a degree of social involvement with others. Second, one may place any specific incident in terms of its position on a social-anomic continuum. Thus, in regard to courtesy expressions, a person may extend courtesies (the social end of the continuum) or withhold them (the anomic end). Anomic conditions, up and down the spectrum, are said to characterize the metropolis in comparison with the small town.

The ultimate adaptation to an overloaded social environment is to totally disregard the needs, interests, and demands of those whom one does not define as relevant to personal need satisfaction, and to develop optimally efficient means of identifying whether an individual falls into the category of friend or stranger. The disparity in treatment of friends and strangers ought to be greater in cities than towns; the time allotment and willingness to become involved with those who can make no personal claim on one's time will be less in cities than in towns.

Bystander Intervention in Crises

The most striking deficiencies in urban social responsibility occur in crisis situations, such as the Genovese murder in Queens. As is well known, in 1964, Catherine Genovese, coming home from a night job in the early hours of an April morning, was stabbed repeatedly over an extended period of time. Thirty-eight residents of a respectable New York City neighborhood admitted to having witnessed at least part of the attack but none went to her aid or called the police until after she was dead. Milgram and Hollander (1964) analyzed the event in these terms:

Urban friendships and associations are not primarily formed on the basis of physical proximity. A person with numerous close friends in different parts of the city may not know the occupant of an adjacent apartment. This does not mean that a city dweller has fewer friends than does a villager, or knows fewer persons who will come to his aid; however, it does mean that his allies are not constantly at hand. Miss Genovese required immediate aid from those physically present. There is no evidence that the city had deprived Miss Genovese of human associations, but the friends who might have rushed to her side were miles from the scene of her tragedy.

Further, it is known that her cries for help were not directed to a specific person; they were general. But only individuals can act, and as the cries were not specifically directed, no particular person felt a special responsibility. The crime and the failure of community response seem absurd to us. At the time, it may well have seemed equally absurd to the Kew Gardens residents that not one of the neighbors would have called the police. A collective paralysis may have developed from the belief of each of the witnesses that someone else must surely have taken that obvious step [p.602].

Latané and Darley (1969) have reported laboratory approaches to the study of bystander intervention and have established experimentally the principle that the larger the number of bystanders the less likely it is that any one of them will intervene in an emergency. In any quantitative characterization of the social texture of city life a first order of business is the application of these experimental methods of field situations set in large cities and small towns. Theorists argue that the indifference shown in the Genovese case would not be present in a small town, but in the absence of solid experimental findings the question remains an open one.

More than just callousness prevents bystanders from participating in altercations between people. A rule of urban life is respect for other people's emotional and social privacy, perhaps because physical privacy is so hard to achieve. And in situations for which the standards are heterogeneous, it is much harder to know whether taking an active role is unwarranted meddling or an appropriate response to a critical situation. If a husband and wife are quarreling in public, at which point should a bystander step in? On the one hand, the heterogeneity of the city produces substantially greater tolerance of behavior, dress, and codes of ethics than does the small town, but this diversity also encourages people to withhold aid for fear of antagonizing the participants or crossing an inappropriate and difficult-to-define line.

Moreover, the frequency of demands present in the city gives rise to norms of noninvolvement. There are practical limitations to the Samaritan impulse in a major city. If a citizen attended to every needy person, if he were sensitive to and acted on every altruistic impulse that was evoked in the city, he could scarcely keep his own affairs in order.

Gaertner and Bickman (1968) have extended the bystander studies to an examination of help across ethnic lines. They arranged for blacks and whites, with clearly identifiable accents, to call strangers through an apparent error in telephone dialing. The caller indicates that he is attempting to contact a garage and that he is stranded on an outlying highway. He has just used his last dime attempting to reach a garage but received the present number instead by mistake. The caller then requests that the subject assist him in his predicament by calling the garage; he provides a telephone number and locational information to pass on to the service station.

The experimenters compared the number of persons who called the garage in response to white as opposed to Negro solicitation. White-accented callers had a significantly better chance of obtaining assistance than black callers. The findings of Gaertner and Bickman suggest that ethnic allegiance may well be another vehicle for coping with overload: The white, city inhabitant can reduce excessive demands and screen out urban heterogeneity by responding along ethnic lines; overload is made more manageable by limiting the "span of sympathy."

Favor Doing Based on Trust

We may now move away from crisis situations to less urgent examples of social responsibility; for it is not only in situations of dramatic need, but in the ordinary, everyday willingness to lend a hand, that the city dweller is said to be deficient relative to his small-town cousin. The comparative method must be employed in any empirical examination of this question. A commonplace social situation is staged both in an urban setting and a small town, a situation to which a subject can respond either by extending help or withholding it. The responses in town and city are then compared.

One factor in the purported unwillingness of urbanites to extend themselves to strangers may well be their heightened sense of physical and emotional vulnerability—a feeling that is supported by urban crime statistics. A key test for distinguishing between city and town behavior, therefore, is how city dwellers compare with town dwellers in offering aid that increases their personal vulnerability and requires some trust of strangers. Altman, Levine, Nadien, and Villena (1969) devised a study to compare city and town dwellers in this respect. The criterion used in their study was the willingness of householders to allow strangers to enter their homes to use the telephone. Individually the investigators rang doorbells, explained that they had misplaced the address of a friend nearby, and asked to use the phone. The investigators (two males and two females) completed a total of 100 requests for entry in the city and 60 in the small towns. The results gleaned from middle-income housing developments in Manhattan were compared with data gathered in several small towns in Rockland County, outside of New York City (Stony Point, Spring Valley, Ramapo, Nyack, New City, and West Clarkstown).

As Table 1 shows, in all cases there was a sharp increase in the proportion of entries gained by an investigator when he moved from the city to a small

TABLE 1. Percentage of entries by investigators for city and town homes.

| Investigator | % entries | |
	City (n = 100)	Small town (n = 60)
Male		
1	16	40
2	12	60
Female		
1	40	87
2	40	100

town. In the most extreme case the investigator was five times more likely to gain admission to a home in a small town than in Manhattan. Although the female investigators had noticeably higher levels of entry in both cities and towns than the male investigators, all four students did at least twice as well in gaining access to small-town homes than they did to city homes, suggesting that the city-town distinction overrides even the predictably greater fear of male strangers than of female ones.

The lower level of helpfulness by city dwellers seems due in part to recognition of the *dangers* of Manhattan living, rather than to mere indifference or coldness. It is significant that 75% of all city respondents received and answered messages either by shouting through closed doors or by peering through peepholes; in the towns, by contrast, about 75% of the respondents opened the doors, with no barriers between themselves and the investigator.

Supporting the investigators' quantitative results was their general observation that the town dwellers were noticeably more friendly and less suspicious than the city dwellers. Even city dwellers who allowed the investigators to use the phone appeared more ill at ease than their town counterparts; city dwellers often refused to answer the doorbell even when they were at home; and in a few cases city residents called the security people of the housing development. In seeking to explain the sense of psychological vulnerability city dwellers feel, above and beyond differences in actual crime statistics, Altman et al. (1969) point out that for a village resident, if a crime is committed in a neighboring village, he may not perceive it as personally relevant, though the geographic distance may be small. But a criminal act committed anywhere in the city, though miles from the city-dweller's home, is still verbally located within the city, "therefore . . . the inhabitant of the city possesses a larger vulnerable space."

Civilities

Even at the most superficial level of involvement, the exercise of everyday civilities, urbanites are reputedly deficient. Persons bump into each other and frequently do not apologize. They knock over another person's packages, and, as often as not, proceed on their way with a grump, rather than taking the time to help the victim. Such behavior, which many visitors to great cities find distasteful, is less common, we are told, in smaller communities where traditional courtesies are more likely to be maintained.

In some instances it is not simply that in the city traditional courtesies are violated; rather, the cities develop *new norms of noninvolvement*. They are so well defined and so deeply a part of city life that *they* constitute the norms people are reluctant to violate. Men are actually embarrassed to give up a seat on the subway for an old woman; they will mumble, "I was getting off anyway," instead of making the gesture in a straightforward and gracious way. These norms develop because everyone realizes that in situations of high-density people cannot implicate themselves in each other's affairs, for to do so would create conditions of continual distraction that would frustrate purposeful action.

The effects of overload do not imply that at every instant the city dweller is bombarded with an unmanageable number of inputs, and that his responses are determined by the input excess at any given instant. Rather, adaptation occurs in the form of the gradual evolution of norms of behavior. Norms are created in response to frequent discrete experiences of overload; they persist and become generalized modes of responding. They are part of the culture of the metropolis, and even newcomers may adapt to these manners in the course of time.

Overload on Cognitive Capacities: Anonymity

It is a truism that we respond differently toward those whom we know and those who are strangers to us. An eager patron aggressively cuts in front of someone in a long movie line to save time only to confront a friend; he then behaves sheepishly. A man gets into an automobile accident caused by another driver, emerges from his car shouting in rage, then moderates his behavior on discovering a friend driving the other car. The city dweller, when moving through the midtown streets, is in a state of continual anonymity vis à vis the other pedestrians. His ability to know everyone he passes is restricted by inherent limitations of human cognitive capacity. A continual succession of faces briefly appears before him then disappears. Minimal scanning for recognition occurs, but storage in long-term memory is avoided. (No one has yet calculated the number of faces scanned in a day by the typical midtown worker.)

The concept of "anonymity" is a shibboleth of social psychology, but few have defined it precisely or attempted to measure it quantitatively in order to compare cities and towns. Anonymity is part of a continuous spectrum ranging from total anonymity at one end to full acquaintance at the other, and it may well be that measurement of the precise degrees of anonymity in cities and towns would help to explain important distinctions between the quality of life in each. Conditions of full acquaintance, for example, offer security and familiarity, but they may also be stifling because the inhabitant is under continuous scrutiny by people who know him. Conditions of complete anonymity, by contrast, provide freedom from routine social ties, but they may also create feelings of alienation and detachment.

One could investigate empirically the proportion of activities in which the city dweller and town dwellers are known by others at given times in their daily lives, and, if known, with what proportion of those the urbanite and town dweller interact. At his job, for instance, the city dweller may know fully as many people as his rural counterpart. While not fulfilling his occupational or family role, however—say, in traveling about the city—the urbanite is doubtlessly more anonymous than his rural counterpart. (One way to measure the difference in degrees of anonymity would be to display the picture of a New York inhabitant at a busy midtown intersection. One could offer a significant reward to any passerby who could identify the person pictured. Calculation of the total number of passersby during a given period, coupled with the proportion who could identify the picture, provides one measure of urban anonymity. Results could then be compared with those gleaned by displaying the picture of a town dweller on the main street in his town. This test could also be used to define a person's "neighborhood boundary," that area within which a high proportion of people could identify the inhabitant's picture.)

Limited laboratory work on anonymity has begun. Zimbardo (1968) has conducted pilot studies testing whether groups asked to perform certain aggressive acts while wearing masks administer more shock than control groups without masks. The results were inconclusive, though Zimbardo's findings suggest that if we could create laboratory conditions of true anonymity, more aggressive behavior would result.

A related experiment by Zimbardo tested whether the social anonymity and impersonality of the big city encourage greater vandalism than found in small towns. Zimbardo arranged for one car to be left for 64 hours near the New York University campus in the Bronx and a counterpart to be left near Stanford University in Palo Alto. The license plates on both cars were removed and the hoods opened, to provide "releaser cues" for potential vandals. The results were as expected: The New York car was

stripped of all moveable parts within the first 24 hours, and was left a hunk of metal rubble by the end of three days. Unexpectedly, however, most destruction occurred during daylight hours usually under scrutiny by observers, and was led by well-dressed, white adults. The Palo Alto car was left untouched (Zimbardo notes that when it started to rain, one bystander even lowered the car's hood to protect the motor).

Zimbardo attributes the difference in the treatment accorded the two cars to the "acquired feelings of social anonymity provided by life in a city like New York," and he supports his study with several other anecdotes illustrating casual, wanton vandalism in the city. Any study comparing the effects of anonymity in city and town, however, must satisfactorily control for other confounding factors: the large number of drug addicts in New York, the higher proportion of slum dwellers in the city, etc.

Another direction for empirical study is the investigation of the beneficial effects of anonymity. Impersonality of city life breeds its own tolerance for the private lives of inhabitants. Individuality and even eccentricity, we may assume, can flourish more readily in the metropolis than in the small town. Stigmatized persons may find it easier to lead comfortable lives without the constant scrutiny of neighbors. To what degree can this assumed difference between city and town be shown empirically? Waters (1969) hypothesized that avowed homosexuals would be more likely to be accepted as tenants in a large city than in small towns. She dispatched letters from homosexuals and normals to real estate agents in cities and towns across the country. The results of her study were inconclusive, but the general idea of examining the protective benefits of city life to the stigmatized ought to be pursued.

Role Behavior in Cities and Towns

Another product of urban "overload" is the adjustment in roles made by urbanites in daily interactions. As Wirth has said: "Urbanites meet one another in highly segmental roles. . . . They are less dependent upon particular persons, and their dependence upon others is confined to a highly fractionalized aspect of the other's round of activity.'' This tendency is particularly noticeable in transactions between customers and those offering professional or sales services: The owner of a country store has time to become well acquainted with his dozen-or-so daily customers; but the girl at the checkout counter of a busy A & P, handling hundreds of customers a day, barely has time to toss the green stamps into one customer's shopping bag before the next customer has confronted her with his pile of groceries.

In his stimulating analysis of the city *A Communications Theory of Urban Growth,* Meier (1962) discusses several adaptations a system may make when confronted by inputs that exceed its capacity to process them. Specifically, Meier states that according to the principle of competition for scarce resources the scope and time of the transaction shrinks as customer volume and daily turnover rise (see Figure 1). This, in fact, is what is meant by the brusque quality of city life. New standards have developed in cities about what levels of services are appropriate in business transactions.

McKenna and Morgenthau (1969), in a seminar at the City University of New York, devised a study

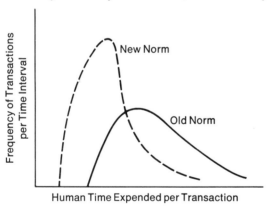

FIGURE 1.   Changes in the demand for time for a given task when overall transaction frequency increases in a social system. (Reprinted with permission from R. L. Meier, *A Communications Theory of Urban Growth,* 1962. Copyrighted by MIT Press, 1962.)

(a) to compare the willingness of city dwellers and small towners to do favors for strangers that entailed a small amount of time and inconvenience but no personal vulnerability, and *(b)* to determine whether the more compartmentalized, transitory relationships of the city would make urban salesgirls less likely than small-town salesgirls to carry out tasks for strangers not related to their customary roles.

To test for differences between city dwellers and small towners, a simple experiment was devised in which persons from both settings were asked to perform increasingly onerous favors for anonymous strangers. It was not possible for the investigators to travel around the country extensively, but by making use of a telephone they were able to reach persons in major cities (Chicago, New York, and Philadelphia) and 37 small towns in the same states in which the cities were located. The average population of the towns was 2,727 people, based on the 1960 census. Typical small towns used in the study were Coxsackie, Ravena, and Wappingers Falls (New York); Chenoa, St. Anne, and Fairbury (Illinois); and Doylestown, Sellersville, and McAdoo (Pennsylvania).

Within the cities, half the calls went to housewives, and the other half to salesgirls in women's apparel shops; the same division was made for the small towns. Each investigator represented herself as a long-distance caller who had mistakenly been connected with the respondent by the operator. The investigator began by asking for simple information about the weather for travel purposes. Next the investigator excused herself on a pretext stating "please hold on," put the phone down for almost a full minute, and then picked it up again and asked the respondent to provide the phone number of a hotel or motel in her vicinity at which the investigator might stay during a forthcoming visit. Scores were assigned to the subjects depending on how helpful they had been. Scores ranged from 1 (meaning that the respondent hung up without giving weather information and without an excuse) to 16 (meaning that the respondent remained on the phone during the delay and carried out all the requests).

McKenna summarizes her results in this manner: "People in the city, whether they are engaged in a specific job or not, are less helpful and informative than people in small towns. . . . People at home, regardless of where they live, are less helpful and informative than people working in shops [p. 8]." Representative quantitative results are shown in Table 2. It is important to note that the relatively high median for urban housewives and salesgirls alike does not jibe with the stereotype of the urbanite as aloof, self-centered, and unwilling to help strangers, and that the quantitative differences obtained by McKenna and Morgenthau are less great than one might have expected. This again points up the need for extensive empirical research on rural-urban differences, research that goes far beyond that provided in the few illustrative pilot studies presented in this paper. At this point we have very limited objective evidence on differences in the quality of social encounters in the city and small town.

The research on this subject needs to be guided by unifying theoretical concepts. As this section of the paper has tried to demonstrate, the concept of overload helps to explain a wide variety of contrasts between city and town behavior: *(a)* the differences in *role enactment* (the urban dwellers' tendency to deal with one another in highly segmented, functional terms; the constricted time and services offered customers by sales personnel); *(b)* the evolution of *urban norms* quite different from traditional town values (such as the acceptance of noninvolvement, impersonality, and aloofness in urban life); *(c)* consequences for the urban dweller's *cognitive processes* (his inability to identify most of the people seen daily; his screening of sensory stimuli; his development of blasé attitudes toward deviant or bizarre behavior; and his selectivity in responding to human demands); and *(d)* the far greater competition for scarce *facilities* in the city (the subway rush, the fight for taxis, traffic jams, standing in line to await services). I would suggest that contrasts between city and rural behavior probably reflect the responses of similar people to very different situations, rather than intrinsic differences between rural personalities and city personalities. The city is a situation to which individuals respond adaptively.

REFERENCES

Altman, D., Levine, M., Nadien, M., & Villena, J. Trust of the stranger in the city and the small town. Unpublished research, Graduate Center, City University of New York, 1969.

Gaertner, S., & Bickman, L. The ethnic bystander. Unpublished research, Graduate Center, City University of New York, 1968.

Latané, B., & Darley, J. Bystander apathy. *American Scientist*, 1969, **57**, 244–268.

McKenna, W., & Morgenthau, S. Urban-rural differences in social interaction: A study of helping behavior. Unpublished research, Graduate Center, City University of New York, 1969.

Meier, R. L. *A communications theory of urban growth.* Cambridge, Mass.: MIT Press, 1962.

Milgram, S., & Hollander, P. Paralyzed witness: The murder they heard. *The Nation,* 1964, **25**, 602–604.

Regional Plan Association (1969). The second regional plan. *The New York Times,* June 15, 1969, 119, Section 12.

Simmel, G. The metropolis and mental life. In K. H. Wolff (Ed.), *The sociology of George Simmel.* New York: The Free Press, 1950. (Originally published: *Die Grosstadte und das Geistesleben die Grossstadt.* Dresden: v. Zahn & Jaensch, 1903.)

Waters, J. The relative acceptance accorded a discreditable person in rural and metropolitan areas. Unpublished research, Graduate Center, City University of New York, 1969.

Wirth, L. Urbanism as a way of life. *American Journal of Sociology,* 1938, **44**, 1–24.

Zimbardo, P. G. The human choice: Individuation, reason and order vs. deindividuation, impulse and chaos. *Nebraska symposium on motivation,* 1969, **17**, 237–307.

TABLE 2. People in each category with scores above overall median.

Category	City	Town
Home	13(11)	17(12.5)
Shop	16(11)	24(14)

Note.—Figures in parentheses indicate the median for that group. $n = 34$ for each cell.

SECTION SUMMARY

The research reported by Latané and Darley in the first article provides strong evidence that social influence and environmental variables can be of considerable importance in determining whether people will intervene in an emergency situation. To evaluate the effect of these social-influence factors, it may be pertinent to look at the model of the emergency-intervention *process* that Latané and Darley (1969, 1970) have developed.

They propose that, when a person is confronted with an emergency situation (defined in terms of the unique characteristics outlined in the Section Introduction), there is a series of decision points through which that person must pass if he or she is going to intervene. Only one particular set of choices will lead the person to take action in the situation. First, the bystander must *notice* the situation. The external event has to break into the person's thinking and intrude into his or her conscious mind. If bystanders are so lost in their own thoughts that the event does not "get through" to them and is therefore not noticed, obviously they are not going to intervene.

If the person does notice the event, she or he must then *interpret* it. Is the man slumped on the street (or in the subway car) suffering a heart attack, or is he simply drunk or asleep? Is the man perched on the ledge of a building trying to decide whether to jump, or is he just a window washer going about his business? Did the flash and buzz indicate a possible dangerous shock to the technician, or was it just the normal operation of the machinery? In other words, is the situation an emergency or not?

The third step involves deciding whether one has a *responsibility* to act in the emergency situation. Perhaps help is already on the way, or perhaps someone else may be better qualified to help. Or perhaps the bystander will decide that the emergency is simply none of his or her business.

According to the model, if the bystander has made the "intervention" choice at each of the three points discussed thus far, she or he will have noticed the event, interpreted it as an emergency, and decided that it is her or his personal responsibility to take action. The last step in this sequence, then, involves more practical questions: *what* to do and *how* to do it. The bystander may take either of two courses of action at this point. The first is the set of behaviors that Latané and Darley (1970, pp. 34–35) call *direct intervention:* swimming out to someone who is drowning, grabbing an extinguisher to put out a fire, or similar personal actions. The second set of acts is labeled "detour" or *indirect intervention,* which involves attempts to report the emergency to the relevant authority (for example, a lifeguard or the fire department) rather than to try to cope with it directly. Obviously, the amount of danger facing the bystander and the degree of skill that he or she has in such situations may be major determinants of which course of action is taken. As the first article in this Section points out, witnesses to the Kitty Genovese murder took *neither* course of action.

Latané and Darley propose that the intervention process is most likely to break down at the second or third step: in interpreting the situation as an emergency or in deciding whether one is responsible for intervention. One of the social processes that they identify is *pluralistic ignorance.* Each member of a group of bystanders may be simultaneously trying to decide how to interpret an ambiguous situation by taking cues from the reactions of others. At the same time, each of the group members is trying to appear calm. Therefore, until or unless someone acts, each bystander sees only "calm," nonresponding bystanders around her or him. The bystander is thus likely to decide that the ambiguous situation must not really be an emergency.

The crucial importance of the variable of the situation's ambiguity is further demonstrated by Clark and Word's study, the second article in this section.

In their earlier study (1972), Clark and Word set up a situation similar to the Latané-Rodin (1969) "fallen woman" experiment described in our first article. Whereas the "emergency" was transmitted via tape recorder in the Latané-Rodin experiment, Clark and Word had their male "victim" actually act out the emergency for each subject or group of subjects. The victim climbed a metal ladder in an adjoining room (door closed), fell from the top of the ladder to the floor, and pulled the ladder over on top of him. He then moaned and groaned in pain. In this situation, presumably much less ambiguous than the Latané-Rodin scenario, Clark and Word found 100% helping—*every* subject went to the victim's aid.

In a second experiment, either one, two, or five persons overheard the same fall without any verbal signs of injury (more ambiguity). In this situation, the lone subject or at least one member of the two- and five-man groups responded to the needs of the victim in only about 30% of the cases. Persons in the two- and five-man groups were less likely to help and intervened more slowly than the solitary subjects did.

In the study reprinted here, Clark and Word once again found that almost everyone (96%) helped in an unambiguous situation, even though the potential danger to helpers was high. Subjects who later reported having either formal training or experiences with electronic equipment ("competent" subjects) were more likely to help the victim and to do so with less risk to themselves than were the "less competent" subjects. Hence, both the characteristics of the situation (ambiguous or unambiguous) and the characteristics of the bystander(s) (competence with electronic equipment) were important determinants of what type of action was taken.

But what of situations that are unambiguous and that are clearly emergencies? Can the presence of other persons decrease the likelihood that any given bystander will react in this situation too? Latané and Darley suggest that it can, through the process of *diffusion of responsibility*. In the first article in this Section they propose that the presence of other people can reduce the "cost" of not acting by reducing the guilt or blame that can be directed to any one individual for inaction. In addition, if others are known to be present, a bystander may assume that someone else has already initiated action to help in the emergency. (This process is illustrated in cases of serious automobile accidents in which an ambulance is not called for some time, apparently because all the bystanders are assuming that someone else has already done so.)

Elsewhere, Latané and Darley (1969, pp. 258–259) have reported a study conducted in the "real world" that supports their model. They staged a series of 96 "robberies" of a discount liquor store over a two-week period. The robberies (of a case of beer) took place when there was either one or two customers (bystanders) in the store and when the cashier was out of sight in the rear of the store. None of the bystanders attempted to intervene in the robbery directly; about one-fifth of the customers spontaneously reported the robbery to the cashier when he returned. After prompting by the cashier ("Hey, what happened to that man who was in here? Did you see him leave?"), about half the remaining subjects (those who had not reported the robbery spontaneously) told the cashier about the theft. The number of robbers (one or two) had no major effect on the pattern of responses.

A total of 65% of the lone customers reported the theft; from this, probability theory would predict that 87% of the two-person groups would include at least one "reporter." However, in only 56% of the two-person groups did *even one* person report the theft. Latané and Darley interpret these results as indicative of the operation of diffusion of responsibility in the two-person groups.

Clark and Word found, to their surprise, that the "cost" of helping (danger of electrocution) did not affect the amount of helping that occurred; virtually everyone helped in the unambiguous situation, whether the apparent danger was high or low.

Nevertheless, other theorists have suggested that costs and rewards for helping and for not helping may be of considerable importance. Piliavin and Piliavin (1972; in press; Piliavin, Rodin, & Piliavin, 1969; Piliavin, Piliavin, & Rodin, 1975) have proposed that witnessing an emergency is physiologically and emotionally arousing. The level of arousal is greatest when the emergency is perceived as severe, when the victim is perceived as similar to the bystander, and when the victim is physically close to the bystander. In most cases, a bystander will respond so as to reduce the arousal as rapidly and completely as possible, with minimal cost to herself or himself.

Costs for helping a victim can include potential danger, effort, time lost, embarrassment, and feelings of inadequacy if the help is ineffective. Costs for *not* helping, on the other hand, could include self-blame for inaction, public censure, and loss of possible rewards (thanks from the victim, feelings of competence, and so on). If costs for helping are low and costs for not helping are high, direct intervention should occur. If both costs are low, however, whether or not a bystander helps may depend on perceived norms in the situation—that is, on perceptions of whether one *should* help or not.

When costs for both helping and not helping are high, the bystander is in a particularly difficult spot. Piliavin and Piliavin (in press) suggest that either of two courses of action is likely. The bystander may intervene indirectly—for example, by calling the police or the fire department. Or the bystander may *redefine* the situation, disparaging the victim and deciding that the victim deserves his or her fate. For example, the bystander might decide that the victim is drunk and therefore not worthy of help. If this happens, the costs for not helping may be reduced, since self-blame is less likely if the victim is perceived as undeserving of help. Finally, if costs for helping are high while costs for not helping are low, the bystander is likely to leave the scene or to ignore or deny the existence of an emergency. (You may want to reinterpret the studies described by Latané and Darley and by Clark and Word in terms of the Piliavins' cost-reward arousal-reduction model. Which approach seems to fit the data most efficiently and closely?)

The discussion of bystander intervention in emergency situations has thus far focused largely on situational variables. You may already have wondered about the influence of attitudinal or personality factors on behavior in such situations. It seems very probable that certain kinds of people will be more likely to intervene in emergency situations than others. To investigate this possibility, Latané and Darley gave a series of personality measures to the subjects who had participated in the "fit to be tried" experiment described in the first article. The subjects filled out the F Scale, a measure of authoritarianism; a scale of Anomie, alienation from social norms and institutions; a scale of Machiavellianism, the tendency to take a tough-minded, cynical, and opportunistic attitude toward others; a scale of Need for Approval, the tendency to try to present a socially desirable picture of oneself; and a Social Responsibility Scale, a measure of the extent to which subjects accept the social-responsibility norm.

Perhaps surprisingly, scores on *none* of these instruments were significantly related to speed of helping in the "fit" experiment. Other researchers (Yakimovich & Saltz, 1971) have reported a similar lack of relationship between responses to personality or attitude questionnaires and helping behavior. In addition, Latané and Darley looked at some demographic characteristics of the subjects (social class, family size, length of stay in New York City, and so on). Out of 11 such variables, only one showed a significant relationship to speed of helping. The smaller the size of the community in which the subject grew up, the more likely she was to help the victim having the "fit" (see Latané & Darley, 1970, pp. 113–120). As the experimenters comment, "This finding may provide comfort for those small town residents who claim 'It couldn't happen here'" (p. 117). Subsequent research will undoubtedly continue to look for personality characteristics that may be related to helping behavior, but it seems likely that in the case of these emergency-related behaviors, situational factors far outweigh personality factors in determining one's responses.

The study of helping behavior in both emergency and nonemergency situations has just begun, and researchers are currently investigating the effects of many variables beyond those mentioned here. For example, several studies have indicated that people who are in a "good mood" may be more generous and helpful to others than people who are not in such a positive state (see, for example, Isen & Levin, 1972; Levin & Isen, 1975; Rosenhan, Underwood, & Moore, 1974). Other research indicates that this is not *always* the case, however (Weyant & Clark, 1976). Although many questions remain to be answered, laboratory and field research like that described in this Section, coupled with investigations of the more general concepts of altruism and helping behavior, may lead to findings that can be translated into social policies to reduce the likelihood that such tragic occurrences will take place in the future.

REFERENCES

Clark, R. D., III, & Word, L. E. Why don't bystanders help? Because of ambiguity? *Journal of Personality and Social Psychology,* 1972, *24,* 392–400.

Isen, A. M., & Levin, P. F. Effect of feeling good on helping: Cookies and kindness. *Journal of Personality and Social Psychology,* 1972, *21,* 384–388.

Latané, B., & Darley, J. M. Bystander "apathy." *American Scientist,* 1969, *57,* 244–268.

Latané, B., & Darley, J. M. *The unresponsive bystander: Why doesn't he help?* New York: Appleton-Century-Crofts, 1970.

Latané, B., & Rodin, J. A lady in distress: Inhibiting effects of friends and strangers on bystander intervention. *Journal of Experimental Social Psychology,* 1969, *5,* 189–202.

Levin, P. F., & Isen, A. M. Further studies of the effect of feeling good on helping. *Sociometry,* 1975, *38,* 141–147.

Piliavin, I. M., Piliavin, J. A., & Rodin, J. Costs, diffusion, and the stigmatized victim. *Journal of Personality and Social Psychology,* 1975, *32,* 429–438.

Piliavin, I. M., Rodin, J., & Piliavin, J. A. Good Samaritanism: An underground phenomenon? *Journal of Personality and Social Psychology,* 1969, *13,* 289–299.

Piliavin, J. A., & Piliavin, I. M. The effect of blood on reactions to a victim. *Journal of Personality and Social Psychology,* 1972, *23,* 253–261.

Piliavin, J. A., & Piliavin, I. M. The Good Samaritan: Why *does* he help? In L. Wispe (Ed.), *Positive forms of social behavior.* Cambridge, Mass.: Harvard University Press, in press.

Rosenhan, D. L., Underwood, B., & Moore, B. Affect moderates self-gratification and altruism. *Journal of Personality and Social Psychology,* 1974, *30,* 546–552.

Weyant, J., & Clark, R. D., III. Dimes and helping: The other side of the coin. Unpublished manuscript, Florida State University, 1976.

Yakimovich, D., & Saltz, E. Helping behavior: The cry for help. *Psychonomic Science,* 1971, *23,* 427–428.

SECTION II
AGGRESSION AND VIOLENCE

INTRODUCTION

The last two decades in the United States have been characterized by a sharp increase in the levels of aggression and violence. Rates of violent crimes such as murder, forcible rape, and aggravated assault have increased dramatically. The nation has been shaken by the assassinations of a President, a Nobel Peace Prize winner, and a popular U. S. Senator, as well as by other violent assaults and attempted assaults on public figures. Mass violence has wracked many of our large urban centers, and college campuses have often been the sites of violent outbursts and tense confrontations between groups. The United States found itself embroiled in an undeclared war halfway across the world—a war that cost more than one and a half million lives, most killed by arms manufactured in the United States. This war also made Americans conscious of the fact that ordinary "American boys" could be involved in brutal massacres of civilian populations.

The scientific study of the causes of aggression and violence and of ways to reduce their prevalence is obviously of crucial importance, in part because all significant human events and behavior should be subjected to scientific scrutiny, but also because techniques and expertise applicable to human survival are badly needed in a world seemingly characterized by increasing aggression, both interpersonal and international. (We will discuss some concepts of international aggression in Section 7.)

Perhaps the most basic question about human aggression concerns its origin. Are aggressive impulses in humans biologically determined, instinctive, and innate, or are they socially determined, the result of learning experiences? The answer to this question has large-scale implications for social policies designed to reduce the level of aggression in society.

This question is directly relevant to a study of the effects derived from observing aggressive behavior in others. If aggressive tendencies are innate, and if each of us carries around a "pool" of aggressive impulses, then the viewing of aggressive behavior by others may serve a very valuable function—it

39

may allow us to release or drain off our pent-up aggressive impulses while watching (and perhaps identifying with) the aggressive action. This release may prevent a future *direct* release of the aggressive energy in socially undesirable activities. This idea goes all the way back to Aristotle, who wrote in *The Art of Poetry* that drama is concerned with "incidents arousing pity and fear in such a way as to accomplish a purgation of such emotions." The term *catharsis,* derived from the Greek word for purgation, has been used to describe this process of releasing aggressive tendencies through viewing the aggressive behavior of others. Freud (1920; reprinted 1959) used the term in a somewhat related sense. He proposed that expressing a particular impulse will reduce its strength. Thus, if you are angry, then acting angrily or aggressively should make you less angry. Even if direct expression is not possible, Freud noted, indirect expression of a feeling should reduce its strength somewhat. Thus, if you feel angry and aggressive, watching someone else behave aggressively may allow you to express your anger indirectly and so feel less angry as a result.

The catharsis position is often applied today as an explanation for the popularity (and perhaps the social value) of professional football in the United States. In essence, the argument holds that the typical male football fan builds up a pool of aggressive potential over the week, having been frustrated and mistreated by his boss, his family, and so on. This potentially harmful aggressiveness is released every Sunday afternoon when he is able to watch and identify with the institutionalized aggression of pro football. He then walks away from the stadium or TV set a less aggressive man, ready to face the next week. Alfred Hitchcock has puckishly offered a similar defense of violent TV programs: "One of television's great contributions is that it brought murder back into the home where it belongs. Seeing a murder on television can be good therapy. It can help work off one's antagonisms. If you haven't any antagonisms, the commercials will give you some" (from Schellenberg, 1970, p. 31).

But what if aggressive urges are not innate or instinctually determined? What if they are the result of socialization and learning experiences? Many social scientists think this latter position is true. They point out that humans are constantly learning from their environment. When people witness acts of aggression, they are provided with models of one way to behave. If the aggression is successful—that is, if the aggressive model obtains what he or she wants by the use of aggression—is it not possible that viewers will be *more* likely to become aggressive when they find themselves in similar situations? If children are constantly exposed to violence on television, will they come to believe that it is commonplace, acceptable, or even desirable? Social psychology has accumulated a wealth of evidence that children learn from and imitate many behaviors that they see other people perform. Will this imitation take place in regard to the aggression viewed on television? Proponents of what is often called the *modeling* position argue that it will. In support of such a position, Berkowitz has commented that "For me at least, it is quite interesting that nobody has ever maintained that sexual desires can readily be satisfied through watching a couple make love. If aggressive urges are drained through seeing aggression, why aren't sexual urges lessened by watching sexual activity?" (in Larsen, 1968, p. 279).

The National Commission on the Causes and Prevention of Violence issued an official statement in September 1969 saying, in part:

Children begin to absorb the lessons of television before they can read or write. . . . In a fundamental way, television helps to create what children expect of themselves and of others, and what constitutes the standards of civilized society. . . . Yet we daily permit our children during their formative years to enter a world of police interrogation, of gangsters beating enemies, of spies performing fatal brain surgery, of routine demonstrations of killing and maiming [from Siegel, 1970, p. 197].

This basic nature/nurture controversy over whether human aggression is largely innate or learned is examined in the first article in this Section, by Leonard Berkowitz of the University of Wisconsin. In discussing this issue, Berkowitz responds to the authors of several recent popular books on human aggression. These authors—Konrad Lorenz, Robert Ardrey, Desmond Morris, and Anthony Storr—all take the general position that human aggressive tendencies *are* largely innate and are parallel to aggressive tendencies in other animal species. Berkowitz, a strong advocate of the learning, or modeling, position, chides them for their "conceptual simplicity."

The two remaining articles in this Section focus on the specific problem of the effect of televised material on viewers, especially children. Our second article focuses on televised "ethnic" aggression and humor that derogate minority groups. John Brigham looks at the "lovable bigot" Archie Bunker, star of the popular television program "All in the Family." As he notes, media "experts" were sharply divided in their opinions concerning whether the show, which features Archie's constant ethnic slurs, insults, and jokes, had a beneficial effect on interracial attitudes and aggression, a harmful effect, or no effect at all. The data presented in this article provide a starting point for finding out which is the case.

One outcome of the growing fears about the impact of televised violence on children was the appointment of the Surgeon General's Scientific Advisory Committee on Television and Social Behavior in June, 1969. In our third article, John P. Murray, then at the National Institute of Mental Health, discusses the impact of the Committee's five-volume report, which was issued in early 1972. The impact and implications of this research will be discussed further in the Section Summary.

REFERENCES

Freud, S. *Beyond the pleasure principle*. New York: Bantam Books, 1959. (Originally published in German, 1920.)

Larsen, O. M. (Ed.), *Violence and the mass media*. New York: Harper & Row, 1968.

Schellenberg, J. A. *An introduction to social psychology*. New York: Random House, 1970.

Siegel, A. E. Violence and aggression are not inevitable. In M. Wertheimer (Ed.), *Confrontation: Psychology and the problems of today*. Glenview, Ill.: Scott, Foresman, 1970. Pp. 196–199.

ARTICLE 4

Simple views of aggression: An essay review

Leonard Berkowitz

The theme of this essay will be drawn from a dust jacket. On the back of the book *Human Aggression* by the British psychiatrist Anthony Storr, we find the following comment by Konrad Lorenz, widely renowned as the "father of ethology": "An ancient proverb says that simplicity is the sign of truth—and of fallacy . . . However, if the simple explanation is in full agreement with a wealth of data, and quite particularly, if it dovetails with data collected in altogether different fields of knowledge, simplicity certainly is indicative of truth." Four of the books reviewed here offer essentially simplistic messages. With the writers represented in the fifth work, I shall argue that the conceptual simplicity advocated by these volumes is definitely *not* "indicative of the truth." All of the books deal with man's capacity for violence, a problem deserving—no, demanding—careful and sophisticated consideration. The four volumes I shall concentrate on, those by Lorenz, Ardrey, Storr, and Morris —and especially the first three—provide only easy formulas readily grasped by a wide audience rather than the necessary close analysis. Being easily understood, their explanation of human aggression helps relieve the anxiety born of the public's concern with war, social unrest, race riots, and student protests, but is an inadequate, and perhaps even dangerous, basis for social policy.

All four voice essentially the same message: Much of human behavior generally, and human aggression in particular, must be traced in large part to man's animal nature. Aggression often arises for innately determined reasons, they say. The authors differ somewhat, however, in how they believe this nature leads to aggression. For Lorenz, Ardrey, and Storr (whom I shall refer to as the Lorenzians), a spontaneously engendered drive impels us to aggression, even to the destruction of other persons. Morris, on the other hand, views many of our aggressive acts as genetically governed responses to certain environmental conditions and to signals sent

Reprinted from *American Scientist,* 1969, **57**(3), 372–383, with the permission of *American Scientist,* Journal of Sigma Xi, The Scientific Research Society of North America.

to us by other people. Nonetheless, over and above their similarities and differences, all four volumes present a highly simplified conception of the causes of and possible remedies for human aggression, and I think it would be well for us to look at a number of these misleading oversimplifications.

THE ROLE OF LEARNING IN HUMAN AGGRESSION

Facing the writers at their own level, one misconception I shall not deal with here is their relative neglect of the role of learning in human aggression. Our behavior is influenced by our experiences *and* our inherited biological characteristics. I have argued elsewhere that innate determinants do enter into man's attacks on others, primarily in connection with impulsive reactions to noxious events and frustrations. These constitutionally governed impulsive responses can be modified by learning, however. The Lorenzians do not appear to recognize this kind of modification in these volumes. They draw a very sharp distinction between learned and innately determined responses, thus ignoring what is now known of the complex interplay between nature and nurture. Lorenz has admitted this on occasion, and the journalist, Joseph Alsop, has recently reported him as saying, "We ethologists were mistaken in the past when we made a sharp distinction between 'innate' and 'learned.'" Of course, there is also an experience-is-all imperialism at the opposite extreme. In sharp contrast to many ethologists and zoologists, social scientists typically have long ignored and even denied the role of built-in, biological determinants. Ashley Montagu's critical discussion of Lorenz in his introduction to *Man and Aggression* is illustrative. "The notable thing about human behavior," he says, "is that it is learned. Everything a human being does as such he has had to learn from other human beings."

Some book reviewers for the popular press, aware of these opposing stances, have approached the present volumes in terms of this kind of polarization. *If* human aggressiveness is learned, Lorenz, *et al.,* are obviously incorrect, but on the other hand, innate determinants to aggression presumably must operate as described by Ardrey, Lorenz, Morris, and Storr. Ardrey, Lorenz, and Storr pose the issue in these simple terms. Critics dispute their views, they maintain, primarily because of a misguided "American optimism"; American social scientists, psychologists and psychiatrists, having a liberal belief in the perfectibility of man, want to attribute social ills—including violence—to environmental flaws which might be remedied rather than to intractable human nature. The critics certainly would recognize the existence of man's innate aggressive drive if they could only shed their honorable but mistaken vision of Utopia.

There are other alternatives, however. Some of human aggressiveness might derive from man's biological properties, characteristics which he shares to some degree with the other animals. He might even be innately "programmed" to respond violently to particular kinds of stimulation, much as other animals do. But his animal characteristics do not have to function the way Lorenz and his associates say they do. The Lorenzian analysis of aggression can be criticized on a logical and empirical basis independently of any general assumptions about the nature of man.

The volume *Man and Aggression,* edited by Montagu, serves as a counterpoise to the Lorenzian books. A number of journalist-reviewers have assumed that Lorenz' views are shared by virtually all students of animal behavior. The Montagu volume clearly shows that there is not the unanimity of support that the laymen believe exists. Many eminent zoologists, as well as comparative psychologists, have taken Lorenz's analysis of aggression seriously to task. *Man and Aggression* is a compilation of generally damning criticisms of the Lorenz and Ardrey books by such authorities as S. A. Barnett, J. H. Crook, T. C. Schneirla, and Sir Solly Zuckerman, as well as Lorenz' old opponent, J. P. Scott. For those people who have read only the Lorenzian analyses, Lorenz may speak for all ethologists; Lorenz is equated with all of ethology in the Storr book, *Human Aggression*. Yet he is not all of the science of animal behavior, and there are many good reasons in the animal as well as human research literature to question the over-all thrust of Dr. Lorenz' argument on grounds besides the "overbold and loose" nature of the Lorenzian contentions generally recognized by many readers.

We need not here review the many objections to the Lorenz and Ardrey volumes that are summarized by the critics included in *Man and Aggression*. However, some of the oversimplifications and errors of reasoning and fact that are characteristic of these two books are also prevalent in the Storr and Morris works, and I think it is important to point out several of these common weaknesses in the extension of popular biology to human aggression.

THE USE OF ANALOGIES

As nearly every critic of these Lorenzian books has pointed out, the writers are excessively free-wheeling in their use of analogies. They frequently attempt to explain various human actions by drawing gross analogies between these behaviors and supposedly similar response patterns exhibited by other animal species. Attaching the same label to these human and animal behaviors, the writers then maintain that they have explained the actions. For Lorenz, man is remarkably similar to the Greylag Goose. The resemblances (that occur to Lorenz but not necessarily to other observers) are supposedly far from superficial ones, and he believes that they can only be explained by the operation of the same mechanisms in man and goose. ". . . highly complex norms of behavior such as falling in love, strife for ranking order, jealousy, grieving, etc. are not only similar but down to the most absurd details the same . . ." and therefore, all of these actions must be governed by instincts.

The analogy emphasized by Ardrey, of course, is based on animal territoriality. Man's genetic endowment supposedly drives him to gain and defend property, much as other animals do, presumably because this territorial behavior provides identity,

stimulation, and security. Basing part of his argument on a study of the lemurs of Madagascar, Ardrey contends that there are two types of societies, noyaux (societies said to be held together by the inward antagonism of the members) and nations (societies in which joint defense of territory has given rise to ingroup leadership and cooperation). The examples of noyaux listed by Ardrey include, in addition to the Madagascar lemurs, herring gull colonies, certain groups of gibbons, and Italy and France.

Morris' analogy, needless to say, is between humans and apes. His theme is that "*Homo sapiens* has remained a naked ape . . . in acquiring lofty new motives, he has lost none of the earthy old ones." We cannot understand the nature of our aggressive urges, he says along with Ardrey, Lorenz, and Storr, unless we consider "the background of our animal origins." Unlike the Lorenzians, however, he doubts the existence of an innate, spontaneous aggressive drive, and emphasizes, to the exclusion of such a drive, the genetically determined signals he believes both apes and people send to their fellows. All four authors make much of the control of aggression by supposedly innate appeasement gestures, although Morris seems to have greater confidence in their efficacy than do the others. He even tells us how we should respond to an angry traffic policeman on the basis of this analogy between human and animal behaviors: The policeman's aggression can (theoretically) be turned off automatically by showing abject submission in our words, body postures, and facial expressions. Moreover, it is essential to "get quickly out of the car and move away from it towards the policeman." This prevents the policeman from invading our territory (our car) and weakens feelings of territorial rivalry. The looks people give each other are very important signals, Morris maintains in accord with a rapidly growing body of experimental-social psychological research, but, in contrast to these investigators, he oversimplifies greatly. Morris contends that prolonged looking at another is an aggressive act. In reality, persistent eye-contact can also be a very intimate, even sexual, encounter, or may arise from a search for information or social support.

This type of crude analogizing is *at best* an incomplete analysis of the behavior the writers seek to explain. Important data are neglected and vital differences are denied. J. H. Crook's excellent paper in *Man and Aggression* (which should be read by every person who has written a favorable review of the Lorenz and Ardrey books) notes the many important considerations omitted by the Lorenzians in general and Ardrey's treatment of territoriality in particular. Where Ardrey, following Lorenz, maintains that territorial behavior is a highly fixed, species-specific action pattern produced by energy accumulating in certain centers in the nervous system, the truth cannot be packaged as easily as this. Many different conditions enter into animal territoriality. The outcome is a complex interaction of ecological and social conditions with internal states so that territorial behavior is far from inevitable as a species characteristic. Territorial maintenance, furthermore, involves different components, such as attack and escape. These components are probably governed by somewhat different, although often interrelated, mechanisms, and appear to be susceptible to different environmental and internal conditions. Given these complexities and the multiplicity of factors involved in the territoriality displayed by birds, we cannot make simple statements about the functions and causes of territoriality even in these species, and it is highly unlikely that human concern with property is controlled by the same processes. Crook's conclusion is certainly reasonable: "The likelihood that the motivation control of territorial behavior is at a different level from that of fishes and birds suggests that human resemblances to the lower animals might be largely through analogy rather than homology." Sixteen years ago, Daniel Lehrman remarked, in an outstanding critique of Lorenzian theory, "it is not very judicious, and actually is rash . . . to assume that the mechanisms underlying two similar response characteristics are in any way identical, homologous, or even similar," merely because the actions of different species or entities seem to resemble each other (in the eyes of the writer, we might add).

THE NOTION OF RITUALIZATION

The same comment can be made about the analogizing involved in Lorenz' and Storr's use of the notion of ritualization. Theorizing that there are evolutionary changes in behavior as well as structure, and that particular action patterns, such as appeasement gestures, have evolved from other behaviors, Lorenz argues that responses originally serving one function can undergo alteration in the course of evolution so that they come to have a different function as well. The drive or energy motivating the original action presumably still powers this altered behavior. According to Lorenz, the appeasement or greetings ceremonies performed by humans and animals alike have become ritualized in this manner through evolutionary developments but still make use of transformed aggressive motivation. Lorenz thinks that the smile of greeting, as an example, might have "evolved by ritualization of redirected threatening." Storr, adopting Lorenz' reasoning, also speaks of "ritualizing the aggressive drive in such a way that it serves the function of uniting" people. For both of these writers, diverted aggressive energy powers the social bonds which tie individuals together in affection and even love. Now, we must ask, is there really good reason to contend, as Lorenz does so authoritatively, that the human smile, the appeasement gesture of the macaques (baring the teeth), and the triumph ceremony of the geese must have evolved in the same way from some original aggressive display? The supposed similarity between the human, monkey, and goose behavior does not mean, as Lehrman pointed out, that the processes underlying these actions are "identical, homologous, or even similar." Elaborating further, in his essay in *Man and Aggression,* Barnett says there is no justification for the "confident, dogmatic assertions Lorenz and his followers have made about the hypothetical process, 'ritualization.' " Harlow's observations regarding monkey development are also troublesome for the Lorenzian analysis of the genesis of social bonds. Affectional patterns generally emerge *before* aggressive ones in these animals, making it unlikely that the earlier, affectional-social acts are "driven" by aggressive motivation.

The dangers of unwarranted analogizing can also be illustrated by referring to another example of "ritualization" mentioned by Storr. It appears that the Kurelu, a primitive people in the heart of New Guinea, engage in frequent intertribal warfare. But instead of killing one another, the warriors shoot arrows at each other from a distance just beyond arrow range and rarely hit each other. Although this type of warfare seems to resemble the threat ceremonies exhibited by a number of animal species, we certainly cannot argue that the Kurelu behavior and animal threats have evolved in exactly the same manner or are based on similar biological mechanisms. Furthermore, both action patterns may ultimately lead to a cessation of attacks—but probably for very different reasons. It is also improper to insist, as the Lorenzians do, that competitive sports are the same type of ritual as the Kurelu warfare and animal threats merely because some writers have applied the same label to all three sets of phenomena; the surface resemblances do not guarantee that all have the same evolutionary causes and that all operate in the same or even in a similar way.

When we come right down to it, there seems to be a kind of "word magic" in this analogizing. The writers appear to believe that they have provided an adequate explanation of the phenomenon at issue by attaching a label to it: a person's smile is an *appeasement gesture;* athletic events are *rituals* comparable to certain animal displays, etc. Storr shows just this kind of thinking in the "proof" he offers for the notion of a general aggressive drive. Aggression is not all bad, Storr insists (in agreement with Lorenz); aggression is necessary to the optimal development of man. It is "the basis of intellectual achievement, of the attainment of independence, and even of that proper pride which enables a man to hold his head high amongst his fellows." The evidence he cites for this statement is word usage: ". . . the words we use to describe intellectual effort are aggressive words. We *attack* problems, or *get our teeth* into them. We *master* a subject when we have *struggled with* and *overcome* its difficulties. We *sharpen* our wits . . ." (Italics in the original.) Waving his words over the particular behavior (in this case, striving for independence and achievement), he has thus supposedly accounted for these actions—and has also swept aside the many studies of achievement motivation by McClelland and his associates suggesting that there is very little similarity between the instigation to aggression and achievement motivation.

Popular discussions of the role of evolution in behavior can also be criticized on this basis. Even if it can be shown that a given behavior pattern has "evolved," such a demonstration does not explain the performance of that action by a particular individual in a specific setting. The application of the word "evolution" does not really help us to understand what mechanisms govern the behavior in this individual or what stimulus conditions affect these mechanisms.

INSTINCTIVE HUMAN ACTIONS

The Lorenzians (and Morris as well) also display this same word magic in the ease with which they refer to human actions as instinctive. Without taking the trouble to specify the criteria they employ in making their designations, they go scattering the label "instinct" around with great relish. As an illustration, in his book *On Aggression,* Lorenz talks about people having an "instinctive need to be a member of a closely knit group fighting for common ideals," and insists that "there cannot be the slightest doubt that militant enthusiasm is instinctive and evolved out of a communal defense response." Doubts must exist, however. The Lorenzians offer neither a precise definition of what they mean by "instinct" nor any substantial evidence that the behavior in question, whether human aggression or militant enthusiasm, is innate even in their vague usage of this term. Several of the writers in *Man and Aggression* (e.g., Barnett and Schneirla), as well as other scientists such as Lehrman, criticize Lorenz severely for his excessively casual employment of the instinct concept. Lorenz elsewhere has acknowledged this imprecision in his popular utterances (see, for example, the previously mentioned article by Alsop), saying that he has used the word only in a shorthand sense.

Nevertheless, the over-simplification regarding "instincts" so prevalent in the Lorenz-Ardrey-Storr writings is difficult to excuse as only shorthand. To say this is not to deny the role of innate processes in human behavior; such determinants apparently exist. Psychologists, together with other students of behavior, have shown, as an example, that human babies have a built-in preference for certain visual stimuli, and do not start with blank neural pages, so to speak, in learning to see and organize complex visual stimulation. The difficulty is that ideas such as Lorenz' "instinctive need to be a member of a closely knit group fighting for common ideals" are, in actuality, extremely drastic departures from the more precise instinct concept found in technical ethological discussions. When they write for an audience of their peers, ethologists generally describe instincts, or better still, instinctive movements, as behavioral sequences culminating in "fixed action patterns." These patterns, which are at the core of the instinct concept, are thought of as rigid and stereotyped species-specific *consummatory* responses generally serving to end a chain of ongoing behavior. Can this definition be applied to "militant enthusiasm"? What is the rigid and stereotyped action that unerringly unfolds to consummate the hypothetical enthusiasm pattern?

SPORTS AS OUTLETS FOR AGGRESSION

We now come to the most important part of the Lorenzian instinct conception, and the feature that has the gravest social implications: the supposed spontaneity of the behavior. The stereotyped instinctive action is said to be impelled by a specific energy that has accumulated in that part of the central nervous system responsible for the coordination of the behavior. The energy presumably builds up spontaneously and is discharged when the response is performed. If the instinctive activity is not carried out for a considerable period of time, the accumulated energy may cause the response to "pop off" *in vacuo*. Aggression, according to Lorenz, Ardrey, and Storr—but not Morris—follows this formula. "It is the spontaneity of the (aggressive) instinct," Lorenz tells us, "that makes it so dangerous." The behavior "can 'explode' without demonstrable external stimulation" merely because the internal accumulating energy has not been discharged by aggressive actions or has not been diverted into other response channels as, for example, in the case of such "ritualized" activities as sports. If violence is to be lessened, suitable outlets must be provided. Lorenz believes that "present-day civilized man suffers from insufficient discharge of his aggressive drive," and together with Ardrey and Storr, calls for more athletic competitions—bigger and better Olympic games. (Denying the Lorenzian formulation, Morris maintains that we do not have an inborn urge to destroy our opponents—only to dominate them—and argues that the only solution is "massive de-population" rather than "boisterous international football.")

This conception can be discussed at various levels. Neurologically, for one thing, Lorenz bases his assertions on observations regarding cardiac and respiratory activities and simple motor coordinations. With such critics as Lehrman and Moltz we must question whether or not these findings can be extended to more complex neural organizations, to say nothing of human aggression. (The Lorenzian interpretation of these observations can also be disputed, as Moltz has shown in the 1965 *Psychological Review*.)

There are empirical difficulties as well as this problem of the long inductive leap. Basing their arguments on a number of studies, Hinde and Ziegler (the latter in an important 1964 *Psychological Bulletin* paper) have proposed that many apparent demonstrations of internally-driven spontaneity can be traced to external stimuli and the operation of associative factors. The responses evidently are evoked by environmental stimuli rather than being driven out by spontaneously accumulating internal excitation. Moltz has also summarized evidence disputing the Lorenzian notion that response performance is necessary if there is to be a reduction in the elicitability of the instinctive action pattern. As Hinde has suggested in several papers, stimulus satiation rather than a response-produced discharge of instinctive action-specific energy may cause a lessening in response elicitability.

COMPLEX ASPECTS OF ANIMAL AND HUMAN AGGRESSION

Going from the simple motor coordinations of the lower animals to the more complex aspects of animal and human aggression, the available data are even less kind to the Lorenzian formulation. Of course Lorenz maintains that his ideas are supported by a substantial body of observations. They are upheld, he says, by the failures of "an American method of education" to produce less aggressive children, even though the youngsters have been supposedly "spared all disappointments and indulged in every way." However, as I have pointed out elsewhere in discussing this argument, excessively indulged children probably expect to be gratified most of the time, so that the inevitable occasional frustrations they encounter are actually relatively strong thwartings for them. There is little doubt that these frustrations can produce aggressive reactions, and Lorenz' criticism of the frustration-aggression hypothesis is a very weak one. Belief in this hypothesis, by the way, does not necessarily mean advocating a completely frustration-free environment for children. Child specialists increasingly recognize that youngsters must learn to cope with and adapt to life's inescapable thwartings, and thus must experience at least some frustrations in the course of growing up. Nor do most contemporary

psychologists believe that frustration is the only source of aggression. Violence can have its roots in pain as well as in obstacles to goal attainment, and can also be learned as other actions are learned.

Aggression, in other words, has a number of different causes, although the Lorenzians seem to recognize (or at least discuss) only one source. Here is yet another erroneous oversimplification: their notion of a unitary drive that is supposedly capable of powering a wide variety of behaviors from ritualized smiling to strivings for independence or dominance. This general drive conception is very similar to the motivational thinking in classical psychoanalysis, but is running into more and more difficulty under the careful scrutiny of biologists and psychologists. Indeed, contrary to Storr's previously cited argument, there is no single instigation to aggression even in the lower animals. Moyer recently has suggested (in the 1968 *Communications in Behavioral Biology*), on the basis of many findings, that there are several kinds of aggression, each of which has a particular neural and endocrine basis.

THE FLOW OF AGGRESSIVE ENERGY

Also like the traditional psychoanalysts, the Lorenzians speak loosely of aggressive energy flowing from one channel of behavior to another. This hypothetical process, mentioned earlier in conjunction with "ritualization," must be differentiated from the more precisely defined response-generalization concept developed by experimental psychologists. Reinforcements provided to one kind of reaction may strengthen other, similar responses. Rewarding a child for making aggressive remarks can increase the likelihood of other kinds of aggressive reactions as well. The reinforcement influence generalizes from one kind of response to another because the actions have something in common. (The actor might regard both types of responses as *hurting* someone.) It is theoretically unparsimonious and even inadvisable to interpret this effect as an energy transfer from one response channel to another. The Lorenz-Storr discussion of ritualization, and the related psychoanalytic concept of sublimation as well, employs just this kind of energy-diversion idea. We cannot here go into the conceptual pitfalls of this analytical model. (The interested reader might wish to read Hinde's article on energy models of motivation in the 1960 *Symposia of the Society for Experimental Biology*.) But there is a fairly obvious flaw in the Lorenzian statement that pent-up aggressive energy can be discharged in competitive sports. Rather than lessening violence, athletic events have sometimes excited supporters of one or both of the competing teams into attacking other persons. This has happened in many countries: in England, as Crook points out and as Storr should have recognized, in this country at times when white and Negro high school basketball teams have competed against each other, and most dramatically, this past March in Czechoslovakia when the Czechs defeated the Russians in hockey. In these cases, the team supporters were so aroused, even when their team won, that they were extremely responsive to aggressive stimuli in the environment.

Experimental tests of the hostility catharsis hypothesis also argue against the energy-diversion idea inherent in both Lorenzian and psychoanalytic theorizing. This well-worn notion maintains, of course, that the display of aggressive behavior in fantasy, play, or real life, will reduce the aggressive urge. Although there is no explicit reference to a catharsis process in Storr's book, his belief that aggressive energy can be sublimated certainly is consistent with the catharsis doctrine. Lorenz comes much closer to a frank acceptance of this idea in his contention that "civilized man suffers from insufficient discharge of his aggressive drive," and in a bit of advice he offers to people on expeditions to the remote corners of the world. Members of socially isolated groups, he says in *On Aggression*, must inevitably experience a build-up of aggressive drive; outsiders aren't available to be attacked and thus provide an outlet for the accumulating aggressive energy. If a person in such an isolated group wishes to prevent the intra-group conflict that otherwise must develop (Lorenz insists), he should smash a vase with as loud and resounding a crash as possible. We do not have to attack other people in order to experience a cathartic reduction in our aggressive urge; it's enough merely to destroy inanimate objects.

SUMMARY

Summarizing (and simplifying) a great many studies, research results suggest that angry people often do (a) feel better, and (b) perhaps even experience a temporarily reduced inclination to attack their tormentors, upon learning that these persons have been hurt. This phenomenon seems to be quite specific, however; the provoked individual is gratified when he finds that the intended target of his aggression has been injured, and does not appear to get the same satisfaction from attacks on innocent bystanders. Besides this, the apparent reduction in the instigation to aggression following an attack is probably often due to guilt- or anxiety-induced restraints evoked by the attack and/or the arousal of other, nonaggressive motives, and is not really the result of an energy discharge. Standard experimental-psychological analysis can do a far better job than the energy-discharge model in explaining the available data. Recent experiments indicate, for example, that the lessening of physiological tension produced by injuring the anger instigator comes about when the aggressor has learned that aggression is frequently rewarded. This tension reduction, or gratification, is evidently akin to a reinforcement effect, and is not indicative of any long-lasting decline in the likelihood of aggression; people who find aggression rewarding are more, not less, likely to attack someone again in the future. The reinforcement process can also account for the appetitive behavior Lorenz and Storr seem to regard as prime evidence for the existence of a spontaneous aggressive drive. Provoked animals will go out of their way to obtain suitable targets to attack, while youngsters who are frequently aggressive toward their peers generally prefer violent TV programs to more peaceful ones. But this search for an appropriate target or for aggressive scenes probably arises from the reinforcing nature of these stimuli rather than from some spontaneous drive, and again, does not mean that there has been an energy discharge when these stimuli are encountered. Quite the contrary. There is some reason to believe that the presence of such aggression-reinforcing stimuli as other people fighting can evoke aggressive responses from those who are ready to act aggressively—much as the sight of food (which is a reinforcement for eating) can elicit eating responses from those who are set to make such responses.

In the end, the Lorenzian analyses must be questioned because of their policy implications as well as because of their scientific inadequacies. Their reliance on casual anecdotes instead of carefully controlled, systematic data, their use of ill-defined terms and gross analogies, and their disregard of hundreds of relevant studies in the interest of an over-simplified theory warrant the disapproval generally accorded them by technical journals. But more than this, the Lorenz-Ardrey-Storr books can also have unfortunate social as well as scientific consequences by impeding recognition of the important roles played by environmental stimuli and learning in aggressive behavior, and by blocking awareness of an important social principle: Aggression is all too likely to lead to still more aggression.

REFERENCES

Ardrey, R. *The territorial imperative.* New York: Atheneum, 1966.

Lorenz, K. *On aggression.* New York: Harcourt Brace Jovanovich, 1966.

Montagu, M. F. A. (Ed.) *Man and aggression.* New York: Oxford University Press, 1968.

Morris, D. *The naked ape.* New York: McGraw-Hill, 1968.

Storr, A. *Human aggression.* New York: Atheneum, 1968.

ARTICLE 5

Verbal aggression and ethnic humor: What is their effect?

John C. Brigham

Probably no American television program in recent years has stirred as much praise and censure as the immensely successful CBS program "All in the Family." Originally aired as a mid-season replacement in January 1971, "All in the Family" became the most popular television program in the country within a few months. It has stayed at or near the top of the ratings for years. Much of the controversy surrounding the program has focused on its treatment of previously taboo subjects: ethnic and sexual bigotry, homosexuality, abortion, death, and other "sensitive" topics.

A number of people have been both intrigued by and concerned over the effect of this blockbuster program on the 50 to 60 million viewers who watch it each week. Particularly controversial are the strident bigotry and verbal aggression of the central character, Archie Bunker, epitomized in his frequent references to "hebes," "dagos," "spicks," "gooks," "polacks," "fruits," "commies," "spades," and so forth. In fact, as Laura Hobson (1971) has pointed out, Archie seems to make use of virtually every derogatory ethnic term that circulates in current American society, with the exception of the explosive term "nigger." What happens to the men, women, and children who are exposed to all this verbal aggression? Do they learn new ways of labeling and perhaps reacting to members of different ethnic groups? Are they provided with further ammunition to use when they feel frustrated or aggressive? Or, on the other hand, might they be shown the folly of such excess, the crudeness, the futility, and the ludicrousness of such bigotry?

Observers have been widely and vocally split on their answers to these questions. Not surprisingly, those persons directly connected with the show, such as Carroll O'Connor, the actor who plays Archie, and Norman Lear, its developer and producer, see it as having a beneficial effect. In an interview in *Ebony*, O'Connor commented "Well, I think we are doing something that needs to be done and that is to show a racist what he is doing. I mean showing him truthfully what he is doing. Now our intention is not to make the racist laugh and enjoy himself. Our intention is to show him just what he is doing. (Sanders, 1972, p. 192).'' In a later interview, O'Connor asserted ''A lot of people write that we are making them understand their own feelings and their own prejudices'' (*Playboy,* 1973).

There seem to be two streams of thought that culminate in predictions that ''All in the Family'' will have a beneficial effect on ethnic relations. On one hand, some writers seem to adopt a modification of the Freudian *catharsis* position described briefly in the Section Introduction—namely, that viewers will become less aggressive from viewing the program, since by observing the hostile ethnic humor that Archie provides they will be able to release their own aggressive tendencies vicariously. In this way, viewers will be less likely to behave in an aggressive manner later on. This claim, of course, parallels arguments supporting the depiction of violence on television.

A second position, the one taken by O'Connor and Lear among others, might be termed a *constructive learning* approach. This is the idea that Archie's expression of his own prejudices and their rebuttal in the program from Mike and other characters highlight the absurdity of such prejudices. Recognition of this absurdity by the viewer could serve as a stimulus for change in the direction of reduced ethnic prejudice and hostility.

But not all observers are willing to accept either of these hypotheses. To many, the likely effect of the program is a negative and frightening one— namely, an increase in the acceptability of verbal aggression, ethnic bigotry, and discriminatory behavior. If Archie provides an attractive or ''lovable'' *model* for viewers, and if the modeling includes racial and ethnic attitudes, then an increase in verbal aggression and prejudice on the part of the viewers could be expected. From the research on the effects of viewed aggression discussed in this Section, we can note the strong evidence that modeling in viewers often does occur, at least for aggressive behavior.

The disparity of opinion about the program's effect can be illustrated by several letters published in the *New York Times Magazine* in April 1972, reacting to an earlier article (Hano, 1972) on ''All in the Family.'' One viewer wrote ''I have watched with great glee as Archie's stupidity is exposed, week after week; and at the same time I realize that after turning off the set what I am going to be left with is a feeling of overwhelming pity. He's pathetic, not hateful.'' Another said ''In spite of the outraged voices of its relatively few critics, no one is inclined to click off the program, because Archie brings humor and ethos into our lives. Humor, the saving grace, puts all temporal vanities into a more objective and realistic light, a light that has been sadly dimmed in the past decade.'' On the other hand, ''[The earlier article] concludes that '50 million Americans are being told, week after week, it does no good to be a bigot.' As Archie in the same issue of the magazine would say, 'Bull ----!' All this highfaluting talk about satire, America laughing at itself, lampooning a way of life is, to repeat, just so much 'Bull ----.' In my opinion, the only meaningful conclusions that can be drawn are that 50 million Americans (excluding Mr. Hano and a few of his friends) are laughing *with,* not *at,* Archie, and that millions of children who are avid viewers, by their very youth, have not attained the necessary sophistication to appreciate the 'satirical' message'' (*New York Times Magazine,* 1972, pp. 20–21).

Yet, despite the anger and outrage on both sides, the data needed for making an objective appraisal of the program's effect simply are not available. As John Rich, a producer-director of the show, has said, ''Nobody knows exactly who watches Archie Bunker—no research!'' Rich's own view is that the controversy is unwarranted: ''Look, it's a 24-minute entertainment and that's all. It would be foolish to put anything so important on such a little section of our lives. It won't contribute to bigotry, or erase it. It won't change things'' (quoted in Woods, 1973, p. 29).

A more complex analysis was suggested by UCLA professor of communications Andrea Rich (cited in Gross, 1975), according to which there are at least five "types" of viewers. The *bristling liberals* are so enraged by Archie's behavior that they hate the show and cannot evaluate it on rational grounds. The *open-minded liberals* see the satire in the show and naïvely assume that everyone else sees the satire too. The *perceptive bigots* also perceive the show's satiric intent but hate the show because of it and will not watch. The *nonperceptive bigots* do not see the satire but rather see Archie as always right and always winning. They are likely to be regular viewers of the show. Finally, the *acculturated bigots* are "society's chameleons," who adopt the attitudes, prejudices, and behaviors of their surroundings. It is these people, Rich suggests, who may possibly change their attitudes and become less prejudiced or less verbally aggressive as a result of viewing the show. Unfortunately, as intriguing as this typology is, there are as yet no data from which to evaluate how accurate it is.

So the battle lines are drawn. Does the program have a beneficial effect in reducing prejudice, as Lear (1971), O'Connor, and others (for example, Hano, 1972) claim, or does the program institutionalize the "lovable bigot," making it easier for potential bigots across the country to act out their bigotry, as still others maintain (for example, Hobson, 1971; Levy, 1972; Sanders, 1972)? Or is John Rich right in arguing that a 24-minute segment of anything, no matter how frequently it is presented or by how many people it is viewed, is not likely to change anything of importance?

What little empirical evidence is available does not allow for any clear-cut answers to these questions. Vidmar and Rokeach (1974) surveyed White adolescents in Canada and the United States and found that racial prejudice was associated with admiration for Archie and with a tendency to see Archie as "winning" in the arguments that occur so often in the program. They also found that frequency of viewing was related to prejudice in their American but not in their Canadian sample. Vidmar

and Rokeach argue that their findings "suggest that the program is more likely reinforcing prejudice and racism than combating it" (p. 46).

Brigham and Giesbrecht (in press) carried out a somewhat similar study in 1973. They questioned both White and Black viewers, including college students and others, in the deep South. It is a reflection of the breadth of the program's appeal that, like Vidmar and Rokeach, they found no relationship between racial attitude and enjoyment of the program. Unlike Vidmar and Rokeach, however, they found no relationship whatsoever between frequency of viewing and racial attitude. For White viewers, high prejudice *was* associated with tendency to like and agree with Archie, to agree that Archie's view of Blacks was valid, and to see the program as having a harmful effect on race relations. Within the Black samples, no such relationships were observed. However, Blacks who most *enjoyed* the program were significantly more likely to see its effect on race relations as more beneficial, and to feel less agreement with Archie and the views he expresses. On the whole, White viewers saw the effect of the program in a somewhat more positive light than did Black viewers, although viewers of both races appeared to enjoy the program equally well. Hence, the results suggested that racial attitude was a significant factor in reacting to the program and its characters for Whites but not for Blacks. Racial attitude was not related to enjoyment of the program or how frequently it was watched for viewers of either race.

In order to gather further data in this area, another survey of Black and White college students was carried out in 1975 (Brigham, 1975). As in the earlier findings of Brigham and Giesbrecht (in press), no relationship between racial attitude and either enjoyment of the program or frequency of viewing was found, for either Whites or Blacks. Hence, there was no support for a "selective exposure" hypothesis—that is, that people with more hostile racial attitudes would be more likely to watch the program. Once again, liking for Archie and agreement with his racial views, and the belief that the program had a harmful effect on race relations, were significantly related to racial prejudice in Whites, as Table 1 indicates. Additionally, perceptions of the program's *intent* were strongly related to racial attitudes. The Vidmar-Rokeach study had provided suggestive evidence that highly prejudiced Whites were significantly less likely to see the program as a satire of Archie or his views. The present data provide strong support for this contention. Furthermore, such highly prejudiced Whites were significantly more likely to see Archie as "winning" and as making more sense in the arguments that characterize the program. None of these relationships were found within the Black sample.

TABLE 1. Correlations between overall favorability of racial attitudes and reactions to "All in the Family" (AITF) for Black and White college students.

	White students		Black students	
	1975	1973	1975	1973
	(N=165)	(N=155)	(N=50)	(N=46)
Frequency of watching AITF	.07	−.02	.05	−.11
Enjoyment of AITF	.13	−.03	.01	.12
Agree with, like Archie (sum of 7 questions)	−.55**	−.60**	.02	−.09
See Archie winning (4 questions)	−.40**	—†	−.09	—†
See show as satire (4 questions)	.46**	—†	−.17	—†
Blacks are as Archie says (2 questions)	−.63**	−.62**	−.13	−.06
AITF helps race relations (4 questions)	.16*	.14*	.18	−.01

*p < .05
**p < .01
†not asked in 1973

The White subjects also completed the Attitudes toward Women scale (AWS) developed by Spence and Helmreich (1972). As Table 2 indicates, the relationships between AWS scores and reactions to the program were strikingly similar to the relationships involving racial attitudes; that is, Whites with favorable attitudes toward women rated the program similarly to the way that Whites with favorable racial attitudes did.

TABLE 2. Correlations between reactions to "All in the Family" and attitudes toward women (AWS) for White students, and Black students' attitudes toward Whites and toward racial integration.

	White students	Black students	
	AWS score†	Att. whites†	Att. integ.†
Frequency of watching AITF	.08	−.08	.05
Enjoyment of AITF	.02	.20	.01
Agree with, like Archie	−.44**	.21	−.31*
See Archie winning	−.41**	.05	−.16
See show as satire	.40**	−.28	−.04
Blacks are as Archie says	−.39**	.16	−.38**
AITF helps race relations	.16*	.31*	

†High scores denote favorable attitudes toward women, Whites, racial integration.
*p < .05
**p < .01

For Black subjects, general reactions to the program were not systematically related to overall racial attitudes (Table 1). However, when the racial-attitude inventory was subdivided into attitude toward Whites and attitude toward racial integration, it was found that Blacks most favorable to integration showed significantly less agreement with Archie and with his racial views (Table 2). Those Blacks with more negative attitudes toward Whites, on the other hand, were more likely to see the program as having a negative effect on race relations in general.

A comparison across races shows that Blacks and Whites did not differ significantly on their degree of agreement with or liking for Archie (a finding also reported by Tate & Surlin, 1975), their feeling about whether Archie wins the arguments, or their agreement with Archie's racial views. Significant between-race differences (p < .001) were found, however, for the two remaining dimensions: Whites were significantly more likely than Blacks to see the show as a satire and to rate it as helpful in race relations.

The results of this survey, in conjunction with earlier research, suggest the following general findings. (1) Contrary to what some have suggested, the viewing audience of "All in the Family" does not appear to contain a disproportionate number of rabidly cheering White racists or of relatively un- prejudiced "White liberals." Frequency of viewing was not related to racial attitude for either Whites or Blacks in this study or in the earlier Brigham- Giesbrecht study. (2) Agreement with Archie and with his racial views can serve as a very potent indicator of racial attitudes of Whites. Neither of these is strongly related to overall racial attitudes for Blacks, although they are somewhat associated with anti-integration attitudes. (3) For both races, posi- tive interracial attitudes are somewhat associated with a favorable orientation toward the program's effects—that is, with the belief that it will be helpful in race relations. (4) As Vidmar and Rokeach and others have suggested, viewers' perception of the program's intent may be strongly related to racial attitudes; that is, highly prejudiced Whites were significantly less likely to perceive the program as a satire and were more likely to feel that Archie, not Mike, is the "winner" in the interactions in the program. In terms of the typology suggested by Andrea Rich, *nonperceptive bigots* seem to out- number *perceptive bigots.*

All of these findings taken together suggest that the effect of the program is not a simple one. Racial attitudes *do* provide a frame of reference for view- ing the program's main character, Archie Bunker, at least for Whites. Indeed, the relationship is so strong that one might be tempted to use reaction to Archie as a disguised measure of the racial attitudes of Whites. The fact that prejudiced Whites are con- siderably less likely to see the show as satire and more likely to see Archie as the victor supports fears that they may "miss the point" and retain their prejudice or become even more hostile (see Leck- enby & Surlin, 1975; Gross, 1975).

The studies briefly described here demonstrate that racial attitudes do play an important part in Whites' perceptions of and identifications with the characters in "All in the Family." Since the pro- gram has led to several "spin-off" programs (also produced by Norman Lear), such as "Maude," "Sanford and Son," and "The Jeffersons," all of which also contain a good deal of verbal aggression

and controversial humor, gathering knowledge about the effects of such humor and verbal aggres- sion remains a point of compelling practical as well as academic interest.

We have already had the benefit of much clever, erudite, and literate speculation concerning the ef- fect of "All in the Family." It is remarkable, how- ever, that there has been so little progress beyond this educated guesswork. Data are badly needed concerning the effects of this and similar programs on viewers, young and old, minority- and majority-group. To gather such data we need to marshal all of the resources at our disposal, includ- ing contributions from media representatives. Only then will we be able to provide some meaningful answers to the questions raised about these pro- grams, programs that are viewed by millions of adults and children every week and that may have important effects upon the ways they behave toward one another.

REFERENCES

Brigham, J. C. Ethnic humor on television: Does it reduce/reinforce racial prejudice? Symposium pre- sentation, American Psychological Association, Chi- cago, 1975.

Brigham, J. C., & Giesbrecht, L. W. The effects of viewed bigotry: Racial attitudes and "All in the Fam- ily." *Journal of Communication,* in press.

Gross, T. Do the bigots miss the message? *TV Guide,* November 8, 1975, pp. 14–18.

Hano, A. Can Archie Bunker give bigotry a bad name? *New York Times Magazine,* March 12, 1972.

Hobson, L. Marketed bigotry. *St. Petersburg Times,* November 22, 1971, p. 1-D.

Lear, N. Bunker booster parries attack. *St. Petersburg Times,* November 23, 1971, p. 1-D.

Leckenby, J. D., & Surlin, S. H. Incidental social learn- ing among Black and White viewers in relation to au- thoritarian characterizations in prime-time entertain- ment programming. Paper presented at the Association for Education in Journalism Convention, Ottawa, 1975.

Levy, F. In defense of prejudice. *New Republic,* August 5/12, 1972, pp. 25–26.

New York Times Magazine, April 9, 1972, pp. 20–21.

Playboy. Carroll O'Connor: A candid conversation with arch-bigot Archie Bunker's better half. January, 1973.

Sanders, C. Nation's new hero is a beer-bellied bigot with 60 million fans. *Ebony,* June, 1972, pp. 186–192.

Spence, J. T. & Helmreich, R. The attitudes toward women scale: An objective instrument to measure attitudes toward the rights and roles of women in contemporary society. *JSAS Catalogue of Research in Psychology,* 1972, *2,* 66.

Tate, E. D., & Surlin, S. H. A cross-cultural comparison of viewer agreement with opinionated television characters. Paper delivered at International Communication Association Meetings, Chicago, April, 1975.

Vidmar, N., & Rokeach, M. Archie Bunker's bigotry: A study in selective perception and exposure. *Journal of Communication,* 1974, *24,* 36–47.

Woods, C. Bunkerism. *New Republic,* December 22, 1973, pp. 29–30.

ARTICLE 6

Television and violence: Implications of the surgeon general's research program

John P. Murray[1]

The magnitude of television's involvement in our daily lives is rather impressive. Recent census figures estimate that 96% of the households in the United States contain at least one television set; many have two or more. In families where there are young children, the television ownership rate approaches total saturation—99%. Moreover, the data available from broadcast rating services indicate that American television sets are turned on for an average of approximately six hours each day. The obvious implication of these rather dry statistics is that virtually every person in the United States has access to television, and some are watching for a considerable length of time. These facts, coupled with the common observation that our youngest citizens are among the heaviest users, have fostered serious concern about television's potential impact on the attitudes, values, and behavior patterns of this vast audience. This concern has been expressed not only by legislators but also by parents, teachers, and a wide range of mental health professionals involved with the growth and development of children.

Throughout television's quarter-of-a-century broadcast history, various commissions and committees have questioned its impact. In the early 1950s, the National Association of Educational Broadcasters surveyed the program content of stations in four major cities (Los Angeles, New York, New Haven, and Chicago) and reported that "crime and horror" drama accounted for 10% of all programming broadcast in these cities.

The first Congressional inquiry was launched in 1954 by Senator Estes Kefauver, Chairman of the Subcommittee to Investigate Juvenile Delinquency. As a result of testimony presented to this commit-

Reprinted from *American Psychologist*, 1972, *28*, 472–478. Copyright 1972 by the American Psychological Association. Reprinted by permission.

[1]The author wishes to acknowledge the contribution of his colleagues at the National Institute of Mental Health, especially Eli A. Rubinstein. Opinions expressed are those of the author and do not necessarily reflect the opinions or official policy of the National Institute of Mental Health.

tee, it was concluded that televised crime and brutality could be potentially harmful to young children. Broadcasters were then urged to take appropriate action to reduce the level of violence portrayed in their programming. A subsequent survey of program content, undertaken by the same Senate subcommittee in 1961, indicated an increase in the level of televised violence over that observed in the 1950s. An additional survey conducted in 1964 again indicated no diminution in the level of portrayed violence. As Chairman of these later hearings, Senator Thomas Dodd noted:

> Not only did we fail to see an appreciable reduction of violence in the new shows, but we also found that the most violent shows of the 1961–62 season have been syndicated and are now being reshown on independent networks and stations [U. S. Senate, 1964, p. 3731].

The committee concluded that, despite its laudable achievement in the fields of education and entertainment, television has also functioned as "a school for violence."

In 1969, the Mass Media Task Force of the National Commission on the Causes and Prevention of Violence concluded, on the basis of a review of existing research, that there was sufficient justification to call for a general reduction in the level of televised violence. The Commission particularly stressed the need to eliminate violence portrayed in children's cartoon programming. The Violence Commission also recommended continued evaluation of television programming, research on the long-term cumulative effects of viewing televised violence, and an analysis of the broad range of television's impact on society (Baker & Ball, 1969).

In response to this mounting concern, Senator John O. Pastore, Chairman of the Subcommittee on Communications of the Senate Commerce Committee, asked the Secretary of Health, Education, and Welfare to request the Surgeon General to conduct a study of the impact of televised violence. In requesting the Surgeon General's participation, Senator

Pastore noted the recent success of the Smoking and Health Study and indicated that he considered television violence to be a similar public health question. As a result of this request, the Surgeon General's Scientific Advisory Committee on Television and Social Behavior, composed of 12 behavioral scientists, was appointed in June 1969. At the same time, $1 million was allocated for research funds, and a staff at the National Institute of Mental Health was appointed to coordinate the research program. During the following two years, a total of 23 independent research projects were conducted by scholars at a number of universities and research institutes. The resulting set of approximately 60 reports and papers was reviewed by the Advisory Committee during the late summer and fall of 1971, and the Committee's report, entitled "Television and Growing Up: The Impact of Televised Violence," was presented to the Surgeon General on December 31, 1971. The Advisory Committee report and five volumes of research reports were published early in 1972.

The studies in this program were focused on three major research questions concerning *(a)* the characteristics of television program content; *(b)* the characteristics of the audience (Who watches what? For how long?); and *(c)* the potential impact of televised violence on the attitudes, values, and behavior of the viewer. Within this framework, let us turn first to the research findings that bear on the nature of the stimulus—the characteristics of television programs viewed in American homes.

TELEVISION CONTENT

One study, conducted by George Gerbner (1972) at the Annenberg School of Communications, was addressed to an analysis of the content of prime time (7:30–10:00 P.M. on weekdays and 9:00–11:00 A.M. on Saturday) television programming broadcast during one week in October for the years 1967, 1968, and 1969. Observers recorded all instances of violence defined by "the overt expression of physical force against others or self, or the compelling of action against one's will on pain of being hurt or killed.'' The results indicated the following:

1. The level of violence did not change from 1967 to 1969. In each of the three years, violent episodes occurred at the rate of five per play or eight episodes per hour, with 8 out of every 10 plays containing some form of violence.
2. Lethal violence (killing) *did* decline over the measured years from 2 in 10 leading characters involved in killing in 1967; to 1 in 10 in 1968; to 1 in 20 in 1969.
3. The level of violence portrayed in programs especially designed for children—cartoons (already the leading violent program format in 1967)—became increasingly violent in 1969. As Gerbner (1972) pointed out: ''Of all 95 cartoon plays analyzed during the three annual study periods, only two in 1967 and one each in 1968 and 1969 did not contain violence'' [p. 36].

On the average, in 1967, one hour of cartoons contained *three* times as many violent episodes as one hour of adult programming. However, in 1969, one hour of cartoons contained *six* times as many violent episodes as an adult hour.

A more recent study, conducted by F. Earle Barcus (1971) at Boston University, was focused on the content of Saturday morning children's programs during the 1971 season. Barcus reported findings that parallel Gerbner's: 71% of all segments had at least one instance of human violence and 3 out of 10 dramatic segments were ''saturated'' with violence.

In one sense, these statistics are merely body counts, significant perhaps, but to ''understand'' televised violence one must look at the qualitative aspects: the time, place, or setting and the characteristics of the aggressors and victims. In the world of television, violence tends to occur in the past or future; in places other than the United States; and frequently in remote, uninhabited, or unidentifiable areas. The means to commit violence are usually weapons, with guns being the most favored weapon. The agents of this violence are usually humans; however, the prevalence of nonhuman agents

has increased each year from 1967 to 1969. The consequences of all this violence are almost negligible. Punching, kicking, biting, even shooting, do not seem to result in much suffering. As Gerbner (1972) pointed out:

Pain and suffering were so difficult to detect that observers could not agree often enough to make the results acceptable. There was no doubt that no painful effect was shown in over half of all violent episodes [p. 41].

Who commits all this mayhem? And who are the unlucky recipients? We noted earlier that the agents of most of the violence are humans—so, too, are the victims. But the aggressors and the victims, the powerful and the weak, the killers and the killed, do not share many common characteristics. Indeed, as Gerbner lyrically indicated: ''The shifting sands of fate have piled a greater burden of victimization on women [p. 50].'' The aggressors are more likely to be male, American, middle-upper class, unmarried, and in the ''prime of life.''

Approximately 70% of all leading characters studied by Gerbner were involved in some form of violence (either as an aggressor or a victim). Of those involved in killing, the odds are two to one in favor of the leading character being a killer rather than being the one killed. Moreover, the odds were also seven to one that the killer would *not* be killed in return.

How ''real'' is this violence? Some researchers have suggested that, in a statistical sense, it is very *un*real. For example, content analyses show that violence in the *television* world occurs between total strangers, but crime statistics indicate that lethal violence in the *real* world is likely to be perpetrated by persons known to the victim. A study conducted by David Clark and William Blankenburg (1972) at the University of Wisconsin failed to find a clear relationship between the level of televised violence broadcast each year and an environmental crime index based on the FBI Uniform Crime Reports. What they were able to demonstrate is that the level of broadcast violence has fluctuated from 1953 to

1969 and seems to run in cycles reaching a peak every four years. In addition, if the audience applauded violent television programs during one season, the viewers were likely to receive an increased dosage during the following season. Thus, Clark and Blankenburg were able to demonstrate a significant correlation between the number of high-violence programs available during a given season and the average Nielsen rating of that type of program during the preceding season.

What are the implications of these content analyses? Foremost is that violence is inherent in television drama and, according to Gerbner (1972), appears to be used to define power and status. In another study, conducted by Cedric Clark (1972) at Stanford University, the author concludes that some members of our society are regularly denied power and status by being continually cast in the role of the helpless victim. Indeed, Clark suggests that the portrayal of specific groups, such as blacks or women, in powerless roles is a form of violence against society.

The overwhelming conclusion that can be drawn from these content analyses is that violent behavior is a common theme in many of the television programs viewed in American homes. Keeping this fact in mind, let us turn next to the topic of viewing.

VIEWING PATTERNS

Who watches television? Virtually everyone does. It was noted earlier that some studies have estimated that the television set is turned on for an average of more than six hours each day. However, it would be a mistake to leave the impression that everyone views extensively. True, almost every home has a television set, but the patterns of use vary according to age, sex, and the family's socioeconomic level. There are, of course, some general guidelines concerning the extent of viewing, such as younger children view more than older children; women more than men; and persons from lower income homes more than middle and upper income families. With regard to children, the de-

velopmental pattern is one of onset of television viewing at 1½–2 years of age, followed by extensive television viewing during preschool and early elementary school years, which is followed by a sharp decline in viewing as the youngster approaches adolescence. Indeed, the extent and duration of viewing remain low from adolescence to early adulthood. For adults, the peak life-span viewing periods occur for persons in their late twenties through early thirties and the elderly.

An idealized curve demonstrating the extent of television viewing across all ages would identify three primary clusters of viewers: young children, young adults, and elderly persons. The most parsimonious explanation for these clusters is the lack of alternative activities: young children have limited physical mobility outside the home; young adults are more likely to be married and have families with young children; and elderly persons frequently report a restricted range of outside activities due to physical limitations.

Our research program has been focused on only one of these three groups: young children. Although this seemed reasonable in terms of limited resources, future research should not neglect the elderly viewer. At present, one can only speculate about the experiences of a person who is physically separated from his or her family, alone and lonely, whose only regular visitor is Johnny Carson.

With regard to children's viewing, we have already suggested that they are among the heaviest users of television. Indeed, several studies (Lyle & Hoffman, 1972a, 1972b; Murray, 1972) have demonstrated that young children spend between two and three hours watching television each day, and they watch more on weekends than during the week. On the average, preschoolers spend approximately half of an adult's workweek sitting in front of the television set.

What kinds of programs do they watch? Universally, the youngest children prefer cartoons and situation comedies to other types of television fare. There is a definite sequence of change in preference patterns during childhood, beginning with cartoons and shifting to situation comedies (e.g., *I Love Lucy*) and child adventure (e.g., *Lassie*), and then to action/adventure programs (e.g., *Hawaii Five-O* and *Mod Squad*). It should *not* be assumed, however, that very young children are only exposed to relatively nonviolent programming. Indeed, we have already noted that cartoons are among the most violent programs on television. Moreover, the three studies cited above, which asked parents to keep a diary of the programs viewed by their children, indicated that even preschoolers spent almost half of their viewing time watching action/adventure programs such as *Mannix, Mod Squad,* and the *FBI*.

IMPACT OF TELEVISED VIOLENCE

Given the fact that there is a considerable amount of violence portrayed on television and that large segments of our society are routinely exposed to such material, one may legitimately question the impact of such programming. In this regard, a considerable body of prior research on imitative behavior (Bandura, 1969), as well as accumulated folk wisdom, has led to the conclusion that children *can* learn from observing behavior of others. The "others" may be their fellow playmates, parents, teachers, or the repairman who visits the child's home. Thus, the boy or girl who mimics the teacher's voice and the youngster who pretends to be the plumber who repaired the family's kitchen sink yesterday are generally considered living proof of this thesis. Can one extend this line of reasoning to include television as one of the "others" from whom a child is likely to learn specific behaviors? (For recent reviews, see Murray, Nayman, & Atkin, 1972; Weiss, 1969.) We know that there have been isolated incidents in which a child has attempted to replicate behavior he has just observed on television—occasionally with tragic consequences. But what about the youngster who is merely surly or inconsiderate toward his brothers and sisters, excessively aggressive or disruptive on the playground, or hostile and cynical about the

value of trust and love in interpersonal relationships? Can these, too, be related to the behaviors the child has observed on the television screen? Perhaps. However, the basic question to which several studies in this program were addressed was, Are children who view televised violence more aggressive than those who do not view such fare? With this question in mind, let us look at some of the findings.

One study, conducted by Aletha Stein and Lynette Friedrich (1972) at the Pennsylvania State University, assessed the effect of exposing preschool children to a "diet" of either antisocial, prosocial, or neutral television programming. The antisocial programs consisted of *Batman* and *Superman* cartoons; prosocial programs were composed of segments of *Misteroger's Neighborhood;* and neutral programming consisted of children's travelogue films. The children were observed throughout a nine-week period which consisted of two weeks of previewing, four weeks of television exposure, and three weeks of follow-up. All observations were conducted while the children were engaged in their daily activities in the nursery school. The observers recorded various forms of behavior that could be described as prosocial (i.e., helping, sharing, cooperative play, tolerance of delay) or antisocial (i.e., arguing, pushing, breaking toys). The over-all results indicated that children who were adjudged to be initially somewhat more aggressive became significantly more aggressive as a result of viewing the *Batman* and *Superman* cartoons. On the other hand, the children who viewed 12 episodes of *Misteroger's Neighborhood* became significantly more cooperative, willing to share toys and to help other children.

In another study, Robert Liebert and Robert Baron (1972), at the State University of New York at Stony Brook, assessed young children's willingness to hurt another child after viewing either aggressive or neutral television programming. The aggressive program consisted of segments drawn from *The Untouchables,* while the neutral program featured a track race. The main findings indicated that the children who viewed the aggressive program demonstrated a greater willingness to hurt another child. The experimental setting provided a situation in which a child could press a button that would either HELP or HURT a child in another room. The youngest children who had viewed the aggressive program pressed the HURT button earlier and for a longer period of time than did their peers who had viewed a track race. Moreover, when the children were later observed during the free-play period, those who had viewed *The Untouchables* exhibited a greater preference for playing with weapons and aggressive toys than did the children who had watched the neutral programming.

In a related study, Paul Ekman (1972) and his associates at the Langley Porter Neuropsychiatric Institute filmed the facial expressions of the children in the Liebert and Baron study and attempted to relate the child's emotional expression while viewing to later hurting or helping behavior. The results indicated that young boys whose facial expressions depicted positive emotions of happiness, pleasure, interest, or involvement while viewing *The Untouchables* were more likely to make hurting responses than were the boys whose facial expressions indicated displeasure or disinterest in such television fare.

An additional series of studies conducted by Aimee Leifer and Donald Roberts (1972) at Stanford University further explored the impact of televised violence in relation to the child's understanding of the motivations and consequences for the portrayed violent acts. The results indicated that as the child grows older, he is more likely to understand the portrayed motives and consequences, but such increased understanding does not seem to modify his postviewing aggressive behavior. Indeed, when a number of variables were assessed, the best predictor of subsequent aggressive behavior was the amount of violence portrayed in the program viewed: children who had viewed the more violent programs produced significantly more aggressive responses.

The several studies we have discussed thus far

have demonstrated some immediate, short-term effects of viewing televised violence. But one may justifiably question the long-range cumulative impact of viewing violence. In this regard, a number of studies in this research program attempted to relate the child's program preference and viewing patterns to the viewer's perception of violence and attitudes concerning the use of violence or force to resolve conflicts. Bradley Greenberg and Thomas Gordon (1972) have suggested, on the basis of a series of studies conducted at Michigan State University, that watching violence on television sensitizes the viewer to perceive more violence in the world around him and increases the likelihood that the viewer will espouse attitudes favorable toward the use of violence as a means of resolving conflicts. Moreover, Steven Chaffee and his associates (Chaffee & McLeod, 1971; McLeod, Atkin, & Chaffee, 1972a, 1972b) at the University of Wisconsin and Jennie McIntyre and James Teevan (1972) at the University of Maryland have noted that there is a consistent and reliable relationship between preference for and viewing of violent television programs and engaging in aggressive or delinquent acts.

Perhaps the most crucial study in this regard was one conducted by Monroe Lefkowitz and his colleagues (Lefkowitz, Eron, Walder, & Huesmann, 1972) at the New York State Department of Mental Hygiene. This study is of particular importance because it was designed to investigate the development of aggressive behavior in children by studying the same boys and girls over a 10-year period, at ages 8 and 18. Ten years ago, the investigators obtained several measures of each child's aggressive behavior and related these to his or her preference for violent television programs (see Eron, 1963). Now, 10 years later, when the subjects were one year out of high school, the investigators obtained similar measures of program preferences and aggressive behavior. For boys, the results indicated that preference for violent programs at age 8 was significantly related to aggressive and delinquent behavior at age 18. For girls, this relationship was in the same direction but was less strong. Thus, one general interpretation of the results of this study is that preferring violent television at age 8 is at least one cause of the aggressive and antisocial behavior these young men displayed 10 years later.

The conclusions that can be drawn from the results of this series of studies are threefold. First, there is considerable violence portrayed on the television screen. And such violence tends not to mirror societal violence, but rather is used as a dramatic punctuation mark—a definer or arbiter of power and status among the performers in each dramatic episode. Second, young children view a considerable amount of television, in the course of which they are exposed to a considerable amount of televised violence. Third, there are a number of studies which point to the conclusion that viewing televised violence causes the viewer to become more aggressive. Indeed, the Surgeon General's Scientific Advisory Committee on Television and Social Behavior (1972) summarized its interpretation of this point as follows:

Thus, there is a convergence of the fairly substantial experimental evidence for *short-run* causation of aggression among some children by viewing violence on the screen and the much less certain evidence from field studies that extensive violence viewing precedes some *long-run* manifestations of aggressive behavior [p. 10].

Thus, the major implication of the results of this research program is the clear need for a reduction in the level of violence portrayed on television. At the same time it is equally important to encourage broadcasters to modify the balance of programming in favor of prosocial content. Indeed, the recommendations stemming from this research program are not merely negative sanctions against televised violence but rather a plea for more beneficial and useful forms of television content.

REFERENCES

Baker, R. K., & Ball, S. J. *Mass media and violence: A staff report to the National Commission on the Causes and Prevention of Violence.* Washington, D. C.: U. S. Government Printing Office, 1969.

Bandura, A. Social learning theory of identificatory processes. In D. A. Goslin (Ed.), *Handbook of socialization theory and research.* Chicago: Rand McNally, 1969.

Barcus, F. E. *Saturday children's television: A report of TV programming and advertising on Boston commercial television.* Boston: Action for Children's Television, 1971.

Chaffee, S., & McLeod, J. Adolescents, parents, and television violence. Paper presented at the annual meeting of the American Psychological Association, Washington, D. C., September 1971.

Clark, C. Race, identification, and television violence. In G. A. Comstock, E. A. Rubenstein, & J. P. Murray (Eds.), *Television and social behavior.* Vol. 5. *Television's effects: Further explorations.* Washington, D. C.: U. S. Government Printing Office, 1972.

Clark, D. G., & Blankenburg, W. B. Trends in violent content in selected mass media. In G. A. Comstock & E. A. Rubinstein (Eds.), *Television and social behavior.* Vol. 1. *Media content and control.* Washington, D. C.: U. S. Government Printing Office, 1972.

Ekman, P., Liebert, R. M., Friesen, W., Harrison, R., Zlatchin, C., Malmstrom, E. J., & Baron, R. A. Facial expressions of emotion while watching televised violence as predictors of subsequent aggression. In G. A. Comstock, E. A. Rubinstein, & J. P. Murray (Eds.), *Television and social behavior.* Vol. 5. *Television's effects: Further explorations.* Washington, D. C.: U. S. Government Printing Office, 1972.

Eron, L. Relationship of TV viewing habits and aggressive behavior in children. *Journal of Abnormal and Social Psychology,* 1963, **67,** 193–196.

Gerbner, G. Violence in television drama: Trends and symbolic functions. In G. A. Comstock & E. A. Rubinstein (Eds.), *Television and social behavior.* Vol. 1. *Media content and control.* Washington, D. C.: U. S. Government Printing Office, 1972.

Greenberg, B. S., & Gordon, T. F. Children's perceptions of television violence: A replication. In G. A. Comstock, E. A. Rubinstein, & J. P. Murray (Eds.), *Television and social behavior.* Vol. 5. *Television's effects: Further explorations.* Washington, D. C.: U. S. Government Printing Office, 1972.

Lefkowitz, M., Eron, L., Walder, L., & Huesmann, L. R. Television violence and child aggression: A follow up study. In G. A. Comstock & E. A. Rubinstein (Eds.), *Television and social behavior.* Vol. 3. *Television and adolescent aggressiveness.* Washington, D. C.: U. S. Government Printing Office, 1972.

Leifer, A. D., & Roberts, D. F. Children's responses to television violence. In J. P. Murray, E. A. Rubinstein, & G. A. Comstock (Eds.), *Television and social behav-*

ior. Vol. 2. *Television and social learning*. Washington, D. C.: U. S. Government Printing Office, 1972.

Liebert, R. M., & Baron, R. A. Short-term effects of televised aggression on children's aggressive behavior. In J. P. Murray, E. A. Rubinstein, & G. A. Comstock (Eds.), *Television and social behavior*. Vol. 2. *Television and social learning*. Washington, D. C.: U. S. Government Printing Office, 1972.

Lyle, J., & Hoffman, H. R. Children's use of television and other media. In E. A. Rubinstein, G. A. Comstock, J. P. Murray (Eds.), *Television and social behavior*. Vol. 4. *Television in day-to-day life: Patterns of use*. Washington, D. C.: U. S. Government Printing Office, 1972. (a)

Lyle, J., & Hoffman, H. R. Explorations in patterns of television viewing by preschool-age children. In E. A. Rubinstein, G. A. Comstock, & J. P. Murray (Eds.), *Television and social behavior*. Vol. 4. *Television in day-to-day life: Patterns of use*. Washington, D. C.: U. S. Government Printing Office, 1972. (b)

McIntyre, J., & Teevan, J. Television and deviant behavior. In G. A. Comstock & E. A. Rubinstein (Eds.), *Television and social behavior*. Vol. 3. *Television and adolescent aggressiveness*. Washington, D. C.: U. S. Government Printing Office, 1972.

McLeod, J., Atkin, C., & Chaffee, S. Adolescents, parents, and television use: Adolescent self-report measures from Maryland and Wisconsin samples. In G. A. Comstock & E. A. Rubinstein (Eds.), *Television and social behavior*. Vol. 3. *Television and adolescent aggressiveness*. Washington, D. C.: U. S. Government Printing Office, 1972. (a)

McLeod, J., Atkin, C., & Chaffee, S. Adolescents, parents, and television use: Self-report and other-report measures from the Wisconsin sample. In G. A. Comstock & E. A. Rubinstein (Eds.), *Television and social behavior*. Vol. 3. *Television and adolescent aggressiveness*. Washington, D. C.: U. S. Government Printing Office, 1972. (b)

Murray, J. P. Television in inner-city homes: Viewing behavior of young boys. In E. A. Rubinstein, G. A. Comstock, & J. P. Murray (Eds.), *Television and social behavior*. Vol. 4. *Television in day-to-day life: Patterns of use*. Washington, D. C.: U. S. Government Printing Office, 1972.

Murray, J. P., Nayman, O. B., & Atkin, C. K. Television and the child: A comprehensive research bibliography. *Journal of Broadcasting*, 1972, **26**(1), 21–35.

Stein, A., & Friedrich, L. K. Television content and young children's behavior. In J. P. Murray, E. A. Rubinstein, & G. A. Comstock (Eds.), *Television and social behavior*. Vol. 2. *Television and social learning*. Washington, D. C.: U. S. Government Printing Office, 1972.

Surgeon General's Scientific Advisory Committee on Television and Social Behavior. *Television and growing up: The impact of televised violence*. Washington, D. C.: U. S. Government Printing Office, 1972.

United States Senate, Committee on the Judiciary. Effects on young people of violence and crime portrayed on television. Part 16. *Investigation of juvenile delinquency in the United States, July 30, 1964*. Washington, D. C.: U. S. Government Printing Office, 1964.

Weiss, W. Effects of the mass media of communication. In G. Lindzey & E. Aronson (Eds.), *The handbook of social psychology*. (2nd ed.) Reading, Mass.: Addison-Wesley, 1969.

SECTION SUMMARY

Murray's article summarizes the results of some 60 reports and papers that were reviewed by the Surgeon General's Scientific Advisory Committee on Television and Social Behavior. Looking at the results of all of the studies on children's imitation of live or film-mediated models that have been carried out over the past 25 years or so, the following points seem established (J. L. Singer, 1971): (1) The evidence seems clear that nursery-school-aged children do imitate the aggressive behavior of adults or cartoon-type figures observed live or on film. (2) This imitation often takes the form of rather direct imitation but also may involve the expression of more general aggressive patterns. (3) The observation of film-mediated aggression leads to imitation especially if: (a) the model is not punished, (b) the model is of the same sex as the child, (c) the child is moderately frustrated, and (d) no disapproval of the model's behavior is provided by adults in the child's presence.

There are a number of limitations on such generalizations, however. First of all, most studies of children have involved nursery-school children from predominantly middle-class backgrounds. Such children may be particularly compliant imitators of adult models. Second, the measures of aggression employed have usually involved play situations and attacks on inanimate objects. It is an open question whether aggressive play is at all the same as direct assault on another child.

Further, a "one-shot" viewing of a film of an aggressive model in the laboratory is simply not the same thing as television viewing over an extended period of time. Not only is there a considerable difference in viewing time, but the complexity of the television stimulus is considerably greater outside the laboratory setting. As reactions to "All in the Family" illustrate, many "messages" come from television viewing; not all are violent, and some may even be antiviolent (see J. L. Singer, 1971, for extended discussions of these points).

Several researchers have attempted to avoid these pitfalls by conducting relatively long-term field studies of television viewing and aggression. One study, carried out by Feshbach and R. Singer (1971) in seven settings involving teenage boys living in residential schools, found results suggesting that viewing a "diet" of aggressive programs for six weeks did *not* increase aggressive tendencies in adolescent boys. But methodological difficulties and shortcomings are more likely to occur in large-scale field studies than in carefully controlled laboratory investigations. For example, is it possible that youths watching a nonviolent "diet" of television programs might become more aggressive because of their frustration at being deprived of their favorite (violent) programs? Feshbach and Singer were forced to include "Batman" (certainly a violent program) among the programs seen by their control groups as well as by their experimental groups because the youths on the "nonviolent diet" protested so loudly when it was initially omitted from their programming. Another factor that makes interpretations of their study difficult is the fact that only six hours per week of television viewing time was controlled by the experimenters. What type of programs were the youths watching on their own time? Although the amount of time they were allowed to watch television varied from school to school, the youths had unlimited viewing privileges in some of the residential schools. Were youths in the nonviolent group more likely to watch violent programs on their own time, to "make up" for the violent programming that they had been "deprived" of?

Data from other field studies do not support the Feshbach-Singer results. Wells (1973), attempting to replicate the Feshbach-Singer study, found significantly *greater* physical aggressiveness in boys who viewed the more violent television programs. Two other recent field studies have found similar evidence that exposure to violent movies increases aggressive behavior (Leyens, Camino, Parke, &

Berkowitz, 1975; Parke, Berkowitz, Leyens, West, & Sebastian, 1975).

The issue of the effect of witnessed hostility and aggression on future behavior is obviously of great complexity. Difficulties in determining a clear-cut answer are perhaps increased by the fact that sociopolitical values and vested interests are of such importance in this area. Television and movie executives are naturally very much concerned with any research and theorizing that may threaten their livelihood. At the other pole, abhorrence of violence or ethnic hostility in any form is an article of faith to many people of particular sociopolitical persuasions, such as the "bristling liberals" described by Andrea Rich. Neither of these orientations is conducive to the operation of solid, objective scientific research, since each is likely to give rise to prejudgments before the facts are in (as the quotations in our second article illustrate) or to nonobjective interpretations of existing findings.

A vivid example of the way in which vested interests and values can hamper scientific research is provided by the case of the Surgeon General's Scientific Advisory Committee on Television and Social Behavior, whose findings were described in Murray's article. In 1969 the chairman of the Senate Subcommittee on Communications asked the Department of Health, Education, and Welfare (HEW) to appoint a blue-ribbon committee "to devise techniques and to conduct a study . . . which will establish scientifically insofar as possible what harmful effects, if any, these (violent) programs have on children" (Boffey & Walsh, 1970, p. 949).

In selecting this committee, a list of 40 knowledgeable persons was drawn up. The list was then sent to the three major television networks—CBS, NBC, and ABC—and to the National Association of Broadcasters for "comment." The result of this procedure was that the broadcasting industry was allowed to veto the appointment of potentially hostile critics (that is, those who might support the modeling position), while the industry was given prominent representation on the panel. For exam-

ple, among the seven rejected candidates were Leonard Berkowitz, Albert Bandura, and Otto Larsen, editor of *Violence and the Mass Media* (1968). Included on the final panel were an NBC vice-president and Joseph Klapper, director of social research for CBS (see Klapper, 1960). Three of the remaining ten committee members were either serving as consultants to the television industry or had previously been employed by or consulted for the industry (Boffey & Walsh, 1970). James Jenkins, chairman of the board of scientific affairs of the American Psychological Association, commented "It looks like an exemplar of the old story of the 'regulatees' running the 'regulators' or the fox passing on the adequacy of the eyesight of the man assigned to guard the chicken coop" (Boffey & Walsh, 1970, pp. 951–952).

As one might predict, the committee's 279-page report, released in early 1972, also stimulated a great deal of controversy. The report's summary seemed to suggest that violence in television programming does not have an adverse effect on the majority of the nation's youth but may influence small groups of youngsters already predisposed by many factors to aggressive behavior. Criticisms of the committee and the report centered on four points: (1) that the selection procedures were biased; (2) that the report softened the findings (of a link between viewed aggression and violence) contained in the five volumes of original research on which it was based; (3) that the summary of the report was made even more equivocal than the report itself, and (4) that, in reporting the outcome, the mass media inadvertently misread the summary in such a way as to largely absolve television violence of any significant effect on children.

The upshot of this controversy is that the Senate Subcommittee on Communications, which had requested the report in the first place, scheduled hearings to investigate the investigations. During these hearings, U. S. Surgeon General Steinfeld made the following statement: "Certainly my interpretation is that there is a causative relationship between televised violence and subsequent anti-social behavior, and that the evidence is strong enough that it requires some action on the part of responsible authorities, the TV industry, the Government, the citizens'' (quoted in Liebert, Neale, & Davidson, 1973, p. 155). The television networks have also initiated their own studies of the effects of violent programming. Such research programs have come under attack from academicians for their possible bias, lack of objectivity, and potential use as a delaying tactic (see Goldsen, 1971).

On the other side of the coin, Berkowitz (1971) has given his view of how the values of ''liberal intellectuals'' may bias their interpretations of research results. He points out that the President's Commission on the Causes and Prevention of Violence concluded that media violence can induce persons to act aggressively (see Lange, Baker, & Ball, 1969), whereas the majority of the President's Commission on Obscenity and Pornography concluded that exposure to pornography might have a temporary stimulating effect but no long-term harmful effect. Berkowitz argues that the research results obtained by the two commissions were actually ''strikingly similar''—that is, that both observed aggression and observed (media) sex have a temporary stimulating effect and that it is largely unknown whether they have long-term consequences independently of other environmental supports.

Yet the policy recommendations of the two commissions were quite different. The Violence Commission urged the television industry to do away with children's cartoons containing ''serious, noncomic violence'' and to lessen the amount and duration of violent episodes in all programs. The Pornography Commission, on the other hand, recommended the repeal of all legislation prohibiting the sale, exhibition, or distribution of sexual materials to consenting adults. Berkowitz suggests that the sociopolitical values of the committee members are responsible for these contrasting policy recommendations. Although it is difficult to evaluate the actual degree of similarity in the tasks of the committees and of the research results they reviewed, Berkowitz' analysis is an intriguing one.

It is obvious that more evidence on the effects of viewing televised hostility, violence, and aggression is needed. Laboratory studies suggest that such viewing may have the deleterious result of increasing aggressive tendencies in young children. Vested interests and sociopolitical values may lead one to question the objectivity and validity of many of the studies presently being carried out and the policy recommendations derived from them. Any conclusions concerning the effect of television on violent behavior must await the results of thoughtful, indepth research programs carried out by objective social scientists. A resolution of the larger issue of whether aggressive tendencies are chiefly innate or learned also must await further research.

REFERENCES

Berkowitz, L. Sex and violence: We can't have it both ways. *Psychology Today,* December 1971, 14 *ff.*

Boffey, P. M., & Walsh, J. Study of TV violence: Seven top researchers blackballed from panel. *Science,* 1970, *168,* 948–952.

Feshbach, S., & Singer, R. D. *Television and aggression: An experimental field study.* San Francisco: Jossey-Bass, 1971.

Goldsen, R. K. NBC's make-believe research on TV violence. *Trans-Action,* October 1971, 28–35.

Klapper, J. T. *The effects of mass communication.* New York: Free Press, 1960.

Lange, D. L., Baker, R. K., & Ball, S. J. *Mass media and violence.* Washington, D. C.: U. S. Government Printing Office, 1969.

Larsen, O. N. (Ed.), *Violence and the mass media.* New York: Harper & Row, 1968.

Leyens, J. P., Camino, L., Parke, R. D., & Berkowitz, L. Effects of movie violence on aggression in a field setting as a function of group dominance and cohesion. *Journal of Personality and Social Psychology,* 1975, *32,* 346–360.

Liebert, R. M., Neale, J. M., & Davidson, E. S. *The early window: Effects of television on children and youth.* New York: Pergamon Press, 1973.

Parke, R. D., Berkowitz, L., Leyens, J. P., West, S. G., & Sebastian, R. The effects of repeated exposure to movie violence on aggressive behavior in juvenile delinquent boys: Field experimental studies. In L. Berkowitz (Ed.), *Advances in experimental psychology* (Vol. 8). New York: Academic Press, 1975.

Singer, J. L. The influence of violence portrayed in television or motion pictures upon overt aggressive behavior. In J. L. Singer (Ed.), *The control of aggression and violence*. New York: Academic Press, 1971. Pp. 19–60.

Wells, W. D. Television and aggression: Replication of an experimental field study. Unpublished manuscript, University of Chicago, 1973.

SECTION III

INTERPERSONAL ATTRACTION

INTRODUCTION

Poets, philosophers, social scientists, and many others have long been interested in what makes people attractive or unattractive to others. Countless factors have been proposed, but on the basis of a half-century of empirical research we can identify several characteristics that appear to be the most powerful determinants of attraction.

One such factor, perhaps surprisingly, is *propinquity,* or closeness. Other things being equal, we tend to like best those people who live and work nearest to us and with whom we have the most chance to interact. There seem to be several reasons for this. One is *availability;* there are more opportunities to get to know people who live or work near to us, and there is less "cost" in terms of effort in getting to know them. A second is the *expectation of continued interaction.* Since people expect to interact more often with those living and working near to them, they may tend to accentuate the positive and minimize the negative aspects of those people so that future interactions will be pleasant and agreeable. A third reason is *predictability.* As you get to

know people, you are better able to predict how they will react to things that you do. Therefore, you are better able to obtain the kinds of reactions you want from them. Finally, *familiarity* seems to play a part. Research indicates that people develop positive feelings toward individuals and objects they see often (Zajonc, 1968) and tend to dislike unfamiliar or unexpected things.

Besides propinquity, another factor in determining attraction is *ability.* Not surprisingly, people who are able, competent, and intelligent seem to be liked more than people who are not. There may be limits to this, however. If a person seems *too* perfect or *too* intelligent, he or she may seem very dissimilar to ourselves and may be disliked for that reason. Therefore, a person who is extremely competent and intelligent might be liked most when he or she shows a few human frailties (Aronson, Willerman, & Floyd, 1966). It has been suggested that this is why President John F. Kennedy became more popular with the American public after his blunder in sponsoring the attempt to invade Cuba at the Bay of

Pigs in 1961 (see also the Janis article in Section 7). Other research, however, indicates that making a blunder does not *always* increase the attractiveness of a highly competent person (Deaux, 1972; Mettee & Wilkins, 1972).

Other people's reactions to us are also important. How much we like someone is often strongly affected by how much that person appears to like us; if our liking appears to be *reciprocated*—that is, returned by the other person—the degree of attraction we feel is likely to increase. Liking begets liking, and friendship usually begets friendship.

Most of us would suspect that people tend to like others whose beliefs, values, and attitudes are *similar* to their own. The results of research strongly support this proposition. Donn Byrne and his colleagues (see, for example, Byrne, 1971) have gathered considerable evidence that similarity in attitudes and values can be a potent predictor of attraction and friendship formation. Other research suggests that much racially discriminatory behavior (see Section 5) may occur partially because prejudiced people *assume* that people of a different race hold attitudes and values *dis*similar to their own (see, for example, Silverman, 1974).

There is still another important determinant of interpersonal attraction, one that has only recently been widely studied: *physical appearance*. Most of us are familiar with the old phrases "you can't judge a book by its cover" and "beauty is only skin deep," which suggest that physical appearance has nothing to do with what one's personality characteristics are. It is becoming increasingly clear that although most of us have heard this, few of us seem to act as if we believe it. In our first article, Karen Dion, Ellen Berscheid, and Elaine Walster investigate the assumptions that people have about the relationship between appearance and personality. They wanted to see whether physically attractive persons are assumed to possess more socially desirable personality traits than unattractive persons and whether they are expected to lead better lives than unattractive individuals are. Their data indicate the presence

of a powerful stereotype: "What is beautiful is good."

The effect of similarity on attraction is investigated in the study by Russell L. Leonard, Jr., of the American Institutes for Research. Leonard points out that self-concept may play an important role in the similarity-attraction relationship. He suggests that only a person with high self-esteem will think highly of those persons similar to himself (and will think less of those dissimilar to himself). Leonard predicts that a person with a negative self-concept may actually be *less* attracted to similar than to dissimilar others.

While most social psychologists would agree that both attitude similarity and physical attractiveness can be important determinants of liking, the two factors are not often compared directly. In our third study, Robert E. Kleck, of Dartmouth College, and Carin Rubenstein, of Smith College, make such a comparison. Their research involves both measures taken within an experimental situation and self-reports from subjects two to four weeks later. The results of this study seem to be troublesome for those who assert that similarity is the primary cause of attraction. We will return to this issue in the Section Summary.

REFERENCES

Aronson, E., Willerman, B., & Floyd, J. The effect of a pratfall on increasing interpersonal attractiveness. *Psychonomic Science,* 1966, *4,* 157–158.

Byrne, D. *The attraction paradigm.* New York: Academic Press, 1971.

Deaux, K. To err is humanizing: But sex makes a difference. *Representative Research in Social Psychology,* 1972, *3,* 20–28.

Mettee, D. R., & Wilkins, P. C. When similarity "hurts": Effects of perceived ability and a humorous blunder on interpersonal attraction. *Journal of Personality and Social Psychology,* 1972, *22,* 246–258.

Silverman, B. I. Consequences, racial discrimination, and the principle of belief congruence. *Journal of Personality and Social Psychology,* 1974, *29,* 497–508.

Zajonc, R. B. Attitudinal effects of mere exposure. *Journal of Personality and Social Psychology,* 1968, *9*(2, part 2), 1–27.

ARTICLE 7

What is beautiful is good[1]

Karen Dion
Ellen Berscheid
Elaine Walster

A person's physical appearance, along with his sexual identity, is the personal characteristic most obvious and accessible to others in social interaction. It is perhaps for this reason that folk psychology has always contained a multitude of theorems which ostensibly permit the forecast of a person's character and personality simply from knowledge of his outward appearance. The line of deduction advanced by most physiognomic theories is simply that "What is beautiful is good . . . [Sappho, Fragments, No. 101]," and that "Physical beauty is the sign of an interior beauty, a spiritual and moral beauty . . . [Schiller, 1882]."

Several processes may operate to make the soothsayers' prophecies more logical and accurate than would appear at first glance. First, it is possible that a correlation between inward character and appearance exists because certain personality traits influence one's appearance. For example, a calm, relaxed person may develop fewer lines and wrinkles than a tense, irritable person. Second, cultural stereotypes about the kinds of personalities appropriate for beautiful or ugly people may mold the personalities of these individuals. If casual acquaintances invariably assume that attractive individuals are more sincere, noble, and honest than unattractive persons, then attractive individuals should be habitually regarded with more respect than unattractive persons. Many have noted that one's self-concept develops from observing what others think about oneself. Thus, if the physically attractive person is consistently treated as a virtuous person, he may become one.

The above considerations pose several questions: (a) Do individuals in fact have stereotyped notions of the personality traits possessed by individuals of varying attractiveness? (b) To what extent are these

Reprinted from the *Journal of Personality and Social Psychology*, 1972, *24*, pp. 285–290. Copyright 1972 by the American Psychological Association. Reprinted by permission.

[1]This research was financed in part by National Institute of Mental Health Grants MH 16729 to Berscheid and MH 16661 to Walster.

stereotypes accurate? *(c)* What is the cause of the correlation between beauty and personality if, in fact, such a correlation exists?

Some observers, of course, deny that such stereotyping exists, and thus render Questions *b* and *c* irrelevant. Chief among these are rehabilitation workers (cf. Wright, 1960) whose clients possess facial and other physical disabilities. These researchers, however, may have a vested interest in believing that physical beauty is a relatively unimportant determinant of the opportunities an individual has available to him.

Perhaps more interestingly, it has been asserted that other researchers also have had a vested interest in retaining the belief that beauty is a peripheral characteristic. Aronson (1969), for example, has suggested that the fear that investigation might prove this assumption wrong has generally caused this to be a taboo area for social psychologists:

> As an aside, I might mention that physical attractiveness is rarely investigated as an antecedent of liking— even though a casual observation (even by us experimental social psychologists) would indicate that we seem to react differently to beautiful women than to homely women. It is difficult to be certain why the effects of physical beauty have not been studied more systematically. It may be that, at some levels, we would hate to find evidence indicating that beautiful women are better liked than homely women—somehow this seems undemocratic. In a democracy we like to feel that with hard work and a good deal of motivation, a person can accomplish almost anything. But, alas (most of us believe), hard work cannot make an ugly woman beautiful. Because of this suspicion perhaps most social psychologists implicitly prefer to believe that beauty is indeed only skin deep— and avoid the investigation of its social impact for fear they might learn otherwise [p. 160].

The present study was an attempt to determine if a physical attractiveness stereotype exists and, if so, to investigate the content of the stereotype along several dimensions. Specifically, it was designed to investigate *(a)* whether physically attractive stimulus persons, both male and female, are assumed to possess more *socially desirable personality traits* than unattractive persons and *(b)* whether they are expected to *lead better lives* than unattrac-

tive individuals. With respect to the latter, we wished to determine if physically attractive persons are generally expected to be better husbands and wives, better parents, and more successful socially and occupationally than less attractive persons.

Because it seemed possible that jealousy might attenuate these effects (if one is jealous of another, he may be reluctant to accord the other the status that he feels the other deserves), and since subjects might be expected to be more jealous of attractive stimulus persons of the same sex than of the opposite sex, we examined the Sex of Subject × Sex of Stimulus Person interactions along the dimensions described above.

METHOD

Subjects

Sixty students, 30 males and 30 females, who were enrolled in an introductory course in psychology at the University of Minnesota participated in this experiment. Each had agreed to participate in return for experimental points to be added to their final exam grade.

Procedure

When the subjects arrived at the designated rooms, they were introduced to the experiment as a study of accuracy in person perception. The experimenter stated that while psychological studies have shown that people do form detailed impressions of others on the basis of a very few cues, the variables determining the extent to which these early impressions are generally accurate have not yet been completely identified. The subjects were told that the purpose of the present study was to compare person perception accuracy of untrained college students with two other groups who had been trained in various interpersonal perception techniques, specifically graduate students in clinical psychology and clinical psychologists. The experimenter noted his belief that person perception accuracy is a general ability varying among people. Therefore, according to the experimenter, college students who are high on this ability may be as accurate as some professional clinicians when making first-impression judgments based on noninterview material.

The subjects were told that standard sets of photographs would be used as the basis for personality inferences. The individuals depicted in the photographs were said to be part of a group of college students currently enrolled at other universities who were participating in a longitudinal study of personality development scheduled to continue into adulthood. It would be possible, therefore, to assess the accuracy of each subject's judgments against information currently available on the stimulus persons and also against forthcoming information.

Stimulus materials. Following the introduction, each subject was given three envelopes. Each envelope contained one photo of a stimulus person of approximately the subject's own age. One of the three envelopes that the subject received contained a photograph of a physically attractive stimulus person; another contained a photograph of a person of average attractiveness; and the final envelope contained a photograph of a relatively unattractive stimulus person.[2] Half of our subjects received three pictures of girls; the remainder received pictures of boys.

To increase the generalizability of our findings and to insure that the general dimension of attractiveness was the characteristic responded to (rather than unique characteristics such as hair color, etc.), 12 different sets of three pictures each were prepared. Each subject received and rated only 1 set. Which 1 of the 12 sets of pictures the subjects received, the order in which each of the three envelopes in the set were presented, and the ratings

made of the person depicted, were all randomly determined.

Dependent variables. The subjects were requested to record their judgments of the three stimulus persons in several booklets.[3] The first page of each booklet cautioned the subjects that this study was an investigation of accuracy of person perception and that we were not interested in the subjects' tact, politeness, or other factors usually important in social situations. It was stressed that it was important for the subject to rate the stimulus persons frankly.

The booklets tapped impressions of the stimulus person along several dimensions. First, the subjects were asked to open the first envelope and then to rate the person depicted on 27 different *personality traits* (which were arranged in random order).[4] The subjects' ratings were made on 6-point scales, the ends of which were labeled by polar opposites (i.e., exciting-dull). When these ratings had been computed, the subject was asked to open the second envelope, make ratings, and then open the third envelope.

In a subsequent booklet, the subjects were asked to assess the stimulus persons on five additional personality traits.[5] These ratings were made on a slightly different scale. The subjects were asked to indicate which stimulus person possessed the "most" and "least" of a given trait. The stimulus person thought to best represent a positive trait was assigned a score of 3; the stimulus person thought to possess an intermediate amount of the trait was as-

[2] The physical attractiveness rating of each of the pictures was determined in a preliminary study. One hundred Minnesota undergraduates rated 50 yearbook pictures of persons of the opposite sex with respect to physical attractiveness. The criteria for choosing the 12 pictures to be used experimentally were *(a)* high-interrater agreement as to the physical attractiveness of the stimulus (the average interrater correlation for all of the pictures was .70); and *(b)* pictures chosen to represent the very attractive category and very unattractive category were not at the extreme ends of attractiveness.

[3] A detailed report of the items included in these booklets is available. Order Document No. 01972 from the National Auxiliary Publication Service of the American Society for Information Science, c/o CCM Information Services, Inc., 909 3rd Avenue, New York, New York 10022. Remit in advance $5.00 for photocopies or $2.00 for microfiche and make checks payable to: Research and Microfilm Publications, Inc.

[4] The subjects were asked how altruistic, conventional, self-assertive, exciting, stable, emotional, dependent, safe, interesting, genuine, sensitive, outgoing, sexually permissive, sincere, warm, sociable, competitive, obvious, kind, modest, strong, serious, sexually warm, simple, poised, bold, and sophisticated each stimulus person was.

[5] The subjects rated stimulus persons on the following traits: friendliness, enthusiasm, physical attractiveness, social poise, and trustworthiness.

signed a score of 2; and the stimulus person thought to least represent the trait was assigned a score of 1.

In a previous experiment (see Footnote 3), a subset of items was selected to comprise an index of the *social desirability* of the personality traits assigned to the stimulus person. The subjects' ratings of each stimulus person on the appropriate items were simply summed to determine the extent to which the subject perceived each stimulus person as socially desirable.

In order to assess whether or not attractive persons are expected to lead happier and more successful lives than unattractive persons, the subjects were asked to estimate which of the stimulus persons would be most likely, and which least likely, to have a number of different life experiences. The subjects were reminded again that their estimates would eventually be checked for accuracy as the lives of the various stimulus persons evolved. The subjects' estimates of the stimulus person's probable life experiences formed indexes of the stimulus person's future happiness in four areas: *(a)* marital happiness (Which stimulus person is most likely to ever be divorced?); *(b)* parental happiness (Which stimulus person is most likely to be a good parent?); *(c)* social and professional happiness (Which stimulus person is most likely to experience deep personal fulfillment?); and *(d)* total happiness (sum of Indexes *a, b,* and *c*).

A fifth index, an occupational success index, was also obtained for each stimulus person. The subjects were asked to indicate which of the three stimulus persons would be most likely to engage in 30 different occupations. (The order in which the occupations were presented and the estimates made was randomized.) The 30 occupations had been chosen such that three status levels of 10 different general occupations were represented, three examples of which follow: Army sergeant (low status); Army captain (average status); Army colonel (high status). Each time a high-status occupation was foreseen for a stimulus person, the stimulus person was assigned a score of 3; when a moderate status occupation was foreseen, the stimulus person was assigned a score of 2; when a low-status occupation was foreseen, a score of 1 was assigned. The average status of occupations that a subject ascribed to a stimulus person constituted the score for that stimulus person in the occupational status index.

RESULTS AND DISCUSSION

Manipulation Check

It is clear that our manipulation of the relative attractiveness of the stimulus persons depicted was effective. The six unattractive stimulus persons were seen as less attractive than the average stimulus persons, who, in turn, were seen as less attractive than the six attractive stimulus persons. The stimulus persons' mean rankings on the attractiveness dimension were 1.12, 2.02, and 2.87, respectively. These differences were statistically significant ($F = 939.32$).[6]

Test of Hypotheses

It will be recalled that it was predicted that the subjects would attribute more socially desirable personality traits to attractive individuals than to average or unattractive individuals. It also was anticipated that jealousy might attenuate these effects. Since the subjects might be expected to be more jealous of stimulus persons of the same sex than of the opposite sex, we blocked both on sex of subject and sex of stimulus person. If jealousy attenuated the predicted main effect, a significant Sex of Subject × Sex of Stimulus Person interaction should be secured in addition to the main effect.

All tests for detection of linear trend and interaction were conducted via a multivariate analysis of variance. (This procedure is outlined in Hays, 1963.)

The means relevant to the hypothesis that attractive individuals will be perceived to possess more socially desirable personalities than others are reported in Table 1. Analyses reveal that attractive individuals were indeed judged to be more socially desirable than are unattractive ($F = 29.61$) persons. The Sex of Subject × Sex of Stimulus Person interaction was insignificant (interaction $F = .00$).

[6]Throughout this report, $df = 1/55$.

Whether the rater was of the same or the opposite sex as the stimulus person, attractive stimulus persons were judged as more socially desirable.[7]

Furthermore, it was also hypothesized that the subjects would assume that attractive stimulus persons are likely to secure more prestigious jobs than those of lesser attractiveness, as well as experiencing happier marriages, being better parents, and enjoying more fulfilling social and occupational lives.

The means relevant to these predictions concerning the estimated future life experiences of individuals of varying degrees of physical attractiveness are also depicted in Table 1. As shown in the table, there was strong support for all of the preceding hypotheses save one. Attractive men and women were expected to attain more prestigious occupations than were those of lesser attractiveness ($F = 42.30$), and this expectation was expressed equally by raters of the same or the opposite sex as the stimulus person (interaction $F = .25$).

The subjects also assumed that attractive individuals would be more competent spouses and have happier marriages than those of lesser attractiveness ($F = 62.54$). (It might be noted that there is some evidence that this may be a correct perception. Kirkpatrick and Cotton (1951), reported that "well-adjusted" wives were more physically attractive than "badly adjusted" wives. "Adjustment," however, was assessed by friends' perceptions, which may have been affected by the stereotype evident here.)

[7]Before running the preliminary experiment to determine the identity of traits usually associated with a socially desirable person (see Footnote 3), we had assumed that an exciting date, a nurturant person, and a person of good character would be perceived as quite different personality types. Conceptually, for example, we expected that an exciting date would be seen to require a person who was unpredictable, challenging, etc., while a nurturant person would be seen to be predictable and unthreatening. It became clear, however, that these distinctions were not ones which made sense to the subjects. There was almost total overlap between the traits chosen as representative of an exciting date, of a nurturant person, and a person of good or ethical character. All were strongly correlated with social desirability. Thus, attractive stimulus persons are assumed to be more exciting dates ($F = 39.97$), more nurturant individuals ($F = 13.96$), and to have better character ($F = 19.57$) than persons of lesser attractiveness.

According to the means reported in Table 1, it is clear that attractive individuals were not expected to be better parents ($F = 1.47$). In fact, attractive persons were rated somewhat lower than any other group of stimulus persons as potential parents, although no statistically significant differences were apparent.

As predicted, attractive stimulus persons were assumed to have better prospects for happy social and professional lives ($F = 21.97$). All in all, the attractive stimulus persons were expected to have more total happiness in their lives than those of lesser attractiveness ($F = 24.20$).

The preceding results did not appear to be attenuated by a jealousy effect (Sex of Subject × Stimulus Person interaction Fs = .01, .07, .21, and .05, respectively).

The subjects were also asked to estimate the likelihood that the various stimulus persons would marry early or marry at all. Responses were combined into a single index. It is evident that the subjects assumed that the attractive stimulus persons

TABLE 1. Traits attributed to various stimulus others

Trait ascription[a]	Unattractive stimulus person	Average stimulus person	Attractive stimulus person
Social desirability of the stimulus person's personality	56.31	62.42	65.39
Occupational status of the stimulus person	1.70	2.02	2.25
Marital competence of the stimulus person	.37	.71	1.70
Parental competence of the stimulus person	3.91	4.55	3.54
Social and professional happiness of the stimulus person	5.28	6.34	6.37
Total happiness of the stimulus person	8.83	11.60	11.60
Likelihood of marriage	1.52	1.82	2.17

[a]The higher the number, the more socially desirable, the more prestigious an occupation, etc., the stimulus person is expected to possess.

were more likely to find an acceptable partner than those of lesser attractiveness ($F = 35.84$). Attractive individuals were expected to marry earlier and to be less likely to remain single. Once again, these conclusions were reached by all subjects, regardless of whether they were of the same or opposite sex of the stimulus person (interaction $F = .01$).

The results suggest that a physical attractiveness stereotype exists and that its content is perfectly compatible with the "What is beautiful is good" thesis. Not only are physically attractive persons assumed to possess more socially desirable personalities than those of lesser attractiveness, but it is presumed that their lives will be happier and more successful.

The results also suggest that the physical attractiveness variable may have a number of implications for a variety of aspects of social interaction and influence. For example, it is clear that physically attractive individuals may have even more advantages in the dating market than has previously been assumed. In addition to an aesthetic advantage in marrying a beautiful spouse (cf. Josselin de Jong, 1952), potential marriage partners may also assume that the beautiful attract all of the world's material benefits and happiness. Thus, the lure of an attractive marriage partner should be strong indeed.

We do not know, of course, how well this stereotype stands up against contradictory information. Nor do we know the extent to which it determines the pattern of social interaction that develops with a person of a particular attractiveness level. Nevertheless, it would be odd if people did not behave toward others in accordance with this stereotype. Such behavior has been previously noted anecdotally. Monahan (1941) has observed that

Even social workers accustomed to dealing with all types often find it difficult to think of a normal, pretty girl as being guilty of a crime. Most people, for some inexplicable reason, think of crime in terms of abnormality in appearance, and I must say that beautiful women are not often convicted [p. 103].

A host of other familiar social psychological dependent variables also should be affected in predictable ways.

In the above connection, it might be noted that if standards of physical attractiveness vary widely, knowledge of the content of the physical attractiveness stereotype would be of limited usefulness in predicting its effect on social interaction and the development of the self-concept. The present study was not designed to investigate the degree of variance in perceived beauty. (The physical attractiveness ratings of the stimulus materials were made by college students of a similar background to those who participated in this study.) Preliminary evidence (Cross & Cross, 1971) suggests that such differences in perceived beauty may not be as severe as some observers have suggested.

REFERENCES

Aronson, E. Some antecedents of interpersonal attraction. In W. J. Arnold & D. Levine (Eds.), *Nebraska Symposium on Motivation*, 1969, **17**, 143–177.

Cross, J. F., & Cross, J. Age, sex, race, and the perception of facial beauty. *Developmental Psychology*, 1971, **5**, 433–439.

Hays, W. L. *Statistics for psychologists*. New York: Holt, Rinehart & Winston, 1963.

Josselin de Jong, J. P. B. *Lévi-Strauss' theory on kinship and marriage*. Leiden, Holland: Brill, 1952.

Kirkpatrick, C., & Cotton, J. Physical attractiveness, age, and marital adjustment. *American Sociological Review*, 1951, **16**, 81–86.

Monahan, F. *Women in crime*. New York: Ives Washburn, 1941.

Schiller, J. C. F. *Essays, esthetical and philosophical, including the dissertation on the "Connexions between the animal and the spiritual in man."* London: Bell, 1882.

Wright, B. A. *Physical disability—A psychological approach*. New York: Harper & Row, 1960.

ARTICLE 8

Self-concept and attraction for similar and dissimilar others

Russell L. Leonard, Jr.

Recent research has focused on the relationship between attitude similarity and interpersonal attraction (Bowditch, 1969; Byrne, 1961, 1965, 1969; Byrne, Clore, & Worchel, 1966; Byrne, London, & Reeves, 1968). These researchers have consistently found that the greater the degree of attitude similarity between two persons, the greater is their attraction for each other.

It is important that effort be directed toward the identification of limiting or boundary conditions where this relationship does not hold, since there are a number of situations where attraction or rejection due to attitude similarity–dissimilarity could result in unfair bias. For example, Golightly, Huffman, and Byrne (1972) found that attitude similarity affects the amount of money one person will approve as a loan to another, even when relevant financial information (debts, income, etc.) is held constant. Personnel decisions to hire, fire, promote, and demote persons in the business world represent another example.

The present study seeks to establish the self-concept as a moderator of the similarity-attraction relationship. Previous research in this area is inconclusive and suffers from methodological limitations. Griffitt (1966) found that subjects are more attracted to others with similar self-concepts but found no effect on attraction for similarity of another's self-concept to a subject's ideal self-concept. Thus, Griffitt was concerned with personality similarity and did not actually test the interaction of self-esteem and similarity as distinct variables. This relationship was tested by Hendrick and Page (1970), who compared the responses of low-, mod-

Reprinted from the *Journal of Personality and Social Psychology*, 1975, *31*, 926–929. Copyright 1975 by the American Psychological Association. Reprinted by permission.

This study was based in part on the author's doctoral dissertation submitted to the graduate school of Ohio State University. The study was supported by National Science Foundation Grant 2355 to Milton D. Hakel. The author would like to thank Donn Byrne, Richard Klimoski, Ronald Carver and Paul Fingerman for their comments on an earlier draft.

erate-, and high-self-esteem subjects to others representing varying degrees of attitude similarity. They found no effect for self-esteem on an attraction measure; however, the Self-Esteem × Similarity interaction approached significance, a finding the authors attributed to the tendency for moderate-self-esteem subjects to respond less negatively to dissimilar others than either the low- or high-self-esteem subjects. One problem with the Hendrick and Page (1970) study is the way in which they chose to define the low-self-esteem group. This group had an average self-ideal correlation of −.05, which is essentially zero. The fact that one's self-description bears no relation to one's ideal description (in contrast to a negative relationship, for example) may or may not mean that one is low in self-esteem. Also, the fact that the subjects in the Hendrick and Page study never saw or interacted with the others they evaluated but only saw their purported responses to an attitude questionnaire may undermine the generalizability of the findings to real-world, face-to-face settings.

It is apparent that the role of the self-concept in the similarity-attraction relationship has not been adequately tested. It is likely, as Griffitt (1966) suggested, that if a person A esteems himself highly, he will also esteem highly those similar to himself and think less of those dissimilar to himself. According to Korman (1970), a negative self-concept develops as a result of a life history of failure to achieve goals. Thus, an individual with a negative self-concept may associate similar others with unpleasant outcomes and be less attracted to them than to dissimilar others.

METHOD

Subjects

Subjects were 36 female and 28 male psychology students who participated to satisfy a course requirement. Four upperclass psychology majors served as confederates.

Instruments

Prior to the experiment, information was obtained about the subjects' education, work experience, and demographic characteristics. Subjects also completed a 14-item attitude scale dealing with salient campus issues (e.g., Viet Nam), and the self-assurance scale of the Ghiselli Self-Descriptive Inventory (Ghiselli, 1971). Scores on this instrument were used to measure self-concept. Scores ranged from 17 to 37 or from the 5th to the 90th percentile on Ghiselli's norm tables for the employed adult population (male and female). The median score was 26, which corresponds to the 60th percentile. Those scores above the median were designated as favorable, those below as unfavorable. The median percentile for the low group was the 33rd, while the high group median was the 86th percentile.

Since the study involved role-played employment interviews, two dependent measures were constructed. The first was a 25-point scale which measured overall attraction to the applicant as a prospective employee. The scale was divided into 5 blocks each containing 5 rating points. Thus, Points 1–5 were labeled poor, 6–10 below average, 11–15 average, 16–20 above average, and 21–25 superior. The second was a 9-point, behaviorally based scale measuring expectation of effort on the job. The lowest point, 1, was anchored by the statement, "This person almost always fails to complete work on time." The highest rating, 9, was anchored by, "This person would take the initiative to see that a job was done right even if he was not personally responsible for it, and even if it meant changing his own immediate plans." The final instrument was a check on the similarity manipulation. It consisted of a 5-point perceived similarity-to-self (of the confederates) scale which subjects filled out at the end of the experiment.

Procedure

Subjects returned in groups of eight for the actual experiment. Small sessions were necessary because of a limited number of confederates (four) to role play as job applicants. Subjects were told the purpose was to relate characteristics of themselves to ratings they would make about persons playing roles as job applicants and that they would each interview another person who would be playing a role as an applicant for the job of "Laboratory Assistant—Department of Psychology." Subjects were given a description of this job, a list of questions to ask the applicant, and a set of materials about the person they were to interview. Included were the applicant's responses to the same attitude scale the subject had completed earlier. The subjects' responses were used to make the applicant appear similar in half of the cases and dissimilar in the other half. Similarity was operationalized to mean that all responses on the 5-point scales were within 1 point of the subject's original ones. Dissimilarity was defined as a discrepancy of 3 points or more on all items except those marked 3. For these a response of 1 or 5 was considered dissimilar.

Also included was the applicant's resume, which provided information concerning education, employment, and demographic factors. This information was also manipulated so as to make the confederates appear similar to the subjects in half of the cases and dissimilar in the other half (similar or dissimilar college majors, work experience, etc.).

After the subjects had studied the applicant materials, they conducted 15-minute interviews with confederates in soundproof cubicles. Confederates were thoroughly trained in how to respond to the subjects' questions so that the interviews would be homogeneous. In addition, they tried to play their roles so as to be as consistent with their responses to the attitude items as possible. Confederates were aware that the study was concerned with the degree of similarity-dissimilarity between themselves and the subjects; however, they had no knowledge of either the self-esteem measures or the specific hypothesis being tested. It was felt that this interview procedure would sharpen the dissimilarity-similarity effect and provide a closer approximation to the real world than if subjects only read the confederates' responses. When the interviews were over, each subject completed the rating scales and the manipulation check described above.

To determine if the manipulation had been successful, the mean ratings of the applicants on the perceived similarity-to-self scale were compared for the designated similar and dissimilar groups. These were 3.91 and 2.56 (1 = very dissimilar, 2 = dissimilar, 3 = ?, 4 = similar, 5 = very similar), respectively, $F (1,62) = 35.08, p < .001$. It was concluded that the manipulation had been successful.

The design was a 2×2 factorial with two levels of subject self-concept (favorable and unfavorable) and two levels of "applicant" similarity (similar and dissimilar).

RESULTS

Table 1 shows the mean ratings of overall attraction toward the applicant and expectation of effort for the four cells. Analyses of variance of these data revealed that the only significant interactions were those which clearly establish the self-concept as a moderator of the attraction relationship. The effect of similarity on attraction holds only among high self-concept subjects; it is reversed among low self-concept subjects. The same moderating effect occurs for the subjects' expectations of the applicants' expenditure of effort on the job. The reversal effect for low-self-concept subjects represents a distinct boundary condition for Byrne's (1971) "law of attraction."

To examine the interactions more carefully, comparisons were made among the cells using the Scheffé procedure described by Winer (1971). For the attraction variable, the high-self-concept-dissimilar applicant cell was significantly different from the high–similar cell, $F (1, 60) = 7.91$, $p < .01$, and the low–dissimilar cell, $F (1, 60) = 7.91, p < .01$. The same cells were different for the expenditure of effort ratings, $F (1, 60) = 12.12$, $p < .01$ and $F (1, 60) = 6.8, p < .05$, respectively. Thus, a large portion of the interaction ap-

TABLE 1. Mean rating of attraction to the applicant and expectation of effort

Self-concept	Similarity			
	Low		High	
	Attraction[a]	Effort[b]	Attraction	Effort
Unfavorable	16.88	7.63	14.94	7.13
Favorable	12.50	5.88	17.00	7.63

[a]Self-Concept $\times$ Similarity F (1, 60) = 8.09, $p < .01$.
[b]Self-Concept $\times$ Similarity F (1, 60) = 10.04, $p < .01$.

pears to be due to two factors: the tendency of subjects with high self-concepts to reject attitudinally dissimilar others and the failure of low self-concept subjects to prefer similar others. These results occurred despite the fact that the overall self-concept level of the subjects was higher than that for the general population of employed adults (Mdn = 60th percentile).

DISCUSSION

These results underscore the importance of the self-concept as a limiting factor or boundary condition to the similarity–attraction relationship. It seems clear that the improved procedures in this study allowed for a more adequate test of the moderating effect of the self-concept than was possible in previous studies (Griffitt, 1966; Hendrick & Page, 1970). The previous studies relied on "paper" others, while the present study involved face-to-face interaction between the participants, a fact which probably served to heighten the saliency of the situation for the subjects. The present study also employed a more subtle, 5-point attitude response format rather than the 2-point agree-disagree scales used earlier. Also, the self-assurance scale of the Ghiselli Self-Descriptive Inventory (Ghiselli, 1971) is probably a better measure of self-esteem than the Q-sort self-ideal discrepancy measure. Fi-

nally, the present study involved a double manipulation of similarity, attitudes *and* life history.

More research is needed to establish additional boundary conditions to the similarity-attraction relationship and to find ways of eliminating its potential biasing effect in critical interpersonal decision making. It has been shown that similarity can influence loan decisions (Golightly, et al., 1972) and hiring decisions (Baskett, 1973). On the positive side, Leonard (Note 1) showed that the similarity bias does not occur in an interview setting when interviewers are given complete and detailed information concerning the relationship between interview-elicited information and future job performance. Such results are encouraging and suggest that the "law of attraction" (Byrne, 1971) is lawful only under certain conditions.

REFERENCES

Baskett, G. D. Interview decisions as determined by competency and attitude similarity. *Journal of Applied Psychology*, 1973, *57*, 343–345.

Bowditch, J. L. Biographical similarity and interpersonal choice. Unpublished doctoral dissertation, Purdue University, 1969.

Byrne, D. Interpersonal attraction and attitude similarity. *Journal of Abnormal and Social Psychology*, 1961, *62*, 713–715.

Byrne, D. Authoritarianism and response to attitude similarity-dissimilarity. *Journal of Social Psychology*, 1965, *66*, 251–256.

Byrne, D. Attitudes and attraction. In L. Berkowitz (Ed.), *Advances in experimental social psychology* (Vol. 4). New York: Academic Press, 1969.

Byrne, D. *The attraction paradigm*. New York: Academic Press, 1971.

Byrne, D., Clore, G., & Worchel, P. Effect of economic similarity-dissimilarity on interpersonal attraction. *Journal of Personality and Social Psychology*, 1966, *4*, 220–224.

Byrne, D., London, O., & Reeves, K. The effects of physical attractiveness, sex, and attitude similarity on interpersonal attraction. *Journal of Personality*, 1968, *36*, 259–271.

Ghiselli, E. E. *Explorations in managerial talent*. Pacific Palisades, Calif.: Goodyear, 1971.

Golightly, C., Huffman, D., & Byrne, D. Liking and loaning. *Journal of Applied Psychology,* 1972, *56*, 521–523.

Griffitt, W. Interpersonal attraction as a function of the self-concept and personality similarity-dissimilarity. *Journal of Personality and Social Psychology,* 1966, *4*, 581–584.

Hendrick, C., & Page, H. A. Self-esteem, attitude similarity and attraction. *Journal of Personality,* 1970, *38,* 588–601.

Korman, A. Toward an hypothesis of work behavior. *Journal of Applied Psychology,* 1970, *54*, 31–41.

Winer, B. J. *Statistical principles in experimental design.* New York: McGraw-Hill, 1971.

ARTICLE 9

Physical attractiveness, perceived attitude similarity, and interpersonal attraction in an opposite-sex encounter

Robert E. Kleck
Carin Rubenstein

Research extending over several decades has largely supported the notion that overt physical characteristics of persons can function as important determinants of the impressions elicited from others. With no more information about a person than that he or she is physically disabled (e.g., Ray, 1946), unusually short and fat (e.g., Dibiase & Hjelle, 1968), or highly physically attractive (e.g., Miller, 1970), individuals are able to formulate rather elaborate impressions which show a high degree of interperceiver agreement.

An important question which follows upon the demonstration of such stereotypical views of physically distinct others is the nature of the relationship between our perceptions of those others and our overt behavior in their presence. If there is continuity between what we think to be true concerning a person and how we behave toward that person, then our expectations may function as self-fulfilling prophecies (e.g., Rosenthal & Jacobson, 1968). Expectations linked to physical appearance may be particularly important in this regard in that they are elicited by cues immediately and continually available in face-to-face encounters (Dion, Berscheid, & Walster, 1972).

Previous research has already documented that social interactions involving persons with negatively valued physical attributes (e.g., the physically deformed) are characterized by a number of consistent behavior biases on the part of the normal (Kleck, 1968, 1969; Kleck, Ono, & Hastorf, 1966). The research reported here is an attempt to extend this analysis to the interaction outcomes experienced by persons with positively valued physical characteristics, in this case, the physically attractive. It is reasonable to expect, consistent with the positive stereotype associated with physically at-

Reprinted from the *Journal of Personality and Social Psychology*, 1975, *31*, pp. 107–114. Copyright 1975 by the American Psychological Association. Reprinted by permission.

This research was supported in part by National Heart and Lung Institute Undergraduate Research Training Grant HE 05303-13.

tractive others (Dion et al., 1972), that interactions involving attractive stimulus persons are characterized by nonverbal behaviors and result in self-reports which connote liking and approach to a greater extent than do interactions involving less attractive stimulus persons.

Considerable recent interest has focused on the relative importance of physical attractiveness and attitudinal similarity as determinants of interpersonal attraction. Studies by Byrne, London, and Reeves (1968) and Stroebe, Insko, Thompson, and Layton (1971), for example, have found that when a photographed stranger of either high or low physical attractiveness is described as attitudinally similar or dissimilar, self-report measures of liking are influenced by both sets of cues. Attitudinal similarity was manipulated within the present study to assess the generality of these previous results to situations involving actual social interaction, but under conditions in which the stimulus person's behavior is independent of the particular combination of attractiveness and similarity which she represents. Although Byrne, Ervin, and Lamberth (1970) have previously addressed a similar issue, their study does not permit an assessment of the behavioral implications of attitudinal similarity or physical attraction per se in that the behavior of the stimulus person was not under the experimenters' control and may have covaried in important ways with these characteristics.

It was expected, consistent with the large body of previous research on similarity (Byrne, 1971), that perceived high similarity to a stimulus person would result in greater self-report and nonverbal indicators of attraction to that person than would low perceived similarity. While the present design is not, strictly speaking, an appropriate test of the relative potency of similarity and physical attractiveness, it was anticipated that the latter variable would have a stronger impact on our dependent measures than the former. This expectation derived from the point noted earlier that physical appearance information is immediately available to another in social interaction and does not depend upon memory for its continued availability.

The dependent measures of central interest consist of a number of self-report indicators of interpersonal attraction, including Byrne's attraction index and three nonverbal measures previously demonstrated to covary with attraction, that is, eye contact (Exline & Winters, 1965), smiling (Rosenfeld, 1966), and interaction distance (Mehrabian, 1969). In addition, person perception measures similar to those employed by Dion, Berscheid, and Walster (1972) to determine the presence of a physical attractiveness stereotype were collected. It was expected that the systematic differences in impressions elicited by these latter investigators on the basis of photographs of attractive and unattractive individuals would also be elicited by actual stimulus persons varying on the physical attractiveness dimension.

METHOD

Overview

Four experimental conditions were defined by the manipulation of the physical attractiveness of a confederate and by a parallel manipulation of perceived attitudinal similarity. Subjects participated in only one cell of the 2 × 2 design and the confederates in all four. The experimental session was divided into two distinct and, from the point of view of the subject, unrelated periods. During the first part of the study the confederate and subject interviewed one another concerning a number of campus issues. In the second phase they participated together in a ''short-term memory task,'' the purpose of which was to provide a less constrained context in which social interaction could take place. The physical attractiveness of the confederate was manipulated through the use of makeup and perceived similarity by having the confederate and subject report on their responses to items drawn from Byrne's (1971) attitude scale.

Subjects

Individuals were recruited during spring and summer terms at Dartmouth College to serve in a "study of interviewlike encounters." The 48 male subjects received either course credit or money for their participation.

Confederates

Five female age peers of the subjects were recruited to serve as confederates. The central criterion for selection was whether or not the facial attractiveness of the person could successfully be controlled through the use of unobtrusive makeup and hair styling. Those potential confederates who were rejected were primarily persons whose facial attractiveness could not be masked without the use of noticeable amounts of makeup. The confederates were not informed regarding the purposes of the study beyond the information that we were interested in the implications of varying physical appearances on social interaction. They were also not informed regarding the dependent measures or that they were being videotaped. The importance of maintaining a constant but natural pattern of behavior across subjects was emphasized during the training of the confederates.

Procedure

Prior to any contact with the confederate each subject responded to 15 attitudinal items selected from Byrne's (1971) 56-item Survey of Attitudes questionnaire. These items require the respondent to indicate which of six alternatives most closely corresponds with his or her position on a given issue (e.g., premarital sex relations). The subset of items taken from the scale was chosen by the authors on the basis of presumed high relevance to undergraduates.

The subject arrived at the experimental room first and was greeted by the experimenter, who introduced herself and asked the subject to take one of two seats placed facing one another at a distance of 5.5 feet in a 18 × 14 foot room. The confederate appeared almost immediately, was introduced to the subject, and was asked to take the other chair. The experimenter identified herself as an undergraduate working on a study of interviewlike situations and explained that it "facilitates interaction in such situations to know something about the other person." She then reminded them that they had both previously completed an attitude survey and handed them the survey form which they had completed. She suggested that, before the interview began, they could exchange information about themselves by reading the attitude items they had endorsed on the survey. The confederate started and alternated with the subject in reading the responses to the 15 attitudinal issues. This procedure resulted in the confederate always giving her opinion on a given item first. In the high-similarity condition, the confederate's responses corresponded with those of the subject on 13 of the 15 items whereas in the low-similarity condition correspondence was present for only 2 of the 15. At the conclusion of the reading of the opinion statements the confederate said, "We seem to agree a lot," (high-similarity condition) or, "We seem to disagree a lot" (low-similarity condition). The experimenter responded by saying "Yes, as matter of fact, you seem to be one of the most similar (dissimilar) pairs we've had."

The experimenter then reiterated her interest in interviewlike encounters and explained that each person would serve as both interviewer and interviewee. Since she wanted the interviews to be as standard as possible across pairs of subjects, she had prepared a standard set of questions (e.g., "How could the social life at the college be improved?") which she wanted each person to ask. The interviewer's task was to pose the question and to record on the interview form what he or she considered to be the central points made by the interviewee. The confederate was always "randomly" chosen to assume the role of interviewer first. As soon as the experimenter handed the interview forms to the confederate and subject, she left the room with the comment that she would be in the adjoining room and someone should come and get her when they were finished.

From the adjoining room the experimenter monitored the video and audio recording equipment. Neither the subjects nor the confederates were aware they were being recorded via hidden television cameras and microphones but were informed of this fact at the conclusion of the study.

At the conclusion of the interview period the subject and confederate were placed in separate rooms and were asked to answer a number of questions concerning the interview situation and the other person. When these were finished, the experimenter asked the subject to go to the same room in which the confederate was filling out the questionnaires. When the subject arrived at this room, the confederate, who had placed her questionnaire face down in front of her, was seated at the side and toward the end of a long table. Six other chairs were placed around the table at equal distances, and several were along the walls of the large (24 × 36 foot) room. The experimenter explained that the second part of the study was unrelated to the first and was a very brief experiment in memory which she was running as a favor to a professor in the department. A list of 10 words was to be shown to the subjects twice, followed by a 10-minute interval. The experimenter stressed that during this 10-minute period the subjects were free to talk or move about the room but that they should not actively rehearse the word list. After starting the projector on an automatic sequence, she left the room with the explanation that she would be back in 10 minutes to test their recall. From an adjoining room she observed the interaction between the subject and confederate without their knowledge. At the end of 10 minutes she returned to the room, asked both persons to write down as many of the items from the word list as they could recall, and explained that she would like them to complete one final questionnaire. The Interpersonal Judgment Scale (Byrne, 1971) required them to rate the other interactant on such dimensions as morality, adjustment, sexual attractiveness, and intelligence.

The primary purpose of the second phase of the study was to provide the subjects with a context in which more spontaneous interaction with the confederate would be possible. The confederate was instructed to not initiate interaction but to respond naturally to conversation initiated with her. Chair placement of the confederate was constant across subjects in order that seating distance could be assessed as a dependent measure.

Between two and four weeks after the initial interaction, the experimenter contacted the subject in his dormitory to complete a postexperimental questionnaire and to debrief the subject concerning the nature of the study. The questionnaire focused on the subject's recall of his partner (the confederate) and probed his impressions of the study and any suspicions he might have had concerning it. At this time it was revealed to him that he had been videotaped during the interview, and his permission was requested to retain that record for analysis purposes.[1]

RESULTS

Manipulation checks

The subjects rated the confederates on perceived attitudinal similarity and physical attractiveness, both during the experimental session and two to four weeks later as part of the follow-up interview. These ratings were done on 7-point scales, with the similarity dimension anchored by very similar and not at all similar and the attractiveness dimension anchored by extremely attractive physically and extremely unattractive physically. Two-way analyses of variance of these ratings revealed the manipulations to be highly effective in determining the perception of similarity, $F (1,40) = 54.4$, $p < .00001$, and attractiveness, $F (1,40) = 36.2$,

[1] No subject refused to have his video records made available for analysis, and only four expressed suspicion regarding the experimental procedures. In two of the cases suspicion focused on the similarity manipulation and in two on the attractiveness manipulation. For the latter, the apparent source of suspicion was that subjects who had been paired with a confederate in the unattractive condition had later seen her on campus in her more typical, and hence more attractive, physical state.

$p < .00001$, at the time of the interaction and also at the time of the follow-up interview (similarity: $F(1,37) = 42.9$, $p < .00001$; attractiveness: $F(1,37) = 16.9$, $p < .0005$). In that three subjects run during the summer term could not be contacted in time for the follow-up interviews, the number is reduced to 41 for the latter two analyses. There are no significant interactions in these analyses, which indicates that the manipulation of the confederate on one dimension did not affect the subjects' perception of her on the other.

As a further check on the effectiveness of the modification of the confederates' appearance, standardized color slides were taken of the confederates each time they were "made up" for the study. Two photographs of each confederate (one from the attractive and one from the unattractive condition) were randomly selected for presentation to independent male judges. Each of two groups of 12 judges saw one photograph of each confederate and rated her physical attractiveness on a 7-point scale. The confederate photographs were embedded in a longer sequence of photographs of females of approximately the same age. For all confederates the high-attractive condition photograph resulted in significantly higher ratings of physical attractiveness than did the low-attractive condition photograph, the t ratios ranging between $t(11) = 8.8$, $p < .00001$ and $t(11) = 3.3$, $p < .005$.

An important aspect of the intended manipulation is obviously the standardization of the confederates' behavior across the experimental conditions. In training the confederates the importance of a natural and consistent behavior pattern had been emphasized, and they were kept blind regarding the experimental hypotheses as well as the specific dependent measures under investigation. Without her awareness each confederate was videotaped during the conversational encounter, and her gaze and smiling behavior were compared across conditions. Because of scheduling difficulties, the participation of the confederates could not be precisely balanced across the design. Four of the confederates each appeared at least twice and not more than three

times in each of the four experimental conditions. The fifth confederate participated once in three of the conditions and twice in the fourth. Since this slightly unequal distribution made it impossible to treat confederates separately in the analyses, each appearance of a confederate was entered as an independent observation, and two-way analyses of variance were conducted with the data. Gaze and smiling behavior were chosen as measures of confederate constancy because they have been demonstrated to be important nonverbal behaviors in the modulation of face-to-face interaction (e.g., Kendon, 1967), and they are also the nonverbal measures of primary concern vis-à-vis the subjects. Thus, if the confederates were found to differ across experimental conditions in regard to the frequencies of these behaviors, such differences could have potential confounding implications for any observed differences in the subjects' behavior.

Scoring of the dependent measures was done by one coder for all of the confederate videotapes and for a random subset by a second coder. Intercoder reliabilities were computed for the overlapping sample and exceeded .90 for all dependent measures. It should be noted, of course, that the coders could not remain blind regarding whether a confederate was in the attractive or unattractive condition, and thus the possibility of coder bias cannot be completely excluded. Since the interaction consisted of two distinct parts during which the confederate was primarily either a listener-interviewer (Part 1) or a speaker (Part 2), the analyses were conducted for each part separately as well as for the total interaction. No significant main effects or interactions were present for percentage of time smiling, frequency of smiling per unit of time, percentage of gaze time, or for the average duration of gaze.

Self-report measures

Subsequent to the interviewlike interaction, subjects completed an impression scale made up of 10 polar adjectives. These were a subset of the items previously employed by Dion et al. (1972) to establish the presence of a physical attractiveness stereotype in young adults. Ratings were summed for those five trait items which had been identified by the previous investigators as traits associated with a socially desirable person (social, interesting, self-assertive, sincere, and warm). An analysis of variance revealed no differences in the ratings received by attractive and unattractive confederates though there was a tendency for the attractive confederate to be perceived as a more socially desirable person, $p < .12$. Similarity had no effect on the ratings, and there was no evidence of an interaction between these variables.

The Byrne (1971) 10-item Interpersonal Judgment Scale was completed by all subjects at the end of the short-term memory portion of the experimental session. The key items are ratings of liking and desirability as a work partner, which Byrne and Nelson (1965) and others have combined into a general attraction index. The data are plotted in Figure 1. An analysis of variance of the ratings reveals a significant effect for physical attractiveness, $F(1,40) = 8.39, p < .01$, but not for perceived similarity, $F = 1.6$, or for the interaction, $F = .9$. Ratings of liking, not combined with ratings on desirability as a work partner, strongly discriminate the attractive from the unattractive conditions, $F(1,40) = 8.9, p < .01$. Three other items on the Interpersonal Judgment Scale are face-valid indicators of approach responses toward others; dating, marriage, and sexual attractiveness. For the first two, the physical attractiveness manipulation again results in more positive ratings, dating: $F(1,40) = 10.4, p < .005$; marriage: $F(1,40) = 12.7, p < .005$, with no effects for similarity and no evidence of an interaction between attractiveness and similarity. In regard to ratings on the sexual attractiveness dimension, neither experimental manipulation has a consistent effect on the subjects' ratings.

The final self-report measures of interest were collected two to four weeks after the experimental session and prior to debriefing the subjects regard-

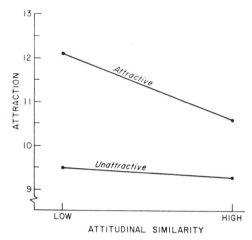

FIGURE 1. Attraction as a function of perceived similarity and physical attractiveness of the confederates. (The data are derived from a summation of ratings on liking and desirability as a work partner, and high numbers correspond to high levels of attraction.)

ing the nature of the study. In addition to the manipulation checks reported earlier, subjects were asked (a) to indicate whether and how frequently they had thought about the person they had interacted with, (b) to describe what their partner had looked like, (c) to indicate their present degree of liking for the partner, and (d) to indicate how much they had enjoyed participating in the study. Analyses of variance of these responses indicate that subjects who had interacted with confederates in the physically attractive condition reported thinking about her more frequently, $F(1,37) = 3.93$, $p = .05$, showed a tendency to remember more aspects of her clothing and appearance, $F(1,37) = 2.7, p = .10$, and continued to like her more, $F(1,37) = 11.64, p < .005$, than did subjects who had interacted with the unattractive confederates. Consistent with the earlier self-report data, perceived confederate similarity had no significant impact on these measures.

Nonverbal measures

Gaze and smiling behaviors were coded from the videotapes for both the talking-interviewee and the listening-interviewer phases of the interaction. The coder was blind regarding the experimental conditions represented by any particular subject, and only one behavior (smiling or gaze) was scored at a time. Since the video cameras were in approximately the same position as the observer in the Exline and Winters (1965) study, it was assumed that this procedure would index actual looking as reliably as their widely used method. A second coder independently scored a randomly selected subset of the videotapes and achieved a reliability of .93 for smiles and .91 for gaze behavior with the first coder. Both smiling scores and gaze scores were converted to percentages to correct for the different interaction times upon which they are based.

During the period in which the subjects were being interviewed, those talking to physically attractive confederates spent more time looking at her, F (1,36) = 6.73, $p < .02$, and smiling, F (1,36) = 5.94, $p < .02$, than did those talking to less attractive confederates.[2] These differences are not present when the subject is in the role of listener-interviewer though the direction of the differences is the same. The absence of an effect when the subject is in the interviewer role can in part be accounted for by the fact that subjects took notes on what the confederate was saying, and thus their gaze was diverted away from the other interactant for much of the time. Neither of the nonverbal measures are related to perceived attitude similarity for either the talking or listening phases of the interaction.

Two final behavioral measures were derived from the short-term memory part of the interaction. No significant effects were obtained in regard to seating distance primarily because 78% of the subjects elected to sit one chair position removed from the confederate. The time required for the subject to initiate verbal interaction with the confederate was also recorded, and again no significant differences as a function of the experimental manipulations were observed.

[2] For these analyses, the total sample is reduced to 40 (10 per cell) due to camera and video recorder malfunctions.

DISCUSSION

In the light of previous research the most striking aspect of the findings reported here is the total absence of an effect of perceived attitudinal similarity on either nonverbal or self-report measures of interpersonal attraction. As the data for the manipulation checks revealed, the absence of such an effect cannot be attributed to a faulty or weak induction of perceived similarity. The lack of continuity between the present results and studies such as those of Stroebe et al. (1971) and Byrne et al. (1968) may be attributable to the fact that, while we used actual persons in face-to-face contact, they employed photographs as stimuli. Situations involving actual interaction may so increase the potency of the physical attractiveness cues that the effect observed for similarity in noninteraction studies is simply overwhelmed.

The discontinuity between the present findings and those of Byrne et al. (1970) are not so easily dismissed, however, in that a similarity effect was obtained with actual stimulus persons, varying in physical attractiveness, subsequent to a "coke date" interaction. The dissimilarities in the two designs need to be taken into account, however, in attempting to compare the results. While the present study focused on the effects of perceived similarity and manipulated physical attractiveness, that of Byrne et al. involved *actual* similarity (both attitudes and personality) and *rated* physical attractiveness. Thus, while much of the effort of the current study was directed toward maintaining constancy in the behavior of the stimulus persons across experimental conditions, the behavior of the stimulus persons in Byrne et al. was free to covary with these stimulus differences. Second, in that the previous authors did not select their subjects on the basis of physical attractiveness, it appears likely that the stimulus persons in the present design represent more extreme points on the physical attractiveness dimension.

It is important to note that evidence for the salience of appearance cues in social interaction, both in regard to stigmatizing cues such as physical deformities and in regard to less striking physical variations such as the attractiveness manipulation employed here, derives from studies involving either little interaction (an evening dance, a coke date, a conversational encounter) or no interaction at all (photographs of "persons you might date"). It has been suggested by several investigators (e.g., Richardson, 1969) that while appearance cues may be very important during the initial phases of an interaction, they probably decrease in importance as interaction time accumulates. Evidence counter to this argument is provided in a recent study by Kleck, Richardson, and Ronald (1974), in which children's friendship choices following two weeks of intense social interaction were strongly and positively related to the physical attractiveness of the stimulus children. Dion and Berscheid (Note 1) have obtained similar results in a nursery school setting. Such results can be accounted for in at least two ways. Either attractiveness cues continue to have an impact on interpersonal attraction responses independent of the particular interpersonal exchanges which take place, or physical attractiveness tends to be highly correlated with behaviors and interaction outcomes which others find reinforcing.

One must be cautious in attempting to generalize from laboratory manipulations of the sort represented here to the operation of physical attractiveness and attitudinal similarity cues in naturalistic interactions. The extrapolation of laboratory findings is particularly problematic in regard to perceived similarity for a number of reasons. In the first place, the manipulation of this variable (via the presentation of relatively large amounts of attitudinal information at the start of an interaction) is at variance with the gradual exchange of such information which takes place in natural settings (Altman & Taylor, 1973). Second, in order to reduce suspicion regarding the similarity manipulation, a fixed order of information exchange was imposed on the interaction such that the subject always gave his opinion on a given issue after he had heard the confederate express hers. A possible implication of such a restriction is that the subject will be made uncomfortable by being placed in a position where the confederate can perceive his behavior as an attempt to ingratiate her, particularly if she is physically attractive. The implications of such uncomfortableness are not obvious, but this factor may help account for the absence of a similarity effect in the present data (see Figure 1). Finally, in the present design the revelation of similarity was independent of the physical attractiveness of the person to whom the similarity was disclosed. There is reason to expect (e.g., Berscheid & Walster, 1973) that in naturalistic situations the physical appearance of an interactant may itself affect whether we choose to reveal attitudinally similar or dissimilar information.

It is important to keep in mind that the present results are based on male-female dyads in which only females serve as stimulus persons. On the basis of previous research (Berscheid & Walster, 1973) one might well expect the effects of physical attractiveness to be greater under these conditions than would be the case in same-sex dyads or when females are responding to males. Clearly, this assumption needs to be investigated in that there is some evidence (e.g., Byrne et al., 1970) to the contrary.

REFERENCE NOTE

1. Dion, K., & Berscheid, E. *Physical attractiveness and social perception of peers in preschool children.* Unpublished manuscript, 1972. (Available from E. Berscheid, Department of Psychology, N309 Elliott Hall, University of Minnesota, Minneapolis, Minnesota 55455.)

REFERENCES

Altman, I., & Taylor, D. A. *Social penetration: The development of interpersonal relationships.* New York: Holt, Rinehart & Winston, 1973.

Berscheid, E., & Walster, E. Physical attractiveness. In L. Berkowitz (Ed.), *Advances in experimental social psychology.* Vol. 7. New York: Academic Press, 1973.

Byrne, D. *The attraction paradigm.* New York: Academic Press, 1971.

Byrne, D., Ervin, C. H., & Lamberth, J. Continuity between the experimental study of attraction and real-life computer dating. *Journal of Personality and Social Psychology,* 1970, *16,* 157–165.

Byrne, D., London, O., & Reeves, K. The effects of physical attractiveness, sex, and attitude similarity on interpersonal attraction. *Journal of Personality,* 1968, *36,* 259–271.

Byrne, D., & Nelson, D. Attraction as a linear function of proportion of positive reinforcements. *Journal of Personality and Social Psychology,* 1965, *1,* 659–663.

Dibiase, W. J., & Hjelle, L. A. Body-image stereotypes and body-type preferences among male college students. *Perceptual and Motor Skills,* 1968, *27,* 1143–1146.

Dion, K., Berscheid, E., & Walster, E. What is beautiful is good. *Journal of Personality and Social Psychology,* 1972, *24,* 285–290.

Exline, R. V., & Winters, L. C. Affective relations and mutual glances in dyads. In S. S. Tomkins & C. E. Izard (Eds.), *Affect, cognition, and personality.* New York: Springer, 1965.

Kendon, A. Some functions of gaze direction in social interaction. *Acta Psychologica,* 1967, *26,* 22–63.

Kleck, R. Physical stigma and nonverbal cues emitted in face-to-face interaction. *Human Relations,* 1968, *21,* 19–28.

Kleck, R. Physical stigma and task interaction. *Human Relations,* 1969, *22,* 53–60.

Kleck, R., Ono, H., & Hastorf, A. H. The effects of physical deviance upon face-to-face interaction. *Human Relations,* 1966, *91,* 425–436.

Kleck, R. E., Richardson, S. A., & Ronald, L. Physical appearance cues and interpersonal attraction in children. *Child Development,* 1974, *45,* 305–310.

Mehrabian, A. Significance of posture and position in the communication of attitude and status relationships. *Psychological Bulletin,* 1969, *71,* 359–372.

Miller, A. G. Role of physical attractiveness in impression formation. *Psychonomic Science,* 1970, *19,* 241–243.

Ray, M. H. The effect of crippled appearance on personality judgments. Unpublished master's thesis, Stanford University, 1946.

Richardson, S. A. The effect of physical disability on the socialization of a child. In D. A. Goslin (Ed.), *Handbook of socialization theory and research.* Chicago: Rand McNally, 1969.

Rosenfeld, H. M. Instrumental affiliative functions of facial and gestural expressions. *Journal of Personality and Social Psychology,* 1966, *4,* 65–72.

Rosenthal, R., & Jacobson, L. *Pygmalion in the classroom.* New York: Holt, Rinehart & Winston, 1968.

Stroebe, W., Insko, C. A., Thompson, V. D., & Layton, B. D. Effects of physical attractiveness, attitude similarity, and sex on various aspects of interpersonal attraction. *Journal of Personality and Social Psychology,* 1971, *18,* 79–91.

SECTION SUMMARY

As Kleck and Rubenstein note in the third article in this Section, the outcome of their study differs from that of several earlier studies, most notably the one conducted by Byrne, Ervin, and Lamberth (1970). They point out that the present study utilized *perceived* similarity (through confederates' attitude responses) and *manipulated* the physical attractiveness of the confederate (through the use of makeup), whereas the Byrne et al. study involved *actual* similarity in both attitudes and personality (based on questionnaire responses) and the *rated* physical attractiveness of each partner by the other. We encourage you to evaluate the other possible reasons Kleck and Rubenstein give for the differences between the results of their study and those of earlier studies.

The Dion, Walster, and Berscheid study, reprinted as the first article in this Section, as well as other studies conducted subsequently, show that physical attractiveness can be a surprisingly potent determinant of liking. But there are limitations to this effect. As Kleck and Rubenstein point out, most research has involved either little interaction (an evening dance, a conversational encounter, a coke date) or no interaction at all (photographs of "persons you might date"). Everyday behavioral situations are often not of this type. Some theorists have suggested that although physical attractiveness may be of major importance in the *initial* contacts between people, its importance may decrease as people get to know each other better and other factors, such as attitude similarity or dissimilarity, become known.

Levinger and Snoek (1972), for example, have depicted different levels that relationships may achieve. At the level of *surface contact,* interaction between people begins but is restricted, and the relationship is somewhat shallow. Each person may begin to probe the relationship more intensely to determine whether to go further in it. At this stage surface characteristics are important, as are any other factors that encourage further contact. Thus, according to Levinger and Snoek, factors such as propinquity, physical attractiveness, perceived competence, and reciprocal liking will all be of considerable importance. If, however, the relationship achieves a deeper level, which they label *mutuality,* attention may be turned away from surface traits and toward less obvious characteristics, such as similarity of values and attitudes and satisfaction of each other's needs.

As the Dion et al. article illustrates, however, the effect of physical attractiveness, at least in initial encounters, is quite powerful. Research has indicated that in a "blind date" or "computer dance" situation, physical attractiveness is a strong predictor of how much a person will like his or her date.

In fact, in computer-dance situations where people are allowed to *choose* from several potential dates, attractiveness appears to be *all-powerful* in determining choices. But there is also some evidence that "matching" according to attractiveness may take place. Berscheid, Dion, Walster, and Walster (1971) found that less physically attractive males and females tended to choose somewhat less physically attractive dates for themselves than did more attractive persons. Another study indicates that such matching may be a lasting phenomenon. Murstein (1972) compared the similarity in attractiveness of couples who were engaged or dating steadily with "couples" created by randomly matching photos of a male and female. It was found that the engaged/dating couples were more similar in attractiveness than the randomly matched couples. There is also evidence that adults may treat physically attractive children differently from the way in which they treat unattractive ones (Dion, 1972). However, there is *no* evidence that a self-fulfilling prophecy may take place—that is, that physically attractive persons might actually develop the attractive personality characteristics they are expected to have (Berscheid & Walster, 1974).

Although there is much research evidence that physical attractiveness usually leads to positive assumptions about personality characteristics and perhaps to more favorable treatment, there can be exceptions to this general trend. For example, what if someone "used" his or her physical attractiveness in order to take advantage of someone else? Might this person be evaluated very negatively by others? Sigall and Ostrove (1975) compared college students' reactions to both attractive and unattractive female defendants who were guilty of either an attractiveness-related crime (a swindle) or a crime unrelated to attractiveness (a burglary). As they had predicted, these researchers found that, when the offense was a burglary, the unattractive defendant was more severely punished (given a longer prison sentence) than was the attractive defendant. However, when the offense was attractiveness-related (the swindle), the attractive defendant was actually treated somewhat *more* harshly than the unattractive one. Hence, this research suggests that, while physical attractiveness is usually beneficial in terms of the treatment one receives from others, there may be times when it is actually a liability.

Other research has identified further negative attributions that may be associated with attractiveness. Dermer and Thiel (1975) found that while more attractive women were expected to have more socially desirable personalities and to achieve more social and professional happiness than less attractive women, they were also seen as more vain and egotistical, more likely to request a divorce and to have an extramarital affair, and more likely to have a "bourgeois orientation"—to be materialistic,

snobbish, and unsympathetic to oppressed peoples. Hence, the stereotype might be restated as: "What is beautiful is good in *most* respects."

The research included in this Section has focused largely on two important determinants of attraction: (1) similarity of beliefs and attitudes and (2) physical appearance. But as we mentioned in the Section Introduction, there are other important determinants of attraction too, such as propinquity, ability, and reciprocated liking. It is all of these factors together, in interaction with our own personality characteristics (such as self-esteem, as illustrated in Leonard's article in this Section), that will determine whom we like and, perhaps, whom we love as well.

REFERENCES

Berscheid, E., Dion, K., Walster, E., & Walster, G. W. Physical attractiveness and dating choice: A test of the matching hypothesis. *Journal of Experimental Social Psychology, 1971, 7,* 173–189.

Berscheid, E., & Walster, E. Physical attractiveness. In L. Berkowitz (Ed.), *Advances in Experimental Social Psychology* (Vol. 7). New York: Academic Press, 1974.

Byrne, D., Ervin, C. H., & Lamberth, J. Continuity between the experimental study of attraction and real-life computer dating. *Journal of Personality and Social Psychology, 1970, 16,* 157–165.

Dermer, M., & Thiel, D. L. When beauty may fail. *Journal of Personality and Social Psychology. 1975, 31,* 1168–1176.

Dion, K. Physical attractiveness and evaluation of children's transgressions. *Journal of Personality and Social Psychology, 1972, 24,* 207–213.

Levinger, G., & Snoek, J. D. *Attraction in relationship: A new look at interpersonal attraction.* Morristown, N.J.: General Learning Press, 1972.

Murstein, B. Physical attractiveness and marital choice. *Journal of Personality and Social Psychology,* 1972, *22,* 8–12.

Sigall, H., & Ostrove, N. Beautiful but dangerous: Effects of offender attractiveness and nature of the crime on juridic judgment. *Journal of Personality and Social Psychology, 1975, 31,* 410–414.

SECTION IV

THEORIES OF ATTITUDE CHANGE: FOCUS ON COGNITIVE CONSISTENCY

INTRODUCTION

Why do people change their attitudes? Are there principles by which we can predict and explain when and why attitude change occurs? Questions such as these have great implications for everyday life. Everyone, from the door-to-door encyclopedia salesman to the juror in the trial of socialite fugitive Patricia Hearst—whose defense was that she had been "brainwashed" into committing illegal acts—is concerned with the processes that form and change attitudes. A decade ago McGuire (1966) noted that the concept of "attitude" received more space in social-psychology textbooks than did any other topic. That is still true. Social psychologists are concerned with the development and organization of attitudes, with the measurement of attitudes and the sampling of opinions, and with the reasons why attitudes do or do not change.

Perhaps the most effective way of approaching the question of why attitudes change is to begin by considering a related point: why do people hold their present attitudes? That is, what *reason* does a person have for holding *any* attitude? The key factor here may be the *function* that the attitude serves. Daniel Katz (1960) and Smith, Bruner, and White (1956) have identified four major types of functions that an attitude can serve for its holder.

One function of attitudes is to give people a frame of reference or standard for evaluating attitude-relevant objects, or a way of structuring the world as they know it. This function can be labeled the *knowledge* function. A rational, information-based appeal to change one's attitude might be effective if the attitude were serving this function.

Attitudes can also allow one to identify with, or gain the approval of, important reference groups. In addition, the expression of appropriate attitudes may be directly rewarded by important persons in one's environment—parents, teachers, friends, and so forth. Attitudes that allow a person to achieve such rewards can be seen as serving the *social adjustment* function. In such a case, an appeal to one's reference-group consciousness or a change in the pattern of rewards and punishments might be an effective attitude-change technique.

A third function is the *value-expressive* function, wherein attitudes are used to give expression to individuals' central values and to their self-concepts. If people can be convinced that new or different attitudes would reflect their central values more accurately than their existing ones, then attitude change may take place.

The fourth general function is the *ego-defensive* function. In this case attitudes are a reflection (or externalization) of unresolved inner problems. As defense mechanisms, such attitudes may allow individuals to protect themselves from acknowledging uncomplimentary basic truths about themselves. Prejudicial attitudes toward minority-group members may serve such a function; the hostility may have little or no relationship to the actual characteristics of the minority-group members; it may instead stem from the holder's unresolved personality problems, such as unexpressed aggression or fear of losing status. Archie Bunker's racial attitudes (described in Section 2) provide an illustration of attitudes that are serving an ego-defensive function.

As we have suggested, knowing which function an attitude is serving in a particular case may indicate which attitude-change stratagems will work best. At a more general level, there are many theories of why attitudes change. These have been extensively reviewed in a number of textbooks (the interested reader may want to see Triandis, 1971; Kiesler, Collins, & Miller, 1969; Himmelfarb & Eagly, 1974; and Fishbein & Ajzen, 1975). In this Section we focus on one popular but controversial theory—cognitive dissonance theory.

Originally formulated by Leon Festinger (1957), cognitive dissonance theory has stimulated an avalanche of research, criticisms, and countercriticisms in social psychology. The theory itself, however, is basically quite straightforward. Festinger proposed that any two "cognitive elements" (any knowledge, opinion, or belief about the environment, about oneself, or about one's behavior) that a person holds can coexist in one of three general forms: irrelevant (no relationship to each other), consonant (consistent with each other), or dissonant (in which the opposite of one element would follow from the other). If two cognitive elements have a dissonant relationship to each other, the existence of dissonance creates psychological tension or discomfort that *motivates* the person to reduce dissonance and achieve consonance. The more important the two elements are, the greater is the dissonance created.

With regard to reasons for changing one's attitude, then, cognitive dissonance theory deals directly with one's internal state. The existence of dissonance describes a state of internal dissatisfaction; to reduce or eliminate this dissatisfaction, one may change an attitude, change a behavior, or expose oneself to new information (add new cognitive elements) to strengthen or bolster one of the cognitive elements.

As Elliot Aronson, then at the University of Texas, states in the first article, this basically simple theory has generated a good bit of hostility within social psychology. Aronson describes the problems inherent in the theoretical imprecision and "conceptual fuzziness" of cognitive dissonance theory and makes his own propositions about modes of analysis that may reduce this fuzziness. You are encouraged to keep these modifications in mind while reading the remaining articles in this Section. In the Section Summary we will briefly outline two other theories that have been developed to explain the same phenomena that dissonance theory is intended to explain.

In the second article, Daryl Bem of Stanford University sounds a cautionary note regarding the abstruse theorizing that cognitive dissonance theory has engendered. His reservations about the "fastidious pool of cognitive clarity" implied by dissonance theory should be carefully considered.

The tremendous range of research issues and scholarly debates that dissonance theory has stimulated is far too broad to even summarize here. Our third article, therefore, focuses on one specific area where the theory might be applied—political persuasion. Joel Cooper, John M. Darley, and James E. Henderson, of Princeton University, point out that information from two types of sources (traditional political wisdom and psychological research) has suggested that face-to-face communication with voters should be most effective in changing attitudes about political issues and, furthermore, that the individuals who make such face-to-face contact should appear well-dressed, clean, and conventional. Cooper, Darley, and Henderson propose, however, that there are situations under which these generalizations might not apply. Deriving their hypotheses from cognitive dissonance theory, they propose that in some cases a deviant-appearing "hippie" individual might actually be more effective in changing attitudes than a "straight" individual would be. Their field experiment tests this possibility.

REFERENCES

Festinger, L. *A theory of cognitive dissonance*. Stanford, Calif.: Stanford University Press, 1957.

Fishbein, M., & Ajzen, I. *Belief, attitude, intention, and behavior*. Reading, Mass.: Addison-Wesley, 1975.

Himmelfarb, S., & Eagly, A. H. (Eds.), *Readings in attitude change*. New York: Wiley, 1974.

Katz, D. The functional approach to the study of attitudes. *Public Opinion Quarterly*, 1960, *24*, 163–204.

Kiesler, C. A., Collins, B. E., & Miller, N. *Attitude change: A critical analysis of theoretical approaches*. New York: Wiley, 1969.

McGuire, W. J. Attitudes and opinions. In P. R. Farnsworth, O. McNemar, and Q. McNemar (Eds.), *Annual review of psychology*, Vol. XVII. Palo Alto, Calif.: Annual Reviews, 1966. Pp. 475–514.

Smith, M. B., Bruner, J. S., & White, R. W. *Opinions and personality*. New York: Wiley, 1956.

Triandis, H. C. *Attitude and attitude change*. New York: Wiley, 1971.

ARTICLE 10

Dissonance theory: Progress and problems

Elliot Aronson

As a formal statement, Festinger's theory of cognitive dissonance (1957) is quite primitive; it lacks the elegance and precision commonly associated with scientific theorizing. Yet its impact has been great. As McGuire has observed in his recent survey in the *Annual Review of Psychology* (1966, p. 492), "Over the past three years, dissonance theory continued to generate more research and more hostility than any other one approach." I will allude to the "hostility" part of this statement from time to time throughout this chapter; but first let us discuss the research.

The research has been as diverse as it has been plentiful; its range extends from maze running in rats (Lawrence & Festinger, 1962), to the development of values in children (Aronson & Carlsmith, 1963); from the hunger of college sophomores (Brehm, Back, & Bogdonoff, 1964), to the proselytizing behavior of religious zealots (Festinger, Riecken, & Schachter, 1956). For descriptive summaries of dissonance experiments, the reader is referred to Festinger, 1957; Festinger and Aronson, 1960; Brehm and Cohen, 1962; Festinger and Bramel, 1962; Festinger and Freedman, 1964.

The proliferation of research testing and extending dissonance theory is due for the most part to the generality and simplicity of the theory. Although it has been applied primarily in social psychological settings, it is not limited to social psychological phenomena such as interpersonal relations or feelings toward a communicator and his communication. Rather, its domain is in the widest of places: the skull of an individual organism.[1]

From "Dissonance Theory: Progress and Problems," by E. Aronson. In R. P. Abelson, E. Aronson, W. J. McGuire, T. M. Newcomb, M. J. Rosenberg, and P. H. Tannenbaum (Eds.), *Theories of Cognitive Consistency: A Sourcebook.* Copyright 1968. Reprinted by permission of the author.

This chapter was prepared while the author's research was being supported by grants from the National Science Foundation (NSF GS 750) and the National Institute of Mental Health (MH 12357), which he gratefully acknowledges.

[1] An additional reason for the great number of experiments on dissonance theory is completely *ad hominem:* Leon Festinger has an unmatched genius for translating interesting hypotheses into workable experimental operations and for inspiring others to do so. He has produced a great deal of research irrespective of any particular theoretical approach.

The core notion of the theory is extremely simple: Dissonance is a negative drive state which occurs whenever an individual simultaneously holds two cognitions (ideas, beliefs, opinions) which are psychologically inconsistent. Stated differently, two cognitions are dissonant if, considering these two cognitions alone, the opposite of one follows from the other. Since the occurrence of dissonance is presumed to be unpleasant, individuals strive to reduce it by adding "consonant" cognitions or by changing one or both cognitions to make them "fit together" better—i.e., so that they become more consonant with each other.[2] To use Festinger's time-worn (but still cogent) example, if a person believes that cigarette smoking causes cancer and simultaneously knows that he himself smokes cigarettes, he experiences dissonance. Assuming that the person would rather not have cancer, his cognition "I smoke cigarettes" is psychologically inconsistent with his cognition "cigarette smoking produces cancer." Perhaps the most efficient way to reduce dissonance in such a situation is to stop smoking. But, as many of us have discovered, this is by no means easy. Thus, a person will usually work on the other cognition. There are several ways in which a person can make cigarette smoking seem less absurd. He might belittle the evidence linking cigarette smoking to cancer ("Most of the data are clinical rather than experimental"); or he might associate with other cigarette smokers ("If Sam, Jack, and Harry smoke, then it can't be very dangerous"); or he might smoke filter-tipped cigarettes and delude himself that the filter traps the cancer-producing materials; or he might convince himself that smoking is an important and highly pleasurable activity ("I'd rather have a shorter but more enjoyable life than a longer, unenjoyable one"); or he might actually make a virtue out of smoking by developing a romantic, devil-may-care image of

himself, flaunting danger by smoking. All of these behaviors reduce dissonance, in effect, by reducing the absurdity involved in going out of one's way to contract cancer. Thus, dissonance theory does not rest upon the assumption that man is a *rational* animal; rather, it suggests that man is a rational*izing* animal—that he attempts to appear rational, both to others and to himself. To clarify the theoretical statement and to illustrate the kind of research generated by the theory, I will briefly describe a few experiments.

Dissonance Following a Decision

One of the earliest experiments testing derivations from dissonance theory was performed by Brehm (1956). Brehm gave individuals their choice between two appliances which they had previously evaluated. He found that following the decision, when the subjects reevaluated the alternatives, they enhanced their liking for the chosen appliance and downgraded their evaluation of the unchosen one. The derivation is clear. After making a difficult choice, people experience dissonance; cognitions about any negative attributes of the preferred object are dissonant with having chosen it; cognitions about positive attributes of the unchosen object are dissonant with *not* having chosen it. To reduce dissonance, people emphasize the positive aspects and deemphasize the negative aspects of the chosen object while emphasizing the negative and deemphasizing the positive aspects of the unchosen object (see also Festinger, 1964).

Dissonance Resulting from Effort

Aronson and Mills (1959) reasoned that, if people undergo a great deal of trouble in order to gain admission to a group which turns out to be dull and uninteresting, they will experience dissonance. The cognition that they worked hard in order to become members of the group is dissonant with cognitions concerning the negative aspects of the group. One does not work hard for nothing. To re-

---

[2] Although dissonance theory is an incredibly simple statement, it is not quite as simple as a reading of this chapter will indicate. Many aspects of the theory (for example, the propositions relevant to the magnitude of dissonance) will not be discussed here because they are peripheral to the major focus of this chapter.

duce dissonance, they will distort their perception of the group in a positive direction. In the Aronson-Mills experiment, college women underwent an initiation in order to become a member of a group discussion on the psychology of sex. For some of the girls the initiation was very embarrassing—it consisted of reciting a list of obscene words in the presence of the male experimenter. For others the initiation was a mild one. For still others there was no initiation at all. All of the subjects then listened to the same tape-recording of a discussion being held by the group they had just joined. As predicted, the girls in the Severe Initiation condition rated the discussion much more favorably than did those in the other two conditions (see also Aronson, 1961; Zimbardo, 1965; Lewis, 1964; Gerard & Mathewson, 1966).

Insufficient Justification

Aronson and Carlsmith (1963) predicted that if threats are used to prevent people from performing a desired activity, the *smaller* the threat, the greater will be the tendency for people to derogate the activity. If an individual refrains from performing a desired activity, he experiences dissonance: The cognition that he likes the activity is dissonant with the cognition that he is not performing it. One way to reduce dissonance is by derogating the activity—in that way he can justify the fact that he is not performing it. However, any threat provides cognitions that are consonant with not performing the activity; and the more severe the threat, the greater the consonance. In short, a severe threat provides ample justification for not performing the activity; a mild threat provides less justification, leading the individual to add justifications of his own in the form of convincing himself that he *doesn't like* to perform the activity. In their experiment, Aronson and Carlsmith found that children who were threatened with *mild* punishment for playing with a desired toy *decreased* their liking for the toy to a greater extent than did children who were severely threatened (see also Turner & Wright, 1965; Freedman, 1965).

WHAT IS PSYCHOLOGICAL INCONSISTENCY?

The very simplicity of the core of the theory is at once its greatest strength and its most serious weakness. We have already discussed the heuristic value of its simplicity. It should be emphasized that many of the hypotheses which are obvious derivations from the theory are *unique* to that theory—i.e., they could not be derived from any other theory. This increases our confidence in dissonance theory as an explanation of an important aspect of human behavior. The weakness occurs primarily in the difficulty involved with defining the limits of the theoretical statement. While at the "center" of the theory it is relatively easy to generate hypotheses that are clear and direct, at its "fringes" it is not always clear whether or not a prediction can be made from the theory and, if so, exactly what that prediction will be.[3] Although investigators who have had experience working with the theory seem to have little difficulty intuiting its boundary conditions, they have had considerable difficulty communicating this to other people; indeed, a situation has evolved which can best be described by the statement: "If you want to be sure, ask Leon." This has proved to be both a source of embarrassment for the proponents of the theory as well as a source of annoyance and exasperation to its critics.

Why is it so difficult to make a more precise theoretical statement? Perhaps the most basic reason has to do with the nature of the inconsistency involved in the core definition of dissonance theory. It would be easy to specify dissonant situations if the theory were limited to *logical* inconsistencies. There exist relatively unequivocal rules of logic which can be applied without ambiguity or fear of contradiction. But recall that the inconsistency that produces dissonance, although it can be logical inconsistency, is not necessarily logical. Rather, it is *psychological* inconsistency. While this aspect of

---

[3]Further along in this chapter some attempt will be made to specify exactly what we mean by "center" and "fringes."

the theory increases its power, range, and degree of interest, at the same time it also causes some serious problems. Thus, returning to our friend the cigarette smoker, the cognition regarding smoking cigarettes is not logically inconsistent with the cognition linking cigarette smoking to cancer; i.e., strictly speaking, having information that cigarette smoking causes cancer does not make it illogical to smoke cigarettes. But these cognitions do produce dissonance because, taken together, they do not make sense psychologically. Assuming that the smoker does not want cancer, the knowledge that cigarettes cause cancer should lead to *not* smoking cigarettes. Similarly, none of the research examples mentioned above deals with logical inconsistency; e.g., it is not illogical to go through hell and high water to gain admission to a dull discussion group; it is not illogical to choose to own an appliance that one considers slightly more attractive than the unchosen alternative; it is not illogical to refrain from playing with a toy at the request of an adult.

Festinger (1957) lists four kinds of situations in which dissonance can arise: (1) logical inconsistency, (2) inconsistency with cultural mores, (3) inconsistency between one cognition and a more general, more encompassing cognition, (4) past experience.

1. Logical inconsistency: Suppose a person believed that all men are mortal but also held the belief that he, as a man, would live forever. These two cognitions are dissonant because they are logically inconsistent. The contrary of one follows from the other on strict logical grounds.

2. Cultural mores: If a college professor loses his patience with one of his students and shouts at him angrily, his knowledge of what he is doing is dissonant with his idea about what is the proper, acceptable behavior of a professor toward his students—in our culture. In some other cultures this might be appropriate behavior and, therefore, would not arouse dissonance.

3. Inconsistency between one cognition and a more encompassing cognition: In a given election, if a person who has always considered himself to be

a Democrat votes for a Republican candidate, he should experience dissonance. The concept ''I am a Democrat'' encompasses the concept ''I vote for Democratic candidates.''

4. Past experience: If a person stepped on a tack while barefoot and felt no pain, he would experience dissonance because he knows from experience that pain follows from stepping on tacks. If he had never had experience with tacks or other sharp objects, he would *not* experience dissonance.

The illustrations presented above are clear examples of dissonance. Similarly, the situations investigated in the experiments I have described above are clearly dissonant. But there *are* situations where for all practical purposes it is not perfectly clear whether two cognitions are dissonant or merely irrelevant. Because dissonance is *not* limited to logical inconsistencies it is occasionally difficult to specify a priori whether or not a cultural more is being violated, whether or not an event is markedly different from past experience, or whether or not it is different from a more general cognition. Recall the basic theoretical statement: Two cognitions are dissonant if, considering these two cognitions alone, the opposite of one follows from the other. The major source of conceptual ambiguity rests upon the fact that Festinger has not clarified the meaning of the words ''follows from.''

For example, if I learn that my favorite novelist beats his wife, does this arouse dissonance? It is difficult to be certain. Strictly speaking, being a wife-beater is not incompatible with being a great novelist.[4] However, there may be a sense in which the term ''great novelist'' implies that such a person is wise, sensitive, empathic, and compassionate—and wise, sensitive, empathic, and compassionate people do not go around beating their wives. This is not a logical inconsistency; nor is it a clear violation

---

[4]If *I* had beaten my wife I might experience dissonance because of *my* violation of a cultural more. But since I know that many people beat their wives, discovering that a particular person beats his wife is not necessarily inconsistent with my cognition about the world and human nature. More will be said about this later.

of a cultural more; moreover, it may have nothing to do with past experience—and it is not *necessarily* imbedded in a more general cognition. Thus, a knowledge of the kinds of situations in which dissonance *can* occur is not always useful in determining whether dissonance *does* occur.

A rule of thumb which I have found useful is to state the situation in terms of the violation of an expectancy. For example, one might issue the following instructions: "Consider Thurgood Marshall. I'm going to tell you something about his beliefs about the native I.Q. of Negroes relative to that of Caucasians. What do you expect these beliefs to be?" I imagine that most people would have a firm expectancy that Justice Marshall would have said that there are no innate differences. Consequently, one could then conclude that if individuals were exposed to a statement by Justice Marshall to the effect that Negroes were innately stupider than Caucasians, most would experience dissonance. Let us try our difficult example: Suppose we confronted a large number of people with the following proposition: "Consider the great novelist X. I am about to tell you something about whether or not he beats his wife. What do you expect me to say?" My guess is that most people would shrug; i.e., they would not have a strong expectancy (but, again, this is an empirical question; I am not certain that it would come out this way). If this occurred, one could conclude that X's wife-beating behavior is irrelevant to his status as a novelist. An empirical rule of thumb may be of practical utility but is, of course, no substitute for a clearer, less ambiguous, more precise theoretical statement. Near the end of this chapter we will elaborate upon this rule of thumb and indicate how it might be used conceptually.

THE "NOTHING BUT" CRITIQUE

Scientists tend to be conservative, parsimonious creatures. This is generally a healthy attitude which most frequently manifests itself in a reluctance to accept a new theory or a novel explanation for a phenomenon if the phenomenon can be squeezed (even with great difficulty) into an existing approach. In this regard, dissonance theory has been referred to as nothing but a new name for an old phenomenon. This has been most persistently stated in regard to that aspect of the theory related to decision making. In this context dissonance theory has been referred to as nothing but another name for conflict theory.

In fact, there are several differences. Conflict occurs before a decision is made, dissonance occurs after the decision. During conflict it is assumed that an individual will devote his energies to a careful, dispassionate, and sensible evaluation and judgment of the alternatives. He will gather all of the information, pro and con, about all of the alternatives in order to make a reasonable decision. Following the decision, a person is in a state of dissonance—all negative aspects of X are dissonant with having chosen X; all positive aspects of Y are dissonant with *not* having chosen Y. Far from evaluating the alternatives impartially (as in conflict), the individual experiencing dissonance will seek biased information and evaluations designed to make his decision appear more reasonable. As in Brehm's (1956) experiment, he will seek to spread the alternatives apart. The more difficulty a person had making a decision, the greater the tendency toward this kind of behavior as a means of justifying his decision.

But how can we be certain that the spreading apart of the alternatives in Brehm's experiment occurred after the decision? Could it not have occurred during the conflict stage? That is, it is conceivable that, in order to make their decision easier, subjects in Brehm's experiment began to reevaluate the appliances in a biased manner *before* the decision. If this were the case, then there is no essential difference between predecisional and postdecisional processes; if so, this behavior can be considered part of conflict—and there is, indeed, no need to complicate matters by bringing in additional terminology.

Brehm's experiment does not allow us to determine whether the evaluation of chosen and un-chosen alternatives was spread apart before or after the decision. Recent experiments by Davidson and Kiesler (1964) and by Jecker (1964) serve to clarify this issue. In Jecker's experiment, subjects were offered their choice between two phonograph rec-ords. In three conditions there was *low conflict;* i.e., subjects were told that there was a very good chance that they would receive *both* records no mat-ter which they chose. In three other conditions, *high conflict* was produced by telling them that the prob-ability was high that they would be given only the record that they chose. All of the subjects rated the records before the instructions; in each of the conflict conditions subjects rerated the records either (a) after they discovered that they received both records, (b) after they discovered that they re-ceived only the one record they chose, or (c) before they were certain whether they would get one or both. The results are quite clear: No spreading apart occurred when there was no dissonance; i.e., when the subject actually received both records or when he was not certain whether he would receive one or both he did *not* reevaluate the alternatives systemat-ically. Where dissonance did occur there was a sys-tematic reevaluation; i.e., subjects spread their evaluation of the alternatives when they received only one record—this occurred independently of the degree of conflict. This experiment provides clear evidence that conflict and dissonance are dif-ferent processes; whatever else dissonance theory might be, it is *not* "nothing but conflict theory."

THE MULTIPLE MODE PROBLEM

As indicated earlier, several problems are central to the theoretical statement. One of the knottiest and most interesting conceptual problems in dissonance theory involves the fact that, in a given situation, there is usually more than one way for a person to reduce dissonance. For example, the cigarette smoker has several techniques at his disposal. He

may use any one, or several simultaneously. Ex-perimentally, this problem can be eliminated by the simple device of blocking alternative techniques of dissonance reduction. This is part of the definition of experimental control; any experimenter worth his salt will attempt to control the environment so that the behavior elicited by his independent variable will occur in a manner which is measurable and at a time and place where the measuring instruments have been set up. To illustrate: In a typical communication-persuasion experiment, if a highly credible communicator states a position which is discrepant from the position of the recipient, the recipient experiences dissonance. He can reduce dissonance in one of four ways: (1) he can change his opinion to make it coincide with the com-municator's; (2) he can attempt to change the com-municator's opinion; (3) he can seek social support from other members of the audience; (4) he can derogate the communicator. If one is interested in measuring opinion change (No. 1), one can elimi-nate No. 2 and No. 3 by making it impossible for the subject to interact either with the communicator or his fellow subjects. Furthermore, one can reduce the subject's ability to derogate the communicator by assigning the latter high enough prestige so that he becomes virtually nonderogatable. Thus, if these four techniques exhaust the universe, the only way that a subject can reduce dissonance is by changing his attitude on the issue. The prudent experimenter will have built his experiment to make it appear reasonable to measure the subject's attitudes after the communication and he will use the most sensi-tive measuring instrument he can construct.

Thus, if the question one asks is "Does disso-nance occur in such a situation and does it get re-duced?" the answer can be easily determined ex-perimentally. But we may have a different question in mind: "In a given situation, how do people gen-erally reduce dissonance?" And the answer to this question may be strikingly different from the mode found in the laboratory experiment. Thus, in the above example, most people might prefer to argue with the communicator rather than change their opinion.

The above argument suggests that the results from carefully controlled laboratory experiments, on occasion, may be somewhat misleading. For example, suppose a young Ph.D. is being considered for a teaching position in a major department at a prestigious Ivy League university. What happens if the members of that department decide not to hire him? If he feels that he is a good and worthy scholar, he will experience cognitive dissonance: His cognition that he is a good scholar is dissonant with his cognition that he was rejected by members of a good department. As I see it, he can reduce dissonance in at least two ways: (a) he can convince himself that his rejectors are, in reality, stupid, defensive, unprofessional, and/or senile people who cannot or will not recognize a good man when they see one; (b) he can convince himself that if they can reject him (as good as he is), then their standards must be astronomically high and therefore they are a fine group of nonsenile professionals. Both of these techniques succeed in reducing dissonance; moreover, they both protect the individual's ego—he leaves for his job at East Podunk State Teacher's College with the conviction that he is a good scholar. But note that the results of his dissonance-reducing behavior can leave him with totally opposite opinions about the members of the staff at the Ivy League university. Thus, if one wanted to arouse dissonance in an individual for the specific purpose of enhancing his impressions of the people at Ivy University, one had better be careful. The same dissonance-producing situation can result in quite the opposite dissonance-reducing behavior.

This is a serious conceptual problem. One way that it can be solved is by coming up with a set of specific propositions that can lead one to state the conditions under which one mode or the other is more likely to occur. I have previously outlined a possible solution in a specific situation. The situation I was concerned with involved alternative modes of dissonance reduction following the un-successful expenditure of effort. If a person struggles to reach a goal and fails, he experiences dissonance. His cognition that he exerted effort to attain the goal is dissonant with his cognition that he did not reach it. He could reduce dissonance by convincing himself that the goal was not worth it anyway; recall that this was the way that Aesop's fox reduced dissonance in the fable of the sour grapes. There is another reasonable way to reduce dissonance; by the person's finding something else in the situation to which he can attach value in order to justify his expenditure of effort without achieving his avowed goal. Thus, the fox might convince himself that he got some much-needed exercise while leaping for the grapes—and that even though he failed to get those luscious, sweet grapes, it was worth the effort because of the muscles he developed while trying.

Under what conditions will an individual take one path rather than the other? In my paper (Aronson, 1961) I suggested that the first solution is probably easier—but only in a situation where the effort expended is of short duration. But if the situation consists of a long and repeated expenditure of effort, it becomes a less viable solution. To use our previous illustration, if the fox made a few leaps at the grapes and failed, he could convince himself that they were probably sour anyway; but if he spent the entire afternoon struggling to reach the grapes, it would not effectively reduce dissonance to maintain that the grapes were sour—for if that were the case, why in the world did he try to reach them over and over and over again? The data from my experiment indicate that, after the repeated expenditure of effort, people *do* attach value to an incidental stimulus; however, the definitive factorial experiment remains to be done.

It is encouraging to note that experimenters are beginning to focus their efforts on this kind of problem. A good example of this trend is described in a very recent article by Walster, Berscheid, and Barclay (1967), who hypothesize that individuals will choose that mode of dissonance reduction which is least likely to be challenged by future events. In their experiment, children were given their choice between two toys. In a situation like this, individuals can reduce dissonance in two ways: by cognitively increasing the attractiveness of the chosen alternative and/or by cognitively decreasing the attractiveness of the unchosen alternative. One-half of the children were led to expect that they would subsequently hear objective information about the toy they chose; one-half of the children were led to expect that they would hear objective information about the rejected toy. The investigators found, as predicted, that individuals reduced dissonance by distorting the attractiveness of that toy which they were not going to hear information about. That is, they opted to reduce dissonance in a manner which was less likely to run up against objective reality.

In order to be of maximum use, such specific solutions should be restated into more general propositions, where possible, and incorporated into the theory. An important step in this direction was taken by Brehm and Cohen (1962) in emphasizing the importance of commitment and volition in determining not only the strength of the dissonance involved, but, perhaps more important, the nature of the dissonance and, hence, the kind of mechanism needed to reduce dissonance. Whether or not a high degree of volition is present can often change the nature of the prediction. For example, as part of one study, Aronson, Turner, and Carlsmith (1963) reasoned that disagreement with a highly credible source produces more dissonance than disagreement with a source having low credibility. The cognition that a highly sentient person believes X is dissonant with the cognition that I believe *not*-X. The higher the credibility of the source, the greater the dissonance—because the less sense it makes to be in disagreement with him. This should lead to greater attitude change in the Highly Credible condition—to reduce dissonance. The results were consistent with this reasoning. On the other hand, Zimbardo (1960) and Brehm and Cohen (1962) rea-

soned that under certain conditions a source having low credibility would produce *greater* attitude change than one having high credibility. Specifically, if a person had chosen of his own volition to go to hear a speech by a low credibility source, he would experience dissonance. The cognition involving volition and commitment is dissonant with the cognition that the credibility of the communicator is low; after all, it is absurd to choose to go out of one's way to hear a low prestige source make a speech which is discrepant with one's own opinion. In order to reduce dissonance, one might convince oneself that there was no essential discrepancy—that one always held the position espoused by the low credibility source. Thus, both Zimbardo and Brehm and Cohen suggested that under conditions of high commitment one might get greater agreement with a low credibility source than with a high credibility source. This prediction made by Zimbardo and by Brehm and Cohen is consistent with other data involving choice and commitment. For example, Smith (1961) found that soldiers who volunteered to eat grasshoppers when induced by an unpleasant leader, came to like the grasshoppers better than did those who volunteered to eat them when induced by an affable leader. Similar results are reported by Zimbardo (1964).

It should be clear that the prediction made by Aronson, Turner, and Carlsmith and that made by Zimbardo and by Brehm and Cohen are not mutually exclusive; rather, they apply to a crucially different set of circumstances. Although both predictions are derived from dissonance theory, they involve different aspects of the theory; the crucial distinction is whether or not a high degree of volition is present. Nonetheless, to avoid confusion, these distinctions should be stated with even greater clarity.

To sum up this section, dissonance theory, as originally stated *does* have some areas of conceptual fuzziness. In my opinion, much of this fuzziness can be eliminated by empirical research. Again, this research should be focused on the conditions and variables which maximize and minimize the occurrence of dissonance and dissonance reduction as well as the conditions which lead to one or another mode of dissonance reduction. This position will be elaborated upon in a moment.

THE "UNDERLYING COGNITION" PROBLEM

The importance of commitment emerges most clearly when we scrutinize the phenomenon of the white lie more thoroughly. Clearly, every time we say something that we do not believe, we do *not* experience dissonance. Under certain conditions there are some underlying cognitions which serve to prevent the occurrence of dissonance. For example, if we stated a counter-attitudinal position in the context of a formal debate, we would not experience dissonance (see Scott, 1957, 1959; Aronson, 1966). It is clearly understood both by the speaker and the audience that a debator's own personal views have nothing to do with the opinions he expresses. The rules of the game of debating provide an underlying cognition which prevents the occurrence of dissonance. Similarly, as teachers we frequently are exposed to a great many stupid ideas from our students. I think that unless we know the student well—know that he is capable of "taking it"—most teachers refrain from tearing the idea to pieces. Instead, we tend to give the student our attention, nod and smile, and suggest that it is not such a bad idea. We do this because we have a general underlying cognition that we should not discourage students early in their careers and that it is wrong to be unkind to people who are relatively powerless to fight back. It would be ludicrous to suggest that teachers begin to believe that a student's poor idea is really a pretty good one simply because the teacher had said "pretty good idea" to the student. The underlying cognition prevents the occurrence of dissonance. But observe how commitment can make it a dissonant situation. If, on the basis of the teacher's statement, the student had decided to read his paper at the state psychological

convention, the teacher might begin to convince himself that it was not such a bad idea—because the teacher has now been committed—he has misled the student into taking some action. This increases the teacher's commitment to the situation and is probably more powerful than the underlying consonant cognition "this is how we treat students." The teacher now seeks additional justification for having misled the student, perhaps by convincing himself that it was not such a bad idea after all.

The general point to be made here is an important one. Inconsistency is said to arise between two cognitive elements if, "considering these two alone, the [opposite] of one element follows from the other" (Festinger, 1957, pp. 260–261). But we know that in most situations two cognitions are almost never taken by themselves. Occasionally, two cognitions which in the abstract would appear to be dissonant fail to arouse dissonance because of the existence of a neutralizing underlying cognition. For example, suppose I know a brilliant fellow who is married to an incredibly stupid woman. These cognitions are inconsistent but I would contend that they do not necessarily produce dissonance. I can tolerate this inconsistency—it does not cause me pain, it does not necessarily lead me to change my opinion about the brilliant fellow or his wife, I do not conclude that he is dumber than I thought or that she is smarter. Why? Because I have a general, underlying, pervasive cognition that there are a multitude of factors which determine mate selection—similarities of intelligence being only one of them. Moreover, I know that it is extremely rare for all of these to be matched in a marital relationship. Therefore, although taken by themselves the above two cognitions are incompatible, I simply do not ever take them by themselves.

Festinger suggests that one way to reduce dissonance is to martial consonant cognitions—thus, he might say that the above reasoning is one way of reducing dissonance. But it is a moot and important point whether I martialed the above cognitions as a result of the inconsistency, or whether I walked around with these cognitions about mate selection before the fact. If the latter is the case, then it can hardly be said that I dredged up this overriding cognition as a means of reducing dissonance. For example, let us look at the finding (Aronson & Carlsmith, 1963; Turner & Wright, 1965; Freedman, 1965) that children threatened with mild punishment for playing with a toy tend to derogate that toy after refraining from playing with it. Suppose that many children entered the situation with the strong feeling that adults must be obeyed always, even when commands are arbitrary and threats are nonexistent ("My mother, right or wrong!"). Put another way (which will become important in a moment), suppose that part of the self concept of these children was "obedience to adult authority." If this were the case there would have been no dissonance—even though, *taken by itself,* the cognition "I like that toy" is dissonant with the cognition "I'm not playing with it." If this were *not* already a part of the person's self concept, it might have become one as a function of the experiment— i.e., developing a belief in the importance of obedience is one way of reducing dissonance in the above situation. But if it were already there—there would have been no dissonance to begin with.

This added complexity should not lead us to throw our hands up in despair. Rather, it should lead us to a more careful analysis of the situations we are dealing with and perhaps even to a greater concern with individual differences.

THE IMPORTANCE OF THE SELF CONCEPT AND OTHER EXPECTANCIES

In discussing the difficulties in making precise predictions from dissonance theory in some situations, we have purposely tiptoed around the problem of individual differences. The fact that all people are not the same presents intriguing problems for dissonance theory as it does for all general motivational theories. Of course, one man's "problem" is another man's primary datum; i.e., psychologists who are interested in personality re-

gard individual differences as being of great interest. For those who are primarily interested in establishing nomothetic laws, individual differences usually constitute nothing more than an annoying source of error variance. Nevertheless, whether or not we are interested in individual differences *per se,* an understanding of the way people differ in dissonant situations can be an important means to clarify and strengthen the theory. Basically, there are three ways that individuals differ which should be of concern to people investigating dissonance theory:

1. People differ in their ability to tolerate dissonance. It seems reasonable to assume that some people are simply better than others at shrugging off dissonance; i.e., it may take a greater *amount* of dissonance to bring about dissonance-reducing behavior in some people than in others.

2. People probably differ in their preferred mode of dissonance reduction. E.g., some people may find it easier to derogate the source of a communication than to change their own opinion. Others may find the reverse resolution easier.

3. What is dissonant for one person may be consonant for someone else; i.e., people may be so different that certain events are regarded as dissonant for some but not for others.

I shall not dwell on the first two here save to say that, earlier in this chapter, I underscored the difficulty of ascertaining the proper conditions for establishing whether or not dissonance exists for *most people* and the conditions for determining which mode of dissonance reduction *most people* will use; the existence of individual differences complicates matters further by adding another important dimension which should eventually be specified. The third case will be discussed here because it is of great relevance for the general theory. Furthermore, I regard it as prior to the other two, for before one can determine (a) whether an individual is experiencing *enough* dissonance to reduce it or (b) *how* he will reduce it, we must first determine whether the events are indeed dissonant, consonant, or irrelevant to him.

Dissonant or consonant with what? Recall the earlier discussion wherein I described a rule of thumb based upon an expectancy (e.g., the Thurgood Marshall and wife-beating novelist illustrations). In my judgment, dissonance theory makes a clear prediction when a firm expectancy is involved as one of the cognitions in question. Thus, our cognition about Thurgood Marshall's *behavior* can be dissonant with our expectancy about how Justice Marshall *will* behave. Dissonance theory is clearer still when that firm expectancy involves the individual's self concept, for—almost by definition—our expectancies about our own behavior are firmer than our expectancies about the behavior of another person. Thus, at the very heart of dissonance theory, where it makes its clearest and neatest prediction, we are not dealing with just any two cognitions; rather, we are usually dealing with the self concept and cognitions about some behavior. If dissonance exists it is because the individual's behavior is inconsistent with his self concept.

As I pointed out several years ago (Aronson, 1960), this point has been elusive because most of the experiments testing dissonance theory have made predictions based upon the tacit assumption that people have a high self concept. Why do people who buy new cars selectively expose themselves to ads about their own make of car (Ehrlich, Guttman, Schönbach, & Mills, 1957) and try to convince themselves that they made the right choice? Because the knowledge that one has bought a junky car is dissonant with a high self concept. But suppose a person had a low self concept? Then, the cognition that he bought a junky car would *not* be dissonant. Indeed, if the theory holds, such a person should engage in all kinds of "bizarre" behavior like exposing himself to ads about other cars, hearing squeaks and rattles that are not even there, and saying, in effect, "Just my luck, I bought a lemon—these things are always happening to me." In short, if a person conceives of himself as a "schnook," he will expect to behave like a schnook; consequently, wise, reasonable, successful, un-schnooky behav-

ior on his part should arouse dissonance. One of the advantages of this kind of statement is that it allows us to separate the effects of dissonance from other hedonic effects. That is, people with *high* self concepts who fail *do* experience dissonance; but they experience many other negative feelings as well—due simply to the fact that failure is unpleasant. No one can deny that success brings pleasant consequences for people with high and low self concepts alike. That is, regardless of a person's self concept, successful achievement is often accompanied by such pleasant things as acclaim, money, fame, admiration, popularity, etc. But dissonance theory allows us to predict that, for people with low self concepts, the "good feelings" aroused by the products of success will be tempered by the discomfort caused by dissonance—the dissonance between a low self concept and cognitions about high performance. Several experiments have demonstrated that people who expect failure are somewhat discomforted by success (Aronson & Carlsmith, 1962; Cottrell, 1965; Brock *et al.*, 1965), but the data are by no means unequivocal.

Thus, although we may not have been fully aware of it at the time, in the clearest experiments performed to test dissonance theory, the dissonance involved was between a self concept and cognitions about a behavior that violated this self concept. In the experiments on counterattitudinal advocacy, for example, I would suggest that it is incorrect to say that dissonance existed between the cognition "I believe the task is dull" and "I told someone that the task was interesting." This is not dissonant for a psychopathic liar—indeed, it is perfectly consonant. What is dissonant is the cognition "I am a decent, truthful human being" and the cognition "I have misled a person; I have conned him into believing something which just isn't true; he thinks that I really believe it and I cannot set him straight because I probably won't see him again." In the initiation experiments, I would maintain that dissonance does not exist between the cognition, "I worked hard to get into a group" and the cognition "The group is dull and stupid.'' Recall that for a ''schnook'' these cognitions are not at all dissonant. What is dissonant in this situation is the cognition ''I am a reasonable and intelligent person'' and the cognition ''I have worked hard for nothing.'' Reasonable, intelligent people usually get a fair return for their investment—they usually do not buy a pig in a poke (unless there is some reasonably implicit guarantee, as in Freedman's [1963] experiment discussed above).

As an empirical refinement this self concept notion is probably trivial. The experimenters who made the tacit assumption that people have high self concepts achieved positive results—which indicates that this assumption is valid for most people in these situations. But it may constitute a valuable and interesting *theoretical* refinement. A theory becomes infinitely more meaningful when its domain is clearly demarcated; i.e., when it states clearly where it does not apply. If it is the case that dissonance theory makes unequivocal predictions only when the self concept or another strong expectancy is involved, then an important set of boundary conditions has been drawn. What I described earlier as a rule of thumb may actually be a conceptual clarification.

I stated early in this chapter that ''at the 'center' of the theory'' predictions are unequivocal, but at the ''fringes'' they are somewhat fuzzy. At this point, we can say that ''at the center'' means situations in which the self concept or other firm expectancies are involved—and in which most people share the same self concepts or other firm expectancies. Thus, most people have self concepts about being truthful and honest so that we can make clear predictions intuitively, as in the Carlsmith, Collins, and Helmreich (1966) experiment. Most people have self concepts involving making reasonable and wise decisions so that we can intuit clear predictions, as in the Brehm (1956) or Jecker (1964) experiments. Also, most people have firm expectancies about what Thurgood Marshall would say about Negro intelligence, so that a dissonance theory pre-

diction makes sense and can be made clearly, even though a self concept is not involved. The prediction about the great novelist who beats his wife gives the theory trouble precisely because people differ tremendously with regard to whether or not they expect a particular novelist to be a gentle and considerate man. In a specific instance, the knowledge of whether or not individual X has this expectancy would increase the accuracy of the prediction. I do not regard this of great importance. What I do regard as important is merely the recognition of the fact that dissonance theory may be best suited for making general predictions in situations where expectancies are firm and nearly universal.

Several years ago, Zajonc (1960) raised a very interesting and reasonable question: If dissonance is bothersome, why do we enjoy magicians? That is, magicians can be thought of as people who arouse dissonance. Should we not experience pain and discomfort when we see rabbits pulled from hats, women sawed in half, or dimes turned into quarters? Perhaps the reason why we are not upset by magicians is because the behavior of a magician is consonant with our expectancy regarding magicians. That is, since we know in advance that magicians use tricks and sleight-of-hand techniques to produce interesting illusions, why should we experience dissonance when we see him do these things? Is this not akin to the schnook who expects to purchase an inferior car?

Before the reader dismisses this as mere sophistry, let me hasten to say that this is an empirical question. What I am suggesting is that we enjoy magicians *only* when they are billed as magicians. If they were not billed as magicians, they would cause quite a bit of discomfort. If the fellow sitting next to us at the bar suddenly ''became'' a fat woman, this would be very upsetting—unless the bartender had forewarned us that we were sitting next to a professional quick-change artist known as ''Slippery Sam, the man of a thousand faces.'' If he then ''became'' a fat woman, we would be thrilled and delighted. It is interesting to note that the bartender could have produced a similar result if he had forewarned us that he had placed some LSD in our drink. In short, either being told a man is a magician or being told we were fed a hallucinogen is consistent with seeing a man "become" a fat woman!

Empirically, this can be tested by finding some young children or some people from a different culture who have never seen or heard of magicians. My guess is that without the expectancy regarding magicians that Zajonc and I share, these subjects would be quite upset by the goings on.

MAN CANNOT LIVE BY CONSONANCE ALONE

The implication of this essay is that dissonant situations are ubiquitous and that man expends a good deal of time and energy attempting to reduce dissonance. It should be obvious that man does many other things as well. Festinger never intended dissonance theory to be imperial or monolithic. In 1957, he clearly recognized the fact that dissonance reduction is only one of many motives and can be counteracted by more powerful drives. We have already discussed how dissonance effects and reward-incentive effects can both occur in the same experimental design. Even more basic is the confrontation that occurs when consonance needs meet utility needs head-on. An extremely high drive to reduce dissonance would lead man to weave a cocoon about himself, never admitting his mistakes and distorting reality to make it compatible with his behavior. But if a person is ever going to grow, improve, and avoid repeating the same errors, he must sooner or later learn to profit from past mistakes. One cannot profit from one's mistakes without first admitting that one has *made* a mistake. And yet, the admission of error almost always arouses some dissonance. The fact is, people frequently *do* profit from their mistakes; thus, people occasionally do not avoid or reduce dissonance.

To illustrate, if a man spends $50,000 for a home, dissonance theory would suggest that he may be the last to notice that, during the rainy season, there is water in the basement. Noticing water would arouse dissonance by making his purchase appear to have been a mistake. But to notice the water has great utility—for he must notice it in order to repair it, prepare for the flood, or check the basement of the next house he buys. Thus, dissonance and utility are in constant tension by virtue of the fact that under certain conditions dissonant information may be extremely useful, and, conversely, useful information can arouse dissonance. Mills, Aronson, and Robinson (1959) suggested that one reason that people frequently do not avoid dissonant information is that it often has great utility. In their experiment, they found that many subjects who had recently committed themselves to taking essay exams as opposed to multiple-choice exams opted to read articles explaining why essay exams were more difficult, anxiety-producing, etc. In this situation, apparently, the utility of the information was considered worth the price to be paid in dissonance. More recent experiments by Canon (1964) and Aronson and Ross (1966) have begun to indicate the requisite conditions for these effects: Basically, as utility increases and dissonance becomes weaker, individuals begin to show a preference for dissonance-arousing but useful information. But as dissonance increases (i.e., immediately after a decision or when commitment is high, etc.), individuals tend to manifest dissonance-reducing behavior in spite of the fact that the future consequences of such behavior tend to be unpleasant.

EPILOGUE

The theory of cognitive dissonance is much more complicated than it was thought to be ten years ago. A good deal of research has been done since 1957. Many of the problems which were specified early have been solved; many new problems have been unearthed, some of which remain to be solved. Hopefully, future research will lead to the emergence of still new problems, which will lead to still more research, which will continue to yield an increased understanding of human behavior. I guess that is what science is all about. In their critique of five years of dissonance theory, Chapanis and Chapanis concluded with the pronouncement "Not proven." Happily, after ten years, it is still not proven; all the theory ever does is generate research!

REFERENCES

Aronson, E. The cognitive and behavioral consequences of the confirmation and disconfirmation of expectancies. Unpublished manuscript, Harvard University, 1960.

Aronson, E. The effect of effort on the attractiveness of rewarded and unrewarded stimuli. *Journal of Abnormal and Social Psychology,* 1961, **63,** 375–380.

Aronson, E. The psychology of insufficient justification: An analysis of some conflicting data. In S. Feldman (Ed.), *Cognitive consistency: Motivational antecedents and behavioral consequences.* New York: Academic Press, 1966. Pp. 109–133.

Aronson, E., & Carlsmith, J. M. Performance expectancy as a determinant of actual performance. *Journal of Abnormal and Social Psychology,* 1962, **65,** 178–182.

Aronson, E., & Carlsmith, J. M. Effect of the severity of threat on the valuation of forbidden behavior. *Journal of Abnormal and Social Psychology,* 1963, **66,** 584–588.

Aronson, E., & Mills, J. The effect of severity of initiation on liking for a group. *Journal of Abnormal and Social Psychology,* 1959, **59,** 177–181.

Aronson, E., & Ross, A. The effect of support and criticism on interpersonal attractiveness. Unpublished data, 1966.

Aronson, E., Turner, J., & Carlsmith, J. M. Communicator credibility and communication discrepancy as determinants of opinion change. *Journal of Abnormal and Social Psychology,* 1963, **67,** 31–36.

Brehm, J. W. Post-decision changes in the desirability of alternatives. *Journal of Abnormal and Social Psychology,* 1956, **52,** 384–389.

Brehm, J. W., & Cohen, A. R. *Explorations in cognitive dissonance.* New York: Wiley, 1962.

Brehm, M. L., Back, K. W., & Bogdonoff, M. D. A physiological effect of cognitive dissonance under stress and deprivation. *Journal of Abnormal and Social Psychology,* 1964, **69,** 303–310.

Brock, T. C., Eidelman, S. K., Edwards, D. C., & Schuck, J. R. Seven studies of performance expectancy as a determinant of actual performance. *Journal of Experimental Social Psychology,* 1965, **1,** 295–310.

Canon, L. Self-confidence and selective exposure to information. In L. Festinger, *Conflict, decision, and dissonance.* Stanford, Calif.: Stanford University Press, 1964. Pp. 83–96.

Carlsmith, J. M., Collins, B. E., & Helmreich, R. L. Studies in forced compliance: I. The effect of pressure for compliance on attitude change produced by face-to-face role playing and anonymous essay writing. *Journal of Personality and Social Psychology,* 1966, **4,** 1–13.

Chapanis, N. P., & Chapanis, A. Cognitive dissonance: Five years later. *Psychological Bulletin,* 1964, **61,** 1–22.

Cottrell, N. B. The effect of expectancy-performance dissonance upon reaction time performance. Paper presented at a meeting of the Midwestern Psychological Association, April 1965.

Davidson, J. R., & Kiesler, S. Cognitive behavior before and after decisions. In L. Festinger, *Conflict, decision, and dissonance.* Stanford, Calif.: Stanford University Press, 1964. Pp. 10–21.

Ehrlich, D., Guttman, I., Schönbach, P., & Mills, J. Post-decision exposure to relevant information. *Journal of Abnormal and Social Psychology,* 1957, **54,** 98–102.

Festinger, L. *A theory of cognitive dissonance.* Evanston, Ill.: Row, Peterson, 1957.

Festinger, L. *Conflict decision, and dissonance.* Stanford, Calif.: Stanford University Press, 1964.

Festinger, L., & Aronson, E. The arousal and reduction of dissonance in social contexts. In D. Cartwright & A. Zander (Eds.), *Group dynamics.* (2nd ed.) Evanston, Ill.: Row, Peterson, 1960. Pp. 214–231.

Festinger, L., & Bramel, D. The reactions of humans to cognitive dissonance. In A. Bachrach (Ed.), *The experimental foundations of clinical psychology.* New York: Basic Books, 1962. Pp. 254–279.

Festinger, L., & Freedman, J. L. Dissonance reduction and moral values. In P. Worchel & D. Byrne (Eds.), *Personality change.* New York: Wiley, 1964. Pp. 220–243.

Festinger, L., Riecken, H., & Schachter, S. *When prophecy fails.* Minneapolis: University of Minnesota Press, 1956.

Freedman, J. L. Attitudinal effects of inadequate justification. *Journal of Personality,* 1963, **31,** 371–385.

Freedman, J. L. Long-term behavioral effects of cognitive dissonance. *Journal of Experimental Social Psychology,* 1965, **1,** 145–155.

Gerard, H. B., & Mathewson, G. C. The effects of severity of initiation on liking for a group: A replication. *Journal of Experimental Social Psychology,* 1966, **2,** 278–287.

110 THEORIES OF ATTITUDE CHANGE

Jecker, J. D. The cognitive effects of conflict and dissonance. In L. Festinger, *Conflict, decision, and dissonance.* Stanford, Calif.: Stanford University Press, 1964. Pp. 21–32.

Lawrence, D. H., & Festinger, L. *Deterrents and reinforcement.* Stanford, Calif.: Stanford University Press, 1962.

Lewis, M. Some nondecremental effects of effort. *Journal of Comparative and Physiological Psychology,* 1964, **57,** 367–372.

McGuire, W. J. Attitudes and opinions. *Annual Review of Psychology,* 1966, **17,** 475–514.

Mills, J., Aronson, E., & Robinson, H. Selectivity in exposure to information. *Journal of Abnormal and Social Psychology,* 1959, **59,** 205–253.

Scott, W. A. Attitude change through reward of verbal behavior. *Journal of Abnormal and Social Psychology,* 1957, **55,** 72–75.

Scott, W. A. Attitude change by response reinforcement: Replication and extension. *Sociometry,* 1959, **22,** 328–335.

Smith, E. E. The power of dissonance techniques to change attitudes. *Public Opinion Quarterly,* 1961, **25,** 626–639.

Turner, E. A., & Wright, J. Effects of severity of threat and perceived availability on the attractiveness of objects. *Journal of Personality and Social Psychology,* 1965, **2,** 128–132.

Walster, E., Berscheid, E., & Barclay, A. M. A determinant of preference among modes of dissonance reduction. *Journal of Personality and Social Psychology,* 1967, **7,** 211–216.

Zajonc, R. B. Balance, congruity and dissonance. *Public Opinion Quarterly,* 1960, **24,** 280–296.

Zimbardo, P. G. Involvement and communication discrepancy as determinants of opinion conformity. *Journal of Abnormal and Social Psychology,* 1960, **60,** 86–94.

Zimbardo, P. G. A critical analysis of Smith's "grasshopper" experiment. Unpublished manuscript, New York University, 1964.

Zimbardo, P. G. The effect of effort and improvisation on self-persuasion produced by role-playing. *Journal of Experimental Social Psychology,* 1965, **1,** 103–120.

ARTICLE 11

The case for nonconsistency

Daryl J. Bem

Up to this point, I have tried to state the strongest possible case for the thesis that men do not merely subscribe to a random collection of beliefs and attitudes but rather possess coherent *systems* of beliefs and attitudes which are internally and psychologically consistent. I have even implied that whenever an individual's beliefs and attitudes appear to be inconsistent, if we would only look deeper into the basic premises of his belief system, consistency will be forthcoming.

We have seen that the consistency theorists themselves have taken the further step of postulating that men possess a drive toward cognitive consistency. As I have done, these theorists emphasize that this consistency is most often psychological rather than logical, and they are alert to the nonrationality of some of the strategies which individuals often employ to attain consistency. In addition, consistency theorists do not claim that individuals need to be aware of the inconsistencies in order to be motivated toward consistency. The consistency theorists are thus quite flexible, and collectively they have marshaled an impressive amount of evidence to document their main hypothesis that inconsistency motivates belief and attitude change. Indeed, a recently published book called *Theories of Cognitive Consistency: A Sourcebook* (known affectionately by the in-group as TOCCAS)* contains 84 chapters, 830 pages of text, 41 pages of references (about 1000 references), and more about cognitive consistency than almost anyone would care to know (Abelson, Aronson, McGuire, Newcomb, Rosenberg, & Tannenbaum, 1968). Inconsistency, they seem to be trying to tell us, motivates belief and attitude change.

But I don't believe it. At least not very much. In my view, a vision of inconsistency as a temporary turbulence in an otherwise fastidious pool of cogni-

*The preceding article, by Aronson, is taken from this book. [Eds.]

tive clarity is all too misleading. My own suspicion is that inconsistency is probably our most enduring cognitive commonplace. That is, I suspect that for most of the people most of the time and for all the people some of the time inconsistency just sits there. I think that we academic psychologists, including the consistency theorists, probably spend too much time with bright college students who are as eager to achieve a respectable overall unity in their cognitions as we, their instructors, are eager to impress them and ourselves with the same admirable coherence of thought. We have already seen that we psychologists are well represented in the population of liberal-intellectuals who are willing to spend restless nights agonizing over the apparent inconsistencies between integration and black power, and you will find us striving for cognitive quiescence on similar dilemmas at any meeting of the American Civil Liberties Union. I believe, in short, that there is more inconsistency on earth (and probably in heaven) than is dreamt of in our psychological theories.

Psychologists and political scientists who have analyzed the public mind outside the laboratory have arrived at similar conclusions. For example, Herbert McClosky, a man who has spent much time trying to understand the political attitudes of Americans, has said, "As intellectuals and students of politics we are disposed by training and sensibility to take political ideas seriously. . . . We are therefore prone to forget that most people take them less seriously than we do, that they pay little attention to issues, rarely worry about the consistency of their opinions, and spend little or no time thinking about the values, presuppositions and implications which distinguish one political orientation from another." (Quoted by Abelson, 1968.) Let me illustrate.

LIBERALS OR CONSERVATIVES?

Lloyd Free, a pollster and political analyst, and Hadley Cantril, a social psychologist, have conducted a large-scale study of the political beliefs of

Americans (1967). Using the resources of the Gallup polling organization, these two men in 1964 interviewed over 3,000 people representing a cross-section of the American public. One of their purposes was to study the nature of liberalism and conservatism, both at a practical, or operational, level and at a more ideological level. First they constructed a five-item questionnaire to identify what they called operational liberalism and conservatism. It covered most of the controversial "welfare" programs of the Democratic administration then in office, including federal aid to education, Medicare, federal low-rent housing programs, urban renewal programs, and federal attempts to reduce unemployment. An individual was then defined as completely or predominantly liberal if he favored all or all but one of the programs on which he had an opinion. To qualify as completely or predominantly conservative, an individual had to oppose all or all but one of the programs on which he had an opinion. Others, providing that they had an opinion on at least three of the programs, were labeled as "middle-of-the-road."

The American public distributed itself as follows:

Completely or predominantly liberal	65%
Middle-of-the-road	21%
Completely or predominantly conservative	14%

In other words, about two thirds of the American public qualified as "liberal" with respect to the favoring of specific government programs; and within the liberal category itself, over two thirds of the individuals were "completely liberal" in that they favored all the government programs about which they had an opinion. As Table 1 shows, only 14% of the American public could be labeled conservative at the operational level.

These results are in line with previous polls which show that the American public has been "liberal" in this sense at least since the days of the New Deal three decades ago. Even though "conservative" shifts of other kinds have occasionally intervened (e.g., with respect to civil rights activity) and though the 1966 and 1968 elections were interpreted by some as a trend toward conservatism, the general liberal trend toward welfare programs has never changed. Thus, a poll in February, 1967, showed that 54% of the American public favored even the controversial Community Action programs to combat poverty. The Head Start schooling program for young children was favored by 67%, and federally financed job training was endorsed by 75% of the American public; majorities also opposed any reduction in current programs involving federal grants for low-income housing and for welfare and relief payments. When it comes right down to the specifics of the welfare state, Americans are, for the most part, "liberals."

But what about ideology? What about the conservatives who supported Barry Goldwater in 1964 or voted for the conservative candidates in 1966 and 1968? Surely more than 14% of the American people are "conservative." And surely they are, as Free and Cantril discovered on a second questionnaire designed to identify not operational, but ideological, liberals and conservatives by asking the following questions:

1. The federal government is interfering too much in state and local matters.
2. The government has gone too far in regulating business and interfering with the free enterprise system.
3. Social problems here in this country could be solved more effectively if the government would only keep its hands off and let people in local communities handle their own problems in their own ways.
4. Generally speaking, any able-bodied person who really wants to work in this country can find a job and earn a living.
5. We should rely more on individual initiative and ability and not so much on governmental welfare programs.

A person had to disagree with all or all but one of the statements on which he had an opinion to qualify as completely or predominantly liberal on this "ideological" scale. To be defined as completely or predominantly conservative, he had to agree with all or all but one of the items on which he had an opinion. Others were classified as middle-of-the-road if they had an opinion on at least three state-

ments. Table 1 shows the results of the ideological part of the survey in comparison with the operational part.

As we see, a very different picture emerges. Half the American public is conservative in ideology, whereas only 14% of the American public would have the government pull out of any of its major welfare activities. Conversely, whereas 65% of Americans are liberal at the operational level, only 16% were either completely or predominantly liberal ideologically. Somebody here has cognitive schizophrenia.

We can identify that "somebody" by combining the results of the survey into a single table which shows how each group on the ideological scale stood on the operational scale.

Table 2 shows that 90% of the ideological liberals also qualified as liberals on the operational scale, but among ideological conservatives almost half (46%) proved to be operational liberals! Another way of stating this result is to say that nearly one out

TABLE 1. Comparison of results on ideological and operational scales. (Adapted from Free & Cantril, 1967, p. 32.)

	Ideological Scale	Operational Scale
Completely or predominantly liberal	16%	65%
Middle-of-the-road	34%	21%
Completely or predominantly conservative	50%	14%

TABLE 2. Operational scale and ideological scale combined. (Adapted from Free & Cantril, 1967, p. 37.)

	Ideological Scale		
	Liberal	Middle-of-the-road	Conservative
Operational Scale			
Liberal	90%	78%	46%
Middle-of-the-road	9%	18%	28%
Conservative	1%	4%	26%

of every four Americans (23%, that is, 46% of 50%) is an ideological conservative and at the same time an operational liberal. Barry Goldwater might have fared much better in 1964 if he could have attacked government programs in general while avoiding mention of any program in particular. The Republicans had apparently learned this lesson well by 1968, when Richard Nixon continued to make many ideologically conservative statements, just like those on the questionnaire, while at the same time proposing such things as increased Social Security benefits.

There is one flaw in the Free-Cantril study. Perhaps you noticed that the way all the questions were worded, anyone who agreed or approved of statements on the operational scale would be classified as "liberal" whereas anyone who agreed with statements on the ideological scale would be classified as "conservative." Consequently, a person who tends to agree with any plausible-sounding statement without examining it critically would automatically end up being inconsistent in this study. Indeed, research shows that such individuals do exist; they are called "yea-sayers" (Couch & Keniston, 1960). I think it is quite likely that many of the individuals in the Free-Cantril study who ended up being classified as both ideological conservatives and operational liberals were simply pleasant people who tended to agree with anything the nice man said that seemed reasonable; they were yea-sayers. Perhaps it is more accurate to say that such people are nonconsistent or nonlogical rather than that they are inconsistent or illogical.

Of course, for purposes of my argument it doesn't matter why so many Americans ended up simultaneously as ideological conservatives and operational liberals. Whether they are truly inconsistent or simply nonconsistent (yea-sayers), the fact remains that at least 23% of the American people, unlike the intellectuals who make up consistency theories, "pay little attention to issues, rarely worry about the consistency of their opinions, and spend little or no time thinking about the values, presuppositions and implications which distinguish one political orientation from another."

Thus, I would suggest that consistency theories are all right in their place, but what we need is a good theory of nonconsistency. And when such needs arise, I consult Robert Abelson, the psychologist with theories for all occasions.[1]

OPINION MOLECULES: TOWARD A THEORY OF NONCONSISTENCY

Abelson (1968) suggests that an individual's beliefs and attitudes are often composed of encapsulated, isolated "opinion molecules." Each molecule is made up of (1) a belief, (2) an attitude, and (3) a perception of social support for them. Or, as Abelson likes to put it, each opinion molecule contains a fact, a feeling and a following. For example: "It's a fact that when my Uncle Charlie had back trouble, he was cured by a chiropractor [fact]. You know, I feel that chiropractors have been sneered at too much [feeling], and I'm not ashamed to say so because I know a lot of people who feel the same way [following]." Or, "Nobody on this block wants to sell to Negroes [following], and neither do I [feeling]. The property values would decline [fact]."

Opinion molecules serve such a simple function that psychologists have usually ignored them. They are conversational units. They give us something coherent to say when a particular topic comes up in conversation. Accordingly, they do not need to have logical interconnections between them, and they are notoriously invulnerable to argument because of their isolated, molecular character. I suspect that the majority of our knowledge comes packed in little opinion molecules like these, just waiting for the topic to come up.

In conclusion: (1) It's a fact that there is more nonconsistency in heaven and earth than is dreamt of in our psychological theories; (2) I feel that the

---

[1]Abelson has already been cited in this book as one of the men who coined the word psycho-logic, as the discoverer of alternative strategies for removing inconsistency, and as an editor of the cognitive consistency sourcebook. He is often considered to be a consistency theorist. Fortunately, he would rather be right than consistent.

"opinion molecule" theory applies even to intellectuals—more often than they would like to think; and (3) I'm not ashamed to say so because I know Robert Abelson feels the same way.

REFERENCES

Abelson, R. P. Computers, polls, and public opinion— Some puzzles and paradoxes. *Trans-action,* September 1968, **5,** 20–27.

Abelson, R. P., Aronson, E., McGuire, W. J., Newcomb, T. M., Rosenberg, M. J., & Tannenbaum, P. H. (Eds.) *Theories of cognitive consistency: A sourcebook.* Chicago: Rand-McNally, 1968.

Couch, A., & Keniston, K. Yeasayers and naysayers: Agreeing response set as a personality variable. *Journal of Abnormal and Social Psychology,* 1960, **60,** 151–174.

Free, L. A., & Cantril, H. *The political beliefs of Americans.* New Brunswick, N.J.: Rutgers University Press, 1967.

ARTICLE 12

On the effectiveness of deviant- and conventional- appearing communicators: A field experiment[1]

Joel Cooper
John M. Darley
James E. Henderson

The various aspects of political persuasion have long been of interest to social scientists (e.g., Abrams, 1970; Campbell et al., 1954, 1960; Katz & Lazarsfeld, 1955; Smith, 1958), but as Abelson & Zimbardo (1970) have pointed out, researchers have not suggested political campaigning techniques that differ greatly from what conventional wisdom or practical politicians would suggest. For instance, one classic technique in political campaigning is to have one's favored candidate, party, or issue endorsed or associated with someone held in high esteem by the electorate. And candidates also go to great lengths to avoid being associatively linked with those whom they suspect are perceived negatively by the electorate. For example, White (1969) reported that during the 1968 elections, diplomatic "illnesses" reached epidemic proportions among segregationist southern Democrats who did not wish to share the platform with the integrationist national Democratic candidates.

Social psychology can provide theories and data that support these tactics. For example, balance theories (e.g., Heider, 1958) suggest that an observer tends to evaluate similarly two concepts that are associatively linked. Moreover, Osgood and Tannenbaum (1955) have suggested that the amount of evaluative change of a concept is inversely proportional to its original polarization. Consequently, assuming that most political candidates are initially rather neutrally rated, an associative linkage with an extremely positive endorser would cause a considerable increase in the evaluation of the candidate, while a negative association would cause a considerable decrease. Cooper and Jones (1969) have demonstrated that individuals are aware of the dangers of being miscast by being perceived as associatively linked with a disliked other and try to avoid this linkage.

Reprinted from the *Journal of Personality and Social Psychology*, 1974, *29*, pp. 752–757. Copyright 1974 by the American Psychological Association. Reprinted by permission.

[1] We are indebted to Mark P. Zanna for his comments on an earlier draft of the manuscript.

Notwithstanding the increasing use of television, face-to-face communication can be expected to produce more opinion change than can most mass communication (McGuire, 1969) and can be expected to remain a major campaign tactic (Kramer, 1970). Droves of doorbell ringers will still be sent out to convince their neighbors of various political courses of action.

In the selection of these workers, an intuitive form of the associative hypothesis is heavily relied on; the individuals who contact voters are required to be well-dressed, clean, and conventional appearing. Those who initially are not either get "clean for Gene" or are relegated to back office work. Again experimental data can be cited to confirm the decisions of practical politicians. Darley and Cooper (1972) found that deviant, hippie-looking students were less effective in influencing people to accept numerous political leaflets than were conventionally dressed students. Keasey and Keasey (1971) found a similar result using deviant-appearing and conventional-appearing individuals as collectors of signatures on political petitions.

Both accepted campaign practices and available data, then, suggest that unconventional-appearing or deviant-appearing campaigners are to be avoided. Considering the number of younger people adopting unconventional appearances, this is a distressing generalization. Are there no conditions under which these campaigners can be effective?

Cognitive dissonance theory (Festinger, 1957) suggests that there are. When a person voluntarily chooses to listen to a message with which he disagrees, he has created dissonance for himself. If he can cite extrinsic reasons for listening, for example, obliging a liked other person, then there will be less dissonance. In the absence of other justification, he may reduce dissonance by thinking that the message itself is more worthy of attention, and thus be more persuaded by it. In fact, Jones and Brehm (1967) found that when subjects voluntarily listened to a communication, a disliked communicator was more effective in producing attitude change than was a positively evaluated communicator. Applying this

to the case of political campaigns, if an anti-hippy voter, for instance, is induced to agree to listen to the political arguments of some army-jacketed, long-haired, bearded "freak," he cannot rationalize his listening by his liking for the hippie. On the other hand, listening to similar arguments from a conventionally dressed person can be justified on the basis of liking and tolerance for that person. From the basis of dissonance theory, then, it can be predicted that deviant-appearing campaigners will produce more voter agreement with their message than will more conventionally dressed campaigners.

A field experiment was designed to test this hypothesis. First, residents of a suburban community were contacted by telephone to ascertain their availability for a personal visit and to obtain a premeasure of their attitudes on a political issue. Second, the residents were visited either by a deviant-appearing or a conventional-appearing individual, who gave a persuasive communication that was opposite to most residents' opinions on the issue. Finally, a different individual contacted the residents to remeasure their opinions. It was predicted that the individuals who received the communication from the hippies would be persuaded more than would the residents visited by the conventionally dressed students.

METHOD

Subjects

Names were drawn at random from a street-listed telephone directory of a suburban middle-class community in eastern Pennsylvania. Subjects were 120 residents who were divided equally into two experimental groups and one control condition.

The Issue

Since no election was in progress, it was decided that a political issue of interest to the local community would be selected. The campaigners were to influence the subjects to favor the introduction of a state income tax as opposed to an increase in the sales tax. This was currently an active political issue in Pennsylvania, and pretesting indicated that almost all voters would initially oppose the introduction of the income tax.

Campaigners

Four male campaigners were selected by an individual having no knowledge of the experimental procedures or hypotheses. He was instructed to find two students who looked like hippies and two who appeared conventional. The conventional campaigners were neatly dressed with tie and jacket, were clean-shaven, and had short hair. The two hippie-looking students wore blue jeans, had beards, and had exceptionally long hair. The four campaigners were paid for their work but were not told of the hypotheses being examined.

Procedure

Stage 1: telephoning. Experimenters phoned until 120 individuals were reached who were willing to participate. About 40% of those reached declined to participate. Time pressures was the most frequently cited reason for their refusals. The purpose of the phone calls was to help gain access for the hippie and conventional interviewers and to assess the subjects' opinions on the tax question. The experimenter stated:

I am representing the Henderson Economic Institute of Scranton, Pa. We're involved right now in a program to discuss with the voting public the relative merits of a state sales tax and a state income tax. Since we are not government affiliated, we think we can arrive at a good base of comparison. Would it be possible for one of my workers to call on you today for about five or ten minutes to explain what we're trying to do and hopefully obtain your support?

Since it has been found that subjects must feel free to decline to participate in a discrepant situation in order for dissonance to be aroused, it was decided to keep the subjects' freedom open until after they had learned that the "worker" would be either a

hippie or a conventional individual. Therefore, the experimenter added, "If you say yes now and change your mind, that's all right. We are just trying to get a prospectus of houses to visit."

Finally, to measure the subjects' opinions on the tax issue, the experimenter added, "By the way, are you in favor, or not in favor, of a state income tax?" After receiving an answer, the experimenter continued, "Would you say you were in favor (opposed) slightly, moderately, or strongly?" This provided a 7-point premeasure (a neutral response was permitted) of subjects' opinions.

Stage 2: campaigning. The 120 subjects were divided equally into three groups. One third of the subjects were randomly assigned to be interviewed by one of the conventional interviewers, one third, by a hippie interviewer, and one third were assigned to a control group and were not interviewed at all.

The campaigner rang at each subject's door, introduced himself, and reinstated the subject's choice whether or not to invite him in. Once a deviant-appearing campaigner was refused entry into a house.[2]

Once inside, the campaigner made a few remarks regarding the merits of the income tax as opposed to the sales tax. The campaigner's comments, carefully rehearsed by all four campaigners, were designed to last three or four minutes. He stated that the Henderson Institute's purpose was to take the case for the income tax to the legislature in Harrisburg and to the people of the state of Pennsylvania. He described the sales tax as one that takes proportionally more money from the lower and middle classes, pushes prices higher, and is deceptively large. By contrast, he described the income tax as more equitable and less inflationary. He was careful to mention that there were some arguments against the income tax but made it clear that the income tax was preferable.

---

[2]The final interview was conducted with this subject. A conservative solution was to include his data on the analyses, so they were retained.

In order to keep each of the interviews as standard as possible, the campaigners were instructed to refrain from answering questions. Instead, they made hasty exits, explaining that they were running behind their schedules and that it was important for them to move on.

Stage 3: polling. Two to four days after the interview, each of the 120 subjects was visited by an experimenter (one male and one female, both dressed in business clothes) who was blind with respect to the treatment given the subject. The experimenter introduced himself by saying:

Hello, I'm involved in a nationwide opinion survey this year because we feel that the public's opinion on vital issues should be felt. Could I ask you to fill out this short questionnaire?

If any questions arose about the previous interviewing, the experimenter replied, "Oh, yes, we heard about that, but that company is not related to ours."

The experimenter then gave the questionnaire to the subject. It contained 25 items of local, national, and international interest, each followed by 7-point response scales. The crucial question that served as the major dependent measure was the statement, "An income tax is to be preferred over a sales tax," followed by a 7-point response scale ranging from strongly in favor to strongly opposed. Seven questions related to the subjects' views of students and young people, while three additional questions assessed subjects' views of hair and clothing styles. The remaining questions served mainly as filler items.

RESULTS

Subjects' opinions on the income tax question were gathered on the telephone prior to any influence attempt. The results of this measure (see Table 1) showed that most subjects favored a sales tax to an income tax. The overall mean was 5.24 (a score of 7 indicated extreme support for the sales tax).

The data from the final questionnaire first were analyzed for any effect due to experimenter within each group. None was found. Similarly, no significant effect was found for whether the male or female experimenter collected the final data.

Table 1 presents the opinions of the three groups on the tax issue after the interview had taken place. It can be seen that the group interviewed by the hippie-looking student became more highly favorable to the income tax than did either of the other groups. An analysis of variance, summarized in Table 2, demonstrated that the differences between the hippie group and each of the other two groups were highly reliable.

Although the conditions did not differ significantly on the tax-attitude premeasure, an analysis of covariance was performed to rule out any possibility that the slight premeasure differences might have contributed to the final results. Again, the group interviewed by the hippie was more in favor of the income tax than were the other groups ($F = 7.59, df = 2/116, p < .001$).

The results also showed that members of the group interviewed by the hippie became more favorable in their attitudes toward students. Seven items in the questionnaire related to this dimension. An example of such an item was "Students are a force for positive change in the U.S." The combined mean for all seven questions is presented in Table 1. A multivariate analysis performed on the data showed that the hippie-interviewed group was more favorable toward students than was each of the other two groups (multivariate $F = 8.34$, $p < .001$). Somewhat surprisingly, this pattern did not apply to questions that directly related to subject's opinions of long hair and deviant clothing. The item, "I think it is wrong for young people to wear long hair and deviant clothing," was among three questions designed to measure attitudes toward hippie attire. No differences were found between groups on these items.

TABLE 1. Means of subjects' attitudes.

Attitude	Interviewed by hippie	Interviewed by conventionalist	Control
Premeasure	4.93	5.63	5.18
Tax question	3.63	4.80	4.95
All student questions	3.78	4.53	4.39

Note. $n = 40$. The higher the number, the more favorable toward sales tax or the less favorable toward students.

TABLE 2. Summary of the analysis of variance on the tax question.

Source	df	MS	F
Treatments	2	21.06	9.34*
Error	117	2.12	
Comparisons			
Hippie versus control		70.22	33.12*
Hippie versus conventional		55.22	26.05*
Conventional versus control		.90	< 1

* $p < .001$.

DISCUSSION

The central prediction of the present study was confirmed; deviant-appearing campaigners were more effective in producing attitudinal shifts than were more conventional campaigners. This prediction was generated within the framework of dissonance theory, but dissonance is not the only theory that would lead to these results; correspondent inference theory (Jones & Davis, 1965) could also predict increased effectiveness for the hippie campaigner. According to that theory, when an actor exhibits out-of-role behavior, the observer is able to make more confident and more specific inferences about the dispositions and intentions of the actor. To the extent that our subjects perceived campaigning on the issue of tax structures to be out of role for radical hippies, the conditions for a confident or correspondent inference are met. In this situation, the inference is that the deviant campaigner is really committed to the income tax position for which he

argues; and he might produce greater influence as a function of his greater sincerity.

To separate the dissonance and correspondent inference analyses requires a complexly structured situation that is probably best created in a laboratory rather than in a field setting. In the laboratory, one might think of manipulating a variable that is known to affect dissonance, such as choice, and to see if the effect diminishes under conditions of low choice. But in the field situation, it is difficult to use such an approach. It is difficult to convince a housewife, for example, that she has no choice but to let a deviant campaigner into her home. In the field, a better solution might be to find a situation in which conventional and unconventional campaigners could be both in role and out of role in the same study. This could provide the nucleus for a factorial design to assess the importance of correspondent inference notions in producing results like those of the present experiment.

As difficult as it might be to separate dissonance from correspondent inference notions in the present context, the separation has some important implications for political persuasion processes. If the dissonance analysis is the correct one, then the specific content of the political attitude—just as long as it is counterattitudinal for the voters—is unimportant. However, to the extent that the effect is mediated by attributional or correspondent inference considerations, the generality of the results is more limited.

As we have already suggested, it probably was out of role, and thus fitted correspondent inference conditions, for a hippie to be introduced by telephone and to argue for the rather abstract principles that recommend a personal income tax over a sales tax. But would it be out of role for him to argue for the election of Gene McCarthy or some other peace candidate? Probably not, and if the increased persuasion were due to inference processes, it would not occur in these circumstances. In fact, in such situations, deviant campaigners might be discounted by the audience (Kelley, 1971). Any actual campaign manager contemplating the use of deviant campaigners would be critically interested in the answer to this question, as would the theoretical psychologist.

There is another problem that faces the campaign manager contemplating sending his unconventional-appearing volunteers into the field. Dissonance theory suggests that bringing individuals to the point of compliance without actually producing compliance causes dissonance-produced attitude change in the direction opposite to that desired (Darley & Cooper, 1972). This applies to door-to-door campaigning in the following way: Residents who make a decision not to allow the deviant entrance to speak because they assume he holds attitudes discrepant from their own (e.g., supports another candidate) need to reduce their dissonance by justifying their decision to bar the campaigner from their house. One way to do this is to become more extreme in their original opinions, the same opinions that the campaigner was hoping to change in the opposite direction. In the present study, the deviant campaigners gained almost perfect access into households. But this was probably due to the initial commitment to see them extracted by the earlier telephone conversation. In an election campaign, this would be a costly and time-consuming procedure but perhaps a necessary one to avoid producing a boomerang attitude change.

The present research has provided field confirmation of the dissonance theory prediction that there are conditions under which deviant communicators can be more effective than can conventional ones in effecting attitude change in their audience. The degree to which this effect is independent of the particular content and context of the communication remains to be investigated, as do the complex trade-offs determining the theory's significance for actual campaign practices.

REFERENCES

Abelson, R. P., & Zimbardo, P. G. *Canvassing for peace.* Ann Arbor, Mich.: Society for the Psychological Study of Social Issues, 1970.

Abrams, M. The opinion polls and the British election of 1970. *Public Opinion Quarterly,* 1970, **34**, 317–324.

Campbell, A., et al. *The voter decides.* Evanston, Ill.: Row, Peterson, 1954.

Campbell, A., et al. *The American voter.* New York: Wiley, 1960.

Cooper, J., & Jones, E. E. Opinion divergence as a strategy to avoid being miscast. *Journal of Personality and Social Psychology,* 1969, **13**, 23–30.

Darley, S., & Cooper, J. Cognitive consequences of forced noncompliance. *Journal of Personality and Social Psychology,* 1972, **24**, 321–326.

Darley, J. M., & Cooper, J. The "Clean for Gene" phenomenon: The effect of students' appearance on political campaigning. *Journal of Applied Social Psychology,* 1972, **2**, 24–33.

Festinger, L. *A theory of cognitive dissonance.* Stanford: Stanford University Press, 1957.

Heider, F. *The psychology of interpersonal relations.* New York: Wiley; 1958.

Jones, E. E., & Davis, K. E. From acts to dispositions: The attribution process in person perception. In L. Berkowitz (Ed.), *Advances in experimental social psychology.* Vol. 2. New York: Academic Press, 1965.

Jones, R. A., & Brehm, J. W. Attitudinal effects of communicator attractiveness when one chooses to listen. *Journal of Personality and Social Psychology,* 1967, **6**, 64–70.

Katz, E., & Lazarsfeld, P. F. *Personal influence.* Glencoe, Ill.: Free Press of Glencoe, 1955.

Keasey, C. B., & Keasey, M. Social influence in a high-ego-involvement situation: A field study of petition signing. Paper presented at the 42nd Annual Meeting of the Eastern Psychological Association, New York, April 1971.

Kelley, H. H. *Attribution in social interaction.* New York: General Learning Press, 1971.

Kramer, G. H. The effect of precinct level canvassing on voter behavior. *Public Opinion Quarterly,* 1970, **34**, 560–572.

McGuire, W. J. The nature of attitudes and attitude change. In G. Lindzey & E. Aronson (Eds.), *Handbook of social psychology.* Vol. 3. Reading, Mass.: Addison-Wesley, 1969.

Osgood, C. E., & Tannenbaum, P. H. The principle of congruity in the prediction of attitude change. *Psychological Review,* 1955, **62**, 42–55.

Smith, M. B. Opinion, personality and political behavior. *American Political Science Review,* 1958, **52**, 1–17.

White, T. H. *The making of the president: 1968.* New York: Bantam, 1969.

SECTION SUMMARY

Analysts have pointed out that cognitive dissonance theory has been "tested, questioned, applied, modified, vilified, accepted, and rejected" by psychologists (Shaw & Costanzo, 1970, p. 215). It has been hailed as the most important theoretical advance in recent social psychology, and it has been criticized as a research area characterized by poor methodology, inadequate definitions, and oversimplification (see Chapanis & Chapanis, 1964; Silverman, 1964; Fishbein & Ajzen, 1975).

Although the research evidence is often very complex and sometimes apparently contradictory, some of the major propositions of cognitive dissonance theory have received solid support. As Aronson mentions in the first article, in "free-choice" situations in which the subject must choose between two alternatives that he or she finds about equally desirable, the subject's evaluation of the chosen alternative tends to rise and that of the unchosen (rejected) alternative tends to drop once he or she has made a choice. Interestingly, there is some evidence that a "regret phase" may sometimes occur, in which the evaluation of the *un*chosen alternative rises immediately after the decision is made (Walster, 1964). However, as dissonance reduction through devaluing the unchosen alternative goes into motion, this phase ends and the evaluation of the unchosen alternative drops.

Research results also indicate that, if people undergo a great deal of trouble to gain admission to a group that turns out to be worthless and dull, they appear to experience dissonance stemming from the *disconfirmed expectancy* that the group would be valuable and interesting. This dissonance may be reduced by deciding that the group really is more interesting than it initially appeared (see Aronson & Mills, 1959; Gerard & Mathewson, 1966).

Cognitive dissonance theory and research have focused on situations involving "internal satisfaction"—more specifically, cognitive consistency. Despite the misgivings Bem expresses in his article, it appears that, for most people in most situations, consistency between cognitive elements is, in some sense, "satisfying." In fact, cognitive inconsistency *can* function as a strong motivation toward attitude change to reduce the inconsistency. Yet it is clear that sometimes inconsistency—in Bem's words—"just sits there." And it may "sit there" more frequently for some people than for others.

As we mentioned in the Section Introduction, two other theoretical approaches have been developed to account for the same phenomena that cognitive dissonance theory seeks to explain. One of these, developed by Daryl Bem (1967, 1972), is called *self-perception theory*. Bem has proposed that, just as we often infer what other people's attitudes are by watching them behave, so we may often infer what our *own* attitudes are by watching ourselves behave. We decide what our attitudes are, in Bem's analysis, on the basis of the things we see ourselves doing. For example, people who choose one object and reject another do not necessarily experience discomfort or dissonance, according to Bem; instead, they simply infer that since they chose one object over the other they must like the chosen object more than the unchosen one. Self-perception theory makes many of the same predictions that cognitive dissonance theory does, but it suggests that the *process* by which attitudes are changed is different. Instead of the state of psychological tension described by dissonance theory, self-perception theory depicts a more neutral, passive process in which individuals simply change their perception of what their attitudes must be. If there is an obvious external reason why a person engaged in a behavior, such as being paid a lot of money or having no choice, the person will infer that he or she engaged in the behavior for *that* reason. If, on the other hand, no such external cause is obvious, then the person may infer that his or her own attitude must be consistent with the behavior, since nothing else would cause the behavior to occur.

Still another way of analyzing such situations is through *impression-management theory* (Tedeschi, Schlenker, & Bonoma, 1971). According to this theory, society teaches people to behave consistently. We learn that behaving inconsistently or foolishly causes us to be punished by others who observe our behavior, so we try to avoid being "caught" behaving in such inconsistent ways. By managing the impressions we create, we look like good, consistent people and avoid being punished or disliked. In contrast to dissonance or self-perception theory, then, impression-management theory views people as actively changing their attitudes when necessary in order to receive rewards and to avoid punishments, and not as being upset by psychological inconsistency or as passively inferring what their attitudes are from their own behaviors.

In addition to conceptual issues suggested by the competing theories of self-perception and impression management, cognitive dissonance theory has its own ambiguities. One problem is that, at least at present, there is no way of measuring dissonance directly. The presence of dissonance must be *inferred* from knowledge of the situations in which people find themselves, the strength and quality of their relevant cognitions, and their behavior. Suppose you set up a study to see whether dissonance causes subjects to change their attitudes in the direction predicted by dissonance theory. You find, however, that the subjects do *not* change their attitudes in your experiment. Does this mean that the theoretical predictions were incorrect—that is, that dissonance did not cause attitude change? Or do your results indicate that your experimental situation simply failed to create the state of dissonance in your subjects that you thought it would? From the results of your study alone, you cannot tell.

As originally proposed, dissonance theory makes no provisions for individual differences (although Festinger was aware of the importance of this issue). It seems reasonable that the same situation can create different levels of dissonance in different people and, furthermore, that individuals will be able to tolerate different amounts of dissonance before feeling the need to reduce it. Finally, as Aronson mentions, in any given situation there is usually more than one way for a person to reduce dissonance. What determines which *mode* of dissonance reduction a particular individual chooses? For further discussion of these points the interested reader should see the textbooks mentioned in the Section Introduction.

One factor that may affect the mode of dissonance reduction chosen, as well as the amount of dissonance induced by any given situation, is the function or functions that the attitudes are serving, as outlined in the Section Introduction. For example, attitudes that are serving a function central to a person's self-concept (an ego-defensive or value-expressive function) may be particularly resistant to change, and a relatively high level of dissonance might have to be present before any change takes place. For attitudes serving a more "mundane" function (knowledge or social adjustment), a much smaller amount of dissonance may be sufficient to create meaningful attitude change.

At least some aspects of cognitive dissonance theory have received impressive research support. But is the theory relevant to everyday life? We think so. One example might be racial attitudes and prejudice (see also Section 5). It is a popular belief that "you can't legislate morality"—that is, that passage of new legislation, such as civil rights laws, will have no effect on the underlying attitudes of hostility and racial prejudice that make such laws necessary. This idea stems originally from William Graham Sumner (1906), one of the pioneers of sociology, who asserted around the turn of the twentieth century that mores and folkways were much stronger than formal laws: "stateways cannot change folkways."

Sumner's stand was clearly dominant in the legal position of the courts on racial matters for most of this country's history. In the 1896 decision of the Supreme Court that set the precedent for the separate-but-equal doctrine *(Plessy vs. Ferguson)*, the Court said: "Legislation is powerless to eradicate racial instincts or to abolish distinctions based upon physical differences, and the attempt to do so can only result in accentuating the difficulties of the present situation. . . . If one race is inferior to the other socially, the constitution of the United States cannot put them on the same plane.'' The argument has raged anew recently in debates about the efficacy of civil rights legislation.

The force of recent law (particularly, but not exclusively, since the Supreme Court's 1954 decision that made *de jure* school segregation illegal) has been to ignore the problem of whether or not attitudes can be changed. Nevertheless, behavior and attitudes *have* changed, partially, at least, as a result of statutes and court decisions. For example, research has found that in areas where parents have little choice about which public school their child attends, White parents whose children are attending integrated schools tend to be much more favorable toward integration than those whose children attend segregated schools, even in the same area of the country (Brigham & Weissbach, 1972, Chapter 7).

Changes in the law are one factor that may lead to attitude change. But what is it that legal change *does* that sometimes results in attitude change? As you may already have realized, both cognitive dissonance theory and self-perception theory suggest mechanisms by which such change may occur. Suppose that parents believe in racial segregation and yet their child is ''forced'' by a court order to attend an integrated school. Suppose also that the parents do have some choice in the matter: through a great deal of financial hardship the parents *could* scrape together enough money to send the child to a segregated private school, but they have decided to use this hard-earned money for other things. A dissonance-theory analysis would be that the two cognitive elements (belief in school segregation and knowledge that the child is attending an integrated school even though they could afford to send him to a segregated school) are in conflict, and the parents are presumably in a state of dissonance. In many cases, the easiest route to dissonance reduction for the parents may be to change their beliefs and attitudes (for example, ''Well, maybe integration isn't so bad after all''). If this type of accommodation takes place on a widespread scale, the attitudes of such parents when measured should show an appreciable change. Data from public-opinion polls suggest that this is indeed the case (see Brigham & Weissbach, 1972, Chapter 1). (You may want to apply a self-perception or impression-management-theory analysis to the same situation.)

Events of the past decade have made it clear that ''forced'' integration does not *always* lead to reduced prejudice, however. In some communities across the nation, desegregation programs initiated by changing the boundaries of school districts, by forced busing, or both, have led to fights, riots, and apparent increases in hostility among both Blacks and Whites. In other communities, such programs have operated smoothly and harmoniously. It is clear that many factors in addition to individual attitudes may play a crucial role in determining the effect of legally ''forced'' behaviors (for example, see Carithers, 1970; Silverman & Shaw, 1973; Hermalin & Farley, 1973).

Theories of how and why attitudes change will necessarily continue to undergo modifications like those suggested by Aronson, Bem, and Tedeschi and associates. As Deutsch and Krauss (1965, p. 76) have stated, ''Undoubtedly Festinger would rather be stimulating than right. . . . This attitude is entirely sensible. In the present stage of development of social psychology, no one is ever 'right' for very long.'' By its simplicity and provocativeness, the theory of cognitive dissonance continues to stimulate new research that adds to our knowledge of how attitudes can be changed.

REFERENCES

Aronson, E., Mills, J. The effect of severity of initiation on liking for a group. *Journal of Abnormal and Social Psychology*, 1959, *59*, 177–181.

Bem, D. J. Self-perception: An alternative interpretation of cognitive dissonance phenomena. *Psychological Review*, 1967, *74*, 183–200.

Bem, D. J. Self-perception theory. In L. Berkowitz (Ed.), *Advances in experimental social psychology*, Vol. 6. New York: Academic Press, 1972.

Brigham, J. C., & Weissbach, T. A. (Eds.), *Racial attitudes in America: Analyses and findings of social psychology.* New York: Harper & Row, 1972.

Carithers, M. W. School desegregation and racial cleavage, 1954–1970: A review of the literature. *Journal of Social Issues,* 1970, *26*(4), 25–47.

Chapanis, N. P., & Chapanis, A. C. Cognitive dissonance: Five years later. *Psychological Bulletin,* 1964, *61*, 1–33.

Deutsch, M., & Krauss, R. M. *Theories in social psychology.* New York: Basic Books, 1965.

Fishbein, M. & Ajzen, I. *Belief, attitude, intention, and behavior.* Reading, Mass.: Addison-Wesley, 1975.

Gerard, H. B. & Mathewson, G. C. The effects of severity of initiation on liking for a group: A replication. *Journal of Experimental Social Psychology,* 1966, *2*, 278–287.

Hermalin, A. I., & Farley, R. The potential for residential integration in cities and suburbs: Implications for the busing controversy. *American Sociological Review,* 1973, *38*, 596–610.

Shaw, M. E. & Costanzo, P. R. *Theories of social psychology.* New York: McGraw-Hill, 1970.

Silverman, I. In defense of dissonance theory: Reply to Chapanis and Chapanis. *Psychological Bulletin,* 1964, *62*, 205–209.

Silverman, I. & Shaw, M. E. Effects of sudden mass school desegregation on interracial interactions and attitudes in one Southern city. *Journal of Social Issues,* 1973, *29*(4), 133–142.

Sumner, W. G. *Folkways.* New York: Ginn, 1906.

Tedeschi, J. T., Schlenker, B. R., & Bonoma, T. V. Cognitive dissonance: Private ratiocination or public spectacle? *American Psychologist,* 1971, *26*, 685–695.

Walster, E. The temporal sequence of post-decision processes. In L. Festinger (Ed.), *Conflict, decision, and dissonance.* Stanford, Calif.: Stanford University Press, 1964. Pp. 112–128.

SECTION V

PREJUDICE AND RACISM

INTRODUCTION

We all know people whose reactions to another person are very much influenced by the racial, ethnic, or religious background of the other person. Such people may even misjudge a person's qualities if they know that he or she belongs to a certain group. Why do some people have these "prejudiced" reactions? Does the fault reside in the racial, ethnic, or religious group that is stigmatized? Or do people reject certain groups because of defects in their own emotional adjustment? Or is this reaction simply a reflection of the environment to which they have been exposed?

In this Section we will discuss some of the factors that contribute to the existence of hostile racial attitudes and, on a broader scale, to the existence of a societal structure that may permit or even encourage mistreatment of minority-group members. We will look at the effects that such mistreatment may have on the minority-group members themselves and at ways in which changes in this situation may be set in motion.

To begin, we should clarify what is usually meant by the terms *prejudice* and *racism*. The traditional social-psychological definition of prejudice has been stated by Gordon Allport (1954, p. 9), who defined ethnic prejudice as:

> . . . an antipathy based upon a faulty and inflexible generalization. It may be felt or expressed. It may be directed toward the group as a whole, or toward an individual because he is a member of that group. The net effect of prejudice, thus defined, is to place the object of prejudice at some disadvantage not merited by his own conduct.

We propose one extension to Allport's definition. That is, not only is prejudice a negative or hostile attitude, as Allport implies, but it is also an attitude that has something *wrong* about it. All of us have negative attitudes at times toward people, but it is doubtful that we would treat *all* these negative attitudes as cases of prejudice. As the term *prejudice* is generally used, it is reserved for a particular kind of negative attitude: one which is considered undesirable or *unjustified* (see Brigham & Weissbach, 1972).

With specific reference to attitudes toward minority ethnic groups, there are several factors that might cause a negative attitude to be regarded as prejudiced. Some of these are as follows: (1) the attitude may serve as the basis for *unjust discriminatory social practices* (as Allport mentions); (2) the beliefs associated with the attitude may be *factually incorrect;* (3) the attitude may be the product of a "faulty" or *illogical thought process;* (4) it may be derived from an *unacceptable source,* such as hearsay or distorted perceptions; (5) it may be characterized by inordinate *rigidity;* (6) the fact that the attitude is widespread within the majority culture may mean that there was a *lack of individual thought* in adopting it; and (7) the attitude may *ascribe to ethnic inheritance* characteristics that are actually *cultural acquisitions.* You can probably think of additional factors that are relevant.

It is obvious that a prejudicial attitude may lead to discriminatory behavior. But, although prejudice and discrimination often go hand in hand, this is not always the case. A person may have prejudiced attitudes and yet not be discriminatory in his behavior. (For example, a White may dislike Blacks intensely yet still serve them as customers in his store.) Or a person may appear unprejudiced in his attitudes and yet behave in a discriminatory manner. (For example, a storeowner who does not himself have a negative attitude toward Blacks might not employ a Black salesperson if he felt that he would lose many customers because of it.) When such a discrepancy between attitudes and behavior exists, there is often a tendency to conclude that the attitudes are unimportant and the behavior crucial. Unfortunately, life is not that simple. Each instance of behavior is determined by a variety of factors, of which attitudes are one. We should not neglect the study of attitudes and prejudice just because they do not always forecast a specific action. The study of attitudes is still useful in that an attitude alone, or in combination with other attitudes, may be predictive of certain actions. The attitude also serves as a way of organizing one's reactions "within one's head" and is thus important to study for that reason, too.

Not all cases of discrimination can be attributed to the hostile attitudes of individuals. Recently a great deal of attention has been paid to the concept of *institutional racism,* as originally identified by Carmichael and Hamilton (1967). The hostile ethnic attitudes of individuals may be described as cases of prejudice or of individual racism. But when some or all of the major societal institutions are structured so that they permit or encourage the subjugation and mistreatment of large groups of people, *institutional* racism exists. It has been convincingly argued that present-day American society is so structured. A vivid example of institutional racism is provided by Carmichael and Hamilton (1967, p. 4): "When White terrorists bombed a Black church and killed five Black children, that was an act of individual racism, widely deplored by most segments of the society. But when in that same city—Birmingham, Alabama—five hundred Black babies die each year because of the lack of proper food, shelter, and medical facilities, and thousands more are destroyed and maimed physically, emotionally, and intellectually because of conditions of poverty and discrimination in the Black community, that is the operation of institutional racism." We will discuss some of the most salient instances of institutional racism in the Summary.

The articles in this Section focus on the effects of prejudice and institutional racism on both minority- and majority-group members and on the conditions that are crucial for changing this situation. In the first article, Thomas F. Pettigrew of Harvard University discusses the question of paramount importance in this complex area of prejudice, discrimination, and institutional racism: shall Americans of the future live racially separate or together? He focuses on five key assumptions often proposed by White and Black separatists. Pettigrew then devotes his attention to the best "route" to "true integration," wherein true personal and group autonomy can be retained in a state of racial togetherness.

In the second article, Dalmas Taylor, a Black psychologist at the University of Maryland, questions some of Pettigrew's propositions. In contrast to Pettigrew, Taylor stresses the importance of minority-group *power* as a precondition for equal status and the achievement of racial justice. However, both Pettigrew and Taylor are concerned with the effect that *interracial contact* may have on prejudice and discrimination. They review research evidence that suggests that interracial contact, *when it is of a particular sort,* may lead to a significant reduction in prejudice for the participants. Allport (1954) and Cook (1970) have specified the conditions of the contact situation that must be met if positive attitude change is likely to occur. These conditions are: (1) The participants in the contact situation must be of *equal status* within the situation. (2) The situation should be structured so that mutual interdependence and cooperation are encouraged. Moreover, such cooperation should lead to a successful outcome. (3) The social norms applicable to the situation should encourage interracial association. (4) The situation should be one that promotes personal, intimate relationships and friendship formation. (5) The attributes of the participants should contradict the prevailing negative ethnic stereotypes. (6) The situation should be one that encourages the participants to generalize their (changed) attitudes to other situations and to other ethnic group members. We will outline a study designed to meet all of these criteria in the Section Summary.

One possible cause of discriminatory behavior is pinpointed by Donald G. Dutton and Vicki Lea Lennox, of the University of British Columbia, in our third article. Dutton and Lennox focus on the *need* in many Whites to maintain an image of themselves as unprejudiced. Dutton's earlier research had indicated that Whites might maintain this self-image by engaging in "reverse discrimination"— that is, by treating Blacks more favorably than Whites (Dutton, 1971; 1973). In the present study, Dutton and Lennox "threatened" Whites by providing physiological "evidence" to them that they might be racially prejudiced. They expected that, once threatened, Whites would seek out opportunities to reinstate their image of themselves as unprejudiced. The authors reasoned that if the White came across an "easy" or "token" way to do this, such as donating money to a Black panhandler, then he or she would no longer feel pressure to "prove" his or her egalitarianism. If, on the other hand, the threatened White does not have the opportunity to reinstate a favorable (unprejudiced) self-image in an "easy" way, then the White should be more ready to undertake more ambitious tasks to reinstate the unprejudiced self-image, such as donating time to work on a "Brotherhood Week" campaign.

We will further discuss the effects of prejudice and institutional racism on members of all ethnic groups in the Summary. While reading the articles that follow, you are encouraged to think about the cumulative psychological and economic consequences of racism for all citizens.

REFERENCES

Allport, G. W. *The nature of prejudice.* Reading, Mass.: Addison-Wesley, 1954.

Brigham, J. C., & Weissbach, T. A. (Eds.) *Racial attitudes in America: Analyses and findings of social psychology.* New York: Harper & Row, 1972.

Carmichael, S., & Hamilton, C. V. *Black power: The politics of liberation in America.* New York: Random House, 1967.

Cook, S. W. Motives in a conceptual analysis of attitude-related behavior. In W. J. Arnold and D. Levine (Eds.), *Nebraska symposium on motivation, 1969.* Lincoln: Univ. of Nebraska Press, 1970. Pp. 179–231.

Dutton, D. G. Reactions of restauranteurs to blacks and whites violating restaurant dress regulations. *Canadian Journal of Behavioural Science,* 1971, *3,* 298.

Dutton, D. G. The relationship of amount of perceived discrimination toward a minority group on behaviour of majority group members. *Canadian Journal of Behavioural Science,* 1973, *5,* 34–45.

ARTICLE 13

Racially separate or together?

Thomas F. Pettigrew

The United States has had an almost perpetual racial crisis for a generation. But the last third of the twentieth century has begun on a new note, a change of rhetoric and a confusion over goals. Widespread rioting is just one expression of this. The nation hesitates: it seems to have lost its confidence that the problem can be solved; it seems unsure as to even the direction in which a solution lies. In too simple terms, yet in the style of the fashionable rhetoric, the question has become: Shall Americans of the future live racially separate or together?

This new mood is best understood when viewed as part of the eventful sweep of recent years. Ever since World War I, when war orders combined with the curtailment of immigration to encourage massive migration to industrial centers, Negro Americans have been undergoing rapid change as a people. The latest products of this dramatic transformation from Southern peasant to Northern urbanite are the second and third generations of young people born in the North. The most significant fact about this "newest new Negro" is that he is relatively released from the principal social controls recognized by his parents and grandparents, from the restraints of an extended kinship system, a conservative religion, and an acceptance of the inevitability of white supremacy.

Consider the experience of the 20-year-old Negro in 1971. He was born in 1951; he was only 3 years old when the Supreme Court ruled against *de jure* public school segregation; he was only 6 years old at the time of disorders over desegregation in Little Rock, Arkansas; he was 9 years old when the student-organized sit-ins began at segregated lunch counters throughout the South; he was 12 when the dramatic march on Washington took place and 15 when the climactic Selma march occurred. He has witnessed during his short life the initial dismantling of the formal structure of white supremacy. Conventional wisdom holds that such an experience should lead to a highly satisfied generation of young black Americans; but newspaper headlines and social-psychological theory tell us that precisely the opposite is closer to the truth.

The young black surveys the current scene and observes correctly that the benefits of recent racial advances have disproportionately accrued to the expanding middle class, leaving the urban lower class ever further behind. While the middle-class segment of Negro America has expanded from roughly 5 to 25 percent of the Negroes since 1940,[1] the vast majority of blacks remain poor. The young Negro has been raised on the proposition that racial integration is the basic solution to racial injustice, but his doubts grow as opportunities open for the skilled while the daily lives of the unskilled go largely unaffected. Accustomed to a rapid pace of events, many Negro young people wonder if integration will ever be possible in an America where the depth of white resistance to racial change becomes painfully more evident: in 1964, the equivocation of the Democratic Party Convention when faced with the challenge of the Mississippi Freedom Democratic Party; in 1965, the brutality at the bridge in Selma; in 1966, the summary rejection by Congress of anti-discrimination legislation for housing; in 1968, the wanton assassinations within ten weeks of two leading symbols of the integration movement; and, finally, the retrogression in Federal action for civil rights under the Nixon administration. These events create understandable doubts as to whether Dr. Martin Luther King's dream of equality can ever be achieved.

It is tempting to project this process further, as many analyses in the mass media unhesitantly have done, and suggest that all of black America has undergone this vast disillusionment, that blacks now overwhelmingly reject racial integration and are instead turning to separatist goals. As we shall note shortly when reviewing evidence from surveys, this is not the case. Strictly separatist solutions for the black ghettos of urban America have been most elaborately and enthusiastically advanced not by Negro writers but by such popular white writers as the newspaper columnist Joseph Alsop and William H. Ferry, formerly of the Center for the Study of Democratic Institutions (Alsop, 1967a, 1967b; Ferry, 1968).[2] These white analysts, like many white spokesmen for three centuries before them, are prepared to abandon the American dream of equality as it should apply to blacks, in the name of "hard realities" and under a conveniently mistaken notion that separatism is what blacks want anyway.

Yet the militant stance and rhetoric have shifted in recent years. In a real sense, integration has not failed in America, for it still remains to be tried as a national policy. Many Negroes of all ages sense this; they feel that the nation has failed integration rather than that integration has failed the nation. Influential black opinion turned in the late 1960s from integration as the primary goal to other goals—group power, culture, identity, integrity, and pride. Only a relatively small segment of blacks see these new goals as conflicting with integration; but this segment and their assumptions are one focus of this chapter, for they play a disproportionately critical role for the two chief concerns of this volume—racial integration and white racism. The principal contention throughout this book has been that *integration is a necessary condition for the eradication of white racism at both the individual and institutional levels.* But no treatment of this thesis in America of the 1970s would be complete unless it included a brief discussion of this new black mood and its apparently separatist fringe.

---

[1] These figures derive from three gross estimates of "middle class" status: annual family income of $6,000 or more, high school graduation, or white-collar occupation. Thus, in 1961 roughly one-fifth of Negro families received in excess of $6,000 (a percentage that now must approach one fourth, even in constant dollars); in 1960, 22 percent of Negroes over 24 years of age had completed high school; and in 1966, 21 percent of employed Negroes held white-collar occupations.

[2] For answers to these articles see: Schwartz, Pettigrew, and Smith (1967, 1968). Ferry even proposes that "black colonies" be formally established in American central cities, complete with treaties enacted with the Federal government. The position of black militants is in sharp contrast to this; they complain of having a colonial status now and do not consider it a desirable state of affairs.

Even much of this fringe of young ideological blacks should be described as ''apparently'' separatist, for the labels that make sense for white Americans necessarily must shift meaning when applied to black Americans. Given the national events that have occurred in their short lives, it is not surprising that this fringe regard racial integration less as an evil than as irrelevant to their preoccupations. They often call for *selective* separatism of one or more aspects of their lives while also demanding their rights of entry into the society's principal institutions. It is no accident that the most outspoken members of this faction are college students in prestigious and predominantly white universities.

Through the eyes of some whites, this behavior seems highly inconsistent; it looks as though they talk separation and act integration. But actually the inconsistency is often, though not always, more apparent than real. Consistent with the new emphasis upon power and pride, these young blacks are attempting to define their situation for themselves with particular attention to group autonomy. They are generally as opposed to forced separatism as were Negroes of past generations, and they reject other imposed doctrines as well. And for many of them, integration appears to be imposed by white liberals. ''Why is it that you white liberals only insist on *racial* integration,'' they often ask, ''when separation by class and ethnicity is a widespread fact of American life? Why is it no one gets upset by Italian separatism or Jewish separatism, only black separatism?'' That the imposed separation of Negroes in America is qualitatively different and more vast than that practiced against or by any other sizable American minority, that integration as a doctrine was a creation not of white liberals but of their own fathers and grandfathers—these answers to the young blacks' insistent question are intellectually sound. But such responses do not relate to the feelings underlying the question, for they ignore the positive functions of the new emphasis which excite many young black Americans today.

The positive functions of the new militancy and ideology are exciting precisely because they go to the heart of many young blacks' personal feelings. If the new ideology's analysis of power at the societal level is incomplete, its analysis of racial self-hate at the individual level is right on the mark. Its attention to positive identity and ''black is beautiful'' is needed and important. Indeed, the abrupt shift from ''Negro'' to ''black'' is an integral part of this movement. Many members of older generations would have taken offense at being called ''black''; it was considered a slur. But in facing the issue squarely, young blacks want to be called by the previously forbidden term in order to externalize the matter and convert it into a positive label. The fact that the historical justification sometimes cited for the shift is thin at best is not the point.[3] The important consideration is psychological, and on this ground there is every reason to believe that the change is healthy.

Racial integration has shifted, then, in much black thought from the status of a principal goal to that of one among other mechanisms for achieving ''liberation.'' ''Liberation,'' in its broadest meaning for American race relations, means the total elimination of racial oppression. Similar to the older usage of ''freedom,'' ''liberation'' means the eradication of the burden of racism that black Americans have borne individually and collectively since 1621. From this particular black perspective, ''racially separate or together'' is not the issue so much as what mix of strategies and efforts can actually achieve liberation.

There are, then, positive functions internal to black communities and individuals which this new stance and line of thought appear to have. Much of the present writing in race relations is devoted to

---

[3] It is sometimes held that ''Negro'' was the term for slaves; but actually both ''Negro'' and ''black'' were frequently used in documents concerning slaves. Some critics argue that the true skin color of Negro Americans is basically brown, not black, and that the term ''black'' is therefore inappropriate. But of course ''white'' Americans are seldom white either; besides, ''Negro'' is simply the Spanish word for ''black.'' The importance of the term ''black'' is in fact basically psychological. I have used both terms interchangeably because surveys indicate each is preferred by different segments of the Negro community.

these positive functions. But what do these trends spell out for the possibility of effectively combating white racism? While accepting the conclusion of the Kerner Commission that this is the basic problem, some recent black thought takes the position that wholly *black* concerns must take such precedence that the fight against white racism is, if not irrelevant, at least of secondary importance. Worse, some elements of the separatist fringe actively contribute to the growth and legitimacy of white racism. Hence, when Roy Innis, the national chairman of the Congress of Racial Equality (CORE), goes on a publicized tour to meet governors of the Deep South in order to advocate his program of separate-but-equal public schools, it hardly helps the effort to eliminate white racism.

This truly separatist fringe, then, is neither necessary to nor typical of the new black thrust. It gains its importance from, and becomes potentially dangerous because of, the way it nourishes white racism at both the individual and institutional levels. And it is for this reason that we need to compare it with white segregationist thought. Obviously, the two groups of separatists have sharply different sources of motivation: the blacks to withdraw, the whites to maintain racial supremacy. Nor are their assumptions on a par for destructive potential. But the danger is that black and white separatism could congeal as movements in the 1970s and help perpetuate a racially separate and racist nation. Because of this danger, it is well to examine the basic assumptions of both groups.

SEPARATIST ASSUMPTIONS

White segregationists, both in the North and in the South, base their position upon three bedrock assumptions. *Assumption 1* is that separation benefits both races because each feels awkward and uncomfortable with the other: *Whites and Negroes are happiest and most relaxed when in the company of "their own kind"* (Armstrong & Gregor, 1964).

Assumption 2 is blatantly racist: *Negroes are inherently inferior to whites, and this is the underly-*

ing reality of all racial problems. The findings of both social and biological science place in serious jeopardy every argument put forward for this assumption, and a decreasing minority of white Americans subscribe to it (Pettigrew, 1964). Yet it remains the essential substratum of the thinking of white segregationists; racial contact must be avoided, according to this reasoning, if standards of whites are not to be lowered. Thus, attendance at a desegregated school may benefit black children, but is deemed by segregationists to be inevitably harmful to white children.[4]

Assumption 3 is derived from this assumption of white superiority: *Since contact can never be mutually beneficial, it will inevitably lead to racial conflict*. The White Citizens' Councils in the Deep South, for example, insist that they are opposed to violence and favor racial separation as the primary means of maintaining racial harmony. As long as Negroes "know their place," as long as white supremacy remains unchallenged, strife will be at a minimum.

Black separatists base their position upon three somewhat parallel assumptions. They agree with Assumption 1, that both whites and Negroes are more at ease when separated from each other. It is a harsh fact that blacks have borne the heavier burden of desegregation and have entered previously all-white institutions where open hostility is sometimes practiced by segregationist whites in order to discourage the process, and this is a partial explanation of agreement among blacks with Assumption 1. Yet some of this agreement stems from more subtle situations: the demands by some black student organizations on interracial campuses for all-black facilities have been predicated on this same assumption.

A second assumption of black separatists focuses directly upon white racism. Supported by the chief conclusion of the National Advisory Commis-

---

[4]Analysis specifically directed on this point shows that this contention is not true for predominantly white classrooms as contrasted with comparable all-white classrooms (United States Commission on Civil Rights, 1967, Vol. 1, p. 160).

sion on Civil Disorders, black separatists consider that white racism is the central problem, and that "white liberals" should confine their energies to eradicating it (National Advisory Commission on Civil Disorders, 1968). Let us call this *Assumption 4: White liberals must eradicate white racism.* This assumption underlies two further contentions: namely, that "white liberals" should stay out of the ghetto except as their money and expertise are explicitly requested, and that it is no longer the job of black militants to confront and absorb the abuse of white racists.

The third assumption of black separatists is the most basic of all, and is in tacit agreement with the segregationist notion that interracial contact as it now occurs makes only for conflict. Interaction between black and white Americans, it is held, can never be truly equal and mutually beneficial until blacks first gain personal and group autonomy, self-respect, and power. This makes *Assumption 5: Autonomy is necessary before contact.* It often underlies a two-step theory of how to achieve meaningful integration: the first step requires separation so that Negroes can regroup, unify, and gain a positive self-image and identity; only when this is achieved can the second step, real integration, take place. Ron Karenga, a black leader in Los Angeles, states the idea forcefully: "We're not for isolation, but interdependence. But we can't become interdependent unless we have something to offer. We can live with whites interdependently once we have black power" (Calame, 1968).[5]

Each of these ideological assumptions deserves examination in the light of social-psychological theory and findings.

SOCIAL-PSYCHOLOGICAL CONSIDERATIONS OF SEPARATIST ASSUMPTIONS

Assumption 1: Whites and Negroes are more comfortable apart than together.

There can be no denying that many black and

[5] Karenga's contention that blacks presently have nothing "to offer" a racially interdependent America strangely echoes similar contentions of white racists.

white Americans initially feel uncomfortable and ill at ease when they encounter each other in new situations. This reality is so vivid and so generally recognized that both black and white separatists use it widely in their thinking, though they do not analyze the nature and origins of the situation.

The literature of social science is replete with examples of the phenomenon. Irwin Katz has described the initial awkwardness in biracial task groups in the laboratory: white partners usually assumed an aggressive, imperious role, black partners a passive role. Similarly, Yarrow found initial tension and keen sensitivity among many Negro children in an interracial summer camp, much of which centered on fears that they would be rejected by white campers (Katz, 1964; Yarrow, 1958). But, more important, such tension does not continue to pervade a truly integrated situation. Katz noted that once blacks were cast in assertive roles, behavior in his small groups became more equalitarian and this improvement generalized to new situations. Yarrow, too, observed a sharp decline in anxiety and sensitivity among the black children after two weeks of successful integration at the summer camp.

This is not to say that new interracial situations invariably lead to acceptance. The *conditions* of the interracial contact are crucial; and even under optimal conditions, the cross-racial acceptance generated by contact is typically limited to the particular situation which created it. A segregated society restricts the generalization effects of even truly integrated situations; and at times like the present, when race assumes such overwhelming salience, the racial tension of the larger society may even poison previously successful interracial settings.

Acquaintance and similarity theory helps to clarify the underlying process. Newcomb (Newcomb, Turner, & Converse, 1965) states the fundamental tenet as follows:

Insofar as persons have similar attitudes toward things of importance to both or all of them, and discover that this is so, they have shared attitudes; under most conditions the experience of sharing such attitudes is rewarding, and thus provides a basis for mutual attraction.

Rokeach has applied these notions to race relations in the United States with some surprising results. He maintains that rejection of black Americans by white Americans is motivated less by racism than by assumed differences in beliefs and values. In other words, whites generally perceive Negroes as holding beliefs contrasting with their own, and it is this perception—not race *per se*—that leads to rejection. Indeed, a variety of subjects have supported Rokeach's ideas by typically accepting in a social situation a Negro with beliefs similar to their own over a white with different beliefs (Rokeach, Smith, & Evans, 1960; Rokeach & Mezei, 1966; Smith, Williams, & Willis, 1967; Stein, 1966; Stein, Hardyck, & Smith, 1965).[6]

Seen in the light of this work, racial isolation has two negative effects, both of which operate to make optimal interracial contact difficult to achieve and initially tense. First, isolation prevents each group from learning of the beliefs and values they do in fact share. Consequently, Negroes and whites kept apart come to view each other as very different; this belief, combined with racial considerations, causes each race to reject contact with the other. Second, isolation leads in time to the evolution of genuine differences in beliefs and values, making interracial contact in the future even less likely.[7]

A number of findings of social-psychological research support this extrapolation of interpersonal-attraction theory. Stein et al. (1965) noted that relatively racially isolated white ninth-graders in California assumed an undescribed Negro teen-

ager to be similar to a Negro teen-ager who was described as being quite different from themselves. Smith et al. (1967) found that similarity of beliefs was more critical than racial similarity in desegregated settings, less critical in segregated settings. And the U.S. Commission on Civil Rights, in its study of *Racial Isolation in the Public Schools,* found that both black and white adults who as children had attended interracial schools were more likely as adults to live in an interracial neighborhood and hold more positive racial attitudes than comparable adults who had known only segregated schools (U.S. Commission on Civil Rights, 1967). Or, to put it negatively, Americans of both races who experienced only segregated education are more likely to reflect separatist behavior and attitudes as adults.

Racial separatism, then, is a cumulative process. It feeds upon itself and leads its victims to prefer continued separation. In an open-choice situation in Louisville, Kentucky, black children were far more likely to select predominantly white high schools if they were currently attending predominantly white junior high schools.[8] From these data, the U. S. Commission on Civil Rights concluded: "The inference is strong that Negro high school students prefer biracial education only if they have experienced it before. If a Negro student has not received his formative education in biracial schools, the chances are he will not choose to enter one in his more mature school years" (U. S. Commission on Civil Rights, 1963). Similarly, Negroes who attended segregated schools, the Civil Rights Commission finds, are more likely to believe as adults that interracial schools "create hardships for Negro children" and are less likely to send their children to desegregated schools than are Negroes who attended biracial schools (U. S. Commission on Civil Rights, 1963). Note that those who most fear discomfort in biracial settings are precisely those who

[6]The resolution (Triandis & Davis, 1965) of the earlier controversy between Triandis and Rokeach takes on added weight when the data from studies favorable to Rokeach's position are examined carefully (Triandis, 1961; Rokeach, 1961). That interpersonal realms lead to varying belief-race weightings is borne out by Table 4 in Stein et al. (1965); that intensely prejudiced subjects, particularly in environments where racist norms even extend into less intimate realms, will act on race primarily is shown by one sample of whites in the Deep South in Smith et al. (1967).

[7]Both black and white observers tend to exaggerate racial differences in basic values. Rokeach and Parker note from data from national surveys that, while there appear to be real value differences between the rich and the poor, once socio-economic factors are controlled there are no sharp value differences between black and white Americans (Rokeach & Parker, 1970).

[8]For twelve junior highs, the Spearman-Brown rank-order correlation between the white junior high percentage and the percentage of Negroes choosing predominantly white high schools is +.82 (corrected for ties)—significant at better than the 1 percent level of confidence.

have experienced such situations *least*. If desegregation actually resulted in perpetual and debilitating tension, as separatists are so quick to assume, it seems unlikely that children already in the situation would willingly opt for more, or that adults who have had considerable interracial contact as children would willingly submit themselves to biracial neighborhoods and their children to biracial schools.

Moreover, in dealing with the fact that some tension does exist, a social-cost analysis is needed. The question becomes: What price comfort? Racially homogeneous settings are often more comfortable for members of both races, though, as we have just noted, this seems to be most true at the start of the contact and does not seem to be so debilitating that those in the situation typically wish to return to segregated living. But those who remain in racial isolation, both black and white, find themselves increasingly less equipped to compete in an interracial world. Lobotomized patients are more comfortable, too, but they are impaired for life.

Moreover, there is nothing inevitable about the tension that characterizes many initial interracial encounters in the United States. Rather, tension is the direct result of the racial separation that has traditionally characterized our society. In short, separation is the cause of awkwardness in interracial contacts, not the remedy for it.

Assumption 2: Negroes are inferior; and Assumption 4: White liberals must eradicate white racism.

These two assumptions, though of vastly different significance, raise related issues; and both also are classic cases of self-fulfilling prophecies. Treat a people as inferior, force them to play subservient roles,[9] keep them essentially separate, and eventually the people produced by this must come to support the initial racist notions. Likewise, assume that whites are unalterably racist, curtail efforts by Negroes to confront racism directly, separate Negroes from whites even further, and the result will surely be a continuation, if not a heightening, of racism.

The core of racist attitudes, the assumption of innate racial inferiority, has been under sharp attack from social science for over three decades.[10] Partly because of this work, attitudes of white Americans have undergone massive change over these years. Yet a sizable minority of white Americans, perhaps still as large as a fifth of the adult population, persist in harboring racist attitudes in their most vulgar and naive form. This is an important fact in a time of polarization, such as the present, for this minority becomes the vocal right anchor in the nation's process of social judgment. Racist assumptions not only are nourished by separatism but in turn rationalize separatism. Equal-status contact is avoided because of the racist stigma placed on black Americans by three centuries of slavery and segregation. But changes are evident both here and in social-distance attitudes. Between 1942 and 1963 the percentage of white Americans who favored racially desegregated schools rose from 30 to 63; the percentage of those with no objections to a Negro neighbor rose from 35 to 63 (Hyman & Sheatsley, 1964; Sheatsley, 1966). This trend did not abate during the mid-1960s of increasing white polarization mistakenly labeled "white backlash." This trend slowed, however, at the very close of the 1960s and in the early 1970s—possibly as a result of less insistence for integration.

The slow but steady erosion of racist and separatist attitudes among white Americans occurred during years of confrontation and change, although the process has been too slow to keep pace with the Negro's rising aspirations for full justice and complete eradication of racism. In a period of confrontation, dramatic events can stimulate surprisingly sharp changes in a short period of time.

The most solid social-psychological evidence about changes in racial attitudes comes from the studies of contact. Repeated research in a variety of newly desegregated situations showed that the attitudes of white and blacks toward each other mark-

---

[9]For a role-analysis interpretation of racial interactions in the United States, see Pettigrew (1964).

[10]One of the first significant efforts in this direction was the classic intelligence study by O. Klineberg (1935). For a summary of current scientific work relevant to racist claims regarding health, intelligence, and crime, see Pettigrew (1964).

edly improved: in department stores, public housing (Deutsch & Collins, 1951; Jahoda & West, 1951; Wilner, Walkley, & Cook, 1955; Works, 1961), the armed services (Stouffer, et al., 1949; MacKenzie, 1948), and the Merchant Marine (Brophy, 1946), and among government workers (MacKenzie, 1948), the police (Kephart, 1957), students (MacKenzie, 1948), and general small-town populations (Williams, 1964). Some of these findings can be interpreted not as results of contact, but as an indication that more tolerant white Americans seek contact with Negro Americans. A number of the investigations, however, restrict this self-selection factor, making the effects of the new contact itself the only explanation of the significant alterations in attitudes and behavior.

Surveys bear out these findings on a national scale. Hyman and Sheatsley found that among whites the most extensive changes in racial attitudes have occurred where extensive desegregation of public facilities had already taken place (Hyman & Sheatsley, 1964).[11] Recall, too, that data from the Coleman Report indicate that white students who attend public schools with blacks are the least likely to prefer all-white classrooms and all-white "close friends"; and this effect is strongest among those who began their interracial schooling in the early grades (Coleman et al., 1966). This fits neatly with the findings of the U. S. Commission on Civil Rights (1967) for both black and white adults who had attended biracial schools as children.

Not all intergroup contact, of course, leads to increased acceptance; sometimes it only makes matters worse. Keep in mind Allport's criteria: prejudice is lessened when the two groups (1) possess equal status in the situation, (2) seek common goals, (3) are cooperatively dependent upon each other,

and (4) interact with the positive support of authorities, laws, or customs (Allport, 1954). These criteria are actually an application of the broader theory of interpersonal attraction. All four conditions maximize the likelihood that shared values and beliefs will be evinced and mutually perceived. Rokeach's belief-similarity factor is, then, apparently important in the effects of optimal contact. Following Triandis and Davis's (1965) findings, we would anticipate that alterations in attitudes achieved by intergroup contact, at least initially, will be greatest in formal areas and least in intimate areas.

From this social-psychological perspective, the assumption of black separatists that "white liberals" should eliminate white racism seems to be an impossible and quixotic hope. One can readily appreciate the militants' desire to avoid further abuse from white racists; but their model for change is woefully inadequate. White liberals can attack racist attitudes publicly, conduct research on racist assertions, set the stage for confrontation. But with all the will in the world they cannot accomplish by themselves the needed push, the dramatic events, the actual interracial contact which have gnawed away at racist beliefs for a generation. A century ago the fiery and perceptive Frederick Douglass phrased the issue pointedly (Douglass, 1962, pp. 366–367):

I have found in my experience that the way to break down an unreasonable custom is to contradict it in practice. To be sure in pursuing this course I have had to contend not merely with the white race but with the black. The one has condemned me for my presumption in daring to associate with it and the other for pushing myself where it takes it for granted I am not wanted.

Assumption 3: Contact must lead to conflict; and Assumption 5: Autonomy is needed before contact.

History reveals that white separatists are correct when they contend that racial change creates conflict, that if only the traditions of white supremacy were to go unchallenged racial harmony might be restored. One of the quietest periods in Amer-

---

[11]This is, of course, a two-way causal relationship. Not only does desegregation erode racist attitudes, but desegregation tends to come first to areas where white attitudes are least racist to begin with. Hyman and Sheatsley's finding, however, specifically highlights the former phenomenon: "In those parts of the South where some measure of school integration has taken place official action has preceded public sentiment, and public sentiment has then attempted to accommodate itself to the new situation."

ican racial history, 1895–1915, witnessed the construction of the massive system of institutional racism as it is known today—the "nadir of Negro American history," as Rayford Logan (1957) calls it. The price of those two decades of relative peace is still being paid by the nation. Even if it were possible now to gain racial calm by inaction, the United States could not afford the enormous cost.

But if inaction is clearly impossible, the types of action necessary are not so clear. Black separatists believe that efforts to further interracial contact should be abandoned or at least delayed until greater personal and group autonomy is achieved by Negroes. This view and the attitudes of white separatists just mentioned are two sides of the same coin. Both leave the struggle against racism in attitudes completely in the hands of "white liberals." And the two assumptions run a similar danger. Racism is reflected not only in attitudes but, more importantly, in institutionalized arrangements that operate to restrict the choices open to blacks. Both forms of racism are fostered by segregation, and both have to be confronted directly by Negroes. To withdraw into the ghetto, psychologically tempting as this may be for many, is essentially to give up the fight to alter the racially discriminatory operations of the nation's chief institutions. The Rev. Jesse L. Jackson, the Chicago black leader of Operation Breadbasket, makes the same point in forceful terms (Jackson & Poussaint, 1970):

Let's use this analogy. Assuming that racism is a hot fire. If we're gonna take over things and run them and destroy racism, we got to get to the core of the fire. You can't destroy it by running away from it. The fact is, at this point in American history, racism is in trouble in terms of the government, economy, political order and even the psychological order.

The issues involved are shown schematically in Figure 1. By varying contact-separation and an ideologically vague concept of "autonomy," four cells may be set up that represent the various possibilities under discussion. Cell A, true integration, refers to institutionalized biracial situations where there is cross-racial friendship, racial interdependence, and a strong measure of personal and group autonomy. Such situations do exist in America today, but they are rare islands in a sea of conflict. Cell B represents the autonomous ghetto postulated by advocates of black separatism, relatively independent of the larger society and far more viable than is commonly the case now. This is an ideologically derived hypothetical situation, for no such urban ghettos exist today. Cell C stands for merely desegregated situations. These are often mistakenly called "integrated." They are institutionalized bi-

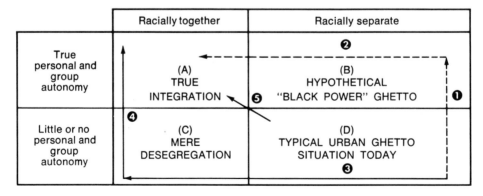

FIGURE 1.   Schematic diagram of autonomy and contact-separation. Dotted lines denote hypothetical paths; solid lines, actual paths. The author is indebted to Professor Karl Deutsch of Harvard University for several stimulating conversations out of which came this diagram.

racial settings which involve little cross-racial ac-ceptance and, often, patronizing legacies of white supremacy. Cell D represents today's typical highly separate urban ghetto with little or no personal or group autonomy.

Definitional confusions may obscure the meaning of Figure 1, especially the definition of "integra-tion." This term became almost a hallowed symbol of the civil rights movement of previous decades, and its present disparagement in newer black thought may be traced in part to this fact. But most disparagement of "integration" is due to defini-tional confusion between it and "assimilation" and between it and desegregation as diagrammed in Figure 1. As Lerone Bennett (1970, pp. 37–38) rightly points out, these confusions among both whites and blacks stem from employing exclusively a white standard of reference:

One of the greatest enemies of integration in America today is the word integration. Contrary to the hopes of some and the fears of others, integration does not mean black elimination. Integration may or may not lead to assimilation, but assimilation does not necessarily mean the disappearance of a minority. . . . Differences can be eliminated in favor of a creative minority. Both "inte-grationists" and "separatists" forget that there is a blackening process as well as a whitening process. Liberationists, who recognize this dialectic, say blacks must assimilate and not be assimilated. . . . Integration is not disappearance; nor is it simple contiguity . . . since men have given the word integration a bad name, we shall use the word transformation to refer to the real thing.

Cell A refers to "the real thing," to the integration of *whites* as well as blacks, to the end product of Lerone Bennett's "transformation."

Except for white separatists, observers of diverse persuasions agree that the achievement of true in-tegration (cell A) should be the ultimate goal. But there are, crudely speaking, three contrasting ways of getting there from the typical current situation (cell D). The black separatist assumes that only one route is possible: from the depressed ghetto of today to the hypothetical ghetto of tomorrow and then,

perhaps, on to true integration (lines 1 and 2 in Figure 1). The desegregationist assumes precisely the opposite route: from the present-day ghetto to mere desegregation and then, hopefully, on to true integration (lines 3 and 4 in Figure 1). But there is a third, more direct route, right across from the cur-rent ghetto to true integration (line 5 in Figure 1). Experience to date combines with a number of social-psychological considerations to favor the last of these possibilities with some important qualifica-tions.

The route favored by black separatists has a sur-prising appeal for an untested theory; besides those whites who welcome any alternative to integration, it seems to appeal to militant black leaders searching for a new direction into which to channel the ghet-to's rage, and to blacks who just wish to withdraw as far away from whites as possible. Yet, on reflection, it can be seen that the argument involves the per-verse notion that the way to bring two groups to-gether is to separate them further. One is reminded of the detrimental consequences of isolation in economics, through "closed markets," and in genetics, through "genetic drift." In social psychology, isolation between two contiguous groups generally leads to: (1) the development of diverse values, (2) reduced intergroup communica-tion, (3) uncorrected perceptual distortions of each other, and (4) the growth of vested interests within both groups for continued separation. Race rela-tions in the United States already suffer from each of these conditions; and the proposal for further sep-aration, even if a gilded ghetto were possible, can only exacerbate them.

In fairness, it should be emphasized again that the criticisms here are directed against the concept of the insulated ghetto, not the shrewder and more sub-tle notions of power and regrouping combined with challenges to the restriction of choice imposed by the nation's leading institutions. As was mentioned at the beginning of this chapter, a much larger seg-ment of militant blacks, judging from their actions, adheres to the latter program. The fascinations of the more romantic notions of a totally self-sufficient black community and even occasional expressions of black chauvinism are apparently diminished by many of the unromantic facts of the situation.

We will not pursue the many economic and political difficulties inherent in the concept of the insulated ghetto, but it should be mentioned that the resources immediately available in the ghetto for the task are meager. Recognizing this limitation, black separatists call for massive Federal aid with no strings attached. But this requires a national consensus. Some separatists consider that the direct path to integration (line 5 in Figure 1) is idealistic dreaming, then turn and assume that the same racist society that resists integration will unhesitatingly pour a significant portion of its treasure into the ghetto. "Local control" without access to the necessary tax base is not control. This raises the question of the political limitations of this route. Irish-Americans entered the mainstream through the political system, and this method is often cited as appropriate to black separatism—but is it really? Faster than any other immigrant group except Jewish Americans, the Irish have assimilated on the direct route of Figure 1. Forced to remain in ghettos at first, the Irish did not settle for "local control" but strove to win city hall itself. Boston's legendary James Michael Curley won "Irish power" not by becoming mayor of the South Boston ghetto, but by becoming mayor of the entire city. Analogies between immigrants and blacks contain serious inaccuracies, however, since immigrants never suffered from slavery and legalized separation. But to the extent an analogy is appropriate, Mayor Carl Stokes of Cleveland, Mayor Richard Hatcher of Gary, and Mayor Kenneth Gibson of Newark are far closer to the Irish-American model than are black separatists.

A critical part of the thinking of black separatists centers on the psychological concept of "fate control"—more familiar to psychologists as Rotter's (1966) internal control of reinforcement variable. "Until we control our own destinies, our own schools and areas," goes the argument, "blacks cannot possibly achieve the vital sense of fate con-

trol." Data from the Coleman Report are cited to show that fate control is a critical correlate of achievement in school for black children (Coleman et al., 1966). But no mention is made of the additional fact that levels of fate control among black children were found by Coleman to be significantly higher in interracial schools than in all-Negro schools. Black separatists brush this important finding aside because all-Negro schools today are not what they envision for the future. Yet the fact remains that interracial schools appear to be facilitating the growth of fate control among Negro students now; the ideological contention that fate control can be developed as well or better in uniracial schools remains an untested and hypothetical assertion.

Despite the problems, black separatists feel that their route (lines 1 and 2 in Figure 1) is the only way to true integration, in part because they regard the indirect route of desegregation (lines 3 and 4) as an affront to their dignity. Anyone familiar with the blatantly hostile and subtly rejecting acts that typify some interracial situations will understand this repudiation of nonautonomous desegregation (cell C).[12] Merely desegregated schools, defined as biracial institutions typified by racial tension and little cross-racial friendship, have scant benefits over segregated schools (U. S. Commission on Civil Rights, 1967).[13]

This finding reflects Allport's conditions for optimal contact. Truly integrated institutions afford the type of contact that maximizes cross-racial acceptance and the similarity of beliefs described by Rokeach.[14] They apparently also maximize the

[12]For extreme examples of this phenomenon in public schools in the Deep South, see Chessler (1967).

[13]More recent evidence for this distinction is provided in Koslin, Koslin, Pargament, and Waxman (1970).

[14]Another white observer enthusiastic about black separatism even denies that the conclusions of the contact studies are applicable to the classroom and other institutions which do not produce "continual and extensive equal-status contact under more or less enforced conditions of intimacy." Stember selectively cites the investigations of contact in public housing and the armed forces to support his point (Stember, 1968); but he has to omit the many

positive and minimize the negative factors which Katz (1964, 1967) has isolated as important for performance of Negroes in biracial task groups. And they also seem to increase the opportunity for beneficial cross-racial evaluations, which may well be critical mediators of the effects of biracial schools (Pettigrew, 1967). Experimental research following up these leads is now called for to detail the precise social-psychological processes operating in the truly integrated situation (Pettigrew, 1968).

The desegregation route (lines 3 and 4 in Figure 1) has been successfully navigated, though the contention of black separatists that Negroes bear the principal burden for this effort is undoubtedly true. Southern institutions that have attained integration, for example, have typically traveled this indirect path. This route, then, is not as hypothetical as the route advocated by black separatists, but it is hardly to be preferred over the route of direct integration (line 5).

Why not the direct route, then? The standard answer is that it is impossible, that demographic trends and resistance from whites make it out of the question in our time. One is reminded of the defenders of slavery in the 1850s, who attacked the Abolitionists as unrealistic dreamers and insisted that slavery was so deeply entrenched that efforts should be limited to making it into a benign institution. If the nation acts on such speculations, of course, they will probably be proven correct. What better way is there to prevent racial change than to act on the assumption that it is impossible?

The belief that integration is impossible, however, is based on some harsh facts of urban racial demography. Between 1950 and 1960, the average annual increment of Negro population in the central cities of the United States was 320,000; from 1960 to 1966 the estimated annual growth climbed to

400,000, though reduced in-migration from the rural South has lowered this annual growth rate considerably since 1966. In the suburbs, however, the average annual growth of the Negro population declined from 60,000 between 1950 and 1960 to an estimated 33,000 between 1960 and 1966, though it has sharply increased since 1966 (U. S. Departments of Labor and Commerce, 1970). In other words, it would require several times the present trend in growth of Negro populations in the suburbs just to maintain the sprawling central-city ghettos at their present size. In the nation's largest metropolitan areas, then, the trend is still pushing in the direction of ever increasing separatism.

But these bleak data are not the whole picture. In the first place, they refer especially to the very largest of the metropolitan areas—to New York City, Chicago, Los Angeles, Philadelphia, Detroit, Washington, D. C., and Baltimore. Most Negro Americans do not live in these places, but rather in areas where racial integration is in fact possible in the short run if attempts in good faith are made. There are more Berkeleys—small enough for school integration to be effectively achieved—than there are New York Cities. In the second place, the presumed impossibility of reversing racial trends in the central city is based on anti-metropolitan assumptions. Without metropolitan cooperation central cities—and many suburbs, too—will find their racial and other basic problems continuing. Do we need to assume such cooperation impossible? We previously proposed effective state and Federal incentives to further this cooperation. Moreover, some large black ghettos are already extending into the suburbs (e.g., east of Pittsburgh and west of Chicago); the first tentative metropolitan schemes to aid racial integration are emerging in a variety of cities (e.g., Boston, Hartford, Rochester, and Portland, Oregon); and several major metropolitan areas have even consolidated (e.g., Miami-Dade County and Nashville-Davidson County). Once the issue is looked at in metropolitan terms, its dimensions become more manageable. Black Americans are found in America's metropolitan areas in almost the

studies from less intimate realms which reached the same conclusions—such as those conducted in schools (Pettigrew, 1968), and employment situations (Harding & Hogrefe, 1952; Kephart, 1957; MacKenzie, 1948; Williams, 1964), and even one involving brief contact between clerks and customers (Saenger & Gilbert, 1950).

same ratio as white Americans: about two-thirds of each group reside in these 212 regions. On a metropolitan basis, therefore, Negroes are not disproportionately metropolitan.

Yet it must be admitted that many young blacks, separatist and otherwise, are simply not convinced by such arguments. Such large-scale proposals as metropolitan educational parks strike them as faraway pipe dreams of no significance to their immediate problems. Contact theory holds little appeal. They rightfully argue that Allport's four conditions do not typify the American national scene. How often, they ask, do blacks actually possess equal status in situations with whites? And in struggles for racial power, as they view it, can there be a cooperative seeking of common goals? And as for the possibility that true integration of cell A will be sanctioned by those in authority, they say ruefully, consider the public images on racial matters of Nixon, Mitchell, Agnew, Carswell. Maybe the demographic arguments against the possibility of integration are overdrawn, they concede, but can one realistically expect Allport's conditions of positive contact to become the rule in the foreseeable future of the United States?

Underlying this criticism is less a theoretical and ideological difference than a sharply contrasting assessment of the probabilities and possibilities of America's race relations. These black spokesmen may well be right. The United States may indeed be so racist both as to individuals and structure that the type of institutional changes advocated throughout this volume will never be achieved. No footnoting of references or social-psychological theory can refute this possibility, but I hope it is wrong. The entire analysis of this book is predicated on the more optimistic view that somehow American society will muddle through. To assume otherwise, once again, is to risk contributing to the problem by engaging in a self-fulfilling prophecy.

Moreover, the attack on contact theory is based in part on a misreading of it. *Situations* meeting Allport's four conditions do exist in the United

States, and we have seen that they are becoming more numerous in such realms as employment. True, as noted, these truly integrated situations are still isolated islands and together do not constitute a critical mass nationally. Yet the status of Negroes is rising in the United States. Indeed, the personal lives of the black critics themselves typically attest to this social mobility, for roughly 90 percent of middle-class blacks today derive from families which were lower class in 1940. But these very gains create rapidly rising expectations and a keen sense of relative deprivation, some of which gets channeled among some blacks into the separatist ideology under discussion.

Nor are power struggles as completely racial and competitive as critics claim. For one thing, power conflicts almost invariably involve class as well as racial interests, and to the extent that class is involved there are at least potential white allies. White Americans, after all, are an even more diverse assortment than black Americans. But actually the theory requires only that blacks and some whites share common goals to the point where coalitions become important to both; one of the coalitions is called the Democratic Party, which since Franklin Roosevelt has consisted of a precarious combination of minorities which together total a registration far larger than that of the rival party.

Finally, concerning Allport's fourth condition on the sanction of laws and authorities, there is solid evidence in civil rights legislation and other institutional changes that we are moving toward the sanctioning of true integration. By and large, of course, America's institutions still do not play this role; they are racist, in the Kerner Commission's plain language, in that their normal operations still act typically to restrict choice for blacks. But positive change is evident from the appearance of Negroes on television to their participation in former bastions of white privilege. True, as far as race is concerned the Nixon Administration is a throwback to the naivete of early twentieth-century administrations; it offers no "authority sanction," nor does it promise to in its remaining years. Yet there are other political alternatives which would willingly offer the racial leadership the nation so desperately needs. To opt out of the opposition, to assume that the Mitchells and Agnews are inevitable and typical products of the American political system, is to ensure that such men will in fact remain in power.

To argue for route 5 in Figure 1 is not to assume that it will be easy to achieve, or that Allport's optimal conditions for intergroup contact apply generally throughout America at present. The direct path does stress that *simultaneous* attention must be given to both integration and individual and collective autonomy, for today's cell D has neither and tomorrow's cell A must have both. And neither the desegregation (paths 3 and 4 of Figure 1) nor the separatist (paths 1 and 2) route gives this simultaneous attention. Once again, Bennett (1970, p. 38) phrases the argument cogently:

It is impossible, Simon de Beauvoir said, to draw a straight line in a curved space. Both "integrationists" and "separatists" are trying to create right angles in a situation which only permits curves. The only option is transformation of a situation which does not permit a clear-cut choice in either direction. This means that we must face the fact that it is impossible to move 30 million African-Americans anywhere.

IMPLICATIONS FOR POLICY

Much of the confusion over policy seems to derive from the assumption that since *complete* integration in the biggest cities will not be possible in the near future, present efforts toward opening opportunities for integration for both Negro and white Americans are premature. This thinking obscures two fundamental issues. First, the democratic objective is not total racial integration and the elimination of black neighborhoods; the idea is simply to provide an honest choice between separation and integration. Today only separation is available; integration is closed to blacks who would choose it. The long-term goal is not a complete obliteration of

cultural pluralism, of distinctive Negro areas, but rather the transformation of these ghettos from racial prisons to ethnic areas freely chosen or not chosen. Life within ghettos can never be fully satisfactory as long as there are Negroes who reside within them only because discrimination requires them to

Second, the integrationist alternative will not become a reality as long as we disparage it or abandon it to future generations. *Exclusive* attention to programs for enriching life in the ghetto is almost certain, to use Kenneth Clark's pointed word, to "embalm" the ghetto, to seal it in even further from the rest of the nation (making line 2 in Figure 1 even less likely). This danger explains the recent interest of conservative whites in enrichment programs for the ghetto. The bribe is straightforward: "Stop rioting and stop demanding integration, and we'll minimally support separatist programs within the ghetto." Even black separatists are understandably ambivalent about such offers, as they come from sources long identified with opposition to all racial change. Should the bargain be struck, however, race relations in the United States will be dealt still another serious blow.

Yet a policy concentrating *exclusively* on integration, like one concentrating exclusively on enrichment, runs its own danger of worsening the situation. As many black spokesmen correctly point out, a single-minded pursuit of integration is likely to blind us to the urgent requirements of today's black ghettos. Either policy followed mechanically and exclusively, then, has serious limitations which the rival strategy is designed to correct. This fact strongly suggests that a national transformation from a racist society to an open society will require a judicious mix of both the strategies.

The outlines of the situation, then, are these: (1) Widespread integration is possible everywhere in the United States except in the largest central cities. (2) It will not come unless present trends are reversed and considerable resources are provided for the process. (3) Big central cities will continue to have significant concentrations of Negroes even with successful metropolitan dispersal. (4) Large Negro ghettos are presently in need of intensive enrichment. (5) Some enrichment programs for the ghetto run the clear and present danger of embalming the ghetto further.

Given this situation and the social-psychological considerations we have been discussing, the overall strategy needed must contain the following elements:

1. A major effort toward racial integration must be mounted in order to provide genuine choice to all Negro Americans in all realms of life. This effort should envisage complete attainment of the goal in smaller communities and cities by the late 1970s and a halting of separatist trends in major central cities, with a movement toward metropolitan cooperation.

2. A simultaneous effort is required to enrich the vast central-city ghettos of the nation, to change them structurally, and to improve life in them. In order to avoid "embalming" them, however, strict criteria must be applied to proposed enrichment programs to ensure that they will not hinder later dispersal and integration. Restructuring the economics of the ghetto, especially by developing urban cooperatives, is a classic example of productive enrichment. Effective job training programs offer another example of productive enrichment. The building of enormous public housing developments within the ghetto presents a good illustration of counterproductive enrichment. Some programs, such as the decentralization of huge public school systems or the encouragement of business ownership by Negroes, can be either productive or counterproductive depending upon how they are focused. A decentralization plan of many small homogeneous school districts for New York City is clearly counterproductive for later integration; a plan involving a relatively small number of heterogeneous school districts for New York City could well be productive. Likewise, black entrepreneurs who are encouraged to open small shops and are expected to prosper with an all-black clientele are not only part of a counterproductive plan, but are probably committing economic suicide. Negro businessmen who are encouraged to pool their resources to establish somewhat larger operations and to appeal to white as well as black customers on major traffic arteries in and out of the ghetto could be an important part of a productive plan.

In short, a mixed strategy is called for—both integration and enrichment—and it must contain safeguards that the two aspects will not impede each other. Results of recent surveys strongly suggest that such a mixed strategy would meet with widespread approval among black Americans.

Young men prove to be the most forthright separatists, but even here the percentages of men aged 16 to 19 who were separatists ranged only from 11 to 28 (Campbell & Schuman, 1968). An interesting interaction between type of separatism and educational level of the respondent appears in Campbell and Schuman's data. Among the 20- to 39-year-olds, college graduates tended to be more separatist in those realms where their training gives them a vested interest in positions free of competition—black-owned stores for black neighborhoods, black teachers in mostly black schools. The poorly educated were most likely to believe that whites should be discouraged from taking part in civil rights organizations and to agree that "Negroes should have nothing to do with whites if they can help it" and that "there should be a separate black nation here" (Campbell & Schuman, 1968).

But if separatism draws little favorable response even in the most politicized ghettos, positive aspects of cultural pluralism attract wide interest. For example, 42 percent endorse the statement that "Negro school children should study an African language." And this interest seems rather general across age, sex, and education categories. Campbell and Schuman regard this as evidence of a broadly supported attempt ". . . to emphasize black consciousness *without* rejection of whites. . . . A substantial number of Negroes want *both* integration and black identity." Or in the terms of this paper, they prefer cell A in Figure 1—"true integration."

When viewed historically, this preferred combination of black consciousness without separation is not a new position for black Americans. It was, for example, their dominant response to the large-scale movement of Marcus Garvey in the 1920s. Garvey, a West Indian, stressed pride in Africa and black beauty and successfully mounted a mass movement throughout the urban ghettos of the day, but his famous ''back to Africa'' separatist appeals were largely ignored as irrelevant.

A FINAL WORD

Racially separate or together? Our social-psychological examination of separatist assumptions leads to the assertion of one imperative: the attainment of a viable, democratic nation, free from personal and institutional racism, requires extensive racial integration in all realms of life as well as vast programs of ghetto enrichment. To prescribe more separation because of discomfort, racism, conflict, or the need for autonomy is like getting drunk again to cure a hangover. The nation's binge of *apartheid* must not be exacerbated but alleviated.

REFERENCES

Allport, G. W. *The nature of prejudice*. Reading, Mass.: Addison-Wesley, 1954.

Alsop, J. No more nonsense about ghetto education! *New Republic*, July 22, 1967, **157,** 18–23. (a)

Alsop, J. Ghetto schools. *New Republic*, Nov. 18, 1967, **157,** 16–19. (b)

Armstrong, C. P., & Gregor, A. J. Integrated schools and Negro character development: Some considerations of the possible effects. *Psychiatry*, 1964, **27,** 69–72.

Bennett, L., Jr. Liberation. *Ebony*, August, 1970, Vol. 25, pp. 36–43.

Brophy, I. N. The luxury of anti-Negro prejudice. *Public Opinion Quarterly*, 1946, **9,** 456–466.

Calame, B. E. A west coast militant talks tough but helps avert racial trouble. *The Wall Street Journal*, July 26, 1968, Vol. 172, No. 1, p. 15.

Campbell, A., & Schuman, H. Racial attitudes in fifteen American cities. In The National Advisory Commission on Civil Disorders, *Supplemental Studies*. Washington, D. C.: U. S. Government Printing Office, 1968. P. 5.

Chessler, M. *In their own words*. Atlanta: Southern Regional Council, 1967.

Coleman, J. S., Campbell, E. Q., Hobson, C. J., McPartland, M., Mood, A. M., Weinfield, F. D., & York, R. L. *Equality of educational opportunity*. Washington, D. C.: U. S. Government Printing Office, 1966.

Deutsch, M., & Collins, M. *Interracial housing: A psychological evaluation of a social experiment*. Minneapolis: University of Minnesota Press, 1951.

Douglass, F. *Life and times of Frederick Douglass: The complete autobiography*. New York: Collier Books, 1962. (original edition in 1892).

Ferry, W. H. Black colonies: A modest proposal. *The Center Magazine*, January 1968, Vol. 1, pp. 74–76.

Harding, J., & Hogrefe, R. Attitudes of white department store employees toward Negro co-workers. *Journal of Social Issues*, 1952, **8,** 18–28.

Hyman, H. H., & Sheatsley, P. B. Attitudes toward desegregation. *Scientific American*, July 1964, **211,** 16–23.

Jackson, J. L., & Poussaint, A. F. A dialogue on separatism. *Ebony*, August 1970, Vol. 25, pp. 62–68.

Jahoda, M., & West, P. Race relations in public housing. *Journal of Social Issues*, 1951, **7,** 132–139.

Katz, I. Review of evidence relating to effects of desegregation on the performance of Negroes. *American Psychologist*, 1964, **19,** 381–399.

Katz, I. The socialization of competence motivation in minority group children. In D. Levine (Ed.), *Nebraska symposium on motivation*. Lincoln: University of Nebraska Press, 1967.

Kephart, W. M. *Racial factors and urban law enforcement*. Philadelphia: University of Pennsylvania Press, 1957.

Klineberg, O. *Negro intelligence and selective migration*. New York: Columbia University Press, 1935.

Koslin, S., Koslin, B., Pargament, R., & Waxman, H. Classroom racial balance and students' interracial attitudes. Unpublished paper, Riverside Research Institute, New York City, 1970.

Logan, R. W. *The Negro in the United States: A brief history*. Princeton, N. J.: Van Nostrand, 1957.

MacKenzie, B. The importance of contact in determining attitudes toward Negroes. *Journal of Abnormal and Social Psychology*, 1948, **43,** 417–441.

National Advisory Commission on Civil Disorders, *U. S. riot commission report*. Washington, D. C.: U. S. Government Printing Office, 1968.

Newcomb, T. M., Turner, R. H., & Converse, P. E. *Social psychology: The study of human interaction*. New York: Holt, Rinehart and Winston, 1965.

Pettigrew, T. F. *A profile of the Negro American*. Princeton, N. J.: Van Nostrand, 1964.

Pettigrew, T. F. Social evaluation theory: Convergences and applications. In D. Levine (Ed.), *Nebraska symposium on motivation.* Lincoln: University of Nebraska Press, 1967.

Pettigrew, T. F. Race and equal education opportunity. *Harvard Educational Review,* 1968, **38,** 66–76.

Riley, R. T., & Pettigrew, T. F. Dramatic events and racial attitude change. Unpublished paper, Harvard University, August 1970.

Rokeach, M. Belief versus race as determinants of social distance: Comment on Triandis' paper. *Journal of Abnormal and Social Psychology.* 1961, **62,** 184–186.

Rokeach, M., & Mezei, L. Race and shared belief as factors in social choice. *Science,* 1966, **151,** 167–172.

Rokeach, M., & Parker, S. Values as social indicators of poverty and race relations in America. *Annals of the American Academy of Political and Social Science,* 1970, **388,** 97–111.

Rokeach, M., Smith, P., & Evans, R. Two kinds of prejudice or one? In M. Rokeach (Ed.), *The open and closed mind.* New York: Basic Books, 1960.

Rotter, J. B. Internal versus external control of reinforcement. *Psychological Monographs,* 1966, **80,** (609).

Saenger, G., & Gilbert, E. Customer reactions to the integration of Negro sales personnel. *International Journal of Opinion and Attitude Research,* 1950, **4,** 57–76.

Schwartz, R., Pettigrew, T., & Smith, M. Fake panaceas for ghetto education. *New Republic,* Sept. 23, 1967, **157,** 16–19.

Schwartz, R., Pettigrew, T., & Smith, M. Is desegregation impractical? *New Republic,* Jan. 6, 1968, **1,** 74–76.

Sheatsley, P. B. White attitudes toward the Negro. In T. Parsons and K. B. Clark (Eds.), *The Negro American.* Boston: Houghton Mifflin, 1966.

Smith, C. R., Williams, L., & Willis, R. H. Race, sex and belief as determinants of friendship acceptance. *Journal of Personality and Social Psychology,* 1967, **5,** 127–137.

Stein, D. D. The influence of belief systems on interpersonal preference. *Psychological Monographs,* 1966, **80** (616).

Stein, D. D., Hardyck, J. A., & Smith, M. B. Race and belief: An open and shut case. *Journal of Personality and Social Psychology,* 1965, **1,** 281–290.

Stember, C. H. Evaluating effects of the integrated classroom. *The Urban Review,* June 1968, **2,** 30–31.

Stouffer, S. A., Suchman, E. A., DeVinney, L. C., Star, S. A., & Williams, R. M., Jr. Studies in social psychology in World War II. Vol. 1, *The American soldier: Adjustment during army life.* Princeton, N. J.: Princeton University Press, 1949.

Triandis, H. C. A note on Rokeach's theory of prejudice. *Journal of Abnormal and Social Psychology,* 1961, **62,** 184–186.

Triandis, H. C., & Davis, E. E. Race and belief as determinants of behavioral intentions. *Journal of Personality and Social Psychology,* 1965, **2,** 715–725.

United States Commission on Civil Rights. *Civil rights USA: Public schools, southern states, 1962.* Washington, D. C.: U. S. Government Printing Office, 1963.

United States Commission on Civil Rights. *Racial isolation in the public schools.* Washington, D. C.: U. S. Government Printing Office, 1967.

U. S. Department of Labor and Commerce. *The social and economic status of Negroes in the United States, 1969.* Washington, D. C.: U. S. Government Printing Office, 1970.

Williams, R. M., Jr. *Strangers next door; Ethnic relations in American communities.* Englewood Cliffs, N. J.: Prentice-Hall, 1964.

Wilner, D. M., Walkley, R., & Cook, S. W. *Human relations in interracial housing; A study of the contact hypothesis.* Minneapolis: University of Minnesota Press, 1955.

Works, E. The prejudice-interaction hypothesis from the point of view of the Negro minority group. *American Journal of Sociology,* 1961, **67,** 47–52.

Yarrow, M. R. (Ed.) Interpersonal dynamics in a desegregation process. *Journal of Social Issues,* 1958, **14**(1), 3–63.

ARTICLE 14

Should we integrate organizations?

Dalmas Taylor

EQUAL-STATUS CONTACT HYPOTHESIS

Allport's (1954) equal-status hypothesis derives its conceptual support from the definition of prejudice as a negative attitude. In essence, it presumes that contact between the prejudiced and the objects of the prejudice will reduce the erroneous perceptions thought to be responsible for the prejudice. It is further assumed that this shift will lead to a positive change in attitude and, hopefully, a change in behavior. Heider's balance theory aids somewhat in the theoretical analysis of the possible effects of contact. Heider (1958) postulates unit relationships (things going together) and liking relationships. Contact with another person would establish a unit relationship. If a dislike relationship existed along with the unit relationship, imbalance would be created and pressures would develop to reduce the imbalance. This imbalance could be reduced by changing the liking relationship from dislike to like, producing the effect predicted by Allport's hypothesis. Alternatively, however, the unit relationship could be dissolved with no change in liking. In instances where the contact cannot be terminated, as in school integration, balance theory would predict increased liking as the only option possible. Dissonance theory, however, would make the opposite prediction. In dissonance theory, forced contact is not a condition that produces dissonance. As Brehm and Cohen (1962) note, volition is an important factor in the development of dissonance. Balance theory, then, would predict the result hypothesized by Allport could occur, but not necessarily. Exchange or reinforcement interpretations (Thibaut and Kelley, 1959; Homans, 1961) also bear on the equal-status contact hypothesis. Homans (1961) specifically suggests that if interaction is frequent, sentiments of liking will grow. However, this outcome will obviously be influenced by the rewards and costs in the situation, in which case there would certainly be occasions when liking would not be expected.

The literature on the relationship between proximity and attractiveness indicates that proximity (which increases contact) will lead to increasingly positive attitudes. Festinger, Schachter, and Back (1950), in a study of relationships within a housing project, found that individuals chose to associate with those with whom they were in close proximity and with whom they had the most opportunity to interact. Whyte (1956) found similar results in relationship to voluntary association (presumably based on attraction); those living close together related more than those who were more distant. In a laboratory study, Freedman, Carlsmith, and Suomi (1969) demonstrated that proximity effects are mediated, at least in part, by simple familiarity and that this produces more attraction. Subjects met and sat silently in the same room for differing numbers of sessions. The more frequently the subjects met, the greater their expressed liking for each other.

Proximity is related to attractiveness for several reasons. First, it is easier to interact with people who are close, and this ease positively reinforces the interaction. In addition, when two people are in proximity, there is more opportunity to exchange information, a condition which leads to increased similarity according to the theories of both Newcomb (1953) and Homans (1950). Newcomb points out that proximity increases attraction in two ways. First, proximity and the continued communication it entails increases similarity of beliefs and values. Secondly, with increased similarity, liking increases. Therefore, there appears to be ample theoretical justification for the conceptual validity of the contact hypothesis. Additionally, there is some empirical evidence that such contact can have a positive effect on attitudes.

A second assumption of the hypothesis, however, is that it is necessary for the contact to be on an equal-status level. Evidence on the relationship between perceived similarity and attraction or liking has relevance to the evaluation of this portion of the hypothesis. This analysis is based on the assumption that perceived similarity is greater in two people of equal status than of unequal status. Balance theory can again offer useful insights here. Balance theory would predict that equal status could produce increased attractiveness via perceived similarity. Balance theory notes that if Y is similar to X and Y dislikes X, imbalance and pressures to change are created. Balance may be restored by liking X. It is also clear, however, in line with the above analysis, that balance may also be restored by reducing the perceived similarity. Similarity is based on perception, and the perception can be distorted to achieve balance.

The importance of similarity in race relations is demonstrated by the research derived from Rokeach's belief congruence hypothesis, which argues that negative racial attitudes are based on the dissimilarity of beliefs assumed by whites. Whether belief is more important than race in determining prejudice is still an unclear issue, but the fact is that whites, if given no other information, assume that blacks hold different beliefs and that this is an influential factor in their negative attitudes toward blacks (Byrne and Wong, 1962; Rokeach and Mezei, 1966; Rokeach, Smith, and Evans, 1960; Triandis and Davis, 1965).

Newcomb's (1961) roommate study is the clearest indication of the general relationship between similarity and attractiveness. Newcomb found that roommates originally matched to be similar liked each other more than those who were dissimilar. In this study, the similarity clearly preceded the liking. However, qualification of the effects of similarity must be made in light of findings by Byrne and Wong (1962) and Byrne and McGraw (1964). These authors demonstrated that contact won't increase belief similarity in prejudiced people unless nearly complete similarity exists at the outset.

The importance of status, per se, has been stressed by attribution theorists. Kelley (1967), for example, notes that status has important implications for the type of attribution made, whether positive or negative, since status has implications for whether the behavior was externally or internally caused. Thibaut and Riecken (1955) demonstrated that an individual who complies with a request is liked more if he is of higher status than the person making the request, rather than if he is of lower status. A study such as this, while not dealing directly with equal status, does appear to have implications for equal-status association by showing how status affects the attribution of positive or negative traits. Since it is probably true that most whites have most of their contacts with black people of lower status, attribution of negative traits is most frequent in interpreting the behavior of blacks. Equal-status contact should, therefore, according to attribution theory, change the type of attribution made to black people in a more positive direction. It would appear, then, that research in the area of attribution provides support for the equal-status contact hypothesis.

It is also suggested that the sharing of common goals is essential for the contact to be successful. The requirement for cooperative interdependence, which is also an important aspect of the equal-status contact hypothesis, is closely related to the goal requirement; hence, the two will be treated together. The prediction of the positive effects of a common goal also receives conceptual support from balance theory. If A wants X (goal), B wants X, and A dislikes B, imbalance exists. This may be reduced by a shift in conditions such that A likes B. (Rejection of the goal by A would also restore balance.) Hence, once again balance theory would predict contact with cooperative interdependence and a common goal may result in increased liking, not that it necessarily will.

Reinforcement theory would predict that shared goals under cooperative interdependence should lead to increased liking. Association of another person with positive reinforcement, as would occur in cooperative interdependence, should create increased liking. A study by Festinger and Kelley (1951) demonstrates the potentially positive aspects of creating common goals and goals of a type which require cooperative interdependence for successful

achievement. These authors found that subjects who were involved in common goals showed reduced hostility for others who participated in and had favorable attitudes toward the endeavor. Both participation and favorable attitudes would appear to be necessary for the establishment of cooperative interdependence. This study, then, demonstrated the potential efficacy of common or shared goals and cooperative interdependence in the reduction of negative attitudes.

Sherif's studies (1936, 1966) are among the clearest indications that both common goals and cooperative interdependence are necessary for contact to work in the reduction of hostility. After creating conflict and negative attitudes between two groups of boys in a camp, Sherif attempted to reduce the conflict in a number of ways. The only successful method found was to bring the groups together (contact) to obtain something they both wanted (common goal) which they could obtain only by working together (cooperative interdependence).

Then the experimenters tried the equivalent of racial integration. They brought the two groups together for movies, meals, and other social events. But instead of serving to reduce hostility, the events merely provided added opportunity for the two groups to assail each other. Finally, a series of crises were arranged to force cooperation between the groups. For example, water came to the camp in pipes from a tank about a mile away. The experimenters arranged to interrupt it and then called the boys together to inform them of the crisis. Both groups promptly volunteered to search the water line for trouble. They worked together harmoniously, and before the end of the afternoon had located and corrected the difficulty. Similar joint endeavors in response to other experimentally created crises resulted in the cessation of hostility and other negative behaviors. Members of the two groups actively sought opportunities to mingle, entertain, and otherwise socialize with each other.

The general literature on similarity, status, contact, and cooperative interdependence strongly suggests that there is a rational basis for Allport's hypothesis, i.e., there is ample evidence to suggest that it *should* work. Yet, in terms of social policy and practice, there has been little encouragement from results. Concerted efforts in the areas of housing, employment, and education have failed to yield outcomes consistent with Allport's prediction.

The classic study by Deutsch and Collins (1951) examined similar housing projects in which the buildings were either integrated or segregated. In the integrated buildings, the authors found more contact and more positive attitudes toward blacks. This study provides fairly strong support for Allport's hypothesis. Stouffer et al. (1949) found that increased contact among soldiers led to decreased stereotyping, indicating once again the successful outcome of contact.

Other studies have not found such positive effects. A study by Campbell (1958) indicated that school desegregation which led to increased contact did indeed have a large effect on attitudes, but the effect operated in both directions, with attitudes not only becoming more positive in some individuals, but becoming more negative in others. Other studies have shown that integration may produce more positive attitudes but that the change is limited only to the situation in which the contact takes place and does not represent a more generalized improvement in attitudes toward the group which is the object of the prejudice (Harding and Hogrefe, 1952; Palmore, 1955). Webster (1961) found that whites' attitudes toward blacks became more negative after integration than they had been previously. Negative effects as a result of housing integration have also been found (Kramer, 1950; Hunt, 1959).

The research results appear to be far more negative than would be expected on the basis of the analysis of the general theoretical and empirical information on various subparts of the hypothesis. In addition, examination of the current social situation suggests that the effects of implementation of social policy in line with Allport's hypothesis have not been as successful as one would hope. Although some positive attitude change has probably taken place, racial tension and conflict are still widespread. In addition, there is evidence that attitudes in some instances have become more negative, e.g., the emotional nature of the busing issue.

Several reasons may be suggested for the failure to achieve as great an improvement in attitudes as expected. In the first case, the laws, while increasing contact, may not fulfill all the conditions of the hypothesis. School desegregation often involves bringing lower-class blacks into middle-class white schools. Additionally, it is not always clear whether or not common goals are involved in many of the situations involving integration. More profoundly, however, many of these situations fail to come to grips with the fact that prejudice is deeply rooted in the character structure of most whites. In this respect, the theoretical analysis of attitudes in terms of their functions has implications for the contact hypothesis.

The functional analysis of attitudes as set forth by Smith, Bruner, and White (1956) posits that there are three primary functions that an attitude can serve. The first is the *object-appraisal* function, which permits the individual to evaluate objects and people in order to obtain a stable picture of the world. The second function is the *social-adjustment* function, in which one's attitudes serve to guide behavior in a way that helps the individual to fit in with his social group. Attitudes serving these first two functions would appear to be amenable to change under conditions of the equal-status hypothesis. If the attitude created an incorrect perception of the world in its object-appraisal function, contact should reveal this error and produce attitude change. In addition, changes in the requirements of the social situation could be affected by increased contact leading to changes in attitudes serving the social-adjustment function. The third function is that of *externalization*, in which the attitude serves to solve personal and psychological problems of the individual. For example, an attitude may be formed which projects one's own unacceptable behavior onto the object of prejudice. Integration would not be likely to change attitudes serving this function, since the contact would not alleviate the individual problems underlying the attitude. It is unclear how widespread this function is in prejudiced attitudes, but to the extent that it exists it decreases the likelihood of contact leading to positive attitude change.

RACIALLY SEPARATE OR TOGETHER?

Pettigrew (1967; 1969) has argued that *only* through contract (integration) can the belief in inferiority and value dissimilarity be eliminated. He further suggests that any separation between the races simply increases forces which support prejudice—including institutional forces. The issues which Pettigrew brings to bear on this argument are delineated in a four-cell model whose dimensions are "contact-separation" and "autonomy" (see Figure 1). The four cells in this model are: Cell "A," true integration which includes institutionalized biracial situations with individual and group (biracial) autonomy; Cell "B," black power ghetto (hypothetical) independent of society; Cell "C," desegregated situations with little cross-racial acceptance; and Cell "D," today's urban ghetto with little or no personal or group autonomy. Pettigrew suggests that "black separatists" see only one route to integration: from the depressed ghetto to the hypothetical ghetto and then, perhaps, true integration (lines 1 and 2 in Fig-

ure 1); whereas desegregationists assume the opposite route: mere desegregation, then true integration (lines 3 and 4 in Figure 1). Pettigrew argues that the only approach to "true integration" is from Cell D directly to Cell A (line 5).

Since I take exception to this model and its hypothesized outcomes, I will discuss my objections in the context of observations already made and an alternative model (see Figure 2). The proposed model takes as its starting point the assertion that the "hypothetical black power ghetto" inadequately depicts the phenomenon which it was devised to explain. Additionally, integration as a strategy and integration as a goal, in the means-end sense, have always lacked conceptual distinction and clarity. Pettigrew's model suffers this same deficiency. Consider, for example:

> The overall *strategy* needed must contain the following elements: (a) A major effort toward racial integration must be mounted. . . . This effort should envisage by the late 1970's complete attainment of the goal . . . (b) . . . strict criteria must be applied to proposed enrichment programs to insure that they are productive for later dispersal and *integration* (Pettigrew, 1969, p. 64, italics added).

The proposed model in Figure 2 provides an analysis that hopefully clarifies this confusion; additionally, its logic evolves from concepts of racism

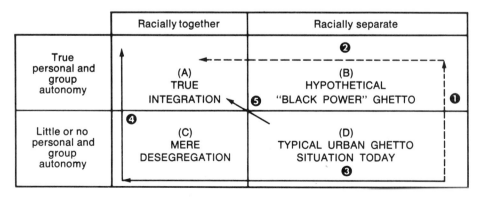

FIGURE 1.   Schematic Diagram of Autonomy and Contact-Separation. From T. F. Pettigrew, Racially separate or together? *Journal of Social Issues,* 1965, *25,* No. 1, 43–69; revised in 1969.
Note: Dotted lines denote hypothetical paths; solid lines, actual paths.

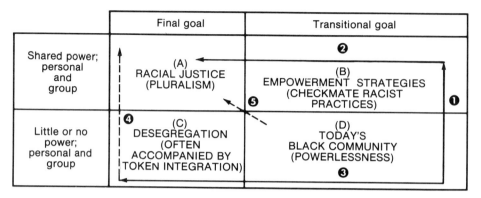

FIGURE 2.   Schematic Diagram of Power and Goals.
Note: Dotted lines denote paths with low probability of successful outcomes, and solid lines denote paths with a high probability of successful outcomes.

as discussed by Carmichael and Hamilton (1967) and Jones (1972). As indicated above, in the study by Sherif (1936; 1966), the validity of the equal-status contact hypothesis is contingent upon conditions of cooperative interdependence to achieve common goals. However, a precondition to equal status which neither Allport nor Pettigrew acknowledge is *power*. Accordingly, the model proposed here permits an examination of the relationship between power and the ultimate goal in race relations. In Cell "A" racial justice refers to inter-group harmony predicated on concepts of equity and fair play irrespective of racial identification; Cell "B" represents the category of strategies instrumental to achieving racial justice. The advantage here is that this conceptualization does not preclude multiple strategies, nor does it prejudge the character of any strategy. It also acknowledges that some *strategy* is necessary to move from today's situation (Cell D) to the desired goal (Cell A), a feature that is missing in Pettigrew's model. Furthermore, it obviates the usage of the provocative and misleading term "separatist." Cell "C" represents the all-too-familiar practice of desegregation, in which racial barriers are relaxed or substituted by token integration—rarely if ever involving the transmittal of power. Cell "D" typifies today's society, in which most blacks are economically deprived and

poorly educated—and powerless to alter these conditions.

Assuming agreement upon the final goal (Cell A), the proposed model in Figure 2 allows multiple strategies but only one route to that end. Movement to desegregation and then racial justice (lines 3 and 4) is virtually impossible, as is movement from today's black community to racial justice (line 5), since neither of these efforts comes to terms with the empowerment of blacks (and other minorities). Giving blacks equal education, equal employment, equal income, equal housing, and so on, will never lead to perceived equality in the eyes of whites, without the addition of power. Carmichael and Hamilton (1967) provide a rather detailed analysis of race relations in Tuskegee, Alabama, where blacks have achieved equal socioeconomic status with whites, but still suffer the ill effects of prejudice and discrimination.

The TCA (Tuskegee Civic Association) held a peculiar position in the black community. Not many people openly supported it (and many wished it would just quiet down), but they recognized that something was wrong with the one-way deferential relationship existing between the races in the community. They knew that it was incongruous for them to have economic and educational achievements and to remain at the political mercy of a white minority. It was, to say the least, embarrassing, and for this reason many black people never talked about it. They withdrew and let the TCA fight their political battles (p. 132).

When the political advantage of the whites became threatened by increases in black voters, whites persuaded the state legislature to pass a law gerrymandering the city of Tuskegee. The result was that only ten black voters were left in the city; no whites were touched by the gerrymandering.

The blacks had achieved education and economic security—both of which are still projected throughout the nation as cure-alls—but the whites continued to lay and collect taxes, rule over the school system, determine law enforcement practices. The reason is obvious enough: blacks did not have *political* power. Economic security or the promise of it may, as we noted in Chapter V, be vital to the building of a strong political force. But in a vacuum it is of no use to black people working for meaningful change (p. 134).

In light of these events, it seems naive to argue that integration, per se, is the solution to the nation's ills. White liberals have always supported an integrated society as a solution to racial problems. The unchallengeable, overriding goal has been integration. The end was critically considered, means were not; yet, integration has become the means. In fact, the commitment to that particular strategy is so ingrained that it freezes or restricts the ability to explore constructive alternatives when considering solutions to racial problems. Blacks have pursued integration strategies by seeking coalitions with the white power structure, rich and upper-class whites, philanthropists, entrepreneurs, middle-class white progressives (liberals), poor whites, and finally radical whites. In all cases, these efforts have met with failure, primarily because (1) internal power relations between blacks and whites were never resolved, (2) hidden conflicts between the interests of poor blacks and middle-class whites were never resolved, and finally, (3) the latent racism of whites has never been adequately confronted.

The 1960s witnessed a crystallization of these issues accompanied by a metamorphosis on the part of many blacks, including members of the black middle class who had separated from their community, divorced themselves from any responsibility to it, yet never gained acceptance by the white community. This marginal class (see E. Franklin Frazier's *Black Bourgeoisie*) is the best evidence of the failure of integration to produce the goals characterized by Cell A in the model in Figure 2.

In a recent issue of *Operations Research*, Ackoff (1970) describes a model that is a fair approximation of the strategy implied in Cell B (Figure 2). Along with two colleagues, Ackoff developed an untried approach to university aid to the ghetto. It is the assumption behind this approach that is of paramount importance, however: *the best way the white community can help the black community is to enable it to solve its problems in the way it, the black community, wants to*. Therefore, leadership selected from the black community submitted a proposal, which was funded by the Anheuser-Busch Charitable Trust and the Ford Foundation, for $50,000 per year for two years. From this beginning, nine manufacturing firms that grossed more than 1.5 million dollars in 1969 and employed 125 people from the community were established. Through university aid, loans from banks have been secured that have enabled the start-up of additional businesses, including technical and managerial assistance. A credit union which permits community individuals to join for only 25 cents was also established to permit personal loans. The university has developed a program in business education for the disadvantaged in the area, scholarships to private suburban schools have been secured, and an Urban Leadership Training Program has been established.

At the time of his article, Ackoff indicated that the leadership in the black community had established their independence from outer influence. Yet their planning required a sensitivity to potential sources of resources from the larger society of which the black community is a part. This undoubtedly required a skillful utilization of power in bringing about ends compatible with aspirations of the black community and yet not compromising their independence. In conclusion, Ackoff indicates that these ghetto leaders have as an ultimate objective the dissolution of the ghetto by having it absorbed into the main current of the culture of which it is a part.

It is with this final conclusion that I would take some exception. One of my key objections to integration per se is that it typically represents an absorption of the black community—culture, values, and all. The implications of such an outcome are psychologically negative. Implicit in such a process is the indication that blackness is inferior and offers nothing of value—or nothing worth preserving.

Black power advocates represent the most encompassing challenge to these psychologically negative dynamics. Before he died, Whitney Young wrote: ''Black power is not a shout of separation. Black power simply means . . . look at me . . . I'm here. I have dignity. I have pride. I have roots. I insist, I demand that I participate in those decisions that affect my life, and the lives of my children. It means that I'm somebody and that's what Black *power* [italics added] means.''

A model that can be cited as an example of these dynamics in action was developed within the context of the Unitarian-Universalist Church. In May, 1968, the Unitarian-Universalist Association, at its General Assembly, voted to fund a Black Affairs Council $250,000 a year for four years. These monies are administered solely by blacks, with no strings, in support of innovation within black communities leading to growth in (1) education, (2) economic development, and (3) political empowerment. Through this funding mechanism, curriculum development and special seminars related to the black community have been supported at major educational institutions; a model of economic development which fosters community control and ownership has been initiated through projects in Newark, New Jersey, and Washington, D.C.; finally, notable examples of political empowerment derive from input to the Committee for a Unified Newark, whose voter registration and educational programs created the atmosphere which enabled the election of Mayor Kenneth Gibson. Similar support and involvement with the National Democratic Party of Alabama witnessed its most dramatic success in Green County, Alabama, where the successful challenge to local voting procedures resulted in a majority of blacks being elected to county office— for the first time in the South!

In summary, it is my contention that the most urgent and pressing task facing the managers of today's organizations is to explore ways of creating avenues for the empowerment of neglected minorities. Any careful analysis of organizations would point both to advantages and oppressive outcomes associated with power. Unfortunately, rarely is power shared or transferred without confrontation and struggle. In that light, one of the most useful functions this volume could serve would be to facilitate managers' awareness of the wisdom in sharing and/or relinquishing power gracefully. It is clear to me that black empowerment cannot be realized without the development of new approaches among whites in dealing with their institutions and new modes and models of relationships between blacks and whites.

Only those who have already experienced a revolution within themselves can reach out effectively to help others.

Malcolm X

REFERENCES

Ackoff, R. L. A black ghetto's research on a university. *Operations Research,* Sept.–Oct., 1970, *18,* 761–771.

Allport, G. W. *The nature of prejudice.* Reading, Mass.: Addison-Wesley, 1954.

Brehm, J. W., and Cohen, A. R. *Explorations in cognitive dissonance.* New York: Wiley, 1962.

Byrne, D., and McGraw, C. Interpersonal attraction toward Negroes. *Human Relations,* 1964, *17,* 201–213.

Byrne, D., and Wong, T. J. Racial prejudice, interpersonal attraction and assumed dissimilarity of attitudes. *Journal of Abnormal and Social Psychology,* 1962, *65,* 246–253.

Campbell, E. Q. Some social psychological correlates of direction in attitude change. *Social Forces,* 1958, *36,* 335–340.

Carmichael, S., and Hamilton, C. V. *Black power: The politics of liberation in America.* New York: Vintage Books, 1967.

Deutsch, M., and Collins, A. E. *Interracial housing.* Minneapolis: University of Minnesota Press, 1951.

Festinger, L., and Kelley, H. H. *Changing attitudes through social contact.* Ann Arbor: University of Michigan, Institute of Social Research, 1951.

Festinger, L., Schachter, S., and Back, K. *Social pressures in informal groups: A study of human factors in housing.* New York: Harper, 1950.

Frazier, E. F. *Black bourgeoisie.* Glencoe, Ill.: Free Press, 1957.

Freedman, J. L., Carlsmith, J. M., and Suomi, S. The effect of familiarity on liking. Unpublished paper, Stanford University, 1969.

Harding, J., and Hogrefe, R. Attitudes of white department store employees toward negro co-workers. *Journal of Social Issues,* 1952, *8,* 18–28.

Heider, F. *The psychology of interpersonal relations.* New York: Wiley, 1958.

Homans, G. C. *Social behavior: Its elementary forms.* New York: Harcourt, 1961.

Homans, G. C. *The human group.* New York: Harcourt, 1950.

Hunt, C. L. Private integrated housing in a medium sized Northern city. *Social Problems,* 1959, *7,* 195–209.

Jones, J. M. *Prejudice and racism.* Reading, Mass.: Addison-Wesley, 1972.

Kelley, H. H. Attribution theory in social psychology. *Nebraska Symposium on Motivation,* 1967, *15,* 192–238.

Kramer, B. M. Residential contact as a determinant of attitudes toward negroes. Unpublished paper, Harvard College Library, 1950.

Newcomb, T. M. An approach to the study of communicative acts. *Psychological Review,* 1953, *60,* 393–404.

Palmore, E. B. The introduction of negroes into white departments. *Human Organizations,* 1955, *14,* 27–28.

Pettigrew, T. F. Racially separate or together? *Journal of Social Issues,* 1969, *25,* 43–69.

Pettigrew, T. F. Social evaluation theory: convergences and applications. In D. Levine (ed.), *Nebraska symposium on motivation.* Lincoln, Neb., University of Nebraska Press, 1967.

Rokeach, M., and Mezei, L. Race and shared belief as factors in social choice. *Science,* 1966, *151,* 167–172.

Rokeach, M., Smith, P. W., and Evans, R. I. *Two* kinds of prejudice or one? In M. Rokeach (ed.), *The open and closed mind.* New York: Basic Books, 1960.

Sherif, M. *In common predicament.* Boston: Houghton Mifflin, 1966.

Sherif, M. *The psychology of social norms.* New York: Harper, 1936.

Smith, M. B., Bruner, J., and White, R. W. *Opinions and personality.* New York: Wiley, 1956.

Stouffer, S. A., Suchman, E. A., Devinney, C. C., Star, S. A., and Williams, R. M., Jr. Adjustment during army life. In *Studies in social psychology in World War II.* Vol. I: *The American Soldier.* Princeton, N. J.: Princeton University Press, 1949.

Thibaut, J. W., and Kelley, H. H. *The social psychology of groups.* New York: Wiley, 1959.

Thibaut, J. W., and Riecken, H. W. Some determinants and consequences of the perception of social causality. *Journal of Personality,* 1955, *24,* 113–133.

Triandis, H. C., and Davis, E. E. Race and belief as determinants of behavioral intentions. *Journal of Personality and Social Psychology,* 1965, *2,* 715–725.

Webster, S. W. The influence of interracial contact on social acceptance in a newly integrated school. *Journal of Educational Psychology,* 1961, *52,* 292–296.

Whyte, W. H., Jr. *The organization man.* New York: Simon and Schuster, 1956.

ARTICLE 15

Effect of prior "token" compliance on subsequent interracial behavior[1]

Donald G. Dutton
Vicki Lea Lennox

In a pair of field studies, Dutton (1971, 1973) has demonstrated a reverse-discrimination effect where majority group members (usually whites) behave more favorably to racial minority group members than they do to other whites in the same situation. Various conditions must be met before this phenomenon occurs: *(a)* The whites involved must want to think of themselves as persons who do not discriminate on a racial basis, *(b)* they must be interacting with others whom they recognize as belonging to a group that has been discriminated against, and *(c)* the situation must be one with legitimate reasons for behaving unfavorably to the other persons involved (Dutton, 1973). It is assumed that under such conditions, egalitarian whites attempt to avoid cues from their own behavior which imply that they might be racially discriminating against the minority group member. One form of avoidance might be to comply with the demands this person makes. When the demands occur in a situation where they have only a moderate probability of being granted to another white (such as panhandling), reverse discrimination may be demonstrated as a difference in compliance rates to the minority and white requests. Previous studies have found: *(a)* higher admission rates to restaurants for improperly dressed blacks compared to improperly dressed whites (Dutton, 1971), *(b)* higher donation rates to a charity when soliciting was done by a black or by a native Indian than when it was done by a white (Dutton, 1973), and *(c)* higher donation rates to a black panhandler than to a white panhandler by subjects who had previously been led to believe that they might be prejudiced (Dutton & Lake, 1973).

This latter finding confirmed the hypothesis that avoidance of threat to the egalitarian self-image was an underlying motive for high compliance rates to minority group members in interaction situations.

Reprinted from the *Journal of Personality and Social Psychology,* 1974, *29,* 65–71. Copyright 1974 by the American Psychological Association. Reprinted by permission.

[1] This research was supported by Canada Council Grant S71-1548 and University of British Columbia Research Committee Grant 26-9672 to the first author.

Through the use of a false autonomic feedback technique (Valins, 1966) to subjects viewing interracial slides, Dutton and Lake (1973) led one group of subjects (high threat) to believe that they gave physiological evidence of possible underlying prejudices toward blacks. Using the same technique, a low-threat group was led to believe that they possessed no such prejudices. Subsequently, all subjects were panhandled by a confederate outside the laboratory. When the panhandler was black, subjects donated 47.25¢ and 16.75¢ in the high-threat and low-threat conditions, respectively ($p < .001$). When the panhandler was white, high-threat and low-threat subjects donated 28.25¢ and 27.75¢, respectively (ns). These results were interpreted as representing an attempt by the threatened subjects who were panhandled by the black to prove to themselves through their behavior that they were not prejudiced despite their prior physiological reactions. Compliance to the requests of the black panhandler provided a way of reestablishing an egalitarian self-image that was inexpensive in that it did not require long-term behavior from the subject. Conversely, when subjects were not threatened, the white panhandler received a significantly higher donation than the black panhandler. This latter finding suggested that when the egalitarian self-image is reconfirmed, motivation to engage in subsequent reconfirming behaviors is diminished.

All of the request-compliance situations investigated in previous studies of reverse discrimination have been "trivial" in nature; that is, they have been of short-term duration and have involved no reduction of social emotional distance between the subject and the person making the request. The aim of the present study was to examine the consequences of compliance in such trivial situations on subsequent compliance in situations requiring more long-term effort and commitment on behalf of the whites involved. If compliance by whites to interracial requests in long-term situations is also partially motivated by a desire to establish an egalitarian self-image and if this motive can be satisfied by compliance in short-term interracial interractions, then such "token" compliance may reduce compliance in subsequent long-term behavioral commitment situations. Interaction with blacks provides the white person with a source of behavioral cues about himself. A white who wants to believe he is egalitarian (or free of racial prejudice) can obtain cues which verify this self-image by complying with requests made by a minority group member. On the other hand, the refusal of such requests carries the implication of possible prejudice, even when the reasons for refusal are not based on the racial membership of the person making the request. Hence, a person may refuse a panhandler for a variety of reasons, but if that panhandler is black, a racially based reason may lead to the inference that the requests of the black were refused because the white person involved is racially prejudiced. To avoid this inference, pressures are created on the would-be egalitarian white to comply to the black's request. Once this request is granted, however, the white may have efficiently "proved" to himself that he is egalitarian. Hence, he may feel a reduced need to comply to a subsequent long-term request. A white who has not had an opportunity to prove his egalitarianism to himself in the trivial interaction situation should still possess this motive for compliance in the subsequent long-term situation and hence should show a greater willingness to comply. Thus, it was predicted that white subjects who want to think of themselves as prejudice free, and who are given an opportunity to comply to a request from a black in a trivial interaction situation, are less likely to demonstrate subsequent compliance to a request for long-term aid than are a similar group of subjects who are not given the opportunity for prior token compliance.

To allow for assessment of the main hypothesis, three experimental groups were run in the present study. All three groups received threat that they might be prejudiced, using false autonomic feedback techniques. Such threat provided a motive for subsequent interracial compliance (Dutton & Lake, 1973). Three trivial compliance groups were then created by having subjects, who had left the laboratory, either panhandled by a black male, a white male, or not panhandled at all. The white control group ensured that only *interracial* compliance led to a subsequent decrease in long-term aid. This long-term-aid opportunity was provided by requesting all subjects at a later date, to donate time to an interracial "brotherhood" campaign. Compliance to this relatively long-term behavioral commitment constituted the dependent variable of this study. The main hypothesis predicted that subjects panhandled by a black would commit themselves to *less* effort on the campaign than subjects who were not panhandled. Subjects panhandled by a white do not satisfy the hypothesized motives for interracial compliance and hence should not demonstrate the same decrease in long-term commitment. Indeed, a previous study by Freedman and Fraser (1966) showed that the elicitation of a small request from a subject led to greater compliance to a subsequent "larger request" than could be obtained from subjects who had not been asked to make the prior, smaller compliance. To the extent that the white panhandler condition in the present study resembled the conditions of the Freedman and Fraser study, one might expect increased compliance to the long-term request, as compared to the nonpanhandled group. Finally, to assess the effect on long-term compliance of the threat treatment itself, a control group who received no prior threat treatment or panhandling also received the brotherhood campaign request.

METHOD

Overview

This experiment involved five phases: *(a)* measurement of subjects' values, attitudes, and beliefs about minority groups, *(b)* establishment of credibility for autonomic feedback provided to subjects in the laboratory, *(c)* creation of threat for subjects through manipulated autonomic feedback, *(d)* creation of experimental groups through panhandling treatment, and *(e)* collection of dependent variable data, that is, the amount of effort donated by the subjects under threat conditions.

Subjects

Two hundred and fifty undergraduate students from eight classes at a college in Vancouver were given a social attitude scale during the spring term of 1972. From these students, 100 subjects (50 males and 50 females) were chosen who *(a)* rated equality as an important value, *(b)* rated themselves between 0 and 10 on a scale where 0 = no prejudice and 100 = great deal of prejudice, and *(c)* rated themselves as less prejudiced than Canadian college students in general. These subjects were then randomly assigned to a control group or one of three experimental groups (12 males, 13 females for two groups and 12 females, 13 males for two groups).

Procedure

Four weeks after initial contact, the subjects in the three experimental groups were telephoned and asked to participate in a laboratory study of voluntary control of autonomic behavior. Each subject was offered a Can$2 fee for participating in the study.

On arriving at the laboratory, the subject was seated in a waiting room and provided with a copy of an article on autonomic control (Lang, 1970) to read. On entering the laboratory, the subject was given an elaborate explanation of the experiment stressing that autonomic control was possible so long as a person had access to feedback about autonomic processes. The subject was told that the present experiment was examining the effects of various forms of feedback on autonomic control and that he was in a group that would receive galvanic skin response (GSR) and pulse rate feedback as they viewed a series of slides. Electrodes which led to an array of polygraph equipment were connected to the subject. Immediately in front of the subject was a GSR dial showing needle deflections. Pulse rate was transmitted to the subject by a tone signal. The measurement techniques were explained to the subject, and each subject was told how an emotional reaction to any particular slide would lead to an increase in pulse and deflection on the GSR meter. The subject was instructed to look at each slide and then to carefully observe the meter and listen to the pulse tone and then to concentrate on decreasing both the pulse rate and the GSR deflection for that particular slide.

The experimenter then stationed himself behind the polygraph equipment and out of sight of the subject "to record your responses" and proceeded to show the slide series. Series 1 contained five neutral slides and five arousal slides. The neutral slides were pictures of everyday objects (i.e., bottles, books, etc., sitting on a table). The arousal slides were color slides of homicide victims graphically depicting the wounds which the victim had received. Each subject was given feedback on the arousal slides that led him to believe he was responding strongly (e.g., noticeable pulse tone increases and GSR meter deflections). No such feedback was given on the neutral slides. The experimenter then repeated the entire series of slides, lowering the arousal feedback slightly on the arousal slides. At this stage, the subject was asked if he had any questions about what had just happened before the experimenter proceeded.

The experimenter now gave the subject further instructions which indicated that the subject would now view a second set of slides of "social scenes." These instructions stated:

Social situations also can provide intense reactions in people such as hatred, prejudice, etc. Sometimes these emotional reactions are buried or repressed because of their unacceptability to a person; however, the physiological representation of the reaction remains. Many psychologists feel that autonomic responses are the truest measures of underlying reactions that we hold about social groups and situations. In the slides you are about to see, some situations and social groups are pictured that you may hold negative attitudes about. If this is so, then the pulse tone and GSR needle will register your reactions just as they did with the other set of slides.

The subject was then told that the experimenter was again interested in the subject's ability to control his or her autonomic responses to these slides.

The subject then saw a set of slides depicting *(a)* three scenes of white riot police beating white students, *(b)* two scenes of sexual intercourse involving a white male and female, *(c)* four interracial scenes (black-white), three of which showed interracial couples and one which showed black children and white children playing together, and *(d)* some neutral scenes of people picnicking, etc. Since such a wide variety of scenes were used, the subject could not have known that the experimenter specifically expected a strong reaction on interracial scenes.

Subjects were given high arousal feedback to the riot and sexual scenes on first viewing. They were also given high arousal feedback to interracial scenes on first viewing. No arousal feedback to neutral scenes was given. On second viewing, arousal feedback to the riot and sexual scenes was slightly diminished, but not to the interracial scenes.

At this point the experimenter disconnected the subject from the electrodes, asked for questions, and signed a "payment for subject" sheet for the subject, which he instructed the subject to take to a psychology department secretary in another part of the building "who is the only one allowed to disburse payment for this study." The experimenter then thanked the subject for participation and advised the subject to collect payment right away since the secretary would be taking a lunch (or coffee) break in about 15 minutes.

When the subject left the laboratory, the experimenter phoned the secretary to notify her that the subject was on his way. The secretary then stepped on a button (located unobtrusively under her desk) which activated a buzzer in another room where a confederate who was to act as a panhandler was situated. From this room, the confederate could see people leaving and entering the secretary's office while not being seen himself. When the subject entered the secretary's office, she buzzed the confederate twice. The confederate then knew that the last person to enter the secretary's office before the buzz was his "target" to be panhandled and left the room and took a position down the hall from the secretary's office. Meanwhile, the secretary spent about one minute looking for the "receipt sheet" for the subject to sign (thus allowing the confederate time to take his position). When the subject signed the sheet, the secretary apologized, saying that all she had left was quarters and would the subject mind taking quarters as payment? This ploy ensured that each subject would, in fact, have some change to give the panhandler. When the subject left the secretary's office he was greeted by the confederate who (a) asked him where a hypothetical room was located and (b) said "Can you spare some change for some food?" The confederate was told to ask the subject only once and if the subject said "How much?" he was to respond with "Whatever you can spare." The confederate, although aware of the experimental hypothesis, did not know what treatment group any subject had been in. Hence, motivation to prove the experimenter's hypothesis could not affect nonverbal transmission of demands (e.g., maintaining eye contact longer with certain subjects).

Two days later, all students in the eight classes which originally served as the subject pool were informed by their instructor that on behalf of a "Brotherhood Society" on campus, he was going to distribute forms requesting students to donate time to a "Brotherhood Week" campaign emphasizing interracial tolerance and good will. These commitment forms contained a short message from the hypothetical organization asking for volunteers and eight possible activities for which the subject could volunteer. These forms had previously been given to 50 students who had been asked to rank each item on a scale of difficulty. The mean ranking for each item was then taken and the items arranged in order, ranging from those requiring little effort to those requiring the most effort. Forms filled out by subjects in the three experimental groups and the control groups were separated from the others and the raw data analyzed. Subjects in all four groups were contacted as soon as possible after the collection of these data and were debriefed.

RESULTS

Check on the Manipulation of Threat

The effectiveness of the threat manipulation was measured first by using a pretest group of subjects who were assigned to the high-threat and low-threat conditions. High-threat subjects rated their "degree of upset" significantly higher than low-threat subjects ($t = 4.2, df = 20, p < .01$). In addition, interviews were conducted with each pretest subject to ensure that threat of being prejudiced was indeed the cause of feeling upset rather than some other aspect of the threat manipulation. Sixteen of 20 subjects in the high-threat group spontaneously offered this reason as the cause of their upset.

No manipulation checks were administered to experimental subjects at the termination of the laboratory segment of the experiment. First, the experimenters felt confident that the manipulation would be effective on the basis of the Dutton and Lake (1973) successful manipulation and because of the success with the current pretest subjects. Also, it was felt that such a strategy might make subjects suspicious that they were not in an experiment in autonomic control but instead were participating in a study that had something to do with racial attitudes. Thus, only after they were debriefed were experimental subjects asked, "How threatened were you by the possibility that you might be prejudiced?" at the end of the laboratory section of the experiment. The average rating by subjects in the threat condition was 82 on a 100-point scale where 100 = extremely threatened, 75 = quite threatened, 50 = somewhat threatened, and 0 = not threatened. Low-threat subjects in the Dutton and Lake (1973) study had made a mean rating of 37 on this scale which differed significantly from the ratings of high-threat subjects in that experiment. Thus, despite a less than optimal measure of the threat manipulation for experimental subjects, the effectiveness of the manipulation procedure does not seem questionable.

Donations to Panhandlers

Twenty-one of the 25 subjects solicited by the black panhandler donated some money. Thirteen of the 25 subjects solicited by the white panhandler donated some money. Thus, a higher percentage of subjects donated to blacks ($x^2 = 5.8$, $p < .02$). Average donations were 68.2¢ to the black panhandler and 35.6¢ to the white panhandler ($t = 8.02$, $df = 24$, $p = .01$). Every subject who was solicited was included in the analysis of the results of the commitment request.

Scale Ratings

Prior to administering the commitment forms to experimental subjects, 50 undergraduates from the same college as the experimental subjects rated each of the eight activities on the scale for difficulty. These ratings were made on a 100-point scale where 0 = extremely easy and 100 = extremely difficult. The mean difficulty ratings assigned to the activities are listed in Table 1.

Compliance to the Commitment Request

Scores for experimental subjects were computed by adding the difficulty ratings of each activity to which they committed themselves on the commitment form. Hence, a subject who checked Items 1 and 2 would receive a total of 20 points. Table 2 shows mean commitment levels for subjects in each group.

Comparisons of relevant means were made using Dunn's multiple-comparison procedure (Kirk, 1968, p. 79). This procedure has an advantage over a one-way analysis of variance in that it allows all planned comparisons among treatment means to be made, whether orthogonal or not. This is done by splitting up an alpha level among a set of comparisons in any proportion (depending upon the undesirability of Type 1 errors for each comparison). The test yields a critical difference statistic (d) based on

TABLE 1. Mean difficulty ratings assigned to commitment form activities by nonexperimental subjects

Activity	Rating
1. Post 100 notices on campus prior to Brotherhood Week.	8
2. Address and seal envelopes one afternoon in student center.	12
3. Post 100 notices around town prior to Brotherhood Week.	22
4. Phone 25 people to be volunteers.	37
5. Help at Organizational Meeting one evening.	51
6. Canvass on campus for 10 hours during week previous to Brotherhood Week.	72
7. Work in booth in student center for 10 hours during Brotherhood Week.	88
8. Canvass in town 5 hours a week for 4 weeks prior to Brotherhood Week.	94

TABLE 2. Average difficulty of activities committed to on the commitment form by subjects in the four groups

Control group	Experimental group		
	Black panhandler condition	No-panhandler condition	White panhandler condition
17.9	31.8	46.2	54.8

alpha, the degrees of freedom for mean square error, and the number of comparisons made. Any difference between means which exceeds the d value can then be considered significant at the appropriate alpha level.

The ds for the dependent variable data were 13.7 (for alpha set at .05) and 17.0 (for alpha set at .01), with a df of 3/96. Hence, it may be seen from Table 2 that the threatened group panhandled by a black committed themselves to significantly more than the control group receiving the commitment request only (d = 13.9, p < .05). However, the threatened group panhandled by a black committed themselves to significantly less than the threatened group which was not panhandled (d = 14.4, p < .05). Finally, the threatened group panhandled by a white tended to commit themselves to more than the threatened nonpanhandled group, but this difference was not significant ($d = 8.6$, ns).

Table 3 shows the mean commitment scores for subjects who either did or did not comply to the initial request from the panhandler. In the black panhandler condition, only four subjects failed to comply with the initial request. Of these, two refused any commitment to the brotherhood campaign and two committed to the least effortful activity. Hence, the mean commitment score for this group was only 4.0. By contrast, those subjects who did comply to the black panhandler had an average commitment score of 37.1 ($t = 2.81$, $df = 23$, $p < .05$, one-tailed). In the white panhandler condition, subjects who complied to the initial request had a mean commitment of 61.3, and those who did not initially comply, 47.8 ($t = 2.06$, $df = 23$, $p < .05$, one-tailed).

TABLE 3. Commitment scores for subjects who did or did not comply to the panhandler's request

Experimental group	n	$\overline{X}$ commitment score
Black panhandler condition		
Did comply	21	37.1
Did not comply	4	4.0
White panhandler condition		
Did comply	13	61.3
Did not comply	12	47.8

DISCUSSION

The main hypothesis of this study was confirmed. The opportunity to comply to a small request by a black served to make subjects who were threatened by the possibility that they might be prejudiced less likely to comply with a subsequent request for relatively long-term aid to an interracial organization. It might be that token compliance to the first request helps reestablish the egalitarian self-concept that subjects desired and which had been disconfirmed by the threat manipulation. This token compliance "freed" these subjects from the pressure created by the threat manipulation (e.g., that they might be prejudiced). The threatened nonpanhandled subjects could only relieve this pressure through greater compliance with the "long-term commitment" demands. Unfortunately, this explanation leaves an important question unanswered. If subjects in the group panhandled by a black could satisfy themselves that they were not prejudiced by merely donating money to a black, why did threatened nonpanhandled subjects have to go to such great lengths to do the same? Why, for example, could they not achieve the same result as the panhandled subjects by committing themselves to post 100 notices on campus? It could be that the verbal request made by the teacher in class may have been partially responsible for the high compliance rate. This request suggested that normally most people agreed to the easier items and stressed the need for people to perform the more difficult items. Although the effect of this request was not overwhelming with nonthreatened subjects whose mean commitment rate was only 17.9, it may have interacted with prior threat to produce substantial commitment. Perhaps, threatened nonpanhandled subjects had to perceive themselves as doing something more for blacks than the ordinary person in order to perceive their behavior as indicating an absence of prejudice. Of course, since subjects in all four groups received the same request from the same person at the same time, the content or manner of delivery cannot account for differences between groups.

The threat treatment itself led subjects to commit themselves to more activities than nonthreatened subjects. This is consistent with previous studies (Dutton, 1971; Dutton & Lake, 1973) and suggests once again that information inconsistent with an ideal self-image may motivate a person to attempt to reestablish that self-image through his behavior. As pointed out in Dutton (1973), publicity given to injustices suffered by racial minority groups may sensitize would-be egalitarian whites so that cues from their behavior in interactions with these minority group members may themselves carry the "threat" of prejudice. So if, for example, a white denies the requests of a person whom he recognizes as belonging to a racial minority that has suffered discrimination, he is faced with the possibility that his own behavior may represent yet another instance of that discrimination. For a would-be egalitarian, such a possibility may be regarded as threatening to his ideal self-image.

The present study is also relevant to the more general question of the effect of prior compliance to a small request on subsequent compliance to a larger request. Freedman and Fraser (1966) found that such prior compliance increased compliance to the subsequent request even when the latter was made three days after the prior request and by a different person than the initial requester. In some ways, the white panhandler condition in the present study fits the requirement for this ''foot-in-the-door'' phenomenon described by Freedman and Fraser. In both studies, subjects received a small initial request and a subsequent larger request. The commitment mean of the group panhandled by a white (54.8) in the present study does not, however, differ significantly from the nonpanhandled group mean (46.2). However, before it is concluded that this constitutes a disconfirmation of the foot-in-the-door hypothesis, several points should be considered. First, all subjects in the present experiment were given a laboratory threat treatment that was absent for Freedman and Fraser's subjects. Although the threat treatment is of diminished relevance in making a comparison of the group panhandled by a white and the nonpanhandled group, it nevertheless introduces a new element that makes direct comparison of the present study with the Freedman and Fraser study more difficult. Second, the initial request made by the white panhandler in the present study had only a 52% probability of being granted (compared to a 66% compliance rate to the initial request in the Freedman and Fraser study). As with the Freedman and Fraser study, subjects who re-fused the first request showed low compliance rates on the second commitment request (see Table 3). Hence, the commitment rate for the group panhandled by a white as a whole is lowered, making it more similar to the commitment rate for the non-panhandled group.

The highest commitment rates (61.3) were obtained from subjects who were panhandled by a white and complied. This raises the possibility that a recent contribution to a white may accentuate the threat to one's self-image brought about by refusing to contribute to a black or to a black cause.[2] One could conceivably excuse a refusal to contribute to a black to a principle of not donating rather than to racial discrimination. Recent compliance to a white makes this excuse less plausible. Data consistent with this notion were obtained by Dutton (1971).

REFERENCES

Dutton, D. G. Reactions of restaurateurs to blacks and whites violating restaurant dress regulations. *Canadian Journal of Behavioural Science*, 1971, **3**, 298.

Dutton, D. G. The relationship of amount of perceived discrimination toward a minority group on behaviour of majority group members. *Canadian Journal of Behavioural Science*, 1973, **5**, 34–45.

Dutton, D. G., & Lake, R. A. Threat of own prejudice and reverse discrimination in interracial situations. *Journal of Personality and Social Psychology*, 1973, **28**, 94–100.

Freedman, J. L., & Fraser, S. C. Compliance without pressure: The foot-in-the-door technique. *Journal of Personality and Social Psychology*, 1966, **4**, 195–202.

Lang, P. J. Autonomic control or learning to play the internal organs. *Psychology Today*, 1970, **4**(5), 37.

Valins, S. Cognitive effects of false heart-rate feedback. *Journal of Personality and Social Psychology*, 1966, **4**, 400–408.

[2] We are indebted to Charles Kiesler for raising this point.

SECTION SUMMARY

Both Pettigrew and Taylor are concerned with ways of reducing the overall levels of prejudice, hostility, and discrimination between ethnic groups that characterize many areas of present-day society. They agree that the condition of "mere desegregation," in which minority-group members have little or no autonomy or power, is not desirable. But they disagree on the best way to proceed from our present situation of minority powerlessness, lack of autonomy, and separation. Pettigrew argues that the most promising route to "true integration" is the direct one, involving a "mixed integration-enrichment strategy," avoiding the possible intermediate steps of "mere desegregation" or the "hypothetical Black Power ghetto." He proposes that such a direct route is *not* impossible; it just hasn't been tried yet.

Taylor, on the other hand, deplores Pettigrew's attention to the "provocative and misleading" concept of separatism and argues instead for the importance of *empowerment strategies*. In the Section Introduction we outlined those characteristics of *equal-status contact* that may lead to reductions in prejudice and hostility between groups, and both Pettigrew and Taylor review some of the evidence illustrating this effect. But Taylor argues that power is a necessary *precondition* for equal status—that without the addition of power, giving Blacks equal education, employment, income, housing, and so forth will never lead to perceived equality in the eyes of Whites. And without perceived equality, equal-status contact may not be possible.

The most clear-cut demonstration of the possible beneficial effects of equal-status contact comes from a long-term study carried out by Cook (1970). Cook created an experimental situation that met the six criteria for a successful interracial contact situation outlined in the Section Introduction. The situation involved three college students—a Black woman, an unprejudiced White woman, and a prejudiced White woman—and two experimenters,

one Black and one White. The first two women were actually experimental confederates, and the prejudiced woman was the only real subject. The experiment consisted of a complex task that continued for two hours a day for four weeks. The results of this long-term study are encouraging. About 40% of the subjects had changed their racial attitudes to a large degree (more than one standard deviation on three separate attitude measures) when they were measured in a completely different setting a month or more after the interracial contact had ended.

Cook also attempted to see whether personality factors could account for the fact that some women drastically changed their attitudes in this situation while other women did not. It was found that a group of measures assessing positive attitudes toward people (low cynicism and low anomie) effectively differentiated the "changers" from the "nonchangers" (Wrightsman & Cook, 1967). The women who became significantly less prejudiced were those who had the most positive attitudes toward people. In addition, the changers also tended to have a higher need for social approval and lower self-esteem than nonchangers. These last two measures probably serve as indices of general "persuasibility."

Subsequent research involving interracial groups in the military has indicated that success on a group task leads to increased liking among *all* group members, Black and White (Blanchard, Adelman, & Cook, 1975), and that the perceived competence of the Black member of the group was of major importance in determining the Whites' reactions to him (Blanchard, Weigel, & Cook, 1975). Still further evidence of the possible beneficial effects of cooperative interethnic contact is provided by a recent study of student work groups involving White, Black, and Mexican-American students in newly desegregated junior and senior high schools (Weigel, Wiser, & Cook, 1975).

One way to gain some perspective on the question

of which strategies may be most effective in reducing prejudice, racism, and discrimination in our society is to examine what *caused* the prejudice in the first place. With regard to prejudice in Whites, we can identify two general classes of causal factors: individual-level and sociocultural-level factors (Ashmore, 1970). Individual-level factors are aspects of an individual's *personality structure* that may lead the person to adopt prejudicial attitudes. Volumes of research attempts have been carried out to identify personality factors that tend to accompany, and perhaps help to cause, prejudicial attitudes in Whites. Although enumeration of all such factors is beyond the scope of this Summary, some of those most often identified are: an authoritarian personality structure (Adorno, Frenkel-Brunswik, Levinson, & Sanford, 1950), excessive cognitive category width (Allport & Ross, 1967), frustration or fear of loss of status and the aggression that this may produce, concreteness (as opposed to abstractness) in cognitive functioning (Brigham & Severy, 1976), and the tendency to assume that people of another race have beliefs, attitudes, and values far different from one's own (Rokeach, 1968; Silverman, 1974).

To change attitudes that are products of personality structures such as those just listed, it may be necessary to induce changes in the personality itself. Techniques of this sort that have been attempted include psychotherapy and self-insight training (see Ashmore, 1970). At a more general level, changes in child-rearing practices so that these practices are not conducive to the development of prejudice-prone personalities might be an important factor. Since the racial attitudes of Whites *are* apparently becoming less prejudiced (Brigham & Weissbach, 1972), the changes in general child-rearing techniques that have taken place in recent years may be one of the factors in this change. Finally, if general conflict-causing aspects of the environment are reduced, individuals' feelings of deprivation and frustration and the accompanying prejudice may also be reduced.

The effects of prejudice and racism on minority-group members can be awesome. The objective standard of living of minority ethnic groups in the United States (Blacks, Mexican-Americans, Asian Americans, Indians, Puerto Ricans) is dismal when compared with that enjoyed by the White majority. Numerous studies and surveys have shown that minority-group members have much lower levels of housing, education, and income, and much higher levels of unemployment, infant mortality, and other undesirable outcomes, than do Whites.

The cumulative *psychological* effects of racism for minority-group members can also be vast. Not only must they deal with everyday rebuffs and personal unpleasantries, but they must also be aware of the structure of society. As has been noted repeatedly, the pressures of such a society may set up a "self-fulfilling prophecy" whereby the minority-group members actually adopt those negative traits ascribed to them, perhaps as a conscious means of adapting and "getting along," perhaps as a "to-hell-with-it" reaction to repeated frustrations, or perhaps simply because of an eventual acceptance of the majority-group and institutional orientation.

As we mentioned in the Introduction, the concept of institutional racism has received increasing attention in the past decade. A very brief outline of some of the causes and manifestations of institutional racism follows. (For more detailed discussion of these phenomena, see Knowles & Prewitt, 1969; Daniels & Kitano, 1970; Brigham & Weissbach, 1972.)

One of the institutions thought by many to have played a decisive role in the formulation of institutional racism in the United States is organized religion. The historical emphasis on "civilizing" the ignorant "heathen" through missionary work, along with the general international policy of manfully shouldering the "white man's burden," of helping our "little brown brothers," certainly connotes a paternalistic assumption of the superiority of the majority American culture.

Another major force has been Social Darwinism. This doctrine, which arose after the acceptance of Charles Darwin's theory of biological evolution, holds that "survival of the fittest" is as applicable to cultures and groups or races of people as it is to species of animals. The implication is that those cultures or races who have "survived best" and gained control (the majority group) must be the "fittest." Ignoring all the mammoth practical barriers that may exist for minority groups, the theory naïvely assumes that the cream (of the culture) will inevitably rise to the top.

United States immigration policies provide another illustration of the nonegalitarian nature of societal institutions. Traditionally, "quotas" were set up so that large numbers of supposedly "desirable" ethnic groups (that is, northern Europeans) were allowed to emigrate to the United States while the immigration of other peoples was drastically limited. Although strict quotas were discontinued in the late 1960s, it is instructive to note that as recently as 1962 less than 5% of the immigrants permitted by the quotas to emigrate were non-European; about 70% were from Great Britain, Germany, and Ireland alone (Berry, 1965).

A conceptual stance similar to Social Darwinism is apparent in the application of the "immigrant analogy" by Whites to the problems faced by Blacks. Basically, the often-heard statement is of the type: "My (immigrant) grandparents made it OK in America! Why can't the Blacks?" The U. S. Riot Commission (Kerner Commission) enumerated several reasons why this analogy is utterly inappropriate. The conditions that Blacks have faced and still face in the United States simply are not parallel to those faced by European immigrants of several generations past. The crucial differences involve the following factors: (1) the maturing economy—unlike the situation several generations ago, today's economy has little use for the unskilled labor that an undereducated group may have to offer; (2) the disability of race—the structure of discrimination faced by Blacks is more pervasive than that ever faced by European immigrants; (3) entry into the political system—such entry, via ward politics or political machines, is much more difficult today than in the past; (4) cultural factors—the

segregation and lack of job opportunities faced by Blacks, and the increasing gap between opportunities and aspirations, have placed great stresses on the Black culture (Kerner et al., 1968, pp. 278–282).

The role of the public schools in contributing to this legacy of discrimination has also been described by many analysts. It has been pointed out that the content of traditional textbooks subtly adds to the flow of racism. In many cases, as you are undoubtedly aware, minority-group members have been presented in a stereotyped, derogatory manner. Although recent attention to these inequities has brought forth a flood of "ethnically balanced" books, the problem remains. A related problem concerns the appropriateness of the content of schoolbooks for minority children. Educators are realizing that stories about trips to Grandmother's farm have no relevance to ghetto Black children who have never even seen a farm. The use of materials that may be of no relevance to minority children necessarily dampens their enthusiasm for education and may contribute to an ongoing pattern of poor academic performance. Such inadequate educational materials, coupled with the use of "ability groupings" in schools, may lead to virtual segregation by socioeconomic status and hence often by ethnic group; and so the cycle is repeated. Traditional "histories" of American society also have utterly ignored the crucial contributions made by minority-group members and by minority cultures to the establishment of present-day American culture. Only during the 1960s did many educators begin to become aware of this glaring omission.

Finally, the influence of the general media (books, radio, television, movies, and so on) is another factor in this pattern. Examples from *Little Black Sambo* and *Amos 'n Andy* to the "Frito Bandito" and "skin-colored" (that is, pink) Band-Aids make it painfully clear how such portrayals can provide material for further stereotyping and derogation by majority-group members. The article by Brigham in Section 2 concerning the popular television program "All in the Family" and the controversy over the strident bigotry of its central character, Archie Bunker, describes another example of the impact of the media.

The forces of institutional racism also continue to affect the perceptions, attitudes, and behavior of majority-group members. Much research has illustrated that if people are "forced" to behave in a nondiscriminatory manner their attitudes may become less prejudiced (see, for example, Section 4; also, Brigham & Weissbach, 1972). A similar effect in the opposite direction can also be postulated. That is, if "forced" to act in a discriminatory manner (by institutionalized racist pressure), majority-group members may develop attitudes to justify such behavior to themselves. The more susceptible to societal conformity pressure they are, the more their behavior may correspond to the institutional sanctions (Pettigrew, 1961). Similarly, a majority-group child may develop negative attitudes through the affectively neutral process of making inferences from available evidence or "putting two and two together" (Ashmore, 1970). If the child becomes aware that the societal institutions encourage racism, he or she is likely to assume that there must be a good reason for this—that is, that the minority group must deserve such treatment. Furthermore, if the minority-group members with whom he or she comes into contact can be perceived (or misperceived) as having some of the expected "bad" traits, perhaps due to the self-fulfilling prophecy effect described earlier, then the child's negative orientation will be strengthened.

Legacies of institutional racism may operate in still more subtle ways. Although many majority-group Americans do not express acceptance of negative ethnic stereotypes, they nevertheless are aware of their existence. When asked to list the most common societal stereotypes of five ethnic groups, for instance, White college students in 1970 were able to do so with remarkable inter-subject agreement (Brigham, 1972). Therefore, even if majority group members do not consciously *believe in* such negative trait attributions, they are still "psychologically available" for use. And people may draw upon them if they are in an uncomfortable situation, seeking to project or displace hostility, or if they see a minority-group member who manifests such a trait.

One way of breaking out of this vicious cycle, we have suggested, is through equal-status contact. But how can such contact be initiated? One analyst has made an imaginative suggestion for establishing contact on a massive scale. Pierce (1969) has proposed that a Children's Domestic Exchange (CDE) program could be set up. Under this program, children between the ages of 10 and 18, of *all* socioeconomic and ethnic backgrounds, would be given travel grants. Ideally, each child would travel at least once a year, always to a situation distinct from his own cultural background. The length of his stay could vary from days to months. For example, a majority-group child from Hendersonville, North Carolina, might stay with a Navajo family in Arizona; a Mexican-American from Los Angeles might go to a farm in Indiana.

Pierce proposed that, given our present technological expertise and computer-aided communications systems, such a program is feasible. It would require a staff cadre modeled after VISTA or the Peace Corps. Pierce suggests, and we concur, that for such volunteer participants, the "transcultural, transethnic experiences . . . would broaden each of them and facilitate meaningful attitude changes" (Pierce, 1969, p. 565). This should hold true for both the children and the volunteer adults in whose homes the children would stay.

But such far-reaching attitude change, even if accomplished, might be inadequate to significantly reduce the degree of oppression of minority groups if major societal institutions continue to support discriminatory behavior. Many analysts have therefore suggested that the most efficient way to reduce oppression is to attempt to eliminate institutional racism.

A thorny problem exists with respect to the eradication of institutional racism, however. The people who are in the most advantageous positions to modify our major societal institutions are those who hold positions of power within them. But they are precisely the people who might be expected to be *least* aware of the ethnic bias in "their" institution. Having worked within the institution for so long, they may completely fail to recognize, or perhaps effectively rationalize, any such bias. In short, such power figures might be "unable to see the forest for the trees." Such a suggestion has even been made about the institution of psychology itself (see Baratz & Baratz, 1970; Thomas, 1970).

It is apparent that if far-reaching progress is to be made toward a truly egalitarian society, massive changes must take place on at least two fronts. The ethnic attitudes, beliefs, and behavioral inclinations (particularly, but not solely) of the American majority must undergo major changes, perhaps partially through equal-status contact and massive reeducation programs. At the same time, the ways in which society and its institutions contribute to oppression of minority-group members must be fully recognized, and drastic measures must be taken to eliminate these societal barriers. Only then will it be possible for the condition of "true integration" and racial justice described by Pettigrew and by Taylor to become a reality in American society.

REFERENCES

Adorno, T. W., Frenkel-Brunswik, E., Levinson, D. J., & Sanford, R. N. *The authoritarian personality.* New York: Harper, 1950.

Allport, G. W., & Ross, J. M. Personal religious orientation and prejudice. *Journal of Personality and Social Psychology,* 1967, *5,* 432–443.

Ashmore, R. D. Prejudice: Causes and cures. In B. E. Collins, *Social psychology.* Reading, Mass.: Addison-Wesley, 1970. Pp. 247–339.

Baratz, S. S., & Baratz, J. C. Early childhood intervention: The social science base of institutional racism. *Harvard Educational Review,* 1970, *40,* 29–50.

Berry, B. *Race and ethnic relations.* (3rd ed.). Boston: Houghton Mifflin, 1965.

Blanchard, F. A., Adelman, L., & Cook, S. W. Effect of group success and failure upon interpersonal attraction in cooperating interracial groups. *Journal of Personality and Social Psychology,* 1975, *31,* 1020–1030.

Blanchard, F. A., Weigel, R. H. & Cook, S. W. The effect of relative competence of group members upon interpersonal attraction in cooperating interracial groups. *Journal of Personality and Social Psychology,* 1975, *32,* 519–530.

Brigham, J. C. Racial stereotypes: Measurement variables and the stereotype-attitude relationship. *Journal of Applied Social Psychology,* 1972, *2,* 63–76.

Brigham, J. C., & Severy, L. J. Personality and attitude determinants of voting behavior. *Social Behavior and Personality: An International Journal,* 1976, *4*(1), 127–139.

Brigham, J. C., & Weissbach, T. A. (Eds.), *Racial attitudes in America: Analyses and findings of social psychology.* New York: Harper & Row, 1972.

Cook, S. W. Motives in a conceptual analysis of attitude-related behavior. In W. J. Arnold and D. Levine (Eds.), *Nebraska symposium on motivation, 1969.* Lincoln: University of Nebraska Press, 1970. Pp. 179–321.

Daniels, R., & Kitano, H. H. L. *American racism: Exploration of the nature of prejudice.* Englewood Cliffs, N. J.: Prentice-Hall, 1970.

Kerner, O. et al. *Report of the national advisory commission on civil disorders.* New York: Bantam Books, 1968.

Knowles, L. L., & Prewitt, K. *Institutional racism in America.* Englewood Cliffs, N. J.: Prentice-Hall, 1969.

Pettigrew, T. F. Social psychology and desegregation research. *American Psychologist,* 1961, *16,* 105–112.

Pierce, C. M. Violence and counterviolence: The need for a Children's Domestic Exchange. *American Journal of Orthopsychiatry,* 1969, *39,* 553–568.

Rokeach, M. *Beliefs, attitudes, and values.* San Francisco: Jossey-Bass, 1968.

Silverman, B. I. Consequences, racial discrimination, and the principle of belief congruence. *Journal of Personality and Social Psychology,* 1974, *29,* 497–508.

Thomas, C. W. Psychologists, psychology, and the black community. In F. F. Korten, S. W. Cook, and J. I. Lacey (Eds.), *Psychology and the problems of society.* Washington, D. C.: American Psychological Association, 1970. Pp. 259–267.

Weigel, R. H., Wiser, P. L., & Cook, S. W. The impact of cooperative learning experiences on cross-ethnic relations and attitudes. *Journal of Social Issues,* 1975, *31*(1), 219–244.

Wrightsman, L. S., & Cook, S. W. The factorial structure of "positive attitudes toward people." Paper presented at the Southeastern Psychological Association Meetings, Atlanta, 1967.

SECTION VI

SEXISM

INTRODUCTION

Consider the following situation: A man and his teenage son are driving in an automobile when they are involved in a very serious accident. The man is killed and the boy is critically injured. He is rushed by ambulance to the local hospital and wheeled into the emergency room. The staff surgeon in charge looks at the boy, shudders, and says "I can't operate on this boy. This is my son."

How can this statement be explained?

If your answer did not indicate that the staff surgeon is a woman and is the boy's mother, it may reflect *sexism*. (Incidentally, it is unlikely that Russian students would have difficulty with this question, since most of the physicians in the USSR are women.)

Sexism can be defined as any attitude, action, or institutional structure that subordinates a person because of his or her sex. In this sense sexism is similar to racism, which was analyzed in Section 5, and the causes and outcomes of racism and sexism are similar in many ways. Although, in the abstract, either men or women could be subordinated because of their sex, the vast majority of sexist attitudes and

acts are in fact directed against women and in favor of men. This type of sexism is reviewed in this Section.

The examples of sexism are numerous. Some are blatant, such as paying women less than men for identical work or denying women access to certain occupations. (Some specifics are given in the first article in this Section.) Sexism permeates our religious heritage and our language, as exemplified by the assumption that God is male and by the use of such words as *chairman* and *mankind,* as well as by reliance on the pronoun *he* when referring to a nonspecific person who could be of either sex.

Sexism is learned at an early age. Although some recent books for children are trying to modify the pattern, most literature for infants and young children depicts girls sewing or playing with dolls and boys playing with toys and mechanical objects. Portrayals of adults in such materials are equally stereotyped. At day's end, Father is pictured as returning from the office or the factory while Mother has stayed home and acted as a domestic worker all day.

Adherents of the Women's Liberation movement have referred to some men as "male chauvinist pigs," implying that they manifest extremely discriminatory behavior against females. ("Chauvinist" derives from Nicolas Chauvin, a soldier-follower of Napoleon I who attained much notoriety for his grotesque displays of attachment for the fallen Napoleon. "Male chauvinism" is an unreasoning, extravagant devotion to the viewpoint that men are superior to women.) But sexism can be manifested unintentionally by both men and women in ways not readily apparent to them. As the feminists tell us, we need to have our "consciousness raised" about the subtle ways in which women are "put down" in contemporary life. In our first article, Sandra and Daryl Bem give examples of the ways in which sexism operates as an insidious, *unconscious ideology* in our society, while the remaining two articles provide empirical evidence of such discrimination.

To some social psychologists, a particularly aggravating manifestation of sexism is found in the theorizing of male psychologists about the nature of feminine personality and behavior. Male theorists have not been reluctant to speculate about the nature of the female psyche and female sexuality, and often their speculations are condescending and paternalistic. Sigmund Freud is a prominent example. Since Freud's theories have had such a profound effect on subsequent ideas about human sexuality and personality development, we will outline portions of his *stage theory* here.

Freud proposed that a child passes through several psychosexual stages of development on the way to adulthood. Freud always used male terms and examples, and he referred to the third of these stages as the "phallic" (the first two were the "oral" and "anal"), even though the vast majority of his patients were women.

During the phallic stage the child "discovers" the presence or absence of a penis, according to Freud. Desires to stimulate the sexual organs are likely to be punished by parents, but this does not dampen the motivation. During this period a boy, according to Freud, "rather naïvely wishes to use his new-found source of pleasure, the penis, to please his oldest source of pleasure, the mother" (Schaeffer, 1971, p. 12). He envies his father, who is occupying the position he craves and is doing the thing he wishes to do. Thus emerges the Oedipus conflict, which Freudian theory sees as being resolved by the boy's gradual identification with his father. The boy says, in effect, "I will get vicarious satisfaction by identifying with my father. Then what he does will bring me some sense of pleasure and satisfaction." In this way Freud handles the important question of how masculine identification develops in boys. Of course, the scenario we have described is an idealized one; many boys will not achieve the identification. Their fathers may be absent or, even if present, may be weak or otherwise not worthy of identification or emulation.

So much for boys. As Schaeffer (1971) indicates, Freudian theory has difficulty with the process of identification in females. The cornerstone of Freud's psychoanalytic theory is the physiological structure and development of humans. Males and females differ in sexual anatomy, and this difference would have to be recognized in a theory that, like Freud's, is built on biological considerations. Additionally, the problem of identification by females is different from that of males because girls have from infancy invested their libidinal energy in their mother, the source of gratification when the girl was hungry or distressed. Does this mean that the process of identification with the parent of the same sex is easier for girls? Not necessarily so, according to Freud. But his accounts of female identification were never as clear or fully developed as were his descriptions of the processes in males (see Hall & Lindzey, 1968, 1970; Hall, 1954).

Some quotations from one of Freud's papers, "Some psychological consequences of the anatomical distinction between sexes" (Freud, 1959; originally published in 1925), illustrate his orientation. Freud speaks of "a momentous discovery which little girls are destined to make. They notice the penis of a brother or playmate, strikingly visible and of large proportions, at once recognize it as the superior counterpart of their own small inconspicuous organ, and from that time forward fall a victim to envy for the penis. . . . The physical consequences of penis-envy . . . are various and far-reaching. After a woman has become aware of the wound to her narcissism, she develops, like a scar, a sense of inferiority.''*

Freud believed that among the results of penis-envy were feelings of inferiority, jealousy (which, he felt, ''plays a far larger part in the mental life of women than of men''), emotionality, and an underdeveloped sense of justice. He stated that the *superego* (conscience) in women ''is never so inexorable, so impersonal, so independent of its emotional origins as we require it to be in men. Character traits which critics of every epoch have brought up against women—that they show less sense of justice than men, that they are less ready to submit to the great necessities of life, that they are more often influenced in their judgments by feelings of affection or hostility—all these would be amply accounted for by the modifications in the formation of their super-ego.'' We will evaluate the validity of some of these hypotheses in the Section Summary.

One of Freud's hypotheses, then, was that females, as well as males, perceive females as inferior. Here again sexism, like racism, may lead to a self-fulfilling prophecy. Just as Blacks may come to internalize Whites' negative stereotypes about them, so may females come to believe that they cannot achieve the levels of success that males can. In the first article in this Section, Sandra and Daryl

Bem describe two empirical studies of this phenomenon. In one (Horner, 1969; 1970) a ''fear of success'' was shown by females in situations in which achievement was under scrutiny. Females who succeeded in achievement-oriented situations were seen as unhappy misfits. The other study, by Goldberg (1968), served as a stimulus for the second article, by Pheterson, Kiesler, and Goldberg. They describe a replication and amplification of the earlier demonstration that females devalue the quality of an artistic product when they believe it has been done by another female. In the third article, Goldberg, Gottesdiener, and Abramson provide further evidence of ways in which women may be ''put down'' both by men and by other women.

REFERENCES

Freud, S. Some psychical consequences of the anatomical distinction between the sexes. In E. Jones (Ed.), *The collected papers of Sigmund Freud.* Vol. 5, Chapter 17. New York: Basic Books, 1959. (First German edition, 1925.)

Goldberg, P. Are women prejudiced against women? *Trans-action,* 1968, *5*(4), 28–30.

Hall, C. S. *A primer of Freudian psychology.* Cleveland: World Publishing Co., 1954.

Hall, C. S., & Lindzey, G. The relevance of Freudian psychology and related viewpoints for the social sciences. In G. Lindzey & E. Aronson (Eds.), *Handbook of social psychology* (Vol. 1). Cambridge, Mass.: Addison-Wesley, 1968. Pp. 245–319.

Hall, C. S., & Lindzey, G. *Theories of personality.* (2nd ed.). New York: Wiley, 1970.

Horner, M. S. Fail: Bright women. *Psychology Today,* 1969, *3*(6), 36–38ff.

Horner, M. S. Femininity and successful achievement: A basic inconsistency. In J. M. Bardwick, E. Douvan, M. S. Horner, & D. Gutmann, *Feminine personality and conflict.* Monterey, Calif.: Brooks/Cole, 1970. Pp. 45–74.

Schaeffer, D. L. (Ed.), *Sex differences in personality: Readings.* Monterey, Calif.: Brooks/Cole, 1971.

*From ''Some Psychical Consequences of the Anatomical Distinction between the Sexes,'' by S. Freud. In Chapter XVII of Volume 5 of *The Collected Papers of Sigmund Freud,* edited by Ernest Jones, M.D. This and all other quotations from this source are reprinted by permission of Basic Books, Inc., Publishers, New York, 1959, and The Hogarth Press Ltd.

ARTICLE 16

Homogenizing the American woman: The power of an unconscious ideology

Sandra L. Bem
Daryl J. Bem

In the beginning God created the heaven and the earth. . . . And God said, Let us make man in our image, after our likeness; and let him have dominion over the fish of the sea, and over the fowl of the air, and over the cattle, and over all the earth. . . . And the rib, which the Lord God had taken from man, made he a woman and brought her unto the man. . . . And the Lord God said unto the woman, What is this that thou has done? And the woman said, The serpent beguiled me, and I did eat. . . . Unto the woman God said, I will greatly multiply thy sorrow and thy conception; in sorrow thou shalt bring forth children; and thy desire shall be to thy husband, and he shall rule over thee [Gen. 1, 2, 3].

There is a moral to that story. St. Paul spells it out even more clearly:

For a man . . . is the image and glory of God, but the woman is the glory of the man. For the man is not of the woman, but the woman of the man. Neither was the man created for the woman, but the woman for the man [1 Cor. 11].

Let the woman learn in silence with all subjection. But I suffer not a woman to teach, nor to usurp authority over the man, but to be in silence. For Adam was first formed and then Eve. And Adam was not deceived, but the woman, being deceived, was in the transgression. Notwithstanding, she shall be saved in childbearing, if they continue in faith and charity and holiness with sobriety [1 Tim. 2].

Now one should not assume that only Christians have this kind of rich heritage of ideology about women. Consider now the morning prayer of the Orthodox Jew:

Blessed art Thou, oh Lord our God, King of the Universe, that I was not born a gentile.
Blessed art Thou, oh Lord our God, King of the Universe, that I was not born a slave.
Blessed art Thou, oh Lord our God, King of the Universe, that I was not born a woman.

Or consider the Koran, the sacred text of Islam:

Men are superior to women on account of the qualities in which God has given them pre-eminence.

Because they think they sense a decline in feminine "faith, charity, and holiness with sobriety," many people today jump to the conclusion that the ideology expressed in these passages is a relic of the past. Not so, of course. It has simply been obscured by an egalitarian veneer, and the same ideology has now become unconscious. That is, we remain unaware of it because alternative beliefs and attitudes about women, until very recently, have gone unimagined. We are very much like the fish who is unaware of the fact that his environment is wet. After all, what else could it be? Such is the nature of all unconscious ideologies in a society. Such, in particular, is the nature of America's ideology about women.

What we would like to do in this paper is to discuss today's version of this same ideology.

When a baby boy is born, it is difficult to predict what he will be doing 25 years later. We can't say whether he will be an artist, a doctor, a lawyer, a college professor, or a bricklayer, because he will be permitted to develop and fulfill his own unique potential—particularly, of course, if he happens to be White and middle-class. But if that same newborn child happens to be a girl, we can predict with almost complete confidence how she is likely to be spending her time some 25 years later. Why can we do that? Because her individuality doesn't have to be considered. Her individuality is irrelevant. Time studies have shown that she will spend the equivalent of a full working day, 7.1 hours, in preparing meals, cleaning house, laundering, mending, shopping, and doing other household tasks. In other words, 43% of her waking time will be spent in activity that would command an hourly wage on the open market well below the federally set minimum for menial industrial work.

Of course, the point is not really how little she would earn if she did these things in someone else's home. She will be doing them in her own home for free. The point is that this use of time is virtually the same for homemakers with college degrees and for homemakers with less than a grade-school education, for women married to professional men and for women married to blue-collar workers. Actually, that's understating it slightly. What the time study really showed was that college-educated women spend slightly *more* time cleaning their houses than their less-educated counterparts!

Of course, it is not simply the full-time homemaker whose unique identity has been rendered largely irrelevant. Of the 31 million women who work outside the home in our society, 78% end up in dead-end jobs as clerical workers, service workers, factory workers, or sales clerks, compared to a comparable figure of 40% for men. Only 15% of all women workers in our society are classified by the Labor Department as professional or technical workers, and even this figure is misleading—for the single, poorly paid occupation of non-college teacher absorbs half of these women, and the occupation of nurse absorbs an additional quarter. In other words, the two jobs of teacher and nurse absorb three-quarters of all women classified in our society as technical or professional. This means, then, that fewer than 5% of all professional women—fewer than 1% of all women workers—fill those positions that to most Americans connote "professional": physician, lawyer, engineer, scientist, college professor, journalist, writer, and so forth.

Even an IQ in the genius range does not guarantee that a woman's unique potential will find expression. There was a famous study of over 1300 boys and girls whose IQs averaged 151 (Terman & Oden, 1959). When the study began in the early 1900s, these highly gifted youngsters were only 10 years old, and their careers have been followed ever since. Where are they today? Of the men, 86% have now achieved prominence in professional and managerial occupations. In contrast, only a minority of the women are even employed. Of those who are,

37% are nurses, librarians, social workers, and non-college teachers. An additional 26% are secretaries, stenographers, bookkeepers, and office workers. Only 11% have entered the higher professions of law, medicine, college teaching, engineering, science, economics, and the like. And even at age 44, well after all their children have gone to school, 61% of these highly gifted women remain full-time homemakers. Talent, education, ability, interests, motivations: all irrelevant. In our society, being female uniquely qualifies an individual for domestic work—either by itself or in conjunction with typing, teaching, nursing, or (most often) unskilled labor. It is this homogenization of America's women that is the major consequence of our society's sex-role ideology.

It is true, of course, that most women have several hours of leisure time every day. And it is here, we are often told, that each woman can express her unique identity. Thus, politically interested women can join the League of Women Voters. Women with humane interests can become part-time Gray Ladies. Women who love music can raise money for the symphony. Protestant women play canasta; Jewish women play mah-jongg; brighter women of all denominations and faculty wives play bridge.

But politically interested *men* serve in legislatures. *Men* with humane interests become physicians or clinical psychologists. *Men* who love music play in the symphony. In other words, why should a woman's unique identity determine only the periphery of her life and not its central core?

Why? Why nurse rather than physician, secretary rather than executive, stewardess rather than pilot? Why faculty wife rather than faculty? Why doctor's mother rather than doctor? There are three basic answers to this question: (1) discrimination, (2) sex-role conditioning, and (3) the presumed incompatibility of family and career.

DISCRIMINATION

In 1968, the median income of full-time women workers was approximately $4500. The comparable figure for men was $3000 higher. Moreover, the gap is widening. Ten years ago, women earned 64% of what men did; that percentage has now shrunk to 58%. Today, a female college graduate working full-time can expect to earn less per year than a male high school dropout.

There are two reasons for this pay differential. First, in every category of occupation, women are employed in the lesser-skilled, lower-paid positions. Even in the clerical field, where 73% of the workers are women, females are relegated to the lowest-status positions and hence earn only 65% of what male clerical workers earn. The second reason for this pay differential is discrimination in its purest form—unequal pay for equal work. According to a survey of 206 companies in 1970, female college graduates were offered jobs that paid $43 per month less than those offered to their male counterparts in the same college major.

New laws should begin to correct both of these situations. The Equal Pay Act of 1963 prohibits employers from discriminating on the basis of sex in the payment of wages for equal work. In a landmark ruling on May 18, 1970, the U.S. Supreme Court ordered that $250,000 in back pay be paid to women employed by a single New Jersey glass company. This decision followed a two-year court battle by the Labor Department after it had found that the company was paying men selector-packers 21.5 cents more per hour than women doing the same work. In a similar case, the Eighth Circuit Court of Appeals ordered a major can company to pay more than $100,000 in back wages to women doing equal work. According to the Labor Department, an estimated $17 million is owed to women in back pay. Since that estimate was made, a 1972 amendment extended the Act to cover executive, administrative, and professional employees as well.

But to enjoy equal pay, women must also have access to equal jobs. Title VII of the 1964 Civil Rights Act prohibits discrimination in employment on the basis of race, color, religion, national origin—and sex. Although the sex provision was treated as a joke at the time (and was originally introduced by a Southern Congressman in an attempt to defeat the bill), the Equal Employment

Opportunities Commission (E.E.O.C.) discovered in its first year of operation that 40% or more of the complaints warranting investigation charged discrimination on the basis of sex (Bird, 1969).

Title VII has served as one of the most effective instruments in helping to achieve sex equality in the world of work. According to a report by the E.E.O.C., nearly 6000 charges of sex discrimination were filed with that agency in 1971 alone, a 62% increase over the previous year.

But the most significant legislative breakthrough in the area of sex equality was the passage of the Equal Rights Amendment by both houses of Congress in 1972. The ERA simply states that ''Equality of rights under the law shall not be denied or abridged by the United States or by any state on account of sex.'' This amendment had been introduced into every session of the Congress since 1923, and its passage now is clearly an indication of the changing role of the American woman. What all of the amendment's various ramifications will be is hard to predict, but it is clear that it will have profound consequences in private as well as public life.

Many Americans assume that the recent drive for equality between the sexes is primarily for the benefit of the middle-class woman who wants to seek self-fulfillment in a professional career. But in many ways, it is the woman in more modest circumstances, the woman who *must* work for economic reasons, who stands to benefit most from the removal of discriminatory barriers. It is *she* who is hardest hit by unequal pay; it is *she* who so desperately needs adequate day-care facilities; it is *her* job which is often dead-ended while her male colleagues in the factory get trained and promoted into the skilled craft jobs. Even if both she and her husband work at unfulfilling jobs eight hours a day just to make an adequate income, it is still *she* who carries the additional burden of domestic chores when they return home.

We think it is important to emphasize these points at the outset, for we have chosen to focus our remarks in this particular paper on those fortunate men and women who can afford the luxury of pursuing self-fulfillment through the world of work and

career. But every societal reform advocated by the new feminist movement, whether it be the Equal Rights Amendment, the establishment of child-care centers, or basic changes in America's sex-role ideology, will affect the lives of men and women in every economic circumstance. Nevertheless, it is still economic discrimination that hits hardest at the largest group of women, and it is here that the drive for equality can be most successfully launched with legislative and judicial tools.

SEX-ROLE CONDITIONING

Even if all job discrimination against women were to end tomorrow, however, nothing very drastic would change. For job discrimination is only part of the problem. It does impede women who choose to become lawyers or managers or physicians. But it does not, by itself, help us to understand why so many women ''choose'' to be secretaries or nurses rather than executives or physicians; why only 3% of 9th-grade girls as compared to 25% of the boys ''choose'' careers in science or engineering; or why 63% of married women ''choose'' not to work at all. It certainly doesn't explain those young women whose vision of the future includes only marriage, children, and living happily ever after—who may, at some point, ''choose'' to take a job, but who almost never ''choose'' to pursue a career. Discrimination frustrates choices already made. Something more pernicious perverts the motivation to choose.

That ''something'' is an unconscious ideology about the nature of the female sex, an ideology that constricts the emerging self-image of the female child and the nature of her aspirations from the very beginning, an ideology that leads even those Americans who agree that a Black skin should not uniquely qualify its owner for janitorial or domestic service to act as if the possession of a uterus uniquely qualified *its* owner for precisely such service.

Consider, for example, the 1968 student rebellion at Columbia University. Students from the radical Left took over some administration buildings in the name of egalitarian ideals that they accused the university of flouting. Here were the most militant spokesmen one could hope to find in the cause of egalitarian ideals. But no sooner had they occupied the buildings than the male militants blandly turned to their sisters-in-arms and assigned them the task of preparing the food, while they—the menfolk—would presumably plan future strategy. The reply these males received was the reply that they deserved—we will leave that to your imagination—and the fact that domestic tasks behind the barricades were desegregated across the sex line that day is an everlasting tribute to the class consciousness of these ladies of the Left. It was really on that day that the campus women's liberation movement got its start—when radical women finally realized that if it was left up to the men they would never get to make revolution, only coffee.

But these "conscious" co-eds are not typical, for the unconscious assumptions about a woman's "natural" talents (or lack of them) are at least as prevalent among women as they are among men. A psychologist named Phillip Goldberg (1968) demonstrated this by asking female college students to rate a number of professional articles from each of six fields. The articles were collated into two equal sets of booklets, and the names of the authors were changed so that the identical article was attributed to a male author (for example, John T. McKay) in one booklet and to a female author (for example, Joan T. McKay) in the other booklet. Each student was asked to read the articles in her booklet and to rate them for value, competence, persuasiveness, writing style, and so forth.

As he had anticipated, Goldberg found that the identical article received significantly lower ratings when it was attributed to a female author than when it was attributed to a male author. He had predicted this result for articles from professional fields generally considered the province of men, like law or city planning, but, to his surprise, these women also downgraded articles from the fields of dietetics and elementary school education when they were attributed to female authors. In other words, the students rated the male authors as better at everything, agreeing with Aristotle that "we should regard the female nature as afflicted with a natural defectiveness." Such is the nature of America's unconscious ideology about women.

When does this ideology begin to affect the life of a young girl? Research now tells us that from the day a newborn child is dressed in pink, she is given "special" treatment. Perhaps because they are thought to be more fragile, 6-month-old infant girls are actually touched, spoken to, and hovered over more by their mothers while they are playing than are infant boys (Goldberg & Lewis, 1969). One study even showed that when mothers and babies are still in the hospital, "mothers smile at, talk to, and touch their female infants more than their male infants at two days of age" (Thoman, Leiderman, & Olson, 1972.) Differential treatment can't begin much earlier than that.

As children begin to read, the storybook characters become the images and the models that little boys and little girls aspire to become. What kind of role does the female play in the world of children's literature? The fact is that there aren't even very many females *in* that world. One survey (Fisher, 1970) found that five times as many males as females appear in the titles of children's books, that the fantasy world of Doctor Seuss is almost entirely male, and that even animals and machines are represented as male. When females do appear, they are noteworthy primarily for what they do *not* do. They do not drive cars; they seldom even ride bicycles. In one story in which a girl does ride a bicycle, it's a two-seater. Guess where the girl is seated! Boys in these stories climb trees, fish, roll in the leaves, and skate. Girls watch, fall down, and get dizzy. Girls are never doctors, and, although they may be nurses or librarians or teachers, they are never principals. The survey uncovered only one children's book about mothers who work, and that one concludes that what mothers love "best of all" is "being your very own Mommy and coming home to you." Although this is no doubt true of many Daddies as well, no book about working fathers has ever found it necessary to apologize for working in quite the same way.

As children grow older, more explicit sex-role training is introduced. Boys are encouraged to take more of an interest in mathematics and science. It is usually boys, not girls, who are given chemistry sets and microscopes for Christmas. Moreover, all children quickly learn that mommy is proud to be a moron when it comes to math and science, whereas daddy is a little ashamed if he doesn't know all about such things. When a young boy returns from school all excited about biology, he is almost certain to be encouraged to think of becoming a physician. A girl with similar enthusiasm is usually told that she might want to consider nurse's training later on, so she can have an interesting job to fall back on in case—God forbid—she ever needs to support herself. A very different kind of encouragement! Any girl who doggedly persists in her enthusiasm for science is likely to find her parents as horrified by the prospect of a permanent love affair with physics as they would be by the prospect of an interracial marriage, or, horror of horrors, no marriage at all. Indeed, our graduate women report that their families seem convinced that the menopause must come at age 23.

These socialization practices take their toll. When they apply for college, boys and girls are about equal on verbal-aptitude tests, but boys score significantly higher on mathematical-aptitude tests —about 60 points higher on the College Board Exams, for example (Brown, 1965). For those who are convinced that this is due to female hormones, it is relevant to know that girls improve their mathematical performance if the problems are simply reworded so that they deal with cooking and gardening, even though the abstract reasoning required for solution remains exactly the same (Milton, 1959). That's not hormones! Clearly, what has been undermined is not a woman's mathematical ability, but rather her confidence in that ability.

But these effects in mathematics and science are only part of the story. The most conspicuous outcome of all is that the majority of America's women

become full-time homemakers. Moreover, of those who do work, nearly 80% end up in dead-end jobs as clerical workers, service workers, factory workers or sales clerks. Again, it is this "homogenization" of America's women that is the major consequence of America's sex-role ideology.

The important point is not that the role of homemaker is necessarily inferior, but rather that our society is managing to consign a large segment of its population to that role—either with or without a dead-end job—solely on the basis of sex just as inexorably as it has in the past consigned the individual with a Black skin to the role of janitor or domestic. The important point is that in spite of their unique identities the majority of American women end up in virtually the *same* role.

The socialization of the American male has closed off certain options for him, too. Men are discouraged from developing certain desirable traits, such as tenderness and sensitivity, just as surely as women are discouraged from being assertive and, alas "too bright." Young boys are encouraged to be incompetent at cooking and certainly at child care, just as surely as young girls are urged to be incompetent at math and science. The elimination of sex-role stereotyping implies that each individual would be encouraged to "do his (or her!) own thing." Men and women would no longer be stereotyped by society's definitions of masculine and feminine. If sensitivity, emotionality, and warmth are desirable *human* characteristics, then they are desirable for men as well as for women. If independence, assertiveness, and serious intellectual commitment are desirable *human* characteristics, then they are desirable for women as well as for men. Thus, we are not implying that men have all the goodies and that women can obtain self-fulfillment by acting like men. That is hardly the utopia implied by today's feminist movement. Rather, we envision a society that raises its children so flexibly and with sufficient respect for the integrity of individual uniqueness that some men might emerge with the motivation, the ability, and the opportunity to stay home and raise children without bearing the stigma of being peculiar. Indeed, if homemaking is as glamorous as women's magazines and television commercials would have us believe, then men, too, should be able to enjoy that option. And even if homemaking isn't all that glamorous, it would probably still be more fulfilling for some men than the jobs into which they now find themselves forced because of their role as bread-winners. Thus, it is true that a man's options are also limited by our society's sex-role ideology, but as the "predictability test" reveals, it is still the woman whose identity is rendered irrelevant by America's socialization practices.

Further Psychological Barriers

But what of the woman who arrives at age 21 still motivated to be challenged and fulfilled by a growing career? Is she free to choose a career if she cares to do so? Or is there something standing even in her way?

There is. Even the woman who has managed to finesse society's attempt to rob her of her career motivations is likely to find herself blocked by society's trump card: the feeling that one cannot have a career and be a successful woman simultaneously. A competent and motivated woman is thus caught in a double bind that few men have ever faced. She must worry not only about failure but also about success.

This conflict was strikingly revealed in a study that required college women to complete the following story: "After first-term finals, Anne finds herself at the top of her medical-school class" (Horner, 1969). The stories were then examined for concern about the negative consequences of success. The women in this study all had high intellectual ability and histories of academic success. They were the very women who could have successful careers. And yet, over two-thirds of their stories revealed an inability to cope with the concept of a feminine, yet career-oriented, woman. The most common "fear-of-success" stories showed fears of social rejection as a result of success. The women in this group showed anxiety about becoming unpopular, unmarriageable, and lonely:

Anne starts proclaiming her surprise and joy. Her fellow classmates are so disgusted with her behavior that they jump on her in a body and beat her. She is maimed for life.

Anne is an acne-faced bookworm. . . .She studies twelve hours a day, and lives at home to save money. "Well, it certainly paid off. All the Friday and Saturday nights without dates, fun—I'll be the best woman doctor alive." And yet a twinge of sadness comes through—she wonders what she really has. . . .

Anne doesn't want to be number one in her class. . . . She feels she shouldn't rank so high because of social reasons. She drops to ninth and then marries the boy who graduates number one.

In the second "fear-of-success" category were stories in which the women seemed concerned about definitions of womanhood. These stories expressed guilt and despair over success and doubts about their femininity and normality:

Unfortunately Anne no longer feels so certain that she really wants to be a doctor. She is worried about herself and wonders if perhaps she is not normal. . . .Anne decides not to continue with her medical work but to take courses that have a deeper personal meaning for her.

Anne feels guilty. . .She will finally have a nervous breakdown and quit medical school and marry a successful young doctor.

A third group of stories could not even face up to the conflict between having a career and being a woman. These stories simply denied the possibility that any woman could be so successful:

Anne is a code name for a nonexistent person created by a group of med students. They take turns writing for Anne. . . .

Anne is really happy she's on top, though Tom is higher than she—though that's as it should be. Anne doesn't mind Tom winning.

Anne is talking to her counselor. Counselor says she will make a fine nurse.

By way of contrast, here is a typical story written not about Anne but about John:

John has worked very hard and his long hours of study have paid off. . . . He is thinking about his girl, Cheri, whom he will marry at the end of med school. He realizes he can give her all the things she desires after he becomes established. He will go on in med school and be successful in the long run.

Nevertheless, there were a few women in the study who welcomed the prospect of success:

Anne is quite a lady—not only is she top academically, but she is liked and admired by her fellow students—quite a trick in a man-dominated field. She is brilliant—but she is also a woman. She will continue to be at or near the top. And . . . always a lady.

We may hope that the day is approaching when as many "Anne" stories as "John" stories will have happy endings. But notice that even this story finds it necessary to affirm repeatedly that femininity is not necessarily destroyed by accomplishment. One would never encounter a comparable story written about John who, although brilliant and at the top of his class, is "still a man, still a man, still a man."

It seems unlikely that anyone in our society would view these "fear-of-success" stories as portraits of mental health. But even our concept of mental health has been distorted by sex-role stereotypes. Here we must indict our own profession of psychology. A recent survey of 79 clinically trained psychologists, psychiatrists, and social workers, both male and female, revealed a double standard of mental health (Broverman, Broverman, Clarkson, Rosenkrantz, & Vogel, 1970). That is, even professional clinicians have two different concepts of mental health, one for men and one for women, and these concepts parallel the sex-role stereotypes prevalent in our society. Thus, according to these clinicians, a woman is to be regarded as healthier and more mature if she is more submissive, less independent, less adventurous, more easily influenced, less aggressive, less competitive, more excitable in minor crises, more susceptible to

hurt feelings, more emotional, more conceited about her appearance, less objective, and more antagonistic toward math and science! But this was the very same description that these clinicians used to characterize an unhealthy, immature man or an unhealthy, immature adult (sex unspecified)! The equation is clear: Mature woman equals immature adult.

Given this concept of a mature woman, is it any wonder that few women ever aspire to challenging and fulfilling careers? In order to have a career, a woman will probably need to become relatively more dominant, independent, adventurous, aggressive, competitive, and objective, and relatively less excitable, emotional and conceited than our ideal of femininity requires. If she were a man (or an adult, sex unspecified), these would all be considered positive traits. But because she is a woman, these same traits will bring disapproval. She must then either be strong enough to have her "femininity" questioned, or she must behave in the prescribed feminine manner and accept second-class status, as an adult and as a professional.

And, of course, should a woman faced with this conflict seek professional help, hoping to summon the strength she will need to pursue her career goals, the advice she is likely to receive will be of virtually no use. For, as this study reveals, even professional counselors have been contaminated by the sex-role ideology.

It is frequently argued that a 21-year-old woman is perfectly free to choose a career if she cares to do so, that no one is standing in her way. But this argument conveniently overlooks the fact that our society has spent 20 years carefully marking the woman's ballot for her, and so it has nothing to lose in that 21st year by pretending to let her cast it for the alternative of her choice. Society has controlled not her alternatives (although discrimination does do that), but more importantly, it has controlled her motivation to choose any but one of those alternatives. The so-called "freedom to choose" is illusory, and it cannot be invoked to justify a society that controls the woman's motivation to choose.

Biological Considerations

Up to this point, we have argued that the differing life patterns of men and women in our society can be chiefly accounted for by cultural conditioning. The most common counter argument to this view, of course, is the biological one. The biological argument suggests that there may really be inborn differences between men and women in, say, independence or mathematical ability. Or that there may be biological factors beyond the fact that women can become pregnant and nurse children that uniquely dictate that they, but not men, should stay home all day and shun serious outside commitment. What this argument suggests is that maybe female hormones really are responsible somehow. One difficulty with this argument, of course, is that female hormones would have to be different in the Soviet Union, where one-third of the engineers and 75% of the physicians are women (Dodge, 1966). In America, by way of contrast, women constitute less than 1% of the engineers and only 7% of the physicians. Female physiology *is* different, and it may account for some of the psychological differences between the sexes, but America's sex-role ideology still seems primarily responsible for the fact that so few women emerge from childhood with the motivation to seek out any role beyond the one that our society dictates.

But even if there really were biological differences between the sexes along these lines, the biological argument would still be irrelevant. The reason can best be illustrated with an analogy.

Suppose that every Black American boy were to be socialized to become a jazz musician on the assumption that he has a "natural" talent in that direction; or suppose that parents and counselors should subtly discourage him from other pursuits because it is considered "inappropriate" for Black men to become physicians or physicists. Most Americans would disapprove. But suppose that it *could* be demonstrated that Black Americans, *on the average,* did possess an inborn better sense of rhythm than White Americans. Would *that* justify ignoring

the unique characteristics of a *particular* Black youngster from the very beginning and specifically socializing him to become a musician? We don't think so. Similarly, as long as a woman's socialization does not nurture her uniqueness but treats her only as a member of a group on the basis of some assumed *average* characteristic, she will not be prepared to realize her own potential in the way that the values of individuality and self-fulfillment imply that she should.

THE PRESUMED INCOMPATIBILITY OF FAMILY AND CAREER

If we were to ask the average American woman why she is not pursuing a full-time career, she would probably not say that discrimination had discouraged her; nor would she be likely to recognize the pervasive effects of her own sex-role conditioning. What she probably would say is that a career, no matter how desirable, is simply incompatible with the role of wife and mother.

As recently as the turn of the century, and in less technological societies today, this incompatibility between career and family was, in fact, decisive. Women died in their forties and they were pregnant or nursing during most of their adult lives. Moreover, the work that a less technological society requires places a premium on mobility and physical strength, neither of which a pregnant woman has a great deal of. Thus, the historical division of labor between the sexes—the man away at work and the woman at home with the children—was a biological necessity. Today it is not.

Today, the work that our technological society requires is primarily mental in nature; women have virtually complete control over their reproductive lives; and most important of all, the average American woman now lives to age 74 and has her last child before age 30. This means that by the time a woman is 35 or so, her children all have more important things to do with their daytime hours than to spend them entertaining some adult woman who has nothing fulfilling to do during the entire second half of her life span.

But social forms have a way of outliving the necessities that gave rise to them. And today's female adolescent continues to plan for a 19th-century life-style in a 20th-century world. A Gallup poll has found that young women give no thought whatever to life after forty (Gallup & Hill, 1962). They plan to graduate from high school, perhaps go to college, and then get married. Period!

The Woman as Wife

At some level, of course, this kind of planning is "realistic." Because most women do grow up to be wives and mothers, and because, for many women, this means that they will be leaving the labor force during the child-rearing years, a career is not really feasible. After all, a career involves long-term commitment and perhaps some sacrifice on the part of the family. Futhermore, as every "successful" woman knows, a wife's appropriate role is to encourage her husband in *his* career. The "good" wife puts her husband through school, endures the family's early financial difficulties without a whimper, and, if her husband's career should suddenly dictate a move to another city, she sees to it that the transition is accomplished as painlessly as possible. The good wife is selfless. And to be seriously concerned about one's own career is selfish—if one is female, that is. With these kinds of constraints imposed upon the work life of the married woman, perhaps it would be "unrealistic" for her to seriously aspire toward a career rather than a job.

There is some evidence of discontent among these "selfless" women, however. A 1962 Gallup poll (Gallup & Hill, 1962) revealed that only 10% of American women would want their daughters to live their lives the way they did. These mothers wanted their daughters to get more education and to marry later. And a 1970 study of women married to top Chicago-area business and professional men (Ringo, 1970) revealed that if these women could live their lives over again, they would pursue careers.

Accordingly, the traditional conception of the husband-wife relationship is now being challenged, not so much because of this widespread discontent among older, married women, but because it violates two of the most basic values of today's college generation. These values concern personal growth, on the one hand, and interpersonal relationships, on the other. The first of these emphasizes individuality and self-fulfillment; the second stresses openness, honesty, and equality in all human relationships.

Because they see the traditional male-female relationship as incompatible with these basic values, today's young people are experimenting with alternatives to the traditional marriage pattern. Although a few are testing out ideas like communal living, most seem to be searching for satisfactory modifications of the husband-wife relationship, either in or out of the context of marriage. An increasing number of young people claim to be seeking fully egalitarian relationships, and they cite examples like the following:

Both my wife and I earned college degrees in our respective disciplines. I turned down a superior job offer in Oregon and accepted a slightly less desirable position in New York where my wife would have more opportunities for part-time work in her specialty. Although I would have preferred to live in a suburb, we purchased a home near my wife's job so that she could have an office at home where she would be when the children returned from school. Because my wife earns a good salary, she can easily afford to pay a housekeeper to do her major household chores. My wife and I share all other tasks around the house equally. For example, she cooks the meals, but I do the laundry for her and help her with many of her other household tasks.

Without questioning the basic happiness of such a marriage or its appropriateness for many couples, we can legitimately ask whether such a marriage is, in fact, an instance of interpersonal equality. Have all the hidden assumptions about the woman's "natural" role really been eliminated? Have our visionary students really exorcised the traditional ideology, as they claim? There is a very simple test. If the marriage is truly egalitarian, then its description should retain the same flavor and tone even if the roles of the husband and wife are reversed:

Both my husband and I earned college degrees in our respective disciplines. I turned down a superior job offer in Oregon and accepted a slightly less desirable position in New York where my husband would have more opportunities for part-time work in his speciality. Although I would have preferred to live in a suburb, we purchased a home near my husband's job so that he could have an office at home where he would be when the children returned from school. Because my husband earns a good salary, he can easily afford to pay a housekeeper to do his major household chores. My husband and I share all other tasks around the house equally. For example, he cooks the meals, but I do the laundry for him and help him with many of his other household tasks.

Somehow it sounds different, and yet only the pronouns have been changed to protect the powerful! Certainly no one would ever mistake the marriage *just* described as egalitarian or even very desirable, and thus it becomes apparent that the ideology about the woman's "natural" place unconsciously permeates the entire fabric of such "pseudo-egalitarian" marriages. It is true the wife gains some measure of equality when she can have a career rather than have a job, and when her career can influence the final place of residence. But why is it the unquestioned assumption that the husband's career solely determines the initial set of alternatives that are to be considered? Why is it the wife who automatically seeks the part-time position? Why is it *her* housekeeper rather than *their* housekeeper? Why *her* household tasks? And so forth throughout the entire relationship.

The important point is not that such marriages are bad or that their basic assumptions of inequality produce unhappy, frustrated women. Quite the contrary. It is the very happiness of the wives in such marriages that reveals society's smashing success in socializing its women. It is a measure of the distance our society must yet traverse toward the goal of full

equality that such marriages are widely characterized as utopian and fully egalitarian. It is a mark of how well the woman has been kept in her place that the husband in such a marriage is almost idolized by women, including his wife. Why? Because he "permits her" to squeeze a career into the interstices of their marriage as long as his own career is not unduly inconvenienced. Thus is the master blessed for exercising his power benignly while his "natural" right to that power forever remains unquestioned. Such is the subtlty of America's ideology about women.

In fact, however, even these "benign" inequities are now being challenged. More and more young couples really are entering marriages of full equality, marriages in which both partners pursue careers or outside commitments that carry equal weight when all important decisions are to be made, marriages in which both husband and wife accept some compromise in the growth of their respective careers for their mutual partnership. Certainly such marriages have more tactical difficulties than more traditional ones: it is simply more difficult to coordinate two independent lives rather than one-and-a-half. The point is that it is not possible to predict ahead of time, *on the basis of sex,* who will be doing the compromising at any given point of decision.

It should be clear that the man or woman who places career above all else ought not to enter an egalitarian marriage. The man would do better to marry a traditional wife, a wife who will make whatever sacrifices his career necessitates. The woman who places career above all else would do better—in our present society—to remain single. For an egalitarian marriage is not designed for extra efficiency, but for double fulfillment.

The Woman as Mother

In all marriages, whether traditional, pseudo-egalitarian or fully egalitarian, the real question surrounding a mother's career will probably continue to be the well-being of the children. All parents want to be certain that they are doing the very best for their children and that they are not depriving them in any important way, either materially or psychologically. What this has meant recently in most families that could afford it was that the mother would devote herself to the children on a full-time basis. Women have been convinced—by their mothers and by the so-called experts—that there is something wrong with them if they even want to do otherwise.

For example, according to Dr. Spock (1963), any woman who finds full-time motherhood unfulfilling is showing "a residue of difficult relationships in her own childhood." If a vacation doesn't solve the problem, then she is probably having emotional problems that can be relieved "through regular counseling in a family social agency, or if severe, through psychiatric treatment. . . . Any mother of a pre-school child who is considering a job should discuss the issues with a social worker before making her decision." The message is clear: if you don't feel that your 2-year-old is a stimulating, full-time companion, then you are probably neurotic.

In fact, research does not support the view that children suffer in any way when the mother works. Although it came as a surprise to most researchers in the area, maternal employment in and of itself does not seem to have any negative effects on the children; and part-time work actually seems to benefit the children. Children of working mothers are no more likely than children of nonworking mothers to be delinquent or nervous or withdrawn or antisocial; they are no more likely to show neurotic symptoms; they are no more likely to perform poorly in school; and they are no more likely to feel deprived of their mothers' love. Daughters of working mothers are more likely to want to work themselves, and, when asked to name the one woman in the world that they most admire, daughters of working mothers are more likely to name their own mothers! (Nye & Hoffman, 1963). This is one finding that we wish every working woman in America could hear, because the other thing that is true of almost every working mother is that she *thinks* she is hurting her children and she feels guilty. In fact, research has

shown that the worst mothers are those who would like to work, but who stay home out of a sense of duty (Yarrow, Scott, de Leeuw, & Heinig, 1962). The major conclusion from all the research is really this: what matters is the quality of a mother's relationship with her children, not the time of day it happens to be administered. This conclusion should come as no surprise; successful fathers have been demonstrating it for years. Some fathers are great, some fathers stink, and they're all at work at least eight hours a day.

Similarly, it is true that the quality of substitute care that children receive while their parents are at work also matters. Young children do need security, and research has shown that it is not good to have a constant turnover of parent-substitutes, a rapid succession of changing baby sitters or housekeepers (Maccoby, 1958). Clearly, this is why the establishment of child-care centers is vitally important at the moment. This is why virtually every woman's group in the country, no matter how conservative or how radical, is in agreement on this one issue: that child-care centers ought to be available to those who need them.

Once again, it is relevant to emphasize that child-care centers, like the other reforms advocated, are not merely for the benefit of middle-class women who wish to pursue professional careers. Of the 31 million women in the labor force, nearly 49% of them are working mothers. In 1960, mothers constituted more than one-third of the total woman labor force. In March, 1971, more than 1 out of 3 working mothers (4.3 million of them) had children under 6 years of age, and about half of these had children under 3 years of age. And most of these women in the labor force—like most men—work because they cannot afford to do otherwise. Moreover, they cannot currently deduct the full costs of child care as a business expense, as the executive can often deduct an expensive car. At the moment, the majority of these working women must simply "make do" with whatever child-care arrangements they can manage. Only 6% of their children under 6 years of age currently receive group care in child-care centers. *This* is why child-care centers are a central issue of the new feminist movement, why they are not just an additional luxury for the middle-class family with a woman who wants to pursue a professional career.

But even the woman who is educationally and economically in a position to pursue a career must feel free to utilize these alternative arrangements for child care. For, once again, America's sex-role ideology intrudes. Many people still assume that if a woman wants a full-time career, then children must be unimportant to her. But of course, no one makes this assumption about her husband. No one assumes that a father's interest in his career necessarily precludes a deep and abiding affection for his children or a vital interest in their development. Once again, America applies a double standard of judgment. Suppose that a father of small children suddenly lost his wife. No matter how much he loved his children, no one would expect him to sacrifice his career in order to stay home with them on a full-time basis—even if he had an independent source of income. No one would charge him with selfishness or lack of parental feeling if he sought professional care for his children during the day.

It is here that full equality between husband and wife assumes its ultimate importance. The fully egalitarian marriage abolishes this double standard and extends the same freedom to the mother. The egalitarian marriage provides the framework for both husband and wife to pursue careers that are challenging and fulfilling and, at the same time, to participate equally in the pleasures and responsibilities of child-rearing. Indeed, it is the egalitarian marriage that has the potential for giving children the love and concern of two parents rather than one. And it is the egalitarian marriage that has the most potential for giving parents the challenge and fulfillment of two worlds—family and career—rather than one.

In addition to providing this potential for equalized child care, a truly egalitarian marriage embraces a more general division of labor that satisfies what we like to call ''the roommate test.''

That is, the labor is divided just as it is when two men or two women room together in college or set up a bachelor apartment together. Errands and domestic chores are assigned by preference, agreement, or flipping a coin, alternated, given to hired help, or—perhaps most often—left undone.

It is significant that today's young people, so many of whom live precisely this way prior to marriage, find this kind of arrangement within marriage so foreign to their thinking. Consider an analogy. Suppose that a White male college student decided to room or set up a bachelor apartment with a Black male friend. Surely the typical White student would not blithely assume that his Black roommate was to handle all the domestic chores. Nor would his conscience allow him to do so even in the unlikely event that his roommate would say: ''No, that's okay. I like doing housework. I'd be happy to do it.'' We suspect that the typical White student would still not be comfortable if he took advantage of this offer, because he and America have finally realized that he would be taking advantage of the fact that such a roommate had been socialized by our society to be ''happy'' with such obvious inequity. But change this hypothetical Black roommate to a female marriage partner, and somehow the student's conscience goes to sleep. At most it is quickly tranquilized by the comforting though that ''she is happiest when she is ironing for her loved one.'' Such is the power of an unconscious ideology.

Of course, it may well be that she *is* happiest when she is ironing for her loved one.

Such, indeed, is the power of an unconscious ideology.

REFERENCES

Bird, C. *Born female: The high cost of keeping women down.* New York: Pocket Books, 1969.

Broverman, I. K., Broverman, D. M., Clarkson, F. E., Rosenkrantz, P. S., & Vogel, S. R. Sex-role stereotypes and clinical judgments of mental health. *Journal of Consulting and Clinical Psychology,* 1970, *34*, 1–7.

Brown, R. *Social psychology.* New York: Free Press, 1965.

Dodge, N. D. *Women in the Soviet economy*. Baltimore: Johns Hopkins Press, 1966.

Fisher, E. The second sex, junior division. *The New York Times Book Review,* May, 1970.

Gallup, G., & Hill, E. The American woman. *The Saturday Evening Post,* Dec. 22, 1962, pp. 15–32.

Goldberg, P. Are women prejudiced against women? *Transaction,* April, 1968, 28–30.

Goldberg, S., & Lewis, M. Play behavior in the year-old infant: Early sex differences. *Child Development,* 1969, *40,* 21–31.

Horner, M. S. Fail: Bright women. *Psychology Today,* November, 1969.

Maccoby, E. E. Effects upon children of their mothers' outside employment. In *Work in the lives of married women.* New York: Columbia University Press, 1958.

Milton, G. A. Sex differences in problem solving as a function of role appropriateness of the problem content. *Psychological Reports,* 1959, *5,* 705–708.

Nye, F. I., & Hoffman, L. W. *The employed mother in America.* Chicago: Rand McNally, 1963.

Ringo, M. The well-placed wife. Unpublished manuscript, John Paisios & Associates, 332 South Michigan Ave., Chicago, Illinois, 60604.

Spock, B. Should mothers work? *Ladies' Home Journal,* February, 1963.

Terman, L. M., & Oden, M. H. *Genetic studies of genius, V. The gifted group at mid-life: Thirty-five years' follow-up of the superior child.* Stanford, Calif.: Stanford University Press, 1959.

Thoman, E. B., Leiderman, P. H., & Olson, J. P. Neonate-mother interaction during breast feeding. *Developmental Psychology,* 1972, *6,* 110–118.

U.S. Department of Labor, Wage and Labor Standards Administration, Women's Bureau. Fact sheet on the earnings gap, February, 1970.

U.S. Department of Labor, Wage and Labor Standards Administration, Women's Bureau. *Handbook on women workers,* 1969. Bulletin 294.

Yarrow, M. R., Scott, P., de Leeuw, L., & Heinig, D. Child-rearing in families of working and non-working mothers. *Sociometry,* 1962, *25,* 122–140.

ARTICLE 17

Evaluation of the performance of women as a function of their sex, achievement, and personal history[1]

Gail I. Pheterson
Sara B. Kiesler
Philip A. Goldberg

One explanation for the apparent failure of women to achieve as much success as men is prejudicial evaluations of their work by men (cf. Klein, 1950; Scheinfeld, 1944). If men undervalue the accomplishments of women, women also may do so. Women's misjudgment of themselves should contribute to an actual lack of achievement. If women devalue their own and each other's work, they should be less willing to try to achieve and less supportive of their fellow women's efforts. The present study investigates the conditions under which women devalue female performance.

Goldberg (1968) designed a study to investigate prejudice among women toward women in the areas of intellectual and professional competence. College women were asked to evaluate supposedly published journal articles on linguistics, law, art history, dietetics, education, and city planning; for each article, half of the subjects saw a male author's name and half saw a female author's name. The results confirmed the hypothesis that college women value the professional work of men more highly than the identical work of women. Women devalued female work for no other reason than the female name associated with the article. Sensitivity to the sex of the author served to distort judgment and thereby prejudice women against the work of other women.

Using the identical procedure, Pheterson (1969) explored prejudice against women among middle-aged, uneducated women. The professional articles were on marriage, child discipline, and special education. The results did not support the findings of Goldberg. Women judged female work to be equal to male work; in fact, evaluations were almost significantly more favorable for female work than for male work.

The differing results of Goldberg and Pheterson were perhaps due to the different subjects used, to the different articles, or to some combination of the two. One plausible explanation might be that the

Reprinted from the *Journal of Personality and Social Psychology*, 1971, *19,* pp. 114–118. Copyright 1971 by the American Psychological Association. Reprinted by permission.
[1]This study was supported, in part, by funds from National Science Foundation Grant GS 27292 to the second author.

printed articles had different significance for the two sets of subjects. College women see the printed word frequently, are taught to be critical, and may take the publication of a paper relatively lightly. They might have viewed the articles simply as vehicles for presenting ideas or proposals. Uneducated women, on the other hand, might regard the publication or, even, writing of an article as a big accomplishment in itself, regardless of the specific ideas presented. Perhaps all women judge women less favorably than men when evaluating their proposals or unfinished work because men are more likely to succeed. That is, given a piece of work which has uncertain status, the man's, rather than woman's, is more likely in our society to eventually be successful. On the other hand, women may judge the recognized accomplishments or already successful work of women to be equal or even better than the same work of men. Success is less common for women. A contrast effect may cause people to overvalue achievement when they expect none. Also, women may overvalue female accomplishment because they assume that women face greater obstacles to success and therefore must exert more energy, display more competence, or make more sacrifices than men.

The present study was designed to investigate the divergent results of Goldberg (1968) and Pheterson (1969) and, further, to test the previously presented arguments. Women were asked to judge paintings created by men and women. Some paintings represented attempts to accomplish—that is, were entries in art competitions. Other paintings represented actual accomplishments—they had already won prizes. The first hypothesis was that women will evaluate male attempts to accomplish more highly than female attempts. The second hypothesis was that women will evaluate female accomplishments as equal to or better than male accomplishments.

The above hypotheses suggest that people judge successful persons more highly when they have more odds against them (as women presumably do). Thus, a woman's accomplishment might be praised more than a man's accomplishment because women face greater obstacles. Our culture shows great admiration for the achievements of the handicapped or underprivileged (Allport, 1958). A third hypothesis was formulated to explore this admiration and its influence on female judgments. It stated that women will evaluate the accomplishments of people with personal odds against them more favorably than the accomplishments of people without such odds.

METHOD

Subjects

The subjects were 120 freshmen and sophomore women students at Connecticut College. College women were used to permit a replication of the Goldberg (1968) study within the experimental design. They volunteered in student dormitories for immediate participation in the 15-minute task.

Experimental Design

There were three experimental manipulations constituting a 2 X 2 X 2 design. Eight paintings were presented to small groups of subjects for evaluation. The sex of the artist, the status of the paintings, and the personal odds faced by the artist were manipulated, such that for each painting half of the subjects thought that it had been created by a male artist, and half thought that it had been created by a female artist; half thought it was a prize-winning painting, and half thought it was just an entry in a show; half thought the artist had faced unusually severe obstacles, and half thought the artist had faced no unusual obstacles. Each subject participated in each experimental condition, evaluating all eight paintings sequentially. The identity of each painting was counterbalanced among subjects, so that all conditions were represented for each painting.

Procedure

Subjects were seated in a room equipped with a slide projector and screen. Each subject was given a booklet and was told to read the directions:

Slides of eight paintings will be shown in conjunction with brief biographical sketches of the artists. After viewing the slide, turn the page and answer five evaluative questions about the painting. No personal information about your identity, talents, or tastes is required. This is a study of the artistic judgments of college students.

The subjects were then instructed to read the first artist sketch, inspect the projected painting, turn the page and answer the appropriate questions, and then proceed in the same manner for each of the eight slides.

Eight slides of unfamiliar modern art painting were used. To accompany them, fictitious artist profiles were composed to include the eight experimental conditions. These profiles appeared in the booklets in different orders for the different subjects. Half of the profiles described a female artist, and half described a male. Their age, residence, and occupations were briefly described (identical for male and female). For example, "Bob (Barbara) Soulman, born in 1941 in Cleveland, Ohio, teaches English in a progressive program of adult education. Painting is his (her) hobby and most creative pastime." Cosss-cutting the sex manipulation, half of the profiles described the painting as a contest entry (e.g., "She has entered this painting in a museum-sponsored young artists' contest"), and half described it as a recognized winner (e.g., "This painting is the winner of the Annual Cleveland Color Competition"). In a third manipulation, half of the profiles described the painter as having had obstacles to success (e.g., "An arm amputee since 1967, he has been amazingly productive as an artist").

After each slide, the subjects turned a booklet page. Five questions asked the subjects to evaluate the paintings on a scale of 1–5, with higher ratings representing more favorable evaluations. After every slide, the following questions were posed: (a) Judging from this painting, how technically competent would you judge Mr. (or Miss) _____ to be? (b) How creative would you judge Mr. (or Miss) _____ to be? (c) What rating would you give to Mr. (or Miss) _____ for the overall quality and content of his (her) painting? (d) What emotional impact has Mr. (or Miss) _____ instilled in his (her) painting? (e) Judging from this painting, what prediction would you make for the artistic future of Mr. (or Miss) _____?

After all eight slides were shown, the study was explained, and the subjects were asked not to discuss it.

RESULTS

The questionnaire data were analyzed using four-way analyses of variance, with three experimental conditions and subjects as the fourth factor. Three questions asked the subjects to evaluate the artists; these were assumed to be directly relevant to the hypotheses.

The first question, technical competence, revealed an overall rating of the male artists as significantly superior to the female artists ($F=3.99$, $df=1/119$, $p<.05$). There was a significant Sex X Painting Status interaction ($F=5.42$, $df=1/119$, $p<.05$). Inspection of the mean ratings of males and females under winner and entry conditions indicates that the main effect of male superiority was attributable to the entry condition and showed no differences in the winner condition. Means in the entry condition differed significantly in favor of men ($t = 1.99$, $p < .05$); means in the winner condition were identical (see Table 1). All other main effects and interactions were not significant.

The question concerning the artistic future of the artist produced results paralleling the competence data (see Table 2). There was a significant Sex X Painting Status interaction ($F=4.52$, $df=1/119$, $p<.05$). Males were evaluated significantly more favorably than females for their entry paintings ($t=1.92$, $p<.06$). Evaluations did not differ significantly for the winning paintings, although evaluations tended to favor the female winners.

A third question, asking about the artist's creativity, yielded no significant differences. (Intui-

TABLE 1. Mean competence ratings of male and female artists with winning or entry paintings.

Status of painting	Sex of artist	
	Male	Female
Winner	3.483	3.483
Entry	3.562	3.354

TABLE 2. Mean ratings of artistic future of male and female artists with winning and entry paintings.

Status of painting	Sex of artist	
	Male	Female
Winner	2.970	2.987
Entry	3.062	2.812

tively, these data are not surprising, given the ambiguity of the term "creative." Also, "creativity" has some feminine connotations which judges may not wish to attribute to men, even when they believe the men are better artists.) In addition, the subjects evaluated the paintings themselves, equally among conditions (their quality and their emotional impact). Bias apparently was directed toward the performer, rather than toward his or her work.

The data presented above support our first and second hypotheses. Women value male work more highly than female work when it is only an attempt or entry; however, this bias dissipates when the work advances from entry to winner. The third hypothesis concerning the odds condition was not confirmed; there were no significant differences among the odds conditions.

DISCUSSION

Some professional women have claimed that their work is evaluated by men less well than it would be if they were men (e.g., Klein, 1950). The recent data of Goldberg (1968) and Pheterson (1969) have added a new dimension to the attitudi-

nal factors inhibiting female success. Under certain conditions, even women are prejudiced against the performance of other women. The present study investigated one aspect of this prejudice. Women evaluated female entries in a contest less favorably than identical male winners.

The implications of this finding are far-reaching. The work of women in competition is devalued by other women. Even work that is equivalent to the work of a man will be judged inferior until it receives special distinction, and that distinction is difficult to achieve when judgment is biased against the work in competition. According to the present data and those of Goldberg, women cannot expect unbiased evaluations until they prove themselves by award, trophy, or other obvious success. Obvious success is perceived differently by some groups than by others. The present research was based on the speculation that uneducated, middle-aged women perceived published articles as signs of obvious success, whereas college women perceived such work simply as a presentation of ideas. Women were prejudiced against female ideas but not against female success. The manipulation of entry and winner in this study permitted controlled examination and confirmation of that speculation.

A question might be raised regarding the strength of the present findings. Of five questionnaire items, only two supported our hypothesis. These were the first question (technical competence of the artist) and the fifth (the artist's future). However, a priori reasoning would suggest that these were the very questions where one would expect bias against women to occur. As mentioned earlier, creativity is ambiguous and may have feminine connotations. The paintings themselves were abstract, unknown, and also difficult to judge on the dimensions covered (quality and emotional impact). If people are expecting men to perform better than women, they should have the strongest expectations about tasks on which society has already labeled men as superior. In everyday life, many professional men are regarded as technically competent and are successful; we see fewer women in these positions (girls are not raised to be engineers or business executives). Thus, the subjects might simply be described as reflecting attitudes in society at large. They assume the men to be more competent and predicted a more successful future for men *unless* there was evidence to the contrary—that is, that the women had, in fact, succeeded. The subjects probably did not have very strong convictions about whether men are more creative than women (husbands usually leave such creative tasks as home decorating and sewing to their wives). The quality and emotional impact of an abstract painting are also unlikely to have aroused strong attitudes favoring men. We argue, then, that our questionnaire data reflected the differing expectations which women (or men) have about men and women. That is, a woman will probably be less competent and her accomplishments fewer than a man's, although she may be as creative (but probably not in science or business) and certainly as "emotional." Such an analysis implies that the subjects were not really judging the artists or paintings at all, but were simply expressing attitudes they held prior to the study. This, of course, was our purpose.

The third hypothesis, which predicted evaluations of paintings by people with odds against them to be more favorable in the winner condition than evaluations of identical paintings by people without odds, was not supported by the data. It is possible that the odds manipulation was too obvious. Perhaps some subjects were immediately aware of their special admiration for achievers with odds and therefore controlled their responses or underrated them, thus masking any positive bias the odds may have instilled. Informal subjects' feedback after the task supports this explanation. No subject suspected the importance of artist sex differences; however, many subjects reported the suspicion that they were expected to overvalue paintings of the handicapped or underprivileged. This suspicion may have caused

a reaction which obscured prejudicial responses. Remaining to be demonstrated, then, is the hypothesis that obstacles make successes seem greater.

Why do women devalue each others' performance? If one accepts women as a group which has important similarities to minority groups in our society, the answer is obvious. The members of minority groups, and women, have less power and fewer opportunities than do the dominant group, white Anglo-Saxon males. Self-defeating as it is, groups feeling themselves to be the target of prejudice nevertheless tend to accept the attitudes of the dominant majority. This process has also been called identification with the aggressor (Allport, 1958). Women, then, when confronted with another woman who is trying to succeed in some endeavor, will assume that she is less motivated, less expert, or simply less favored by others than a man would be (all these assumptions may be perfectly true).

Our data suggest that women do not devalue another woman when she has attained success. Without evidence, we think men do not either. In fact, a woman who has succeeded may be overevaluated. The present study apparently did not afford a proper test of this hypothesis. Perhaps if the artists had been identified as famous and really superior, women would have been rated more highly than men.

REFERENCES

Allport, G. W. *The nature of prejudice.* New York: Addison-Wesley, 1958.

Goldberg, P. A. Are women prejudiced against women? *Trans-action,* April 1968, 28–30.

Klein, X. V. The stereotype of femininity. *Journal of Social Issues,* 1950, **6,** 3–12.

Pheterson, G. I. Female prejudice against men. Unpublished manuscript, Connecticut College, 1969.

Scheinfeld, A. *Women and men.* New York: Harcourt, Brace, 1944.

ARTICLE 18

Another put-down of women? Perceived attractiveness as a function of support for the feminist movement

Philip A. Goldberg
Marc Gottesdiener
Paul R. Abramson

It is a matter of easy observation to note that the feminist movement has aroused strong feelings, negative and positive. It is also a matter of easy observation to note that physical attractiveness is an important element in interpersonal attractiveness (cf. Berscheid & Walster, 1972; Jourard & Secord, 1955).

Imputing unfavorable characteristics to people whose attitudes we do not like very much is simply one well-evidenced halo effect. An amusing example of this phenomenon as it applies to physical characteristics is provided by Kassarjian (1963). In his study, Kassarjian found that during the 1960 presidential election campaign, partisans overestimated the height of their candidate and underestimated the height of the opposing candidate.

This present study attempts to investigate the stereotypic view of the physical attractiveness of young women identified as supporters of the women's liberation movement. The specific questions that guided this research were: (a) How does the perception of attractiveness affect the attribution of feminist attitudes; (b) How well does this attribution correspond to reality; (c) To what extent are these judgments influenced by the person's own feminist attitudes; and (d) What differences, if any, are there in the judgments of men and women?

STUDY 1

Method

Subjects. The subjects were 40 male and 29 female introductory psychology students from the University of Connecticut who volunteered as part of their course requirement.

Reprinted from the *Journal of Personality and Social Psychology*, 1975, *32*, pp. 113–115. Copyright 1975 by the American Psychological Association. Reprinted by permission.

This research was supported in part from a National Science Foundation Grant from the University of Connecticut Computer Center gj 9 and the Connecticut College Psychology Department Research Fund.

The authors are indebted to Michael Morgan, Cleary Smith, and Phil Biscuti who served as the photographers and Linda C. Abramson who assisted in data preparation and analysis.

Procedure. Thirty female undergraduates were haphazardly selected from the campus of Connecticut College to participate in a study about women's liberation. These young women filled out a questionnaire ascertaining their attitudes toward the women's liberation movement and they were photographed. The questionnaire assessed whether they strongly supported the movement, supported the movement with little reservation, supported the movement but had serious reservations about it, did not support the movement, or strongly opposed the movement. The photographs were portraits, including in addition to the face only the shoulders of the female.

The 30, 7 x 5 inch (17.8 x 12.7 cm), black and white photographs were encased in plastic and bound into a booklet. Two complete booklets were used. Each photograph was numbered, and the number assigned was recorded on the women's movement questionnaire which corresponded to the female in the photograph.

The 69 introductory psychology students from the University of Connecticut judged the attractiveness of these photographs. The 69 subjects were individually administered a booklet and rated the attractiveness of the 30 photographs on a 5-point Likert scale. The raters were instructed to keep in mind that, in the general population, a score of 5 (extremely good looking) would be obtained by 8% of the population, a score of 4 (better than average looking) by about 17%, a score of 3 (average) by about 50%, a score of 2 (somewhat below average) by about 17%, and a score of 1 (considerably below average) by about 8% of the population. These rating procedures were identical to those used by Murstein (1972) in a study of physical attractiveness and marital choice.

Results

The results indicated that there were no significant sex differences in the ratings of any of the photographs. In addition, the data illustrated that the male and female mean ratings of attractiveness of the overall photographs were highly correlated ($r = .93$). Since there were no pronounced sex differences in the photo ratings, the scores of all the raters were pooled.

The mean attractiveness rating of all of the photographs was 2.81, with a standard deviation of .34. The ratings ranged from a mean of 3.59 ($SD = .87$) to a mean of 1.85 ($SD = .79$).

To investigate whether there were any real differences existing in attractiveness between women who support the women's liberation movement and those who do not, the 30 photographed females were split at the median into high and low support for the women's liberation movement groups. (The actual data indicated that 15 females strongly supported the movement, 14 had serious reservations about it, and 1 female did not support it at all.) Using the mean attractiveness ratings of these females, the results indicated that there were no significant differences in attractiveness ($t = 1.24$) between the high ($M = 2.69$, $SD = .50$) and low ($M = 2.92$, $SD = .49$) women's liberation movement support groups.

STUDY 2

Method

Subjects. The subjects were 41 male and 41 female introductory psychology students at the University of Connecticut who volunteered as part of their course requirement.

Procedure. The subjects were individually administered a booklet containing the 30 photographs described in the Procedure section of Study 1. They were informed that 15 of the women very strongly supported the women's liberation movement and 15 did not. The subjects were instructed to look at the photographs and put the numbers of the women who they believe supported the women's liberation movement in a column marked *Support* and the numbers of the women who did not support the women's liberation movement in a column marked *Not Support*. It was stressed that they make sure that there were 15 numbers in each column. In addition, each subject filled out the women's liberation questionnaire.

Results

The mean attractiveness ratings obtained in Study 1 for each of the numbered photographs were substituted for the numbers for which the subjects assigned to either supporting or not supporting the women's liberation movement columns. A one-way analysis of variance was performed for the difference between the mean attractiveness ratings of the perceived support versus perceived not support photographed women. The data strongly indicated that the women perceived as supporting the women's liberation movement $(M = 2.75, SD = .12)$ were rated significantly less attractive than the women perceived as not supporting the women's liberation movement $(M = 2.86, SD = .11; F = 33.36, p < .001)$.

The data were also analyzed separately by the sex of subject. Females rated those women they perceived as supporting the women's liberation movement $(M = 2.77, SD = .10)$ as significantly less attractive than the women they perceived as not supporting the movement $(M = 2.85, SD = .10; F = 11.65, p < .001)$. Males also rated the women they perceived as supporting the women's liberation movement $(M = 2.74, SD = .13)$ as significantly less attractive than the women they perceived as not supporting the movement $(M = 2.87, SD = .13; F = 21.73, p < .001)$.

The present findings also indicate that the subjects' own attitudes toward the women's liberation movement were uncorrelated with their mean attractiveness ratings. Female subjects' attitudes toward the women's liberation movement were uncorrelated with their mean attractiveness rating of women whom they perceived as not supporting the movement $(r = .07)$ and their mean attractiveness rating of women whom they perceived as supporting the movement $(r = -.11)$. Similar findings were obtained for male subjects. Their attitudes toward the women's liberation movement were uncorrelated with their mean attractiveness rating of women they perceived as not supporting the movement $(r = .19)$ and their mean attractiveness rating of women they perceived as supporting the movement $(r = -.20)$.

GENERAL DISCUSSION

The general results seem clear: Women who support the feminist movement are believed to be less attractive physically than their sisters who do not support the movement, though the evidence is that there is no true difference in attractiveness between the two groups.

The variables that did not yield differences are, perhaps, the most interesting. *Both* men and women responded similarly in associating unattractiveness with support for the women's liberation movement. This finding is, perhaps, consistent with the findings of Goldberg (1968) and Pheterson, Kiesler, and Goldberg (1971) who found that women shared in the general cultural prejudice against women.

Do the results represent further evidence of prejudice against women? One could argue that the data suggest that the subjects accepted a widely shared cultural stereotype, which is not, however, a prejudice. Or, that the derogation involved was directed against specific kinds of women from which one could not reasonably infer a more general misogyny.

Perhaps, we understand that expressions of concern for "law and order" often cloak racist attitudes and that opposition to "zionists" often means opposition to Jews generally. So too, it may be suggested, that the put-down of feminists might very well serve as a cover for a more generally misogynous attitude.

The finding that one's personal attitudes toward the women's liberation movement were uncorrelated with the categorization of supporters of the movement was unexpected, yet it is consistent with previous research on stereotyping with ethnic groups. Bettleheim and Janowitz's (1964) data, which were based on extensive interviews, found no significant relationship between personal stereotypes made about blacks or Jews and an individual's own attitudes toward these two groups. Similar results were obtained by Karlins, Coffman, and Walters (1969) with college students' stereotypes of 10 national and ethnic groups. They conclude that individuals possess stereotypes even though they may not often express them or feel affected by them.

Fishbein (1967) argues that it is a misconception to assume that an individual's attitude toward an object is a major determinant of his behavior with respect to that object. He summarizes research which indicates that attitudes were not related to behavior in any consistent fashion, but appear to be consequences or determinants of beliefs or behavioral intentions, rather than predictors of overt behavior.

The potential for trouble inherent in the ethnic stereotype is well-known (cf. Allport, 1954). Ethnic prejudice and prejudice toward women are not identical phenomena, but there is an increasing literature attesting to uncomfortable parallels. The results from this study may provide one more example for the pervasive social put-down to which women are subject.

REFERENCES

Allport, G. W. *The nature of prejudice*. Cambridge, Mass.: Addison-Wesley, 1954.

Berscheid, E., & Walster, E. Beauty and the best. *Psychology Today*, March 1972, 42–46.

Bettleheim, B., & Janowitz, M. *Social change and prejudice*. New York: Free Press, 1964.

Fishbein, M. A consideration of beliefs and their role in attitude measurement. In M. A. Fishbein (Ed.), *Readings in attitude theory and measurement*. New York: Wiley, 1967.

Goldberg, P. A. Are women prejudiced against women? *Trans-action*, 1968, *5*, 28–30.

Jourard, S. M., & Secord, P. F. Body cathexis and personality. *British Journal of Psychology*, 1955, *46*, 130–138.

Karlins, M., Coffman, T. L., & Walters, G. On the fading of social stereotypes: Studies in three generations of college students. *Journal of Personality and Social Psychology*, 1969, *13*, 1–16.

Kassarjian, H. H. Voting intentions and political perception. *Journal of Psychology*, 1963, *56*, 85–88.

Murstein, B. I. Physical attractiveness and marital choice. *Journal of Personality and Social Psychology*, 1972, *22*, 8–12.

Pheterson, G. I., Kiesler, S. B., & Goldberg, P. A. Evaluation of the performance of women as a function of their sex, achievement, and personal history. *Journal of Personality and Social Psychology*, 1971, *19*, 114–118.

SECTION SUMMARY

Freud's theory of sex differences seems to include five central hypotheses (Schaeffer, 1971):

1. Males and females both perceive females as inferior.
2. Females have a weaker superego than males.
3. Females identify with the mother less than males identify with the father.
4. Females are more jealous than males.
5. Masturbation, particularly during puberty, is much less common in girls than in boys.

The second article in this Section offers some clarifications of the first hypothesis. Previous studies (Goldberg, 1968: MacBrayer, 1960) had indeed supported Freud's hypothesis that females viewed themselves as inferior to men. But the more recent work of Pheterson, Kiesler, and Goldberg indicates that there are limits to this reaction; for example, if an artistic product has been recognized as exemplary, such a designation outweighs the "fact" that it has been done by a woman. Women do not devalue the *successful* products of another woman. However, recent research also indicates that accomplishments on "masculine" tasks are seen as better, by both men and women, than are (equally difficult) accomplishments on "feminine" tasks (Deaux & Emswiller, 1974). Our third article provides still further evidence that women may share in a "general cultural prejudice" against women.

Freud's second hypothesis was that the superego in men is more *internalized* than the superego in women; Freud felt that women do not incorporate the superego in their personality to the degree that men do (Hall, 1964). The supposedly less-internalized superego is more dependent on the outside world (parents, peers, authority figures, society in general) for sources of "correct" behavior. The more-internalized superego is more independent of such sources—more self-reliant. Using the content of dreams as material by which to judge strength of superego, Hall finds confirmation of Freud's hypothesis. However, there are several debatable

assumptions in Hall's use of dream content. For example, it is assumed that dreams in which the dreamer is a *victim of aggression* reflect an externalized superego, whereas dreams in which the dreamer is a *victim of misfortune* show an internalized superego, the latter supposedly reflecting a greater acceptance of guilt and self-blame. The reasoning is certainly tenuous.

Other research (Sears, Maccoby, & Levin, 1957; Rempel & Signori, 1964) finds the opposite, when the variable under study is the child's conscience. Sears and associates report that 29% of the girls observed had strong consciences, compared to 20% of the boys. Freud's hypothesis of retarded moral development in females, then, lacks consistent support at this time.

Do females identify with their mothers less than males identify with their fathers, as Freud's third hypothesis proposes? Blum (1949), using data from a projective test, concludes that Freud's hypothesis was correct, but Blum's study has been severely criticized (Seward, 1950). More recent research (Lynn, 1966) questions the accuracy of this hypothesis.

Freud also hypothesized that females are more jealous than males. The operational definition of jealousy was not specified, and the topic has apparently not been investigated by psychologists.

Freud's fifth hypothesis—dealing with sex differences in extent of masturbation—receives confirmation in the famous Kinsey studies of sexual behavior (Kinsey, Pomeroy, & Martin, 1948; Kinsey, Pomeroy, Martin, & Gebhard, 1953). Less than two-thirds (62%) of Kinsey's adult female sample reported that they had ever masturbated, whereas 93% of adult males reported having done so. Even more pronounced are sex differences in first masturbatory experience; 61% of the boys but only 8% of the girls reported having had their first such experience during puberty. Although Kinsey's data are self-reports, are subject to faking, and come from all-volunteer samples, more recent self-report studies of female college students confirm the differential rates reported by Kinsey (Davis, 1971; Kaats & Davis, 1970).

So the majority of Freud's hypotheses regarding female sexuality have not been supported by further research. And even the generality of the initial hypothesis—that both males and females perceive females as inferior—has its limits, as our second article shows. Yet Freud's largely unsupported hypotheses have been used for decades as a "scientific" sanction for sexism.

A belief in some "different status" of female sexuality dies hard, as do many other assumptions about female dependence and weakness. For example, Erik Erikson, a highly regarded contemporary neo-Freudian, has beneficially extended Freud's thinking in many areas. (For example, he is not content to see the stages of psychological development ending at puberty; instead he theorizes that they continue through adolescence, maturity, and even old age.) But although Erikson is quite critical of Freud's theory of sexual identification in women, he views women as relatively passive and masochistic. And Erikson, like Freud, bases his conclusion primarily on anatomical and physiological differences; he states that "there are aspects of the body . . . in which women are basically so different from men that the feminine ego has a very specific task to perform in integrating body, role, and individuality" (quoted in Evans, 1969, p. 47).

It is Erikson's view, rather than Freud's, that is most often invoked today by those who emphasize innate differences between the sexes. But Erikson himself, despite his condescending neo-sexist orientation, advocates some of the same changes that feminists do; he argues that women must be given positions of power in our society. But, paradoxically, he does so precisely because of what he calls their "feminine qualities" and the possible new directions he believes they have to offer (Erikson, 1965). So Erikson is right for the wrong reasons, and the unconscious ideology of sexism remains alive and intransigent in contemporary psychoanalytic thinking.

Traditional views of women's nature and role may be found elsewhere in contemporary literature. *The Prisoner of Sex* (1971), by Norman Mailer, contains a highly articulate exploration of this novelist's attitudes toward sex. Mailer is aware that he has been the recipient of violent attacks by many feminists because of the ways in which he has portrayed women and sexual relationships in his writings; hence he struggles in this book to understand his feelings toward women—their nature, their role in society, and their relationship to him.

And yet the outcome is not a step toward liberation for anyone. Mailer ends his analysis with the question he posed at the beginning: when a man and a woman live together, who finally does the dishes? Should the household work be equally divided? He reprints a "Marriage Agreement" developed by Shulman (1970) that includes the following preamble:

> We reject the notion that the work which brings in more money is more valuable. The ability to earn more money is already a privilege which must not be compounded by enabling the larger earner to buy out his/her duties and put the burden on the one who earns less, or on someone hired from outside. . . .
> As parents we believe we must share all responsibilities for taking care of our children and home—not only the work, but the responsibility [Shulman, 1970, p. 6].

Then follow a set of detailed procedures that operationalize the agreement. Mailer finds the following ones the most bothersome:

10. Cleaning: Husband does all the house-cleaning, in exchange for wife's extra childcare (3:00 to 6:30 daily) and sick care.
11. Laundry: Wife does most home laundry. Husband does all dry cleaning delivery and pick up. Wife strips beds, husband remakes them [Shulman, 1970, p. 6].

Mailer refuses to buy such an agreement. No, he would not be married to such a woman. He would not be happy about helping her "if his work should suffer, no, not unless her work was as valuable as his own" (Mailer, 1971, p. 165). But it is sadly clear that for Mailer *women's work could never be as valuable as his own*. He is a man, and man's work is "meaningful." After three months of self-analysis and 165 pages of print, the unconscious ideology remains: women's work is inferior. Truly this does reflect male chauvinism; it affirms that "my" work, just because I think it more creative or because it is more financially remunerative, is more "valuable" than hers (see Deaux & Emswiller, 1974).

One reason for the pervasiveness of the unconscious ideology of sexism is that sex-role stereotyping begins at such an early age. Boys learn early that they are more important than girls. As Bem and Bem indicate, parents respond differentially to male and female infants, and the kinds of clothing and toys that are given to boys are different from those given to girls. Girls are taught early to serve in menial roles, and parents assume that girls are more dependent and tied to the home.

Despite these parental behaviors, the evidence that male infants are less dependent than female infants is not that clear. Maccoby and Jacklin (1971), in reviewing the research, conclude that *ratings* (by observers) attribute more dependence to females, but actual recording of behavior does not show any greater level of dependent behavior in females. It is the *expectation* of observers that is different for each sex. Maccoby and Jacklin conclude:

It is our opinion that the bulk of evidence indicates that dependency and attachment behavior are characteristic of all human children, and that there is little or no differentiation by sex in this behavior from infancy through the preschool period. There may be some situations that elicit more of the behavior from one sex than the other, but so far we do not have a clear picture as to what the important situational factors are. Meanwhile, we cannot accept the generalization that girls are more passive-dependent than boys in early childhood [p. 7].

At present we cannot say whether any significant sex differences in dependence exist during infancy. If female infants *are* no more dependent than male infants, despite efforts of parents to make them so,

an implication is that as adults they need not manifest a greater degree of such behavior than do men. Thus, even if adult females should tend to be more dependent than males, this is a product of their learning of certain expectations and roles.

We are not advocating the position that there are no irrevocable sex differences in personality or temperament. The structural and physiological differences between the sexes are not to be denied, and they may influence one's response. For example, Maccoby and Jacklin conclude that the male sex is more aggressive than the female sex and speculate that this difference has biochemical, if not instinctual, causes.

The menstrual cycle in the female has a potential effect on changes in her temperament. Judith Bardwick (1970), after reviewing the relevant research, suggests that "there are regular predictable changes in the personality of sexually mature women that correlate with changes in the menstrual cycle. These personality changes are extreme, they occur in spite of individual personality differences, and they are the result of the endocrine or other physical changes that occur during the cycle" (p. 21).

In line with this evaluation, self-reports of irritability, depression, and anxiety quite consistently occur in women just before the onset of menstruation. Are these feelings physiologically determined, or are they the result of learning a stereotype about the expected behavior of females? A large proportion of the suicides and criminal acts of violence committed by women occur during the premenstrual and menstrual phases of the cycle (Dalton, 1964), which indicates that the physiological changes may be at least part of the cause.

But we need to recognize that men, too, may undergo changes in mood that are influenced by physiological changes. Men do not experience menstrual changes, but the fluctuations in their energy level, mood, and well-being from day to day and month to month may still be heavily influenced by physiological shifts (Luce, 1971). More body-based mood changes exist than most of us realize; to base explanations of female temperament changes on menstrual cycles, while avoiding any understanding of the causes of mood changes in men, reflects *scientific* male chauvinism!

Also, we need to recognize that the mood shift resulting from menstrual changes is not so great in some women as in others. We must reject a conclusion that the menstrual cycle strongly determines temperamental changes in *all* females. As Bem and Bem remind us, the most important difference is not the difference between the sexes but the difference *within* each sex.

Even if males as a group are more aggressive, there are large variations in degree of aggressiveness within that group. Although males as a group are physically stronger than females, there are some women who are physically stronger than some men. And even though it is the female sex that is capable of childbearing, not all females are able to do so. Our goal is a society in which these *individual* variations in personality and behavior are recognized and allowed to develop.

For this goal to be realized, we must shift our focus away from "the nature of women" to an understanding of the socialization of sex roles in our society. We must consider not only how women learn their "proper place" but also how men learn theirs. We need to consider the changing conceptions of "feminine" and "masculine." What do these terms mean now? What should they mean in the future? What reforms are necessary to liberate women—and men?

REFERENCES

Bardwick, J. M. Psychological conflict and the reproductive system. In J. M. Bardwick, E. Douvan, M. S. Horner, and D. Gutmann, *Feminine personality and conflict*. Monterey, Calif.: Brooks/Cole, 1970.

Blum, G. S. A study of psychoanalytic theory of psychosexual development. *Genetic Psychology Monographs*, 1949, *33*, 3–99.

Dalton, K. *The premenstrual syndrome*. Springfield, Ill.: Charles C Thomas, 1964.

Davis, K. E. Sex on campus: Is there revolution? *Medical Aspects of Human Sexuality*, 1971, *5*, 128–142.

Deaux, K., & Emswiller, T. Explanations of successful performance on sex-linked tasks: What is skill for the male is luck for the female. *Journal of Personality and Social Psychology*, 1974, *29*, 80–85.

Erikson, E. Reflections of womanhood. In R. J. Lifton (Ed.), *The woman in America*. Boston: Houghton Mifflin, 1965. Pp. 1–26.

Evans, R. I. *Dialogue with Erik Erikson*. New York: Dutton, 1969.

Freud, S. Some psychological consequences of the anatomical distinction between the sexes. In E. Jones (Ed.), *The collected papers of Sigmund Freud*. Vol. 5, Chapter 17. New York: Basic Books, 1959. (Originally published in German in 1925.)

Goldberg, P. Are women prejudiced against women? *Trans-action*, 1968, *5*(4), 28–30.

Hall, C. A modest confirmation of Freud's theory of a distinction between the superego of men and women. *Journal of Abnormal and Social Psychology*, 1964, *69*, 440–442.

Kaats, G. R., & Davis, K. E. The dynamics of sexual behavior of college students. *Journal of Marriage and the Family*, 1970, *32*, 390–399.

Kinsey, A. C., Pomeroy, W. B., & Martin, C. E. *Sexual behavior in the human male*. Philadelphia: Saunders, 1948.

Kinsey, A. C., Pomeroy, W. B., Martin, C. E., & Gebhard, P. H. *Sexual behavior in the human female*. Philadelphia: Saunders, 1953.

Luce, G. G. *Body time*. New York: Pantheon, 1971.

Lynn, D. B. The process of learning parental and sex-role identification. *Journal of Marriage and the Family*, 1966, *28*, 466–470.

MacBrayer, C. T. Differences in the perception of the opposite sex by males and females. *Journal of Social Psychology*, 1960, *52*, 309–314.

Maccoby, E. E., & Jacklin, C. N. Sex differences and their implications for sex roles. Paper presented at the meeting of the American Psychological Association, Washington, D.C., September, 1971.

Mailer, N. *The prisoner of sex*. New York: New American Library, 1971.

Rempel, H., & Signori, E. I. Sex differences in self-rating of conscience as a determinant of behavior. *Psychological Reports*, 1964, *15*, 277–278.

Schaeffer, D. L. (Ed.), *Sex differences in personality: Readings*. Monterey, Calif.: Brooks/Cole, 1971.

Sears, R. R., Maccoby, E., & Levin, H. *Patterns in child rearing*. Evanston, Ill.: Row-Peterson, 1957.

Seward, J. P. Psychoanalysis, deductive methods, and the Blacky test. *Journal of Abnormal and Social Psychology*, 1950, *45*, 529–535.

Shulman, A. Marriage agreement. *Off Our Backs*, Nov. 8, 1970, p. 6.

GROUP PROCESSES: DEINDIVIDUATION, GROUPTHINK, AND WAR

INTRODUCTION

The material we have covered so far has dealt largely with the behavior of separate individuals. In this Section we look at the behavior of individuals in *groups*. A group can be described as a *unitary entity* that is held together by the *common interests* and *goals* of the group members and that is *organized* to a greater or lesser degree. All of us are members of numerous groups at any particular time. Although there are a great number of interesting and important areas for study within this general area, we will focus on three particular aspects of group interactions: deindividuation, decision-making, and war.

Why should one join a group? There seem to be two general types of reasons (Schachter, 1959). First, a person can join a group as a means to an end, in order to achieve things that he or she could not achieve alone. Second, groups may represent goals in and of themselves; things such as approval, prestige, praise, love, and friendship can only be received from other people.

An additional process that can occur only with the presence of other people has been called *dein-*

dividuation (Festinger, Pepitone, & Newcomb, 1952). Deindividuation refers to a state of relative anonymity wherein group members do not feel singled out or identifiable. Deindividuation may lead to both (1) changes in how people perceive themselves, and (2) lowered restraints on behavior. These two changes in turn could be expected to cause an increase in antisocial or unusual behaviors. If people feel that they are anonymous members of the group, might they not commit acts that they would never commit if they were alone?

Research suggests that persons may indeed commit socially undesirable acts when they feel deindividuated and unidentifiable—acts that they would be less likely to commit if they felt identifiable (for example, Zimbardo, 1970; Cannavale, Scarr, & Pepitone, 1970). Although it seems possible that deindividuation could also lead to socially acceptable behaviors that are often inhibited, such as crying or expressions of joy, this possibility has not received as much research attention.

One way of increasing feelings of deindividuation is to make individuals unidentifiable by having them wear identical uniforms and hats and even reflector sunglasses (so that their eyes cannot be seen). Philip G. Zimbardo and his colleagues at Stanford University have suggested that in our society the prison situation is one in which feelings of deindividuation are likely to be strong. Guards may wear identical uniforms, and in some cases prisoners are given numbers and may also have to wear identical uniforms. In our first article, Zimbardo and his colleagues describe a *simulation study* in which they attempted to simulate the conditions of a prison in the basement of the Psychology building at Stanford University. In particular they attempted to re-create conditions of time disorientation, enforced child-like dependence, an oppressive physical environment, and anonymity.

All subjects in the prison study were "normal" college students who were paid $15 a day for their participation and randomly assigned to being either prisoners or guards. As you will see, Zimbardo and his co-workers went to a good deal of trouble to make the "arrest" and "prison" situation as realistic as possible. Nevertheless, neither the researchers nor the subjects were at all prepared for the intensity of the experience that followed.

What happens when a group gets together to make a decision? Many writers have argued that the decision resulting from the "team approach" in business enterprises, for example, will result in a reduced level of involvement and in a conservative course of action (Whyte, 1956). Yet research indicates that this is not necessarily the case. In fact, the so-called *risky shift* effect indicates that group decisions are often likely to be *more* risky or extreme than decisions made by comparable individuals who are working separately. While this "shift to risk" does not take place under all circumstances, it is still a very widespread occurrence (see, for example, Myers & Lamm, 1976).

One group decision that had terribly negative effects for many United States citizens was the decision is to sponsor the Bay of Pigs invasion of President John F. Kennedy's Executive Committee in 1961 that the United States should sponsor an invasion of Cuba by Cuban refugees. The invasion was a complete disaster. Of the 1400 Cuban exiles who were trained, equipped, and sent on the invasion mission, 200 died. The remaining 1200, who had landed at the Bay of Pigs in Cuba, spent seven months in Cuban prisons and were finally ransomed by the United States government for food and drugs worth 53 million dollars. This incident also pushed Cuban Premier Fidel Castro into closer interaction with the Soviet Union and perhaps set up the Cuban "missile crisis" of 1962, during which the U.S. and the Soviet Union came frighteningly close to nuclear war.

The decision to sponsor the Bay of Pigs invasion was a disastrous one, and, in retrospect, downright stupid. Yet it was made by a group of very bright, talented government officials. How could these talented persons have come to such a bad decision?

Irving Janis, at Yale University, has studied the accounts of what went on at the meetings leading to this decision as well as to other similarly disastrous governmental decisions. He has proposed that a process that he calls *groupthink* took place. Groupthink, according to Janis, represents a way to maintain the self-esteem of group members who are confronted by a challenging, important decision. Group members strive for consensus and unanimity so that they can feel more secure in their decision. Unfortunately, this striving rules out critical, independent thinking, checking of information, attention to moral concerns, and self-doubts about the wisdom of the group's decision. The group seals itself off from the outside and rationalizes the worth of its decision. The phenomena of groupthink and risky shift may often interact in a decision situation. Once a group has decided on a riskier decision than they would have advocated as individuals (for example, sponsoring the invasion of Cuba), then the process of groupthink may operate as a way of *justifying* the decision. In our second article Janis outlines the salient characteristics of groupthink as they were apparent in the decision to sponsor the Bay of Pigs invasion.

It has been proposed by many political writers (for example, Halberstam, 1972) that United States conduct of the Vietnam War in the 1960s and early 1970s was characterized by a whole series of poorly thought-out, unwise decisions. In our third reading, Ralph K. White outlines some of the delusions and misconceptions that can lead to incorrect decisions in wars such as the Vietnam conflict.

White has had a long career in international affairs. He worked for the Central Intelligence Agency (1947 to 1951) and the Voice of America (1951 to 1954) and directed the Division of Research and Reference Service for the United States Information Agency (1954 to 1964). He has traveled widely in both the Soviet Union and Vietnam.

In his article, White focuses on the difficulties in international communication. As he notes, there is often a "mirror image" in the way that the people of different nations view one another (see Bronfenbrenner, 1961). He also discusses the effect of territorial self-image and the "pro-us illusion"—the tendency to see people in the other country as more friendly to one's own side than they actually are.

(One of the mistaken views of those sponsoring the Bay of Pigs invasion was that the Cuban people would rise up to help the invaders overthrow Castro. Such a local revolt never materialized.)

REFERENCES

Bronfenbrenner, U. The mirror-image in Soviet-American relations. *Journal of Social Issues,* 1961, *17*(3), 45–56.

Cannavale, F. J., Scarr, H. A., & Pepitone, A. Deindividuation in the small group: Further evidence. *Journal of Personality and Social Psychology,* 1970, *16,* 141–147.

Festinger, L., Pepitone, A., & Newcomb, T. Some consequences of deindividuation in groups. *Journal of Abnormal and Social Psychology,* 1952, *47,* 382–389.

Halberstam, D. *The best and the brightest.* New York: Random House, 1972.

Myers, D. G., & Lamm, H. The group polarization phenomenon. *Psychological Bulletin,* 1976, *83,* 602–627.

Schachter, S. *The psychology of affiliation.* Stanford, Calif.: Stanford Univ. Press, 1959.

Whyte, W. H., Jr. *The organization man.* New York: Simon & Schuster, 1956.

Zimbardo, P. G. The human choice: Individuation, reason, and order versus deindividuation, impulse, and chaos. In W. J. Arnold and D. Levine (Eds.), *Nebraska symposium on motivation, 1969.* Lincoln, Neb.: Univ. of Nebraska Press, 1970. Pp. 237–307.

ARTICLE 19

The psychology of imprisonment: Privation, power and pathology[1]

Philip G. Zimbardo
Craig Haney
W. Curtis Banks
David Jaffe

In prison, those things withheld from and denied to the prisoner become precisely what he wants most of all.

Eldridge Cleaver, *Soul on Ice* (1968)

Our sense of power is more vivid when we break a man's spirit than when we win his heart.

Eric Hoffer, *The Passionate State of Mind* (1954)

Every prison that men build is built with bricks of shame, and bound with bars lest Christ should see how men their brothers maim.

Oscar Wilde, *The Ballad of Reading Gaol* (1898)

Wherever any one is against his will, that is to him a prison.

Epictetus, *Discourses* (2nd. cent.).

The quiet of a Sunday morning in Palo Alto, California was shattered by a screeching squad car siren as police swept through the city picking up college students in a surprise mass arrest. Each suspect was charged with a felony, warned of his constitutional rights, spread-eagled against the police car, searched, handcuffed and carted off in the back seat of the squad car to the police station for booking. In some cases, curious neighbors who witnessed these arrests expressed sympathy and concern to the families of these unfortunate young men. Said one alarmed mother of an 18-year-old college sophomore arrested for armed robbery, ''I felt my son must have done something; the police have come to get my son!''

After being fingerprinted and having identification forms prepared for his ''jacket'' (central infor-

[1]This research was funded by ONR grant N00014–67–A–0112–0041 to P. G. Zimbardo. The ideas expressed here are those of the authors and are not necessarily endorsed by ONR or any sponsoring agency. We wish to acknowledge the invaluable contributions to this research of Carlo Prescott, our prison consultant, who generously shared with us his insights into the nature of imprisonment. Greg White helped immeasurably in the data-reduction phase of this research, and we are indebted to him and to the many other students, Palo Alto Police, and Stanford University personnel who assisted in the various stages of creating and operating this mock prison, as well as collecting and analyzing the data it generated.

mation file), each prisoner was left isolated in a detention cell to wonder what he had done to get himself into this mess. After a while, he was blindfolded and transported to the "Stanford County Prison." Here he began the induction process of becoming a prisoner—stripped naked, skin searched, deloused, and issued a uniform, bedding, soap, towel, toothpaste and toothbrush.

The prisoner's uniform was a loosely fitting smock with an ID number on front and back. A chain was bolted around one ankle and had to be worn at all times. In place of having his head shaved, the prisoner had to wear a nylon stocking cap over his head to cover his hair. Orders were shouted at him and the prisoner was pushed around by the guards if he didn't comply quickly enough. By late afternoon, when all the arrests were completed, and each prisoner had been duly processed, the warden greeted his new charges with an impromptu welcome:

As you probably already know I'm your Warden. All of you have shown that you are unable to function outside in the real world for one reason or another—that somehow you lack a responsibility of good citizens of this great country. We of this prison, your correctional staff, are going to help you learn what your responsibilities as citizens of this country are. Here are the rules. Sometime in the very near future there will be a copy of the rules posted in each of the cells. We expect you to know them and to be able to recite them by number. If you follow all of these rules and keep your hands clean, repent for your misdeeds and show a proper attitude of penitence, you and I will get along just fine.

There followed a reading off of the sixteen basic rules of prisoner conduct (which the warden and his staff of eleven correctional officers had compiled):

Rule Number One: Prisoners must remain silent during rest periods, after lights out, during meals, and whenever they are outside the prison yard. *Two:* Prisoners must eat at mealtimes and only at mealtimes. *Three:* Prisoners must not move, tamper, deface or damage walls, ceilings, windows, doors, or other prison property. . . . *Seven:* Prisoners must address each other by their ID number only. *Eight:* Prisoners must address the guards as "Mr. Correctional Officer". . . . *Sixteen:* Failure to obey any of the above rules may result in punishment.

Most of the nine prisoners, all "first-offenders," sat on the cots in their barren cells dazed and shocked by the unexpected events which had transformed their lives so suddenly.

Something out of the ordinary *was* indeed taking place. For the police, the arrests they had made were of a routine sort and had been executed with their usual efficiency. But what was unusual were the blindfolds, the ankle chains, the stocking caps, smocks—and the long-haired, hippie-looking *guards*. Just what kind of prison was this?

We're all of us guinea pigs in the laboratory of God. Humanity is just a work in progress.

Tennessee Williams, *Camino Real*

It was, in fact, a very special kind of prison—an experimental, mock prison—created specifically for the purpose of investigating the psychological effects of imprisonment upon volunteer research subjects. When we planned our two-week-long simulation of prison life, we sought answers to a number of questions of social and academic interest. How do men adapt to the novel and alien situation in which those called "prisoners" lose their liberty, civil rights and their privacy, while those called "guards" gain power and social status? What is responsible for the alleged brutality and violence in American prisons—is it the nature of the prison population (presumably filled with sociopathic criminals and sadistic guards), or is it the social-psychological environment of the prison experience? Under what conditions can a role-playing simulation achieve a sufficient level of reality to become more than just a game (in this instance, one of "cops and robbers"), so that it is both a source of new self-knowledge for the participants and one of socially relevant knowledge for the researchers studying it?

Our mock prison represented an attempt to simulate *functionally* some of the significant features of the psychological state of imprisonment. We did this by first making an intensive conceptual analysis of the variables involved in the prison situation after spending hundreds of hours in discussions with ex-convicts, parole officers, and correctional personnel, and after reviewing much of the existing literature on prisons and concentration camps. We then formulated a set of procedures to operationalize these variables so they would be maximally effective given the limitations and constraints of the setting available to us. We did not intend to generate a *literal* simulation of "real" prison details or standard operational practices. Rather, our primary concern was to achieve some equivalent psychological effects despite differences between the form and structure of the particular operations employed in the "Stanford County Prison" and those in "real" prisons. We did, however, try to introduce enough "mundane realism" (Aronson & Carlsmith, 1969) into the experience so that the role-playing participants might be able to go beyond the superficial demands of their assigned roles into the deep structure of the prisoner and guard mentality. This was accomplished in part through the cooperation of the local Police Department, who made the unexpected arrests appear as part of a routine raid. A local TV station sent a cameraman to film the "arrests," which furthered the illusion of a newsworthy event actually taking place and encouraged the arresting officers to act their roles convincingly. Realism was enhanced by a visit to the prison from a Catholic priest who had been a prison chaplain, by a public defender who discussed bail and trial procedures with the prisoners, and by parents, relatives and friends during several scheduled visitors' hours. There were parole board meetings as well as disciplinary meetings headed by an ex-convict and staffed by "adult authorities" who were strangers to the prisoners. Small details, such as stationery imprinted with the name of the prison, also helped to carry some of the burden of realism. Thus, for example, the mother of prisoner 5486 reported to the Prison Superintendent that she had felt guilty when the mailman, delivering a letter from her imprisoned son, asked her what was the charge against him and whether his case had gone to trial yet.

The prison was physically constructed in the basement of Stanford University's Psychology building, which was deserted after the end of the summer school session. A long corridor was converted into the prison "Yard" by partitioning off both ends. Three 6 ft. × 9 ft. laboratory rooms opening onto this corridor were made into cells by replacing their doors with barred ones and replacing existing furniture with three cots (to a cell). A small, dark storage closet opposite the cells served as solitary confinement, and was posted with an appropriate sign, "THE HOLE." Adjacent offices were refurnished as guards' quarters, interview-testing rooms and bedrooms for the "Warden" (Jaffe) and the "Superintendent" (Zimbardo). Toilet facilities (without showers) were available in a nearby corridor. A concealed video camera and hidden microphones recorded much of the verbal and nonverbal interactions between and among guards and prisoners. The physical environment was one in which prisoners could always be observed by the staff, except when they were secluded in solitary confinement.

These quarters, although clean and neat, were rather small, stark and without aesthetic appeal. No unplanned interruptions or distractions were possible, and the natural variation in sensory stimulation was minimal. The lack of windows resulted in poor air circulation, and persisting odors arose from the unwashed bodies of the prisoners. After 10 P.M. lockup, toilet privileges were denied, so prisoners who had to relieve themselves would have to urinate and defecate in buckets provided by the guards. Sometimes, the guards refused permission to have them cleaned out and this made the prison smell.

We are aware of the content of experience, but unaware that it is illusion. We see the shadows, but take them for substance.

R. D. Laing, *Self and Others*

"Real" prisoners typically report feeling powerless, arbitrarily controlled, dependent, frustrated, hopeless, anonymous, dehumanized and emasculated. It is not possible, pragmatically or ethically, to create such chronic states in volunteer subjects who realize that they are in an experiment for only a short time. Racism, physical brutality, indefinite confinement and enforced homosexuality were not features of our mock prison (see Davis, 1968, regarding sexual assaults). Instead, we created symbolic manifestations of those variables presumably fundamental to the experience of being imprisoned.

Anonymity was promoted through a variety of operations to minimize each prisoner's uniqueness and prior identity (see Zimbardo, 1970). Their uniforms, ID numbers and caps, as well as removal of their personal effects and their being housed in barren cells, all made the subjects appear similar to each other, often indistinguishable to observers, and forced upon them the situational group identity of "prisoner." Having to wear smocks, which were like dresses, without undergarments caused the prisoners to be more restrained in their physical actions and to move in ways which were more feminine than masculine. Forcing the prisoners to obtain permission from the guards for routine and simple activities such as writing letters, smoking a cigarette or even going to the toilet elicited from them a child-like dependency.

The oppressiveness of the environment was exaggerated by the absence of clocks or windows to mark the passage of time, by the constant surveillance of the guards, the total lack of privacy, and also by the significance of having always to wear the ankle chain.

Above all, "real" prisons are time machines for playing tricks with the human conception of time. In our prison, the prisoners often did not even know whether it was day or night, or what hour it was. A few hours after falling asleep, they were rousted by shrill whistles for their "count." The ostensible purpose of the count was to provide a public test of the prisoners' knowledge of the rules and of their ID numbers. But more importantly for us, the counts, which occurred at least once on each of the three different guard shifts, provided a regular occasion for the guards to relate to the prisoners under conditions where these interactions could be recorded and

subsequently analyzed. Over the course of the study, the duration of the counts was gradually and spontaneously increased by the guards from their initial perfunctory ten minutes to a seemingly interminable several hours. During these interactions, guards who were bored could find ways to amuse themselves, recalcitrant prisoners could be ridiculed, arbitrary rules could be enacted, and any dissension among the prisoners could be openly exacerbated by the guards.

The experience of going to sleep after a day of continual harassment, being awakened abruptly a few hours later, going through the tedium of the count, returned to sleep, awakened in the morning to start another day of imprisonment, had the effect of stretching time out, making it pass slowly in a seemingly unending circular, rather than linear flow. Thus, for the prisoners the subjective duration of their imprisonment was much greater than that reckoned by objective, clock time, which ceased to have much validity for them in this prison.

The time slips away from me. . . .There is no rest from it even at night. . . . The days, even the weeks lapse into each other, endlessly into one another. Each day that comes and goes is exactly like the one that went before.

George Jackson, *Soledad Brother*

The guards were also "deindividuated" by virtue of wearing identical khaki uniforms and silver reflector sunglasses which made eye contact with them impossible. Their symbols of power were billy clubs, whistles, handcuffs and the keys to the cells and the "main gate." Although our guards received no formal training from us in how to be guards, for the most part they moved with apparent ease into their roles. Movies, TV, novels, and all of our mass media had already provided them with ample models of prison guards to emulate.

Said one of the toughest guards, "I didn't plan things out ahead of time. It was all spur of the moment, ad lib, so to speak, and well I guess there's enough information in me that was taken from plays that I've read and movies that I've seen that enabled me to come out with a lot of things. . .'' Just as ''real'' correctional officers subjected to these very same cultural influences, our mock guards had available to them behavioral templates of what it means to be a guard, upon which they could build their role performances. So, too, with the mock prisoners.

Our guards were told that they must maintain ''law and order'' in this prison, that they were responsible for handling any trouble which might break out, and they were cautioned as to the seriousness and potential dangers of the situation they were about to enter. Surprisingly, in most prison systems, ''real'' guards are not given much more psychological preparation than this for what is one of the most difficult, demanding and dangerous jobs imaginable. They are expected to learn how to adjust to their new employment from on-the-job experience, as documented in the Orientation Manual for correctional personnel at San Quentin Prison (July, 1970):

The only way you really get to know San Quentin is through experience and time. Some of us take more time and must go through more experiences than others to accomplish this; some really never do get there.

The confrontation between our mock guards and prisoners was motivated initially by the desire to earn the money we were paying for their participation in this experiment—$15 per day for an eight-hour guard duty and the same amount for each twenty-four-hour period of prisoner confinement. However, over time, the money became an abstraction, a remote source of extrinsic justification which was much less compelling than the intrinsic sources of motivation which evolved from the dynamics of the prisoner-guard relationship itself. For example, guards often worked overtime, never asking to be paid for it, were never late nor called in sick, nor did they demand more money after realizing how difficult, exhausting and tedious their job was. The prisoners did not complain of the inequity between their payment and that of the guards, and by the end of the study, all but two were willing to forfeit the

money they had earned working as inmates if we would parole them. There is considerable evidence from a variety of self-reports and observational measures to indicate that these subjects were deeply into the experience of being guards and prisoners, much more so than we had thought was possible in an experiment.

The symbolic interaction between guards and prisoners requires each to play his own role while also forcing the others to play their role appropriately. You cannot be a prisoner if no one will be your guard, and you cannot be a prison guard if no one takes you or your prison seriously. Therefore, over time a perverted symbiotic relationship developed. As the guards became more aggressive, prisoners became more passive; assertion by the guards led to dependency in the prisoners; self-aggrandizement was met with self-deprecation, authority with helplessness, and the counterpart of the guards' sense of mastery and control was the depression and hopelessness witnessed in the prisoners. As these differences in behavior, mood and perception became more evident, the need for the now ''righteously'' powerful guards to rule the obviously inferior and powerless inmates became sufficient justification to support almost any further indignity of man against man.

Power takes as ingratitude the writhing of its victims.

Rabindranath Tagore, *Stray Birds*.

Consider the following typical comments by different members of our ''correctional staff'' taken from their diaries, post-experimental interviews and ''critical incident report files'':

Guard: I was surprised at myself. . .I made them call each other names and clean the toilets out with their bare hands. I practically considered the prisoners cattle, and I kept thinking I have to watch out for them in case they try something.
Guard: During the inspection, I went to cell 2 to mess up a bed which the prisoner had made and he grabbed me, screaming that he had just made it, and he wasn't going to let me mess it up. He grabbed my throat, and although he

was laughing I was pretty scared. I lashed out with my stick and hit him in the chin (although not very hard) and when I freed myself I became angry.

Guard: I was tired of seeing the prisoners in their rags and smelling the strong odors of their bodies that filled the cells. I watched them tear at each other on orders given by us.

Guard: (Preparing for the first Visitors' Night). After warning the prisoners not to make any complaints unless they wanted the visit terminated fast, we finally brought in the first parents. I made sure I was one of the guards on the yard, because this was my first chance for the type of manipulative power that I really like—being a very noticed figure with almost complete control over what is said or not. While the parents and prisoners sat in chairs, I sat on the end of the table dangling my feet and contradicting anything I felt like. This was the first part of the experiment I was really enjoying.

Guard: Acting authoritatively can be fun. Power can be a great pleasure.

It was not long before the guards began to demonstrate their inventiveness in the application of arbitrary power. They made the prisoners obey petty, meaningless and often inconsistent rules, and forced them to engage in tedious, useless work, such as moving cartons back and forth between closets and picking thorns out of their blankets for hours on end. Not only did the prisoners have to sing songs or laugh or refrain from smiling on command, but they were also encouraged to curse and vilify each other publicly during some of the counts. They sounded off their numbers endlessly, and were repeatedly made to do pushups, on occasion with a guard stepping on them or a prisoner sitting on them. Pushups were the most common form of physical punishment employed by the guards for infractions of the rules or displays of improper attitudes toward them or the institution. When we observed the guards doing this, we thought it was an appropriate form of punishment in a prison, too, much like fraternity hazing. However, we have learned from the drawings and account of a former inmate (A. Kantor, 1971) that pushups were often used in Nazi concentration camps as mass punishment for men already at the point of physical exhaustion.

Not only did the prisoners become resigned to their fate; they even behaved in ways which actually helped to justify their dehumanizing treatment at the hands of the guards. Analysis of the tape-recorded private conversations between prisoners and of remarks made by them to interviewers revealed that fully half could be classified as non-supportive of other prisoners. More dramatic is the significant finding that 85% of the evaluative statements by prisoners about their fellow prisoners were uncomplimentary and deprecating!

Prisoner: That 2093, the rest of us use him as a scapegoat. . . . We couldn't understand how he could mentally comply with everything asked of him.

This result should be taken in the context of an even more suprising one. What do you imagine the prisoners talked about when they were alone in their cells with each other, given a temporary respite from the continual harassment and surveillance by the guards? Girl friends, career plans, hobbies, politics, home town, and so on, were what we assumed would be the major topics of conversation. But instead, their concerns were almost exclusively riveted to prison topics. Their monitored conversations revealed only 10% of the time was devoted to "outside" topics, while 90% of the time they discussed escape plans, the food, grievances, opinions about ingratiation tactics to use with specific guards in order to get a cigarette, permission to go to the toilet, or some other favor. Becoming obsessed with these immediate survival concerns made talk about past and future an idle luxury. But doing so had a doubly negative effect upon the prisoners' adjustment. First, by voluntarily allowing prison topics to occupy their thoughts even when they did not have to continue playing their roles, the prisoners themselves extended the oppressiveness and reality of the experience. Secondly, since the prisoners were all strangers to each other to begin with, they could only know what the others were really like by observing how they behaved and by evaluating their stated ideas, opinions, values, past experiences and expectations. But what each prisoner observed was his fellow prisoners allowing the guards to humiliate them, acting like compliant sheep, carrying out mindless orders with total obedience and even being cursed by these fellow prisoners (at a guard's command). Then when they were alone, these same prisoners spent their free time complaining and planning how to best get through some imminent prison event, rather than comparing backgrounds and sharing information about their true identities. After days of living confined together in this tight environment, many of the prisoners did not even know the names of most of the others, where they came from, or even the most basic information about what they were like when they were not "prisoners." Under such circumstances, how could a prisoner have respect for his fellows, or any self-respect for what *he* obviously was becoming in the eyes of all those evaluating him?

> Life is the art of being well deceived; and in order that the deception may succeed it must be habitual and uninterrupted.
>
> Wm. Hazlitt, "On Pedantry," *The Round Table*.

Thus, the combination of realistic and symbolic elements in this experiment fused to create a vivid illusion of imprisonment. This illusion merged inextricably with reality for at least some of the time for every individual who became part of the improvisational drama we were staging—prisoners, guards, administrative staff, experimenters, and even visitors. It was remarkable how readily we all slipped into our roles, temporarily gave up our identities, and allowed these assigned roles and the social forces in the situation to guide, shape and eventually to control our freedom of thought and action.

But precisely where does one's "identity" end and one's "role" begin? When the private self and the public role behavior clash, what direction will attempts to impose consistency take? In our simulated prison such distinctions became blurred as we reacted in ways characterized by the following comments from various participants in this simulation.

Prisoner 416, harassed for refusing to eat, which he did as an act of independence and also as an attempt to get sick so he would have to be released, reported:

> I began to feel that I was losing my identity, the person I call (*name*), the person who put me into this place, the person who volunteered to go into this prison . . . was distant from me, was remote until finally, I wasn't that. I was #416—I was really my number, and 416 was going to have to decide what to do. . . .

The cruelest guard of all, nicknamed "John Wayne" by the prisoners (because of his tough, violent, domineering style) led the assault on prisoner 416 for his disobedience of Prison Rule Two: "Prisoners must eat at mealtimes, and only at mealtimes." He punished him, as well as his cell mates, forced him to sleep with the cold, dirty sausages, kept him in solitary hours longer than our imposed limit allowed, made the other prisoners choose between keeping their blankets or having him released from solitary (the majority voted to keep their blankets), and finally asserted (without conferring with the staff) that visiting privileges for everyone would be curtailed if 416 didn't eat. The prisoners reacted not by objecting to this arbitrary rule but by verbally and almost physically attacking 416.

This guard's reaction to the situation he created was to get indignant and angry at 416 because "he was so callous to the people around him it was really shocking . . . his fellow prisoners were pleading with him and he was just thinking about his own petty reason for attempting something so foolish as starving himself." He was also disgusted with the other prisoners because they were so obedient: "This was another experiment of mine, to see if I could get them to say things against each other and really mean it, and they really meant it against 416 today. . . . I told them to say and do some pretty obscene things, and they did."

The torment experienced by our "good guard" (the one the prisoners liked most), who shared shift duties with this "bad" guard, is obvious in his perceptive analysis of what it felt like to be responded to as a "guard":

What made the experience most depressing for me was the fact that we were continually called upon to act in a way that just was contrary to what I really feel inside. I don't feel like I'm the type of person that would be a guard, just constantly giving out shit and forcing people to do things, and pushing and lying—it just didn't seem like me, and to continually to keep up and put on a face like that is just really one of the most oppressive things you can do. It's almost like a prison that you create yourself—you get into it, and it's just, it becomes almost the definition you make of yourself, it almost becomes like walls, and you want to break out and you want just to be able to tell everyone that "this isn't really me at all, and I'm not the person that's confined in there—I'm a person who wants to get out and show you that I am free, and I do have my own will, and I'm not the sadistic type of person that enjoys this kind of thing."

Not only was he a "good" guard because of the little favors he did for the prisoners when contrasted with the indifference or hostility of most other guards; he was "good" from the guards' point of view as well—he let them do their thing without ever directly intervening on behalf of the prisoners. Bruno Bettleheim, in a personal communication, reported that this pattern was common in his concentration camp experience, namely, of the "good" guard who managed to be liked by everyone, while privately dissenting yet never publicly disobeying. Indeed, it is just such "good" people who inadvertently suppress rebellion of the powerless by proffering hope which never materializes.

In another instance, prisoner 819, who had gone into a rage followed by an uncontrollable crying fit, was about to be prematurely released from the prison when a guard lined up the prisoners and had them chant in unison, "819 is a bad prisoner. Because of what 819 did to prison property we all must suffer. 819 is a bad prisoner," over and over again. When the Superintendent realized 819 might be overhearing this, he rushed into the room where 819 was supposed to be resting, only to find him in tears, prepared to go back into the prison because he could not leave as long as the others thought he was a "bad prisoner." Sick as he felt, he had to prove to them he was not a "bad" prisoner. He had to be persuaded that he was not a prisoner at all, that the others were also just students, that this was just an experiment and not a prison and the Prison Superintendent and his staff were only research psychologists.

These assurances to him were necessary reminders to us as well, because we were by this time so much into our prison roles that we were losing the distance and objectivity critical for our other role as experimental social psychologists. A report from the Warden notes, "While I believe that it was necessary for *staff* [me–italic added to highlight the unconscious depersonalization] to enact the Warden role, at least some of the time, I am startled by the ease with which I could turn off my sensitivity and concern for others for 'a good cause.'"

When a former prison chaplain was invited to talk with the prisoners (in order to offer us his evaluation of the validity of our prison setting) he puzzled everyone by disparaging the inmates for not taking any constructive action in order to get released. "Don't you know you must have a lawyer in order to get bail, or to appeal to charges against you?" Several of them accepted his pastoral invitation to contact their parents in order to secure the services of an attorney. The next night one of the parents stopped at the Superintendent's office before visiting time was scheduled to begin and handed him the name and phone number of her cousin, who was a public defender. A priest had called her and suggested the need for a lawyer's services! We called the lawyer. He came, interviewed the prisoners, discussed sources of bail money and promised to return again after the weekend. But at that point we realized that we had to end this experiment because it was no longer just an experiment.

We've travelled too far, and our momentum has taken over; we move idly towards eternity, without possibility of reprieve or hope of explanation.

Tom Stoppard, *Rosencrantz and Guildenstern are Dead*

We were no longer dealing with an intellectual exercise in which an hypothesis was being evaluated in the dispassionate manner dictated by the canons of the scientific method. We were caught up in the passion of the present, the suffering, the need to control people not variables, the escalation of power and all of the unexpected things which were erupting around and within us. So our planned two-week simulation was aborted after only six (was it only six?) days and nights.

But even before this study was officially terminated, we had already been ''forced'' to release four prisoners because of extreme emotional depression or acute anxiety attacks, and in another case, because of a psychosomatic rash over the prisoner's entire body. They had not made an adequate adjustment to ''prison life''! What distinguished the five subjects who endured the prison experience to the end from those who had to be released early were differences in their scores on the F-scale of authoritarianism (Adorno et al., 1950). The higher a prisoner's F-scale score, the more likely he was to remain functioning longer in the authoritarian environment of our prison ($r = .898$). Incidentally, there was *no* group difference between prisoners and guards in their mean scores on this measure of acceptance of authority and adherence to conventional values, nor was there on Machiavellianism-scale scores (Christie & Geis, 1970).

The description of our prison as ''authoritarian'' is substantiated by a detailed analysis of the nature of the interaction between prisoners and guards as video-recorded over twenty-five separate behavioral units (such as counts, meals, and so on). These data are presented in Figure 1. The pattern of results which emerges is remarkably analogous to that reported by White and Lippitt (1960) in their classic study comparing autocratic and democratic forms of group leadership. They found authoritarian role leaders were differentiated from others in the marked frequency with which they gave orders, commands and information. Similarly, in our study there was a high degree of differentiation in social behavior between the mock guards and prisoners. The guards' most typical mode of response, over

which they had exclusive prerogative, was to give commands (which included orders), and next most was to insult the prisoners. Their emphasis on coercive control is further evidenced by: the relatively high frequency with which they threatened, were physically aggressive, used instruments (night sticks, fire extinguishers, etc.) to keep the prisoners in line, and referred to them in impersonal, anonymous, deprecating ways to reduce their individuality, such as ''Hey, you'' or ''You ass hole, 5401, come here.'' From the first to the last day's observations there was a significant increase in the guards' use of most of these domineering, abusive tactics.

Every guard at some time engaged in these abusive, authoritarian behaviors, since *power* was the major dimension on which everyone and everything was defined in this situation. To be a guard who did not take advantage of this institutionally sanctioned use of power was to appear ''weak,'' ''out of it,'' ''wired up by the prisoners,'' or simply a deviant from the established norms of appropriate guard behavior. Three sub-groups of guards could be distinguished. At one extreme, there were a few ''good guy'' guards who occasionally did little favors for the prisoners and were reluctant to punish them. About a third of the guards were ''tough but fair''; their orders were usually within the prescribed rules of prison operation, and they made it clear to the prisoners that they were just doing their job. And finally, over a third of the guards were extremely hostile, arbitrary and cruel in the forms of degradation and humiliation they invented. They appeared to thoroughly enjoy the power they wielded whenever they put on their uniforms and were transformed from their routine everyday existence into ''guards'' with virtually total power over other people.

Each prisoner coped with the frustration, novel experience of being powerless, and growing sense of hopelessness in his own way after a concerted attempt to rebel was crushed by the guards on the

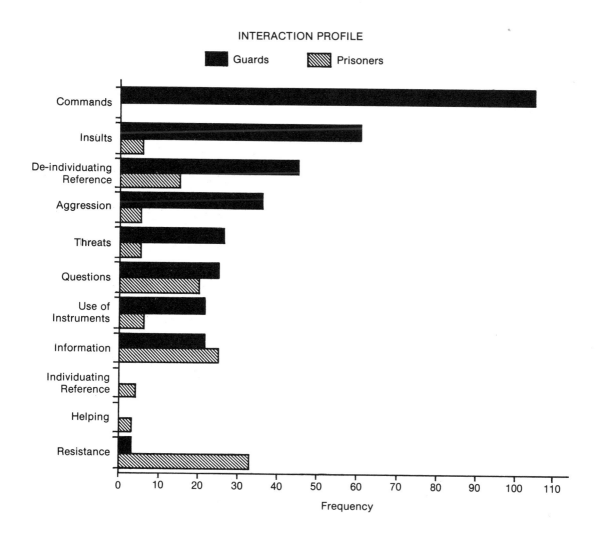

FIGURE 1.   Interaction profile of guard and prisoner behavior across 25 occasions over six days in the simulated prison environment.

second day. As noted, half of them reacted emotionally, breaking down as a legitimate way of passively escaping by forcing us to release them. 416 went on his hunger strike. Some tried to be good prisoners, doing whatever they were told; one of them was nicknamed "Sarge" because of his total obedience in executing all commands. One of the leaders of the prisoner revolt said:

> If we had gotten together then, I think we could have taken over the place. But when I saw the revolt wasn't working, I decided to toe the line. Everyone settled into the same pattern. From then on, we were really controlled by the guards.

Other prisoners simply withdrew into an introverted, protective shell.

From Figure 1 it is obvious that the prisoners *reacted* rather than acted. Initially, they resisted the guards, answered their questions and asked some. Over time, however, as they began to "toe the line," they stopped resisting, questioning and indeed, almost ceased responding altogether. There was a general decrease in all categories of response as they learned the safest strategy to use in an unpredictable, capricious threatening environment from which there is no physical escape: do nothing, except what is required. Act not, want not, feel not and you will not get into trouble in prison-like situations.

When our mock prisoners asked questions, about half the time they got answers, but the rest of the time they got insulted and punished—and it was not possible for them to predict which would be the outcome. So, they became the human analogue of the "learned helplessness phenomenon" in animals reported by Seligman and his associates (1974). Passivity as a reaction to a traumatic, capricious environment is the result of having learned that responding bears no relationship to controlling reinforcers in that situation. Another companion response to passivity in a threatening environment, revealed in a recent study by Maslach (1974), is to avoid doing anything which might call attention to oneself. By choosing instead to behave in ways

which help deindividuate them, powerless people can at least seek the security of anonymity and nonexistence in the eyes of their oppressors.

> And the only way to really make it with the bosses [in Texas prisons] is to withdraw into yourself, both mentally and physically—literally making yourself as small as possible. It's another way they de-humanize you. They want you to make no waves in prison and they want you to make no waves when you get out.
>
> Mike Middleton, Ex-Con, *Christian Science Monitor* Series.

In institutions charged with the "management" of deviants and the outcasts of society—the mentally ill, the retarded, the aged, the unfit of all kinds—treatment moves from concern for humanity to "detached concern" (Lief & Fox, 1963), to indifference, and finally, to depersonalization (Rosenhan, 1973). Individuals are stripped of the attributes that have come to represent their uniqueness and singularity and even of their freedom to respond emotionally because emotions are too spontaneous, idiosyncratic and human. Curiously, over time, the "patients" participate in their own psychological destruction, first making themselves "small" and then, as one prisoner in Rhode Island Adult Correctional Institution told us, "by beating the system and cutting off your emotions so nothing they do to you will ever get to you and then they can't break you."

> I have made some giant steps toward acquiring the things I personally will need if I can be successful in my plans. . . . I have repressed all emotion.
>
> George Jackson, *Soledad Brother*

SOME CONCLUSIONS AND IMPLICATIONS

In this brief article we can but touch upon a few of the most salient issues and questions raised by this simulation experiment, among them: how to explain the power and pathology which emerged; whether the results of such a role-playing study have any meaningful generalizability; and what the ethics are of performing experiments of this kind where people are made to suffer.

Who Were the Guards and Prisoners?

Had the reactions we observed been reported as those of actual prison inmates and correctional officers, the explanation for why they occurred would probably center upon some personality characteristics peculiar to these two populations— typically, sadistic-aggression tendencies within the guards and sociopathic, defective character structures among the prisoners. To account for the observed differences between them and indeed, from our own standards of what constitutes "normal" behavior, we typically focus upon personality traits as internal dispositions for individuals to respond in particular ways.

The probability of invoking such a *dispositional hypothesis* increases as the behavior in question is more aberrant or repulsive to us, as the individuals involved are perceived as more non-comparable to us, and as the situation they are in is more unfamiliar to us. Given this orientation, the solution to social problems is always directed toward specific "problem people"—the vandals, the Black militants, the revolutionaries, the under-achieving school children, the welfare cheats, etc. Remedies then involve changing the people, by motivating them, isolating them, imprisoning them, committing them, executing them, cutting off aid to them, and so on. Such an analysis ignores the variation in behavior attributable to the operation of *situational*, social forces upon the individual or group.

In a real prison, it is impossible to separate out what each individual brings into the prison from what the prison brings out in each person. The research strategy we employed was designed to partial out the confounding effects of chronic personality dispositions from those attributable to the prison environment itself. Therefore, at the start of our study we made certain that every one of our subjects was "normal-average" on a variety of personality

dimensions and was representative of educated, Caucasian, middle-class America.

Our final sample of subjects (11 guards and 10 prisoners in all) were selected from over 75 college-student volunteers recruited through newspaper ads for a study on prison life. They came from more than a dozen different colleges throughout the U.S. and Canada. After all applicants were given an intensive clinical interview and completed an extensive background questionnaire, we selected only those who were judged to be emotionally stable, physically healthy, mature, law-abiding citizens to participate. On each of eight sub-tests of the Comrey Personality Scale (1970) their scores fell within the middle range (40–60 percentile) of the normative male population. Then they were randomly assigned to the experimental treatment of either role-playing a prisoner or a guard. Thus, it is important to note that at the beginning of our study there were no measurable differences between those students assigned to be guards and those to be prisoners, nor for that matter, any differences between either of them and a "normal" comparison population (to which the reader probably belongs).

What is most surprising, therefore, about the outcome of this simulated role-playing experience is the relative ease with which sadistic behavior could be elicited from normal, non-sadistic people, and the extent of the emotional disturbance which emerged in young men selected precisely on the basis of their emotional stability. The pathology observed in this study cannot be attributed to any pre-existing personality differences of the subjects. Rather, their abnormal social and personal reactions were a product of their *transaction* with an environment whose norms and contingencies supported the production of behavior which would be pathological in other settings, but were "appropriate" in this prison.

Milgram's (1965) classic research has demonstrated the power of specifiable situational forces in causing good men to perform evil deeds. Mischel (1968, 1969) has convincingly argued that personality trait scores have limited predictive utility and that what we perceive as personality consistency is really consistency in the situations people voluntarily choose to enter and consistency of response imposed by others in those situations. Argyle and Little (1972) have experimentally shown that relatively little variation in a model social interaction is attributable to "person variance" (16%); "situation variance" accounts for most (44%), and the situation × person interaction next most (40%). Therefore, it is time psychologists stopped offering legislators, lawmen and lay people "traits," "dispositions" and "individual differences" as reasonable solutions to existing problems in our society.

To change behavior we must discover the institutional supports which maintain the existing undesirable behavior and then design programs to alter these environments.[2] As an instance of this principle, we learned that in our mock prison the existence of so many rules to govern prisoner behavior promoted coercive rather than positive forms of responding by the guards. When behavior is under rule control, if the person follows and obeys the rule, he or she is behaving as expected, and naturally, there is no reward for doing what one ought to. But if the rule is broken, punishment results. The more extensive the control by rules in any situation from prison to school to home, the greater the likelihood that the dominant strategy of interpersonal control will be coercive and punitive.

Reality of Role-Playing and Significance of Simulation

It was obvious to every one of us that what went wrong in this study was that it became too real, that we had to end it before the seventh day because it

[2]We recognize, of course, that the physical institution of prison is but a concrete and steel metaphor for the existence of more pervasive, albeit less obvious, prisons of the mind which each of us daily create, populate, and perpetuate. We speak here of the prisons of racism, sexism, ageism, despair, social conventions, shyness and the like. The social convention of marriage, as one example, becomes for many couples a state of imprisonment in which one partner agrees to be prisoner or guard, forcing or allowing the other to play the reciprocal role. Programs of social change designed to alter the environment of imprisonment must also be addressed to these less formal, more subtle social-psychological prisons.

was working "too well." Any experienced encounter-group leader can attest to the creation of "reality" out of even a relatively transient though intense role-playing situation (Aronson, 1972). When people live in a situation, eat, sleep, work there, have all their social contacts and sources of reinforcement there, it becomes a primary, present-tense reality. Janis (1971) poignantly reveals how the phenomenon of "groupthink" can distort existing reality and create a new reality when decision makers in the President's cabinet form an insulated, cohesive group to handle crises (such as the Cuban Bay of Pigs invasion).

The most directly relevant extension of the ideas in this prison simulation comes from a recent "mock hospital" study (Orlando, 1973). Personnel from Elgin State Hospital in Illinois role-played either mental patients or staff in a weekend simulation on a ward in the hospital. The mock mental patients soon displayed behavior indistinguishable from that which we usually associate with the chronic pathological syndromes of actual mental patients: incessant pacing, uncontrollable weeping, depression, hostility, fights, stealing from each other, complaining. Of the 29 mock patients, 93% reported feeling incarcerated, 89% felt an identity loss, and three fourths of them felt that at times nobody cared about them or treated them like a "person." A mental health specialist turned mock patient reported: "I began to feel very much like an animal, with no identity or true worth. I felt defenseless and frightened. There was no privacy, not even in the bathroom." These reactions, so similar in appearance to those of actual patients, could not easily be attributed to the internal disposition or "mental illness" of the participants, since in reality they were themselves charged with the care of the patients. Many of the "mock staff" took advantage of their power to act in ways comparable to our mock guards by dehumanizing their powerless victims.

Recently, a military tribunal in Belgium heard a case of a simulated NATO army exercise in which some Belgian soldiers were taken "prisoner" by Belgian paracommandos. These mock prisoners were bound hand and foot, beaten, given electric shocks, hung from beams and abused in other ways. Why did this occur? According to a report in the *New York Times* (11/5/72):

During the hearing, the accused stated that they did not consider their actions to have been unusual. Said one: "I thought we had to do it. It was the only method to get needed information."

Ethical Considerations

The reader should be disturbed by the ethical dilemma posed in the present research—we certainly are. Some experimental subjects were made to suffer physically and mentally as prisoners, others were forced to realize that as guards they could delight in their abuse of arbitrary power and could so readily dehumanize other human beings. Moreover, these experiences were endured for nearly a week, not merely for the 50 minutes (one college class period) typical in most psychological experiments. But the potential social value of this study derives precisely from the fact that normal, healthy, educated young men could be so radically transformed under the institutional pressures of a "prison environment." The argument runs, if this could happen in so short a time, without the excesses that are possible in real prisons, in the "cream-of-the-crop" of American youth, then one can only shudder at imagining what society is doing to the actual guards and prisoners who are at this very moment participating in that unnatural "social experiment."

Prior to participating, the subjects did give their informed consent to be under surveillance, to be harassed and to have their civil rights abridged. And every one of the 75 applicants stated on a questionnaire that he believed with 100% certainty he could endure the full two-week treatment without difficulty. This common illusion of personal invulnerability, of dispositional power, caused them to underestimate the subtle power of situational forces to control and reshape their behavior. We too, were susceptible to this attribution error.

During a full day of debriefing sessions at the conclusion of our simulation, (first with the ex-prisoners, then with the ex-guards, and finally, together with all participants) we all vented our strongly felt emotions, made it a time to reflect upon the moral and ethical issues each of us faced and discussed how we might react more morally in future "real-life" analogues to this situation. Year-long follow-ups via questionnaires, diaries, personal interviews and group reunions indicate that the mental anguish was transient and situationally specific, but the self-knowledge gained has persisted. For every one of the subjects and researchers, it was a profound learning experience we could not have believed possible were we only observers in the audience and not actors in the drama.

We have begun to try to maximize the social value of the implications of this study by presenting the findings to a Congressional Subcommittee on Prison and Prison Reform (Zimbardo, 1971), to those in corrections, to student groups,[3] and to average citizens who continue to pay taxes to support the status quo of prison operation ignorant of the toll prisons take daily from all those inside their walls, as well as from the society in general into which ex-cons pass for a time before becoming prisoners again.

I was recently released from 'solitary confinement' after being held therein for 37 months [months!]. A silent system was imposed upon me and to even 'whisper' to a man in the next cell resulted in being beaten by guards, sprayed with chemical mace, black-jacked, stomped, and thrown into a 'strip-cell' naked to sleep on a concrete floor without bedding, covering, wash basin, or even a toilet. The floor served as toilet and bed, and even there the 'silent system' was enforced. To let a 'moan' escape your lips because of the pain and discomfort . . . resulted in another beating. I spent not days, but months there during my 37 months in solitary. . . . I have filed every writ possible against the administrative acts of brutality. The State Courts have all denied the petitions. Because of my refusal to let the 'things die down' and 'forget' all that happened during my 37 months in solitary. . . . I am the most hated prisoner in ——— Penitentiary, and called a 'hard-core incorrigible.'

[3]For information about a 50-minute slide show with synchronized taped narration and sound effects portraying the dramatic features of this mock prison study, write to: P. G. Zimbardo Inc., Box #4395, Stanford University, Stanford, California 94305.

Professor Zimbardo, maybe I am an incorrigible, but if true, it's because I would rather die than to accept being treated less than a human being. I have never complained of my prison sentence as being unjustified except through legal means of appeals. I have never put a knife on a guard's throat and demanded my release. I know that thieves must be punished and I don't justify stealing, even though I am a thief myself. But now I don't think I will be a thief when I am released. No, I'm not rehabilitated. It's just that I no longer think of becoming wealthy by stealing. I now only think of 'killing.' Killing those who have beaten me and treated me as if I were a dog. I hope and pray for the sake of my own soul and future life of freedom, that I am able to overcome the bitterness and hatred which eats daily at my soul, but I know to overcome it will not be easy.

CONCLUSION

Yet, in spite of the profoundly negative characterization of prisons drawn by our results and the reports of others, there is cause for guarded optimism about the possibility of their constructive reform. If, indeed, the pathology of prisons can be isolated as a product of the power relations in the social-psychological structure of the institution itself, change is conceivable. Social institutions being the creations of human beings—our experiments in social and political control—are susceptible to modification when confronted by a human consciousness protesting their inadequacy and evils, supported by an informed electorate concerned about eliminating all forms of injustice. Institutionalized prisons can be changed so that human values are promoted and celebrated rather than crushed and perverted—but "it will not be easy."

REFERENCES

Adorno, T. W., Frenkel-Brunswik, E., Levinson, D. J., & Sanford, R. N. *The authoritarian personality.* New York: Harper, 1950.

Argyle, M., & Little, R. Do personality traits apply to social behavior? *Journal of the Theory of Social Behaviour,* 1972, *2,* 1–35.

Aronson, E. *The social animal.* San Francisco: W. H. Freeman, 1972.

Aronson, E., & Carlsmith, M. J. Experimentation in social psychology. In G. Lindzey & E. Aronson (Eds.), *Handbook of social psychology.* Vol. II. Reading, Mass.: Addison-Wesley, 1969. Pp. 1–79.

Christie, R., & Geis, F. L. (Eds.). *Studies in machiavellianism.* New York: Academic Press, 1970.

Comrey, A. L. *Comrey personality scales.* San Diego: Educational and Industrial Testing Service, 1970.

Davis, A. J. Sexual assaults in the Philadelphia prison system and sheriff's vans. *Trans-action Magazine,* 1968, *6,* 8–16.

Janis, I. J. Group think among policy makers. In N. Sanford, C. Comstock (Eds.), *Sanctions for evil.* San Francisco: Jossey-Bass, 1971.

Kantor, A. *Book of Alfred Kantor.* New York: McGraw-Hill, 1971.

Lief, H. I., & Fox, R. C. Training for "detached concern" in medical students. In Harold I. Lief and others (Eds.), *Psychological basis of medical practice.* New York: Harper and Row, 1963. Pp. 12–35.

Maslach, C. The social bases of individuation. *Journal of Personality and Social Psychology,* 1974, *29,* 411–425.

Milgram, S. Some conditions of obedience and disobedience to authority. *Human Relations,* 1965, *18* (1), 57–76.

Mischel, W. *Personality and assessment.* New York: Wiley, 1968.

Mischel, W. Continuity and change in personality. *American Psychologist,* 1969, *24,* 1012–18.

New York Times. 'Torture' Case in NATO weighed. November 5, 1972, p. 3.

Orlando, N. J. The mock ward: A study in simulation. In O. Milton & R. G. Wahler, *Behavior disorders: Perspectives and trends.* Philadelphia: J. B. Lippincott, 1973.

Rosenhan, D. On being sane in insane places. *Science,* 1973, *179,* 250–258.

Seligman, M. E. P. Depression and learned helplessness. In R. J. Friedman & M. M. Katz (Eds.), *The psychology of depression: Contemporary theory and research.* Washington, D. C.: Winston and Sons, 1974.

White, R., & Lippitt, R. *Autocracy and democracy.* New York: Harper and Row, 1960.

Zimbardo, P. G. The human choice: Individuation, reason, and order versus deindividuation, impulse, and chaos. In W. J. Arnold & D. Levine (Eds.), *1969 Nebraska symposium on motivation.* Lincoln, Nebraska: University of Nebraska Press, 1970.

Zimbardo, P. G. Hearings before Subcommittee No. 3 of the Committee on the Judiciary House of Representatives Ninety-Second Congress First Session on Corrections, Part II, *Prisons, prison reform, and prisoners' rights: California.* October 25, 1971. Serial No. 15. Washington: U.S. Government Printing Office, 1971.

ARTICLE 20

Groupthink

Irving L. Janis

"How could we have been so stupid?" President John F. Kennedy asked after he and a close group of advisers had blundered into the Bay of Pigs invasion. For the last two years I have been studying that question, as it applies not only to the Bay of Pigs decision-makers but also to those who led the United States into such other major fiascos as the failure to be prepared for the attack on Pearl Harbor, the Korean War stalemate and the escalation of the Vietnam War.

Stupidity certainly is not the explanation. The men who participated in making the Bay of Pigs decision, for instance, comprised one of the greatest arrays of intellectual talent in the history of American Government—Dean Rusk, Robert McNamara, Douglas Dillon, Robert Kennedy, McGeorge Bundy, Arthur Schlesinger Jr., Allen Dulles and others.

It also seemed to me that explanations were incomplete if they concentrated only on disturbances in the behavior of each individual within a decision-making body: temporary emotional states of elation, fear, or anger that reduce a man's mental efficiency, for example, or chronic blind spots arising from a man's social prejudices or idiosyncratic biases.

I preferred to broaden the picture by looking at the fiascos from the standpoint of group dynamics as it has been explored over the past three decades, first by the great social psychologist Kurt Lewin and later in many experimental situations by myself and other behavioral scientists. My conclusion after poring over hundreds of relevant documents— historical reports about formal group meetings and informal conversations among the members—is that the groups that committed the fiascos were victims of what I call "groupthink."

"Groupy"

In each case study, I was surprised to discover the extent to which each group displayed the typical

Reprinted from *Psychology Today*, Nov. 1971, pp. 43 *ff*. Copyright © 1971 by Ziff-Davis Publishing Company. Reprinted by permission of *Psychology Today Magazine*.

phenomena of social conformity that are regularly encountered in studies of group dynamics among ordinary citizens. For example, some of the phenomena appear to be completely in line with findings from social-psychological experiments showing that powerful social pressures are brought to bear by the members of a cohesive group whenever a dissident begins to voice his objections to a group consensus. Other phenomena are reminiscent of the shared illusions observed in encounter groups and friendship cliques when the members simultaneously reach a peak of ''groupy'' feelings.

Above all, there are numerous indications pointing to the development of group norms that bolster morale at the expense of critical thinking. One of the most common norms appears to be that of remaining loyal to the group by sticking with the policies to which the group has already committed itself, even when those policies are obviously working out badly and have unintended consequences that disturb the conscience of each member. This is one of the key characteristics of groupthink.

1984

I use the term groupthink as a quick and easy way to refer to the mode of thinking that persons engage in when *concurrence-seeking* becomes so dominant in a cohesive ingroup that it tends to override realistic appraisal of alternative courses of action. Groupthink is a term of the same order as the words in the newspeak vocabulary George Orwell used in his dismaying world of *1984*. In that context, groupthink takes on an invidious connotation. Exactly such a connotation is intended, since the term refers to a deterioration in mental efficiency, reality testing and moral judgments as a result of group pressures.

The symptoms of groupthink arise when the members of decision-making groups become motivated to avoid being too harsh in their judgments of their leaders' or their colleagues' ideas.

They adopt a soft line of criticism, even in their own thinking. At their meetings, all the members are amiable and seek complete concurrence on every important issue, with no bickering or conflict to spoil the cozy, ''we-feeling'' atmosphere.

Kill

Paradoxically, soft-headed groups are often hard-hearted when it comes to dealing with outgroups or enemies. They find it relatively easy to resort to dehumanizing solutions—they will readily authorize bombing attacks that kill large numbers of civilians in the name of the noble cause of persuading an unfriendly government to negotiate at the peace table. They are unlikely to pursue the more difficult and controversial issues that arise when alternatives to a harsh military solution come up for discussion. Nor are they inclined to raise ethical issues that carry the implication that *this fine group of ours, with its humanitarianism and its high-minded principles, might be capable of adopting a course of action that is inhumane and immoral.*

Norms

There is evidence from a number of social-psychological studies that as the members of a group feel more accepted by the others, which is a central feature of increased group cohesiveness, they display less overt conformity to group norms. Thus we would expect that the more cohesive a group becomes, the less the members will feel constrained to censor what they say out of fear of being socially punished for antagonizing the leader or any of their fellow members.

In contrast, the groupthink type of conformity tends to increase as group cohesiveness increases. Groupthink involves nondeliberate suppression of critical thoughts as a result of internalization of the group's norms, which is quite different from deliberate suppression on the basis of external threats of social punishment. The more cohesive the group, the greater the inner compulsion on the part of each member to avoid creating disunity, which inclines him to believe in the soundness of whatever proposals are promoted by the leader or by a majority of the group's members.

In a cohesive group, the danger is not so much that each individual will fail to reveal his objections to what the others propose but that he will think the proposal is a good one, without attempting to carry out a careful, critical scrutiny of the pros and cons of the alternatives. When groupthink becomes dominant, there also is considerable suppression of deviant thoughts, but it takes the form of each person's deciding that his misgivings are not relevant and should be set aside, that the benefit of the doubt regarding any lingering uncertainties should be given to the group consensus.

Stress

I do not mean to imply that all cohesive groups necessarily suffer from groupthink. All ingroups may have a mild tendency toward groupthink, displaying one or another of the symptoms from time to time, but it need not be so dominant as to influence the quality of the group's final decision. Neither do I mean to imply that there is anything necessarily inefficient or harmful about group decisions in general. On the contrary, a group whose members have properly defined roles, with traditions concerning the procedures to follow in pursuing a critical inquiry, probably is capable of making better decisions than any individual group member working alone.

The problem is that the advantages of having decisions made by groups are often lost because of powerful psychological pressures that arise when the members work closely together, share the same set of values and, above all, face a crisis situation that puts everyone under intense stress.

The main principle of groupthink, which I offer in the spirit of Parkinson's Law, is this: *The more amiability and esprit de corps there is among the members of a policy-making ingroup, the greater the danger that independent critical thinking will be replaced by groupthink, which is likely to result in irrational and dehumanizing actions directed against outgroups.*

Symptoms

In my studies of high-level governmental decision-makers, both civilian and military, I have found eight main symptoms of groupthink.

1. Invulnerability. Most or all of the members of the ingroup share an *illusion* of invulnerability that provides for them some degree of reassurance about obvious dangers and leads them to become over-optimistic and willing to take extraordinary risks. It also causes them to fail to respond to clear warnings of danger.

The Kennedy ingroup, which uncritically accepted the Central Intelligence Agency's disastrous Bay of Pigs plan, operated on the false assumption that they could keep secret the fact that the United States was responsible for the invasion of Cuba. Even after news of the plan began to leak out, their belief remained unshaken. They failed even to consider the danger that awaited them: a worldwide revulsion against the U. S.

A similar attitude appeared among the members of President Lyndon B. Johnson's ingroup, the "Tuesday Cabinet," which kept escalating the Vietnam War despite repeated setbacks and failures. "There was a belief," Bill Moyers commented after he resigned, "that if we indicated a willingness to use our power, they [the North Vietnamese] would get the message and back away from an all-out confrontation. . . . There was a confidence—it was never bragged about, it was just there—that when the chips were really down, the other people would fold."

A most poignant example of an illusion of invulnerability involves the ingroup around Admiral H. E. Kimmel, which failed to prepare for the possibility of a Japanese attack on Pearl Harbor despite repeated warnings. Informed by his intelligence chief that radio contact with Japanese aircraft carriers had been lost, Kimmel joked about it: "What, you don't know where the carriers are? Do you mean to say that they could be rounding Diamond Head (at Honolulu) and you wouldn't know it?" The carriers were in fact moving full-steam toward Kimmel's command post at the time. Laughing together about a danger signal, which labels it as a purely laughing matter, is a characteristic manifestation of groupthink.

2. Rationale. As we see, victims of groupthink ignore warnings; they also collectively construct rationalizations in order to discount warnings and other forms of negative feedback that, taken seriously, might lead the group members to reconsider their assumptions each time they recommit themselves to past decisions. Why did the Johnson ingroup avoid reconsidering its escalation policy when time and again the expectations on which they based their decisions turned out to be wrong? James C. Thompson, Jr., a Harvard historian who spent five years as an observing participant in both the State Department and the White House, tells us that the policymakers avoided critical discussion of their prior decisions and continually invented new rationalizations so that they could sincerely recommit themselves to defeating the North Vietnamese.

In the fall of 1964, before the bombing of North Vietnam began, some of the policymakers predicted that six weeks of air strikes would induce the North Vietnamese to seek peace talks. When someone asked, "What if they don't?" the answer was that another four weeks certainly would do the trick.

Later, after each setback, the ingroup agreed that by investing just a bit more effort (by stepping up the bomb tonnage a bit, for instance), their course of action would prove to be right. *The Pentagon Papers* bear out these observations.

In *The Limits of Intervention,* Townsend Hoopes, who was acting Secretary of the Air Force under Johnson, says that Walt W. Rostow in particular showed a remarkable capacity for what has been called "instant rationalization." According to Hoopes, Rostow buttressed the group's optimism about being on the road to victory by culling selected scraps of evidence from news reports or, if necessary, by inventing "plausible" forecasts that had no basis in evidence at all.

Admiral Kimmel's group rationalized away their warnings, too. Right up to December 7, 1941, they convinced themselves that the Japanese would never dare attempt a full-scale surprise assault against Hawaii because Japan's leaders would realize that it would precipitate an all-out war which the United States would surely win. They made no attempt to look at the situation through the eyes of the Japanese leaders—another manifestation of groupthink.

3. Morality. Victims of groupthink believe unquestioningly in the inherent morality of their ingroup; this belief inclines the members to ignore the ethical or moral consequences of their decisions.

Evidence that this symptom is at work usually is of a negative kind—the things that are left unsaid in group meetings. At least two influential persons had doubts about the morality of the Bay of Pigs adventure. One of them, Arthur Schlesinger, Jr., presented his strong objections in a memorandum to President Kennedy and Secretary of State Rusk but suppressed them when he attended meetings of the Kennedy team. The other, Senator J. William Fulbright, was not a member of the group, but the President invited him to express his misgivings in a speech to the policymakers. However, when Fulbright finished speaking the President moved on to other agenda items without asking for reactions of the group.

David Kraslow and Stuart H. Loory, in *The Secret Search for Peace in Vietnam,* report that during 1966 President Johnson's ingroup was concerned primarily with selecting bomb targets in North Vietnam. They based their selections on four factors—the military advantage, the risk to American aircraft and pilots, the danger of forcing other countries into the fighting, and the danger of heavy civilian casualties. At their regular Tuesday luncheons, they weighed these factors the way school teachers grade examination papers, averaging them out. Though evidence on this point is scant, I suspect that the group's ritualistic adherence to a standardized procedure induced the members to feel morally justified in their destructive way of dealing with the Vietnamese people—after all, the danger of heavy civilian casualties from U. S. air strikes was taken into account on their checklists.

4. Stereotypes. Victims of groupthink hold stereotyped views of the leaders of enemy groups: they are so evil that genuine attempts at negotiating differences with them are unwarranted, or they are too weak or too stupid to deal effectively with whatever attempts the ingroup makes to defeat their purposes, no matter how risky the attempts are.

Kennedy's groupthinkers believed that Premier Fidel Castro's air force was so ineffectual that obsolete B-26s could knock it out completely in a surprise attack before the invasion began. They also believed that Castro's army was so weak that a small Cuban-exile brigade could establish a well-protected beachhead at the Bay of Pigs. In addition, they believed that Castro was not smart enough to put down any possible internal uprisings in support of the exiles. They were wrong on all three assumptions. Though much of the blame was attributable to faulty intelligence, the point is that none of Kennedy's advisers even questioned the CIA planners about these assumptions.

The Johnson advisers' sloganistic thinking about "the Communist apparatus" that was "working all around the world" (as Dean Rusk put it) led them to overlook the powerful nationalistic strivings of the North Vietnamese government and its efforts to ward off Chinese domination. The crudest of all stereotypes used by Johnson's inner circle to justify their policies was the domino theory ("If we don't stop the Reds in South Vietnam, tomorrow they will be in Hawaii and next week they will be in San Francisco," Johnson once said). The group so firmly accepted this stereotype that it became almost

impossible for any adviser to introduce a more sophisticated viewpoint.

In the documents on Pearl Harbor, it is clear to see that the Navy commanders stationed in Hawaii had a naive image of Japan as a midget that would not dare to strike a blow against a powerful giant.

5. Pressure. Victims of groupthink apply direct pressure to any individual who momentarily expresses doubts about any of the group's shared illusions or who questions the validity of the arguments supporting a policy alternative favored by the majority. This gambit reinforces the concurrence-seeking norm that loyal members are expected to maintain.

President Kennedy probably was more active than anyone else in raising skeptical questions during the Bay of Pigs meetings, and yet he seems to have encouraged the group's docile, uncritical acceptance of defective arguments in favor of the CIA's plan. At every meeting, he allowed the CIA representatives to dominate the discussion. He permitted them to give their immediate refutations in response to each tentative doubt that one of the others expressed, instead of asking whether anyone shared the doubt or wanted to pursue the implications of the new worrisome issue that had just been raised. And at the most crucial meeting, when he was calling on each member to give his vote for or against the plan, he did not call on Arthur Schlesinger, the one man there who was known by the President to have serious misgivings.

Historian Thomson informs us that whenever a member of Johnson's ingroup began to express doubts, the group used subtle social pressures to "domesticate" him. To start with, the dissenter was made to feel at home, provided that he lived up to two restrictions: 1) that he did not voice his doubts to outsiders, which would play into the hands of the opposition; and 2) that he kept his criticisms within the bounds of acceptable deviation, which meant not challenging any of the fundamental assumptions that went into the group's prior commitments. One such "domesticated dissenter" was Bill Moyers.

When Moyers arrived at a meeting, Thomson tells us, the President greeted him with, "Well, here comes Mr. Stop-the-Bombing."

6. Self-censorship. Victims of groupthink avoid deviating from what appears to be group consensus; they keep silent about their misgivings and even minimize to themselves the importance of their doubts.

As we have seen, Schlesinger was not at all hesitant about presenting his strong objections to the Bay of Pigs plan in a memorandum to the President and the Secretary of State. But he became keenly aware of his tendency to suppress objections at the White House meetings. "In the months after the Bay of Pigs I bitterly reproached myself for having kept so silent during those crucial discussions in the cabinet room," Schlesinger writes in *A Thousand Days*. "I can only explain my failure to do more than raise a few timid questions by reporting that one's impulse to blow the whistle on this nonsense was simply undone by the circumstances of the discussion."

7. Unanimity. Victims of groupthink share an *illusion* of unanimity within the group concerning almost all judgments expressed by members who speak in favor of the majority view. This symptom results partly from the preceding one, whose effects are augmented by the false assumption that any individual who remains silent during any part of the discussion is in full accord with what the others are saying.

When a group of persons who respect each other's opinions arrives at a unanimous view, each member is likely to feel that the belief must be true. This reliance on consensual validation within the group tends to replace individual critical thinking and reality testing, unless there are clear-cut disagreements among the members. In contemplating a course of action such as the invasion of Cuba, it is painful for the members to confront disagreements within their group, particularly if it becomes apparent that there are widely divergent views about whether the preferred course of action is too risky to

undertake at all. Such disagreements are likely to arouse anxieties about making a serious error. Once the sense of unanimity is shattered, the members no longer can feel complacently confident about the decision they are inclined to make. Each man must then face the annoying realization that there are troublesome uncertainties and he must diligently seek out the best information he can get in order to decide for himself exactly how serious the risks might be. This is one of the unpleasant consequences of being in a group of hardheaded, critical thinkers.

To avoid such an unpleasant state, the members often become inclined, without quite realizing it, to prevent latent disagreements from surfacing when they are about to initiate a risky course of action. The group leader and the members support each other in playing up the areas of convergence in their thinking, at the expense of fully exploring divergencies that might reveal unsettled issues.

"Our meetings took place in a curious atmosphere of assumed consensus," Schlesinger writes. His additional comments clearly show that, curiously, the consensus was an illusion—an illusion that could be maintained only because the major participants did not reveal their own reasoning or discuss their idiosyncratic assumptions and vague reservations. Evidence from several sources makes it clear that even the three principals—President Kennedy, Rusk and McNamara—had widely differing assumptions about the invasion plan.

8. Mindguards. Victims of groupthink sometimes appoint themselves as mindguards to protect the leader and fellow members from adverse information that might break the complacency they shared about the effectiveness and morality of past decisions. At a large birthday party for his wife, Attorney General Robert F. Kennedy, who had been constantly informed about the Cuban invasion plan, took Schlesinger aside and asked him why he was opposed. Kennedy listened coldly and said, "You may be right or you may be wrong, but the President has made his mind up. Don't push it any further. Now is the time for everyone to help him all they can.''

Rusk also functioned as a highly effective mindguard by failing to transmit to the group the strong objections of three ''outsiders'' who had learned of the invasion plan—Undersecretary of State Chester Bowles, USIA Director Edward R. Murrow, and Rusk's intelligence chief, Roger Hilsman. Had Rusk done so, their warnings might have reinforced Schlesinger's memorandum and jolted some of Kennedy's ingroup, if not the President himself, into reconsidering the decision.

Products

When a group of executives frequently displays most or all of these interrelated symptoms, a detailed study of their deliberations is likely to reveal a number of immediate consequences. These consequences are, in effect, products of poor decision-making practices because they lead to inadequate solutions to the problems under discussion.

First, the group limits its discussions to a few alternative courses of action (often only two) without an initial survey of all the alternatives that might be worthy of consideration.

Second, the group fails to reexamine the course of action initially preferred by the majority after they learn of risks and drawbacks they had not considered originally.

Third, the members spend little or no time discussing whether there are nonobvious gains they may have overlooked or ways of reducing the seemingly prohibitive costs that made rejected alternatives appear undesirable to them.

Fourth, members make little or no attempt to obtain information from experts within their own organizations who might be able to supply more precise estimates of potential losses and gains.

Fifth, members show positive interest in facts and opinions that support their preferred policy; they tend to ignore facts and opinions that do not.

Sixth, members spend little time deliberating about how the chosen policy might be hindered by bureaucratic inertia, sabotaged by political opponents, or temporarily derailed by common accidents. Consequently, they fail to work out contingency plans to cope with foreseeable setbacks that could endanger the overall success of their chosen course.

Support

The search for an explanation of why groupthink occurs has led me through a quagmire of complicated theoretical issues in the murky area of human motivation. My belief, based on recent social psychological research, is that we can best understand the various symptoms of groupthink as a mutual effort among the group members to maintain self-esteem and emotional equanimity by providing social support to each other, especially at times when they share responsibility for making vital decisions.

Even when no important decision is pending, the typical administrator will begin to doubt the wisdom and morality of his past decisions each time he receives information about setbacks, particularly if the information is accompanied by negative feedback from prominent men who originally had been his supporters. It should not be surprising, therefore, to find that individual members strive to develop unanimity and esprit de corps that will help bolster each other's morale, to create an optimistic outlook about the success of pending decisions, and to reaffirm the positive value of past policies to which all of them are committed.

Pride

Shared illusions of invulnerability, for example, can reduce anxiety about taking risks. Rationalizations help members believe that the risks are really not so bad after all. The assumption of inherent morality helps the members to avoid feelings of shame or guilt. Negative stereotypes function as stress-reducing devices to enhance a sense of moral righteousness as well as pride in a lofty mission.

The mutual enhancement of self-esteem and morale may have functional value in enabling the members to maintain their capacity to take action, but it has maladaptive consequences insofar as concurrence-seeking tendencies interfere with critical, rational capacities and lead to serious errors of judgment.

While I have limited my study to decision-making bodies in Government, groupthink symptoms appear in business, industry and any other field where small, cohesive groups make the decisions. It is vital, then, for all sorts of people—and especially group leaders—to know what steps they can take to prevent groupthink.

Remedies

To counterpoint my case studies of the major fiascos, I have also investigated two highly successful group enterprises, the formulation of the Marshall Plan in the Truman Administration and the handling of the Cuban missile crisis by President Kennedy and his advisers. I have found it instructive to examine the steps Kennedy took to change his group's decision-making processes. These changes ensured that the mistakes made by his Bay of Pigs ingroup were not repeated by the missile-crisis ingroup, even though the membership of both groups was essentially the same.

The following recommendations for preventing groupthink incorporate many of the good practices I discovered to be characteristic of the Marshall Plan and missile-crisis groups:

1. The leader of a policy-forming group should assign the role of critical evaluator to each member, encouraging the group to give high priority to open airing of objections and doubts. This practice needs to be reinforced by the leader's acceptance of criticism of his own judgments in order to discourage members from soft-pedaling their disagreements and from allowing their striving for concurrence to inhibit critical thinking.

2. When the key members of a hierarchy assign a policy-planning mission to any group within their organization, they should adopt an impartial stance instead of stating preferences and expectations at the beginning. This will encourage open inquiry and impartial probing of a wide range of policy alternatives.

3. The organization routinely should set up several outside policy-planning and evaluation groups to work on the same policy question, each deliberating under a different leader. This can prevent the insulation of an ingroup.

4. At intervals before the group reaches a final consensus, the leader should require each member to discuss the group's deliberations with associates in his own unit of the organization—assuming that those associates can be trusted to adhere to the same security regulations that govern the policymakers—and then to report back their reactions to the group.

5. The group should invite one or more outside experts to each meeting on a staggered basis and encourage the experts to challenge the views of the core members.

6. At every general meeting of the group, whenever the agenda calls for an evaluation of policy alternatives, at least one member should play devil's advocate, functioning as a good lawyer in challenging the testimony of those who advocate the majority position.

7. Whenever the policy issue involves relations with a rival nation or organization, the group should devote a sizable block of time, perhaps an entire session, to a survey of all warning signals from the rivals and should write alternative scenarios on the rivals' intentions.

8. When the group is surveying policy alternatives for feasibility and effectiveness, it should from time to time divide into two or more subgroups to meet separately, under different chairmen, and then come back together to hammer out differences.

9. After reaching a preliminary consensus about what seems to be the best policy, the group should hold a "second-chance" meeting at which every

member expresses as vividly as he can all his residual doubts, and rethinks the entire issue before making a definitive choice.

How

These recommendations have their disadvantages. To encourage the open airing of objections, for instance, might lead to prolonged and costly debates when a rapidly growing crisis requires immediate solution. It also could cause rejection, depression and anger. A leader's failure to set a norm might create cleavage between leader and members that could develop into a disruptive power struggle if the leader looks on the emerging consensus as anathema. Setting up outside evaluation groups might increase the risk of security leakage. Still,

inventive executives who know their way around the organizational maze probably can figure out how to apply one or another of the prescriptions successfully, without harmful side effects.

They also could benefit from the advice of outside experts in the administrative and behavioral sciences. Though these experts have much to offer, they have had few chances to work on policy-making machinery within large organizations. As matters now stand, executives innovate only when they need new procedures to avoid repeating serious errors that have deflated their self-images.

In this era of atomic warheads, urban disorganization and ecocatastrophes, it seems to me that policymakers should collaborate with behavioral scientists and give top priority to preventing groupthink and its attendant fiascos.

ARTICLE 21

Three not-so-obvious contributions of psychology to peace

Ralph K. White

There are two things in this world that don't quite fit together. One is that mushroom cloud. We try not to think about it—but it's *there,* rising, enormously, behind everything else we do. And then there's the other thing: the whole complicated spectacle of all the old causes of war going on as usual. There's the arms race, and ABM, and—much worse than ABM—that hydra-headed monster, MIRV. Most of all, there's the war in Vietnam. It stands there as a continual, glaring reminder that the United States—our own peace-loving United States—is capable of the kind of bungling that got us into that war. And then comes the thought: *if* even the peace-loving United States could bungle itself into a little war like Vietnam, what guarantee is there that we won't bungle ourselves into a big war—a nuclear war? It might be possible to exorcize the specter of that mushroom cloud if the Vietnam war did not exist. But it does exist.

The sense of bafflement is especially great perhaps among psychologists, because a good many psychologists feel that the bungling that got us into the Vietnam war, and could get us into a nuclear war, consists largely of ignoring certain fundamental *psychological* truths. Most of our American policy-makers (both Johnson and Nixon, for instance) behave as if they don't recognize certain things that we psychologists take for granted—things such as the necessity of empathy (including empathy with our own worst enemies), the dangers of black-and-white thinking, and the role of the self-fulfilling prophecy in the vicious spiral of the arms race.

Communicating with Policy-Makers

All of this strengthens the case for better communication—better communication directly between us and the policy-makers in Washington, and better communication also between us and other scholars (historians, political scientists, area

Reprinted from the *Journal of Social Issues,* 1969, 25(4), pp. 23–39, by permission of the author and the Society for the Psychological Study of Social Issues.

specialists) who in turn influence the policy-makers a good deal more than we do.

One difficulty in communicating with these people is that from their standpoint we often sound like a little boy trying to teach Grandma to suck eggs. Many of them are experts in their own fields, people from whom we really could learn a great deal. And then we come up with these ideas that they think they have heard many times already, ideas that they often think we have dressed up in pretentious new terminology but that they regard as essentially old, familiar, and in a sense obvious ideas.

The paradox is that it is precisely these so-called obvious ideas that we often see the top policy-makers ignoring when it comes to concrete action decisions. We see that mushroom cloud coming closer because they *act* as if they couldn't see what to *us* seems obvious. So, in order to define the problem accurately, it looks as if we need three categories. First, there are the things that really are obvious, on the verbal level *and* on the action level. Second, there are the things that seem obvious on the verbal level but that are often ignored on the action level. And third, there are the things that are not obvious on either the verbal or the action level.

Difficulties in Communicating the "Obvious"

The second category, although it won't be my main focus in this paper, does seem to me the most important: namely, the things that seem obvious on the general, abstract, verbal level, but that are often ignored on the specific, concrete, action level. As examples, let's take the three ideas I've already mentioned: the necessity of empathy, the dangers of black-and-white thinking, and the role played by the self-fulfilling prophecy in the vicious spiral of the arms race.

When empathy is defined in common-sense terms like "understanding the other fellow's point of view," any policy-maker is likely to say: "Sure, I believe in that, and I try to do it all the time." The chances are he takes pride in understanding the other fellow's point of view—even when he doesn't really understand it.

Or take the black-and-white picture. Anybody who has ever seen a Western movie, and knows about the bad guys and the good guys, the black hats and the white hats, is likely to have some notion, on the verbal level, of the dangers of black-and-white thinking, even if in practice he engages in black-and-white thinking most of the time.

Or take the role of the self-fulfilling prophecy in the vicious spiral of the arms race. To some, the self-fulfilling prophecy may be a new and interesting idea—Senator Fulbright found it a new and interesting idea when he heard it from Jerome Frank—but the vicious spiral of the arms race is an old idea that has been heard many times and might be accepted in theory even by people like Melvin Laird who in practice ignore it. What can we do then? The things that we feel are being most dangerously ignored in practice are the things most likely to make our listeners yawn.

The answer, as I see it, is *not* to stop talking about these fundamental things. It is, rather, to get right down onto the concrete action level and to talk not about these abstractions as such, but about concrete examples of them.

Bombing and Empathy

For instance, take again the notion of empathy. It seems to me that a flagrant concrete example of violation of the principle of empathy was our bombing of North Vietnam. That bombing was urged and continually supported by our most flagrant non-empathizers—the military. But its effects included a continual solidifying of opposition to us among the people in North Vietnam. It was as if we were doing our best to persuade every man, woman, and child in North Vietnam that America really *is* the devil, the wanton cruel aggressor that Communist propaganda has always said it was. Most of our military men in active service not only failed to empathize with the North Vietnamese; it looks as if they actively, though unconsciously, resisted the temptation to empathize. They shut their eyes to the best evidence available: the first-hand testimony of people like Harrison Salisbury (1967), Cameron (1966), Gerassi (1967), Gottlieb (1965), and the Quakers of the ship, *Phoenix,* who went to North Vietnam and came back saying that our bombing was solidifying opposition to us (Zietlow, 1967). They shut their eyes also to the evidence that the bombing was tending to alienate from us most of the other people in the world. And, most surprisingly, they shut their eyes to the evidence of history, represented by our own strategic bombing survey after World War II (Over-all report, 1945) which described how our bombing of Germany and Japan had had the same solidifying effect.

This kind of concrete example may jolt and antagonize some people, but it won't make them yawn. And focusing on such examples should help to make abstract concepts like empathy become more and more a part of the reality-world of the listener, on the concrete action level. It matters very little whether a policy-maker talks about empathy. It matters a great deal whether the impulse to empathize keeps coming up in his mind, at those particular moments when wisdom in action requires that he should at least try to understand the other fellow's point of view.

Communicating the "Not-So-Obvious"

Then there is that third category of psychological ideas and psychological facts that really are relatively unfamiliar to the decision-makers on both levels. I'm going to talk about three of them today: "three not-so-obvious contributions of psychology to peace." (Of course when I say "contributions" I mean potential contributions. What we have done is to learn certain things about the psychological causes of war. Whether these insights and the facts that support them ever actually contribute to peace depends on our own effort and our own skill as communicators.) Also it should be clear that these are not necessarily the most important of the not-

so-obvious contributions. There are others that seem to me just as important or more so: Charles Osgood's (1962) GRIT proposal, for instance, and the experimental work Morton Deutsch has been doing (Deutsch and Krauss, 1962), and the monumental job Herbert Kelman did editing that big volume, *International Behavior* (1965). But those are pretty well known. I'm going to focus here on three that are not very well known.

THE HOVLAND PRINCIPLE IN COMMUNICATING WITH COMMUNISTS

First, there is a corollary of the Hovland principle that a two-sided presentation of an argument is more persuasive than a one-sided presentation when you are talking with people who initially disagree with you. The corollary is that *we Americans should publicly accept as much as we can honestly accept of the Communist point of view*.

To some psychologists this may seem obvious, but most of our politicians and foreign-policy makers are likely to regard it as far from obvious. To many of them it must sound like subversive doctrine—like being "soft on Communism." That is precisely why we psychologists, *if* we think the evidence supports it, ought to be saying so—clearly, and often, and with all the research evidence that we can bring to bear.

Let's look at the evidence. You are probably familiar with the impressive body of experimental data accumulated by Hovland and his colleagues (Hovland, Janis, & Kelley, 1953), on the general advantages of a "two-sided" form of persuasion —defining a two-sided argument not as a neutral position but as a genuine argument that candidly takes the stronger arguments on the other side into account. And "candidly taking them into account" means not only stating them fairly before trying to refute them, but also acknowledging any elements in them that the speaker honestly regards as elements of truth. You are probably also familiar with their more specific findings, including the finding that the two-sided approach is not always more effective. It is likely to be more effective if the audience is intelligent, or initially hostile to the viewpoint of the speaker, or both intelligent and hostile. Now comes the corollary, which is especially interesting from the standpoint of our relations with the Communist world. The Communist leaders fit exactly the Hovland prescription for the kind of people with whom one should use the two-sided approach. They are intelligent. They could hardly have maintained stability in a vast nation like the USSR if they were not at least fairly intelligent. And, to put it mildly, they are initially in disagreement with us. So it would follow that in communicating with them we should use the two-sided approach.

What is Right in Communism?

What would it mean, concretely? It would *not* mean soft-pedaling any of the things we believe to be wrong and dangerous on the Communist side: the invasion of Czechoslovakia, for instance, or the recent regression toward Stalinism in the Soviet Union, or the anarchy and cruelty of the "great cultural revolution" in Communist China, or the assassination of village leaders in Vietnam. But it would mean coupling candor about what we think is wrong with candor about what we think is right. That raises the question: what *is* right in Communism? Is anything right? Each of us would probably have a different answer, but just to make the main point concrete I'm going to go out on a limb and mention some of the things that I personally think are right.

Most important, probably, is the depth and intensity of the Russians' desire for peace. They hate and fear war at least as much as we do. How could they not hate war, after the searing experience they went through in World War II? We can also give them credit for bearing the brunt of World War II—and winning, on that crucial Eastern Front. I know from my own experience in Moscow that nothing touches the heart of a Russian more than real appreciation,

by an American, of what they suffered and what they accomplished in our common struggle against Hitler. There is real common ground here, both when we look back on World War II and when we look ahead to the future. We and the Communists, looking ahead, find ourselves on the same side in the rather desperate struggle that both they and we are waging against the danger of nuclear war.

Some other things that I personally would acknowledge include Soviet space achievements, which really are extraordinary, considering how backward Russia was in 1917; the case for Communist Chinese intervention in Korea after MacArthur crossed the 38th Parallel; the case for Communist China in the matter of Quemoy and Matsu; the Vietnamese Communist case against Diem and his American supporters; a very large part of their case against what we have been doing in Vietnam since the death of Diem. And, more basically, the proposition that the Communist countries are ahead of us in social justice. In spite of striking inequalities, my reading of the evidence is that they are definitely ahead of us in eliminating unearned income—"surplus value"—and somewhat ahead of us in diminishing the gap between rich and poor. (This and related problems are spelled out more fully in White, 1967–8.)

Research on the Need to Seek Common Ground

If all this has a subversive sound, please recall again the Hovland experiments, and also the rather large number of other experiments that bring out, in one way or another, the desirability of discovering common ground if conflict is to be resolved. For instance, there are the experiments of Blake and Mouton (see Sawyer and Guetzkow, 1965) on how each side in a controversy ordinarily underestimates the amount of common ground that actually exists between its own position and that of its adversary. There is all the research on the non-zero-sum game, and the need to keep the players on both sides from treating a *non*-zero-sum game, in which the adversaries actually share some common interests, as if it were a zero-sum game in which loss for one side always means gain for the other. There is the so-called Rapoport Debate (actually originated by Carl Rogers, apparently), in which neither side is permitted to argue for its position until it has stated, to the other side's satisfaction, what the other side is trying to establish. There is Sherif's Robbers' Cave experiment in which conflict was replaced by cooperation and friendliness when a superordinate goal—an overriding common goal—demanded cooperation (Sherif, 1958). There is Rokeach's work (1960) on the importance of common beliefs as a basis for good will. There is Kenneth Hammond's recent work on the harm done by implicit assumptions that differ on the two sides of an argument, and that are never really challenged or examined. All of these have as a common element the idea of common goals or common ground, and the desirability of common ground for conflict-resolution.

The "Modal Philosophy" and East-West Convergence

There is also my own content-analysis (White, 1949) of the values in various ideologies (American, Nazi, and Communist) using the value-analysis technique (White, 1951)—a project carried a good deal further recently by William Eckhardt (Eckhardt and White, 1967). The main upshot of that analysis was that there has apparently been a convergence of the value-systems of the Communist East and the non-Communist West. From a study of opinion and attitude surveys in a number of non-Communist countries, and of behavior data and political speeches and writings on both sides of the East-West conflict, a picture emerged of a good deal more common ground, shared by us and the Communists, than the embattled partisans on either side have ever recognized. Neither they nor we depart very far from the most commonly held political philosophy—I call it the "modal philosophy"—which with minor variations seems to characterize most of the politically conscious

people in the world (White, 1957). (It is the great piling up of people in the middle zone—a very large "mode" in the statistical sense of the word "mode"—that justifies the term "modal philosophy.")

It includes three main elements. First, a preference for private ownership and free enterprise in at least the smaller economic units: the grocery store, the laundry, the repair shop, the small farm. In that respect the global majority seems to lean more toward our American way of life than toward that of the thoroughgoing socialists, or the Communists. A second element, though, is a strong emphasis on social welfare—helping the poor. In that respect the modal philosophy is more like Communism. And third, there is a belief in political democracy, including free speech. Most of the people in the global majority reject dictatorship, and most of them reject the word "communism" because to them it implies dictatorship, while they more or less accept the term "socialism," which to them implies democracy. In fact, the term "democratic socialism" probably comes closer than any other single term to representing what this modal philosophy is. This pattern of values and beliefs, or some not-very-wide variation from it, constitutes the great common ground that liberal Americans share, not only with millions of people who call themselves Communists but also with an actual majority of the politically conscious members of the human race.

MIRROR-IMAGE WARS AND TERRITORIAL SELF-IMAGES

A second not-so-obvious proposition is *the frequency of mirror-image wars, and the importance of overlapping territorial self-images as causes of such wars.*

There are two kinds of war. There is the mirror-image war in which each side really believes that the other side is the aggressor (Bronfenbrenner, 1961). And there is the non-mirror-image war in which one side really believes that the other side is the aggressor, while the other side, though feeling justified, doesn't really literally believe that it is the victim of aggression.

An example of a mirror-image war would be World War I. A great many Americans don't realize how well Bronfenbrenner's term, the "mirror-image," applies to what happened in 1914. A great many still picture that war as a case of outright German aggression, comparable to Hitler's aggression in 1939. The historical facts, as we know them now, do not support that belief. The Germans believed, with some factual justification, that they were the victims of aggression. They pictured Russia, France, and England as ganging up on them, and felt that unless they struck first they would be overwhelmed by enemies on two fronts. Ole Holsti and Robert North (1965) with their content-analysis of the documents of 1914, have confirmed what historians such as Fay (1928) and Gooch (1938) had already showed—that when the war actually broke out the Germans were motivated mainly by fear.

Another mirror-image war is the Vietnam war. The militants on each side clearly believe that the other side is the aggressor. The North Vietnamese see the United States as aggressing against the soil of their homeland, and, in mirror-image fashion, militant Americans see the North Vietnamese as aggressing against South Vietnam, both by a campaign of assassination in the villages and by actual troops invading the South.

There is a supreme irony in this mirror-image type of war. It seems utterly ridiculous that *both* sides should be fighting because of real fear, imagining the enemy to be a brutal, arrogant aggressor, when actually the enemy is nerving himself to fight a war that he too thinks is in self-defense. Each side is fighting, with desperate earnestness, an imagined enemy, a bogey-man, a windmill. But you can't laugh at this kind of joke. It's too bloody, too tragic. You can only stand aghast, and ask: how is it possible, psychologically, for one country, or perhaps both, to be *that* much deluded?

Then there is the other kind of war: a non-mirror-image war. Any conflict regarded by neutral onlookers as outright aggression is a case in point:

Hitler's attack on Poland, for instance. He must have known, and other Germans must have known, that Poland was not attacking or threatening to attack Germany. Whatever their other justifications may have been, in this respect the German perception of the war was not a mirror-image of the perception in the minds of Germany's victims.

Since most people probably assume that the Hitler type of outright aggression is the typical way for wars to start, I did a rough check to see whether that is actually true, looking at thirty-seven wars that have occurred since 1913, and putting each of them, to the best of my ability, in one category or the other. The result was surprisingly even: 21 of the 37 wars (a little more than half) were in my judgment the mirror-image type, and 16 (a little less than half) were the non-mirror-image type. The method was rough, but it does seem clear that mirror-image wars, such as World War I and the Vietnam war, are not unusual exceptions. Their frequency is at least comparable with the frequency of non-mirror-image wars.

Overlapping and Conflict of Territorial Self-Images

Now, what can psychology contribute to an understanding of mirror-image wars, aside from applying to them Bronfenbrenner's apt and vivid term, "mirror-image"?

Actually it can contribute a number of things, several of which I've discussed in a book called *Nobody Wanted War* (White, 1968).[1] In this paper I want to focus on just one of them: the notion of the overlapping and conflict of territorial self-images.

It was a striking fact that most of the mirror-image wars in my list—16 out of 21—grew out of territorial conflicts in which there was reason to think that each side *really* believed that the disputed territory was part of itself. The surface of the world

[1] This book is an expanded version of "Misperception and the Vietnam War," *Journal of Social Issues*, 1966, **22**(3). *Nobody Wanted War* in a further updated edition was published in paperback in April, 1970 (Anchor Books).

is dotted with ulcerous spots that have been the source of an enormous amount of bad blood and, often, of war: Bosnia, Alsace-Lorraine, the Sudetenland, the Polish Corridor, Northern Ireland, Algeria, Israel, Kashmir, the Sino-Indian border, South Korea, Taiwan, Quemoy, South Vietnam. Every one of these ulcerous spots is a zone of overlap, where one country's territorial image of itself overlaps with another country's territorial image of *it*self.

The historians and political scientists are in general quite aware of this as a cause of war, and, under labels such as "irrendentism," or simply "territorial disputes," they have given it a fair amount of emphasis. But I don't think they have given it nearly enough emphasis, and as far as I know they have never suggested an adequate psychological explanation of it. Their favorite formula, the international struggle for power, does not adequately cover it, because what needs to be explained is the special emotional intensity of the desire for power over a certain piece of territory when that territory is perceived as part of the national *self,* even though it may make little contribution to the overall power of the nation. Taiwan is a good case in point. The Chinese Communists seem fanatically intent on driving the invaders out of Taiwan—the "invaders" being us and Chiang Kai-shek—even though Taiwan would add only a little to their national power.

Identification and the Self-Image

But psychologists can offer some useful clues to an understanding of such territorial conflict. One is the notion of the self-image itself, and of how, by a process of identification, the self-image comes to include many things that were not originally part of it. We use a variety of names in referring to the self-image: many would call it simply "the self"; Kurt Lewin called it the "person." (His use of the term was broader, but I won't go into these complexities here.) But whatever we call it, I think most of us would agree that the concept of self-image

plays a central role in psychology, and that the process of identification, by which other things come to be incorporated in the self-image, is also very important. Lewin, for instance, spoke of how a person's clothes come to be psychologically a part of the "person." If clothes are identified with to such an extent that they seem to be part of the person or part of the "self," then surely the territory that represents one's own nation on the map can also be part of it.

Territory in Animal Behavior

Another clue is the analogy with the territorial fighting of animals. Lorenz (1966), Ardrey (1963), Carpenter (1934), and others have described how an animal will spring to the defense of territory that it has identified with and that it seems to regard as its own. Now of course we need to be on our guard against over-hasty parallels between animal behavior and complex human behavior such as war making, but at this point the parallel seems valid, since the mechanism of identification is involved in both. In both cases, too, there is emotional disturbance when strangers—alien, unpredictable, presumably hostile strangers—are seen as impinging on land that is regarded as one's own, and therefore as part of the self.

Territorial Overlap and Intolerance of Ambiguity

Still another clue lies in the notion of intolerance of ambiguity. What calls for explanation, you remember, is the rigidity of overlapping territorial claims, usually on both sides, and the special emotional intensity of those claims. Usually each side refuses to grant for one moment that there could be a particle of validity in the other side's claim. There is a clean-cutness, a simplicity, an all-or-none quality in these territorial perceptions that is clearly a gross oversimplification of the complexity of reality. In each side's reality-world that land just *is* its own; that's all there is to it.

As an example let's take Dean Rusk, and his perception of what land belongs to whom in Vietnam. Of course Secretary Rusk didn't see South Vietnam as belonging to America, but he did apparently see it as self-evidently part of something called the "Free World," and he did assume an American responsibility to resist any Communist encroachment on the Free World. If he had not seen the problem in these simplistic terms, he would hardly have kept coming back, as he did, to the simple proposition that the Communists have to be taught to "let their neighbors alone." To him it apparently seemed self-evident that South Vietnam was a "neighbor" of North Vietnam rather than, as the Communists apparently perceive it, a part of the very body of an independent nation called "Vietnam," into which American invaders have been arrogantly intruding. To Mr. Rusk the notion that American troops might be honestly regarded by anyone as invaders was apparently an intensely dissonant thought, and therefore unthinkable.

Territorial Self-Images in Vietnam

South Vietnam, I think, is almost a classical case of an area in which territorial self-images overlap and in which, therefore, each side honestly feels that it *must* expel the alien intruders. On both sides ideology is to a large extent rationalization; the chief underlying psychological factor is pride—the virile self-image—defined as having the courage to defend one's "own" land when foreigners are perceived as attacking it. In a sense you could also say that fear is a fundamental emotion in wars of this type, but it is important to recognize that the fear is mobilized by cognitive distortion—by the mistaken assumption that the land in dispute is self-evidently one's own, and that therefore anyone else who has the effrontery to exist on that land, with a gun in his hand, must be a diabolical alien "aggressor." Neither fear nor pride would be intensely mobilized—as both of them are   if it were not for this cognitive distortion. Each side feels that its manhood is at stake in whether it has the courage

and the toughness to see to it that every last one of those intruders is thrown out of *its* territory. To Ho Chi Minh this proposition was apparently as self-evident and elemental as the mirror-image of it is to Dean Rusk. Neither one of them, apparently, would tolerate overlapping, and therefore ambiguous, territorial images. Frenkel-Brunswik (1949) would probably say that neither could tolerate ambiguity. We have, then, in the concept of intolerance of ambiguity, another clue to an understanding of why it is that territorial claims have such rigidity and emotional intensity. And we have the implication that *pulling apart* these overlapping images—clarifying boundaries and getting agreement on them—is one of the things that most needs to be done if we want peace. It may be, too, that deliberate withdrawal from certain hotly contested areas would on balance contribute to peace.

THE "PRO-US ILLUSION"

A third not-so-obvious proposition is that *there is a tendency to see the people in another country as more friendly to one's own side than they actually are.* Let's call this the Pro-us Illusion. It's a form of wishful thinking, obviously, but like various other forms of wishful thinking, it is seldom recognized as such by those who indulge in it.

. . . in American Perception of the USSR

One major example of it would be the long-lasting, hard-dying delusion of many Americans that most of the people in the Soviet Union are against their present rulers and on the American side in the East-West conflict. From 1917, when the Communists first came to power, until perhaps the middle 1950's this was a very widespread belief in the United States, and it contributed much to the rigidity of the militant anti-Communist policy of American policy-makers such as John Foster Dulles. The Harvard research by Bauer, Inkeles, Kluckhohn, Hanfmann, and others (1956) did a lot to put an end to this delusion, but it lingers on in some quarters. Not so very long ago a prominent United States Senator declared that the Soviet Union is "seething with discontent" and hostility to its present rulers.

. . . in Our Perception of the Bay of Pigs

Another example was the belief of many Americans, at the time of our Bay of Pigs adventure, that most of the Cuban people were intensely hostile to Castro in the same way we were, and perhaps ready to rise up against him. It is hard to tell just what was in the minds of our policy-makers at that time, but it looks as if they thought there was a good chance of some kind of uprising if we could just provide the spark to ignite it. The sad thing is that they could have known better. They had easy access to the research of Lloyd Free, a good solid piece of public-opinion survey work indicating that most of the Cuban people, less than a year earlier, were quite favorable to Castro (Cantril, 1968). But Free's evidence was ignored. According to Roger Hilsman, the policy-makers just didn't try to find out what real evidence existed on the attitudes of the Cuban people (Hilsman, 1968). They made no genuine effort to get evidence that was free from obvious bias. (The testimony of refugees in Miami, which they apparently did get, was obviously biased.) That much seems clear: their curiosity was inhibited. As to the reasons for their inhibition of curiosity, one can speculate along various lines. Perhaps it was a defense against dissonance; Festinger might say that they were embarked on an enterprise, and any doubts about the wisdom of that enterprise would have been cognitively dissonant. Or perhaps it was a defense of their black-and-white picture; they may have sensed that the information they didn't inquire into would have impaired their all-black image of Castro's diabolical tyranny over the Cuban people, and their all-white image of themselves as liberating the Cuban people from a diabolical tyrant. Heider might say they were preserving psychological harmony or balance. In any

case it looks as if they shut their eyes because they were unconsciously or half-consciously afraid of what they might see. They cherished too fondly the Pro-us Illusion—and we know the fiasco that resulted.

. . . in Our Perception of Vietnam

Now, more disastrously, there is the case of Vietnam. There, too, we more or less kidded ourselves into believing that the people were on our side. In some ways it is very much like the case of Cuba. In both cases there has been a great overestimation of the extent to which the people were pro-us, and consequently a gross overestimate of the possibility of achieving a quick military victory. In both cases, too, there has been a striking lack of interest, on the part of top policy-making officials, in the best evidence that social and political science could provide.

The irony is increased by our solemn official dedication to the great objective of enabling the people of South Vietnam to determine their own destiny. President Johnson, McNamara, Rusk, President Nixon, and others have continually talked about helping "the Vietnamese" to defend themselves against the Viet Cong and invaders from the north—as if the Viet Cong were not Vietnamese, and as if it were self-evident that most of "the Vietnamese" were gallantly resisting these attacks from within and without, and eager for our help in doing so.

Actually that was always far from self-evident. Some of you may have read my long article, "Misperception and the Vietnam War," nearly three years ago in the *Journal of Social Issues* (White, 1966). If so, you may remember the twenty-five pages of the article (pp. 19–44) that were devoted to a rather intensive effort to cover the evidence on both sides of that question and to find out how the people of South Vietnam really felt about the war. The upshot of that analysis was pessimistic; I estimated that probably there were at that time more

South Vietnamese leaning in the direction of the Viet Cong—or NLF[2]—than leaning in our direction.

Since then I have revised and updated the analysis, on the basis of three more years of accumulating evidence. The new information includes all that I was able to glean during two months on the spot in Vietnam, where I had an unusual opportunity to interview well-informed Vietnamese. It includes the Columbia Broadcasting System-Opinion Research Corporation survey, in which more than 1500 South Vietnamese respondents were interviewed (1967), the writings of Douglas Pike (1966), the outstanding authority on the Viet Cong, and a good deal of other miscellaneous evidence. None of this information is conclusive. For instance, the CBS-ORC survey obviously never solved the problem of getting peasants to speak frankly with middle-class, city-bred interviewers. But by putting together all of the various sorts of information, which is what I did in the book *Nobody Wanted War,* (pp. 29–84), we can, I think, make some fairly educated guesses.

The general upshot of the revised analysis differed from the earlier one chiefly in giving a good deal more emphasis to sheer indifference on the part of a great many of the South Vietnamese. It looks as if a large majority are now so disillusioned with both sides that their main preoccupations are simply the effort to survive, and a fervent hope that peace will come soon, regardless of which side wins. It's a plague-on-both-your-houses attitude. But the results of the earlier analysis did seem to be confirmed in that it still looks as if, among those who do care intensely about which side wins, the Viet Cong has the edge. My own very rough and tentative estimates, representing the situation in 1967, were these: something like twenty percent really dedi-

[2] The common term "Viet Cong" seems preferable to "National Liberation Front" here, since the core of the group is unquestionably Communist (which is all that "Cong" means) and the term "liberation" is question-begging Communist propaganda.

cated on the side of the Viet Cong, something like ten percent equally dedicated on the anti-Viet-Cong side, and the remainder, something like seventy percent, relatively indifferent. Since in any political conflict the people who count are the people who care, what matters here is the estimate that, among those who *are* dedicated to one side or the other, more are against the position of the United States than for it. The upshot still seems to be that the psychological balance tips *against* the Saigon government and the intervening Americans. That is probably true even now, in 1969, and in previous years it was apparently much more true. For instance, my estimate is that in early 1965, when we first became very heavily involved, it was more like 40 to 10, not 20 to 10, in favor of the Viet Cong.

If Our Policy-Makers Had Known . . .

Suppose our policy-makers had known that most of the emotionally involved people were against us, and had known it clearly, at the time they were making those fateful commitments and staking American prestige on the outcome. Suppose that in 1961–2 when John Kennedy made his major commitment, or in 1964–5 when Johnson made his, they had said to themselves: "Of course we know that if we fight in Vietnam we will be supporting a small minority against a much larger minority." Would they have done it? Would we now have all the tragedy of the Vietnam War? All the blood, all the guilt, all the moral ignominy in the eyes of most of the rest of the world, all the sensitive intelligent young people here at home estranged from their own country? I doubt it. The American superego—*if* well informed—is too genuinely on the side of national self-determination, too genuinely against any clear, naked form of American domination over little countries on the other side of the world, even in the name of anti-Communism. If Kennedy and Johnson had clearly realized that the attitudes of the South Vietnamese people at that time were much more anti-us than pro-us, would this whole Vietnam mess have been avoided? I think so.

Vietnam was avoidable, just as the Bay of Pigs was avoidable. The one essential factor in avoiding both of these tragedies would have been to look hard and honestly at the best available evidence (not social-science data, in the case of Vietnam, but the testimony of the best-informed area experts, such as Joseph Buttinger). Our policy-makers in 1962 and 1965 did not look hard and honestly at the best available evidence; and the chief reason they didn't, it seems to me, was that they were clinging to an image of America as helping a beleaguered and grateful South Vietnam—not intervening in a nasty civil war in which most of those who were emotionally involved would be against us. Like the adventurers who planned the Bay of Pigs they were not really curious, because they half-knew what the answer would be if they did look honestly at the facts. They too shut their eyes and put their hands over their ears because they were cherishing too fondly the Pro-us Illusion. And we know now the disaster that resulted.

SUMMARY

The three not-so-obvious contributions (or potential contributions) of psychology to peace are:

First, a corollary of the Hovland two-sided approach: namely, that we Americans should strenuously seek common ground with the Communists, and publicly accept all we can honestly accept of the Communist point of view.

Second, the proposition that the mirror-image type of war is most likely to break out when there is overlapping and conflict of territorial self-images. It follows that reducing such overlap by clarifying boundaries, or even by deliberate withdrawal at certain points, would contribute to peace.

And third, the Pro-us Illusion, with the further proposition that if we Americans had not been indulging in it, neither the Bay of Pigs nor the Vietnam war would have occurred.

REFERENCES

Ardrey, R. *African genesis.* New York: Atheneum Publishers, 1963.

Bauer, R. A., Inkeles, A., & Kluckhohn, C. *How the Soviet system works.* Cambridge: Harvard University Press, 1956.

Bronfenbrenner, U. The mirror-image in Soviet-American relations. *Journal of Social Issues,* 1961, **17**(3), 45–56.

Cameron, J. *Here is your enemy.* New York: Holt, Rinehart, & Winston, 1966.

Cantril, H. *The human dimension.* Rutgers, 1968.

Carpenter, C. R. Behavior and social relations of the Howler monkey. *Comparative Psychological Monographs.* Johns Hopkins University, 1934.

Columbia Broadcasting System. *The people of South Vietnam: How they feel about the war.* Privately printed, March 13, 1967.

Deutsch, M., & Krauss, R. M. Studies of interpersonal bargaining. *Journal of Conflict Resolution,* 1962, **6,** 52–76.

Eckhardt, W., & White, R. K. A test of the mirror-image hypothesis: Kennedy and Khrushchev. *Journal of Conflict Resolution,* 1967, **11,** 325–332.

Fay, S. B. *The origins of the world war.* New York: Macmillan, 1928.

Frenkel-Brunswik, E. Intolerance of ambiguity as an emotional and perceptual variable. *Journal of Personality,* 1949, **18,** 108–143.

Gerassi, J. Report from North Vietnam. *New Republic,* March 4, 1967.

Gooch, G. P. *Before the war: Studies in diplomacy.* London: Longmans, Green, 1936–38. 2 vols.

Gottlieb, S. Report on talks with NLF and Hanoi. *Sane World,* September 1965, 1–6.

Hilsman, R. *To move a nation.* New York: Delta, 1968.

Holsti, O., & North, R. C. The history of human conflict. In E. B. McNeil (Ed.), *The nature of human conflict.* Englewood Cliffs: Prentice-Hall, 1965.

Hovland, C. I., Janis, I. L., & Kelley, H. H. *Communication and persuasion.* New Haven: Yale University Press, 1953.

Kelman, H. C. (Ed.). *International behavior: A social-psychological analysis.* New York: Holt, Rinehart, & Winston, 1965.

Lorenz, K. *On aggression.* New York: Harcourt, Brace, & World, 1966.

Osgood, C. *An alternative to war or surrender.* Urbana: University of Illinois Press, 1962.

Pike, D. *Viet Cong.* Cambridge: M.I.T. Press, 1966.

Rokeach, M. *The open and closed mind.* New York: Basic Books, 1960.

Salisbury, H. E. *New York Times,* January 15, 1967.

Sawyer, J., & Guetzkow, H. Bargaining and negotiation in international relations. In H. C. Kelman (Ed.), *International behavior,* New York: Holt, Rinehart, & Winston, 1965.

Sherif, M. Superordinate goals in the reduction of intergroup conflicts. *American Journal of Sociology,* 1958, **63,** 349–356.

United States Strategic Bombing Survey. *Over-all report (European war).* Washington, D. C., Government Printing Office, September 30, 1945.

White, R. K. Hitler, Roosevelt and the nature of war propaganda. *Journal of Abnormal and Social Psychology,* 1949.

White, R. K. *Value Analysis: The nature and use of the method.* SPSSI, 1951, p. 87.

White, R. K. The cold war and the modal philosophy. *Journal of Conflict Resolution,* 1957.

White, R. K. Misperception and the Vietnam war. *Journal of Social Issues,* 1966, **22**(3).

White, R. K. Communicating with Soviet communists. *Antioch Review,* 1967–8, **27**(4).

White, R. K. *Nobody wanted war: Misperception in Vietnam and other wars.* New York: Doubleday, 1968.

Zietlow, C. P. *Washington Post.* April 27, 1967.

SECTION SUMMARY

The three articles in this Section all focus on aspects of behavior in groups and of decisions made in and by groups. The Stanford prison study provides chilling evidence of the impact that roles and factors such as deindividuation can have on an individual's behavior in a group setting. Other researchers, however, have questioned how successful Zimbardo and his colleagues actually were in "functionally simulating" a real prison. Banuazizi and Movahedi (1975; Mohvahedi & Banuazizi, 1975) suggest that the *demand characteristics* of the mock prison (subjects' expectations of how they were *supposed* to behave) may have been so strong that "prisoners" and "guards" alike were just playing stereotypic roles in what they saw as a "scientific game." They claim that within the experimental context itself there were numerous cues pointing to the experimental hypothesis and the experimenters' expectations. Hence, subjects were complying with the actual or perceived demands in the experimental situation and acting on the basis of their own role-related expectancies. Other psychologists have suggested, in turn, that while demand characteristics may have been operating to some extent, there still was much more going on than simple role-playing alone (DeJong, 1975; Doyle, 1975; Thayer & Saarni, 1975).

The prison study also raises ethical questions. As the article states, the researchers had expected to carry out a two-week study but were forced to end their experiment after only six days and nights. By this time they had already released four of the nine prisoners because of extreme emotional depression or acute anxiety attacks. Questions could certainly be raised about the well-being of the participants in Zimbardo's study. Even though they were volunteers and were being paid, might they have suffered some unanticipated permanent negative effects from their participation? Zimbardo and his co-workers carried out a full-day *debriefing* session at the end of the study to work through problems that had arisen during the experiment. In addition, they carried out a year-long follow-up by means of questionnaires, personal interviews, and discussions. The researchers believe that the mental anguish felt by the participants was transient and situationally specific but that the self-knowledge gained in the experiment persisted. We will discuss these ethical issues in greater detail in the Summary to Section 8.

While the prison study focuses on the behavior of persons in a deindividuated state, Janis' article discusses the case in which individuals must band together to reach an important *group* decision. Janis discusses eight main symptoms of groupthink: (1) an illusion of invulnerability, (2) construction of rationalizations, (3) belief in the inherent morality of the ingroup, (4) stereotyped views of the leaders of enemy groups, (5) the application of pressure on individuals who express doubts or question the validity of arguments, (6) self-censorship, (7) the illusion of unanimity, and (8) the existence of "mindguards." Although Janis wrote this article before the Watergate scandal of 1973 and 1974, it is interesting to analyze the behavior of President Nixon and his associates in terms of the same eight symptoms.

Many of the Nixon administration's decisions that became part of the Watergate scandal and that, in retrospect, were bad ones may have come out of the sort of groupthink atmosphere described by Janis. Certainly there appears to have been an illusion of invulnerability on the part of the President and his top advisers. Warnings of impending disaster were ignored or soft-pedaled; the ethical or moral consequences of decisions were often ignored (presidential aide Charles Colson remarked that he would "walk over my grandmother" if it would help the reelection of President Nixon); and political opponents were seen as "enemies" (recall the infamous "enemies list" made up by White House staffers). Later accounts of the series of meetings that led to the approval of the ill-fated Watergate burglary provide clear evidence of self-censorship and of pressure applied to those who did not agree (for example, see *Washington Post* staff, 1974).

Janis also points out what factors often lead to such successful group decisions as the formulation of the Marshall Plan and the handling of the Cuban missile crisis by President John F. Kennedy and his advisers. If President Nixon and his advisers had read Janis' article and followed his suggestions, might the series of decisions that led up to the Watergate scandal have been much different?

The articles by Janis and White (see also White, 1970) illustrate that there is a good deal of social-psychological knowledge that can be of considerable value in understanding and perhaps changing political behavior and decisions that affect all of us. Charles Osgood (1962, 1966) has made a further suggestion concerning how international conflict might be avoided or reduced. His plan, which he has labeled *GRIT* or "graduated reciprocation in tension reduction," is drawn from the results of social-psychological research on conflict. Osgood's plan calls for one party (such as a nation) to announce in advance an intention to make a cooperative conciliatory gesture—for example, a reduction in the production of some sort of arms. The first gesture should be relatively small so that, if it is exploited by the other side, no serious harm will befall the party that made it. The first side should then provide its opponent with an opportunity to reciprocate with a cooperative gesture. Hopefully a step-by-step program can be initiated in which each side makes increasingly cooperative gestures. Certainly, the first steps taken by each side might be viewed with suspicion by the other, but if several such tension-reducing steps take place, the seeds of trust might be planted. Ultimately, this might continue until large-scale acts of cooperation and disarmament take place.

Some have proposed (for example, Etzioni, 1967) that this procedure *was* being tried by the Kennedy administration after the Cuban missile crisis. It appeared that the U. S. government's efforts to reduce tensions did lead to some reciprocation of cooperative gestures between the United States and the Soviet Union, but Kennedy's assassination brought an end to the "experiment." It may be that the "detente" policies of the Nixon and Ford administrations also contained elements of GRIT. Laboratory studies of conflict situations suggest that the GRIT procedures will be effective. It remains to be seen if and when this system can be applied on a large scale to international behaviors. If social psychology can contribute to a policy that increases the chances of world peace, it will have made a significant contribution indeed.

REFERENCES

Banuazizi, A., & Movahedi, S. Interpersonal dynamics in a simulated prison: A methodological analysis. *American Psychologist*, 1975, *30*, 152–160.

DeJong, W. Another look at Banuazizi and Movahedi's analysis of the Stanford Prison experiment. *American Psychologist*, 1975, *30*, 1013–1015.

Doyle, C. Interpersonal dynamics in role playing. *American Psychologist*, 1975, *30*, 1011–1013.

Etzioni, A. The Kennedy experiment. *Western Political Quarterly*, 1967, *20*, 361–380.

Movahedi, S., & Banuazizi, A. Reply. *American Psychologist*, 1975, *30*, 1016–1018.

Osgood, C. E. *An alternative to war or surrender.* Urbana, Ill.: University of Illinois Press, 1962.

Osgood, C. E. *Perspectives in foreign policy* (2nd ed.). Palo Alto, Calif.: Pacific Books, 1966.

Thayer, S., & Saarni, C. Demand characteristics are everywhere (anyway). *American Psychologist*, 1975, *30*, 1015–1016.

Washington Post staff. *The fall of a president.* New York: Dell, 1974.

White, R. K. *Nobody wanted war.* New York: Doubleday, 1970.

SECTION VIII

OBEDIENCE AND COMPLIANCE

INTRODUCTION

Throughout our lives we are subjected to external pressures to comply with many different, and sometimes conflicting, norms and standards. Similarly, there are countless cases in which we are urged to obey the wishes or commands of another person. This person may be one's boss, parent, lover or spouse, college professor, commanding officer in the Army, experimenter in a psychological study, and so on.

The question of when *compliance* with, or obedience to, standards or requests is likely to be greatest has increasingly interested social psychologists in the last three decades. Under what conditions will someone be most likely to comply with a request? Are there conditions under which some people will obey an order even when it appears cruel and inhumane? If so, is such obedience limited to people who already have such inhumane tendencies, or are "normal, everyday people" likely to obey also? The research endeavors described in this Section examine such questions.

One seemingly obvious way in which compliance may be increased is through the operation of *norms*

concerning *social justice* and *reparation*. For instance, if someone does you a favor, you will probably be more likely to help that individual in return than if he or she had not helped you. If the person asks you to do something, therefore, you will be more likely to comply with the request. Several studies have supported this common-sense notion —people will tend to "restore equity" by returning the favor and complying with a request (for example, Regan, 1971). The tendency to comply is particularly strong if the original favor is perceived as being entirely voluntary, rather than suggested or made compulsory by someone else (Goranson & Berkowitz, 1966). Interestingly, although people are more likely to comply with a request from a "favor-doer," it is apparently not because of any increase in liking for the favor-doer (Lerner & Lichtman, 1968; Schopler & Thompson, 1968; Regan, 1971).

Another method by which compliance might be increased is through the arousal of *guilt*. When people feel guilty because they have done something they consider wrong, they generally will try to do something to reduce that guilt. They may perform a good act to "balance" the bad (guilt-inducing) act; they may subject themselves to some kind of unpleasantness and thereby punish themselves for their misbehavior; or they may attempt to minimize the negative aspects of the guilt-arousing situation. The first two of these techniques might make the (guilty) person more likely to comply with an appropriate request (Freedman, Wallington, & Bless, 1967; Carlsmith & Gross, 1969).

Still another method of getting someone to comply with a large request is to get him or her to comply first with a smaller request. This *foot-in-the-door technique* has probably been known to salespeople for a long time, but social psychology has recently provided empirical validation of its effectiveness. As an example, Freedman and Fraser (1966) had experimenters go from door to door asking housewives to sign a petition sponsored by the Committee for Safe Driving that asked their senators to work for legislation to encourage safe driving. Almost all of the housewives signed the petition. Several weeks later, different experimenters went from door to door in the same neighborhood asking each housewife to agree to put a large, unattractive sign saying "Drive Carefully" in her front yard. More than half of the women who had previously agreed to sign the petition (the small request) agreed to post the sign (the larger request). In contrast, only 17% of the women who had not been approached before (with the petition) agreed to post the sign.

This general technique was used in a destructive fashion in the Chinese Communist *brainwashing* attempts on prisoners of war during the Korean War. Schein (1956) has described their technique as the "pacing of demands." In his words:

In the various kinds of responses that were demanded of the prisoners, the Chinese always started with trivial, innocuous ones and, as the habit of responding became established, gradually worked up to more important ones. Thus, after a prisoner had been 'trained' to speak or write out trivia, statements on more important issues were demanded of him. This was particularly effective in eliciting confessions, self-criticism, and information during interrogation [p. 163].

Thus, asking for a small favor before one asks for a larger favor may increase the chances that the larger favor will be granted. There is evidence, however, that precisely the *opposite* technique may also be effective. In our first article, Robert B. Cialdini and his colleagues at Arizona State University describe three experiments illustrating what they call the "rejection-then-moderation" effect. These researchers found that when a requester first asked for an extreme favor (which was refused) and then for a smaller favor, this procedure produced more compliance with the smaller favor than a procedure in which the requester asked solely for the smaller favor.

The research and theory described thus far refer to methods by which the tendency to comply with a specific request can be increased. But what of cases in which the entire situation is structured toward obedience—in which compliance with *any* request by those in charge is expected? There are certain situations, such as the military chain of command or the prison environment, that seem to demand obedience. (The situation of the psychological experiment itself is one that seems to be perceived by many subjects as demanding their cooperation or obedience.) A relevant research question, then, is: how powerful are the pressures toward obedience in such situations? Are they so powerful that even "normal, everyday people" will obey inhumane or cruel demands?

In the second article in this Section, Stanley Milgram, then at Yale University, describes a study that addressed these questions directly. The results of this study and others like it have proved shocking and disturbing to most persons who have read them. (We will describe Milgram's subsequent studies in the Section Summary.) Their relevance in adding to our understanding of how societal "atrocities" can occur has been, and still is, hotly debated.

Our third study relates to a somewhat different type of societal "atrocity"—the Watergate scandal. Stephen G. West, Steven P. Gunn, and Paul Chernicky, all then at Florida State University, designed a situation to parallel one aspect of the Watergate situation—namely, the pressure to stage illegal break-ins and steal information. Their results, like those of Milgram's studies, suggest that such "undesirable" behavior is much more situationally controlled than most of us would like to think.

There are serious ethical questions raised by studies in which deception is used and people are exposed to stress and perhaps induced to behave in ways they would prefer not to. We will discuss these ethical issues in the Summary.

REFERENCES

Carlsmith, J. M., & Gross, A. E. Some effects of guilt on compliance. *Journal of Personality and Social Psychology,* 1969, *11,* 232–239.

Freedman, J. L., & Fraser, S. C. Compliance without pressure: The foot-in-the-door technique. *Journal of Personality and Social Psychology,* 1966, *4,* 195–202.

Freedman, J. L., Wallington, S. A., & Bless, E. Compliance without pressure: The effect of guilt. *Journal of Personality and Social Psychology,* 1967, *7,* 117–124.

Goranson, R. E., & Berkowitz, L. Reciprocity and responsibility reactions to prior help. *Journal of Personality and Social Psychology,* 1966, *3,* 227–232.

Lerner, M. J., & Lichtman, R. R. Effects of perceived norms on attitudes and altruistic behavior toward a dependent other. *Journal of Personality and Social Psychology,* 1968, *9,* 226–232.

Regan, D. T. Effects of a favor and liking on compliance. *Journal of Experimental Social Psychology,* 1971, *7,* 627–639.

Schein, E. H. The Chinese indoctrination program for prisoners of war. *Psychiatry,* 1956, *19,* 149–172.

Schopler, J., & Thompson, V. D. Role of attribution processes in mediating amount of reciprocity for a favor. *Journal of Personality and Social Psychology,* 1968, *10,* 243–250.

ARTICLE 22

Reciprocal concessions procedure for inducing compliance: The door-in-the-face technique

Robert B. Cialdini
Joyce E. Vincent
Stephen K. Lewis
José Catalan
Diane Wheeler
Betty Lee Darby

The foot-in-the-door technique has been investigated by Freedman and Fraser (1966) as a procedure for inducing compliance with a request for a favor. They demonstrated that obtaining a person's compliance with a small request substantially increases the likelihood of that person's compliance with a subsequent, larger request. Freedman and Fraser suggest that the mediator of the foot-in-the-door effect is a shift in the self-perception of the benefactor. After performing or agreeing to perform an initial favor, a person "may become, in his own eyes, the kind of person who does this sort of thing, who agrees to requests made by strangers, who takes action on things he believes in, who cooperates with good causes. . . . The basic idea is that the change in attitude need not be toward any particular person or activity, but may be toward activity or compliance in general." Thus, one effective way to obtain a favor is to begin by making a *minimal* first request which is sure to produce *compliance* and then to *advance* to a larger favor (the one which was desired from the outset). It may well be, however, that an equally effective method for getting a favor done involves the exact opposite procedure. What would be the result of making an *extreme* first request which is sure to be *rejected* and then asking for a more *moderate* second favor (the one which was desired from the outset)? There are two lines of evidence suggesting that such a technique would be efficacious in producing compliance with the second request.

This first sort of evidence comes from work investigating the concept of reciprocation. Gouldner (1960) maintains that a norm of reciprocity exists in all societies. Gouldner states the norm of reciprocity in its simple form as: "You should give benefits to those who give you benefits." (p. 170) There is considerable experimental evidence attesting to the workings of such a rule in our culture (e.g., Brehm

Reprinted from the *Journal of Personality and Social Psychology*, 1975, *31*, pp. 206–215. Copyright 1975 by the American Psychological Association. Reprinted by permission.

& Cole, 1966; Goranson & Berkowitz, 1966; Pruitt, 1968; Regan, 1971; Wilke & Lanzetta, 1970). In each case, receipt of a favor has been shown to increase the likelihood that the favor will be returned, although not necessarily in kind. While Gouldner (1960) speaks of the norm of reciprocity almost exclusively in terms of the reciprocation of benefits and services, it seems likely that a norm for reciprocity governs other types of social exchange also. Specifically, we would like to postulate a reciprocal concessions corollary to the general norm of reciprocity: "You should make concessions to those who make concessions to you." Such a rule can be seen as having an important societal function. Very often in social interaction participants begin with requirements and demands which are unacceptable to one another. In order for the interaction to continue and hence for common goals to be achieved, compromise must be struck. *Mutual* concession is crucial. If there is no implicit prescription that retreat from an initial position by one participant should be reciprocated by the other participant, then it is unlikely that compromise attempts would be initiated and, consequently, that the interaction would continue. However, given a principle for reciprocation of concessions, an interaction participant could instigate compromise attempts with little fear of exploitation by his partner.

Evidence for the existence of a reciprocal concessions relationship in our society can be seen in numerous terms and phrases of the language: "give and take," "meeting the other fellow halfway," etc. Much more compelling, however, are the data which come from a number of studies of negotiation behavior. An experiment by Chertkoff and Conley (1967) demonstrated that the number of concessions a subject makes in a bargaining situation is significantly affected by the number of his opponent's concessions; more frequent concessions by the opponent elicited more frequent concessions from the subject. In a somewhat similar context, Komorita and Brenner (1968) had subjects bargain as buyers against opponent-sellers. In one condition, the op-

ponent initially proposed what was a perfectly equitable selling price and refused to move from that price throughout the course of the negotiations; in other conditions, the opponent began with an extreme offer and then gradually retreated from that price as bargaining progressed. The consistent result was that the former condition elicited the least amount of yielding on the part of the subjects. Komorita and Brenner conclude that, "in a bargaining situation, if one party wishes to reach an agreement at a 'fair' price, clearly a strategy of making an initial offer at that level and remaining firm thereafter is not an effective means of reaching an agreement." (p. 18) Finally, an experiment by Benton, Kelley, and Liebling (1972) had subjects negotiate the allocation of funds with a preprogrammed opponent in a mixed-motive game. One condition of the experiment saw subjects faced with an opponent who repeatedly made an extreme demand during the first two minutes of the bargaining session and who then reduced this demand during the next two minutes. The number of subjects' own extreme demands was drastically reduced by this strategy. In contrast, another condition, in which the opponent remained intransigently extreme, produced almost no reduction in the number of extreme subject demands during this second two-minute period. In sum, it seems that the likelihood of a concession by one party is positively related to the occurrence of a concession by another party.

Let us now return to the original question, "How might we enhance the probability that another will comply with our request for a favor?" The analysis above suggests that if we were to begin by asking for an extreme favor which was sure to be refused by the other, and then we were to move to a smaller request, the other would feel a normative strain to match our concession with one of his own. Since the situation is such that the other's response to our request involves an essentially dichotomous choice—yes or no—the only available reciprocation route for him would be to move from his position of initial noncompliance to one of compliance.

So, by means of an illusory retreat from our initial position, we should be able to obtain another's agreement to the request that we desired from the outset.

In line with the formulation we have proposed, two things are crucial to the success of such a procedure. First, our original request must be rejected by the target person; once this has occurred, the target will have taken a position and an apparent concession on our part will pressure him to meet us halfway and hence to yield to our smaller request. Second, the target must perceive that we have conceded in some way. Thus, the size of our second favor must be unambiguously smaller than that of the first; only then can the action of a reciprocal concessions norm come into play.

EXPERIMENT 1

In order to test the effectiveness of this procedure for inducing compliance, an experiment was conducted. It was expected that a person who followed a refused initial request with a smaller request would obtain more agreement to the smaller request than a person who made *only* the smaller request. Such a result could be explained, however, in a way quite apart from the theoretical account we have proposed. Rather than through the action of a reciprocal concessions mechanism, the superiority of the technique we have described could be seen as occurring through the action of a contrast effect. Exposure to an initial, large request could cause subjects to perceive a subsequent, smaller request as less demanding than would subjects who had never been exposed to the large request; consequently, the former type of subject might be expected to comply more with the critical request. It was necessary, therefore, to include in our experimental design a condition which differentiated these two theoretical explanations.

One point of departure for the two accounts lies in the requirement of the reciprocal concessions explanation for the target's refusal of and the request-

er's moderation of the initial, larger favor. The contrast effect explanation does not demand this sequence of refusal and moderation; rather, it requires only that the target person be previously exposed to the larger request. An experiment was performed, then, which included three conditions. In one condition, subjects were asked to perform a favor. In a second condition, subjects were asked to perform the critical favor after they had refused to perform a larger favor. In a final condition, subjects heard the larger favor described to them before they were asked to perform the critical one.

Method

Subjects.   Subjects were 72 people of both sexes who were moving along university walkways during daylight hours. Only those individuals who were walking alone were selected, and no subjects were selected during the 10-minute break period between classes.

Procedure.   A subject meeting the conditions above was approached by a student-experimenter[1] who initiated interaction by introducing him- or herself as being with the County Youth Counseling Program. At this point, the experimenter made (for the Youth Counseling Program) either an extreme request followed by a smaller request or made just the smaller request.

The extreme request asked subjects to perform as counselors to juvenile delinquents for a period of at least two years. Specifically, the experimenter said:

We're currently recruiting university students to work as voluntary, nonpaid counselors at the County Juvenile Detention Center. The position could require two hours of your time per week for a minimum of two years. You would be working more in the line of a Big Brother (Sister) to one of the boys (girls) at the detention home. Would you be interested in being considered for one of these positions?

[1]The experimenters were three college age students, one female and two male. Experimenters approached only subjects of the same sex as themselves.

The smaller request asked subjects to perform as chaperones for a group of juvenile delinquents on a two-hour trip to the zoo. Specifically, the experimenter said:

We're recruiting university students to chaperone a group of boys (girls) from the County Juvenile Detention Center on a trip to the zoo. It would be voluntary, non-paid, and would require about two hours of one afternoon or evening. Would you be interested in being considered for one of these positions?

Subjects were randomly assigned to one of three conditions.

Rejection-moderation condition. Subjects in this condition heard the experimenter first make the extreme request. After subjects refused the large request, the experimenter said, "Well, we also have another program you might be interested in then." At this point the experimenter made the smaller request.

Smaller request only control. Subjects in this condition were asked by the experimenter only to perform the smaller request.

Exposure control. In this condition the experimenter first described the extreme and then the smaller favor and requested that the subjects perform *either* one. Specifically, subjects in the exposure only control heard the experimenter give the standard introduction and then say:

We're currently recruiting university students for two different programs. In the first, we're looking for voluntary, nonpaid counselors to work at the County Juvenile Detention Center. The position would require two hours of your time per week for a minimum of two years. You would be working more in the line of a Big Brother (Sister) to one of the boys (girls) at the detention center. In the other program, we're looking for university students to chaperone a group of boys (girls) from the detention center on a trip to the zoo. It would also be voluntary, nonpaid, and would require two hours of one afternoon or evening. Would you be interested in being considered for either of these two programs?

No subject during the course of the experiment ever agreed to perform the initial, large favor. However, when a subject agreed to the smaller request, the experimenter took his or her name and phone number. The experimenter promised to call if the subject was needed but explained that "there is a chance that you won't be called because of the large number of people who have already volunteered to help." At this point, the experimenter thanked the subject and moved on.

Predictions. Two predictions derived from the reciprocal concessions model were made. First, it was expected that the subjects in the rejection-moderation condition would comply with the smaller request more than would subjects in the two control conditions. Second, it was predicted that the amount of compliance with the smaller request would not differ between the two controls.

Results

No subject in the present experiment agreed to perform the extreme favor. The percentage of subjects who complied with the smaller request in each of the treatment conditions can be seen in Table 1.

Planned orthogonal contrasts designed to test the two experimental predictions were performed on the data. The first contrast, comparing the compliance rates of the two control groups, found no difference, $\chi^2 = .50$, *ns*. The second contrast tested the combined control conditions against the rejection-moderation condition; this analysis produced a highly significant difference, $\chi^2 = 6.42$, $p = .011$. All tests in this and subsequent experiments are two-tailed.

Additional analyses investigating the extent to which the pattern of results above was affected by such factors as the sex of the subject and the identity of the experimenter provided no statistic which approached conventional levels of significance; the same pattern obtained for all three experimenters and for male and female subjects. In all, then, it

TABLE 1. Percentage of subjects complying with the smaller request.

Treatment	% Compliance
Rejection-moderation condition	50.0
Exposure control	25.0
Smaller request only control	16.7

Note. The *n* for each condition = 24.

seems that the only factor which enhanced the amount of agreement to the smaller request was the procedure of moving to the smaller request *after* the larger request had been refused.

Discussion

It is clear from the findings above that making an extreme initial request which is sure to be rejected and then moving to a smaller request significantly increases the probability of a target person's agreement to the second request. Moreover, this phenomenon does not seem mediated by a perceptual contrast effect; simply exposing the target to the extreme request beforehand does not affect compliance.

While the results of this first experiment lend some support to the reciprocal concessions explanation, they do not, of course, necessarily confirm the validity of the interpretation. If we are to gain confidence in such a model, additional predictions derivable from it must be proposed and demonstrated. To this end, it was decided to replicate and extend our findings in a second experiment.

EXPERIMENT 2

The reciprocal concessions formulation we have described suggests that a target person feels pressure to change from his initial position of noncompliance after it is seen that the requester has changed from his own initial position. It is not enough that the target has been asked to comply with a large then a smaller request, the target must perceive the request for the smaller favor as a concession *by the requester*. If this is in fact the case, a target person who is asked an extreme favor by one individual and a smaller favor by some other individual in a second interaction context should not experience a reciprocation-mediated tendency to agree to the smaller request. The second requester should not be perceived as conceding and thus, according to our model, the target should not be spurred to reciprocate via compliance. On the other hand, if, as in Experiment 1, the requests are made by the same person, compliance with the smaller request should be enhanced.

To test the importance of the perception of concession, an experiment was conducted which included three conditions. In one condition, subjects were asked to perform a favor by a single requester. In a second condition, subjects were asked by a single requester to perform the critical favor after they had refused to perform a larger favor for that requester. In the third condition, subjects were asked to perform the critical favor by one requester after they had refused to perform a larger favor for a different requester. An additional benefit of this third condition was that it afforded another test of the perceptual contrast explanation for the obtained effect and thus provided a conceptual replication of one aspect of Experiment 1.

Method

Subjects. Subjects were 58 males who were selected for participation in a fashion identical to that of Experiment 1.

Procedure. A subject meeting the conditions above was approached by two student-experimenters, one male and one female; we call them Experimenters A and B, respectively. Experimenter A initiated interaction by introducing both himself and Experimenter B to the subject. At this point, a second male experimenter (Experimenter C) who was apparently an acquaintance of Experimenter B, approached the group and engaged Experimenter B in conversation about an upcoming exam they both would be taking. This procedure uniformly distracted the subject's attention for a second, so Experimenter A waited for the subject to turn back to him. Here the three treatment conditions of the study differed.

Rejection-moderation condition. Subjects in this condition next heard Experimenter A ask for the extreme favor. The extreme favor was the same as that used in Experiment 1. After the subject had refused to comply, Experimenter A made the smaller request, which in this experiment asked subjects to chaperone a group of "low-income children" to the zoo. Specifically, he said:

Oh. Well. I'm also with the Campus Volunteer Service Organization in another program that has nothing to do with the Juvenile Detention Center. It involves helping to chaperone a group of low-income children on a trip to the zoo. We can't give you any money for it, but it would only involve about two hours of one afternoon or evening. Would you be willing to help us with this?

Two requester control. The procedures of this condition were similar to those of the rejection-moderation condition except that, upon refusal of the extreme request, Experimenter A thanked the subject and walked away from the group with Experimenter B; this left Experimenter C alone with the subject. At this point, Experimenter C made the smaller request. He prefaced the request by saying,

Excuse me, I couldn't help overhearing you say that you would not be able to be a counselor to juvenile delinquents for two years. [If a subject had given a reason for refusing the extreme request, Experimenter C mentioned that he had overheard the stated reason as well.[2]] But

[2]A replication of Experiment 2 was subsequently performed by the authors. The only difference between the original and replicated versions was that in the replication Experimenter C's performance in the two requester control did not include a claim that he had overheard the target's conversation with Experimenter A. The data of the two versions of Experiment 2 were virtually identical.

maybe you can help *me*. My name is _____, and I'm with the Campus Volunteer Service Organization in a program that has nothing to do with the Juvenile Detention Center. [The remainder of the request was identical to that made in the rejection-moderation condition.]

Smaller request only control. The procedures of this condition were similar to those of the rejection-moderation condition except that the extreme request was not made. The events in this condition were as follow: Experimenters A and B approached the subject; Experimenter A introduced himself and Experimenter B; Experimenter C joined the group and engaged Experimenter B in conversation; Experimenter A made the smaller request. It should be noted that in this and both other conditions the roles of Experimenter A and Experimenter C were alternated between the two male experimenters of the study.

Predictions. The predictions of the present experiment were similar to those of Experiment 1. It was expected, first, that the two control conditions would not differ from one another in amount of compliance with the smaller request. Second, it was thought that the rejection-moderation condition would produce more compliance with the smaller request than would the controls.

The experimenters in this instance were not aware of the nature of these predictions; in fact, they were led by the principal investigator to expect opposite results. As in Experiment 1, the experimenters were undergraduate research assistants. Because of evidence indicating that undergraduate experimenters have in the past produced results consistent with prediction via experimenter expectancy effects (Rosenthal, 1966) or conscious data fixing (Azrin, Holz, Ulrich, & Goldiamond, 1961), a test of such explanations for the obtained effect in Experiment 1 seemed in order. Hence, the experimenters of Experiment 2 were told that the principal investigator was predicting that the smaller request only control would produce the most compliance. This would supposedly be so because of an "irritation or reactance tendency in people who have been asked for favors twice in succession.'' If the pattern of results nonetheless appeared as predicted by the reciprocal concession formulation, experimenter bias could no longer be offered as a possible explanation for the superiority of the rejection-moderation condition.

Results

Three subjects in Experiment 2 complied with the extreme request, two in the rejection-moderation condition and the other in the two requester control. These subjects were removed from the analysis and replaced by three other subjects.[3] The percentage of subjects who complied with the smaller request in each of the treatment conditions of Experiment 2 can be seen in Table 2.

Again, a priori orthogonal contrasts were used to test the experimental predictions. One contrast compared the amounts of compliance with the smaller request within the two control conditions; no conventionally significant difference occurred, $\chi^2 = 2.53$, $p = .111$. The other comparison, which tested the rejection-moderation condition against the combined control conditions, did produce a clearly significant difference at conventional levels, $\chi^2 = 6.85, p = .009$.

Discussion

It appears from the results of Experiment 2 that the target's perception of concession by the requester is a crucial factor in producing compliance with the smaller request. Only when the extreme and the smaller favors were asked by the same requester was compliance enhanced. This finding provides further evidence for a reciprocal concessions mediator of the rejection-then-moderation effect. It seems that our subjects increased the frequency of

---

[3]It was necessary to discard the data of the original three subjects because of the likelihood that their responses to the second request would be mediated by a foot-in-the-door effect rather than a reciprocal concessions effect; thus our results would have been artificially inflated in the direction of prediction.

TABLE 2. Percentage of subjects complying with the smaller request in experiment 2.

Treatment	% Compliance
Rejection-moderation condition	55.5
Two requester control	10.5
Smaller request only control	31.5

Note. The n for the rejection-moderation condition = 20; the n for each of the two control conditions = 19.

assent to the smaller request only in response to what could be interpreted as concession behavior on the part of the requester; such assent, then, would seem best viewed as reciprocal concession behavior.

It might be noted that compliance in the two requester control was inhibited relative to that in the small request only control. This finding replicates quite closely a result obtained by Snyder and Cunningham (1975) and fits very well with evidence suggesting that in most cases, people are quite consistent in their responses to requests for favors (Freedman & Fraser, 1966; Snyder & Cunningham, 1975). Unless there was a pressure to reciprocate a concession, 89.5% of the subjects in our experiment who said, "No" to an initial request said, "No" to a subsequent one.

EXPERIMENT 3

While the data of Experiments 1 and 2 are wholly consistent with the reciprocal concessions formulation, an alternative explanation for these results is applicable as well. It may have been that the heightened compliance in our rejection-moderation conditions was due to the fact that only in these conditions did one requester persist in making a second request after his first had been refused. Perhaps subjects in these conditions acquiesced to the critical, zoo trip request not because of pressure to reciprocate a concession but because they were dunned into accession by a tenacious requester or because they wanted to avoid the requester's perception of them as having a generally antisocial or unhelpful nature.

In order to test this type of explanation, a third experiment was performed. Included in Experiment 3 was a procedure in which subjects were asked to perform an initial favor and then were asked by the same requester to perform a second favor (the critical request) of *equivalent* size. Since the proposal of an equivalent second favor does not constitute a concession on the part of the requester, the reciprocal concessions model would predict no increased compliance with the critical request from this procedure. However, if the persistance of a single requester is the mediator of enhanced compliance, then such a procedure should produce heightened agreement to perform the critical request. A second function of Experiment 3 was to provide a conceptual replication of Experiment 2. As in Experiment 2, one group of subjects received two requests but should not have construed the second request as a concession on the part of the person who made it. In Experiment 2, the perception of concession was avoided by having a second requester make the smaller, critical request; in Experiment 3, it was done by making the initial request equivalent in size to the critical one. For both procedures, the results should be similar—no enhancement of compliance.

Method

Subjects.   Subjects were 72 people of both sexes who were selected for participation in a fashion identical to that of Experiments 1 and 2.

Procedure.   A subject meeting the conditions above was approached by a student-experimenter in a fashion identical to that of Experiment 1.[4] Subjects were randomly assigned to one of three conditions.

Rejection-moderation condition.   Subjects in this condition were treated identically to subjects in the comparable condition of Experiment 1; that is,

[4]In the present experiment there were four experimenters, three female and one male. Experimenters approached only subjects of the same sex as themselves.

after hearing and rejecting an extreme request (to perform as a counselor to a juvenile delinquent for a minimum of two years), a subject heard the same requester make a smaller request (to perform as a chaperone for a group of juvenile delinquents on a two-hour trip to the zoo).

Smaller request only control.   Subjects in this condition were treated identically to subjects in the comparable condition of Experiment 1; that is, a subject heard the requester make only the smaller request to chaperone a group of juvenile delinquents on a trip to the zoo.

Equivalent request control.   Subjects in this condition heard a requester initially request that they perform as chaperones for a group of juvenile delinquents on a two-hour trip to the city museum; after the subjects responded to this first request, the experimenter then requested that they chaperone a group of juvenile delinquents on a two-hour trip to the zoo.

Predictions.   As in the previous experiments, it was predicted on the basis of the reciprocal concessions model that, first, the two control conditions would not differ from one another in amount of compliance with the critical request (the zoo trip) and, second, that the rejection-moderation condition would produce more compliance with the critical request than would the controls.

Results

No subject in Experiment 3 complied with the extreme request in the rejection-moderation condition. However, eight subjects complied with the initial request in the equivalent request control. The percentage of subjects who complied with the critical request in each of the treatment conditions of Experiment 3 can be seen in Table 3.

As before, two planned orthogonal comparisons were used to test the predictions. The first contrasted the two control conditions; no significant

TABLE 3. Percentage of subjects complying with the smaller request in Experiment 3.

Treatment	% Compliance
Rejection-moderation condition	54.1
Equivalent request control	33.3
Smaller request only control	33.3

Note. The *n* for each condition = 24.

difference resulted, $\chi^2 = 0.0$, *ns*. The second tested the rejection-moderation condition against the combined controls; a marginally significant difference occurred, $\chi^2 = 2.88$, $p = .091$. Two features of the data from this experiment argue against the interpretation that a requester's persistence in making requests accounts for the superiority of the rejection-moderation condition. First, the equivalent request control, which involved successive requests from the same requester, produced exactly the same amount of compliance as the smaller request only control. Second, of the eight subjects who agreed to perform the critical request in the equivalent request control, only one had refused to perform the similar-sized initial request. Clearly, then, it is not the case that a persistent requester induces compliance to a second request solely through the act of making a second request. Indeed, in the equivalent request control, subjects were stoutly consistent in the nature of their responses to the two requests. Twenty-two of the 24 subjects in that group responded similarly to both requests.

GENERAL DISCUSSION

Taken together, the findings of Experiments 1, 2, and 3 seem to support the reciprocal concessions model. Each experiment indicated that proposing an extreme request which is rejected and then moving to a smaller request increases compliance with the smaller request. The results of Experiment 1 suggested that the target person's rejection of the initial, extreme request is crucial to the effectiveness of this technique. Through his refusal to perform the large favor, the target puts himself in a position from which virtually his only possible re-

treat is accession to the smaller request. Thus when the requester moves from his extreme proposal to a smaller one, the target must agree to the second proposal in order to relieve any felt pressure for reciprocation of concessions. As was shown in Experiment 1, if movement to a smaller request occurs without the target's initial rejection of the extreme request, compliance with the smaller request will not be significantly enhanced. Experiment 1 demonstrated further, as did Experiment 2, that merely exposing a target person to an extreme request does not increase the likelihood of his compliance with a subsequent smaller request; such results tend to disconfirm a perceptual contrast explanation of the phenomenon. Experiments 2 and 3 demonstrated the importance of concession. Simply presenting a target person with a smaller request after he had rejected a larger one or simply presenting a target person with a second request of equivalent size, does not increase agreement to the second request. Only when the proposal of the second favor can be considered a concession on the part of the requester is compliance increased.

Several aspects of the phenomenon we have investigated suggest that its use would be highly functional for someone in need of a favor. First, it is clear that the effect is quite a powerful one for inducing compliance. Averaging over all three studies and comparing against the small request only control conditions, we were able to double the likelihood of compliance through the use of the rejection-then-moderation procedure. The strength of this procedure is further evidenced when it is realized that it is working in a direction counter to any tendency for the target to be consistent in his responses to requests for favors. It should be remembered that Freedman and Fraser (1966) found such a tendency for consistency to be a potent one in their foot-in-the-door study, and we found a similar tendency in the two requester control of Experiment 2 and the equivalent request control of Experiment 3. Seemingly, then, the size of the effect is such that it overwhelmed a strong propensity in our subjects for constancy in their reactions to compliance requests.

Second, the technique does not limit a requester to the receipt of small favors. It is only necessary that the critical request be *smaller* than the initial one for a reciprocal concessions mechanism to come into play. Evidence that a requester can use this technique to gain assent to a substantial request can be seen in the data of Experiment 1. The smaller request in that study might well be seen, objectively, as an extreme one in itself; it asked subjects to be responsible for an unspecified number of juvenile delinquents of unspecified age in a public place for a period of two hours outdoors in winter.[5] Only 16.7% of our population was willing to agree to such a request when it was the only one made. Yet, the proposal of this request after the rejection of a still more extreme favor produced 50% compliance.

Another benefit of the rejection-then-moderation procedure is that its force seems to derive from the existence of a social norm. Thus, a requester wishing to use the procedure need have little reward or coercive power over his target to be effective. Thibaut and Kelley (1959) speak of a norm in any two-person interaction as a third agent exercising power over each member but whose "influence appeal is to a supraindividual value ('Do it for the group' or 'Do it because it's good') rather than to personal interests. . . ." (p. 129) A recognition of this kind of normative influence in concession making may help explain some of the bargaining literature on the subject, in addition to the data of the present study. For instance, Pruitt and Drews (1969) report with some surprise their subjects' failure to try to maximize their outcomes when faced with a bargaining opponent who made a large, constant concession on each game trial. Even though this sort of opponent was perceived as significantly weaker and less demanding than one who made constant but small concessions on each trial, no advantage was taken of the vulnerable opponent. Every time an opponent made a standard conces-

sion, no matter what the size, a subject responded with a standard concession of his own. Pruitt and Drews admit to being mystified by the lack of "rationality" on the part of their subjects and describe "them as 'automatons' tuning out external stimuli and new ideas, and moving mechanically a standard distance from the position adopted on the first trial." (p. 57) Perhaps much of the mystery can be eliminated by assuming that the subjects were reacting to the pressures of a norm requiring that regular concessions be reciprocated.

A final advantage of a compliance induction procedure which uses concessions involves the feelings of the target person toward the outcome of the interaction. Benton, Kelley, and Liebling (1972) present evidence suggesting that not only will someone who applies such a procedure be quite effective in obtaining favorable payoffs for himself but that the person to whom it is applied will feel more responsible for and satisfied with the outcome. In an allocation of resources situation, subjects faced a bargaining opponent who intransigently demanded the maximum payoff for himself, intransigently demanded a moderately favorably payoff for himself, or retreated from the maximum payoff demand to the moderate payoff demand. In each condition, failure to reach an allocation agreement resulted in a loss of all money by both participants. It was found that the retreat strategy produced the highest average earning for the opponent. Moreover, not only did subjects concede the greatest payoffs to an opponent using this tactic, they felt significantly more responsible for and satisfied with the outcome than did subjects faced with an intransigent opponent. The results of this study when coupled with those of our experiments suggest some intriguing implications. One who feels responsible for the terms of an agreement should be more likely to meet his commitments concerning that agreement. Thus, someone who uses concession to produce compliance with a request for a favor is likely to see the favor actually performed. Second, one who feels fairly satisfied with the outcome of an interaction with another person should be willing to enter into interaction with

---

[5] Only Experiment 1 was conducted in the winter of the year. Experiments 2 and 3 were conducted in the spring or summer which may account for the somewhat higher compliance rates in the small request only controls of these experiments.

that person again. Thus, the target person of a rejection-then-moderation moderation procedure may well be vulnerable to subsequent requests by the same requester. In all, then, it appears that the rejection-then-moderation procedure can be an extremely valuable technique for the elicitation of compliance.

A note of caution should probably be interjected at this point lest we make too much of the potential implications of the present findings. It is the case that the rejection-then-moderation procedure has been shown to work under a fairly limited set of conditions. The extent to which the effect is generalizable to other contexts and situations remains to be seen. For example, we have tested the effectiveness of the procedure only in situations in which the interaction was face-to-face, the interactants were of the same sex, and the requests were prosocial in nature. Moreover, it would be well to remember that, while the present research appears to support a reciprocal concessions interpretation of the effect, it in no way ultimately confirms that interpretation. Other explanations may exist which account completely for the data of this study; and to the extent that they do exist, they should be tested in subsequent work.

Future research on the reciprocal concessions procedure might also profitably investigate the nature of the concept of concession. In the present studies, a concession by a requester was operationalized as moderation from a large request to a smaller one. Involved in such moderation, however, are two separate components: the target will no doubt perceive the move from the large to the smaller request as *more* desirable for himself but *less* desirable for the requester and his cause. While these two aspects of concession usually occur together, there is no good reason to assume that both are necessary for the enhancement of compliance. It may be the proposal of a more desirable arrangement for the target—rather than the proposal of a less desirable arrangement for the requester—that is the crucial, compliance-producing aspect of con-

cession; or the opposite may be the case. Stated otherwise, a concession involves two normally correlated but conceptually separate features: the granting of a more favorable situation to one's interaction partner and the surrendering of a more favorable position for oneself. It remains for further investigation to determine whether the aspect of concession which induces compliance involves the granting of something, the surrendering of something, or both.

REFERENCES

Azrin, N. H., Holz, W., Ulrich, R., & Goldiamond, I. The control of the content of conversation through reinforcement. *Journal of the Experimental Analysis of Behavior*, 1961, *4*, 25–30.

Benton, A. A., Kelley, H. H., & Liebling, B. Effects of extremity of offers and concession rate on the outcomes of bargaining. *Journal of Personality and Social Psychology*, 1972, *24*, 73–83.

Brehm, J. W., & Cole, A. H. Effect of a favor which reduces freedom. *Journal of Personality and Social Psychology*, 1966, *3*, 420–426.

Chertkoff, J. M., & Conley, M. Opening offer and frequency of concession as bargaining strategies. *Journal of Personality and Social Psychology*, 1967, *7*, 185–193.

Freedman, J. L., & Fraser, S. Compliance without pressure: The foot-in-the-door technique. *Journal of Personality and Social Psychology*, 1966, *4*, 195–202.

Goranson, R. E., & Berkowitz, L. Reciprocity and responsibility reactions to prior help. *Journal of Personality and Social Psychology*, 1966, *3*, 227–232.

Gouldner, A. W. The norm of reciprocity: A preliminary statement. *American Sociological Review*, 1960, *25*, 161–178.

Komorita, S. S., & Brenner, A. R. Bargaining and concession making under bilateral monopoly. *Journal of Personality and Social Psychology*, 1968, *9*, 15–20.

Pruitt, D. G. Reciprocity and credit building in a laboratory dyad. *Journal of Personality and Social Psychology*, 1968, *8*, 143–147.

Pruitt, D. G., & Drews, J. L. The effect of time pressure, time elapsed, and the opponent's concession rate on behavior in negotiation. *Journal of Experimental Social Psychology*, 1969, *5*, 43–60.

Regan, D. T. Effects of a favor and liking on compliance. *Journal of Experimental Social Psychology*, 1971, *7*, 627–639.

Rosenthal, R. *Experimenter effects in behavioral research*. New York: Appleton-Century-Crofts, 1966.

Snyder, M., & Cunningham, M. R. To comply or not comply: Testing the self-perception explanation of the "foot-in-the-door" phenomenon. *Journal of Personality and Social Psychology*, 1975, *31*, 64–67.

Thibaut, J. W., & Kelley, H. H. *The social psychology of groups*. New York: Wiley, 1959.

Wilke, H., & Lanzetta, J. T. The obligation to help: The effects of amount of prior help on subsequent helping behavior. *Journal of Experimental Social Psychology*, 1970, *6*, 488–493.

ARTICLE 23

Behavioral study of obedience

Stanley Milgram

Obedience is as basic an element in the structure of social life as one can point to. Some system of authority is a requirement of all communal living, and it is only the man dwelling in isolation who is not forced to respond, through defiance or submission, to the commands of others. Obedience, as a determinant of behavior, is of particular relevance to our time. It has been reliably established that from 1933–45 millions of innocent persons were systematically slaughtered on command. Gas chambers were built, death camps were guarded, daily quotas of corpses were produced with the same efficiency as the manufacture of appliances. These inhumane policies may have originated in the mind of a single person, but they could only be carried out on a massive scale if a very large number of persons obeyed orders.

Obedience is the psychological mechanism that links individual action to political purpose. It is the dispositional cement that binds men to systems of authority. Facts of recent history and observation in daily life suggest that for many persons obedience may be a deeply ingrained behavior tendency, indeed, a prepotent impulse overriding training in ethics, sympathy, and moral conduct. C. P. Snow (1961) points to its importance when he writes:

> When you think of the long and gloomy history of man, you will find more hideous crimes have been committed in the name of obedience than have ever been committed in the name of rebellion. If you doubt that, read William Shirer's "Rise and Fall of the Third Reich." The German Officer Corps were brought up in the most rigorous code of obedience . . . in the name of obedience they were party to, and assisted in, the most wicked large scale actions in the history of the world [p. 24].

While the particular form of obedience dealt with in the present study has its antecedents in these episodes, it must not be thought all obedience entails acts of aggression against others. Obedience serves numerous productive functions. Indeed, the very life of society is predicated on its existence.

Obedience may be ennobling and educative and refer to acts of charity and kindness, as well as to destruction.

General Procedure

A procedure was devised which seems useful as a tool for studying obedience (Milgram, 1961). It consists of ordering a naive subject to administer electric shock to a victim. A simulated shock generator is used, with 30 clearly marked voltage levels that range from 15 to 450 volts. The instrument bears verbal designations that range from Slight Shock to Danger: Severe Shock. The responses of the victim, who is a trained confederate of the experimenter, are standardized. The orders to administer shocks are given to the naive subject in the context of a "learning experiment" ostensibly set up to study the effects of punishment on memory. As the experiment proceeds the naive subject is commanded to administer increasingly more intense shocks to the victim, even to the point of reaching the level marked Danger: Severe Shock. Internal resistances become stronger, and at a certain point the subject refuses to go on with the experiment. Behavior prior to this rupture is considered "obedience," in that the subject complies with the commands of the experimenter. The point of rupture is the act of disobedience. A quantitative value is assigned to the subject's performance based on the maximum intensity shock he is willing to administer before he refuses to participate further. Thus for any particular subject and for any particular experimental condition the degree of obedience may be specified with a numerical value. The crux of the study is to systematically vary the factors believed to alter the degree of obedience to the experimental commands.

The technique allows important variables to be manipulated at several points in the experiment. One may vary aspects of the source of command, content and form of command, instrumentalities for its execution, target object, general social setting, etc. The problem, therefore, is not one of designing increasingly more numerous experimental conditions, but of selecting those that best illuminate the *process* of obedience from the socio-psychological standpoint.

Related Studies

The inquiry bears an important relation to philosophic analyses of obedience and authority (Arendt, 1958; Friedrich, 1958; Weber, 1947), an early experimental study of obedience by Frank (1944), studies in "authoritarianism" (Adorno, Frenkel-Brunswik, Levinson, & Sanford, 1950; Rokeach, 1961), and a recent series of analytic and empirical studies in social power (Cartwright, 1959). It owes much to the long concern with *suggestion* in social psychology, both in its normal forms (e.g., Binet, 1900) and in its clinical manifestations (Charcot, 1881). But it derives, in the first instance, from direct observation of a social fact; the individual who is commanded by a legitimate authority ordinarily obeys. Obedience comes easily and often. It is a ubiquitous and indispensable feature of social life.

METHOD

Subjects

The subjects were 40 males between the ages of 20 and 50, drawn from New Haven and the surrounding communities. Subjects were obtained by a newspaper advertisement and direct mail solicitation. Those who responded to the appeal believed they were to participate in a study of memory and learning at Yale University. A wide range of occupations is represented in the sample. Typical subjects were postal clerks, high school teachers, salesmen, engineers, and laborers. Subjects ranged in educational level from one who had not finished elementary school, to those who had doctorate and other professional degrees. They were paid $4.50 for their participation in the experiment. However, subjects were told that payment was simply for coming to the laboratory, and that the money was theirs no matter what happened after they arrived. Table 1 shows the proportion of age and occupational types assigned to the experimental condition.

TABLE 1. Distribution of age and occupational types in the experiment.

Occupations	20-29 years n	30-39 years n	40-50 years n	Percentage of total (occupations)
Workers, skilled and unskilled	4	5	6	37.5
Sales, business, and white-collar	3	6	7	40.0
Professional	1	5	3	22.5
Percentage of total (age)	20	40	40	

Note—Total $N = 40$.

Personnel and Locale

The experiment was conducted on the grounds of Yale University in the elegant interaction laboratory. (This detail is relevant to the perceived legitimacy of the experiment. In a further variation, the experiment was dissociated from the university, with consequences for performance.) The role of experimenter was played by a 31-year-old high school teacher of biology. His manner was impassive, and his appearance somewhat stern throughout the experiment. He was dressed in a gray technician's coat. The victim was played by a 47-year-old accountant, trained for the role; he was of Irish-American stock, whom most observers found mild-mannered and likable.

Procedure

One naive subject and one victim (an accomplice) performed in each experiment. A pretext had to be devised that would justify the administration of electric shock by the naive subject. This was effectively accomplished by the cover story. After a general introduction on the presumed relation between punishment and learning, subjects were told:

But actually, we know *very little* about the effect of punishment on learning, because almost no truly scientific studies have been made of it in human beings.

For instance, we don't know how *much* punishment is best for learning—and we don't know how much difference it makes as to who is giving the punishment, whether an adult learns best from a youngster or an older person than himself—or many things of that sort.

So in this study we are bringing together a number of adults of different occupations and ages. And we're asking some of them to be teachers and some of them to be learners.

We want to find out just what effect different people have on each other as teachers and learners, and also what effect *punishment* will have on learning in this situation.

Therefore, I'm going to ask one of you to be the teacher here tonight and the other one to be the learner.

Does either of you have a preference?

Subjects then drew slips of paper from a hat to determine who would be the teacher and who would be the learner in the experiment. The drawing was rigged so that the naive subject was always the teacher and the accomplice was always the learner. (Both slips contained the word "Teacher.") Immediately after the drawing, the teacher and learner were taken to an adjacent room and the learner was strapped into an "electric chair" apparatus.

The experimenter explained that the straps were to prevent excessive movement while the learner was being shocked. The effect was to make it impossible for him to escape from the situation. An electrode was attached to the learner's wrist, and electrode paste was applied "to avoid blisters and burns." Subjects were told that the electrode was attached to the shock generator in the adjoining room.

In order to improve credibility the experimenter declared, in response to a question by the learner: "Although the shocks can be extremely painful, they cause no permanent tissue damage."

Learning Task. The lesson administered by the subject was a paired-associate learning task. The subject read a series of word pairs to the learner, and then read the first word of the pair along with four terms. The learner was to indicate which of the four terms had originally been paired with the first word. He communicated his answer by pressing one of four switches in front of him, which in turn lit up one of four numbered quadrants in an answer-box located atop the shock generator.

Shock Generator. The instrument panel consists of 30 lever switches set in a horizontal line. Each switch is clearly labeled with a voltage designation that ranges from 15 to 450 volts. There is a 15-volt increment from one switch to the next going from left to right. In addition, the following verbal designations are clearly indicated for groups of four switches going from left to right: Slight Shock, Moderate Shock, Strong Shock, Very Strong Shock, Intense Shock, Extreme Intensity Shock, Danger: Severe Shock. (Two switches after this last designation are simply marked XXX).

Upon depressing a switch: A pilot light corresponding to each switch is illuminated in bright red; an electric buzzing is heard; an electric blue light, labeled ''voltage energizer,'' flashes; the dial on the voltage meter swings to the right; various delay clicks are sounded.

The upper left-hand corner of the generator is labeled Shock Generator, Type ZLB, Dyson Instrument Company, Waltham, Mass. Output 15 volts–450 volts.

Details of the instrument were carefully handled to insure an appearance of authenticity. The panel was engraved by precision industrial engravers, and all components were of high quality. No subject in the experiment suspected that the instrument was merely a simulated shock generator.[1]

[1] A related technique, making use of a shock generator, was reported by Buss (1961) for the study of aggression in the laboratory. Despite the considerable similarity of technical detail in the experimental procedures, both investigators proceeded in ignorance of the other's work. Milgram provided plans and photographs of his shock generator, experimental procedure, and first results in a report to the National Science Foundation in January 1961. This report received only limited circulation. Buss reported his procedure 6 months later, but to a wider audience. Subsequently, technical information and reports were exchanged. The present article was first received in the Editor's office on December 27, 1961; it was resubmitted with deletions on July 27, 1962.

Sample Shock. Each naive subject is given a sample shock on the shock generator, prior to beginning his run as teacher. This shock is always 45 volts, and is applied by pressing the third switch of the generator. The shock is applied to the wrist of the naive subject, and has its source in a 45-volt battery wired into the generator. This further convinces the subject of the authenticity of the generator.

Shock Instructions. The subject is told to administer a shock to the learner each time he gives a wrong response. Moreover—and this is the key command—the subject is instructed to ''move one level higher on the shock generator each time the learner flashes a wrong answer.'' He is also instructed to announce the voltage level before administering a shock. This serves to continually remind subjects of the increasing intensity of shocks administered to the learner.

Preliminary and Regular Run. Pretests revealed that the procedure of reading words and administering shocks requires some practice before it can be handled smoothly. Therefore, immediately preceding the regular run, the teacher is given a preliminary series of 10 words to read to the learner. There are 3 neutral words in the practice series (i.e., words that the learner answers correctly), so that shocks are administered for 7 of the words, with the maximum shock at 105 volts (moderate shock). Almost all subjects master the procedure by the time the preliminary run is over.

Subjects are then presented with a second list, and are told that the procedure is the same as for the first list; the experimenter adds, however:

When you get to the bottom of the list, repeat it over again, and continue giving shocks, until the learner has learned all the pairs correctly.

The experimenter instructs the subject to

start from 15 volts and increase the shock level one step each time the learner gives a wrong answer.

Feedback from the Victim.   In all conditions the learner gives a predetermined set of responses to the word pair test, based on a schedule of approximately three wrong answers to one correct answer. In the present experimental condition no vocal response or other sign of protest is heard from the learner until Shock Level 300 is reached. When the 300-volt shock is administered, the learner pounds on the wall of the room in which he is bound to the electric chair. The pounding can be heard by the subject. From this point on, the learner's answers no longer appear on the four-way panel.

At this juncture, subjects ordinarily turn to the experimenter for guidance. The experimenter instructs the subject to treat the absence of a response as a wrong answer, and to shock the subject according to the usual schedule. He advises the subjects to allow 5–10 seconds before considering no response as a wrong answer, and to increase the shock level one step each time the learner fails to respond correctly. The learner's pounding is repeated after the 315-volt shock is administered; afterwards he is not heard from, nor do his answers reappear on the four-way signal box.

Experimenter Feedback.   At various points in the experiment the subject may turn to the experimenter for advice on whether he should continue to administer shocks. Or he may indicate that he does not wish to go on. It was important to standardize the experimenter's responses to these inquiries and reactions.

If the subject indicated his unwillingness to go on, the experimenter responded with a sequence of "prods," using as many as necessary to bring the subject into line.

Prod 1: Please continue. *or* Please go on.
Prod 2: The experiment requires that you continue.
Prod 3: It is absolutely essential that you continue.
Prod 4: You have no other choice, you *must* go on.

The prods were always made in sequence: Only if Prod 1 had been unsuccessful, could Prod 2 be used.

If the subject refused to obey the experimenter after Prod 4, the experiment was terminated. The experimenter's tone of voice was at all times firm, but not impolite. The sequence was begun anew on each occasion that the subject balked or showed reluctance to follow orders.

Special prods. If the subject asked if the learner was liable to suffer permanent physical injury, the experimenter said:

Although the shocks may be painful, there is no permanent tissue damage, so please go on. [Followed by Prods 2, 3, and 4 if necessary.]

If the subject said that the learner did not want to go on, the experimenter replied:

Whether the learner likes it or not, you must go on until he has learned all the word pairs correctly. So please go on. [Followed by Prods 2, 3, and 4 if necessary.]

Dependent Measures

The primary dependent measure for any subject is the maximum shock he administers before he refuses to go any further. In principle this may vary from 0 (for a subject who refuses to administer even the first shock) to 30 (for a subject who administers the highest shock on the generator). A subject who breaks off the experiment at any point prior to administering the thirtieth shock level is termed a *defiant* subject. One who complies with experimental commands fully, and proceeds to administer all shock levels commanded, is termed an *obedient* subject.

Further Records.   With few exceptions, experimental sessions were recorded on magnetic tape. Occasional photographs were taken through one-way mirrors. Notes were kept on any unusual behavior occurring during the course of the experiments. On occasion, additional observers were directed to write objective descriptions of the subjects' behavior. The latency and duration of shocks were measured by accurate timing devices.

Interview and Dehoax.   Following the experiment, subjects were interviewed; open-ended questions, projective measures, and attitude scales were employed. After the interview, procedures were undertaken to assure that the subject would leave the laboratory in a state of well being. A friendly reconciliation was arranged between the subject and the victim, and an effort was made to reduce any tensions that arose as a result of the experiment.

RESULTS

Preliminary Notions

Before giving an account of the experimental results, it is instructive to consider how persons predict others will perform when commanded to administer powerful shocks to another person. Fourteen Yale seniors, all psychology majors, were provided with a detailed description of the experimental situation. They were asked to reflect carefully on it, and to predict the behavior of 100 hypothetical subjects. More specifically, they were instructed to plot the distribution of obedience of "100 Americans of diverse occupations, and ranging in age from 20 to 50 years," who were placed in the experimental situation.

There was considerable agreement among the respondents on the expected behavior of hypothetical subjects. All respondents predicted that only an insignificant minority would go through to the end of the shock series. (The estimates ranged from 0 to 3%; i.e., the most "pessimistic" members of the class predicted that of 100 persons, 3 would continue through to the most potent shock available on the shock generator—450 volts.) The class mean was 1.2%. The question was also posed informally to colleagues of the author, and the most general feeling was that few if any subjects would go beyond the designation Very Strong Shock.

Result of Experiment I

Subjects Accept Situation.   With few exceptions subjects were convinced of the reality of the experimental situation, that they were administering shocks to another person, and the most potent shocks were extremely painful. In the post-experimental interview subjects were asked: "How painful to the learner were the last few shocks that you administered to him?" Subjects were instructed to indicate their answers on a printed 14-point scale ranging from "Not at all painful" to "Extremely painful." The modal response was 14 (Extremely painful) with the mean at 13.42.

Signs of Extreme Tension.   Many subjects showed signs of nervousness in the experimental situation, and especially upon administering the more powerful shocks. In a large number of cases the degree of tension reached extremes that are rarely seen in sociopsychological laboratory studies. Subjects were observed to sweat, tremble, stutter, bite their lips, groan, and dig their fingernails into their flesh. These were characteristic rather than exceptional responses to the experiment.

One sign of tension was the regular occurrence of nervous laughing fits. Fourteen of the 40 subjects showed definite signs of nervous laughter and smiling. The laughter seemed entirely out of place, even bizarre. Full-blown, uncontrollable seizures were observed for 3 subjects. On one occasion we observed a seizure so violently convulsive that it was necessary to call a halt to the experiment. The subject, a 46-year-old encyclopedia salesman, was seriously embarrassed by his untoward and uncontrollable behavior. In the post-experimental interviews subjects took pains to point out that they were not sadistic types, and that the laughter did not mean they enjoyed shocking the victim.

Distribution of Scores.   It had been conjectured that persons would not, in general, agree to administer shocks beyond the level designated as Very

Strong Shock. The distribution of maximum shocks for this experiment is shown in Table 2. The obtained distribution of scores deviates radically from the prediction.

Upon command of the experimenter, each of the 40 subjects went beyond the expected breakoff point. No subject stopped prior to administering Shock Level 20. (At this level—300 volts—the victim kicks on the wall and no longer provides answers to the teacher's multiple-choice questions.)

Of the 40 subjects, 5 refused to obey the experimental commands beyond the 300-volt level. Four more subjects administered one further shock, and then refused to go on. Two broke off at the 330-volt level, and 1 each at 345, 360, and 375 volts. Thus a total of 14 subjects defied the experimenter. It is instructive to reprint their remarks at the point of defiance, as transcribed from the tape recordings:

[0124] I think he's trying to communicate, he's knocking. . . . Well it's not fair to shock the guy . . . these are terrific volts. I don't think this is very humane. . . . Oh, I can't go on with this; no, this isn't right. It's a hell of an experiment. The guy is suffering in there. No. I don't want to go on. This is crazy. [Subject refused to administer more shocks.]

[0123] He's banging in there. I'm gonna chicken out. I'd like to continue, but I can't do that to a man. . . . I'm sorry I can't do that to a man. I'll hurt his heart. You take your check. . . . No really, I couldn't do it.

These subjects were frequently in a highly agitated and even angered state. Sometimes, verbal protest was at a minimum, and the subject simply got up from his chair in front of the shock generator, and indicated that he wished to leave the laboratory.

Of the 40 subjects, 26 obeyed the orders of the experimenter to the end, proceeding to punish the victim until they reached the most potent shock available on the shock generator. At that point, the experimenter called a halt to the session. (The maximum shock is labeled 450 volts, and is two steps beyond the designation: Danger: Severe Shock.) Although obedient subjects continued to administer shocks, they often did so under extreme stress. Some expressed reluctance to administer

TABLE 2. Distribution of breakoff points.

Verbal designation and voltage indication	Number of subjects for whom this was maximum shock
Slight shock	
15	0
30	0
45	0
60	0
Moderate shock	
75	0
90	0
105	0
120	0
Strong shock	
135	0
150	0
165	0
180	0
Very strong shock	
195	0
210	0
225	0
240	0
Intense shock	
255	0
270	0
285	0
300	5
Extreme intensity shock	
315	4
330	2
345	1
360	1
Danger: severe shock	
375	1
390	0
405	0
420	0
XXX	
435	0
450	26

shocks beyond the 300-volt level, and displayed fears similar to those who defied the experimenter; yet they obeyed.

After the maximum shocks had been delivered, and the experimenter called a halt to the proceedings, many obedient subjects heaved sighs of relief, mopped their brows, rubbed their fingers over their eyes, or nervously fumbled cigarettes. Some shook their heads, apparently in regret. Some subjects had remained calm throughout the experiment, and displayed only minimal signs of tension from beginning to end.

DISCUSSION

The experiment yielded two findings that were surprising. The first finding concerns the sheer strength of obedient tendencies manifested in this situation. Subjects have learned from childhood that it is a fundamental breach of moral conduct to hurt another person against his will. Yet, 26 subjects abandon this tenet in following the instruction of an authority who has no special powers to enforce his commands. To disobey would bring no material loss to the subject; no punishment would ensue. It is clear from the remarks and outward behavior of many participants that in punishing the victim they are often acting against their own values. Subjects often expressed deep disapproval of shocking a man in the face of his objections, and others denounced it as stupid and senseless. Yet the majority complied with the experimental commands. This outcome was surprising from two perspectives: first, from the standpoint of predictions made in the questionnaire described earlier. (Here, however, it is possible that the remoteness of the respondents from the actual situation, and the difficulty of conveying to them the concrete details of the experiment, could account for the serious underestimation of obedience.)

But the results were also unexpected to persons who observed the experiment in progress, through one-way mirrors. Observers often uttered expressions of disbelief upon seeing a subject administer more powerful shocks to the victim. These persons had a full acquaintance with the details of the situation, and yet systematically underestimated the amount of obedience that subjects would display.

The second unanticipated effect was the extraordinary tension generated by the procedures. One might suppose that a subject would simply break off or continue as his conscience dictated. Yet, this is very far from what happened. There were striking reactions of tension and emotional strain. One observer related:

I observed a mature and initially poised businessman enter the laboratory smiling and confident. Within 20 minutes he was reduced to a twitching, stuttering wreck, who was rapidly approaching a point of nervous collapse. He constantly pulled on his earlobe, and twisted his hands. At one point he pushed his fist into his forehead and muttered: "Oh, God, let's stop it." And yet he continued to respond to every word of the experimenter, and obeyed to the end.

Any understanding of the phenomenon of obedience must rest on an analysis of the particular conditions in which it occurs. The following features of the experiment go some distance in explaining the high amount of obedience observed in the situation.

1. The experiment is sponsored by and takes place on the grounds of an institution of unimpeachable reputation, Yale University. It may be reasonably presumed that the personnel are competent and reputable. The importance of this background authority is now being studied by conducting a series of experiments outside of New Haven, and without any visible ties to the university.

2. The experiment is, on the face of it, designed to attain a worthy purpose—advancement of knowledge about learning and memory. Obedience occurs not as an end in itself, but as an instrumental element in a situation that the subject construes as significant, and meaningful. He may not be able to see its full significance, but he may properly assume that the experimenter does.

3. The subject perceives that the victim has voluntarily submitted to the authority system of the experimenter. He is not (at first) an unwilling captive impressed for involuntary service. He has taken the trouble to come to the laboratory presumably to aid the experimental research. That he later becomes an involuntary subject does not alter the fact that, initially, he consented to participate without qualification. Thus he has in some degree incurred an obligation toward the experimenter.

4. The subject, too, has entered the experiment voluntarily, and perceives himself under obligation to aid the experimenter. He has made a commitment, and to disrupt the experiment is a repudiation of this initial promise of aid.

5. Certain features of the procedure strengthen the subject's sense of obligation to the experimenter. For one, he has been paid for coming to the laboratory. In part this is canceled out by the experimenter's statement that:

Of course, as in all experiments, the money is yours simply for coming to the laboratory. From this point on, no matter what happens, the money is yours.[2]

6. From the subject's standpoint, the fact that he is the teacher and the other man the learner is purely a chance consequence (it is determined by drawing lots) and he, the subject, ran the same risk as the other man in being assigned the role of learner. Since the assignment of positions in the experiment was achieved by fair means, the learner is deprived of any basis of complaint on this count. (A similar situation obtains in Army units, in which—in the absence of volunteers—a particularly dangerous mission may be assigned by drawing lots, and the unlucky soldier is expected to bear his misfortune with sportsmanship.)

7. There is, at best, ambiguity with regard to the prerogatives of a psychologist and the corresponding rights of his subject. There is a vagueness of expectation concerning what a psychologist may require of his subject, and when he is overstepping acceptable limits. Moreover, the experiment occurs in a closed setting, and thus provides no opportunity for the subject to remove these ambiguities by discussion with others. There are few standards that seem directly applicable to the situation, which is a novel one for most subjects.

8. The subjects are assured that the shocks administered to the subject are "painful but not dangerous." Thus they assume that the discomfort caused the victim is momentary, while the scientific gains resulting from the experiment are enduring.

9. Through Shock Level 20 the victim continues to provide answers on the signal box. The subject may construe this as a sign that the victim is still willing to "play the game." It is only after Shock Level 20 that the victim repudiates the rules completely, refusing to answer further.

These features help to explain the high amount of obedience obtained in this experiment. Many of the arguments raised need not remain matters of speculation, but can be reduced to testable propositions to be confirmed or disproved by further experiments.[3]

The following features of the experiment concern the nature of the conflict which the subject faces.

10. The subject is placed in a position in which he must respond to the competing demands of two persons: the experimenter and the victim. The conflict must be resolved by meeting the demands of one or the other; satisfaction of the victim and the experimenter are mutually exclusive. Moreover, the resolution must take the form of a highly visible action, that of continuing to shock the victim or breaking off the experiment. Thus the subject is forced into a public conflict that does not permit any completely satisfactory solution.

11. While the demands of the experimenter carry the weight of scientific authority, the demands of the victim spring from his personal experience of pain and suffering. The two claims need not be regarded as equally pressing and legitimate. The experimenter seeks an abstract scientific datum; the victim cries out for relief from physical suffering caused by the subject's actions.

12. The experiment gives the subject little time for reflection. The conflict comes on rapidly. It is only minutes after the subject has been seated before the shock generator that the victim begins his protests. Moreover, the subject perceives that he has gone through but two-thirds of the shock levels at the time the subject's first protests are heard. Thus he understands that the conflict will have a persistent aspect to it, and may well become more intense as increasingly more powerful shocks are required. The rapidity with which the conflict descends on the

---

[2]Forty-three subjects, undergraduates at Yale University, were run in the experiment without payment. The results are very similar to those obtained with paid subjects.

[3]A series of recently completed experiments employing the obedience paradigm is reported in Milgram (1965).

subject, and his realization that it is predictably re-current may well be sources of tension to him.

13. At a more general level, the conflict stems from the opposition of two deeply ingrained behavior dispositions: first, the disposition not to harm other people, and second, the tendency to obey those whom we perceive to be legitimate authorities.

REFERENCES

Adorno, T., Frenkel-Brunswik, E., Levinson, D. J., & Sanford, R. N. *The authoritarian personality.* New York: Harper, 1950.

Arendt, H. What was authority? In C. J. Friedrich (Ed.), *Authority.* Cambridge: Harvard University Press, 1958. Pp. 81–112.

Binet, A. *La suggestibilité.* Paris: Schleicher, 1900.

Buss, A. H. *The psychology of aggression.* New York: Wiley, 1961.

Cartwright, S. (Ed.) *Studies in social power.* Ann Arbor: University of Michigan, Institute for Social Research, 1959.

Charcot, J. M. *Oeuvres complètes.* Paris: Bureaux du Progrès Médical, 1881.

Frank, J. D. Experimental studies of personal pressure and resistance. *Journal of General Psychology,* 1944, **30,** 23–64.

Friedrich, C. J. (Ed.) *Authority.* Cambridge: Harvard University Press, 1958.

Milgram, S. Dynamics of obedience. Washington, D. C.: National Science Foundation, January 25, 1961. (Mimeo).

Milgram, S. Some conditions of obedience and disobedience to authority. *Human Relations,* 1965, **18,** 57–76.

Rokeach, M. Authority, authoritarianism, and conformity. In I. A. Berg and B. M. Bass (Eds.), *Conformity and deviation.* New York: Harper, 1961. Pp. 230–257.

Snow, C. P. Either-or. *Progressive,* Feb. 1961, 24.

Weber, M. *The theory of social and economic organization.* Oxford: Oxford University Press, 1947.

ARTICLE 24

Ubiquitous Watergate: An attributional analysis

Stephen G. West
Steven P. Gunn
Paul Chernicky

During the past 2 years, the news media have spent a large amount of time and effort investigating the series of political crimes that have been termed Watergate. The media have been very troubled by these crimes, which do not fit the usual explanations (e.g., greed) for political crimes. Consequently, they have been forced to search for new explanations of the Watergate crimes. The press has proposed such explanations as the paranoid style of the Nixon administration, the recruitment of an amoral staff of nonpolitical administrators, and even such fanciful explanations as that members of the Nixon administration had been injected with "moral penicillin." On the other hand, several members of the Nixon administration have proposed a very different set of explanations for the Watergate burglary and cover-up. They have suggested that these activities were a natural result of the potentially violent plans of the radical left and that given the available alternative courses of action, such activities were demanded by circumstances. These divergent explanations of the same event by the press and those who were involved may strike one as unusual, defensive, or possibly even reflecting psychodynamic thought disturbances on the part of one group or the other, but such a result is consistent with recent research and theorizing in social psychology.

Jones and Nisbett (1971) have argued that actors (i.e., those actively involved) and observers often have very different perceptions of the causes of the behavior of the actor in a given situation. They point out that while the actor and observer may have identical information concerning the action and its environmental outcomes, the actor generally has more information about his intentions, his emotional state, and the events leading up to the action. Furthermore, the actor's attention is also focused on the

Reprinted from the *Journal of Personality and Social Psychology*, 1975, *32*, pp. 55–65. Copyright 1975 by the American Psychological Association. Reprinted by permission.

We thank Russell D. Clark, III, William Haythorn, Michael Nash, and Lee Sechrest for their comments on the manuscript and Judi Black for her secretarial assistance.

environment from which he selects cues to guide his behavior, while the observer's attention is focused on the actor and his behavior. According to Jones and Nisbett, the result of these differences is a tendency for the actor to attribute the cause of his behavior to the environment, while the observer tends to attribute the actor's behavior to dispositional characteristics of the actor.

Supporting Jones and Nisbett's (1971) position are two notable cases in which the press, society's professional observers, have inferred that an extreme action was due to the dispositional characteristics of the people involved, only to discover later through social-psychological research that the behavior in question is, under similar conditions, controlled primarily by a variety of situational factors. These two cases are the blind obedience to authority observed in the German army during World War II and the failure of bystanders to help in dramatic emergency situations.

The first case, blind obedience to authority, provides a good example of the disparity between the conclusions of the press and research. Authors such as Shirer (1960) have suggested that the specialized obedience training of the German army, particularly the officer corps, or some aspect of "German national character" was responsible for the horrible actions carried out on the orders of authorities during World War II. However, in a series of experiments, Milgram (1963, 1964a, 1965, 1974) has demonstrated that situational factors such as the proximity of the subject to the victim, the proximity of the experimenter to the subject, the setting in which the experiment takes place, and group pressure are important determinants of obedience. Thus, consistent with the Jones and Nisbett formulation, observers have ignored the possibility of strong situational pressures within the Germany army that may have been in large part responsible for the actions perpetrated in World War II.

A second case that led to similar public outrage and press coverage was the murder of Kitty Genovese in Queens, New York, in front of 38 witnesses who did not attempt to intervene. The press

and other observers pointed to personal factors such as feelings of apathy, dehumanization, and alienation from one's fellow man. However, research by Latané and Darley and their co-workers (Darley & Latané, 1968; Latané & Darley, 1968, 1969; Latané & Rodin, 1969) has shown that groups of bystanders frequently do not help in a wide variety of experimental situations and that the amount of helping is determined by such situational factors as the number of other bystanders (Latané & Darley, 1968, 1969), the others' ability to help (Bickman, 1971; Korte, 1969), the similarity of prior acquaintanceship of the others (Latané & Rodin, 1969; Smith, Smythe, & Lien, 1972), and the ambiguity of the emergency situation (Clark & Word, 1972, 1974). Thus, once again, situational factors are a major determinant of a phenomenon that initially seemed to outside observers to be due to dispositional factors of the actors involved.

Given the possibility of situational determinants of behavior, a very different set of causes for Watergate crimes may be proposed. It may be the case that the Watergate crimes were due to enormous situational pressures on those involved, such as normative expectations within the Nixon administration, the payoff matrix for engaging versus not engaging in these illegal activities, and other pressures that may not have been known or salient to outside observers. If situational factors were important in the Watergate case, then several implications may be drawn from Jones and Nisbett's (1971) theory and recent research on compliance (Allen, 1965; Kiesler & Kiesler, 1969). First, under similar high situational pressures, a significant percentage of a sample of subjects (actors) should agree to engage in similar illegal activities. Second, the percentage of subjects who agree to engage in illegal activities should be a function of situational factors related to compliance. And finally, the subjects, whether they agree or do not agree to engage in illegal activities, should attribute their decision primarily to situational factors, such as potential costs or rewards. However, outside observers should perceive dispositional characteristics rather than situational factors as the cause of the actor's decision.

The derivations were tested in two studies: an experiment and a subsequent interpersonal simulation with observers (Bem, 1967). In the experiment (Study 1), conducted in a field setting, actor subjects were led to believe that they had an opportunity to participate in an illegal burglary. The rationale for the burglary was varied so that some possible situational determinants of compliance in this setting, suggested by the Watergate investigations (Gold, 1973), could be investigated. Three factors considered to be possible determinants of agreement in this situation were studied: (a) sponsorship of the crime by a United States government agency, (b) an offer of a relatively large amount of money for committing the crime, and (c) an offer of immunity from prosecution when the crime is supposedly sponsored by a United States government agency. A control group in which the crime was not sponsored by any agency and the subject could not expect any reward or immunity from prosecution was also included in the design to provide a baseline compliance rate. Since the primary focus of the present experiment was not compliance, it should be sufficient merely to demonstrate differences between experimental conditions. However, based on the testimony during the Watergate hearings and the conformity literature (Allen, 1965; Endler, 1966; Kiesler & Kiesler, 1969), it was predicted that the control condition should have the lowest compliance rate, the government-sponsorship plus immunity-from-prosecution condition should have the highest compliance rate, and the other groups should be intermediate in compliance.

The second study involved comparing the reasons given for participating in the crime by the subjects (actors) in the field experiment and the observers in the interpersonal simulation. Based on Jones and Nisbett's (1971) theory, it was predicted that subjects would tend to attribute their actions to situational factors, while observers would tend to attribute their actions to dispositional characteristics of the subjects.

METHOD

Field Experiment: Study 1

Subjects (actors). The subjects were 80 students (56 males and 24 females) selected at random from a list of undergraduate majors in criminology. Two restrictions were placed on random sampling: Subjects who were close friends of either the experimenter or the confederate were eliminated, and the percentage of males and females was held constant across conditions.

Procedure. Each subject was initially approached by the experimenter, who was known to most of the subjects as a local private investigator. The experimenter told the subject that he had "a project you might be interested in" and suggested to the subject that they meet at the experimenter's home or at a local restaurant. If the subject asked about the reason for the meeting, he (she) was assured that it would be fully discussed at the later time. Every person approached did make an appointment to meet with the experimenter.

At the later meeting, the experimenter was accompanied by the confederate. The experimenter carried a briefcase that contained elaborate plans for the commission of a burglary of a local advertising firm. Except for the changes in the rationale for the crime, the procedure was constant across experimental conditions.

Subjects were randomly assigned to one of four experimental conditions. In the first two conditions, in which the burglary was to be committed for a government agency (the Internal Revenue Service), the subjects were told that the burglary was for the purposes of microfilming an allegedly illegal set of accounting records maintained by the firm to defraud the United States Government out of 6.8 million tax dollars per year. It was further explained that the company was in reality a front for a Miami investment corporation and that a dual set of records was being kept. The microfilmed records were described as being necessary to get a search warrant and subpoena so that the original records could be seized. In the first condition, the subjects were told that the government had guaranteed them immunity from prosecution if apprehended, while in the second condition, the subjects were warned that there would be no immunity from prosecution if apprehended.

In the third condition, the subjects were told that another local advertising firm had offered $8,000 for a copy of a set of designs prepared by the first firm. The subjects were told that they would be paid $2,000 for their participation in the crime.

In the fourth condition (control) the subjects were told that the crime was being committed merely to determine whether the burglary plans designed by the experimenter would work. The subjects were further told that while an illegal act of burglary would be committed, absolutely nothing would be stolen from the office.

Upon meeting the subject, the experimenter introduced him (her) to the confederate, who played the role of a member of the burglary team. The experimenter gave the rationale for the commission of the crime and revealed the details of the plan in a standard order. If the subject protested that he did not want to discuss the crime, he was asked to listen to the plans on their full detail prior to making a final decision. No subject attempted to leave the situation, nor did any ask that the experimenter leave.

The subjects in all conditions were told that the burglary of an advertising firm located in a local office building had been carefully planned and that a four-person team was necessary to carry it out. This team was to consist of (a) the experimenter, who would monitor police calls in an office inside the building; (b) the confederate, who would serve as an outside lookout; (c) a lock-and-safe expert (not present in the experimental situation), who was described as having an extensive background in military intelligence; and (d) the subject, who was to serve as an inside lookout and who was also to microfilm the advertising agency records. The crime was presented to the subject in elaborate detail, including aerial photographs of the building and the

surrounding area, lists of city and state patrol cars, their routes and times, and blueprints of the advertising office. The total effect of the situation was to create as great an impact as possible and to convince the subject that it was a well-planned, professional job with only a minimal chance of being caught.

The subjects were then encouraged to ask questions; these questions were answered by the experimenter. Virtually all of the questions concerned technical details of the plan. The subjects were then asked to come to the final planning meeting, which would take place at the experimenter's office. If the subject refused, the experimenter reemphasized that the plan was foolproof and asked the subject to reconsider his decision. If the subject refused a second time, the experiment was terminated. The confederate, who was blind to the hypotheses, recorded the subject's decision to agree or refuse to participate and summarized the subject's rationale for his decision. The subject's agreement or refusal to participate in the burglary and his reasons for the decision were the major dependent variables. At the conclusion of the experiment, subjects were extensively debriefed, and the nature and the reasons for the deceptions were explained in detail.

Interpersonal Simulation: Study 2

Subjects (observers). The subjects were 238 students from the introductory psychology classes (92 males and 146 females) who volunteered to participate in partial fulfillment of their course requirements. Subjects were run in groups of 30–50 subjects per session; all experimental conditions were represented within each session.

Procedure. Each subject received a mimeographed booklet describing in great detail one of the four conditions used in the field experiment. The subject then answered three sets of dependent measures. The first set (estimations) asked the subject, "If 100 students were presented with this proposal, how many [number] would you guess would agree to participate?" The subject was also asked,

"Would you do it?" and was given the opportunity to respond yes, maybe, or no and to write comments.

The second set (attributions) consisted of a free-response measure and a forced-choice measure. For the free-response measure, the following question was used: "Suppose John, an undergraduate student at FSU [Florida State University], after listening to the proposal described above, agreed [refused] to participate. In two or three sentences, briefly describe why John made this decision." For half of the subjects, John was described as agreeing to participate, while for the other half, John was described as refusing to participate in the burglary.[1]

The above two sets of dependent measures constituted the primary dependent measures for the present experiment. In order to eliminate any effects of the order of presentation of the measures, the order in which these two sets of measures were presented was counterbalanced across subjects.

Finally, a third set of measures (personality impressions) was given to the subjects to provide supplemental information as to their perceptions of the personalities of John and the private investigator. Each subject rated both John and the private investigator on the same fifteen 5-point scales, which were anchored with an adjective at each end (e.g., intelligent-unintelligent). For eight of the pairs, the left side of the scale was anchored with the more socially desirable adjective; while for six of the pairs, the left side of the scale was anchored with the less socially desirable adjective.[2]

In summary, a $4 \times 2 \times 2$ design was used with the factors being the four experimental treatments (government sponsorship, reward, immunity, and control), the order in which the estimation measures and attribution measures were presented, and

whether John agreed or refused to participate in the burglary.

RESULTS

Compliance Rates

Field Experiment: Study 1. The percentage of subjects in each condition agreeing and refusing to participate in the proposed burglary is presented in Table 1. The data were first analyzed using an overall chi-square test,[3] which showed an overall difference in the agreement rates as a function of the four experimental conditions, $\chi^2(3) = 11.8$, $p < .01$. Male and female subjects did not differ in their compliance rates, with Yates's correction, $\chi^2(1) = .63$, *ns*.

The data were further analyzed to investigate the compliance rates of the four experimental groups. Neither the sponsorship by a U. S. government agency nor the offer of a large amount of money for participation led to an appreciable increase in compliance over that in the control condition (Fisher's exact test, both nonsignificant). However, given sponsorship by a U. S. government agency, the offer of immunity from prosecution significantly increased compliance over the rate obtained when no immunity from prosecution was offered, with Yates' correction, $\chi^2(1) = 6.53$, $p < .02$.

Interpersonal Simulation: Study 2. The observer subjects' estimations of the number of college students who would participate in the burglary were subjected to a $4 \times 2 \times 2$ (Conditions $\times$ Decision $\times$ Order) analysis of variance. Of most interest, none of the effects of conditions, namely, the Con-

---

[1] The forced-choice measure adapted from McArthur (1972) was unaffected by the experimental manipulations and is therefore not discussed.

[2] The social desirability of the adjective pairs had been previously assessed in a pilot study by the first author. One pair, liberal-conservative, did not have a clear-cut socially desirable end.

[3] The expected frequencies in the present chi-square analysis are equal to 4 in four cells (agree to participate). While early writers (e.g., Cochran, 1954; Siegel, 1956) suggested that the use of chi-square was questionable when more than 20% of the cells had expected values between 1 and 5, recent work (Good, Gover, & Mitchell, 1970; Yarnold, 1970; Zahn & Roberts, 1971) has shown that the chi-square test is robust so long as the critical cells have equal expected frequencies that are greater than 1.

ditions × Order, Conditions × Decision, and Conditions × Order × Decision interactions were significant $(p > .20)$. Female observers did estimate that a larger number of students (out of a possible 100) would agree to participate than did male observers (for females, $\overline{X} = 27.3$; for males, $\overline{X} = 20.3$), $F(1,194) = 4.81, p < .03$.

The observer subjects' reports of their personal decisions to agree or refuse to participate are also presented in Table 1. These data were subjected to an overall chi-square analysis paralleling that computed for the actor subjects. Due to the small number of observer subjects who reported that they would agree to participate, subjects who responded "maybe" were included in the agreement category for the purposes of the analysis. The analysis showed a slight tendency for an overall difference in the compliance rates as a function of the four experimental conditions, $\chi^2(3) = 5.75, p < .20$.

To determine whether the obtained pattern of results differed for the actor and observer subjects, the data were subjected to a 4 × 2 × 2 multidimensional chi-square analysis (Winer, 1971, pp. 855–859). The appropriate test for actor–observer differences is the Conditions × Actor–Observer × Decision interaction, which failed to reach significance, $\chi^2(3) = 4.70, p < .20$. Once again the Conditions × Decision (Agree to Participate vs. Refuse to Participate) interaction was significant, $\chi^2(3) = 13.48, p < .005$. These effects taken together indicate that the observer subjects are generally able to produce the same pattern of compliance data as the actor subjects but that the effect of the conditions for the observer subjects is much weaker than for the actor subjects.

Contrary to subjects' estimation for other students, fewer females than males said that they would agree to participate in the proposed burglary (13% of females agreed vs. 27.5% of males), with Yates's correction, $\chi^2(1) = 6.37, p < .025$. This finding contrasts with the results of the field study in which there was actually no difference in compliance between males and females.

TABLE 1. Compliance rates of actors and self-estimated compliance rates of observers.

Decision	Government sponsorship		Reward	Control
	Immunity	No immunity		
Actor[a]				
Agree	45	5	20	10
Refuse	55	95	80	90
Observer[b]				
Agree	28.1	14.0	12.2	18.2
Refuse	71.9	76.0	87.8	82.8

Note. Data are given in percentages.
[a]For all experimental conditions, $n = 20$.
[b]For experimental conditions $n = 57$, except for the control condition, where $n = 55$.

Attribution Data

The free-response answers of the actor and observer subjects to the question "Why did you [John] make this decision?" were first reworded into the third person (e.g., "*He* made his decision because . . .") by a secretary who was blind to the experimental hypothesis. The answers were then typed on slips of paper and coded by two raters who were blind as to the subject's condition, the subject's sex, and whether the subject was an actor or observer. The raters coded each response into one of three mutually exclusive categories: (a) A *disposition* of the actor (attitude or personality trait) caused the decision, (b) a dispositional factor in *combination* with an environmental factor caused the decision, or (c) an *environmental factor* caused the decision.[4] The intercorrelation of the ratings of the two raters indicated a satisfactory level of reliability $(r = .95)$.

The attributions of the actors and observers as to the cause of the decision (i.e., dispositional, en-

[4]For example, "He is the type of person who likes adventure and taking risks" was coded as dispositional, while "The amount of money involved and that the plan was foolproof are why he made his decision" was coded as environmental. For further details on the coding system, contact the first author.

TABLE 2. Attributions of actors and observers.

Decision	Actor	Observer
Agree	2.25	1.76
Refuse	2.39	2.05

Note. Responses were coded according to the following scale: 1 = a dispositional factor caused the decision, 2 = a combination of dispositional and environmental factors caused the decision, and 3 = an environmental factor caused the decision.

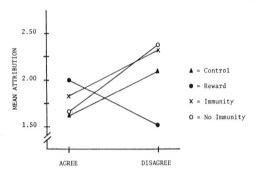

FIGURE 1. Mean attributions of observers on free-response measure ("Suppose John . . ."). The scale of responses is as follows: 1 refers to a personal (dispositional) factor, 2 refers to a combination of dispositional and environmental factors, and 3 refers to an environmental factor.

vironmental, or combination) as a function of the actor's decision to participate in the proposed burglary are presented in Table 2. The analysis of variance showed that as predicted, the actors made more environmental attributions than the observers, $F(1,304) = 12.05, p < .001$. A tendency was also noted for both actors and observers to make more dispositional attributions when the actor agreed than when he refused to participate, $F(1,304) = 3.54$, $p < .10$.

The observer attribution data were further analyzed taking into account the four experimental conditions. The mean attributions made by the observers as a function of the four experimental conditions and the actor's decision to participate or not to participate in the burglary are presented in Figure 1. A 2 × 4 (Decision × Conditions) analysis of variance showed an effect of the actor's decision,

$F(1,220) = 6.41, p < .01$, modified, however, by a Condition × Decision interaction, $F(3,220) = 4.43, p < .01$. In the control, government sponsorship, and immunity conditions, the mean attribution was more dispositional if the actor agreed to participate; whereas in the reward condition, the mean attribution was less dispositional if the actor agreed to participate.

A subsequent analysis that examined possible sex differences in attributions showed one effect of interest, a significant Sex × Agreement interaction, $F(1,196) = 7.02, p < .01$. While the attributions of male observers were strongly affected by whether John agreed or refused to participate (for agree, $\overline{X} = 1.54$; for refuse, $\overline{X} = 2.24$), female observers were affected to a lesser degree by this factor (for agree, $\overline{X} = 1.85$; for refuse, $\overline{X} = 2.00$).

Although analyses paralleling those for the observer data were originally planned for the actor data, the small number of subjects who agreed to participate in two of the conditions precluded a finer statistical breakdown of the actor data.

Personality Impressions

The observer subjects' data for each of the 15 personality impression adjective pairs for both the student and private investigator were subjected to a 4 × 2 × 2 (Conditions × Decision × Order) analysis of variance. The results for the student showed a significant effect for decision in nearly every case. When John was described as agreeing to participate in the burglary, he was rated by the observers as more outgoing, less intelligent, less wealthy, more insecure, less happy, less trustworthy, less generous, more liberal, lower in status, possessing less social poise, less sophisticated, more thrill seeking, and more impulsive than when he was described as refusing to participate in the burglary.[5]

A different pattern of results emerged for the observer's impression of the personality of the pri-

[5]$p < .001$ in each case.

vate investigator. When the student agreed to participate in the burglary, the private investigator was described as more intelligent, higher in status, more socially poised, and less impulsive.[6] In addition, several effects of the experimental conditions emerged. When the burglary was described as being committed for the government agency (immunity and government sponsorship conditions), the private investigator was rated by the observers as being happier, more generous, and more conservative.

In summary, based on the present results and previous pilot research on the social desirability of these adjective pairs, it would seem that when the student is described as agreeing to participate in the burglary, he is perceived by the observers as a less socially desirable and more easily persuaded person than when he refuses to participate. In addition, when the student is described as agreeing to participate, the results suggest that the private investigator is perceived as a more effective persuader than when the student is described as refusing to participate.

DISCUSSION

Compliance Rates

In general, the results of the field experiment tended to support the compliance predictions. Subjects offered immunity from prosecution showed the highest rate of compliance, subjects in the control condition showed a low rate of compliance, and subjects in the reward condition showed an intermediate compliance rate. The low rate of compliance in the government sponsorship condition was unexpected but may have been due to the particular agency chosen, the Internal Revenue Service. Several subjects indicated during the debriefing session that they had ambivalent attitudes toward this agency. While on the one hand, they admired the agency's work in the enforcement of laws pertaining to crime and big business, on the other hand, they expressed hostility toward the

[6] $p < .05$ in each case.

agency's role in collecting personal income tax. Thus, several of the students indicated that they would not take any risk to help this particular agency. Whether students would take such risks for a more esteemed government agency is an empirical question.

It should be emphasized that the high compliance rates obtained in two of the conditions are a reflection of the strong situational pressures in the experiment. Several techniques were used in the present experiment that have been shown in previous research to increase compliance rates. For example, subjects made an initial commitment to come to a meeting (Freedman & Fraser, 1966) where they faced a unanimous majority (Asch, 1956) with a high level of expertise (Freedman, Carlsmith, & Sears, 1974). While no personality measures were obtained on the subjects in the present experiment, based on the failures of personality measures to predict behavior in other situations in which strong situational pressures were placed on the subject, for example, Milgram's obedience research (Elms & Milgram, 1966) and Latané and Darley's bystander intervention research (Darley & Batson, 1973; Darley & Latané, 1968), it seems unlikely that personality variables would predict a significant portion of the variance in the present experimental situation (also see Mischel, 1973).

The limited success of the observer subjects in reproducing the results of the field experiment is consistent with recent research that directly compares actual subjects with role-playing subjects (Darroch & Steiner, 1970; Horowitz & Rothschild, 1970; West & Brown, 1975; Willis & Willis, 1970). Contrary to the optimism of some earlier writers (Brown, 1965; Greenberg, 1967; Kelman, 1967), in general, role playing has not been entirely successful in replicating the results of laboratory or field experiments with involved subjects. In the present experiment, the observer data taken by themselves, even with a much larger number of subjects than in the field experiment, do not show significant condition differences. In addition, if the maybe category had not been fortuitously included along with the yes and no categories as a possible response to the self-estimation question, the weak condition difference trends observed in the data probably would not have been obtained. The failure of the observers to show even similar condition difference trends when estimating how many subjects would participate further demonstrates the fragile nature of the role-playing data. In conclusion, the failure of role playing in the present research and the other failures of role playing to reproduce the results of experiments in a variety of areas, together with the epistemological questions raised by Freedman (1969), lead us to conclude with Freedman (1969, p. 207) that "role playing is not a substitute for experimental research."

Attribution Data

The results of the experiment supported the prediction derived from Jones and Nisbett's (1971) theory. Actors attributed their behavior to environmental factors, while observers attributed the actor's behavior to dispositions of the actor. This finding is consistent with other recent research comparing the attributions of actors and observers (Nisbett, Caputo, Legant, & Marecek, 1973) and other experimental evidence that attributions follow the focus of attention (Duval & Wicklund, 1973; Storms, 1973).

The effect on the observer's attributions of the actor's decision to agree or refuse to participate in the burglary is consistent with Jones and Davis's (1965) theory of correspondent inferences. According to this theory, if an action is out of role or socially undesirable, the observer is more likely to attribute the action to a disposition of the actor than if the action is in role or socially desirable. Since the observers' impression ratings of a student who agreed to participate were less socially desirable than their ratings of a student who refused to participate, most of the observers probably viewed the burglary as being rather socially undesirable. In support of the above interpretation, previous research (Jones, Davis, & Gergen, 1961; Messick &

Reeder, 1972) has demonstrated that observers' attributions become more dispositional as an actor's behavior is perceived as more socially undesirable or out of role.

The Condition × Decision interaction obtained for observer subjects was not predicted, since previous research on other-attribution has not investigated the effects of different types of environmental pressures. However, based on research in the area of self-attribution (Bem, 1967; Deci, 1971; Lepper, Greene, & Nisbett, 1973), it may be that monetary rewards are an especially salient type of environmental pressure that is given greater weight in the attribution process. Other types of rewards such as verbal reinforcement (Deci, 1971) or, in the present case, withdrawal of possible consequences may not be as salient to the observer of behavior, thus leading to dispositional attributions. Those classes of environmental pressure that are salient to observers and, more important, differentially salient to actors and observers can only be determined through future research.

Implications

The present research suggests that when outside observers, including the press, view an action, they tend to give too much weight to dispositional factors as the cause of behavior. In addition, observers seem to be relatively poor role players, so that in some cases, even attempting to put themselves in the role of the actor may not completely eliminate the attributional biases of the observer. Consequently, if an observer is to understand the causes of an actor's behavior, he should try to ascertain the precise situational pressures operating on the actor. In addition, following Jones and Nisbett (1971), the observer should try to understand the past history of the events leading up to the action, the actor's emotional state, and the actor's intentions in choosing to pursue the particular course of action. To the extent that the observer can do these things, he should be able to increase his understanding of the causes of the actor's behavior.

A final point should be made concerning the relative accuracy of the attributions made by actors and observers. It may be argued that the subjects in the field experiment and the members of the Nixon administration did not accurately perceive the "true" causes of their own behavior. This may or may not be the case (see Jones & Nisbett, 1971). However, it is more important, in terms of understanding the causes of the events and in predicting future behaviors, to attempt to understand the situational pressures that the actor perceives to be bearing upon him. For it is the actor's and not the observer's perception of reality that determines the actor's behavior.

UBIQUITOUS WATERGATE: ETHICAL ISSUES

The field experimental portion of the present study involved elaborate deceptions in which some subjects indicated an implicit agreement to become involved in a potentially illegal and possibly immoral activity. During the experiment and following disclosure of the experimental deceptions, it is possible that some subjects may have experienced some temporary loss of self-esteem: They may have felt embarrassed, guilty, or anxious when confronted with the full meaning of their implied agreement to participate in the alleged break-in. It is precisely this kind of experiment that has raised prior controversy concerning ethics in psychological research (e.g., Baumrind, 1964; Kelman, 1967; Milgram, 1964b). Therefore, we feel that it is important to address the ethical issues posed by the present experiment and to state our position on these issues (see also Cook, 1975).

A number of procedural aspects of the field experiment reported here reflect our concern with ethical considerations. First, the actual experimental manipulations were carried out in a controlled setting so that the subjects could not leave the situation feeling that they had, in fact, become involved in an illegal activity. Second, the experimental manipulations were not forced on any of the subjects. Following an initial information contact by the experimenter, all of the subjects agreed to and attended the experi-

mental "meeting" by their own choice. Third, the present procedure was selected only after alternative procedures such as role playing had been carefully considered. Various alternative research methodologies were discussed with colleagues from several different areas of psychology and were ultimately rejected. The failure of the interpersonal simulation in the present case supports the decision not to rely on role-playing methodology. Fourth, a lawyer-psychologist served as a legal consultant during the planning and implementation of the field experiment in order to protect the legal status of the subjects and experimenters. A review of the field experiment by the State Attorney's Office (in Florida) also found the procedures employed to be legally acceptable.[7] Finally, all subjects were thoroughly debriefed *immediately* after the collection of the dependent variables.

The debriefing procedure closely followed the recommendations of Aronson and Carlsmith (1968, pp. 29–36; 70–73). These involve the gradual revelation of the true purpose of the experiment and a discussion with the subject of the necessity for, and the experimenter's regret in having to use, deception in studying problems of this nature. The subject was encouraged to express his (her) feelings, whether positive or negative, about both the importance of the study and the deceptions employed. Finally, the discussion was conducted in a manner that facilitated the restoration of equality to the experimenter–subject relationship.

While post hoc declarations of experimenter innocence are less noteworthy than the experimental precautions discussed above, none of the subjects appeared to suffer any form of psychological trauma as a result of their participation in the field experiment. On the contrary, during debriefing, many subjects spontaneously commented that they found the experiment to be an interesting and even enlightening experience.

We agree, in principle, with Cook (1975) concerning the desirability of long-term postexperimental follow-ups. In that part of our more recent

---

[7]Copies of the legal statement of the State Attorney's Office are available from the first author.

research involving possible mental, physical, or emotional stress to the subjects, such follow-up data have been routinely collected. As Cook has noted, such a procedure will assist in identifying and ameliorating the long-term effects, if any, of the experimental manipulations. In addition, such results, if published, will provide some *empirical* information upon which to base future ethical codes. Follow-ups of previous research have uniformly failed to demonstrate long-term negative consequences of the experimental manipulations (Clark & Word, 1974; Milgram, 1974; Ring, Walston, & Corey, 1970; Zimbardo, 1974), even though the manipulations may have led to greater potential stress on the part of the subjects than the procedures used in the present experiment. In addition, Resnick and Schwartz (1973) have demonstrated that strict adherence to current (American Psychological Association, 1973) ethical standards in a verbal conditioning experiment led to results that were *opposite* to those usually obtained in such studies and resulted in an increase in the negativity of the subjects' attitudes toward the experiment. We argue, as did Gergen (1973), that "what is needed is factual advice about the possible harmful consequences of various research strategies" (p. 912), both to the subject and to the quality of the research results.

In designing and conducting social-psychological research, experimenters are faced with the task of balancing the value of the information gained from their research against concern for the rights and dignity of their subjects (Aronson & Carlsmith, 1968; American Psychological Association, 1973). From our viewpoint, the present experiment addresses questions of vital importance in contemporary American society: What are some of the situational factors which significantly increase the probability that normally law-abiding citizens will agree to involvement in illegal activities that may violate the civil rights of others? To what extent can the press be considered a veridical source of information concerning the causes of certain actions by governmental leaders? The preceding paragraphs delineate our attention to the rights and dig-

nity of the subjects in this experiment. We have attempted to make every effort to achieve the appropriate balance.

REFERENCES

Allen, V. L. Situational factors in conformity. In L. Berkowitz (Ed.), *Advances in experimental social psychology* (Vol. 2). New York: Academic Press, 1965.

American Psychological Association. *Ethical principles in the conduct of research with human participants.* Washington, D. C.: Author, 1973.

Aronson, E., & Carlsmith, J. M. Experimentation in social psychology. In G. Lindzey & E. Aronson, *Handbook of social psychology* (Vol. 2). Reading, Mass.: Addison-Wesley, 1968.

Asch, S. E. Studies of independence and conformity. A minority of one against a unanimous majority. *Psychological Monographs,* 1956, *70*(9, Whole No. 416).

Baumrind, D. Some thoughts on ethics of research: After reading Milgram's "Behavioral study of obedience." *American Psychologist,* 1964, *19*, 421–423.

Bem, D. J. Self-perception. An alternative interpretation of dissonance phenomena. *Psychological Review,* 1967, *74*, 183–200.

Bickman, L. The effect of another bystander's ability to help on bystander intervention in an emergency. *Journal of Experimental Social Psychology,* 1971, *7*, 367–379.

Brown, R. *Social psychology.* New York: Free Press, 1965.

Clark, R. D., III, & Word, L. E. Why don't bystanders help? Because of ambiguity? *Journal of Personality and Social Psychology,* 1972, *24*, 392–400.

Clark, R. D., III, & Word, L. E. Where is the apathetic bystander? Situational characteristics of the emergency. *Journal of Personality and Social Psychology,* 1974, *29*, 279–287.

Cochran, W. G. Some methods for strengthening common χ^2 tests. *Biometrics,* 1954, *10*, 417–451.

Cook, S. W. A comment on the ethical issues involved in West, Gunn, and Chernicky's "Ubiquitous Watergate: An attributional analysis." *Journal of Personality and Social Psychology,* 1975, *32*, 66–68.

Darley, J. M., & Batson, C. D. "From Jerusalem to Jericho'': A study of situational and dispositional variables in helping behavior. *Journal of Personality and Social Psychology,* 1973, *27*, 100–108.

Darley, J. M., & Latané, B. Bystander intervention in emergencies: Diffusion of responsibility. *Journal of Personality and Social Psychology,* 1968, *8*, 377–383.

Darroch, R. K., & Steiner, I. D. Role playing: An alternative to laboratory research? *Journal of Personality*, 1970, *38*, 302–311.

Deci, E. L. Effects of externally mediated rewards on intrinsic motivation. *Journal of Personality and Social Psychology*, 1971, *18*, 105–115.

Duval, S., & Wicklund, R. A. Effects of objective self awareness on the attribution of causality. *Journal of Experimental Social Psychology*, 1973, *9*, 17–31.

Elms, A. C., Milgram, S. Personality characteristics associated with obedience and defiance towards authoritative command. *Journal of Experimental Research in Personality*, 1966, *1*, 282–289.

Endler, N. S. Conformity as a function of different reinforcement schedules. *Journal of Personality and Social Psychology*, 1966, *4*, 175–180.

Freedman, J. L. Role playing: Psychology by consensus. *Journal of Personality and Social Psychology*, 1969, *13*, 107–114.

Freedman, J. L., Carlsmith, J. M., & Sears, D. O. *Social psychology* (2nd ed.). Englewood Cliffs, N. J.: Prentice-Hall, 1974.

Freedman, J. L., & Fraser, S. C. Compliance without pressure: The foot-in-the-door technique. *Journal of Personality and Social Psychology*, 1966, *4*, 195–202.

Gergen, K. J. The codification of research ethics: Views of a doubting Thomas. *American Psychologist*, 1973, *28*, 907–912.

Gold, G. (Ed.) *The Watergate hearings: Break-in and cover-up*. New York: Bantam, 1973.

Good, I. J., Gover, T. N., & Mitchell, G. J. Exact distributions for χ^2 and for the likelihood-ratio statistic for the equiprobable multinomial distribution. *Journal of the American Statistical Association*, 1970, *65*, 267–283.

Greenberg, M. S. Role playing: An alternative to deception? *Journal of Personality and Social Psychology*, 1967, *7*, 152–157.

Horowitz, I. A., & Rothschild, B. H. Conformity as a function of deception and role playing. *Journal of Personality and Social Psychology*, 1970, *14*, 224–226.

Jones, E. E., & Davis, K. B. From acts to dispositions: The attribution process in person perception. In L. Berkowitz (Ed.), *Advances in experimental social psychology* (Vol. 2). New York: Academic Press, 1965.

Jones, E. E., Davis, K. B., & Gergen, K. J. Role playing variations and their informational value for person perception. *Journal of Abnormal and Social Psychology*, 1961, *63*, 302–310.

Jones, E. E., & Nisbett, R. E. *The actor and the observer: Divergent perceptions of the causes of behavior*. Morristown, N.J.: General Learning Press, 1971.

Kelman, H. C. Human use of human subjects: The problem of deception in social psychological experiments. *Psychological Bulletin*, 1967, *67*, 1–11.

Korte, C. Group effects on help giving in an emergency. *Proceedings of the 77th Annual Convention of the American Psychological Association*, 1969, *4*, 383–384. (Summary)

Kiesler, C. A., & Kiesler, S. B. *Conformity*. Reading, Mass.: Addison-Wesley, 1969.

Latané, B., & Darley, J. M. Group inhibition of bystander intervention in emergencies. *Journal of Personality and Social Psychology*, 1968, *10*, 215–221.

Latané, B., & Darley, J. M. Bystander apathy. *American Scientist*, 1969, *57*, 244–268.

Latané, B., & Rodin, J. A lady in distress: Inhibiting effects of friends and strangers on bystander intervention. *Journal of Experimental Social Psychology*, 1969, *5*, 189–207.

Lepper, M. R., Greene, D., & Nisbett, R. E. Undermining children's intrinsic interest with extrinsic reward: A test of the "overjustification" hypothesis. *Journal of Personality and Social Psychology*, 1973, *28*, 129–137.

McArthur, L. A. The how and what of why? Some determinants and consequences of causal attribution. *Journal of Personality and Social Psychology*, 1972, *22*, 171–193.

Messick, D. M., & Reeder, G. Perceived motivation, role variations, and the attribution of personal characteristics. *Journal of Experimental Social Psychology*, 1972, *8*, 482–491.

Milgram, S. Behavioral study of obedience. *Journal of Abnormal and Social Psychology*, 1963, *67*, 371–378.

Milgram, S. Group pressure and action against a person. *Journal of Abnormal and Social Psychology*, 1964, *69*, 137–143. (a)

Milgram, S. Issues in the study of obedience: A reply to Baumrind. *American Psychologist*, 1964, *19*, 848–852. (b)

Milgram, S. Some conditions of obedience and disobedience to authority. *Human Relations*, 1965, *18*, 57–76.

Milgram, S. *Obedience to authority*. New York: Harper & Row, 1974.

Mischel, W. Towards a cognitive social learning reconceptualization of personality. *Psychological Review*, 1973, *80*, 252–283.

Nisbett, R. E., Caputo, C., Legant, P., & Marecek, J. Behavior as seen by the actor and as seen by the observer. *Journal of Personality and Social Psychology*, 1973, *27*, 154–164.

Resnick, J. H., & Schwartz, T. Ethical standards as an independent variable in psychological research. *American Psychologist*, 1973, *28*, 134–139.

Ring, K., Walston, K., & Corey, M. Mode of debriefing as a factor affecting subjective reaction to a Milgram-type obedience experiment: An ethical enquiry. *Representative Research in Social Psychology*, 1970, *1*, 67–88.

Shirer, W. *The rise and fall of the Third Reich*. New York: Simon & Schuster, 1960.

Siegel, S. *Non-parametric statistics*. New York: McGraw-Hill, 1956.

Smith, R. E., Smythe, L., & Lien, D. Inhibition of helping behavior by a similar or dissimilar nonreactive fellow bystander. *Journal of Personality and Social Psychology*, 1972, *23*, 414–419.

Storms, M. D. Videotape and the attribution process: Reversing actors' and observers' points of view. *Journal of Personality and Social Psychology*, 1973, *27*, 165–175.

West, S. G., & Brown, T. J. Physical attractiveness, the severity of the emergency and helping: A field experiment and interpersonal simulation. *Journal of Experimental Social Psychology*, 1975, *11*, 531–538.

Willis, R. H., & Willis, Y. A. Role playing versus deception: An experimental comparison. *Journal of Personality and Social Psychology*, 1970, *16*, 472–477.

Winer, B. J. *Statistical principles in experimental design* (2nd ed.). New York: McGraw-Hill, 1971.

Yarnold, J. K. The minimum expectation in χ^2 goodness of fit tests and the accuracy of approximations to the null distribution. *Journal of the American Statistical Association*, 1970, *65*, 864–886.

Zahn, D. A., & Roberts, G. C. Exact χ^2 criterion tables with cell expectancies one: An application to Coleman's measure of consensus. *Journal of the American Statistical Association*, 1971, *66*, 145–148.

Zimbardo, P. G. On the ethics of intervention in human psychological research: With special reference to the Stanford prison experiment. *Cognition*, 1974, *2*, 243–256.

SECTION SUMMARY

Milgram's study provides a dramatic example of the extent to which human behavior can be dictated when people are in a situation in which they feel they should or must obey. Would you have predicted that more than 60% of Milgram's subjects would have gone "all the way" and delivered the highest shock intensity? If you are like most people, you would not have. Milgram described his procedure in detail to 40 psychiatrists at a leading medical school; they predicted that less than 1% of the subjects would deliver the highest shock. A sample of college undergraduates made similar predictions (Milgram, 1965b).

Even though the average degree of obedience was much higher than most people had anticipated, the overall amount of obedience is still strongly dependent on different characteristics of the situation. In a later series of experiments, Milgram (1965a, 1965b) varied four aspects of the experimental situation to see how they would affect the degree of obedience: (1) immediacy of the victim, (2) immediacy of the authority figure, (3) prestige of the sponsoring institution, and (4) effects of group pressure.

In the remote-feedback condition—the one described in the article in this Section—the learner was in another room and could not be heard or seen by the subject until he pounded on the wall at the 300- and 315-volt levels. In another condition, the voice-feedback condition, the learner made vocal protests that could be heard through the wall and through a slightly opened doorway between the rooms. In a third, proximity condition, the learner was only 1½ feet from the teacher and in the same room. In this case, both visual and audible cues indicating the victim's pain were given. Finally, there was a touch-proximity condition. This condition was similar to the proximity condition, except that beyond the 150 volt level the victim would refuse to put his hand on the shock plate; so for every subsequent trial the experimenter ordered the subject to *force* the victim's hand onto the shock plate. A plastic shield prevented the teacher from receiving the shock.

In each of the four conditions, a different set of 40 adult males participated. The percentage of men who obeyed the experimenter and administered the high shocks were: in the remote-feedback condition, 65%; voice feedback, 62.5%; proximity, 40%; and touch-proximity, 30%. Thus, when the victim was less distant, more subjects refused to obey.

In another series of studies, Milgram found that the more physically distant the authority figure (the experimenter) was, the less likely the subjects were to obey. In fact, obedience was almost three times more frequent when the experimenter remained physically present (as he was in the article in this Section) than when the experimenter was present to give the initial instructions but then left the room and used the telephone for further instructions.

As Milgram mentions in his article in this Section, a large part of the obedience he found might be accounted for by the fact that the research took place on the grounds of Yale University—in Milgram's words, "an institution of unimpeachable reputation." To see if this was the case, Milgram (1965b) conducted the experiment in downtown Bridgeport, Connecticut. The sponsor of the study was supposedly Research Associates of Bridgeport, and the three-room office suite was in a somewhat rundown commercial building located in the downtown shopping area. Even under these conditions, almost half (48%) of the subjects delivered the maximum shock possible. Therefore, it does not appear that the prestige of the sponsoring institution was of crucial importance.

To assess the effects of *group pressure*, Milgram ran two additional studies that employed three confederates instead of one. The experimenter explained that three teachers and one learner would be required. The (real) subject became teacher 3; two of the confederates became teachers 1 and 2, and the other became the learner. In one study both confederate-teachers were *obedient*—they followed the experimenter's commands and did not show sympathy for the victim or comment on his apparent discomfort. Did such obedient models increase the number of real subjects willing to deliver the maximum shock? Not much. In this experiment 29 of the 40 subjects went all the way; this proportion is not significantly greater than the 26 of 40 found in Milgram's original study.

In the second variation of this paradigm, the two teacher-confederates were *defiant*. One confederate refused to continue after the shocks reached the 150-volt level, and the other refused to continue past the 210-volt level. The defiance of the confederates apparently had a major effect on the real subjects. In this study only 10% (4/40) of the real subjects delivered the maximum shock. Yet, interestingly enough, three-fourths of the 36 subjects who refused to go all the way claimed that they would have stopped even without the other teachers' (confederates') example. The results of Milgram's other studies strongly suggest that this is not so, although the subjects may have honestly believed that it was.

Milgram (1974) varied still other aspects of the situation in other studies. In one study he used women as subjects; the obedience rate was precisely the same (65%) as it had been with men (the learner was still male). In another study, in which the teacher could *choose* the level of shock to deliver, only one of 40 subjects used the 450-volt level at all. Finally, Milgram carried out a study in which the subject himself did not have to press the shock level but was assigned to a subsidiary role helping another teacher (actually a confederate). Here over 90% of the real subjects stayed with the experiment through the 450-volt level. So most adults seemed quite willing to participate in this situation as long as *they* were not the ones who inflicted the pain.

Although Milgram's studies highlight the situational factors that may increase or decrease the overall rate of obedience, they unfortunately do not provide many insights on a conceptual or theoretical level (Wrightsman, 1974). *Why* do some subjects obey in the same situation in which others are defiant? *Why* do some situational factors have a stronger effect on obedience than others? Answers to these questions will depend on future research.

As we mentioned in the Section Introduction, the Milgram and West et al. studies, as well as some of the studies discussed in Sections 1 and 7, raise ethical questions. Most observers would agree that the data gathered from these studies are valuable indeed. But what about the unsuspecting subjects? What do they get out of the research? Some critics (for example, Baumrind, 1964; 1971) have argued that they may have gotten more than they bargained for or deserved. Many of the subjects in the Milgram and West et al. experiments (as well as those in the Zimbardo prison study in Section 7) found out that they would agree to engage in negative behaviors that they may not have thought themselves capable of.

What is the effect of such knowledge on a person's self-concept? It might be devastating. Subjects in these studies did not volunteer to find out negative things about themselves; yet this may be what they received. Are social psychologists justified in providing such knowledge for subjects, even when they don't ask for it? Milgram, Zimbardo, and many other social psychologists argue that such knowledge can be tremendously valuable. Milgram (1974) notes that at least one of his subjects applied for and received conscientious objector status during the Vietnam War partly because of his participation in one of Milgram's studies and his realization of what he might do under authority pressure. Zimbardo reports that some participants in his prison study later volunteered vacation time to work in local prisons and became advocates of prison reform.

The "ethical principles in the conduct of research with human participants" adopted by the American Psychological Association (APA, 1973) focus on the unavoidable conflict between the potential risks of research to persons who participate and the benefits that such research may have in advancing knowledge about humanity. The basic tenor of the guidelines under which psychologists operate is given in the following passage:

First, given the initial ethical obligation of the psychological scientist to conduct the best research of which he is capable, ethical conflict is sometimes unavoidable. We therefore are concerned with conflict resolution, not with the advocacy of ethical absolutes. The general ethical question always is whether there is a negative effect upon the dignity and welfare of the participants that the importance of the research does not warrant. Second, in weighing the pros and cons of conducting research involving ethical questions, priority must be given to the research participant's welfare. The nearest that the principles in this document come to an immutable 'thou shalt' or 'thou shalt not' is in the insistence that the human participants emerge from their research experience unharmed—or at least that the risks are minimal, understood by the participants, and accepted as reasonable. If possible, participants should enjoy an identifiable benefit. In general, after research participation, the participants' feelings about the experience should be such that they would willingly take part in further research. The requirements of the research should be ones that research psychologists would find acceptable were members of their immediate families to participate [pp. 10–11].

Both Zimbardo (along with his co-workers) and Milgram carried out extensive follow-up studies to try to assess whether participation in their experiments had had any long-lasting effects on the subjects involved. Of the subjects Milgram contacted, 84% indicated that they were glad to have taken part in the research, 15% reported neutral feelings, and 1% reported that they regretted having participated. Four-fifths of the subjects felt that more experiments of this sort should be carried out. Some caution should be employed in interpreting these figures, however. Persons who have administered shocks to others may be motivated later to justify their behavior to themselves regardless of what they initially thought of the experiment. A university psychiatrist also interviewed a sample of experimental subjects; he was unable to uncover possible injurious effects resulting from participation in the studies (Milgram, 1964, 1965b). Regarding the West et al. study, Cook (1975) has commented directly on how the ethical issues involved relate to the APA's ethical principles.

The potential importance of Milgram's results and the apparent concern for the welfare of his subjects have led some social scientists to propose that this research is among the most powerful and important programs carried out in social psychology. For example, Etzioni (1968, p. 279) has commented "Milgram's experiment seems to be one of the best carried out in this generation. It shows that the often-stated opposition between meaningful, interesting, humanistic study and accurate, empirical quantitative research is a false one: the two perspectives can be combined to the benefit of both." Another social psychologist, Roger Brown, has called this research "the most important social psychological research done in this generation" (Milgram, 1974).

The question that remains is: how far can the results of Milgram's studies be generalized? Has he identified the "latent Eichmann" that resides in most of us, as Etzioni (1968) proposes? Or can much of the variance in his results be attributed to the "demand characteristics" of an unusual research situation? It could be cogently argued that "obedience" is an expected behavior in research subjects, who in other circumstances, such as complying with traffic laws, might not so readily obey. To many persons "science" has become a sacred cow; we take seriously our responsibilities as participants in a particular situation where—contrary to real life—a subject's behavior is closely monitored by an authority figure. (Obedience to traffic regulations would be much greater if we always had a policeman sitting in the car with us.) Do laboratory results mean that we can or cannot generalize Milgram's findings to real-life situations in which we are forced to violate our values under the close supervision of an authority figure? Social scientists are not in agreement with one another; the interested reader should see Orne and Holland (1968) and Milgram (1972) for two opposing positions on this issue.

Baumrind (1964) believes that there may be no relationship between the phenomenon demonstrated in Milgram's laboratory subjects and the behavior of Adolf Eichmann and other Nazi German officers. Milgram (1964), in a reply to Baumrind, disagrees. He states that a soldier's obedience is "no less meaningful" just because it occurs in a military context. The shocking atrocities apparently committed by "ordinary" United States soldiers in Vietnam in the late 1960s provide compelling evidence of the possible relevance of Milgram's findings. For example, columnist Stanley Karnow (1971) has suggested that Milgram's original experiment was "remarkably prescient. He demonstrated in the laboratory what Lt. William Calley and his unit would later dramatize at My Lai—that man's behavior is almost invariably dominated by authority rather than by his own sense of morality." Karnow quotes Milgram as commenting "If we now recoil at our own conduct, it is because we are just as capable as the Nazis of committing crimes in the name of obedience." We encourage you to think about whether or not our behavior is "almost always" dominated by authority and whether the persons you know would be "just as capable as the Nazis" of committing such crimes.

There is some additional evidence suggesting that these findings can be generalized, however. In a study of former Nazi SS concentration camp personnel and members of Gestapo units, Dicks (1972) found many of the same psychological processes (for example, feelings of being a "helpless cog" who is required to follow orders) that Milgram's subjects showed. In addition, in a nationwide survey carried out shortly after Lt. Calley's conviction in 1971, people were asked "What would most people do if ordered to shoot all inhabitants of a Vietnamese village suspected of aiding the enemy, including old men, women, and children?" Two-thirds of the respondents answered "Follow orders and shoot" (Kelman & Lawrence, 1972). The researchers concluded that "We have found that a

large segment of the population . . . regards Calley's actions as normal. They believe that most people would do what Calley did under similar circumstances, that they themselves would do so, that Calley did what he should have done, that his action was right and in keeping with his duty . . . These findings suggest that this large segment of the population is potentially available for rather extreme forms of violence under conditions of orders from legitimate authority" (p. 210).

The extent to which the Milgram and West et al. findings can be generalized is still open to debate. Nevertheless, they have provided a new and sobering frame of reference for the evaluation of human behavior under conditions of extreme authority pressure.

REFERENCES

American Psychological Association. *Ethical principles in the conduct of research with human participants.* Washington, D.C.: American Psychological Association, 1973.

Baumrind, D. Some thoughts on the ethics of research: After reading Milgram's "Behavioral study of obedience." *American Psychologist,* 1964, *19,* 421–423.

Baumrind, D. Principles of ethical conduct in the treatment of subjects: Reaction to the draft report of the Committee on Ethical Standards in Psychological Research. *American Psychologist,* 1971, *26,* 887–896.

Cook, S. W. A comment on the ethical issues involved in West, Gunn, and Chernicky's "Ubiquitous Watergate: An attributional analysis." *Journal of Personality and Social Psychology,* 1975, *32,* 66–68.

Dicks, H. V. *Licensed mass murder: A socio-political study of some S.S. killers.* New York: Basic Books, 1972.

Etzioni, A. A model of significant research. *International Journal of Psychiatry,* 1968, *6,* 279–280.

Karnow, S. Calley, Eichmann both obedient. *St. Petersburg Times,* March 30, 1971.

Kelman, H. C., & Lawrence, L. H. Assignment of responsibility in the case of Lt. Calley: Preliminary report on a national survey. *Journal of Social Issues,* 1972, *28*(1), 177–212.

Milgram, S. Issues in the study of obedience: A reply to Baumrind. *American Psychologist,* 1964, *19,* 848–852.

Milgram, S. Liberating effects of group pressure. *Journal of Personality and Social Psychology,* 1965, *1,* 127–134. (a)

Milgram, S. Some conditions of obedience and disobedience to authority. *Human Relations,* 1965, *18,* 57–76. (b)

Milgram, S. Interpreting obedience: Error and evidence. In A. G. Miller (Ed.), *The social psychology of psychological research.* New York: Free Press, 1972. Pp. 138–154.

Milgram, S. *Obedience to authority.* New York: Harper & Row, 1974.

Orne, M. T., & Holland, C. H. On the ecological validity of laboratory deceptions. *International Journal of Psychiatry,* 1968, *6,* 282–293.

Wrightsman, L. S. The most important social psychological research of this generation? *Contemporary Psychology,* 1974, *19,* 803–805.

SECTION IX

THE ATTRIBUTION OF ATTITUDES AND EMOTIONAL STATES

INTRODUCTION

In social situations each of us is constantly attempting to understand the behaviors of others and to infer from these behaviors the underlying characteristics of the other person. As Fritz Heider (1944, 1958) has pointed out, all of us would like to be able to structure our worlds so that interactions with others would be more likely to have favorable outcomes for us. The success of such structuring depends at least in part on our ability to infer other people's dispositions (for example, attitudes, personality traits) and hence to predict their behavior. When a customer approaches a used-car salesman, the salesman may "size up" the person, making judgments about his or her degree of gullibility or sophistication (as well as how much cash the customer has) on the basis of his or her behavior. The salesman then designs the specific "sales pitch" to use with that customer.

Attribution theory has been developed by social psychologists to deal with this process of analyzing the actions of others. One of the purposes of this Section is to investigate the ways in which social psychologists have studied the attribution of others' attitudes from their behavior.

But is not just the behavior of *others* that people are always trying to understand. We also seek an explanation for *our own reactions.* Suppose that a male college student, as a part of a campus dramatic production, has to play a love scene with a young woman he does not particularly like. As he does so, his fiancée and many others in the audience watch. He finds that he is sweating, his face is flushed, his heart is beating fast. Clearly his behavior is emotional. But what emotion is he experiencing? Embarrassment? Guilt? Lust? Anxiety? Or a combination of several of these?

We could ask this young man to label the emotion. He doubtless could do so, and his labeling would represent a second type of attribution: the attribution of one's own emotional state. In recent years there has been a large body of research, generated by the work of Stanley Schachter (1964; Schachter & Singer, 1962; Schachter & Wheeler, 1962), that seeks to understand how we determine the particular label we use for our own behavior, particularly our emotional behavior. This Section will explore this topic also.

Much of the relevant research concerning how

people make attributions about their own emotional states has dealt with situations in which a person is aware of experiencing bodily changes but is unaware of *why* he or she is experiencing them. That is, the individual knows that physiological changes associated with emotion are occurring—he or she can feel them—but has no appropriate label for them. An explanation, an attribution of a label is sought. One way of resolving such a dilemma is illustrated in the first article in this Section, by Stuart Valins, now at the State University of New York at Stony Brook. Valins' study of subjects' reactions to false information about the speed of their heartbeats stems from Schachter's cognitive-physiological theory of emotion, which Valins reviews in the introduction to his article.

More recently, Schachter's own interest has moved from the attribution of emotional states to a related topic: the self-attribution of hunger and the determinants of eating behavior. Introductory psychology textbooks inform us that we are hungry when the hypothalamus, a small structure in the brain, tells us that we are, and that the hypothalamus bases its conclusion on its continuous analysis of the changing properties of the blood passing through the brain. Yet there appear to be vast individual differences in reliance on this signal—and on stomach contractions, too—as a stimulus to eating. Schachter, now at Columbia University, proposes that obese people are much less sensitive to internal triggers to hunger than are people of normal weight. In the second article in this Section he reviews an ingenious set of experiments that illustrate this phenomenon. We will mention some later studies on this same topic in the Section Summary.

We have noted that people tend to look for the causes of other people's behavior. Thus, we seek to understand the causes of events so that we are better prepared to predict future events. If the behavior of someone else (usually referred to as the "stimulus person" or "actor") can be seen as caused by a disposition that he or she has (such as a tendency to be shy or a way of always disagreeing with others), then knowledge of this disposition enables the observer to predict the actor's behavior in subsequent situations in which that disposition may be relevant.

Of course, one's behavior is affected not only by dispositions but also by external, environmental conditions. In Heider's model the resultant behavior is seen as a function of environmental forces plus personal forces. Environmental forces are those characteristics present in the situation that "press" for a specific type of behavior. Personal force is seen as the product of ability (or power) and of the effort that one exerts. Since this relationship is hypothesized to be a multiplicative one (amount of ability × amount of effort = amount of personal force), if either ability or effort is lacking, the entire strength of personal force will be zero.

But the attribution of environmental forces and personal forces may depend on the observer. Some behaviors may cause us to attribute more influence to environmental forces and some less. Jones and Nisbett (1971) note that, when a freshman at the state university comes to discuss his poor grades with his faculty adviser, a fundamental difference in attribution by the two participants may occur. The student may point to environmental forces (such as a noisy dormitory or a heavy course load) to account for his difficulties. Although the faculty member would like to agree, he is more likely not to, because he will attribute the deficient behavior to personal forces in the student. He will believe instead "that the failure is due to enduring qualities of the student—to lack of ability, to irremediable laziness, to neurotic ineptitude" (Jones & Nisbett, 1971, p. 1).

Our third reading, an excerpt from a book by Kelly G. Shaver of the College of William and Mary, summarizes the attribution process. Shaver notes that, in employing processes of attribution to explain action and to predict whether it will be repeated in the future, one typically goes through several steps: the observation of action, a judgment of the intentions underlying the action, and a dispositional attribution. Shaver then provides illustrations of several areas in which such processes are likely to take place.

REFERENCES

Heider, F. Social perception and phenomenal causality. *Psychological Review,* 1944, *51,* 358–374.

Heider, F. *The psychology of interpersonal relations.* New York: Wiley, 1958.

Jones, E. E., & Nisbett, R. E. *The actor and the observer: Divergent perceptions of the causes of behavior.* New York: General Learning Corporation, 1971.

Schachter, S. The interaction of cognitive and physiological determinants of emotional state. In L. Berkowitz (Ed.), *Advances in experimental social psychology,* Vol. 1. New York: Academic Press, 1964. Pp. 49–80.

Schachter, S., & Singer, J. E. Cognitive, social and physiological determinants of emotional state. *Psychological Review,* 1962, *69,* 379–399.

Schachter, S., & Wheeler, L. Epinephrine, chlorpromazine, and amusement. *Journal of Abnormal and Social Psychology,* 1962, *65,* 121–128.

ARTICLE 25

Cognitive effects of false heart-rate feedback

Stuart Valins

Although there is considerable evidence that emotional states are accompanied by physiological changes (Duffy, 1962; Woodworth & Schlosberg, 1962), until recently there was little indication that these internal events facilitate the development of emotional behavior. Several experiments have now shown that emotional behavior is affected by the experimental manipulation of sympathetic activity. Emotional behavior is more readily learned when the sympathetic nervous system is intact than when it is surgically enervated (Wynne & Solomon, 1955), and more readily manifested during epinephrine-induced states of sympathetic activation than during states of relative inactivation (Latané & Schachter, 1962; Schachter & Singer, 1962; Schachter & Wheeler, 1962; Singer, 1963).

In an attempt to account for the influence of autonomic arousal on emotional behavior, Schachter (1964) has emphasized the importance of the cognitive effects of internal events. Within his cognitive-physiological theory of emotion, physiological changes are considered to function as stimuli or cues and are represented cognitively as feelings or sensations. These feelings, in turn, arouse further cognitive activity in the form of attempts to identify the situation that precipitated them. Emotional behavior results when the feeling state is attributed to an emotional stimulus or situation. The optimum conditions for the development of an emotion are thus present when an individual can say, "That stimulus (emotional) has affected me internally." In accord with these notions, it has been found that when subjects are pharmacologically aroused and exposed to stimuli designed to induce emotion, more emotional behavior is manifested when the arousal state is attributed to the emotional situation than when it is attributed to the injection (Schachter & Singer, 1962). Furthermore, the results of a recent experiment suggest that the effects of internal cues on emotional behavior may be mediated by an alteration in the perceived intensity of the

Reprinted from the *Journal of Personality and Social Psychology*, 1966, *4*, pp. 400–408. Copyright 1966 by the American Psychological Association. Reprinted by permission.

emotional stimulus. Nisbett and Schachter (1966) found that when a series of electric shocks were administered to subjects who were in a mild state of fear, the shocks were judged to be more painful by those subjects who correctly attributed their internal symptoms to the shocks than by subjects who incorrectly attributed their symptoms to a pill.

Once it is granted that internal events can function as cues or stimuli then these events can now be considered as a source of cognitive information. They can, for example, result in cognitions such as, "My heart is pounding," or "My face is flushed." As potential cognitive information, however, these events are subject to the same mechanisms that process any stimulus before it is represented cognitively. Such mechanisms can result in their being denied, distorted, or simply not perceived. It is thus plausible that the cognitive representation of an internal event can be nonveridical; a particular reaction can fail to register or can be misperceived, and a nonexistent reaction can be represented cognitively. Mandler (1962) also has questioned the veridicality of internal sensations and suggests that:

. . . someone may learn to make statements about his internal private events under the control of environmental stimuli or irrelevant internal stimuli. Thus, I could say, "I am blushing," in an embarrassing situation without showing any signs of peripheral vasodilation. Or I may have learned to talk about tenseness in my stomach in a stress situation without stomach events exerting any influence on such a remark [p. 317].

If cognitive representations of internal events are important for emotional behavior, then these nonveridical representations of physiological changes should have the same effects as veridical ones. They will be evaluated by reference to a precipitating situation and result in emotional behavior if the situation is an emotional one. Using Mandler's example, his "symbolic" blusher should be equally embarrassed with or without the presence of peripheral vasodilation. He should be less embarrassed, however, if he now has a mirror at his disposal and observes that he is not blushing. Embarrassment

should be greatest only when he *thinks* that he has blushed in response to the situation.

The present experiment represents an attempt to determine the effects of nonveridical cognitive cues concerning internal reactions on the labeling of emotional stimuli. This will be accomplished by manipulating the extent to which a subject believes his heart has reacted to slides of seminude females and by observing the effects of his "liking" for the slides. The research of Schachter and his associates suggests that if a subject were covertly injected with epinephrine and shown a slide of a nude female, he would interpret his internal sensations as due to the nude stimulus and he would label the girl as more attractive than if he had been injected with placebo and he had experienced no internal sensations. If, however, it is the cognitive effect of internal events that influences emotional behavior, then this same influence should be observed when subjects think that they have reacted to a given stimulus, regardless of whether they have indeed reacted. As such, it is hypothesized that the cognition, "That girl has affected my heart rate," will induce subjects to consider the girl more attractive or appealing than the cognition, "That girl has not affected my heart rate."

These effects are predicted regardless of whether the heart-rate feedback matches the subjects' stereotyped expectations. Most of us would expect that, if anything, our heart rates would increase in response to photographs of nude females. How would we interpret our heart-rate changes, however, if the rate remained normal to some photographs but decreased substantially to others? If all of the photographs were of attractive females, we could not interpret a decrease as indicating that a girl is a "dog." If we felt it necessary to evaluate these reactions at all, it is likely that we would interpret any change in our heart rates as indicating greater attraction or appeal. Only if all of the photographs were relatively unattractive would we expect that a decrease in heart rate be interpreted as less attraction. Thus, under the appropriate cognitive conditions (highly attractive females), feedback indicating that heart rate has decreased should affect the labeling of emotional stimuli in a manner similar to that of feedback indicating that heart rate has increased.

PROCEDURE

Male introductory psychology students, whose course requirements included 6 hours of participation in experiments, volunteered for a psychophysiological experiment. When the subjects arrived at the laboratory, the experiment was described as a study of physiological reactions to sexually oriented stimuli. These reactions were allegedly being recorded while the subjects viewed 10 slides of seminude females. Two groups of subjects were led to believe that they were hearing an amplified version of their hearts beating while watching the slides and heard their "heart rate" change markedly to half of them. Two other groups of subjects heard the identical sounds, but did not associate them with their own heart beats. Several measures of the attractiveness of each slide were subsequently obtained from all subjects and used to evaluate the effects of the heart-rate feedback.

Bogus Heart-Rate Conditions

Subjects in these conditions thought that the experiment was investigating vasomotor reactions to to sexually oriented stimuli. It was explained that:

Most of our research is conducted over at the Bell Medical Research Building. We have all sorts of electronic wizardry and sound proof chambers over there. Right now there are several experiments being conducted and our facilities at Bell are too overcrowded. Because of this situation, we are doing this experiment here, and are forced to use a fairly crude but adequate measure of heart rate. In our other lab we record heart rate using electrodes which are taped to the chest. They pick up the electrical impulses from the heart which are then recorded on a polygraph. Here we are recording heart rate the way they used to do it 30 years ago. I will be taping this fairly sensitive microphone to your chest. It picks up each major

heart sound which is amplified here, and initiates a signal on this signal tracer. This other microphone then picks up the signal and it is recorded on this tape recorder (the signal tracer, amplifier, and tape recorder were on a table next to the subject). By appropriately using a stop watch and this footage indicator, I can later determine exactly where each stimulus occurred and evaluate your heart rate reaction to it.

Unfortunately, this recording method makes it necessary to have audible sounds. They would be a serious problem if we were employing a task which required concentration. Since our procedure does not require concentration, it won't be too much of a problem and it is not likely to affect the results. All that you will be required to do is sit here and look at the slides. Just try to ignore the heart sounds. I will be showing the slides from the next room through this one-way screen. I'll tape this microphone to your chest and after recording your resting heart rate for a while, I will present 10 slides to you at regular intervals. Then I will record your resting heart rate again for several minutes and I will repeat the same slides again in the same order.

After taping the microphone to the subject's chest, the experimenter started the tape recorder and left the room. The sounds which these subjects were hearing were in reality prerecorded. A concealed wire from the tape recorder fed these sounds into the signal tracer speaker. Twenty subjects heard a tape recording which indicated that their heart rates had increased substantially to five slides, but had not changed to five others (heart-rate increase group); 20 other subjects heard a tape recording which indicated that their heart rates had decreased substantially to five of the slides, but had not changed to the other five (heart-rate decrease group).[1]

[1]It should be mentioned that Gerard and Rabbie (1961) and Bramel (1963) have used a similar technique in order to make subjects think that they were more or less frightened or homosexual. They accomplished this by allowing subjects to see dial readings which purportedly indicated internal reactions to experimental stimuli, but which were actually under the control of the experimenter. These investigators, however, were not primarily concerned with the evaluation and labeling of internal states. Their manipulations included detailed explanations of the "meaning" of the dial readings, so that subjects had no choice but to later indicate that they were or were not frightened or homosexual. In contrast, subjects in the present experiment were

Extraneous Sound Conditions

Subjects in these conditions thought that the experiment was investigating vasomotor reactions to sexually oriented stimuli. They were told that:

Most of our research is conducted over at the Bell Medical Research Building. We have all sorts of electronic wizardry and sound proof chambers over there. I am doing this experiment now because of the conflicting results which we have obtained in two other identical experiments which we have done over at Bell. One experiment was done in a completely sound proof chamber. Another one was done in an office in which extraneous sounds could be heard, bells ringing in the hallway, people walking up and down, etc. Well, the results in these two experiments were not the same. We feel that it is possible that the results may have been different due to the extraneous sounds which were heard in the experiment where the subject was in an office. To determine whether extraneous sounds can affect finger temperature reactions to sexual stimuli, throughout this experiment you will hear sounds from this tape recorder, sounds that are completely meaningless but are just our way of controlling and producing extraneous sound. Later I will compare your finger temperature reactions to sexual stimuli with those of subjects who do not hear any sounds. I can then assess the physiological effects of the extraneous sounds and determine whether they were the reason why we obtained directionally different results in the two other experiments.

These sounds have absolutely no meaning for you. Just try to ignore them. I will be showing the slides from the next room through this one-way screen. I'll tape this thermistor to your finger and after recording your resting finger temperature for a while, I will present 10 slides to you at regular intervals. Then I will record your resting finger temperature again for several minutes and I will repeat the same slides again in the same order.

A dummy thermistor was then taped to the subject's finger, the tape recorder started, and the experimenter left the room. Ten of these subjects

(sound increase group) heard the same tape recording as the heart-rate increase group, and 10 (sound decrease group) heard the same recording as the heart-rate decrease group. The sounds emanated from the signal tracer as in the experimental conditions, but the subjects were now told that it was just an elaborate speaker.

Tape Recordings

The tape recordings were made by recording square wave pulses produced by a Hewlett-Packard low-frequency signal generator, a signal tracer used as a capacitance network, and an external speaker. Pulses of a given frequency per minute could be varied over a wide range.

Heart Beat and Sound Increase Recording. This recording began with the pulse rate varying every 5 seconds between 66 and 72 beats per minute (BPM). At the start of the third minute the rate increased in 5-second segments from 72 to 84 and then to 90 BPM. It then decreased to 84, 78, and to 72 BPM, and subsequently continued to vary between 66 and 72 BPM. The identical rate increase was recorded at minutes 5, 8, 10, 11, 15, 17, 20, 22, and 23. The rate continued to vary between 66 and 72 BPM at minutes 4, 6, 7, 9, 12, 13, 14, 16, 18, 19, 21, and 24.

Heart Beat and Sound Decrease Recording. This recording was the same as the previous one except for the minutes at which the rate increased. At the start of the third minute for this recording, the rate decreased from 66 to 54 and then to 48 BPM. It then increased to 54, 60, and to 66 BPM, and subsequently continued to vary between 66 and 72 BPM. This same decrease in rate was recorded whenever an increase had been recorded on the other tape.

(a) specifically instructed to ignore the bogus heart sounds, (b) told nothing about the meaning of heart-rate changes, and (c) told that the experimenter could not hear the heart sounds and thus would not know for some time how the subject had reacted. It is the purpose of the present experiment to determine whether subjects will *spontaneously* label their feelings toward a stimulus by reference to their knowledge of how their hearts have reacted.

Coordination of Slides with Tape Recordings

Ten color slides were made from photographs of seminude females which had been published by *Playboy* magazine. The slides were projected at 1-minute intervals, each for 15 seconds. The first slide was presented approximately 1 minute, 58 seconds after the tape-recorded sounds had begun so that a marked change in the rate of the sounds was evident 2 seconds afterward. Since the remaining nine slides were presented at 1-minute intervals, this same slide-sound change contingency was apparent for slides 3, 6, 8, and 9. Slides 2, 4, 5, 7, and 10 were presented at the minutes when no change in the rate of the sounds occurred. After the tenth slide (Minute 12 on the tape recording), there was a 3-minute break during which the rate of the sounds varied between 66 and 72 BPM. The slides were then repeated in the same manner starting at Minute 15. The slide order was also systematically rotated within conditions so that each slide was followed by a sound change as often as it was not.

To further clarify the procedure, consider the experimental situation as viewed by a subject who thought he was hearing his heart beating. For 2 minutes, he hears it beating at what appears to be a normal and reasonable rate. The first slide is then presented, and shortly afterward he notices a marked change in his heart rate. After 15 seconds of observing the slide, his heart rate gradually returns to what has been established as normal. The second slide is presented, but there is not any noticeable effect on his heart rate. It continues to vary between 66 and 72 BPM. After seeing all 10 slides, it is apparent that 5 of them have affected his heart rate, but the other 5 have not. This conclusion is reinforced when, after a 3-minute period of normal heart rate, the slides are shown again, and the same ones affect his heart rate, while the others have no effect.

Attractiveness Measures

The effects of heart-rate feedback were assessed by determining the extent to which it influenced the subject's opinions of how attractive the girls were. Three measures of these opinions were obtained: (a) attractiveness ratings which were made immediately after the bogus feedback, (b) choice of photographs as remuneration, (c) attractiveness rankings made several weeks after the experiment.

Slide Ratings. After the second presentation of the slides, the experimenter disengaged the apparatus and briefly discussed the slides with the subject. The subject was then told that 12 slides were originally being used but that 2 were eliminated in order to shorten the procedure. It was explained that the experimenter was now considering reducing the number of slides to 7 or 8. He was asking a number of subjects to rate the slides so that only the 7 or 8 most attractive or appealing ones would be included. The slides were quickly shown again to the subject and, using a 100-point scale ranging from "Not at all" to "Extremely," he rated them as to: "How attractive or appealing each girl is to you."

Photograph Choices. The subject then completed a short questionnaire which was followed by an intensive interview to determine whether he had accepted the experimental deceptions. The physiology of sexual arousal was also discussed, but no mention was ever made of the true purpose of the experiment or of the experimental deceptions. The experimenter apologized for being unable to pay the subject and offered to give him some photographs of the girls which had been donated by the publisher. The 10 photographs from which the slides had been made were casually spread on a table, and the subject was told to take 5. The experimenter left the room and thanked the subject before he made his choices. As the subject was leaving, he was intercepted and the photographs taken back. It was explained that the photographs had been offered to the subject only to determine if there were differences in attractiveness estimates relating to slide versus photograph modes of presentation.

Delayed Photograph Rankings. Three weeks after participating in the experiment, the subject received a letter from a fictitious "social scientist."

The letter requested the subject's cooperation for an attitude survey and asked him to permit an interviewer to question him. Approximately 1 week later an interviewer arrived at the subject's dormitory room and described the survey as a study of undergraduate attitudes toward the psychological and physical characteristics of members of the opposite sex. The subjects first ranked three sets of photographs, each consisting of a model in 12 different dresses, according to how attractive the girl was in each photograph. He then ranked 12 photographs of seminude females on the same dimension. Ten of the photographs were those which he had seen in the experiment proper. After ranking these photographs, the interviewer questioned the subject as to whether he had previously seen them and determined whether he had associated the interview with the original experiment. It should be emphasized that throughout these interviews,[2] the subjects were totally unaware that the feedback in the original experiment was nonveridical.

RESULTS

Adequacy of the Experimental Manipulations

In order to be effective, the manipulation of differential heart-rate feedback must be accurately perceived by the subjects and adequately accepted as a reflection of their internal reactions. Although they were instructed to ignore the bogus heart sounds, the subjects' interest in their reactions and the amplification of the sounds resulted in all subjects being aware of the different slide-sound change contingencies. The bogus heart beats were also accepted as veridical. None of the 40 experimental subjects had substantial suspicions that the sounds might not be their heart beats. Several had what they described as momentary doubts when first hearing the sounds, but these were quickly forgotten or dispelled. The slightly varying sound rate during the first 2 minutes seemed quite reasonable and served, as intended, to convince the subjects of the

veridicality of the bogus beats. The bogus heart-rate reactions to the different slides were also accepted as veridical. Although the heart-rate decrease subjects were overwhelmingly surprised by this feedback, they simply considered as wrong their previous expectations of how they react to these stimuli. Suspicions concerning the veridicality of the feedback were also not increased when the subjects were confronted with a marked discordance between their presumed heart-rate reactions and their initial "liking" for a slide. This discordance was apparently reconciled by many subjects in precisely the manner which was predicted. They changed their estimates of how attractive the girls were.

Heart-Rate Feedback and Attractiveness Measures

It was hypothesized that the cue function of internal events affects the labeling of emotional stimuli. A nonveridical cognitive cue which indicates that one has reacted markedly to a slide of a seminude female should, in this situation, be interpreted as indicating that the stimulus object is attractive or appealing.

Slide Ratings. The prerecorded sounds were played throughout the first two presentations of the slides. During the third presentation, the tape recorder was turned off, and the subjects rated the attractiveness or appeal of each girl. If heart-rate feedback has had the predicted effect, the experimental subjects, in comparison to the control subjects, should rate the slides followed by a change in the sound rate (reinforced) as more attractive than the slides not followed by a change (nonreinforced). Table 1 presents the mean ratings of the reinforced and nonreinforced slides for each of the experimental groups and for the combined control groups.[3] When the sounds were not considered heart beats they had virtually no effect on the subjects' ratings.

---

[2] These interviews were skillfully conducted by Joseph Mancusi.

[3] The data of the control groups were combined to facilitate presentation. Their means did not differ significantly on any measure, and both were always in a direction opposite to that of the experimental groups.

TABLE 1. Mean slide attractiveness ratings.

Slides	Conditions		
	Heart-rate increase (N = 20)	Heart-rate decrease (N = 20)	Sound increase + sound decrease (N = 10 + 10)
Reinforced	72.42	69.26	60.86
Nonreinforced	54.11	62.57	63.76
Difference	18.31	6.69	− 2.90

Note.—All p values reported are 2-tailed. p value of difference score comparisons (t tests): heart-rate increase versus sound increase and decrease, $p < .001$; heart-rate decrease versus sound increase and decrease, $p < .05$; heart-rate increase versus heart-rate decrease, $p < .05$.

Since the control groups rated the reinforced and nonreinforced slides similarly, it is evident that the sounds alone did not have any differential excitatory effects.

It can be seen, however, that when subjects thought the sounds were their heart beats, there was a substantial effect of differential feedback on their ratings. Subjects in the heart-rate decrease condition rated the reinforced slides 6.69 points higher than the nonreinforced ones; subjects in the heart-rate increase condition rated the reinforced slides 18.31 points higher than the nonreinforced ones. Each of these differences is significantly greater than that of the combined control groups. The heart-rate increase feedback also had a greater effect than the decrease feedback. Subjects in the former condition apparently lowered their ratings of the nonreinforced slides as well as raising their ratings of the reinforced ones. The effects of the manipulations are more clearly portrayed in Table 2 which presents the number of subjects in each condition who rated the reinforced slides higher than the nonreinforced ones. This analysis shows that the bogus feedback affected the ratings of the majority of the subjects in the experimental conditions, whereas extraneous sounds had little effect in the control conditions.

Photograph Choices. Differential heart-rate feedback has obviously affected the subjects' ratings of the slides. It may be asked, however, to what

extent these ratings are truly indicative of the way subjects feel about these stimuli. Will they now, for example, choose more photographs of the reinforced nudes than the nonreinforced ones as remuneration for participating in the experiment? It will be recalled that each subject selected five photographs. Table 3 tabulates the number of subjects in each condition who chose three or more of the previously reinforced nudes and the number choosing two or less. It can be seen that a significant number of experimental subjects chose more of the photographs that had been reinforced than photographs that had not been reinforced. The data for the heart-rate decrease condition alone are not quite significant, whereas that of the control groups appear just as strong, but in the opposite direction. An analysis of the mean number of reinforced nudes chosen by each group, however, shows that the heart-rate decrease subjects chose significantly more than that expected on a chance basis, but the control groups did not choose significantly less. The control groups chose an average of 2.25 reinforced photographs ($t = 1.55$, ns), whereas the heart-rate decrease subjects chose 3.10 reinforced photographs ($t = 2.41$, $p < .05$), and the heart-rate increase subjects chose 3.20 reinforced photographs ($t = 2.45$, $p < .05$). With the exception that on this measure the experimental groups did not differ from one another, the analysis of photograph choices clearly supports that of the ratings. A marked change in heart rate which is considered as effected by a nude female is interpreted as attraction and results in greater liking for the stimulus.

Delayed Photograph Rankings. It may also be asked whether the observed effects of the heart-rate feedback are temporary or whether they are sufficiently substantial to result in relatively long-lasting cognitive change. In order to answer this question, interviews were conducted with the subjects 4–5 weeks after the experiment proper. During the course of these interviews, the subjects were asked to rank, from most to least attractive, 12 photographs of seminude females. Since 10 of these photographs were used in the experiment proper, an analysis of these rankings permits an evaluation of the relative permanency of the feedback effects. It should be mentioned that the interviewer made every effort to avoid allowing the subjects to associate the interview procedure with the original experiment. Since the source of the photographs was identified as *Playboy* magazine, the subjects did not think it unusual that two experiments would be using similar stimuli. The subjects were, in fact, quite surprised when subsequently informed of the true purpose of the interview. In addition, most of the subjects appeared to rank the photographs on the basis of how they felt at the moment. They were not aware of, or at least did not verbalize, any tendency to rank them according to their previous attractiveness estimates.

It can be seen in Table 4 that the analysis of the delayed photograph rankings is generally consistent

TABLE 2. Number of subjects rating reinforced slides higher and number rating them lower than nonreinforced slides.

Reinforced slides rated	Conditions			
	Heart-rate increase (N = 20)	Heart-rate decrease (N = 19)[a]	Heart-rate increase + decrease (N = 20 + 19)[a]	Sound increase + sound decrease (N = 10 + 10)
Higher	17	15	32	9
Lower	3	4	7	11
p value (sign test)	.002	.02	.001	ns

[a]One subject rated the reinforced and nonreinforced stimuli identically.

TABLE 3. Number of subjects choosing three or more reinforced photographs and number choosing two or less.

No. of reinforced photographs chosen	Conditions			
	Heart-rate increase (N = 20)	Heart-rate decrease (N = 20)	Heart-rate increase + decrease (N = 20 + 20)	Sound increase + sound decrease (N = 10 + 10)
3 or more	15	14	29	6
2 or less	5	6	11	14
p value (sign test)	.04	ns	.007	ns

TABLE 4. Number of subjects ranking reinforced photographs higher and number ranking them lower than nonreinforced photographs.

Reinforced photographs ranked	Conditions			
	Heart-rate increase (N = 20)	Heart-rate decrease (N = 20)	Heart-rate increase + decrease (N = 20 + 20)	Sound increase + sound decrease (N = 10 + 9)[a]
Higher	14	14	28	7
Lower	6	6	12	12
p value (sign test)	ns	ns	.02	ns

[a]One subject could not be contacted for the interview.

with the previous analyses. In comparison to the control subjects, more of the experimental subjects ranked the reinforced photographs as more attractive than the nonreinforced ones ($X^2 = 4.57$, $p < .05$). Thus, differential heart-rate feedback has had effects which are relatively long lasting (mean delay = 31.25 days). Presumed internal reactions have served as cues and have resulted in distinctly different evaluations of emotional stimuli.

DISCUSSION

The major hypothesis of this study has received considerable experimental support. When a subject thought that his heart had reacted markedly to certain slides of seminude females, he rated these slides as more attractive and chose them more often than slides that he thought had not affected his heart rate. These results are exactly what one would have expected had heart-rate changes and veridical feelings of palpitation been pharmacologically induced to some slides but not to others. The mechanism operating to produce these effects is presumably the same regardless of the veridicality of the feedback. Internal events are a source of cognitive information and, as Schachter has proposed, individuals will want to evaluate and understand this kind of information. When an emotional explanation is prepotent, they will label their reactions accordingly. This process is apparently what has been observed in the present experiment. The subjects did attempt to evaluate their reactions, and, having done so, the conditions were such that it was most appropriate for them to explain their reactions by referring to the slides and to interpret them as indicating varying degrees of attraction.

A given heart-rate reaction, however, was not always evaluated as attraction. Post-experimental interviews revealed that, at times, a particular reaction was attributed to surprise, since the subject was daydreaming, and the presentation of the slide shook him out of his reverie, or to a sudden fit of coughing or sneezing, or to a slight resemblance to a former girl friend. It was often evident that these

alternative explanations were sought when subjects could not convince themselves that they liked a particular slide. In such cases, it was apparently necessary for them to explain their reactions by referring to other causes. The subjects' attempts to label their reactions suggest that the attractiveness estimates reflected more than shallow verbal definitions of internal reactions. A number of subjects seemed to actively persuade themselves that a reinforced nude was attractive. They reported looking at the slide more closely, and it was evident that they attempted to justify the feedback by magnifying the girl's positive characteristics. Although these subjects realized that they were looking for an explanation for the feedback, they did not feel that they were distorting the slide. Closer inspection simply showed them what their "subconscious" knew all the time. The girl's breasts or buttocks were indeed nicer than they originally thought. Although there is no systematic evidence available, it would be difficult to explain how the feedback could still have effects after several weeks were it not for a process similar to this active self-persuasion.

It is of some interest to consider whether the heart-rate feedback had a direct physiological excitatory effect. If the bogus heart-rate changes resulted in actual physiological change, the differential attractiveness ratings might be attributed to veridical internal cues rather than nonveridical ones. Although physiological variables were not measured there is little reason to suspect that the bogus feedback had any direct effects other than cognitive ones. If these auditory stimuli had excitatory effects that were not due to their "meaning," then the extraneous-sound subjects should have manifested differential attractiveness ratings depending upon the slide-sound change contingencies. However, the differences observed for these subjects, between their ratings of the reinforced and nonreinforced stimuli, were slight and in a direction opposite to that which would be expected. Furthermore, when subjects rated their awareness of palpitations of actual *feeling* of heart beating during the experiment (4-point scale, ranging from "Not at all" to "An intense amount"), the experimental subjects reported experiencing *fewer* palpitations than did the control subjects. This effect was significant for the heart-rate increase versus extraneous-sound comparison (.6 versus 1.10, $p < .05$) and has subsequently been replicated ($p < .06$). Analysis of the data of this replication, which include galvanic skin response and heart-rate measurements, also reveals that subjects exposed to the heart-rate increase and sound increase manipulations react alike physiologically.[4] It is thus likely that the observed effects of bogus heart-rate feedback are primarily a result of cognitive factors and not physiological ones. In fact, the bogus feedback appears to mask veridical feedback by diverting the subject's attention from his actual internal reactions.

The cognitive manipulations and processes which have been emphasized in the present experiment bear some similarity to current techniques and theory concerned with the extinction of maladaptive emotional behavior. Using systematic desensitization therapy (Wolpe, 1958) phobic patients have been treated by teaching them to perform responses to phobic objects that are incompatible with the fear responses usually generated. In an experimental study, Lang and Lazovik (1963) trained snake-phobic subjects in deep muscle relaxation. The subjects were subsequently hypnotized during each of 11 therapeutic sessions and instructed to relax while imagining a number of situations in which a snake was involved. Subjects participating in this treatment were later observed to be less frightened by snakes and approximately half of them could even be induced to touch or pick up a live snake. The extinction of these well-established behaviors is presumably due to the resulting incompatibility between the induced muscular relaxation and the physiological changes ordinarily accompanying states of fear. Consider the treatment, however, from a subject's point of view. Whereas in the past he has been physiologically upset when thinking about snakes, he can now think about them without

experiencing as many marked internal sensations. His musculature is now completely relaxed and results in his being able to say, "Thinking about snakes no longer affects me internally." Similar cognitions concerning internal events have effectively influenced the labeling of emotional stimuli in the present experiment. It would seem reasonable that such cognitions are also induced during desensitization therapy and might be the primary factor contributing to the successful treatment of phobic patients. If this is so, the rather tedious muscular relaxation procedure could be replaced with another manipulation of the cognitive representation of internal events. It may be possible to eliminate phobic behaviors solely by inducing nonveridical cognitions concerning internal reactions. Such cognitions could be manipulated so that they would be incompatible with the knowledge of how one usually reacts when frightened. Snake-phobic subjects, for example, who are led to believe that thinking about or seeing snakes does not affect them internally, might reevaluate their attitudes toward snakes and become less frightened by them.

REFERENCES

Bramel, D. Selection of a target for defensive projection. *Journal of Abnormal and Social Psychology,* 1963, **66,** 318–324.

Duffy, E. *Activation and behavior.* New York: Wiley, 1962.

Gerard, H., & Rabbie, J. Fear and social comparison. *Journal of Abnormal and Social Psychology,* 1961, **62,** 586–592.

Lang, P. J., & Lazovik, A. D. Experimental desensitization of a phobia. *Journal of Abnormal and Social Psychology,* 1963, **66,** 519–525.

Latané, B., & Schachter, S. Adrenalin and avoidance learning. *Journal of Comparative and Physiological Psychology,* 1962, **65,** 369–372.

Mandler, G. Emotion. In *New directions in psychology.* New York: Holt, Rinehart & Winston, 1962. Pp. 267–343.

Nisbett, R., & Schachter, S. Cognitive manipulation of pain. *Journal of Experimental Social Psychology,* 1966, **2,** 227–236.

Schachter, S. The interaction of cognitive and physiological determinants of emotional state. In L. Berkowitz

[4] S. Valins, unpublished data.

(Ed.), *Advances in experimental social psychology,* Vol. 1. New York: Academic Press, 1964. Pp. 49–80.

Schachter, S., & Singer, J. E. Cognitive, social, and physiological determinants of emotional state. *Psychological Review,* 1962, **69,** 379–399.

Schachter, S., & Wheeler, L. Epinephrine, chlorpromazine, and amusement. *Journal of Abnormal and Social Psychology,* 1962, **65,** 121–128.

Singer, J. E. Sympathetic activation, drugs, and fright. *Journal of Comparative and Physiological Psychology,* 1963, **56,** 612–615.

Wolpe, J. *Psychotherapy by reciprocal inhibition.* Palo Alto, Calif.: Stanford University Press, 1958.

Woodworth, R. S., & Schlosberg, H. *Experimental psychology.* New York: Holt, Rinehart & Winston, 1962.

Wynne, L. C., & Solomon, R. L. Traumatic avoidance learning: Acquisition and extinction in dogs deprived of normal peripheral autonomic function. *Genetic Psychology Monographs,* 1955, **52,** 241–284.

ARTICLE 26

Some extraordinary facts about obese humans and rats

Stanley Schachter

Several years ago, when I was working on the problem of the labeling of bodily states, I first became aware of Stunkard's (Stunkard & Koch, 1964) work on obesity and gastric motility. At that time, my students and I had been working on a series of studies concerned with the interaction of cognitive and physiological determinants of emotional state (Schachter, 1964). Our experiments had all involved manipulating bodily state by injections of adrenaline or placebo and simultaneously manipulating cognitive and situational variables that were presumed to affect a subject's interpretation of his bodily state. In essence, these experiments had demonstrated that cognitive factors play a major role in determining how a subject interprets his bodily feelings. Precisely the same set of physiological symptoms—an adrenaline-induced state of sympathetic arousal—could be interpreted as euphoria, or anger, or anxiety, or indeed as no emotional state at all, depending very largely on our cognitive and situational manipulations. In short, there is not an invariant, one-to-one relationship between a set of physiological symptoms and a psychological state.

This conclusion was based entirely on studies that manipulated bodily state by the exogenous administration of adrenaline or some other agent. My interest in Stunkard's research was generated by the fact that his work suggested that the same conclusion might be valid for endogenous physiological states. In his study, Stunkard had his subjects do without breakfast and come to his laboratory at 9:00 A.M. They swallowed a gastric balloon, and for the next four hours, Stunkard continuously recorded stomach contractions. Every 15 minutes, he asked his subjects, "Do you feel hungry?" They answered "Yes" or "No," and that is all there was to the study. He has then a record of the extent to which stomach contractions coincide with self-reports of hunger. For normally sized subjects, the two coincide closely. When the stomach contracts, the nor-

Reprinted from *American Psychologist*, 1971, *26*, pp. 129–144. Copyright 1971 by the American Psychological Association. Reprinted by permission.

mal subject is likely to report hunger; when the stomach is quiescent, the normal subject is likely to say that he does not feel hungry. For the obese, on the other hand, there is little correspondence between gastric motility and self-reports of hunger. Whether or not the obese subject describes himself as hungry seems to have almost nothing to do with the state of his gut. There are, then, major individual differences in the extent to which this particular bodily activity—gastric motility—is associated with the feeling state labeled "hunger."

To pursue this lead, we (Schachter, Goldman, & Gordon, 1968) designed an experiment in which we attempted to manipulate gastric motility and the other physiological correlates of food deprivation by the obvious technique of manipulating food deprivation so that some subjects had empty stomachs and others full stomachs before entering an experimental eating situation. The experiment was disguised as a study of taste, and subjects had been asked to do without the meal (lunch or dinner) that preceded the experiment.

When a subject arrived, he was, depending on condition, either fed roast beef sandwiches or fed nothing. He was then seated in front of five bowls of crackers, presented with a long set of rating scales and told, "We want you to judge each cracker on the dimensions (salty, cheesy, garlicky, etc.) listed on these sheets. Taste as many or as few of the crackers of each type as you want in making your judgments; the important thing is that your ratings be as accurate as possible."

The subject then tasted and rated crackers for 15 minutes, under the impression that this was a taste test, and we simply counted the number of crackers that he ate. There were, of course, two types of subjects: obese subjects (from 14% to 75% overweight) and normal subjects (from 8% underweight to 9% overweight).

To review expectations: If it is correct that the obese do not label as hunger the bodily states associated with food deprivation, then this manipulation should have no effect on the amount eaten by obese subjects; on the other hand, the eating behav-

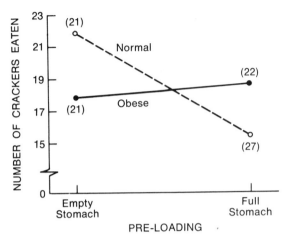

FIGURE 1.   The effects of preloading on eating.

ior of normal subjects should directly parallel the effects of the manipulation on bodily state.

It will be a surprise to no one to learn, from Figure I, that normal subjects ate considerably fewer crackers when their stomachs were full of roast beef sandwiches than when their stomachs were empty. The results for obese subjects stand in fascinating contrast. They ate as much—in fact slightly more—when their stomachs were full as when they were empty. Obviously, the actual state of the stomach has nothing to do with the eating behavior of the obese.[1]

In similar studies (Schachter, 1967; Schachter et al., 1968), we have attempted to manipulate bodily state by manipulating fear and by injecting subjects with epinephrine. Both manipulations are based on Cannon's (1915) and Carlson's (1916) demonstrations that both the state of fear and the injection of epinephrine will inhibit gastric motility and increase blood sugar—both peripheral physiological changes associated with low hunger. These manipulations have no effect at all on obese subjects, but do affect the amounts eaten by normal subjects.

[1]The obese subject's failure to regulate when preloaded with sandwiches or some other solid food has now been replicated three times. Pliner's (1970) recent work, however, indicates that the obese will regulate, though not as well as normals, when preloaded with liquid food.

It seems clear that the set of bodily symptoms the subject labels "hunger" differs for obese and normal subjects. Whether one measures gastric motility as Stunkard did, or manipulates motility and the other physiological correlates of food deprivation, as I assume my students and I have done, one finds, for normal subjects, a high degree of correspondence between the state of the gut and eating behavior and, for obese subjects, virtually no correspondence.

Whether or not they are responsive to these particular visceral cues, the obese *do* eat, and the search for the cues that trigger obese eating occupied my students' and my attention for a number of years. Since the experimental details of this search have been published (Schachter, 1967, 1968, 1971), and I believe are fairly well known, I will take time now only to summarize our conclusions—eating by the obese seems unrelated to any internal, visceral state, but is determined by external, food-relevant cues such as the sight, smell, and taste of food. Now, obviously, such external cues to some extent affect anyone's eating behavior. However, for normals these external factors clearly interact with internal state. They may affect what, where, and how much the normal eats, but chiefly when he is in a state of physiological hunger. For the obese, I suggest, internal state is irrelevant, and eating is determined largely by external cues.

As you may know, there have been a number of experiments testing this hypothesis about the external sensitivity of the obese. To convey some feeling for the nature of the supporting data, I will describe two typical experiments. In one of these, Nisbett (1968a) examined the effects of the sight of food. He reasoned that if the sight of food is a potent cue, the externally sensitive, obese person should eat just as long as food is in sight, and when, in effect, he has consumed all of the available cues, he should stop and make no further attempt to eat. In contrast, the amounts eaten by a normal subject should depend on his physiological needs, not on the quantity of food in sight. Thus, if only a small amount of food is in sight but the subject is given the opportunity to forage for more, the normal subject should eat more than the obese subject. In contrast, if a large amount of food is in sight, the obese should eat more than the normal subject.

To test these expectations, Nisbett provided subjects, who had not eaten lunch, with either one or three roast beef sandwiches. He told them to help themselves and, as he was leaving, pointed to a refrigerator across the room and said, "There are dozens more sandwiches in the refrigerator. Have as many as you want." His results are presented in Table 1. As you can see, obese subjects ate significantly more than normals when presented with three sandwiches, but ate significantly less than normals when presented with only one sandwich.

In another study, Decke (1971) examined the effects of taste on eating. She reasoned that taste, like the sight or smell of food, is essentially an external cue. Good taste, then, should stimulate the obese to eat more than normals, and bad taste, of course, should have the reverse effect.

In a taste test context, Decke provided her subjects with either a decent vanilla milk shake or with a vanilla milk shake plus quinine. The effects of this

TABLE 1.   Effect of quantity of visible food on amounts eaten.

Subjects	No. sandwiches	
	One	Three
Normal	1.96	1.88
Obese	1.48	2.32

Note.—From Nisbett (1968a).

TABLE 2.   Effect of taste on eating.

Subjects	Ounces consumed in	
	Good taste	Bad taste
Normal	10.6	6.4
Obese	13.9	2.6

Note.—From Decke (1971).

taste manipulation are conveyed in Table 2 where, as you can see, obese subjects drank more than normals when the milk shake was good and drank considerably less when the milk shake had been laced with quinine.

Now, anyone who sees Decke's milk shake data and who is familiar with physiological psychology will note that this is precisely what Miller, Bailey, and Stevenson (1950) found and what Teitelbaum (1955) found in the lesioned hyperphagic rat. For those of you who are unfamiliar with this preparation, let me review the facts about this animal. If you make bilateral lesions in the ventromedial nuclei of the hypothalamus, you are likely to get an animal that will eat prodigious amounts of food and will eventually achieve monumental weight—a creature of nightmares. This has been demonstrated for rats, cats, mice, monkeys, rabbits, goats, dogs, and sparrows. Classic descriptions of these preparations portray an animal that immediately after the operation staggers over to its food hopper and shovels in food. For several weeks, this voracious eating continues, and there is, of course, very rapid weight gain. This is called the dynamic phase of hyperphagia. Finally, a plateau is reached, at which point the animal's weight levels off, and its food intake drops to a level only slightly above that of the normal animal. This is called the static phase. During both the static and the dynamic stages, the lesioned animal is also characterized as markedly inactive, and as irascible, emotional, and generally bitchy.

Now it turns out that though the lesioned animal is normally a heavy eater, if you add quinine to its food it drastically decreases its intake to levels far below that of a normal animal's whose food has been similarly tainted. On the other hand, if to its normal food you add dextrose, or lard, or something that is apparently tasty to a rat, the lesioned animal increases its intake to levels considerably above its regular intake and above the intake of a control rat whose food has also been enriched.

The similarity of these facts about the finickiness of the lesioned rat to Decke's findings in her milk shake experiment is, of course, striking, and many people (notably Nisbett, 1968a, 1971) have pointed to this and other similarities between our data on obese humans and the physiologist's data on the obese rat. In order to determine if there was anything more to this than an engaging, occasional resemblance between two otherwise remotely connected sets of data, Judith Rodin and I decided to treat the matter dead seriously and, where possible, to make a point-for-point comparison of every fact we could learn about the hypothalamic, obese rat with every fact we could learn about the obese human. Before describing the results of our work, I would like, however, to be sure that you are aware of the areas of my expertise. I am not a physiological psychologist. Though I am pretty sure that I've eaten a hypothalamus, I doubt that I've ever seen one. When I say something like "bilateral lesions of the ventromedial nuclei of the hypothalamus," you can be sure that I've memorized it. I make this personal confession because of the dilemma that Rodin, also a physiological innocent, and I faced in our work. Though we couldn't have succeeded, we attempted to read *everything* about the ventromedial lesioned rat. If you've ever made this sort of attempt, you may have been seized by the same despair as were we when it sometimes seemed as if there were no such thing as a fact that *someone* had not failed to confirm. (I include in this sweeping generalization, by the way, the apparent fact that a ventromedial lesion produces a hyperphagic, obese animal—see Reynolds, 1963, and Rabin and Smith, 1968.) And it sometimes seemed as if there were no such thing as an experiment which *someone* had not failed to replicate. Since I happen to have spent my college physics lab course personally disproving most of the laws of physics, I cannot say that I find this particularly surprising, but if one is trying to decide what is the fact, it is a depressing state of affairs. In our own areas of expertise, this probably isn't too serious a problem. Each of us in our specialties knows how to evaluate a piece of work. In a field in which you are not expert, you simply cannot, except in the crudest of cases, evaluate. If several experimenters have different results, you just don't know which to believe. In order to cope with this dilemma, Rodin and I decided to treat each of our facts in batting average terms. For each fact, I will inform you of the number of studies that have been concerned with the fact and the proportion of these studies that work out in a given direction. To be included in the batting average, we required only that a study present all or a substantial portion of its data, rather than report the author's impressions or present only the data of one or two presumably representative cases. I should also note that in all cases we have relied on the data and not on what the experimenter said about the data. It may seem silly to make this point explicit, but it is the case that in a few studies, for some perverse reason, the experimenter's conclusions simply have nothing to do with his data. Finally, I should note that in all comparisons of animal and human data, I will consider the data only for animals in the static phase of obesity, animals who, like our human subjects, are already fat. In general, however, the results for dynamic and static animals are quite similar.

As a shorthand method of making comparisons between studies and species, I shall throughout the rest of this article employ what we can call a Fat to Normal (F/N) ratio in which we simply get an index by dividing the magnitude of the effect for fat subjects by the magnitude of the effect for normal control subjects. Thus, if in a particular study the fat rats ate an average of 15 grams of food and normal rats ate 10 grams, the F/N ratio would be 1.50, indicating that the fat rats ate 50% more food than normal rats.

To begin our comparisons, let us return to the effects of taste on eating behavior. We know that fat human beings eat more of a good-tasting food than do normal human beings and that they eat less of bad-tasting food than do normals. The physiologists have done almost identical experiments to ours, and in Line 1 of Table 3 we can compare the effects of good-tasting food on lesioned animals and on men. You will notice on the left that Rodin and I found six studies on lesioned animals, in this case largely rats.

TABLE 3. Effects of taste on eating.

Condition	Animals		Humans	
	Batting average	Mean F/N	Mean F/N	Batting average
Good food	5/6	1.45	1.42	2/2
Bad food	3/4	.76	.84	1/2

Note.—F/N = Fat to normal ratio.

Batting average: five of the six studies indicate that lesioned, static, obese animals eat more of a good-tasting food than do their normal controls. The average F/N ratio for these six studies is 1.45, indicating that fat rats on the average eat 45% more of good-tasting food than do normal rats. On the right side of the table, you can see that there have been two human studies, and that both of these studies indicate that fat humans eat more of good-tasting food than do normal humans. The average F/N ratio for humans is 1.42, indicating that fat humans eat 42% more of good-tasting food than do normally sized humans.[2]

Incidentally, please keep in mind throughout this exercise that the left side of each table will always contain the data for lesioned animals, very largely rats, that have been abused by a variety of people named Epstein, and Teitelbaum, and Stellar, and Miller, and so on. The right side of each table will always contain the data for humans, mostly Columbia College students, nice boys who go home every Friday night, where, I suppose, they too are abused by a variety of people named Epstein, and Teitelbaum, and Stellar, and Miller.

In line 2 of Table 3, we have the effects of bad taste on consumption. For both animals and men, in all of these studies bad taste was manipulated by the addition of quinine to the food. There are four animal studies; three of the four indicate that fat ani-

[2] The technically informed reader undoubtedly will wish to know precisely which studies and what data are included in Tables 3 and 4. There are so many studies involved that, within the context of this paper, it is impossible to supply this information. Dr. Rodin and I are preparing a monograph on this work which will, of course, provide full details on such matters.

mals eat less than normal animals, and the average F/N ratio is .76. There are two human studies: one of the two indicates that fats eat considerably less bad food than normals; the other indicates no significant difference between the two groups, and the mean F/N ratio for these two studies is .84. For this particular fact, the data are more fragile than one would like, but the trends for the two species are certainly parallel.

To continue this examination of parallel facts: the eating habits of the lesioned rats have been thoroughly studied, particularly by Teitelbaum and Campbell (1958). It turns out that static obese rats eat on the average slightly, not considerably, more than normal rats. They also eat fewer meals per day, eat more per meal, and eat more rapidly than do normal animals. For each of these facts, we have parallel data for humans. Before presenting these data, I should note that for humans, I have, wherever possible, restricted myself to behavioral studies, studies in which the investigators have actually measured how much their subjects eat. I hope no one will be offended, I assume no one will be surprised, if I say that I am skeptical of the self-reports of fat people about how much they eat or exercise.[3] For those of you who feel that this is high-handed selection of studies, may I remind you of Stunkard's famous chronic fat patients who were fed everything that, in interviews, they admitted to eating daily, and who all steadily lost weight on this diet.

Considering first the average amount eaten per day when on ad-lib feeding of ordinary lab chow or pellets, you will note in Line 1 of Table 4 that consistently static obese rats eat somewhat (19%) more than do their normal counterparts. The data for humans are derived from all of the studies I know of in which eating is placed in a noshing, or ad-lib, context; that is, a bowl of ordinary food, usually nuts or crackers, is placed in the room, the experiment presumably has nothing to do with eating, and the subject is free to eat or not, as he chooses, just as is a rat

[3]In three of four such self-report studies, fat people report eating considerably less food than do normals.

TABLE 4. Eating habits.

Variable	Animals		Humans	
	Batting average	Mean F/N	Mean F/N	Batting average
Amount of food eaten ad lib	9/9	1.19	1.16	2/3
No. meals per day	4/4	.85	.92	3/3
Amount eaten per meal	2/2	1.34	1.29	5/5
Speed of eating	1/1	1.28	1.26	1/1

Note.—F/N = Fat to normal ratio.

in its cage. In two of the three experiments conducted in this context, obese subjects eat slightly more than do normals; in the third experiment, the two groups eat precisely the same number of crackers. For both humans and rats, then, the fat subject eats only slightly more than the normal subject.

Turning next to the number of meals per day, we note on Line 2 of Table 4 that for both rats and humans, fatter subjects consistently eat fewer meals per day. (A rat meal is defined by Teitelbaum and Campbell, 1958, as "any burst of food intake of at least five pellets separated by at least 5 min. from any other burst [p. 138].") For humans, these particular data are based on self-report or interview studies, for I know of no relevant behavioral data. In any case, again the data for the lesioned rat and the obese human correspond very closely indeed.

From the previous two facts, it should, of course, follow that obese subjects will eat more per meal than normal subjects, and, as can be seen in Line 3 of Table 4, this is the case for both lesioned rats and obese humans. The data for rats are based on two experiments that simply recorded the amount of food eaten per eating burst. The data for humans are based on all experiments in which a plate of food, usually sandwiches, is placed before a subject, and he is told to help himself to lunch or dinner.

Our final datum on eating habits is the speed of eating. Teitelbaum and Campbell (1958) simply recorded the number of pellets their animals ate per minute. Since there is nothing else to do when you are sitting behind a one-way screen watching a subject eat, Nisbett (1968b—data not reported in paper) recorded the number of spoonfuls of ice cream his subjects ate per minute. The comparison of the two studies is drawn in Line 4 of Table 4, where you will note an unsettling similarity in the rate at which lesioned rats and obese humans outspeed their normal counterparts.[4]

All told, then, in the existing literature, Rodin and I found a total of six items of behavior on which it is possible to make rather precise comparisons between lesioned rats and obese humans. These are mostly nonobvious facts, and the comparisons drawn between the two sets of experiments do not attempt to push the analogies beyond the point of common sense. I do not think there can be much debate about pellets versus spoonfuls of ice cream consumed per minute as equivalent measures of eating rate. For all six facts in the existing literature, the parallels between the species are striking. What the lesioned, fat rat does, the obese human does.

In addition to these facts, we identified two other areas of behavior in which it is possible to draw somewhat more fanciful, though still not ridiculous, comparisons between the species. These are the areas of emotionality and of activity. Though there has been little systematic study of emotionality, virtually everyone who has worked with these animals agrees that the lesioned animals are hyperexcitable, easily startled, overemotional, and generally bitchy to handle. In addition, work by Singh (1969) and research on active avoidance learning do generally support this characterization of the lesioned animal as an emotional beast.

For humans, we have two experiments from which it is possible to draw conclusions about emotionality. In one of these (Schachter et al., 1968), we manipulated fear by threat of painful electric shock. On a variety of rating scales, fat subjects acknowledged that they were somewhat more frightened and anxious than did normal subjects. In a second experiment, Rodin (1970) had her subjects listen to an audio tape while they were working at

either a monitoring or a proofreading task. The tapes were either neutral (requiring the subject to think about either rain or seashells) or emotionally charged (requiring the subject to think about his own death or about the bombing of Hiroshima). The emotionally charged tapes produced dramatic differences between subjects. On a variety of rating scales, the obese described themselves as considerably more upset and disturbed than did normal subjects; they reported more palpitations and changes in breathing rate than did normals; and performance, at either the proofreading or monitoring tasks, deteriorated dramatically more for obese than for normal subjects. Again, then, the data are consistent, for both the lesioned animal and the obese human seem to react more emotionally than their normal counterparts.

Finally, on activity, numerous studies using stabilimeter cages or activity wheels have demonstrated that the lesioned animal is markedly less active than the normal animal. This is not, I should add, a totally trivial fact indicating only that the lesioned animal has trouble shlepping his immense bulk around the cage, for the dynamic hyperphagic rat—who though not yet fat, will be—is quite as lethargic as his obese counterpart. On the human side, Bullen, Reed, and Mayer (1964) have taken movies of girls at camp during their scheduled periods of swimming, tennis, and volleyball. They categorize each camper for her degree of activity or exertion during these periods, and do find that the normal campers are more active than are the obese girls.

All told, then, Rodin and I found a total of eight facts, indicating a perfect parallel between the behavior of the lesioned rat and the obese human. We have, so far, found no fact on which the two species differ. Now all of this has proved such an engaging exercise that my students and I decided to play "real" scientist, and we constructed a matrix. We simply listed every fact we could find about the lesioned animals and every fact we could find about obese humans. I have told you about those facts for which parallel data exist. There are, however, nu-

[4]Fat rats do not drink more rapidly than do normals. There are no comparable data for humans.

merous holes in the matrix—facts for rats for which no parallel human data have yet been collected, and vice versa. For the past year, we have been engaged in filling in these holes—designing for humans, experiments that have no particular rhyme or reason except that someone once did such an experiment on lesioned rats. For example, it is a fact that though lesioned rats will outeat normal rats when food is easily available, they will not lift a paw if they have to work to get food. In a Skinner box setup, Teitelbaum (1957) finds that at FR1, when one press yields one pellet, fat lesioned rats outpress normal. As the payoff decreases, however, fat rats press less and less until at FR256, they do not manage to get a single pellet during a 12-hour experimental session, whereas normal rats are still industriously pressing away. Similarly, Miller et al. (1950) found that though lesioned rats ate more than normal controls when an unweighted lid covered the food dish, they ate less than did the controls when a 75-gram weight was fastened to the lid. They also found that the lesioned rats ran more slowly down an alley to food than controls did and pulled less hard when temporarily restrained by a harness. In short, fat rats will not work to get food.

Since there was no human parallel to these studies, Lucy Friedman and I designed a study in which, when a subject arrived, he was asked simply to sit at the experimenter's desk and fill out a variety of personality tests and questionnaires. Besides the usual student litter, there was a bag of almonds on the desk. The experimenter helped herself to a nut, invited the subject to do the same, and then left him alone with his questionnaires and nuts for 15 minutes. There were two sets of conditions. In one, the nuts had shells on them; in the other, the nuts had no shells. I assume we agree that eating nuts with shells is considerably more work than eating nuts with no shells.

The top half of Table 5 presents for normal subjects the numbers who do and do not eat nuts in the two conditions. As you can see, shells or no shells has virtually no impact on normal subjects. Fifty-five percent of normals eat nuts without shells, and

TABLE 5. Effects of work on the eating behavior of normal and fat subjects.

Nuts have	Number who	
	Eat	Don't eat
Normal subjects		
Shells	10	10
No shells	11	9
Fat subjects		
Shells	1	19
No shells	19	1

50% eat nuts with shells. I am a little self-conscious about the data for obese subjects, for it looks as if I were too stupid to know how to fake data. I know how to fake data, and were I to do so, the bottom half of Table 5 certainly would not look the way it does. When the nuts have no shells, 19 of 20 fat subjects eat nuts. When the nuts have shells on them, 1 out of 20 fat subjects eats. Obviously, the parallel to Miller's and to Teitelbaum's rats is perfect. When the food is easy to get at, fat subjects, rat or human, eat more than normals; when the food is hard to get at, fat subjects eat less than normals.

Incidentally, as a casual corollary of these and other findings, one could expect that, given acceptable food, fat eaters would be more likely than normals to choose the easiest way of eating. In order to check on this, Lucy Friedman, Joel Handler, and I went to a large number of Chinese and Japanese restaurants, categorized each patron as he entered the restaurant as obese or normal, and then simply noted whether he ate with chopsticks or with silverware. Among Occidentals, for whom chopsticks can be an ordeal, we found that almost five times the proportion of normal eaters ate with chopsticks as did obese eaters—22.4% of normals and 4.7% of the obese ate with chopsticks.

In another matrix-hole-filling experiment, Patricia Pliner (1970) has demonstrated that obese humans, like lesioned rats, do not regulate food consumption when they are preloaded with solids but, again like the rats, do regulate when they are pre-loaded with liquids.

In addition to these experiments, we are currently conducting studies on pain sensitivity and on passive versus active avoidance learning—all designed to fill in more holes in our human-lesioned rat matrix. To date, we have a total of 12 nonobvious facts in which the behaviors of lesioned rats parallel perfectly the behaviors of obese humans. Though I cannot believe that as our matrix-hole-filling experiments continue, this perfect parallelism will continue, I submit that even now these are mind-boggling data. I would also submit, however, that we have played this enchanting game just about long enough. This is, after all, science through analogy—a sport I recommend with the same qualifications and enthusiasms with which I recommend skiing—and it is time that we asked what on earth does it all mean? To which at this point I can only answer ruefully that I wish to God I really knew.

On its most primitive level, I suppose that I would love to play doctor and issue pronouncements such as, ''Madam, you have a very sick hypothalamus.'' And, indeed, I do know of one case of human obesity (Reeves & Plum, 1969) accompanied by a precisely localized neoplasm that destroyed the ventromedial hypothalamus. This is an astonishing case study, for the lady reads like a lesioned rat—she ate immense amounts of food, as much as 10,000 calories a day, grew impressively fat and was apparently a wildly emotional creature given to frequent outbursts of laughing, crying, and rage. Now I am not, of course, going to suggest that this lady is anything but a pathological extreme. The only vaguely relevant study I know of is a morphological study (Maren, 1955) of the hypothalami of genetically obese mice, an animal whose behavior also resembles the lesioned rat's, which found no structural differences between obese and normal mice.

Mrosovsky (1971) has been developing a more sober hypothesis. Comparing the hibernator and the ventromedial lesioned rat, Mrosovsky has been playing much the same analogical game as have I, and he, too, has noted the marked behavioral similarities of his two species to the obese human. He hypothesizes that the unlesioned, obese animal, rodent or human, has a ventromedial hypothalamus that is functionally quiescent. Though I would be willing to bet that when the appropriate biochemical and electrophysiological studies are done, Mrosovsky will be proven correct, I do not believe that this is a fact which is of fundamental interest to psychologists. Most of us, I suspect, have long been convinced, psychodynamics notwithstanding, that there is *something* biologically responsible for human obesity, and to be able suddenly to point a finger at an offending structure would not really put us much ahead. After all, we've known about the adrenal medulla and emotion for more than 50 years, and I doubt that this particular bit of knowledge has been of much help in our understanding of aggression, or fear, or virtually any other emotional state.

If it is true that the ventromedial hypothalamus is functionally quiescent, for us the question must be, for what function, psychologically speaking, is it quiescent? What processes, or inputs, or outputs are mediated by this particular structure? Speculation and theorizing about the functions of this area have tended to be cautious and modest. Essentially, two suggestions have been made—one that the area is a satiety center, and the other that the area is an emotionality center. Both Miller (1964) and Stellar (1954) have tentatively suggested that the ventromedial area is a satiety center—that in some fashion it monitors the signals indicating a sufficiency of food and inhibits the excitatory (Eat! Eat!) impulses initiated in the lateral hypothalamus. This inhibitory-satiety mechanism can account for the hyperphagia of the lesioned animals and, consequently, for their obesity. It can also account for most of the facts that I outlined earlier about the daily eating habits of these animals. It cannot by itself, however, account for the finickiness of these animals, nor can it, as I believe I can show, account for the apparent unwillingness of these animals to work for food. Finally, this hypothesis is simply irrelevant to the demonstrated inactivity and hyperemotionality of these animals. This irrelevance, however, is not critical if one assumes, as does Stellar, that discrete neural centers, also located in the ventromedial area, control activity and emotionality. The satiety theory, then, can account for some, but by no means all, of the critical facts about eating, and it has nothing to say about activity or emotionality.

As a theoretically more ambitious alternative, Grossman (1966, 1967) has proposed that the ventromedial area be considered the emotionality center and that the facts about eating be derived from this assumption. By definition, Grossman's hypothesis accounts for the emotionality of these animals, and his own work on active avoidance learning certainly supports the emotionality hypothesis. I must confess, however, that I have difficulty in understanding just why these emotional animals become fat. In essence, Grossman (1966) assumes that "lesions in or near the VMH sharply increase an animal's affective responsiveness to apparently all sensory stimuli [p. 1]." On the basis of this general statement, he suggests that "the 'finickiness' of the ventromedial animal might then reflect a change in its affective response to taste." This could, of course, account for the fact that lesioned animals eat more very good- and less very bad-tasting food than do normals. However, I simply find it hard to believe that this affective hypothesis can account for the basic fact about these animals—that for weeks on end, the lesioned animals eat grossly more of ordinary, freely available lab chow.

Grossman (1967) attributes the fact that lesioned animals will not work for food to their "exaggerated response to handling, the test situation, the deprivation regimen, and the requirement of having to work for their daily bread [p. 358]." I suppose all of this is possible, I simply find it farfetched. At the very least, the response to handling and to the deprivation regime should be just as exaggerated whether the reinforcement schedule is FR1 or FR256 and the lesioned animals do press more than the normals at FR1.

My skepticism, however, is irrelevant, and Grossman may be correct. There are, however, at least two facts with which, it seems to me, Grossman's hypothesis cannot cope. First, it would seem to me that an animal with an affective response to food would be likely to eat more rather than less often per day, as is the fact. Second, it is simply common sense to expect that an animal with strong "affective responsiveness to all sensory stimuli" will be a very active animal indeed, but the lesioned animal is presumably hypoactive.

None of the existing theories, then, can cope with all of the currently available facts. For the remainder of this article, I am going to try my hand at developing a hypothesis that I believe can cope with more of the facts than can the available alternatives. It is a hypothesis that derives entirely from our work on human obesity. I believe, however, that it can explain as many of the facts about ventromedial-lesioned rats as it can about the human obese. If future experimental work on animals proves this correct, it would certainly suggest that science by analogy has merits other than its entertainment value.

The gist of our findings on humans is this—the eating behavior of the obese is under external, rather than internal, control. In effect, the obese seem stimulus-bound. When a food-relevant cue is present, the obese are more likely to eat and to eat a great deal than are normals. When such a cue is absent, the obese are less likely to try to eat or to complain about hunger. Though I have not, in this article, developed this latter point, there is evidence that, in the absence of food-relevant cues, the obese have a far easier time fasting than do normals, while in the presence of such cues, they have a harder time fasting (Goldman, Jaffa, & Schachter, 1968).

Since it is a little hard to believe that such stimulus-binding is limited to food-relevant cues, for some time now my students and I have been concerned with the generalizability of these facts. Given our starting point, this concern has led to some rather odd little experiments. For example, Judith Rodin, Peter Herman, and I have asked subjects to look at slides on which are portrayed 13 objects or words. Each slide is exposed for five seconds, and the subject is then asked to recall what he saw. Fat subjects recall more objects than do normal subjects. The experiment has been replicated, and this appears to be a reliable phenomenon.

In another study, Rodin, Herman, and I compared fat and normal subjects on simple and on complex or disjunctive reaction time. For simple reaction time, they are instructed to lift their finger from a telegraph key as soon as the stimulus light comes on. On this task, there are no differences between obese and normal subjects. For complex reaction time, there are two stimulus lights and two telegraph keys, and subjects are instructed to lift their left finger when the right light comes on and lift their right finger when the left light comes on. Obese subjects respond more rapidly and make fewer errors. Since this was a little hard to believe, this study was repeated three times—each time with the same results—the obese are simply better at complex reaction time than are normals. I do not pretend to understand these results, but they do seem to indicate that, for some reason, the obese are more efficient stimulus or information processors.

At this stage, obviously, this is shotgun research which, in coordination with the results of our eating experiments, seems to indicate that it may be useful to more generally characterize the obese as stimulus-bound and to hypothesize that any stimulus, above a given intensity level, is more likely to evoke an appropriate response from an obese than from a normal subject.

Our first test of implications of this hypothesis in a noneating setting is Rodin's (1970) experiment on the effects of distraction on performance. She reasoned that if the stimulus-binding hypothesis is correct, distracting, irrelevant stimuli should be more disruptive for obese than for normal subjects when they are performing a task requiring concentration. Presumably, the impinging stimulus is more likely to grip the attention of the stimulus-bound obese subject. To test this guess, she had her subjects work at a simple proofreading task. In one condition, the

subjects corrected proof with no distractions at all. In the three other conditions, they corrected proof while listening to recorded tapes that varied in the degree to which they were likely to grip a subject's attention, and therefore distract him. The results are presented in Figure 2, where, as you can see, the obese are better at proofreading when undistracted but their performance seriously deteriorates as they are distracted until, at extreme distraction, they are considerably worse than normals. Rodin finds precisely the same pattern of results, by the way, in a similar study in which she uses the complex reaction time task I have already described rather than the proofreading task. For humans, then, there is evidence, outside of the eating context, to support the hypothesis.

Let us return to consideration of the ventromedial lesioned animal and examine the implications of the hypothesis that any stimulus, above a given intensity level, is more likely to evoke an appropriate response from a lesioned than from an intact animal. This is a hypothesis which is, in many ways, similar to Grossman's hypothesis and, on the face of it, would appear to be vulnerable to exactly the same criticisms as I have leveled at his theory. There are, however, crucial differences that will become evident as I elaborate this notion. I assume it is self-

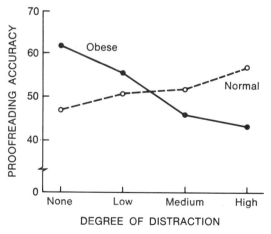

FIGURE 2. The effects of distraction on performance (from Rodin, 1970).

evident that my hypothesis can explain the emotionality of the lesioned animals and, with the exception of meal frequency—a fact to which I will return—can account for virtually all of our facts about the daily eating habits of these animals. I will, therefore, begin consideration of the hypothesis by examining its implications for those facts that have been most troubling for alternative formulations and by examining those facts that seem to most clearly contradict my own hypothesis.

Let us turn first to the perverse and fascinating fact that though lesioned animals will outeat normals when food is easily available, they simply will not work for food. In my terms, this is an incomplete fact which may prove only that a remote food stimulus will not evoke a food-acquiring response. It is the case that in the experiments concerned with this fact, virtually every manipulation of work has covaried the remoteness or prominence of the food cue. Food at the end of a long alleyway is obviously a more remote cue than food in the animal's food dish. Pellets available only after 256 presses of a lever are certainly more remote food stimuli than pellets available after each press of a lever. If the stimulus-binding hypothesis is correct, it should be anticipated that, in contrast to the results when the food cue is remote, the lesioned animal will work harder than the normal animal when the food stimulus is prominent and compelling. Though the appropriate experiment has not yet been done on rats, to my delight I have learned recently that such an experiment has been done on humans by William Johnson (1970), who independently has been pursuing a line of thought similar to mine.

Johnson seated his subject at a table, fastened his hand in a harness, and, to get food, required the subject for 12 minutes to pull, with his index finger, on a ring that was attached by wire to a seven-pound weight. He received food on a VR50 schedule—that is, on the average, a subject received a quarter of a sandwich for every 50 pulls of the ring. Obviously, this was moderately hard work.

To vary stimulus prominence, Johnson manipulated food visibility and prior taste of food. In "food visible" conditions, he placed beside the subject one desirable sandwich covered in a transparent wrap. In addition, as the subject satisfied the VR requirements, he placed beside him quarter sandwiches similarly wrapped. In "food invisible" conditions, Johnson followed exactly the same procedures, but wrapped the sandwiches in white, nontransparent shelf paper. Subjects, of course, did not eat until they had completed their 12 minutes of labor.

As a second means of varying cue prominence, half of the subjects ate a quarter of a very good sandwich immediately before they began work. The remaining subjects ate a roughly equivalent portion of plain white bread.

In Figure 3, you can see the effects of these manipulations on effort. I have arranged the conditions along the dimension of food cue prominence—ranging from no prominent food cues to two promi-

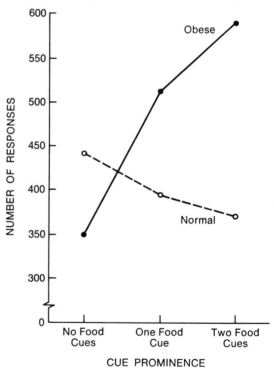

FIGURE 3.   The effect of food cue prominence on effort (from Johnson, 1970).

nent food cues—that is, the subjects ate a quarter sandwich and the food was visible. As you can see, the stimulus prominence manipulations have a marked effect on the obese, for they work far harder when the food cues are prominent and compelling than when they are inconspicuous. In contrast, cue prominence has relatively little effect on normal subjects.

Please note also that these results parallel Miller's and Teitelbaum's results with lesioned rats. When the food cues are remote, the obese human works less hard for food than the normally sized human. The fact that this relationship flips when the cues are prominent is, of course, a delight to me, and wouldn't it be absorbing to replicate this experiment on lesioned rats?

Let us turn next to the fact that lesioned rats are hypoactive. If ever a fact were incompatible with a hypothesis, this one is it. Surely an animal that is more responsive to any stimulus should be hyper-, not hypoactive. Yet this is a most peculiar fact—for it remains a fact only because one rather crucial finding in the literature has been generally overlooked and because the definition of activity seems restricted to measures obtained in running wheels or in stabilimeter-type living cages.

Studies of activity have with fair consistency reported dramatically less activity for lesioned than for normal rats. With one exception, these studies report data of total activity per unit time, making no distinction between periods when the animal room was quiet and undisturbed and periods involving the mild ferment of animal-tending activities. Gladfelter and Brobeck (1962), however, report activity data separately for the "43-hour period when the constant-temperature room was dark and quiet and the rats were undisturbed" and for the "five-hour period when the room was lighted and the rats were cared for [p. 811]." During the quiet time, these investigators find precisely what almost everyone else does—lesioned rats are markedly less active. During the animal-tending period, however, lesioned animals are just about as active as normal animals. In short, when the stimulus field is rela-

tively barren and there is little to react to, the ventromedial animal is inactive; when the field is made up of the routine noises, stirrings, and disturbances involved in tending an animal laboratory, the lesioned animal is just about as active as the normal animal.

Though this is an instructive fact, it hardly proves my hypothesis, which specifies that above a given stimulus intensity the lesioned animal should be *more* reactive than the normal animal. Let us, then, ask—is there any evidence that lesioned animals are more active than normal animals? There is, if you are willing to grant that specific activities such as lever pressing or avoidance behavior are as much "activity" as the gross, overall measures obtained in stabilimeter-mounted living cages.

In his study of activity, Teitelbaum (1957) has distinguished between random and food-directed activity. As do most other investigators, he finds that in their cages, lesioned rats are much less active than are normals. During a 12-hour stint in a Skinner box, however, when on an FR1 schedule, the lesioned animals are more active; that is, they press more than do normals. Thus, when the food cue is salient and prominent, as it is on an FR1 schedule, the lesioned animal is very active indeed. And, as you know, when the food cue is remote, as it is on an FR64 or FR256 schedule, the lesioned animal is inactive.

Since lever pressing is activity in pursuit of food, I suppose one should be cautious in accepting these data as support for my argument. Let us turn, then, to avoidance learning where most of the experiments are unrelated to food.

In overall batting average terms,[5] no area could

---

[5] Of all the behavioral areas so far considered, avoidance learning is probably the one for which it makes least sense either to adopt a batting average approach or to attempt to treat the research as a conceptually equivalent set of studies. Except in this area, the great majority of experiments have used, as subjects, rats with electrolytically produced lesions. In the avoidance learning area, the subjects have been mice, rats, and cats; the lesions are variously electrolytically produced, produced by gold thioglucose injections, or are "functional" lesions produced by topical application of atropine or some other agent.

be messier than this one, for in three of six studies, lesioned animals are better and in three worse at avoidance than normals. However, if one distinguishes between passive and active avoidance, things become considerably more coherent.

In active avoidance studies, a conditioned stimulus, such as a light or buzzer, precedes a noxious event such as electrifying the floor grid. To avoid the shock, the animal must perform some action such as jumping into the nonelectrified compartment of a shuttle box. In three of four such studies, the lesioned animals learn considerably more rapidly than do normal animals. By this criterion, at least, lesioned animals are more reactive than normal animals.[6] Parenthetically, it is amusing to note that the response latencies of the lesioned animal are smaller (Grossman, 1966) than those of the normal animal, just as in our studies of complex reaction time, obese humans are faster than normal humans.

In contrast to these results, lesioned animals do considerably worse than normal animals in passive avoidance studies. In these studies, the animal's water dish or the lever of a Skinner box are electrified so that if, during the experimental period, the animal touches these objects he receives a shock. In both of the studies we have so far found on passive learning, the lesioned animals do considerably worse than normal animals. They either press the lever or touch the water dish more than do normals and accordingly are shocked far more often. Thus, when the situation requires a response if the animal is to avoid shock, the lesioned animal does better

than the normal animal. Conversely, if the situation requires response quiescence if the animal is. to avoid shock, the lesioned animal does far worse than the normal animal. This pair of facts, I suggest, provides strong support for the hypothesis that beyond a given stimulus intensity, the lesioned animal is more reactive than the normal animal. I would also suggest that without some variant of this hypothesis, the overall pattern of results on avoidance learning is incoherent.

All in all, then, one can make a case of sorts for the suggestion that there are specifiable circumstances in which lesioned animals will be more active. It is hardly an ideal case, and only an experiment that measures the effects of systematically varied stimulus field richness on gross activity can test the point.

These ruminations on activity do suggest a refinement of the general hypothesis and also, I trust, make clear why I have insisted on inserting that awkward phrase "above a given intensity level" in all statements of the hypothesis. For activity, it appears to be the case that the lesioned animal is less active when the stimulus is remote and more active when the stimulus is prominent. This interaction between reactivity and stimulus prominence is presented graphically in Figure 4. This is a formulation which I believe fits almost all of the available data, on both animals and men, remarkably well. It is also a formulation which for good ad-hoc reasons bears a striking resemblance to almost every relevant set of data I have discussed.

For human eating behavior, virtually every fact we have supports the assertion that the obese eat more than normals when the food cue is prominent and less when the cue is remote. In Johnson's study of work and cue prominence, the obese do not work as hard as normals when there are no prominent food cues, but work much harder when the food cues are highly salient. In Nisbett's one- and three-sandwich experiment, the obese subjects eat just as long as food cues are prominent—that is, the sandwiches are directly in front of the subject—but when these immediate cues have been consumed,

---

[6]Reactive, yes, but what about activity in the more primitive sense of simply moving or scrambling about the experimental box? Even in this respect, the lesioned animals appear to outmove the normals, for Turner, Sechzer, and Liebelt (1967) report that: "The experimental groups, both mice and rats, emitted strong escape tendencies prior to the onset of shock and in response to shock. Repeated attempts were made to climb out of the test apparatus. This group showed much more vocalization than the control group. . . . In contrast to the behavior of the experimental animals, the control animals appeared to become immobilized or to "freeze" both before and during the shock period. Thus, there was little attempt to escape and little vocalization" [p. 242].

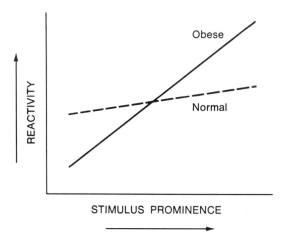

FIGURE 4.   Theoretical curves of relationship of reactivity to stimulus prominence.

they stop eating. Thus, they eat more than normals in the three-sandwich condition and less in the one-sandwich condition. We also know that the obese have an easy time fasting in the absence of food cues and a hard time in the presence of such cues, and so on.

About eating habits we know that the obese eat larger meals (what could be a more prominent cue than food on the plate?), but eat fewer meals (as they should if it requires a particularly potent food cue to trigger an eating response). Even the fact that the obese eat more rapidly can be easily derived from this formulation.

For rats, this formulation in general fits what we know about eating habits, but can be considered a good explanation of the various experimental facts only if you are willing to accept my reinterpretation, in terms of cue prominence, of such experiments as Miller et al.'s (1950) study of the effects of work on eating. If, as would I, you would rather suspend judgment until the appropriate experiments have been done on lesioned rats, mark it down as an engaging possibility.

Given the rough state of what we know about emotionality, this formulation seems to fit the data for humans and rats about equally well. The lesioned rats are vicious when handled and lethargic when left alone. In the Rodin (1970) experiment which required subjects to listen to either neutral or emotionally disturbing tapes, obese subjects described themselves (and behaved accordingly) as less emotional than normals when the tapes were neutral and much more emotional than normals when the tapes were disturbing.

All in all, given the variety of species and behaviors involved, it is not a bad ad-hoc hypothesis. So far there has been only one study deliberately designed to test some of the ideas implicit in this formulation. This is Lee Ross's (1969) study of the effects of cue salience on eating. Ross formulated this experiment in the days when we were struggling with some of the data inconsistent with our external-internal theory of eating behavior (see Schachter, 1967). Since the world is full of food cues, it was particularly embarrassing to discover that obese subjects ate less frequently than normals. Short of invoking denial mechanisms, such a fact could be reconciled with the theory only if we assumed that a food cue must be potent in order to trigger an eating response in an obese subject—the difference between a hot dog stand two blocks away and a hot dog under your nose, savory with mustard and steaming with sauerkraut.

To test the effects of cue prominence, Ross simply had his subjects sit at a table covered with a variety of objects among which was a large tin of shelled cashew nuts. Presumably, the subjects were there to take part in a study of thinking. There were two sets of experimental conditions. In high-cue-saliency conditions, the table and the nuts were illuminated by an unshaded table lamp containing a 40-watt bulb. In low-saliency conditions, the lamp was shaded and contained a 7½-watt red bulb. The measure of eating was simply the difference in weight of the tin of nuts before and after the subject thought his experimentally required thoughts. The results are presented in Figure 5, which needless to say, though I will say it, bears a marked resemblance to our theoretical curves.

So much for small triumphs. Let us turn now to some of the problems of this formulation. Though I

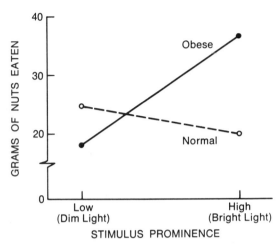

FIGURE 5.   The effects of stimulus intensity on amount eaten (from Ross, 1969).

do not intend to detail a catalog of failings, I would like to make explicit some of my discomforts.

1. Though there has been no direct experimental study of the problem, it seems to be generally thought that the lesioned rat is hyposexual, which, if true, is one hell of a note for a theory which postulates superreactivity. It is the case, however, that gonadal atrophy is frequently a consequence of this operation (Brooks & Lambert, 1946; Hetherington & Ranson, 1940). Possibly, then, we should consider sexual activity as artifactually quite distinct from either gross activity or stimulus-bound activity such as avoidance behavior.

2. I am made uncomfortable by the fact that the obese, both human and rat, eat less bad food than do normals. I simply find it difficult to conceive of nonresponsiveness as a response. I suppose I could conceptually pussyfoot around this difficulty, but I cannot imagine the definition of response that would allow me to cope with both this fact and with the facts about passive avoidance. I take some comfort from the observation that of all of the facts about animals and humans, the fact about bad taste has the weakest batting average. It may yet turn out not to be a fact.

3. Though the fact that obese humans eat less often is no problem, the fact that obese rats also eat less often is awkward, for it is a bit difficult to see how food stimulus intensity can vary for a caged rat on an ad-lib schedule. This may seem farfetched, but there is some experimental evidence that this may be due to the staleness of the food. Brooks, Lockwood, and Wiggins (1946), using mash for food, demonstrated that lesioned rats do not outeat normals when the food is even slightly stale. Only when the food was absolutely fresh and newly placed in the cage did lesioned rats eat conspicuously more than normal rats. It seems doubtful, however, that this could be the explanation for results obtained with pellets.

4. As with food, one should expect from this formulation that the animal's water intake would increase following the lesion. There does not appear to have been much systematic study of the problem, but what data exist are inconsistent from one study to the next. Several studies indicate decreased water intake; at least one study (Krasne, 1964) indicates no change following the operation; and there are even rare occasional case reports of polydipsia. Possibly my interactional hypothesis can cope with this chaos, and systematically varying the salience of the water cue will systematically affect the water intake of the ventromedial animal. It is also possible that under any circumstance, water, smell-less and tasteless, is a remote cue.

There are, then, difficulties with this formulation. These may be the kinds of difficulties that will ultimately damn the theory, or at least establish its limits. Alternatively, these may mostly be apparent difficulties, and this view of matters may help us clarify inconsistent sets of data, for I suspect that by systematically varying cue prominence we can systematically vary the lesioned animal's reactivity on many dimensions. We shall see. Granting the difficulties, for the moment this view of matters does manage to subsume a surprisingly diverse set of facts about animals and men under one quite simple theoretical scheme.

Since I have presented this article as a more or less personal history of the development of a set of ideas, I would like to conclude by taking a more formal look at this body of data, theory, and speculation, by examining what I believe we now know, what seems to be good guesswork, and what is still out-and-out speculation.

1. With some confidence, we can say that obese humans are externally controlled or stimulus-bound. There is little question that this is true of their eating behavior, and evidence is rapidly accumulating that eating is a special case of the more general state.

I have suggested that stimulus prominence and reactivity are key variables in understanding the realms of behavior with which I have been concerned, and Figure 4 represents a first guess as to the nature of the differential functions involved for obese and normal humans. The specific shapes of the curves are, of course, pure guesswork, and the only absolute requirement that I believe the data impose on the theory is that there be an interaction such that at low levels of stimulus prominence, the obese are less reactive, and at high levels of prominence more reactive, than normals.

2. With considerably less confidence, I believe we can say that this same set of hypotheses may explain many of the differences between the ventromedial lesioned rat and his intact counterpart. This conclusion is based on the fact that so much of the existing data either fit or can be plausibly reinterpreted to fit these ideas. Obviously, the crucial experiments have yet to be done.

3. Finally, and most tentatively, one may guess that the obesity of rats and men has a common physiological locus in the ventromedial hypothalamus. I must emphasize that this guess is based *entirely* on the persistent and tantalizing analogies between lesioned rats and obese humans. There is absolutely no relevant independent evidence. However, should future work support this speculation, I suspect, in light of the evidence already supporting the stimulus-binding hypotheses, that

we are in for a radical revision of our notions about the hypothalamus.

REFERENCES

Brooks, C. McC., & Lambert, E. F. A study of the effect of limitation of food intake and the method of feeding on the rate of weight gain during hypothalamic obesity in the albino rat. *American Journal of Physiology,* 1946, **147,** 695–707.

Brooks, C. McC., Lockwood, R. A., & Wiggins, M. L. A study of the effect of hypothalamic lesions on the eating habits of the albino rat. *American Journal of Physiology,* 1946, **147,** 735–741.

Bullen, B. A., Reed, R. B., & Mayer, J. Physical activity of obese and nonobese adolescent girls appraised by motion picture sampling. *American Journal of Clinical Nutrition,* 1964, **14,** 211–223.

Cannon, W. B. *Bodily changes in pain, hunger, fear and rage.* (2nd ed.) New York: Appleton, 1915.

Carlson, A. J. *The control of hunger in health and disease.* Chicago: University of Chicago Press, 1916.

Decke, E. Effects of taste on the eating behavior of obese and normal persons. Cited in S. Schachter, *Emotion, obesity, and crime.* New York: Academic Press, 1971.

Gladfelter, W. E., & Brobeck, J. R. Decreased spontaneous locomotor activity in the rat induced by hypothalamic lesions. *American Journal of Physiology,* 1962, **203,** 811–817.

Goldman, R., Jaffa, M., & Schachter, S. Yom Kippur, Air France, dormitory food, and the eating behavior of obese and normal persons. *Journal of Personality and Social Psychology,* 1968, **10,** 117–123.

Grossman, S. P. The VMH: A center for affective reactions, satiety, or both? *International Journal of Physiology and Behavior,* 1966, **1,** 1–10.

Grossman, S. P. *A textbook of physiological psychology.* New York: Wiley, 1967.

Hetherington, A. W., & Ranson, S. W. Hypothalamic lesions and adiposity in the rat. *Anatomical Record,* 1940, **78,** 149–172.

Johnson, W. G. The effect of prior-taste and food visibility on the food-directed instrumental performance of obese individuals. Unpublished doctoral dissertation, Catholic University of America, 1970.

Krasne, F. B. Unpublished study cited in N. E. Miller, Some psycho-physiological studies of motivation and of the behavioural effects of illness. *Bulletin of the British Psychological Society,* 1964, **17,** 1–20.

Maren, T. H. Cited in J. L. Fuller & G. A. Jacoby, Central and sensory control of food intake in genetically obese mice. *American Journal of Physiology,* 1955, **183,** 279–283.

Miller, N. E. Some psycho-physiological studies of motivation and of the behavioural effects of illness. *Bulletin of the British Psychological Society,* 1964, **17,** 1–20.

Miller, N. E., Bailey, C. J., & Stevenson, J. A. F. Decreased "hunger" but increased food intake resulting from hypothalamic lesions. *Science,* 1950, **112,** 256–259.

Mrosovsky, N. *Hibernation and the hypothalamus.* New York: Appleton-Century-Crofts, 1971.

Nisbett, R. E. Determinants of food intake in human obesity. *Science,* 1968, **159,** 1254–1255. (a)

Nisbett, R. E. Taste, deprivation, and weight determinants of eating behavior. *Journal of Personality and Social Psychology,* 1968, **10,** 107–116. (b)

Nisbett, R. E. Eating and obesity in men and animals. In press, 1971.

Pliner, P. Effects of liquid and solid preloads on the eating behavior of obese and normal persons. Unpublished doctoral dissertation, Columbia University, 1970.

Rabin, B. M., & Smith, C. J. Behavioral comparison of the effectiveness of irritative and non-irritative lesions in producing hypothalamic hyperphagia. *Physiology and Behavior,* 1968, **3,** 417–420.

Reeves, A. G., & Plum, F. Hyperphagia, rage, and dementia accompanying a ventromedial hypothalamic neoplasm. *Archives of Neurology,* 1969, **20,** 616–624.

Reynolds, R. W. Ventromedial hypothalamic lesions with hyperphagia. *American Journal of Physiology,* 1963, **204,** 60–62.

Rodin, J. Effects of distraction on performance of obese and normal subjects. Unpublished doctoral dissertation, Columbia University, 1970.

Ross, L. D. Cue- and cognition-controlled eating among obese and normal subjects. Unpublished doctoral dissertation, Columbia University, 1969.

Schachter, S. The interaction of cognitive and physiological determinants of emotional state. In L. Berkowitz (Ed.), *Advances in experimental social psychology,* Vol. 1. New York: Academic Press, 1964.

Schachter, S. Cognitive effects on bodily functioning: Studies of obesity and eating. In D. C. Glass (Ed.), *Neurophysiology and emotion.* New York: Rockefeller University Press and Russell Sage Foundation, 1967.

Schachter, S. Obesity and eating. *Science,* 1968, **161,** 751–756.

Schachter, S. *Emotion, obesity, and crime.* New York: Academic Press, 1971.

Schachter, S., Goldman, R., & Gordon, A. Effects of fear, food deprivation, and obesity on eating. *Journal of Personality and Social Psychology,* 1968, **10,** 91–97.

Singh, D. Comparison of hyperemotionality caused by lesions in the septal and ventromedial hypothalamic areas in the rat. *Psychonomic Science,* 1969, **16,** 3–4.

Stellar, E. The physiology of motivation. *Psychological Review,* 1954, **61,** 5–22.

Stunkard, A., & Koch, C. The interpretation of gastric motility: I. Apparent bias in the reports of hunger by obese persons. *Archives of General Psychiatry,* 1964, **11,** 74–82.

Teitelbaum, P. Sensory control of hypothalamic hyperphagia. *Journal of Comparative and Physiological Psychology,* 1955, **48,** 156–163.

Teitelbaum, P. Random and food-directed activity in hyperphagic and normal rats. *Journal of Comparative and Physiological Psychology,* 1957, **50,** 486–490.

Teitelbaum, P., & Campbell, B. A. Ingestion patterns in hyperphagic and normal rats. *Journal of Comparative and Physiological Psychology,* 1958, **51,** 135–141.

Turner, S. G., Sechzer, J. A., & Liebelt, R. A. Sensitivity to electric shock after ventromedial hypothalamic lesions. *Experimental Neurology,* 1967, **19,** 236–244.

ARTICLE 27

Interpersonal and social consequences of attribution

Kelly G. Shaver

Attribution theory is founded on the presumption that people actively search for meaning in the social world around them. Another nation abruptly changes a long-standing policy toward our country, and we want to know *why*. A militant organization engages in acts of political terrorism, and we wonder what motivates them to do so. On my bachelor friend's first date with a woman, he attends to every remark she makes, looking for its meaning. We are not content merely to be passive observers of action. Whether the behavior in question is that of a nation, a group, or a single person, and whether its consequences for us are positive or negative, if that behavior is important to us, we will try to interpret it. We employ processes of attribution to *explain* action and to *predict* whether it will be repeated in the future.

In the course of this book we have discovered a great deal about the ways in which perceivers come to understand their own behavior and the behavior of other people. Although the attribution process is a complex one, it can (with some risk of oversimplification) be summarized as follows: The first element in the attribution process is the *observation of action,* broadly conceived so as to include reports of action as well as first-hand observation. Not surprisingly, the first evidence that attribution is a dynamic and social process can be seen at this stage. For example, the stimulus person (the object of an attribution) is not merely behaving, in most cases he is engaging in self-presentation, revealing to observers only what he does not mind their seeing. For his part, the perceiver is not just passively encoding all of the information available to him. He is, instead, actively constructing an impression consistent with his needs and social categories. The degree of selectivity involved in deciding *what* has happened is illustrated by the discrepancies often found in the testimony of various eyewitnesses to an incident. The courtroom setting is designed to produce the greatest possible accuracy in description, and the eyewitnesses are asked only to describe—not interpret—the incident, yet disagreements still arise.

How can you use your knowledge of the factors involved to guard against bias in your own observations of action? Since it is impossible for you to encode all the relevant information, you must first remember that your view of the situation is just that—your viewpoint. Try to take the role of the actor, to see whether he would describe the action in the same terms that you have chosen; try to put aside your expectations and prejudices, so that you can describe what did happen rather than what should have occurred; compare your description of the situation with the views of others to see if they agree with you. As a second line of defense against observational bias, try to form your impression on the basis of a complete segment of behavior. Be aware of the pervasiveness of order effects, and try to give the "late bloomers" the same consideration, based on their overall performance, that you would be tempted to give the early starters. Knowing that there are differences in viewpoint and order effects in attribution should help you to keep from being misled into thinking that your version of the situation is the "truth." Admittedly, these suggestions sound like the first chapter in a book on how to become more interpersonally sensitive, but they are thoroughly grounded in attribution theory and research.

The second element in the attribution process is the *judgment of intention*. Let us suppose that you have been a careful observer and have arrived at a relatively accurate picture of what has taken place. Now, as you begin to wonder about the possible reasons for the occurrence, you must first decide whether the action was intended. We have seen that intentional action can be distinguished from habit, reflex, or accident in several ways, and you can apply these criteria to aid in your judgment. First, since intentional actions are supposed to be goal-directed, you should be able to identify at least some objectives that the actor could plausibly have had.

Your interest at this point is only to establish the *existence* of possible objectives, not to try to choose which one you think was the actor's objective. It is precisely because we cannot find plausible goals that we call some events "accidental." For example, we assume that a driver whose automobile crashes into the concrete support for an overpass has had an accident, since we cannot imagine any plausible goals that might be served by his intentionally aiming at the abutment. Should we discover that two days earlier the driver had taken out a huge life insurance policy, we immediately become suspicious. We have identified a possible objective for an intentional crash.

Existence of possible goals, though necessary, is not sufficient for a judgment of intention. As Heider (1958) points out, there are other factors involved in the determination of intention. The action must occur in the immediate vicinity of the actor (local causality), and the perceiver must believe that if the actor's present behavior were thwarted, he would choose an alternate path to the same goal (equifinality of outcome). In addition to these requirements, there is also the necessity for *exertion*. Not only must the actor be thought to have some identifiable goal, he must also appear to be trying to achieve that objective. So, in your judgment of intention, you should ask yourself whether plausible goals exist for the action, and whether the actor appears to be exerting himself in the direction of one or more of these goals. If all of the necessary conditions are present—possible goals, local causality, equifinality, and exertion—you will conclude that the action was intentionally caused.

The final step in the attribution process is the *making of a dispositional attribution*. You have observed the action and decided that it was intentionally produced, so now you are ready to try to answer the fundamental question, "Why?" As we have seen, at this point there are basically two possibilities. Either the action should be attributed to some factor in the environment (such as a characteristic of the situation or the presence of coercion), or it should be attributed to a specific underlying disposition of the actor. If you have ruled out the environment as a possible cause of an aggressive action, you don't stop with "He acted aggressively because of some [unspecified] personal disposition." You conclude that "he acted aggressively *because he is an aggressive person.*" Your choice of attribution possibilities is not between the environment in general and the person in general, but rather between a specific force in the environment and a specific personal disposition.

In making this choice you will probably employ a combination of the attributional criteria suggested by Jones and Davis (1965) and by Kelley (1967). In order to evaluate the contribution of the environment, you need to have some idea of the degree to which anyone in the same situation would respond as the actor did. If all of the effects are high in assumed desirability (or, in Kelley's terms, if there is no distinctiveness between actors in that situation) you suspect that the environment accounts for most of the action. If, on the other hand, the actor has behaved in a distinctive manner (lack of consistency among actors suggests a low assumed desirability), and if there are few noncommon effects of the action, you are in a good position to guess that the action (say, an act of aggression) should be attributed to a personal disposition of the same name ("he is an aggressive person").

As we have suggested before, this entire process of attribution seldom takes long enough for us to point to each of its components. Only in a jury setting are we likely to find ourselves taking the time to ask: "What could have been gained by that action?" "Was it intended?" "Why did he do it?" We do not often find ourselves actually speaking of things like environmental coercion, assumed desirability, or even consensus among observers unless we are called upon to defend an attribution already made. Nevertheless, a thorough specification of the possible components of an attribution may help us understand the process more fully. And we should not be misled by the time usually required for an attribution into believing that the scientific explanation of attribution is necessarily a simple one. After all, it

takes calculus to explain how the batter in a baseball game is able to have his bat in the correct place when the pitch comes sailing in.

By focusing our attention upon the process of dispositional attribution, we have learned a good deal about the ways in which perceivers might come to understand both their own behavior and the actions of other people. But dispositional attribution is not a perceptual exercise performed in a social vacuum. When attributions are being shaped they are influenced by behavior and motivation; and completed attributions, in turn, help guide subsequent behavior. In the remainder of this chapter we will illustrate some of the ways in which the attributions you make might influence your own self-conception, your actions toward others, and your view of social problems. In each of these brief examples we will try to distinguish between the consequences that might follow an environmental attribution and the consequences that might follow an attribution of the same action to an underlying personal disposition.

SELF-AWARENESS

The attribution principles that we have discussed should enable you to arrive at a more accurate understanding of your own behavior. To what extent is it true that you do not know what you believe until you hear what you say? Is the amount of credit that you demand for success greater than the amount of blame you accept for failure? Can you regard yourself objectively, as another person would see you?

A recently popular technique for increasing self-awareness is the personal growth group. Whether these groups are designed to enhance awareness of sensory experience (encounter groups), to remove barriers to effective interpersonal communication (T-groups), or to identify the sources and effects of discrimination (consciousness-raising groups), they may all be characterized in attributional terms. If you should decide to join such a group, you will find that some of the time you will be a *perceiver* of the other members and some of the time you will be the *stimulus person* who is being perceived. In your role as a stimulus person, you agree to minimize self-presentation ("behave naturally"), and in your role as a perceiver, you agree to give your honest impressions of other participants. The personal and environmental attributions made under these circumstances may have substantial impact on your own self-esteem and on your impressions of other people.

Suppose that through feedback from the other persons in the group you discover that they believe you to be quite a courageous person. For years you have made environmental attributions for your courageous-appearing actions on the grounds that "the situation demanded no less." Now you discover that by virtue of their different viewpoints and experience, the others do not agree with this environmental attribution. Because they realize that many people would not behave as you have, they see your actions as *distinctive,* and make their attributions to your personal disposition. Naturally, this revelation will enhance your self-worth.

Unfortunately, veridicality in attribution is a sword that cuts both ways. After discovering the "truth" (the *consensus* of your peers), you may find that you preferred your attributional defense mechanisms. Suppose that for a long time you have held a job in which you supervise a number of other people. Further suppose that you have never been able to get along with your employees. Now you have always attributed this unpleasantness to your position (an environmental attribution). After all, who likes the boss? But in the group, where no outside statuses are permitted, you *still* find that nobody seems to care for you. It is not your position but rather your personal characteristics that people find distasteful. This sort of change from an environmental to a personal attribution can obviously be a threat to your self-esteem.

Why are the discoveries made in personal growth groups potentially so crucial to self-worth? Perhaps because of another sort of attribution, one dictated by the initial ground rules. Remember when you agreed to give, and to accept, nothing but the truth? Doing so establishes *the only possible attribution*

for a statement made in the group: the person making the assertion believes it to be true. Now if someone congratulated you for being courageous *outside* the group, where truth is not the only ground rule, there could be multiple sufficient causes for the congratulatory statement. It could be flattery, it could be mistaken identity, or it could even be true. The last interpretation would, of course, be *discounted* in direct proportion to the number of other alternatives possible. Although you might like to take the statement at face value, you could not be certain that it would be correct to do so. On the other hand, when a threatening personal attribution is made outside of the group, the same discounting principle can be used to save face. It is not really that you are a bad person, only that your employee is in an angry mood, lashing out at whoever is available; or perhaps the situation has caused him to misperceive your actions. Outside the group, the uncertainty from discounting will mean that you miss an occasional compliment, but it will permit you to maintain your composure in the face of harsh criticism. Inside the group, no discounting is possible —the only available attribution is "truth"—so what is said about you will have a significantly greater effect on your self-worth.

PSYCHOTHERAPY

If separating the personal attributions from the environmental ones is important in producing self-awareness under normal circumstances, it is even more vital in many kinds of psychotherapy. This is so because the avowed goal of classic psychotherapy (as opposed to some more recent behavioristic techniques) is to relieve emotional disorder by helping the client gain "insight" into the source of his anxiety. Whether this goal is achieved with extensive participation and interpretation by the therapist (as in Freudian psychoanalysis), or through a supportive atmosphere in which the client can make the discovery for himself, the outcome can be described as a more veridical attribution. After all, what is "insight" if not a correct attribution of the causes of behavior? Once this veridical attribution is achieved, the client is helped to deal directly with the real causes of his problem, rather than with the false causes erected by his defenses. It should be noted, however, that while veridical attribution can be valuable, it is not desirable for all psychotherapy (any more than it is completely desirable in self-awareness).

One significant exception involves the often highly successful therapeutic procedures collectively known as *behavior modification*. In a situation in which a classic psychotherapist might ask, "What sort of faulty psychological development might have produced these symptoms?" a behavior modifier would wonder, "What are the environmental reinforcements supporting this behavior?" The focus is not on the client's psychological history, but on the circumstances of his present environment. Behavior modification does not presume that there are deep psychodynamic influences on the client's behavior, only that the environment is providing some rewards for his symptoms. If these rewards are removed, the symptoms should disappear. There has been substantial controversy over the psychological, as opposed to the behavioral, results of such treatment. Has the client really been "cured," or will another symptom spring up to replace the one that is no longer being reinforced? Since any further consideration of this problem is well beyond the scope of our discussion, we should only note that behavior modification is an apparently successful therapeutic technique for which cognitive processes, such as attributions, are assumed to be irrelevant.

A second exception to the characterization of psychotherapy as a process designed to increase the veridicality of attribution consists of some of the newly developed misattribution therapies first mentioned in Chapter 6. As noted then, the purpose of these techniques is to derive therapeutic benefits from experimentally induced *mis*attribution of arousal to emotionally irrelevant stimuli. For example, Storms and Nisbett (1970) report partial cures of insomnia based on an induced external attribution

of wakefulness. As they suggest, insomnia may be one sort of psychological problem that can be characterized as a vicious cycle: "occurrence of symptoms, worry about symptoms, consequent exacerbation of symptoms" (p. 326). Such problems should be most amenable to an attribution therapy that would externalize the cause of the symptoms. Storms and Nisbett gave some of their insomniac subjects placebo pills described as a drug capable of producing alertness, high temperature, and heart rate increases. Since all of these symptoms typically accompany insomnia, those subjects receiving the placebo could readily attribute their arousal to the pill (an external and worry-free attribution). And as anticipated, these experimental subjects reported getting to sleep earlier on nights when they took the pills than on nights when they did not. In this case an induced *mis*attribution of internally caused arousal to emotionally irrelevant external causes brought improvement. Thus, depending upon the particular psychological problem and upon the therapeutic method employed, both veridical and nonveridical separation of personal causes from environmental causes can be aids to psychotherapy.

INTERPERSONAL ATTRIBUTIONS AND TRUSTWORTHINESS

Familiarity with the principles and problems of attribution should also enhance the accuracy of your perceptions of others. If you know that the attributions of stable dispositional properties are affected by primacy, you may want to guard against possible bias by giving a closer look to the performance of "late bloomers." If you thoroughly understand how your own motivation can influence your attributional judgments, you may be more careful in forming first impressions of others, especially when the circumstances are ambiguous but important to you. If you are aware of the extent to which behavior can engulf the field, obscuring the environmental constraints on action, you may try to differentiate more carefully between the personal causes of action internal to the actor and the environmental causes also involved.

Throughout this book we have argued that you have two objectives as a perceiver: to explain actions of interest to you and to predict the likelihood of their recurrence. Now what about an actor whose behavior makes these objectives either difficult or easy to attain? We might guess that you would try to avoid a totally unpredictable actor, because some of his unpredictable actions may have bad consequences for you. But predictability alone is not enough. In our friendships, in our love affairs, and in our business dealings, we want to be involved with people we can trust. Interpersonal trust is perhaps the most fundamental characteristic of interaction—not only difficult to achieve, but easy to destroy. An attributional analysis of trustworthiness may help us to understand why this is the case.

As a beginning, we must determine that a person is acting on the basis of his "principles," rather than changing his behavior like a chameleon as the situation and persons involved vary. In terms of Kelley's model, we must observe the actor's behavior in a variety of situations with a number of different other persons present and see that it is relatively constant in order to arrive at a personal (entity) attribution for his actions. We have conducted our exercise in applied social science and have concluded that the environment can be ruled out as a cause of his behavior. Now, however, the attributional task becomes more difficult. We have succeeded in eliminating environmental causes, but we are left not with a single internal cause, but with several possible internal causes. The actions from which trustworthiness is to be inferred are most typically socially desirable. Whether these actions are conceptualized in Jones and Davis's terms as a large number of non-common highly desirable effects (concentrating on the effects produced), or in Kelley's terms as multiple sufficient facilitative causes (concentrating on the possible causes), attribution to a unique disposition of trustworthiness is obviously difficult. It is unfortunate but true that our attributions of negatively valued dispositions like

hostility can be made with more certainty than attributions of positively valued dispositions, because of the great differences in assumed desirability. Since trustworthiness is only one of the possible explanations of the stimulus person's behavior, it must be discounted in proportion to the number of other alternatives. What this means for the perceiver is that there must be still more observations, under different situations, to rule out these alternatives.

Now we can begin to see why trustworthiness is such a difficult matter to establish, and why it can be so easily destroyed. The perceiver must first determine that action was based on internal principles, next that the principles are good (e.g., not manipulative) ones, and only at this point that trustworthiness is the most important principle involved. This can be a lengthy attributional process. More importantly, the perceiver's applied social science has the same limitations as formal social science—each successive confirmation makes the hypothesis of trustworthiness more tenable, but perfect certainty can never be achieved. And it takes only one counterexample to disconfirm.

SOME SOCIAL CONSEQUENCES OF ATTRIBUTION

Where does the responsibility lie for the occurrence of crime? Is it the fault of individuals who commit single acts of criminal behavior? Or should some of the blame be shared by an economic and social system that induces high expectations in all of its people, regardless of their ability to obtain promised rewards through accepted channels? What about drug abuse? Are addicts personally responsible for their fate, or have the usually deplorable conditions of their daily lives led them to seek this sort of escape? When welfare rolls rise dramatically, is it because more and more individual people are refusing to work, or could it be that the advancing technocracy has less need for unskilled and marginal labor?

You will recognize that the answers to these questions of social policy could be phrased in terms consistent either with personal attribution or with situational attribution. More importantly, the sort of attribution chosen will to a large degree determine the solutions proposed. Personal attributions about the reasons for welfare lead to political speeches about "welfare chiselers," appeals for return to simpler days of the Protestant ethic, and laws designed to make needed financial assistance more difficult to obtain. Situational attributions, on the other hand, are likely to suggest that expanded government-supported employment, better job training, and increased educational opportunity for all will provide more lasting reductions in public assistance.

Unfortunately, especially for the people who happen to be in the problem groups, overemphasis on personal causes is as common with social problems as it is with other more individual behaviors. It is not simply that behavior engulfs the field, or even that personal attributions for social problems are more satisfying to the perceivers. Social conditions are less accessible to influence and more resistant to constructive change than are individual people. At the most elementary level, people are more easily identified than are conditions. If you violate a law, you are a criminal by definition; if you are physically dependent upon a drug, you are an addict; if your income is below an established level, you are officially poor. There are no problems of interpretation, no differences of opinion among experts to deal with, no necessity for determining relative weightings of possible causes. All that is necessary is knowledge of the defining characteristic.

This emphasis upon personal attribution has the added advantage of specifying not only the problem, but also the solution: change the people. Punish the criminal (or remove him from society) and the crime problem will go away. Put all the addicts on methadone (an addictive synthetic drug which eliminates the craving for heroin and is usually administered by hospitals) and there will be no more addiction. Sterilize people on welfare and you will break the cycle of poverty. The most appealing aspect of this kind of approach is that it promises to correct the social problem by acting on the indi-

vidual person. There is, however, some reason to believe that solutions to social problems based on correction of assumed personal dispositions will probably be futile. As long as the environmental conditions persist, they will probably lead to similar "personal dispositions" in other people. This sort of interaction between environmental conditions and personal dispositions can be illustrated, on an interpersonal rather than societal level, by the phenomenon of the self-fulfilling prophecy.

A CONCLUDING NOTE: THE SELF-FULFILLING PROPHECY

An important aspect of the way in which our attributions affect our interpersonal behavior—which, in turn, affects our attributions—has been described by Merton (1957) as the *self-fulfilling prophecy*. This term refers to the fact that our expectations about an interaction can produce behavior on our part that will guarantee that the expectation is fulfilled. Let us consider some attributional examples. Suppose that you are a policeman in a large city and are in charge of maintaining order in the ghetto. You know that the crime rate is higher there than in any other part of the city, and in your patrols you frequently must deal with people behaving in a violent way. If we asked you to make an attribution for this violent behavior, you would probably say that it occurred "because they are just violent people." The result of this *personal* attribution is that you expect a violent response from anyone you stop, even for a routine traffic offense. The consequence? In order to establish your dominance at the beginning of the interaction, you, yourself, behave as violently as the laws and regulations permit. When you stop someone for a possible traffic violation, you approach the person's car with your gun drawn, you roughly pull the driver out of his seat, make him put his hands on top of the car, and only after you have thoroughly searched him do you ask to see his driver's license. If we pointed out to you that this is a pretty high-handed way to deal with the public, you would reply that your own behavior is dictated entirely by the *situation,* particularly by your attribution of potential violence to every individual living in the ghetto.

Now take the viewpoint of the ghetto resident. You know that to protect your family, to make sure that your child gets to school without losing his lunch money, to safeguard your few possessions, is to demonstrate your own willingness to take necessary revenge. In fact, perhaps the very best way to insure your family's safety in the harsh environment is to be known as a "bad dude" who had better be left alone. Your attribution for your own violent behavior would, therefore, be made entirely to the *situation.* It is not that you enjoy being tough, but rather that being so is the only way to survive in that environment. And what do you think of the police? They are an occupying force composed of individuals who enjoy throwing their weight around by hassling you and the people you know. Notice that this involves *personal* attributions of hostility to individual police officers. As Jones and Nisbett (1971) would say, each has emphasized the situational influences on his own behavior while emphasizing the importance of personal dispositions in producing the other's actions.

So what happens when the policeman (who attributes his own toughness to the situation, but attributes a disposition of violence to each resident) arrests a ghetto resident (who sees his own behavior as determined by the situation, but views the policeman's toughness as the product of a personal disposition)? Each one is likely to act in a way that will lead to a response by the other which confirms the incorrect attributions. The policeman may be arrogant and overly rough (leading the resident to fight back to protect himself), or the resident may be abusive and threatening (leading the policeman to be rough in order to protect himself). Each one obtains the expected response, and neither realizes that it is his own behavior at the time which produces that response. Each one's behavior fulfills the other's prophecy and strengthens the other's incorrect attribution for the causes of that behavior. The only way out of this situation is to provide an oppor-

tunity for police and residents to meet on neutral territory, under conditions that are designed to help both discover the mistaken attributions that they are making. If each can be made to realize that the other's violence is produced by the situation, rather than by a personal disposition, their adversary relationship might cool a great deal.

In passing, it should be noted that an adversary relationship is not an essential prerequisite for self-fulfilling misattribution. Such misattribution may occur even when the formal social relationship between the parties is one of concern or caring. One of the best examples of this sort of misattribution can be found in mental hospitals. There are always stories about the back-ward patients whose condition seems to improve around a new ward attendant who, for some reason, has not been told just how disturbed the patients on that ward really are. In this instance, the attendant's lack of expectations is clearly reflected in the apparently improved behavior of the patients.

Of all the attributions made to mental patients, none is more important and potentially harmful than the initial attribution made upon admission to the hospital, particularly if the admission has not been by choice. If you are involuntarily committed to a mental hospital, the legal system has formally attributed to you a personal disposition of *mental disorder,* for which you need treatment. The great extent to which hospital staff are likely to rely on this attribution, without determining its actual validity, is indicated in a series of studies reported by Rosenhan (1973). He arranged to have a number of willing graduate students committed by a court to mental hospitals for a short time as part of their clinical training. Although the real patients soon recognized the students for what they were, the staff members continued to believe that they were patients. Indeed, some of the students had substantial difficulty in securing their release at the appropriate time. Given that I have already made a personal attribution of mental disorder to you, what am I likely to think when you tell me that you really are not crazy, that you are a graduate student in clinical psychology, and that you were involuntarily committed as part of your clinical training? My, my, what an interesting delusional system! Imagine, I say to my colleagues, he claims that he is a student who is in here for training.

As we have noted before, once an attribution of mental disorder has been made it is likely to persist, even after all of the behaviors that originally led to attribution have vanished. Even if all of the psychologists and psychiatrists available assert that you have been "cured," I may still believe that some residue of the disposition remains, and I may misattribute your future eccentricities (actions that I would excuse or ignore in "normal" people) to a resurgence of the disorder. If we did not commonly make such attributions, why would employers want to know whether you have ever been hospitalized for a mental disorder (or to broaden the perspective, ever convicted of a crime)? Do they ask you if you have ever had appendicitis? And should you be hired, would you be treated as just another employee, or would you be expected to "do something crazy" (or criminal) at any moment? Will we, by our expectations, put you under sufficient strain to make our original misattribution self-fulfilling? These are questions that must be answered if we are ever to make real progress in returning patients (or prisoners) to a society that will permit them to achieve their full potential as individuals unencumbered by attributions of personal dispositions that no longer exist.

From the examples cited in this chapter, we can get some idea of the importance that attribution plays in our everyday lives. Our social behavior is based in large part upon our knowledge of the interpersonal world, and that knowledge is obtained through attribution processes. A thorough understanding of how these processes function—and how they may be in error—will help us to become more accurate perceivers of our own actions and of the behavior of other people.

REFERENCES

Heider, F. *The psychology of interpersonal relations.* New York: Wiley, 1958.

Jones, E. E., and Davis, K. E. From acts to dispositions: The attribution process in person perception. In L. Berkowitz (Ed.), *Advances in experimental social psychology.* Vol. 2. New York: Academic Press, 1965.

Jones, E. E., and Nisbett, R. E. *The actor and the observer: Divergent perceptions of the causes of behavior.* Morristown, N. J.: General Learning Press, 1971.

Kelley, H. H. Attribution theory in social psychology. In D. Levine (Ed.), *Nebraska Symposium on Motivation, 1967.* Vol. 15. Lincoln, Neb.: University of Nebraska Press, 1967.

Merton, R. *Social theory and social structure.* Glencoe, Ill.: Free Press, 1957.

Rosenhan, D. On being sane in an insane place. *Science,* 1973, *179,* No. 4070.

Storms, M. D., and Nisbett, R. E. Insomnia and the attribution process. *Journal of Personality and Social Psychology,* 1970, *16,* 319–328.

SECTION SUMMARY

As Shaver points out, Heider's (1958) general approach to the attribution process has been extended by Harold H. Kelley (1967), by Daryl Bem (1972), and by Edward E. Jones and his colleagues (Jones & Davis, 1965; Jones & Nisbett, 1971). Jones and his co-workers are more concerned with personal forces than with environmental forces in the attribution of causes to behavior. They analyze conditions that give rise to *correspondent inferences*—that is, cases in which a judgment is made by an observer that a disposition (or dispositional characteristic) of a stimulus person (actor) is a *sufficient* explanation of the actor's behavior. For example, a college English professor is faced with the fact that Eddie, one of her freshman students, continually comes 10 to 15 minutes late to class. If the professor concludes that Eddie's behavior is simply the result of his intense dislike of English classes, her attribution would indicate a correspondent inference. The correspondent-inference approach predicts that, the more often a behavior occurs, and the more it appears to be a matter of free choice (rather than forced on the behaver), the more likely the observer is to attribute an attitude, or disposition, as the cause of the behavior.

One direction taken by research and speculation on this topic is a study of factors that influence the *confidence* with which such correspondent inferences are made. Why is the professor so *sure* that Eddie "dislikes English classes"? One such influence is the degree to which the action could have been *expected* on the basis of roles and social norms. Jones and Davis (1965) propose that the greater the *social desirability* of the behavior, or the degree to which an action conforms to social norms, the *less* information it yields about the intentions of the actor. But if an action violates one's role or the appropriate norms—as coming late to class may violate norms for students—it is more likely that the action will be attributed to personal forces, or dispositions, than to environmental ones.

Another class of factors concerns the degree to which the action affects the observer. One such factor is the *hedonic relevance* of the action, or the degree to which it proves rewarding or costly to the observer (irrespective of the actor's intentions). An act of strong hedonic relevance is one that has direct and important effects on the observer, and the observer is more likely to rely on such actions as sources in his or her inferences concerning the actor. Thus, if the professor sees Eddie's late appearance day after day as detracting from the effectiveness of her lecture, his actions will have strong hedonic relevance for her, and she will be more confident in attributing a *personal* cause to Eddie's behavior. ("He must dislike English classes.") A second factor, *personalism,* refers to the extent to which the actor's behavior is perceived as *intended* to affect or influence the observer in some way. If the professor sees Eddie's behavior as directed specifically toward her, she will give even greater weight to personal forces (as opposed to environmental ones) in attributing causes to Eddie's behavior.

Given this theoretical framework, then, what types of actions are most likely to serve as bases for inferences concerning the dispositional attributes of the actor? That is, what types of behavior are most likely to lead you as an observer to feel confident that you can infer what the actor is "really like" or what he or she "really feels"?

According to Jones and his colleagues, the most fruitful behavior is (1) that which is seen as *not* caused by roles or social norms or other social-desirability pressures (that is, not externally caused), (2) that which has real consequences for you (hedonic relevance), and (3) that which is seen as directed intentionally toward you (personalism). Since social-desirability pressures are usually toward mature, rational, and positive behaviors, one consequence of this analysis is that immature, irrational, or negativistic behaviors will be the ones from which people will draw the most inferences about underlying attributes!

One tendency that has been noticed by several researchers (for example, Nisbett, Caputo, Legant, & Maracek, 1973) is that people are more likely to make dispositional attributions in interpreting *others'* behavior than in interpreting their own behavior. Recall that West, Gunn, and Chernicky in their "Watergate break-in" article (reprinted in Section 8) found this to be the case.

The first article in this Section demonstrates that there is also a strong human tendency to seek some attribution or explanation for one's *own* bodily states. Male subjects who thought that their heartbeat rates changed in response to their looking at certain *Playboy* nudes came to like *those* photos more than other, similar ones. Thus the subjects used their internal sensations—or what they *thought* were their internal sensations—as sources of information about the causes of their own behavior. We seek in this way to make sense out of our actions as well as our bodily states.

But there appear to be individual differences in our reliance on internal sensations in attributing causes to our own behavior. The thesis of the second article in this Section is that, in the case of eating behavior, obese persons are less responsive to internal factors—and more influenced by environmental forces—than are normal-weight persons. If we may exaggerate, we can say that chronically obese people do not know when they are physiologically hungry. Instead, they eat when the clock says it's mealtime or when food is present. Are there also group differences like these in the responsiveness of subjects to the false information about their heartbeat rates?

In a study subsequent to the one reprinted in this Section, Valins (1967) sought to answer this question. He hypothesized that male students who were classified as unemotional on the basis of responses to personality tests would make less use of the information about their heartbeat rates than would male students whose responses to the tests classified them as emotional. Two paper-and-pencil measures of emotionality were given to students during freshman orientation meetings. Those who scored in the extreme direction on each of the two measures

were selected to participate in the false heart-rate feedback procedure. Just as in the previous study, all subjects viewed ten color slides of *Playboy* nudes. But this time *all* of the subjects were told that the sounds they were hearing were their heartbeats. For half of the subjects, the rate was intensified for some of the pictures; for the remaining subjects, the heart rate slowed down when these same photos were viewed.

As in the previous study, male students liked those nudes best to which they thought their heartbeats had reacted. But it was also apparent that the more-emotional subjects were influenced more by the false feedback than were the less-emotional subjects: more-emotional subjects chose more of the pictures associated with changed heart rate. For example, given the task of choosing the five most attractive photographs, highly emotional subjects who had heard their "heart rates" increase chose an average of 3.7 of those pictures, whereas the less-emotional subjects under the same treatment chose 3.2 of those pictures. Corresponding differences in choice occurred for emotional versus unemotional subjects in the "decreased heart-rate" condition.

Why are certain persons more in tune with their internal sensations than others? The reasons are still being sought. But Schachter's program of research offers one fascinating hypothesis. It is noteworthy that, when Schachter began his work on the utilization of external cues by obese persons (Schachter, 1964, 1967), his speculation focused on environmental causes. Using the observations of a psychoanalyst who had worked with obese patients (Bruch, 1961), Schachter wondered if some adults were chronically obese because they had never learned as children to separate feelings of hunger from feelings of discomfort. According to this explanation, the parents of some infants would respond to every anxious wail by sticking food in the child's mouth. The infant comes to label "almost any aroused state as hunger, or, alternatively, labeling no internal state as hunger" (Schachter, 1967, p. 127).

But more recently Schachter has turned to other

possibilities. A major portion of his article in this Section documents the striking resemblance of the behaviors of obese humans to those of rats with damage to the ventromedial nuclei of the hypothalamus. Can it be that most cases of chronic human obesity are at least partly caused by some physiological malfunction or defect in the brain? At present that is only an educated guess, as Schachter indicates; the study of this question has only begun.

Other research has indicated that Schachter's findings about eating behavior may be a special case of a much broader phenomenon of generalized stimulus selectivity. Schachter and Rodin (1974) have gathered evidence that, even in contexts unrelated to eating, obese persons are far more reactive than normal-weight individuals to prominent external cues that affect their pain perception and ideation, emotionality, and distractibility. In addition, Rodin (1975) found the "time perception" of obese persons (judgments of how much time has passed) much more variable and sensitive to external stimuli (such as boredom) than the time perception in normal-weight subjects. Thus these studies suggest that the phenomenon originally identified by Schachter affects much more than just eating behavior.

The work of Schachter, Rodin, and others shows how a line of research originally begun with one goal in mind—self-labeling of bodily states—can branch into many different areas: personality differences between normal and overweight subjects, the role of the hypothalamus in eating behavior, factors affecting time perception, and so forth.

Analyses based on attribution theory can be used to interpret and explain many of the aspects of human behavior covered in this book, such as helping behavior, aggression, obedience, and prejudice. Attribution theory can also provide an alternative way of viewing attitude change (for example, see Miller, Brickman, & Bolen, 1975). As more studies are done employing this framework, our knowledge about human behavior will continue to expand.

REFERENCES

Bem, D. J. The cognitive alteration of feeling states: A discussion. In H. London and R. E. Nisbett (Eds.), *Cognitive alteration of feeling states*. Chicago: Aldine, 1972.

Bruch, H. Transformation of oral impulses in eating disorders: A conceptual approach. *Psychiatric Quarterly,* 1961, *35,* 458–481.

Heider, F. *The psychology of interpersonal relations.* New York: Wiley, 1958.

Jones, E. E., & Davis, K. E. From acts to dispositions. In L. Berkowitz (Ed.), *Advances in experimental social psychology,* Vol. II. New York: Academic Press, 1965. Pp. 219–266.

Jones, E. E., & Nisbett, R. E. *The actor and the observer: Divergent perceptions of the causes of behavior.* New York: General Learning Corporation, 1971.

Kelley, H. H. Attribution theory in social psychology. In D. Levine (Ed.), *Nebraska symposium on motivation,* 1967, Lincoln: University of Nebraska Press, 1967. Pp. 192–238.

Miller, R. L., Brickman, P., & Bolen, D. Attribution versus persuasion as a means for modifying behavior. *Journal of Personality and Social Psychology,* 1975, *31,* 430–441.

Nisbett, R. E., Caputo, C., Legant, P., & Maracek, J. Behavior as seen by the actor and as seen by the observer. *Journal of Personality and Social Psychology,* 1973, *27,* 154–164.

Rodin, J. Causes and consequences of time perception differences in overweight and normal weight people. *Journal of Personality and Social Psychology,* 1975, *31,* 898–904.

Schachter, S. The interaction of cognitive and physiological determinants of emotional state. In L. Berkowitz (Ed.), *Advances in experimental social psychology,* Vol. I. New York: Academic Press, 1964. Pp. 49–80.

Schachter, S. Cognitive effects on bodily functioning: Studies of obesity and eating. In D. C. Glass (Ed.), *Neurophysiology and emotion.* New York: Rockefeller University Press and Russell Sage Foundation, 1967. Pp. 117–144.

Schachter, S., & Rodin, J. *Obese humans and rats.* Washington, D. C.: Erlbaum/Halsted, 1974.

Valins, S. Emotionality and information concerning internal reactions. *Journal of Personality and Social Psychology,* 1967, *6,* 458–463.

SECTION X

RACIAL SIMILARITIES AND DIFFERENCES IN INTELLIGENCE

INTRODUCTION

The term *race* is laden with emotion. Throughout the world, people are classified on the basis of their racial appearance, and often decisions of monumental consequences are made on the basis of a person's apparent race. But how viable is the term *race*? Are different racial groups equal in their *innate* mental abilities? Do the racial groups that comprise the population of the United States and Canada—Caucasian, Negro, North American Indian, Asian American, and Latin American—possess the same potential for mental development? Is heredity or environment a more important determinant of mental ability?

These are among the most complex and controversial questions in social science today. In using theoretical concepts like *race* and *mental ability,* they deal with matters that are central to a variety of social sciences, including anthropology and genetics as well as social psychology. In addition, the answers to these questions have ramifications for solving one of the most urgent domestic problems in the United States and Canada—the integration of minority groups into contemporary life in such a

way as to make available all the opportunities and benefits offered to members of the majority group.

As we reformulate these questions in more researchable terms, we need to look carefully at the meanings given to the terms we use. There are cautions to be followed in interpreting such terms as *intelligence* or *race*. When we speak of intelligence, for example, we are referring to an *abstract unobservable quality*. We *infer* a person's level of intelligence from his or her score on an IQ test, but it must be emphasized that one's level of abstract intelligence and one's IQ-test performance (or IQ score) *are not the same thing*. Levels of performance on IQ tests are also influenced by many environmental factors, including the quality and length of schooling, the type of home life, the opportunities to travel, and so on, as well as by possible genetic factors. Any differences in test performance between racial groups may be the result of such environmental factors, or of differences in motivation to perform well on the test, rather than the result of genetic determinants. The fact that most members of minority groups in the United

States and Canada have been brought up in restricted environments must always be kept in mind when we interpret any racial differences in tested IQ score. Moreover, it is quite likely that some members of minority groups are not as motivated to do well on intelligence tests as are most middle-class Whites; they have not been rewarded for achieving in the past. Again, this factor could cause the mean scores of racial groups to differ from each other, even if these groups do not differ in abstract intelligence.

The term *race* has, of course, been used throughout history as a way of distinguishing among groups of people who appear to be different. But different in what way? Early definitions of race were based on variations in skin color alone. That approach proved unsatisfactory because, among other reasons, it was recognized that there was great variety in skin shading even between members of a group that had completely inbred for many generations.

A later approach, still using surface characteristics (called *phenotypes*), used a number of different features—body physique, skin color, texture of the hair, and facial characteristics—to classify races. This *physical approach* is still used by many sociologists and social anthropologists, even though approaches of this type have led to proposals of as few as two races in the world and as many as 63. The physical approach rejects the use of cultural, or nonbiological, attributes in the determination of races. (In fact, every type of technical definition of race does so.) If two groups differ in customs, language, and location but *are similar in physical characteristics,* we say that their members belong not to different races but rather to different *ethnic groups.* Therefore there is no Jewish *race,* no Chinese *race,* no Italian *race.*

Most recently, a third approach has been formulated. Geneticists and physical anthropologists use *genetic* similarities and differences between people as a way of differentiating races. This *genetic approach* defines races as "populations which differ in the frequencies of some gene or genes" (Dunn & Dobzhansky, 1952, p. 118). For example, one's blood type is determined by genes inherited from his or her ancestors. The blood of every person throughout the world may be classified into one of four general types: O, A, B, or AB. Groups in different parts of the world can be differentiated on the basis of the percentages that possess each type. For example, almost no North American Indians have type AB or B, whereas the blood of about 45% of Chinese is one of these types. But while the genetic approach offers the benefits of greater objectivity and a *genotypic* approach (focusing on underlying characteristics), it still does not permit us to assign with confidence a specific individual to a particular race.

Such technical definitions of race often have little in common with the definitions of race used by people in everyday life. Why do we categorize one person as Black, another as White? Such labels are often determined by the people themselves or by society, although they are also influenced by the person's physical characteristics, his or her family traditions, customs, and the law. As we consider "racial" similarities and differences in intelligence, we must realize that studies have used a *popular* definition of race rather than one of the technical definitions. The category system used by the man on the street does not permit consideration of the fact that most of us are not pure in our racial ancestry; instead it is literally a black-or-white classification. Yet it has been estimated that 70% of those United States citizens classified as Negro according to the popular definition possess some Caucasian background (Roberts, 1955). Some "Negroes" in the United States have almost complete Caucasian ancestry but are classified as Negro because of state laws that so label any person with *any* Negro ancestry.

Similarly, it is estimated that approximately 20% of those United States citizens classified as Caucasian according to the popular definition possess some genetic background of Negro origin as a result of intermarriage or other interbreeding. Truly, when we attempt to compare Black and White groups in the United States and Canada, we are comparing groups that are partly different and partly alike in genetic background, culture, and environment. Nevertheless, numerous comparisons (in fact, more than 250 published ones) have been done. The first article in this Section indicates that the studies have been generally consistent in finding that the average intelligence-test *performance* of Blacks in the United States is below that of Whites. Does this finding mean that Blacks are innately different from Whites? Some psychologists consider this a possibility. For example, Arthur Jensen (1969) of the University of California at Berkeley has suggested that genetic differences in ability between races may exist. Jensen's 1969 article in the *Harvard Educational Review* was highly publicized, even though he was not really saying anything new. Jensen's position is hereditarian; he interprets the data on family resemblances in IQ to mean that about 80% of the variation in IQ scores between persons is hereditary in origin. If this were the case, it would mean that one's environment contributes relatively little. (It should be noted that Jensen has always granted that environmental differences do have *some* influence in determining each individual's IQ.)

We have chosen in this Section to present Jensen's position in detail, along with a sample of critical reactions to it. Jensen's *Harvard Educational Review* article is 123 pages in length; rather than selecting an appropriate excerpt, we have included a more recent article that will give you both an understanding of Jensen's viewpoint and a sample of his reactions to criticisms of his earlier analysis.

The second article, by Leon J. Kamin of Princeton University, is a review of two recent books by Jensen. We have chosen to include this book review for two reasons: first, it provides succinct criticisms not only of Jensen's hereditarian position but also of the data on which Jensen based his conclusions; and second, the author, Leon Kamin, has written a book entitled *The Science and Politics of IQ* (1974) that illustrates the way in which IQ-test results have been used to foster the passage of eugenic sterilization laws and overtly discriminatory immigration policies.

But Kamin's evaluation of Jensen's position has not gone without criticism either. The third article in this Section is a review of Kamin's book by David Layzer.

REFERENCES

Dunn, L. C., & Dobzhansky, T. *Heredity, race and society*. (Rev. ed.) New York: New American Library, 1952.

Jensen, A. R. How much can we boost IQ and scholastic achievement? *Harvard Educational Review*, 1969, *39*, 1–123.

Kamin, L. J. *The science and politics of IQ*. Potomac, Md.: Erlbaum, 1974.

Roberts, D. F. The dynamics of racial intermixture in the American Negro: Some anthropological considerations. *American Journal of Human Genetics*, 1955, *7*, 361–367.

ARTICLE 28

Race, intelligence and genetics: The differences are real

Arthur Jensen

In 1969, in the appropriately academic context of *The Harvard Educational Review* I questioned the then and still prevailing doctrine of racial genetic equality in intelligence. I proposed that the average difference in IQ scores between black and white people may be attributable as much to heredity as environment. Realizing that my views might be wrongly interpreted as conflicting with some of the most sacred beliefs of our democracy, I emphasized the important distinction between individual intelligence and the average intelligence of populations. Moreover, I presented my research in a careful and dispassionate manner, hoping that it would stimulate rational discussion of the issue as well as further research.

Much to my dismay, however, my article set off an emotional furor in the world of social science. Amplified by the popular press, the furor soon spread beyond the confines of academia. Almost overnight I became a *cause célèbre,* at least on college campuses. I had spoken what Joseph Alsop called "the unspeakable." To many Americans I had thought the unthinkable.

Science Vs. the Fear of Racism

For the past three decades the scientific search for an explanation of the well-established black IQ deficit has been blocked largely, I feel, by fear and abhorrence of racism. In academic circles doctrinaire theories of strictly environmental causation have predominated, with little or no attempt to test their validity rigorously. The environmentalists have refused to consider other possible causes, such as genetic factors. Research into possible genetic influence on intelligence has been academically and socially taboo. The orthodox environmental theories have been accepted not because they have stood up under proper scientific investigation, but because they harmonize so well with our democratic belief in human equality.

The civil-rights movement that gained momentum in the 1950s "required" liberal academic adherence to the theory that the environment was responsible for any individual or racial behavioral differences, and the corollary belief in genetic equality in intelligence. Thus, when I questioned such beliefs I, and my theories, quickly acquired the label "racist." I resent this label and consider it unfair and inaccurate.

The Real Meaning of Racism

Since the horrors of Nazi Germany, and Hitler's persecution of the Jews in the name of his bizarre doctrine of Aryan supremacy, the well-deserved offensiveness of the term "racism" has extended far beyond its legitimate meaning. To me, racism means discrimination among persons on the basis of their racial origins in granting or denying social, civil or political rights. Racism means the denial of equal opportunity in education or employment on the basis of color or national origin. Racism encourages the judging of persons not each according to his own qualities and abilities, but according to common stereotypes. This is the real meaning of racism. The scientific theory that there are genetically conditioned mental or behavioral differences between races cannot be called racist. It would be just as illogical to condemn the recognition of physical differences between races as racist.

When I published my article in 1969, many critics confused the purely empirical question of the genetic role in racial differences in mental abilities with the highly charged political-ideological issue of racism. Because of their confusion, they denounced my attempt to study the possible genetic causes of such differences. At the same time, the doctrinaire environmentalists, seeing their own position threatened by my inquiry, righteously and dogmatically scorned the genetic theory of intelligence.

Thankfully, the emotional furor that greeted my article has died down enough recently to permit sober and searching consideration of the true intent and substance of what I actually tried to say. Under fresh scrutiny stimulated by the controversy, many scientists have reexamined the environmentalist explanations of the black IQ deficit and found them to be inadequate. They simply do not fully account for the known facts, in the comprehensive and consistent manner we should expect of a scientific explanation.

The Black IQ Deficit

First of all, it is a known and uncontested fact that blacks in the United States score on average about one standard deviation below whites on most tests of intelligence. On the most commonly used IQ tests, this difference ranges from 10 to 20 points, and averages about 15 points. This means that only about 16 percent of the black population exceeds the test performance of the average white on IQ tests. A similar difference of one standard deviation between blacks and whites holds true for 80 standardized mental tests on which published data exist [see chart, page 84].

A difference of one standard deviation can hardly be called inconsequential. Intelligence tests have more than proved themselves as valid predictors of scholastic performance and occupational attainment, and they predict equally well for blacks as for whites. Unpleasant as these predictions may seem to some people, their significance cannot be wished away because of a belief in equality. Of course, an individual's success and self-fulfillment depends upon many characteristics *besides* intelligence, but IQ does represent an index, albeit an imperfect one, of the ability to compete in many walks of life. For example, many selective colleges require College Board test scores of 600 (equivalent to an IQ of 115) as a minimum for admission. An average IQ difference of one standard deviation between blacks and whites means that the white population will have about seven times the percentage of such potentially talented persons (i.e., IQs over 115) as the black population. At the other end of the scale, the 15-point difference in average IQ scores means that mental retardation (IQ below 70) will occur about seven times as often among blacks as among whites.

The IQ difference between blacks and whites, then, clearly has considerable social significance. Yet the environmentalists dismiss this difference as artificial, and claim it does not imply any innate or genetic difference in intelligence. But as I shall show, the purely environmental explanations most commonly put forth are faulty. Examined closely in terms of the available evidence, they simply do not sustain the burden of explanation that they claim. Of course, they may be *possible* explanations of the IQ difference, but that does not necessarily make them the *most probable*. In every case for which there was sufficient relevant evidence to put to a detailed test, the environmental explanations have proven inadequate. I am not saying they have been proven 100 percent wrong, only that they do not account for *all* of the black IQ deficit. Of course, there may be other possible environmental explanations as yet unformulated and untested.

Arguments for the Genetic Hypothesis

The genetic hypothesis, on the other hand, has not yet been put to any direct tests by the standard techniques of genetic research. It must be seriously considered, however, for two reasons: 1) because the default of the environmentalist theory, which has failed in many of its most important predictions, increases the probability of the genetic theory; 2) since genetically conditioned physical characteristics differ markedly between racial groups, there is a strong *a priori* likelihood that genetically conditioned behavioral or mental characteristics will also differ. Since intelligence and other mental abilities depend upon the physiological structure of the brain, and since the brain, like other organs, is subject to genetic influence, how can anyone disregard the obvious probability of genetic influence on intelligence?

Let us consider some of the genetically conditioned characteristics that we already know to vary between major racial groups: body size and proportions; cranial size and shape; pigmentation of the hair, skin and eyes; hair form and distribution; number of vertebrae; fingerprints; bone density; basic-metabolic rate; sweating; consistency of ear wax; age of eruption of the permanent teeth; fissural patterns on the surfaces of the teeth; blood groups; chronic diseases; frequency of twinning; male-female birth ratio; visual and auditory acuity; color-blindness; taste; length of gestation period; physical maturity at birth. In view of so many genetically conditioned traits that do differ between races, wouldn't it be surprising if genetically conditioned mental traits were a major exception?

The Heritability of Intelligence

One argument for the high probability of genetic influence on the IQ difference between blacks and whites involves the concept of *heritability*. A technical term in quantitative genetics, heritability refers to the proportion of the total variation of some trait, among persons within a given population, that can be attributed to genetic factors. Once the heritability of that trait can be determined, the remainder of the variance can be attributed mainly to environmental influence. Now intelligence, as measured by standard tests such as the Stanford-Binet and many others, does show very substantial heritability in the European and North American Caucasian populations in which the necessary genetic studies have been done. I don't know of any geneticists today who have viewed the evidence and who dispute this conclusion.

No precise figure exists for the heritability of intelligence, since, like any population statistic, it varies from one study to another, depending on the particular population sampled, the IQ test used, and the method of genetic analysis. Most of the estimates for the heritability of intelligence in the populations studied indicate that genetic factors are about twice as important as environmental factors as a cause of IQ differences among individuals.

I do not know of a methodologically adequate determination of IQ heritability in a sample of the

U. S. black population. The few estimates that exist, though statistically weak, give little reason to suspect that the heritability of IQ for blacks, when adequately estimated, should differ appreciably from that for whites. Of course the absence of reliable data makes this a speculative assumption.

What implication does the heritability *within* a population have concerning the cause of the difference *between* two populations? The fact that IQ is highly heritable within the white and probably the black population does not by itself constitute formal proof that the difference between the populations is genetic, either in whole or in part. However, the fact of substantial heritability of IQ within the populations does increase the *a priori* probability that the population difference is partly attributable to genetic factors. Biologists generally agree that, almost without exception throughout nature, any genetically conditioned characteristic that varies among individuals within a subspecies (i.e., race) also varies genetically between different subspecies. Thus, the substantial heritability of IQ within the Caucasian and probably black populations makes it likely (but does not prove) that the black population's lower average IQ is caused at least in part by a genetic difference.

What about the purely cultural and environmental explanations of the IQ difference? The most common argument claims that IQ tests have a built-in cultural bias that discriminates against blacks and other poor minority groups. Those who hold this view criticize the tests as being based unfairly on the language, knowledge and cognitive skills of the white "Anglo" middle class. They argue that blacks in the United States do not share in the same culture as whites, and therefore acquire different meanings to words, different knowledge, and a different set of intellectual skills.

Culture-Fair Vs. Culture-Biased

However commonly and fervently held, this claim that the black IQ deficit can be blamed on culture-biased or "culture-loaded" tests does not

stand up under rigorous study. First of all, the fact that a test is culture-*loaded* does not necessarily mean it is culture-*biased*. Of course, many tests do have questions of information, vocabulary and comprehension that clearly draw on experiences which could only be acquired by persons sharing a fairly common cultural background. Reputable tests, called "culture-fair" tests, do exist, however. They use nonverbal, simple symbolic material common to a great many different cultures. Such tests measure the ability to generalize, to distinguish differences and similarities, to see relationships, and to solve problems. They test reasoning power rather than just specific bits of knowledge.

Surprisingly, blacks tend to perform relatively better on the more culture-loaded or verbal kinds of tests than on the culture-fair type. For example, on the widely used Wechsler Intelligence Scale, comprised of 11 different subtests, blacks do better on the culture-loaded subtests of vocabulary, general information, and verbal comprehension than on the nonverbal performance tests such as the block designs. Just the opposite is true for such minorities as Orientals, Mexican-Americans, Indians, and Puerto Ricans. It can hardly be claimed that culture-fair tests have a built-in bias in favor of white, Anglo, middle-class Americans when Arctic Eskimos taking the same tests perform on a par with white, middle-class norms. My assistants and I have tested large numbers of Chinese children who score well above white norms on such tests, despite being recent immigrants from Hong Kong and Formosa, knowing little or no English, and having parents who hold low-level socioeconomic occupations. If the tests have a bias toward the white, Anglo, middle-class, one might well wonder why Oriental children should outscore the white Anglos on whom the tests were originally standardized. Our tests of Mexican-Americans produced similar results. They do rather poorly on the culture-loaded types of tests based on verbal skills and knowledge, but they do better on the culture-fair tests. The same holds true for American Indians. All these minorities perform on the two types of tests much as one might expect from the culture-bias hypothesis. Only blacks, among the minorities we have tested, score in just the opposite manner.

Intelligence Tests Are Colorblind

Those who talk of culture bias should also consider that all the standard mental tests I know of are colorblind, in that they show the same reliability and predictive validity for blacks and whites. In predicting scholastic achievement, for example, we have found that several different IQ tests predict equally well for blacks and whites. College-aptitude tests also predict grades equally well for blacks and whites. The same equality holds true for aptitude tests which predict job performance.

We have studied culture bias in some standard IQ tests by making internal analyses to see which kinds of test items produce greater differences in scores between blacks and whites. For example, we made such an item-by-item check of the highly culture-loaded Peabody Picture Vocabulary Test, on which blacks average some 15 points lower than whites. The PPVT consists of 150 cards, each containing four pictures. The examiner names one of the pictures and the child points to the appropriate picture. The items follow the order of their difficulty, as measured by the percentage of the children in the normative sample who fail the item.

California Vs. England; Boys Vs. Girls

To illustrate the sensitivity of this test to cultural differences in word meanings, we compared the performance of white schoolchildren in England with children of the same age in California. Although the two groups obtained about the same total IQ score, the California group found some culture-loaded words such as "bronco" and "thermos" easy, while the London group found them difficult. The opposite occurred with words like "pedestrian" or "goblet." Thus the difficulty of some items differed sharply depending on the child's cultural background. A similar "cultural" bias shows up when comparing the performance of boys and girls, both black and white. Though boys and girls score about equally well over all, they show significant differences in the rank order of item difficulty; specific items, e.g., "parachute" versus "casserole" reflect different sexual biases in cultural knowledge.

Yet when we made exactly the same kind of comparison between blacks and whites in the same city in California, and even in the same schools, we found virtually no difference between the two groups in the order of items when ranked for difficulty, as indexed by the percent failing each item. Both groups show the same rank order of difficulty, although on each item a smaller percentage of blacks give the correct answer. In fact, even the differences between adjacent test items, in terms of percent answering correctly, show great similarity in both the black and white groups.

If this kind of internal analysis reflects cultural bias between different national groups, and sexual bias *within* the same racial group, why does it not reflect the supposed bias *between* the two racial groups? If the tests discriminate against blacks, why do blacks and whites make errors on the same items? Why should the most and least common errors in one group be the same as in the other?

Another way internal analysis can be used to check for bias involves looking for different patterns of item intercorrelations. For example, if a person gets item number 20 right, he may be more likely to get, say, item 30 right than if he had missed item 20. This follows because the test items correlate with one another to varying degrees, and the amount of correlations and the pattern of intercorrelations should be sensitive to group differences in cultural background. Yet we have found no significant or appreciable differences between item intercorrelations for blacks and whites.

In summary, we have found no discriminant features of test items that can statistically separate the test records of blacks and whites any better than chance, when the records are equated for total number correct. We could do so with the London versus California groups, or for sex differences within the same racial group. Thus, even when using the PPVT, one of the most culture-loaded tests, black and white performances did not differ as one should expect if we accept the culture-bias explanation for the black IQ deficit. I consider this strong evidence against the validity of that explanation.

The Effect of the Tester

What about subtle influences in the test situation itself which could have a depressing effect on black performance? It has been suggested, for example, that a white examiner might emotionally inhibit the performance of black children in a test situation. Most of the studies that have attempted to test this hypothesis have produced no substantiation of it. In my own study in which 9,000 black and white children took a number of standard mental and scholastic tests given by black and white examiners, there were no systematic differences in scores according to the race of the examiners. What about the examiner's language, dialect, or accent? In one study, the Stanford-Binet test, a highly verbal and individually administered exam, was translated into black ghetto dialect, and administered by a black examiner fluent in that dialect. A group of black children who took the test under these conditions obtained an average IQ score less than one point higher than the average IQ score of a control group given the test in standard English.

The Question of "Verbal Deprivation"

To test the popular notion that blacks do poorly on IQ tests because they are "verbally deprived," we have looked at studies of the test performances of the most verbally deprived individuals we know of: children born totally deaf. These children do score considerably below average on verbal tests, as ex-

pected. But they perform completely up to par on the nonverbal culture-fair type of tests. Their performances, then, turns out to be just the opposite of the supposedly verbally deprived blacks, who score higher on the verbal than on the nonverbal tests.

If one hypothesizes that the black IQ deficit may be due to poor motivation or uncooperative attitudes of blacks in the test situation, then one must explain why little or no difference in scores occurs between blacks and whites on tests involving rote learning and memory. Such tests are just as demanding in terms of attention, effort and persistence, but do not call upon the kinds of abstract reasoning abilities that characterize the culture-fair intelligence tests. We have devised experimental tests, which look to pupils like any other tests, that minimize the need for reasoning and abstract ability, and maximize the role of nonconceptual learning and memory. On these tests black and white children average about the same scores. Therefore, the racial difference clearly does not involve all mental abilities equally. It involves mainly conceptual and abstract reasoning, and not learning and memory.

Another factor often cited as a possible explanation for the black IQ deficit is teacher expectancy—the notion that a child's test score tends to reflect the level of performance expected by his or her teacher, with the teacher's expectation often based on prejudice or stereotypes. Yet numerous studies of teacher expectancy have failed to establish this phenomenon as a contributing factor to the lower IQ scores of blacks.

Testing the Environmental Hypothesis

To test the environmentalist hypothesis, we have examined the results of those tests that most strongly reflect environmental sources of variance, and they turn out to be the very tests that show the least difference between blacks and whites in average scores. The greatest difference in scores between the two racial groups occurs on the tests we infer to be more strongly reflective of genetic variance. If the cultural-environmental hypothesis were correct, just the opposite would be true.

The "Sociologist's Fallacy"

In an attempt to disprove the genetic hypothesis for the black IQ deficit, environmentalists frequently cite studies that compare IQs of socioeconomically matched racial groups, and find considerably less difference in test scores than the usual 15-point difference between races. Here we have a good example of the "sociologist's fallacy." Since whites and blacks differ in average socioeconomic status (SES), the matching of racial groups on SES variables such as education, occupation, and social class necessarily means that the black group is more highly selected in terms of whatever other traits and abilities correlate with SES, including intelligence. Therefore the two groups have been unfairly matched in terms of IQ.

Those who cite the socioeconomic matching studies also fail to take account of the well-established genetic difference between social classes, which invalidates their comparison. For example, when the two races are matched for social background, the average skin color of the black group runs lighter in the higher SES groups. This difference indicates that genetic characteristics do vary with SES. Thus, SES matching of blacks and whites reduces the IQ difference not only because it controls for environmental differences, but because it tends to equalize genetic factors as well.

Variables That Don't Behave

A host of other environmental variables don't behave as they ought to according to a strictly environmentalist theory of the black IQ deficit. For example, on practically all the socioeconomic, educational, nutritional and other health factors that sociologists point to as causes of the black-white differences in IQ and scholastic achievement, the American Indian population ranks about as far below black standards as blacks do below those of whites. The relevance of these environmental indices can be shown by the fact that within each ethnic group they correlate to some extent in the expected direction with tests of intelligence and scholastic achievement. Since health, parental education, employment, family income, and a number of more subtle environmental factors that have been studied are all deemed important for children's scholastic success, the stark deprivation of the Indian minority, even by black standards, ought to be reflected in a comparison of the intelligence and achievement-test performance of Indians and blacks. But in a nationwide survey reported in the Coleman Report, in 1966, Indians scored *higher* than blacks on all such tests, from the first to the 12th grade. On a nonverbal test given in the first grade, for example, before schooling could have had much impact, Indian children exceeded the mean score of blacks by the equivalent of 14 IQ points. Similar findings occur with Mexican-Americans, who rate below blacks on socioeconomic and other environmental indices, but score considerably higher on IQ tests, especially on the nonverbal type. Thus the IQ difference between Indians and blacks and between Mexican-Americans and blacks, turns out opposite to what one would predict from purely environmental theory, which of course, assumes complete genetic equality for intelligence. No testable environmental hypothesis has as yet been offered to account for these findings.

Does Malnutrition Affect Intelligence?

What about malnutrition, another factor frequently cited by the environmentalists to disprove the genetic hypothesis? Malnutrition has indeed been found to affect both physical and mental development in a small percentage of children in those areas of the world that suffer severe protein deficiencies: India, South America, South Africa, and Mexico. But few blacks in the U. S. show any history or signs of severe malnutrition, and I have

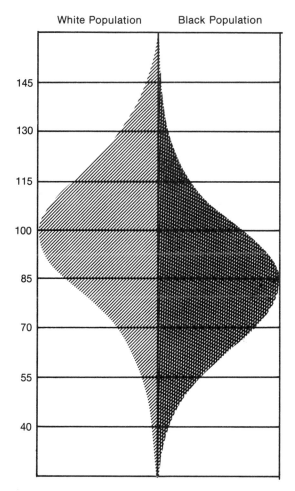

White Population   Black Population

145

130

115

100

85

70

55

40

FIGURE 1. Distribution of IQ scores. On most intelligence tests, black scores average about 15 points lower than do white scores.

found no evidence that the degree of malnutrition associated with retarded mental development afflicts any major segment of the U. S. population.

Nor do I know of any evidence among humans that maternal malnutrition, by itself, can have pre- or postnatal effects on a child's mental development. The severe famine in the Netherlands during the last years of World War II provided an excellent case study of such a possibility. Thousands of men conceived, gestated, and born during the period of most severe famine, were later tested, as young adults, on Raven's Standard Progressive Matrices, a nonverbal reasoning test. Their scores did not differ significantly from the scores of other Dutch youths of the same age who had not been exposed to such maternal nutritional deprivation.

If further research should definitely establish the existence of genetically conditioned differences in intelligence between certain races, what would be the practical implications? It would take several articles to consider the question adequately, but the only morally tenable position in human relations would remain unchanged: that all persons should be treated according to their own individual characteristics, and not in terms of their group identity. Let me stress that none of the research I have discussed here allows one to conclude anything about the intelligence of any individual black or white person.

Equality of rights and opportunities is clearly the most beneficial condition for any society. Acceptance of the reality of human differences in mental abilities would simply underline the need for equality of opportunity in order to allow everyone to achieve his or her own self-fulfillment. In order to take account and advantage of the diversity of abilities in the population, and truly to serve all citizens equally, the public schools should move beyond narrow conceptions of scholastic achievement. They should offer a much greater diversity of ways for children of whatever aptitude to benefit from their education.

Environment Vs. Genetics: Still an Open Question

I have tried to emphasize the uncertainty of our knowledge of the causes of race differences in mental abilities. I do not claim any direct or definite evidence, in terms of genetic research, for the existence of genotypic intelligence differences between races or other human population groups. I have not urged acceptance of a hypothesis on the basis of insufficient evidence. I have tried to show that the evidence we now have does not support the environmentalist theory, which, until quite recently, has been accepted as scientifically established. Social scientists have generally accepted it without question, and most scientists in other fields have given silent assent. I have assembled evidence which, I believe, makes such complacent assent no longer possible, and reveals the issue as an open question, calling for much further scientific study.

Politicizing a Scientific Issue

Most of the scientists and intellectuals with whom I have discussed these matters in the past few years see no danger in furthering our knowledge of the genetic basis of racial differences in mental or behavioral traits. Nor do they fear general recognition of genetic differences in such traits by the scientific world, if that should be the eventual outcome of further research. They do see a danger in politicizing a basically scientific question, one that should be settled strictly on the basis of evidence.

Most of the attempts to politicize the issue, I have found, come from the radical left. True liberals and humanists, on the other hand, want to learn the facts. They do not wish to expend their energies sustaining myths and illusions. They wish to face reality, whatever it may be, because only on the level of reality can real problems be effectively confronted. This means asking hard questions, and seeking the answers with as much scientific ingenuity and integrity as we can muster. It means examining all reasonable hypotheses, including unpopular ones. It means maintaining the capacity to doubt what we might most want to believe, acknowledging the uncertainties at the edge of knowledge, and viewing new findings in terms of shifting probabilities rather than as absolute conclusions.

ARTICLE 29

Is IQ heritable? (A review of two books by Arthur Jensen)

Leon J. Kamin

These two books [*Genetics and Education* and *Educability and Group Differences*] by Jensen form a package. The 1972 collection of reprinted journal articles marshals evidence in support of the assertion that "four times as much of the variance in measured intelligence is attributable to heredity as environment" (p. 301). This earlier work is relatively cautious with respect to Black-White differences in IQ. The "possible importance of genetic factors in racial behavioral differences has been . . . a tabooed subject, just as were the topics of venereal disease and birth control" (p. 159), but it is "a not unreasonable hypothesis that genetic factors are strongly implicated in the average Negro-white intelligence difference" (p. 163).

The second volume takes as an established fact an IQ heritability of about .80 within the White population. Though Jensen recognizes that a high within-group heritability does not formally imply a heritable basis for a between-group difference in means, he argues that it does increase "the *plausibility,* or the *a priori* probability, that genetic differences exist between the groups. Plausibility is a subjective judgment of *likelihood*" (p. 144; italics in the original). The numerous studies of race differences in IQ, and of "racial hybrids," are reviewed at length, and the second shoe finally falls with a clatter: "something between one-half and three-fourths of the average IQ difference between American Negroes and whites is attributable to genetic factors, and the remainder to environmental factors and their interaction with the genetic differences" (p. 363).

These remarkable quantitative estimates presumably depend upon empirical data, and the two volumes are stuffed with numbers that lend an aura of quantitative precision to Jensen's assertions. The numbers, however, are not beyond challenge. They are sometimes cited erroneously, and often with a partisan selectivity. To take a few examples from the 1972 volume, Jensen indicates (p. 124) that the

Reprinted from *Contemporary Psychology,* 1975, *20,* pp. 545–547. Copyright 1975 by the American Psychological Association. Reprinted by permission.

"obtained median" IQ correlation for siblings reared apart in three (unnamed) studies is .47. That is strikingly close to the value of about .50, which would be predicted by an exclusively genetic model of IQ determination. The Jensen table that reports this "obtained median" has been modified since its original appearances in *Harvard Educational Review*. The .47 median had originally been said to be based on no fewer than 33 separate studies. This had clearly been taken from Burt's 1966 paper, and Burt later informed Jensen that the correct number of studies should have been 3, not 33. There are in fact three published studies of siblings reared apart. They are by Hildreth (1925), who reported a correlation of .23; by Freeman, Holzinger, and Mitchell (1928), who reported a correlation of .25; and by Burt (1966), who reported .46. The "obtained median" of these studies is not .47, but .25. That is as easily attributable to the demonstrable tendency to place "separated" sibs into similar environments as to the genetic similarity between sibs.

The same Jensen table indicates that the median correlation for opposite-sexed dizygotic (DZ) twins, based on nine studies, is .49. There do not appear to exist nine studies of opposite-sexed DZ's that produce so low a median as .49. The "median" has again been taken from Burt (1966), who had said it was based on six (unnamed) studies. The use of medians in any event weights small and large studies of representative and unrepresentative samples equally. The most representative and largest sample of opposite-sexed DZ's was obtained from the national Scottish Mental Survey by Mehrota and Maxwell (1950). For 182 pairs of 11-year-olds they reported a correlation of .63. Probably the best sample of same-sexed DZ's was obtained in Sweden by Husen (1959), who examined 416 pairs of males reporting for possible military service and found a correlation of .70. These large-scale studies, reporting correlations far in excess of the genetic expectation of about .50, provide less grist for the hereditarian mill than do the "obtained medians." The Jensen mill, however, grinds exceedingly fine. Thus, on the page following his table of median correlations, he publishes a figure purporting to indicate the median correlation (about .40) obtained in studies of DZ twins reared apart. That median, if true, might have theoretical import, but in fact there does not exist a single study of DZ twins reared apart.

This kind of slipshod "citation" is at times compensated for by a passion for the communication of precise numerical detail. To demonstrate that the pooled data from four studies of separated identical twins form a normal distribution, a chi-square test is performed. The value of chi-square is reported as "only 3.08, $p = 0.80$. (Chi-square with 7 degrees of freedom must exceed 14.07 for significance at the 0.05 level.)" (p. 314). Then, to demonstrate that the variances of twin IQ differences are homogeneous across the four studies (and thus to justify pooling), "Bartlett's test was performed on the standard deviations . . . and revealed that on this parameter the differences among the studies are nonsignificant at the 0.01 level" (p. 318). The skeptical reader may wonder why in this latter instance neither the obtained value of chi-square, nor the value significant at the 0.05 level, is provided. The fact that calculation reveals Bartlett's test to yield a chi-square value that is significant at the 0.02 level may be coincidental, but I suspect not.

There are similar problems with many of the "numbers" cited in the 1973 volume: "Every study of Negroes tested with the Wechsler scales reported in the literature, except for those involving nonrepresentative samples such as delinquents and prisoners, show [sic] higher Verbal IQ than Performance IQ (Shuey, 1966, pp. 295, 359–60, 371)" (p. 278). The Shuey pages cited by Jensen in fact refer to five Wechsler studies of adult samples, none involving delinquents or prisoners. For three of the five Black samples ("every"), Verbal IQ is higher than Performance IQ—in one case by less than one-third of an IQ point. The Shuey volume elsewhere cites eight Wechsler studies of normal Black school children; in seven cases the black children had higher Verbal than Performance IQ's. However, only three of these studies examined

White children as well. Two of these three studies reported larger Verbal-Performance differentials for the Whites than for the Blacks.

There is not space to review the caliber of the studies cited by Jensen, but at least one case should be mentioned. The work of De Lemos (1969), who gave Piaget's conservation tasks to "full-blooded" and "part Caucasian" Australian aboriginal children, is cited as follows: "The results appear almost as if the admixture of Caucasian genes, even so few as one-eighth, introduces mental structures otherwise lacking, that permit the individual to reach higher levels of mental development than normally occurs [sic] in the majority of full-Aboriginals" (p. 316). The tested children lived in "a single integrated community," into which Caucasian genes had been introduced by "laborers and sailors" who "never lived among the tribe." The genealogies had been constructed by the local mission. The De Lemos paper first indicates that for a total of 80 subjects aged 8 to 15 achievement of conservation increased with age. The number of subjects achieving conservation is then given separately for only 38 full- and 34 part-Aboriginal children, with the full-Aboriginals doing worse. There is no indication of why the remaining 8 children were excluded from this analysis, or of whether the age distributions of part- and full-Aboriginals were similar, or of whether the part-Aboriginals had distinctive physical appearances, or of whether the examiner was aware of the child's ancestry. There is an explicit assurance that the "flexibility of Piaget's clinical method" was retained in the scoring procedure. Those who do not share Jensen's subjective estimate of the a priori likelihood that Caucasian genes introduce potent new mental structures will not be surprised to learn that a recent attempt to replicate the De Lemos finding in the same community failed entirely (Dasen, 1972).

The second Jensen volume assiduously gathers any shreds of evidence that might be made to point toward Black genetic inferiority, while ignoring qualifications and contradictions. Thus, for example, much is made of the fact that American Blacks do at least as poorly on "culture-free" tests (specifically, Raven's Progressive Matrices) as on verbal tests. This is said to point toward a genetic, rather than sociocultural, interpretation of low Black scores. The fact is, however, that studies of White twins have failed to demonstrate a substantial genetic basis for the Raven test. For that test, Clark, Vandenberg, and Proctor (1961) obtained an MZ twin correlation of .58, and a DZ twin correlation of .53. For the same test, Husen (1959) reported MZ and DZ correlations of .63 and .52. Thus, even under the dubious assumption that twin correlations reflect heritability, the evidence for a heritable component of the Raven test is minimal—but it is sufficient for Jensen to attribute low Black scores to deficient genes.

The final two pages of the 1973 book contain three educational recommendations that might increase "the benefits of education to the majority of Negro children" once it is recognized that racial differences in ability "are not mainly the result of discrimination and environmental conditions." The educators should search for aptitude × training interactions, they should pay attention to learning readiness, and they should provide greater diversity of curricula and goals. This rich harvest of 69 years of psychometric research had been foreseen clearly, and phrased more provocatively, by Lewis Terman in 1916. Terman indicated that an IQ in the 70–80 range "is very, very common among Spanish-Indian and Mexican families of the Southwest and also among Negroes. Their dullness seems to be racial. . . . They cannot master abstractions, but they can often be made efficient workers."

Terman went on to observe, "There is no possibility at present of convincing society that they should not be allowed to reproduce, although from a eugenic point of view they constitute a grave problem because of their unusually prolific breeding." Fifty-six years later Jensen (1972, pp. 177–179) similarly views with concern the possibility that "Negro lower-class families" may be reproducing at a dysgenic rate. He wonders whether "current welfare policies, unaided by eugenic foresight, could lead to the genetic enslavement of a substantial segment of our population?''

To me, at least, the similarity in the views of Terman and Jensen is both remarkable and depressing. Throughout its history, a recurrent theme in American psychometrics has been a concern with the supposed social menace of Black genetic inferiority. The assumed genetic inferiority, however, is undemonstrated and undemonstrable. To put matters as charitably as I can, policy recommendations based upon the assumption of genetic inferiority seem misguided. (There are others who may put it less charitably.)

The relations between psychology and politics are such that Jensen's two books may be the most significant American psychological work since Carl Brigham's *A Study of American Intelligence* appeared in 1923. That book interpreted World War I intelligence testing of foreign-born draftees as having demonstrated the genetic superiority of ''Nordics'' to Italian, Polish, Russian, and Jewish immigrants from southeastern Europe. The work helped to rationalize the overtly racist Immigration Act of 1924, with its ''national origin quotas.'' The Jensen books will have—have had—a major political impact, although they merely document anew that IQ scores run in families, and that Whites have a higher average score than Blacks. The critical reader who troubles to examine the studies reviewed by Jensen will not, I believe, agree that either of these phenomena has been demonstrated to have any genetic basis. The question we ought to ask is why, especially of late, we have been so ready to believe that they do.

REFERENCES

Brigham, C. C. *A study of American intelligence.* Princeton, N. J.: Princeton University Press, 1923.

Burt, C. The genetic determination of differences in intelligence: A study of monozygotic twins reared together and apart. *British Journal of Psychology,* 1966, *57,* 137–153.

Clark, P., Vandenberg, S., & Proctor, C. On the relationship of scores on certain psychological tests with a number of anthropometric characters and birth orders in twins. *Human Biology,* 1961, *33,* 167–170.

Dasen, P. R. The development of conservation in aboriginal children: A replication study. *International Journal of Psychology,* 1972, *7*(2), 75–85.

DeLemos, M. M. The development of conservation in aboriginal children. *International Journal of Psychology,* 1969, *4,* 255–269.

Freeman, F. N., Holzinger, K. J. & Mitchell, B. C. The influence of environment on the intelligence, school achievement, and conduct of foster children. *27th yearbook of the National Society for the Study of Education,* part 1, pp. 103–217. Bloomington, Ind.: Public School Publishing Co., 1928.

Hildreth, G. The resemblance of siblings in intelligence and achievement. *Contributions to education,* no. 186. New York: Teacher's College, 1925.

Husén, T. *Psychological twin research, 1, A methodological study.* Stockholm: Almqvist and Wiksell, 1959.

Jensen, A. R. *Genetics and education.* New York: Harper & Row, 1972.

Jensen, A. R. *Educability and group differences.* New York: Harper & Row, 1973.

Mehrota, S. N., & Maxwell, J. The intelligence of twins: A comparative study of eleven-year-old twins. *Population Studies,* 1950, *3,* 295–302.

Shuey, A. M. *The testing of Negro intelligence.* (2nd ed.) New York: Social Science Press, 1966.

Terman, L. M. *The measurement of intelligence.* New York: Houghton Mifflin, 1916.

ARTICLE 30

Is there any real evidence that I.Q. test scores are heritable? (A book review of *The Science and Politics of I.Q.,* by Leon J. Kamin)

David Layzer

Conventional wisdom has it that each of us comes into the world equipped with a set of more or less highly differentiated capacities for mental and physical development. These capacities vary greatly from one individual to another—but so do the opportunities our society affords for their development. Inequalities in occupational status and economic rewards therefore reflect environmental as well as genetic differences among individuals. Which of the two sources of inequality is more important? The question obviously has profound social and political implications. If genetic differences are the chief source of social inequalities, one might argue (as many have argued) that efforts to reduce them are misguided. If, on the other hand, environmental factors are to blame, democratic principles would seem to demand far-reaching (and expensive) social reforms. Until recently there was no objective basis for deciding between these two explanations of social inequality, but now (I am still quoting conventional wisdom), thanks to the efforts of psychometricians and quantitative geneticists, the issue can at last be resolved in a scientific way.

Two technical developments are said to be responsible for this breakthrough. One is the I.Q. test, which an American psychologist, Richard J. Herrnstein, calls "psychology's most telling accomplishment." The other is heritability analysis, a statistical technique for analyzing biometric and psychometric data. The I.Q. test (it is maintained) assesses the innate capacities that underlie the acquisition of "higher" cognitive skills: abstract reasoning and problem solving. Heritability analysis is an analytic machine that accepts as inputs statistical correlations between the I.Q. scores of genetically related individuals and yields as output the "heritability of I.Q.," a numerical measure of the relative importance of genetic and environmental sources of the variation of I.Q. within a given population.

Several independent studies of I.Q. heritability have been carried out in recent years, and most of

Reprinted from *Scientific American*, 1975, *233*(1), pp. 126–128.

them have concluded that its value is very high: about .8. This implies that no more than 20 percent of the observed variation in I.Q. can be attributed to nongenetic factors, including some, such as intrauterine experience, that are insensitive to education and social forms of intervention. Early in 1969 Arthur R. Jensen, a professor of educational psychology at the University of California at Berkeley, published a summary of the data supporting this conclusion and a discussion of their educational and social implications. He concluded that children who score low on I.Q. tests lack the capacity for abstract reasoning and that efforts to teach them problem-solving skills are not only futile but also unkind; such children, he suggested, should be taught mainly by rote. Jensen also concluded that reported differences between the average I.Q.'s of black children and white children probably reflect genetic differences between the two groups. The article aroused widespread interest, among public officials charged with formulating and implementing educational and social policies as well as among social scientists and educators. Two years later Herrnstein published a popular account of Jensen's discussion of I.Q. heritability, along with his own assessment of its implications (*The Atlantic Monthly,* September, 1971). Herrnstein argued that the elimination of artificial barriers to social and economic mobility would lead to the emergence of hereditary socioeconomic stratification based on I.Q.

Leon Kamin's book is directed against these arguments and the conventional wisdom in which they are rooted. It reaches two major conclusions. "The first stems from a detailed examination of the empirical evidence which has been adduced in support of the idea of heritability, and it can be stated simply. There exist no data which should lead a prudent man to accept the hypothesis that I.Q. test scores are in any degree heritable."

Kamin's second major conclusion represents his answer to the obvious question raised by the first: If the belief in I.Q. heritability has no empirical support, how has it come to be so widely accepted by the experts? Here is Kamin's answer: "The I.Q. test

in America, and the way in which we think about it, has been fostered by men committed to a particular social view. That view includes the belief that those on the bottom are genetically inferior victims of their own immutable defects. The consequence has been that the I.Q. test has served as an instrument of oppression against the poor—dressed in the trappings of science, rather than politics. The message of science is heard respectfully, particularly when the tidings it carries are soothing to the public conscience."

The data that have been used to support conventional estimates of I.Q. heritability are of two main kinds: I.Q. correlations between genetically related individuals (particularly identical twins) reared separately and I.Q. correlations between genetically unrelated children reared together. Under certain idealized conditions correlations of the first kind would be produced entirely by genetic similarities and those of the second kind would be produced entirely by environmental similarities. If genetic factors play a major role in the genesis of I.Q. differences, as Jensen asserts and Kamin denies, then the I.Q. correlation between separated identical twins should be large, that between separated fraternal twins somewhat smaller and that between separated first cousins smaller still. And the correlation between the I.Q.'s of unrelated children reared together should provide a direct measure of the environmental contribution to the variation of I.Q.

The problem is more complex than these naive considerations suggest. One cannot safely assume that genetically related children who have been reared separately have had uncorrelated environments, since such children are often reared by close relatives living in similar neighborhoods. Nor can one assume that the environments of unrelated children reared together are identical, or even that their genotypes are uncorrelated. These are merely the most obvious of the difficulties one encounters when one comes to grips with the actual data.

Both Jensen and Herrnstein relied heavily on the work of the late Sir Cyril Burt, which, as Kamin remarks, "has had a major impact on all facets of the study of I.Q. heritability. There are, for example, various categories of kinship for which the only existing I.Q. correlations have been provided in Burt's publications. Those publications, and those of his colleagues and students, are almost limitless in number. They furnish us with a veritable treasure of I.Q. data." Kamin has subjected this "treasure" to careful critical scrutiny—and found it to be worthless. Consider, for instance, the IQ correlation for separated identical twins, a statistic commonly assumed to furnish the single most direct and reliable estimate of I.Q. heritability. The value reported by Burt in his last paper on the subject, published in 1966, is .771. Now, Burt's twin sample grew over the years as new subjects were added to it. In 1955 it contained 21 pairs, in 1958 "over 30" pairs and in 1966 53 pairs. Yet in all three years the reported I.Q. correlation had the same value, .771! Kamin points out a number of similar coincidences in Burt's reported data. These intimations of subjectivity, disconcerting as they are, are less so than inconsistencies in the procedures by which Burt and his colleagues assessed I.Q. and various environmental factors. Jensen has reported that Burt's original data files have been destroyed, so that it is not now possible to ascertain the sources of the inconsistencies, contradictions and numerical coincidences that abound in the work published since 1955, but Kamin's conclusion seems inescapable: "The numbers left behind by Professor Burt are simply not worthy of our current scientific attention."

The three remaining studies of separated identical twins, all of which deal with adult subjects, are not particularly informative, although the two larger studies (one carried out in the U.S., the other in Britain) do provide clear evidence that the degree of resemblance between the I.Q.'s of separated twins is profoundly influenced by the degree of resemblance between their environments.

Having demolished the central edifice of hereditarian doctrine, Kamin next trains his critical artillery on some of the outbuildings: studies of I.Q.

correlations between genetically related people who are not identical twins and studies of adopted children. The difference between the I.Q. correlation for identical twins reared together and that for same-sex fraternal twins reared together enables one to estimate I.Q. heritability under certain simplifying (and, as Kamin rightly points out, unjustified) assumptions. Jensen's review of what he described as "all the major twin studies using intelligence tests" yielded heritability estimates ranging from 47 to 91 percent. Kamin notes, however, that Jensen omitted a number of studies, with "sample sizes comparable to the included studies," that seem equally sound methodologically. When some of these are included, the estimates of I.Q. heritability range from an impossible −7 percent to +153 percent. As for the studies of adopted children, the observation that "adopted children's I.Q.'s are very much higher than those of their biological parents forces hereditarians to concede some role to environment. There do not appear to be any equivalent data that compel a similar concession by environmentalists. The hypothesis of zero heritability stands unscathed."

Kamin has made a strong negative case. He has gone back to the primary sources and demonstrated with a wealth of circumstantial detail that the data they contain cannot support the interpretation that Burt, Jensen and other hereditarians have placed on them. He has, I think, been less successful in explaining the widespread acceptance of hereditarian arguments by the scientific community. It is undeniable (and understandable) that the most indefatigable students of the genetics of human intelligence, from Sir Francis Galton to Sir Cyril Burt and from Lewis M. Terman to Arthur R. Jensen, have been strongly motivated by a belief in biological determinism and by a Platonic view of what constitutes a just society. It is also true, as Kamin forcefully reminds us in a brilliant chapter titled "Psychology and the Immigrant," that many American psychologists and geneticists have supported and are continuing to support questionable social legislation with even more questionable scientific judgments. Yet Kamin himself states that I.Q. heritability poses "a straightforward scientific question, one which can be answered by a logical analysis of the data." If the scientific issues are as straightforward as all that, why do they seem so ambiguous and value-laden to so many psychologists and geneticists who have no strong political commitments?

I suggest that the perceived ambiguity does not result from (although it may be nourished by) a conflict between class loyalties and scientific objectivity but rather is implicit in the framework within which the issues have usually been discussed—by Kamin as well as by those whose work he criticizes. Both hereditarians and environmentalists accept, implicitly or explicitly, a view expounded by B. F. Skinner in *Science and Human Behavior*: that the scientific study of behavior has no need of a theoretical framework, that it should make do with the weakest possible hypotheses. Kamin considers the weakest possible hypothesis that could account for observed differences in I.Q. to be the "null hypothesis," which attributes all such differences to nongenetic causes. He then argues, in my opinion convincingly, that published experimental data do not compel one to abandon this hypothesis; that is, the data do not establish a causal link between genetic differences and observed I.Q. differences. So far, so good. Let us, however, look at the other side of the coin. Suppose we take as our starting point the hypothesis that 80 percent of the variation in I.Q. is genetic in origin. Are there any data that would compel us to abandon that hypothesis—data establishing a causal link between specific environmental differences and differences in I.Q. scores? As far as I know there are none. (This may help to explain why the views of hereditarians on I.Q. heritability have not been visibly shaken by the collapse of the principal component of their ostensible data base, the work of Burt.) Hereditarians and environmentalists thus hold positions that are equally impregnable.

From another point of view the two positions are equally untenable. I refer to the point of view shared by the two giants of 20th-century psychology, Freud and Piaget: that a science of human behavior must be firmly rooted in biology. It seems to me that both the environmentalist and the hereditarian approach to the problem of human intelligence and its variation are profoundly unbiological. A biological approach would at the very outset recognize these three aspects of the problem:

1. Intelligence is a biological adaptation whose most distinctive characteristic is plasticity. Intelligence manifests itself in the ability to devise effective responses to new and unforeseen environmental challenges and to make creative use of relevant past experience. Criteria for assessing and comparing intelligent behavior must therefore necessarily vary from one culture or subculture to another. In seeking to devise "culture-free" tests of intelligence psychometricians are pursuing a chimera.

2. Intelligence, like every phenotypically plastic biological character, is not the realization of a genetic blueprint but the outcome of an exceedingly complex interaction of a genetically encoded developmental strategy and a unique environmental history. The outcome of this interaction will of course be affected by variations in both the genotype and its milieu, but there is no reason to suppose a given genotypic variation would produce the same variation in outcome under all environmental conditions, or that a given environmental variation would produce the same variation in outcome for all genotypes. Just such similarity of outcome, however, is the biological meaning of the principal assumption underlying conventional heritability analysis.

3. Heritability is a concept that cannot meaningfully be applied to just any set of numbers someone decides to call measurements. It applies to a certain class of phenotypic characters in populations that satisfy certain rather restrictive conditions. I.Q. scores are not measurements of a character belonging to this class. Although they are valid psychological "measures," they fail to meet the requirements

of a biological measurement. And it has recently been shown that, for technical mathematical and biological reasons, the concept of heritability probably does not apply to any phenotypically plastic trait in natural human populations.

In the light of these considerations the debate between environmentalists and hereditarians seems a bit unreal, centering as it does on analyses of inadmissible data by means of an inapplicable theory. Yet the social and educational implications of current hereditarian doctrines are real enough, and Kamin has performed an important service by exposing their scientific inadequacy.

SECTION SUMMARY

In order to put the position expressed by Arthur Jensen in the first article into its proper context, we need to review some chronology. For many years *a few* social scientists have argued for the existence of innate racial differences in intelligence. In the last 30 years, these conclusions have been based primarily on studies that found racial differences in tested IQ scores even after the researchers had purportedly "equated" the environments of Blacks and Whites (see, for example, Garrett, 1962, 1964, and 1969). The *equated environment strategy* was originally used in the 1930s and 1940s, when studies by Tanser (1939), Bruce (1940), and others attempted to create environmentally comparable groups of Blacks and Whites by making sure to use subjects from the same socioeconomic level. These studies found that the average differences of 10 to 15 points still occurred between economically deprived Whites and economically deprived Blacks. The researchers concluded that, since the environments of the two racial groups were equivalent, the difference in tested IQ must be due to innate differences. But it is more appropriate to question whether there were *any* Whites in the United States in the 1940s whose environment was comparable to that of Blacks. We may even ask, as Gallo and Dorfman (1970) do, whether *at present* in the United States and Canada the environment of Blacks is equivalent to that of Whites, even at the same income level.

Jensen approaches the issue in a different way by looking at the degree to which *any one person's* heredity determines his or her level of mental development. Jensen then speculates about the existence of many types of group differences in intelligence, including social-class and sex differences as well as racial ones.

Jensen's basic viewpoint on the origin of individual differences may be expressed through the following statements:

1. Individual differences in intelligence are *predominantly* attributable to heredity, although environmental factors can play some role.

2. There are socioeconomic-status differences in measured IQ, upper-middle-class children having higher tested IQs than lower-class children. Jensen proposes that part of this difference may be attributable to hereditary factors.

3. The *causes* of tested IQ differences between racial or ethnic groups are "scientifically still an open question" (1969b, p. 6). Jensen speculates, however, that an innate difference between races may exist:

The fact that different racial groups in this country have widely separated geographic origins and have quite different histories which have subjected them to different selective social and economic pressures makes it highly likely that their gene pools differ from some genetically conditioned behavioral characteristics including intelligence [1969b, p. 6].

Jensen's article in the *Harvard Educational Review* has stimulated a wide range of reactions, both emotional and issue-oriented. Most of the published reactions have been generally critical, although, as Layzer indicates in our third article, some have supported and even extended Jensen's conclusions. (See, for example, Richard Herrnstein's 1973 book *IQ in the Meritocracy* or his article in the September 1971 issue of the *Atlantic* magazine.) The selection by Jensen in this Section takes into account many of these criticisms. (The Spring 1969 and Summer 1969 issues of the *Harvard Educational Review* contained many of the early comments, as well as an article in which Jensen responded to them.)

Beyond the criticisms mentioned by Kamin and Layzer, we believe that the primary limitation in Jensen's approach is the implicit assumption that one's tested IQ score is an accurate and complete representation of one's abstract-intelligence level. There is ample evidence that characteristics of the testing situation cause certain persons' tested scores to differ from their true levels of intelligence (Katz, 1964, 1967; Forrester & Klaus, 1964; Sattler, 1970). An examiner may have expectations about how well a subject will perform, and such expectations often have effects on actual performance. A Black child, tested by a White examiner, may be so apprehensive that he or she does not perform up to his or her level of ability. A Puerto Rican or a French Canadian may be hampered by language difficulties. An American Indian child may be constrained by the expectation of his or her tribe that no member seek to stand out from the crowd. Jensen, however, seems to assume that we can take tested IQ differences and use them as 100%-pure indications of intellectual differences.

Beyond this limitation, we believe that Jensen puts too much reliance on the concept of heritability. As even he points out, the heritability of a given population is very much dependent on the extent of environmental differences in that population. If all the persons in a given population are relatively *similar* in the quality of their environment (for example, the relatively affluent Whites living in the Republic of South Africa), the heritability estimate for the population will be relatively high because the variability in environments is limited. In the article reprinted in this Section, Jensen claims that hereditary differences account for 80% of the difference in IQ scores among middle-class Whites. He assumes that these *heritability estimates* would be equally high in Black and lower-class populations—that is, that in these latter populations as well, individual differences in IQ arise much more from hereditary than from environmental differences. But important research by Scarr-Salapatek (1971a, 1971b) has provided us with heritability estimates for these latter groups. She found that in lower-class White and Black populations, the heritability values were lower (from 50% to 60%) than they were for either her middle-class samples or those used by Jensen.

In other words, differences in environment have more of an effect on differences in IQ between two lower-class children or two Black children than they do on IQ differences between two White middle-class children. Her results cause us to question the applicability of Jensen's conclusions when they are applied to lower-class or Black children. Beyond this, Scarr-Salapatek's findings imply that the tested IQ differences between social classes (or between races) "may be considerably larger than the genotypic differences" (1971a, p. 1225). Improvement in the quality of the environment will have the effect of increasing the heritability of intelligence in Black and lower-class groups, but it will also increase their average IQs.

Thus environmental deprivation accounts for much of the difference in average tested IQ between Negroes and Caucasians. Included under the rubric of "environmental deprivation" are such conditions as unstable family life, crowded homes, lower family income, poorer health care, attendance at older schools with less-experienced teachers and fewer teaching aids, fewer opportunities for travel, and many others. Discrimination and environmental deprivation may lead members of minority groups in the United States to believe that they *are* less capable, which influences their motivation to perform well on intelligence tests. Such self-fulfilling prophecies may even serve as sources of support for those minority-group members who do not succeed in life.

We know that an enriched environment can raise the tested IQ of Black children. Those children whose families moved from the Southern part of the United States to the North in the 1930s and 1940s showed year-by-year increases in IQ as they attended the better Northern schools (Lee, 1951; Klineberg, 1935). The Coleman report (Coleman, Campbell, Hobson, McPartland, Mood, Weinfield, & York, 1966) shows that achievement-test performance and IQ scores of Black children improve if the children are placed in racially mixed classes. Attempts to provide a stimulating kindergarten experience for lower-class Black children (Gray & Klaus, 1965, 1970) have increased measured IQs on the average of six to nine points.

So we know that environmental deprivation plays a role in determining tested IQ scores. What about the effects, if any, of heredity? We agree with Gallo and Dorfman (1970) that this is an unanswerable question at this time, for it is impossible to control the relevant variables. What kind of a study would be necessary to do this? Gallo and Dorfman suggest one in which Black and White children are taken at birth and are randomly assigned to families who have been equated on all possible variables. But even this procedure would not suffice. First, there would still be the differences in prenatal environments of the children stemming from differences in the nutrition and health care of the mother. And second, the parents would probably respond differently to a child if the child belonged to a different race. The environment can exact its cost in subtle ways.

In fact, the earlier research on racial similarities and differences in IQ had often ignored major environmental factors by assuming that a gross measurement of socioeconomic status was enough. Tulkin, for example, points out that "a great deal of the variance that has been attributed to social class and race might be traced, more specifically, to differences in experiences from as early as the first year of life" (1970, p. 29). The previously mentioned comprehensive research project on children in Philadelphia (Scarr-Salapatek, 1971a, 1971b) also indicates that we need a refinement of what constitutes *race* or *social class*.

If hereditary racial differences do exist, they are probably meaningless in any practical sense. Even when two groups differ in *average* score by 10–15 points, many members of the "inferior" group score higher than the average of the other group. If we consider that 50% of Whites are above 100 in measured IQ, we need to recognize that in most studies anywhere from 15% to 50% of Blacks are also above the average White in measured IQ.

Any classification of persons into mental-ability groups on the basis of race should be discouraged. Hicks and Pellegrini (1966) reviewed 27 studies of racial comparisons and concluded that knowing a person's race reduces by only 6% the uncertainty in estimating the person's IQ score. Even if racial segregation were not in conflict with the democratic value systems of the United States and Canada, such segregation would not be an efficient way to place children into homogeneous mental-ability groups. But more importantly, the enforcement of segregation places respect for the tested IQ score above respect for the individual. As Dreger writes, "the brutalizing effects of a system of segregation on both segregated and segregators are not worth keeping any race 'pure'" (1967, p. 50).

There is one further matter of great importance that is relevant to the topic of this Section. What are the ethical responsibilities of scientists when they are aware that their data, findings, and conclusions may be used to achieve outcomes that they or society consider undesirable?

For example, Jensen (1969a; also in the article reprinted in this book) has explicitly stated that any possible innate racial differences should not be used to segregate schoolchildren by race. But a scant five days after Jensen's *Harvard Educational Review* article appeared, it was quoted by lawyers in a court case attempting to delay the desegregation of Virginia public schools (Brazziel, 1969). Hunt (1969, p. 149) has reminded scientific practitioners that they "must learn to think of political and social consequences of how and what they write and say." In replying to such charges, Jensen (1969c) has stated:

I would plead for more faith in the wisdom of the First Amendment. To refrain from publishing discussions on socially important issues because possibly there will be some readers with whose interpretations or use of the material we may disagree is, in effect, to give these persons the power of censorship over the publication of our own questions, findings, and interpretations [pp. 239–240].

By reprinting Jensen's article, we affirm our belief that scientific speculations need to be aired, even if their implications may run counter to accepted values of our society. (The publication of Milgram's research on obedience in Section 8 also reflects this view.) Our goal is to critically evaluate speculations such as Jensen's, so that fair and wise decisions can be made from them.

REFERENCES

Brazziel, W. F. A letter from the South. *Harvard Educational Review*, 1969, *39*, 200–208.

Bruce, M. Factors affecting intelligence test performance of Whites and Negroes in the rural South. *Archives of Psychology*, New York, 1940 (No. 252).

Coleman, J., Campbell, E., Hobson, C., McPartland, J., Mood, A., Weinfield, F., & York, R. *Equality of educational opportunity*. Washington, D. C.: U. S. Government Printing Office, 1966.

Dreger, R. M. Hard-hitting hereditarianism. *Contemporary Psychology*, 1967, *12*, 49–51.

Forrester, B. J., & Klaus, R. A. The effect of race of the examiner on intelligence test scores of Negro kindergarten children. *Peabody Papers in Human Development*, 1964, *2*(7), 1–7.

Gallo, P.S., Jr., & Dorfman, D. D. Racial differences in intelligence: Comment on Tulkin. *Representative Research in Social Psychology*, 1970, *1*, 24–28.

Garrett, H. E. The SPSSI and racial differences ("Comment" section). *American Psychologist*, 1962, *17*, 260–263.

Garrett, H. E. McGraw's need for denial ("Comment" section). *American Psychologist*, 1964, *19*, 815.

Garrett, H. E. Reply to Psychology Class 338 (Honors Section). *American Psychologist*, 1969, *24*, 390–391.

Gray, S. W., & Klaus, R. A. An experimental preschool program for culturally deprived children. *Child Development*, 1965, *36*, 887–898.

Gray, S. W., & Klaus, R. A. The Early Training Project. A seventh year report. *Child Development*, 1970, *41*, 909–924.

Herrnstein, R. I.Q. *Atlantic*, 1971, *228*(3), 44–64.

Herrnstein, R. *I.Q. in the meritocracy*. Boston: Atlantic Monthly Press and Little, Brown, 1973.

Hicks, R.A., & Pellegrini, R. J. The meaningfulness of Negro-White differences in intelligence test performance. *Psychological Record*, 1966, *16*, 43–46.

Hunt, J. McV. Has compensatory education failed? Has it been attempted? *Harvard Educational Review*, 1969, *39*, 130–152.

Jensen, A. R. How much can we boost IQ and scholastic achievement? *Harvard Educational Review*, 1969, *39*, 1–123. (a)

Jensen, A. R. Input: Arthur Jensen replies. *Psychology Today*, 1969, *3*(5), 4–6. (b)

Jensen, A. R. Reducing the heredity-environment uncertainty: A reply. *Harvard Educational Review*, 1969, *39*, 449–483. (c)

Katz, I. Review of evidence relating to effects of desegregation in the intellectual performance of Negroes. *American Psychologist*, 1964, *19*, 381–399.

Katz, I. Some motivational determinants of racial differences in intellectual achievement. *International Journal of Psychology*, 1967, *2*, 1–12.

Klineberg, O. *Negro intelligence and selective migration*. New York: Columbia University Press, 1935.

Lee, E. S. Negro intelligence and selective migration: A Philadelphia test of the Klineberg hypothesis. *American Sociological Review*, 1951, *16*, 227–233.

Sattler, J. M. Racial "experimenter effects" in experimentation, testing, interviewing, and psychotherapy. *Psychological Bulletin*, 1970, *73*, 137–160.

Scarr-Salapatek, S. Unknowns in the IQ equation. *Science*, 1971, *174*, 1223–1228. (a)

Scarr-Salapatek, S. Race, social class, and IQ. *Science*, 1971, *174*, 1285–1295. (b)

Tanser, H. A. *The settlement of Negroes in Kent County, Ontario, and a study of the mental capacity of their descendants*. Chatham, Ont.: Shepherd, 1939.

Tulkin, S. Environmental influences on intellectual achievement: A reply to Gallo and Dorfman. *Representative Research in Social Psychology*, 1970, *1*, 29–32.

GLOSSARY

Adrenaline: See Epinephrine.

Aggression: Behavior that is designed to hurt or cause injury or death to another organism or to oneself.

Altruism: Helping behavior; behavior carried out to benefit another person; done without anticipation of rewards from external sources.

Ambiguity: In the study of helping in emergency situations, the degree to which it is clear that a situation is indeed an emergency and that help is needed. The more ambiguous a situation, the less likely it is that help will be given, especially if a large number of bystanders are present.

Analysis of variance: A statistical test to determine whether the average scores for several groups of subjects (or the average scores resulting from differing treatments) are different enough to permit ruling out chance as a likely cause of the differences. If an analysis of variance is statistically significant, the conclusion is that a true difference exists between groups or treatments. The analysis of variance is expressed by an *F* test.

Anomie: A feeling of being alienated, disoriented, and disassociated from any system of social norms and beliefs.

Anonymity: A condition of urban life in which an individual is surrounded by strangers. This provides freedom from social ties but may also create feelings of alienation and detachment. Similar to deindividuation.

Anthropomorphic: The attribution of human characteristics to inanimate objects or subhuman processes.

Anti-Semitism: A generalized negative attitude toward Jews; may include specific beliefs that are contradictory with each other.

Attitude: The internal response or affect felt for or against a psychological object; usually this affect predisposes its holder toward certain actions. Some researchers see attitudes as having three components—feelings (affect), cognitions (beliefs), and action tendencies.

Attribution theory: A minitheory of social psychology dealing with the causes subjects give to their behavior or the behavior of others. Attribution theory seeks to understand the factors that determine the reasons we give for actions.

Authoritarianism: A basic personality style that includes a set of organized beliefs, values, and preferences, including submission to authority, identification with authority, denial of feelings, cynicism, and others.

Balance theory: A theory of attitude change that hypothesizes that people like to hold consistent, compatible beliefs and dislike holding inconsistent, incompatible beliefs.

Belief-similarity theory: Rokeach's theory that much White rejection of Blacks arises not because of race per se but because Whites assume that Blacks hold values and beliefs very different from their own.

Brainwashing: A massive (and largely unsuccessful) attitude-change program used on prisoners of war during the Korean War; chiefly utilizes the arousal of guilt and the foot-in-the-door technique.

Catharsis: The unleashing of feelings; the hypothesized reduction in the intensity of an emotion, such as aggression, resulting from the direct or indirect expression of the emotion. In the debate over the effects of witnessing violence on the expression of aggression, the catharsis theory proposes that watching violent acts "drains off" aggression in the viewer.

Cathexis: An attachment to objects that are gratifying or a rejection of those that are unpleasant.

Children's Domestic Exchange (CDE): A proposed program in which minority- and majority-group children would live in one another's homes for a period of time; theorized to lead to a reduction in ethnic prejudice.

Cognitive approach: One that focuses on mental rather than emotional or physiological determinants of behavior.

Cognitive dissonance: The state in which two beliefs are held and one is opposite to, or in conflict with, the other; one theory of attitude change.

Compliance: Overt conformity, or the act of openly acceding to another's wishes; or, the act of doing what another wants you to, whether or not you are aware of the other's wishes.

Confederate: In a psychological experiment, a participant who appears to be a naïve subject but who is actually an accomplice of the experimenter.

Conformity: Behavior that is in agreement with that of the others in a group and that is influenced by that of the others.

Correlation: An indication of the degree of relationship between two variables in the same population. Correlations can range from +1.00 (perfect positive correlation) through 0.00 (no relationship) to −1.00 (perfect negative correlation). The term *r* is used as a symbol for the Pearson product-moment correlation coefficient. A correlation of .40, for example, would indicate a moderate positive relationship between the two variables in question. If the two variables were aggression and obedience, one could conclude that there is a moderate relationship between aggression and obedience—that is, that *more* aggressive people tend to be *more* obedient. Correlation alone does *not* indicate whether either variable causes the other.

Correspondent inference: The case in which an observer judges that a disposition of a stimulus person (actor) is sufficient explanation of his or her behavior. The opposite case would be one in which the observer decides that an actor's behavior can be explained by aspects of the situation in which the person behaved.

Costs for helping: Factors in an emergency situation that may discourage bystanders from intervening directly. These include potential danger, effort, time lost, embarrassment, and feelings of inadequacy if the help should be ineffective.

Costs for not helping: Factors in an emergency situation that may motivate bystanders to intervene. These include the possibility of self-blame or public censure for inaction and the loss of possible rewards, such as thanks from the victim and feelings of competence.

Debriefing (or dehoaxing): The procedure wherein, at the completion of a study involving deception, the true purpose of the study is explained to each subject, who is given a chance to express his or her feelings.

De facto segregation: Racial separation that is not supported by laws but arises because of housing patterns, income differences, and so on.

Deindividuation: A condition of reduced self-identity, whereby conventional restraints are lessened.

De jure segregation: Racial separation that is enforced by law; now illegal in the United States.

Demand characteristics: The expectations that the subjects bring to psychological experiments; the "demands" that they perceive are put upon them to "cooperate," to "look good," and so on.

Derogation of the victim: A reaction by observers in some emergency situations in which the observers decide that the victim deserved his or her fate. Most likely in situations involving high costs for helping and high costs for not helping.

Diffusion of responsibility: The situation in which the felt responsibility for action may be shared among all participants or onlookers, so that the more bystanders there are, the less is the amount of responsibility for action felt by any single bystander.

Discrimination: Behavior that shows unfair treatment of others and is based on the other person's membership in a specific group rather than on his or her individual actions or characteristics.

Disposition, or dispositional property: An internal characteristic of a person, such as a personality trait or an attitude or an ability, which may be used as an explanation (or partial explanation) of his or her behavior.

Dyad: A two-person group.

Egalitarian marriage: A marriage that provides the framework for both husband and wife to pursue careers that are challenging and fulfilling and, at the same time, to participate equally in the pleasures and responsibilities of child-rearing.

Egalitarian view of race differences: The belief that two races do not differ in their innate mental ability.

Ego: According to Freud, that part of the personality oriented toward acting reasonably and realistically; the "executive" part of personality.

Ego-alien: Irrational; not in tune with what is sensible or realistic or real.

Ego-defensive function: The function of an attitude in which the attitude is a reflection of the holder's unresolved personal problems; often applied to prejudicial attitudes.

Empowerment strategies: Strategies that will achieve power for minority groups in U. S. society. Taylor proposes that without such power, equal education, equal employment, equal income, equal housing, and so forth, will never lead to perceived equality of minority-group members in the eyes of Whites. However, power is rarely shared or transferred without confrontation and struggle.

Epinephrine: A drug that has the effect of triggering the sympathetic nervous system and causing increased heart rate, increased blood pressure, and other physiological reactions to emotion; also called adrenaline.

Equal-status contact: The situation in which ethnic-group members and majority-group members interact in a situation in which their statuses are defined as equal; may lead to a reduction in prejudice.

Equated-environment strategy: In studying racial differences in intelligence, the approach that seeks to find groups that have the same degree of environment yet differ in race. According to this approach, any resultant difference in the average IQ scores of the two groups must be due to differences in heredity.

Equity theory: A minitheory concerned with the tendency to return a favor or comply with the request of a favor-doer because of the norms of social justice and reparation.

Ethnocentrism: A rejection of foreigners, aliens, and all out-groups, accompanied by a belief that one's own group or nationality is the best in all respects.

Ethnic group: A group sharing a common culture, customs, language, religious heritage, or race.

Ethology: The study of the behavior of animals in field situations.

Evaluation apprehension: An experimental subject's fear that his behavior is being observed and evaluated by the experimenter; may lead to changes in behavior within an experiment.

Experimenter expectancy: The ways that experimenters expect their subjects to respond to the experimental manipulation; these expectancies may unconsciously affect the subjects' behaviors.

Externalization function: See Ego-defensive function.

F-scale: A widely used measure of authoritarianism.

F test: The statistical test used in conjunction with an analysis of variance. Also used to see if the distributions of two groups are different (*see* Analysis of variance).

Fate control: The degree to which an individual is able, or thinks he is able, to control his own destiny.

Field study: A study that is done not in a structured laboratory situation but in a natural setting. Often the participants do not even know that they have participated in research. Such studies may be either experimental or correlational.

Foot-in-the-door technique: The technique wherein the likelihood of an individual's agreeing to a large request is increased by getting him or her to agree to a smaller request first.

Forced-compliance paradigm: The experimental situation in which the subject is pressured to undertake a counterattitudinal behavior. A paradigm used to test the cognitive dissonance theory of attitude change.

Functions of attitudes: Reasons why a person may hold the attitudes he does. Four major functions are theorized: knowledge, social adjustment, ego-defensive, and value-expressive.

Gene: An element that determines, along with other genes, the transmission of hereditary characteristics.

Genotype: An underlying characteristic; often a causal factor.

GRIT (Graduated reciprocation in tension reduction): Osgood's plan for reducing conflicts in a step-by-step manner through cooperative conciliatory gestures. The first gesture should be relatively small so that, if it is exploited by the other party, no serious harm will befall the party originally making the gesture. After several such steps, mistrust and suspicion of motives may be lessened.

Group: A unitary entity that is held together by common interests and goals of the group members and that is organized to a greater or lesser degree.

Groupthink: Janis' term for cases in which group norms develop that bolster morale at the expense of critical thinking and concurrence-seeking becomes so dominant that it can override realistic appraisal of alternative courses of action. Most likely to take place when the group is highly cohesive, the group members share the same set of values, and they face a crisis situation that puts everyone under intense stress.

Hedonic relevance: The degree to which another person's behavior has a rewarding or costly effect on an observer. If an act has hedonic relevance, it has more use in attributing causes to the other person's behavior.

Heritability estimate or coefficient: A measure of the degree to which differences in heredity account for differences in some characteristic; for example, if in a group the heritability coefficient for height is .90, the indication is that 90% of the difference in height between group members is accounted for by differences in their heredity.

Hypothesis of genetic equality: Assumption that two groups (racial groups, for instance) possess equivalent heredities; that is, there is no genetic reason for the groups to differ in measured performance.

Id: According to Freud, a set of drives that is the repository for man's basic unsocialized impulses, including sex and aggression.

Identification: The general process by which one person takes on the attributes of another; often involves modeling and imitation.

Immigrant analogy: The naïve assumption that present-day ethnic-group members (especially Blacks) should be able to succeed in the majority culture just as well as European immigrants of past generations.

Immigration quotas: System employed by the U. S. Immigration Service to limit the number of immigrants from various nations, especially nations seen as "undesirable." A prime example of institutional racism.

Impression-management theory: A theory of attitude change that views people as actively changing their attitudes in order to receive rewards (such as being seen as good, consistent people) and to avoid punishments.

Individual racism: Prejudice toward an ethnic group, usually Blacks.

Innate: That which is due to inheritance, as opposed to that which is acquired through learning and the environment.

Innate differences: Those resulting from genetic factors or from different heredities.

Institutional racism: The situation in which major societal institutions are structured to permit or encourage the subjugation or mistreatment of ethnic groups.

Invariant: Irreversible; in only one order.

Knowledge function: The function of an attitude in which it allows the holder to gain new frames of reference or standards for evaluating objects relevant to the attitude.

Latency: The time it takes a person to respond to a stimulus.

Learned helplessness: A phenomenon, originally noticed in animal research, wherein organisms become passive when they learn that their responses give them no control in a situation.

Libido: A basic psychic energy. According to Freud, a person possesses only a certain amount of libido, parts of which he directs toward different concerns.

Likert-type: A specific type of attitude scale in which the format includes a series of definite (that is, not neutral) statements. The subject indicates (usually on a five- or six-point scale) how much he agrees or disagrees with each statement. His answers are summed to give his position or score on this attitude.

Machiavellianism: A set of beliefs held by a person who values the manipulation of others for his or her own purposes.

Manipulation check: An assessment done to determine whether the researcher's attempted manipulation of an independent variable in an experiment has been successful. That is, checking whether subjects undergoing different treatments perceived the situation differently in the direction the experimenter intended. If the manipulation check is unsuccessful, then the portion of the experiment involving that independent variable is no longer valid.

Mean (or mean score): The average for a set of scores, determined by adding up all the scores and dividing by the number of scores. Symbolized by M or $\overline{X}$.

Mediating variable: One that links two other variables and affects the influence of one on the other.

Mindguards: One of the symptoms of groupthink, wherein one or more persons take it upon themselves to become mindguards and protect the group leader and fellow members from adverse or critical information.

Mirror-image wars: Wars in which each side really believes that the other side is the aggressor. Most likely to break out when there are overlapping and conflicting territorial self-images.

Modeling: The tendency of persons, particularly children, to imitate the witnessed behavior of others (models).

Monotonic relationship: A linear relationship; one in which, as one variable increases, the other does so correspondingly.

Morale: Extent to which group members find the group personally satisfying and the extent to which they believe the group is successfully progressing toward its goals.

Mores: Cultural standards defining those behaviors that are morally acceptable or unacceptable.

Mutuality: A relationship that is at a deeper level than that of surface contact. Similarity of values and attitudes and satisfaction of each other's needs may be particularly important in a relationship at this level.

Native differences: Differences between racial (or other) groups not attributable to environment or learning but rather innate or hereditary.

Nonconformity: Behavior that is intended to facilitate the attainment of some goal other than that of fulfilling the normative group expectations.

Object-appraisal function: See Knowledge function.

Opinion molecule: Abelson's term for incapsulated, isolated beliefs and attitudes. Each molecule is made up of a belief, an attitude, and a perception of social support for them.

Overlap: The percentage of Black children whose IQs exceed the average IQ of White children. If the two groups are equal in average IQ, we would expect 50% of the Black children to have IQs exceeding the average for White children.

Overload: The inability of a person in an urban environment to process inputs from the environment because there are too many inputs or because successive inputs come too rapidly after one another.

p < .05: This statement, read as "probability of less than .05," means that the correlation or mean difference is so great that it could have occurred by chance, or coincidence, fewer than 5 times out of every 100 comparisons. Therefore it is concluded that the relationship or the mean difference is a true one, not simply a coincidental finding.

Paradigm: A specific type of research design or methodology.

Personalism: In attributing causes to the acts of another, personalism deals with the degree to which the presence or the attributes of the observer contribute to the target person's intent to produce certain outcomes.

Phenotype: A surface or observable characteristic; often a resultant rather than a causal factor.

Physical-attractiveness stereotype: The tendency of many people to assume that persons who are physically attractive also have many desirable personality characteristics and are, therefore, desirable in many respects.

Pilot study: In research, a small study, or series of studies, carried out prior to the actual research, in order to pretest methodology, procedures, and so on.

Pluralistic ignorance: The process by which, in an ambiguous emergency situation, each bystander is led by the apparent lack of concern of the others to interpret the situation as being less serious than he or she would if alone.

Post hoc analysis: A statistical analysis that is decided on and done after the experimental data have been collected; therefore, not a part of the original design or purpose of the experiment.

Prejudice: An unjustified negative attitude toward all members of a group, based on overgeneralization, lack of information, or misinformation about the group.

Propinquity: Nearness. One of the factors that increase the likelihood of attraction between persons.

Prosocial behavior: Behavior toward others that reflects the desired values of one's society (for example, helpfulness, charity, sympathy, dependability).

Pro-us illusion: The tendency to see people in another country as more friendly to one's side than they actually are.

r: See Correlation.

Race: A controversial term that has several different meanings. A *physical* definition differentiates between groups of people who differ markedly in physical appearance (phenotypes) from each other. A *genetic* approach defines races as populations that differ in the frequencies of some gene or genes.

Racial justice (pluralism): Taylor's term for the ideal state of intergroup relations, involving intergroup harmony predicated on concepts of equity and fair play, irrespective of racial identification.

Racism: A negative orientation toward an ethnic group; differentiated into individual racism and institutional racism.

Reciprocal-concessions model: A means for increasing the likelihood of compliance to a request by first making an extreme request that is rejected and then moving to a smaller request, which is more likely to be granted. The target is likely to agree to the second proposal in order to relieve any felt pressure for reciprocation of concessions.

Reference group: A group with which an individual identifies or aspires to belong.

Rejection-then-moderation procedure: See Reciprocal concessions model.

Risk-benefit approach: Approach to research ethics wherein the potential risks to the well-being of research participants are weighed against the possible benefits to society of the knowledge that would derive from the research.

Risky shift: The observed tendency for group decisions to be more risky than decisions made separately by comparable individuals.

Role enactment: For urban dwellers, the tendency to deal with one another in highly segmented, functional terms.

S.D.: See Standard deviation.

Selective-exposure hypothesis: The hypothesis that people will deliberately expose themselves to stimuli with which they agree and avoid stimuli with which they disagree. A point of debate for persons interested in the effect of controversial media presentations involving violence, verbal aggression, and ethnic hostility.

Selective migration: A point of view that explains the improved IQ performance of Northern Black children in terms of tendencies for brighter children to leave the South and emigrate to the North.

Self-attitudes: Attitudes toward, and feelings about, oneself and the ethnic group to which one belongs.

Self-fulfilling prophecy: The situation in which a minority-group member may come to manifest those negative traits constantly applied to him or her by the majority culture.

Self-perception theory: A theory of attitude development and change proposed by Daryl Bem that suggests that people may often infer what their attitudes are by watching themselves behave. According to self-perception theory, our judgments of our own attitudes and emotions develop in a way similar to the way in which we infer what other people's attitudes are by watching their behavior.

SES: Socioeconomic status. *See* Social class.

Sexism: An attitude or behavior by a person or institution that reflects an unwarranted belief that one sex is inferior to the other.

Sex role: The expectations society holds concerning what is acceptable behavior for each sex.

Simulation: A research procedure that attempts to reproduce in a laboratory context the important aspects of a real-life situation. A literal simulation attempts to reproduce *actual* details and practices, whereas a functional simulation attempts to reproduce the significant *psychological* features of the situation.

Social-adjustment function: The function of an attitude through which the holder can identify with, or differentiate himself from, various reference groups.

Social class: A grouping of persons who share common values, interests, income level, and educational level.

Social-comparison theory: A point of view that states that one evaluates his or her own attitudes and abilities by comparing them with those of other people similar to himself or herself.

Social Darwinism: The application of Darwin's notion of "survival of the fittest" to cultures and races; seen as a component of racism.

Social desirability: A response set to answer questions about oneself in a manner that makes one look "good" or acceptable.

Social desirability of a behavior: The degree to which a certain action is in keeping with what society in general says is appropriate, right, correct, and so on.

Social-distance scale: A measure of how close (physically, socially, psychologically) one wishes to be to members of a particular ethnic group; a measure of prejudice.

Socialization: A "growing-up" process in which the child acquires his or her distinctive values, attitudes, and personality characteristics.

Social mobility: The extent to which a society permits its members to move upward or downward in the social hierarchy according to their own efforts.

Society for the Psychological Study of Social Issues (SPSSI): An organization of psychologists and other social scientists who are concerned with applying the skills and knowledge from the behavioral sciences to the solution of important human problems.

Span of sympathy: The range of people to whom sympathy is likely to be granted, if appropriate; urban overload may cause a reduction in this range.

Stage theory (of social development): A theory that proposes that a child must pass through a series of stages as he or she develops into adulthood. Each stage has a different set of operations or concerns, and the stages must be passed through in a definite sequence.

Standard deviation (S.D.): A measure of how much variability (or spread) is present in a set of scores. A group with a larger standard deviation is more heterogeneous and possesses a wider spread of scores.

Standard error of a score: The amount of inaccuracy (or "error") to be expected in a score a person receives on a mental test, In general, IQ tests have a standard error of five points or more.

Statistically significant: A finding or a difference that is not likely to have been caused by coincidence or chance; hence a true difference.

Stereotype: An unjustified generalization about a group or its members.

Stigma: A charcteristic that is often taken to indicate that a person is substandard or abnormal.

Superego: According to Freud, the part of personality oriented toward doing what is morally proper; the conscience. The superego also includes one's ego-ideal, or ideal self-image.

Surface contact: The initial stages of a relationship between people. Factors such as propinquity, physical attractiveness, perceived competence, and reciprocal liking may be particularly important at this level.

Symbolic aggression: Aggression presented through a medium, such as movies or television.

t test: A statistical test to determine whether the average scores for two groups of subjects are different enough to permit ruling out chance as a likely cause of the difference.

True integration: Pettigrew's term for the situation in which interracial togetherness is possible while true personal and group autonomy are maintained.

Unconscious ideology: A philosophy that is usually unquestioned because alternative beliefs and attitudes have not been imagined. Used to describe the traditional ideology of the "woman's place" in North American society.

Value-expressive function: The function of an attitude wherein the attitude gives expression to the holder's central values and self-concept.

Verbal tests: Those that employ vocabulary and language in their administration or completion.

Yea-sayers: Persons who tend to agree with an attitude statement regardless of the nature of its content.

Zeitgeist: The "spirit of the times."

ARTICLE-AUTHOR INDEX

SUBJECT INDEX